The Complete Book of Maps & Geography

Table of Contents

Section 1:

Introduction to Maps and Map Skills

Floor Plans 4-13
Map Keys 14-24
Map Routes 25-36
Compasses 37-61
City/State/National Maps 62-74
Map Scales 75-86
Population Maps 87-88

Section 2:

United States Geography

Introduction to the U.S. and States 91-112
Boundaries and Rivers 113-121
Kinds of Maps 122
Political Maps 123-127
Physical Maps 128-137
Product Maps 138-147
Climate Maps 148-150

Section 3:

United States Regions

Pacific States 152-159
Mountain States 160-170
North Central States 171-180
South Central States 181-186
Midwest States 187-193
Northeastern States 194-206
Southeastern States 207-220

Section 4:

North and South America

Introduction to North and South America 222-225
Canada 226-230
Mexico 231-233
Central America 234-237
South America 238-240

Section 5:

Grid Maps 242-250

Section 6:

Global Geography

The Globe 252-255
Continents and Oceans 256-267
Hemispheres 268-275
Meridians of Longitude 277-285
Lines of Latitude 286-293
Latitude and Longitude 294-310
Time Zones 311-316

Map and Geography Review Sheets 317-322

Section 1

Introduction to Maps & Map Skills

Name ____________________

The Mole Family

A floor plan shows where things are placed in a room. The Mole Family has just had all of their new living room furniture delivered. Now they have to arrange it. Help them decide where to put each piece of furniture. Color and cut out the pictures of the furniture. Glue the pictures on the drawing of the Mole Family's living room to make a floor plan.

Mole Family's Floor Plan

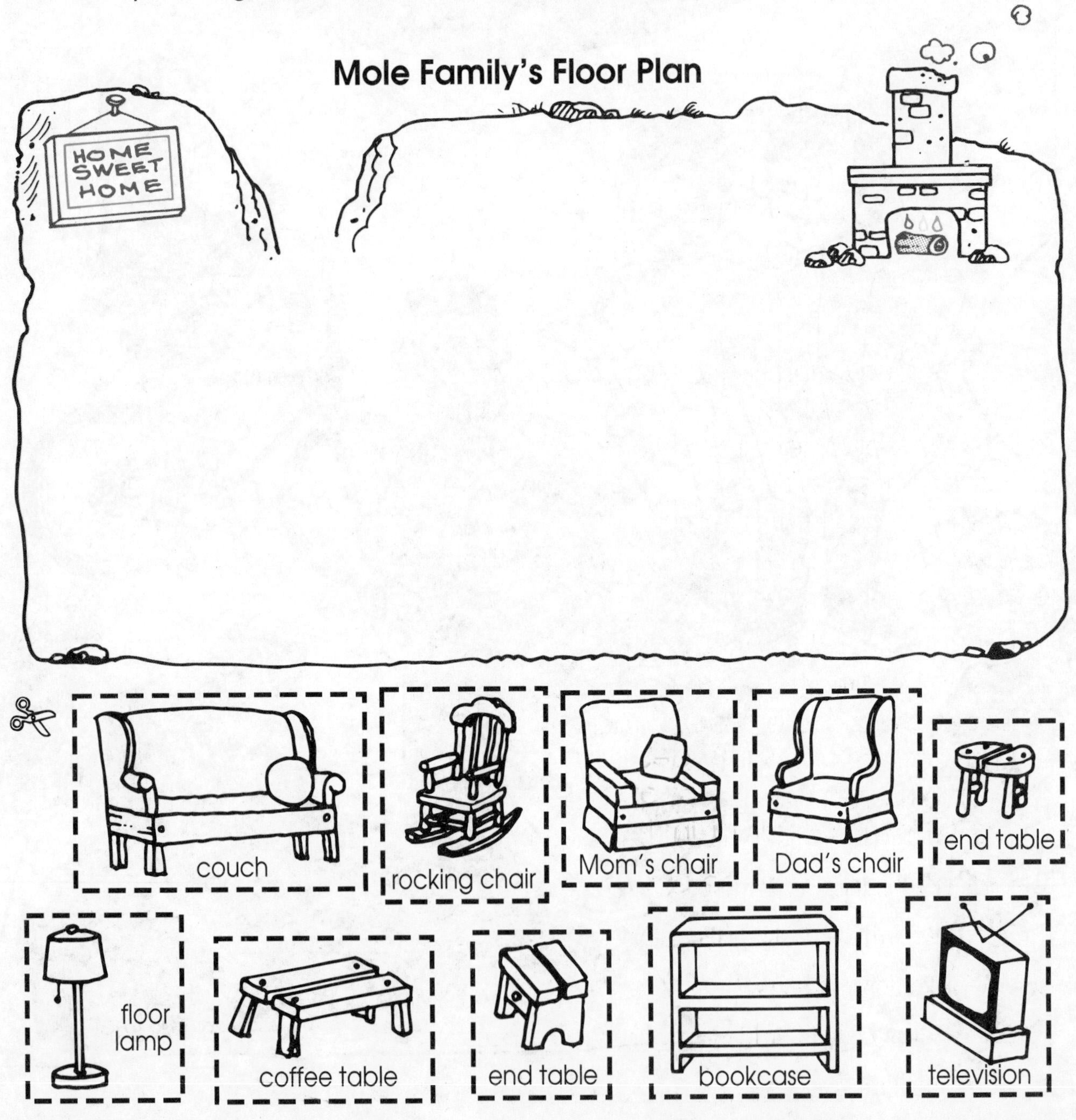

Name________________________________

A Picture From Above

A floor plan looks like a picture someone drew looking down from the sky. It shows you where things are.

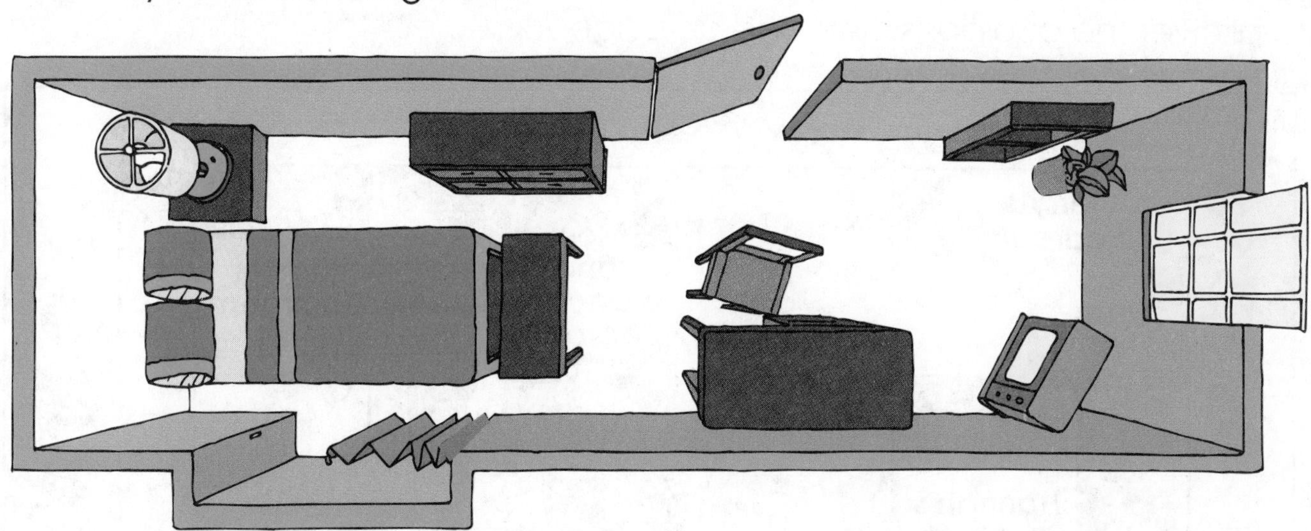

Circle the word which correctly completes each statement.

1. The TV is near the...	a. door	b. window	c. bed
2. The dresser is near the...	a. window	b. door	c. TV
3. Next to the bed is a...	a. TV	b. window	c. table
4. The bench is at the end of the...	a. bed	b. bookshelf	c. closet
5. The plant is by the...	a. dresser	b. bed	c. bookshelf
6. The bookshelf is next to the...	a. bed	b. closet	c. door
7. The lamp is on the...	a. table	b. TV	c. dresser

Follow these directions.

1. Draw a red circle around the TV.
2. Draw a black **X** on the desk.
3. Draw an oval rug in front of the bench using a color of your choice.
4. Draw a stuffed animal in the center of the bed.

Fill in these blanks with the correct word.

1. Between the closet and the TV is a ________________.
2. The window is between the ________________ and the TV.
3. When you walk in the door, the ________________ is to your right.
4. There is/are ________________ lamp(s) in the room.

Name Stephanie Rocha

Hannah's New House

Hannah's family just moved into a new house. It is very different from their other house. Hannah drew a floor plan of her new house. Use the floor plan to answer the questions here and on page 7.

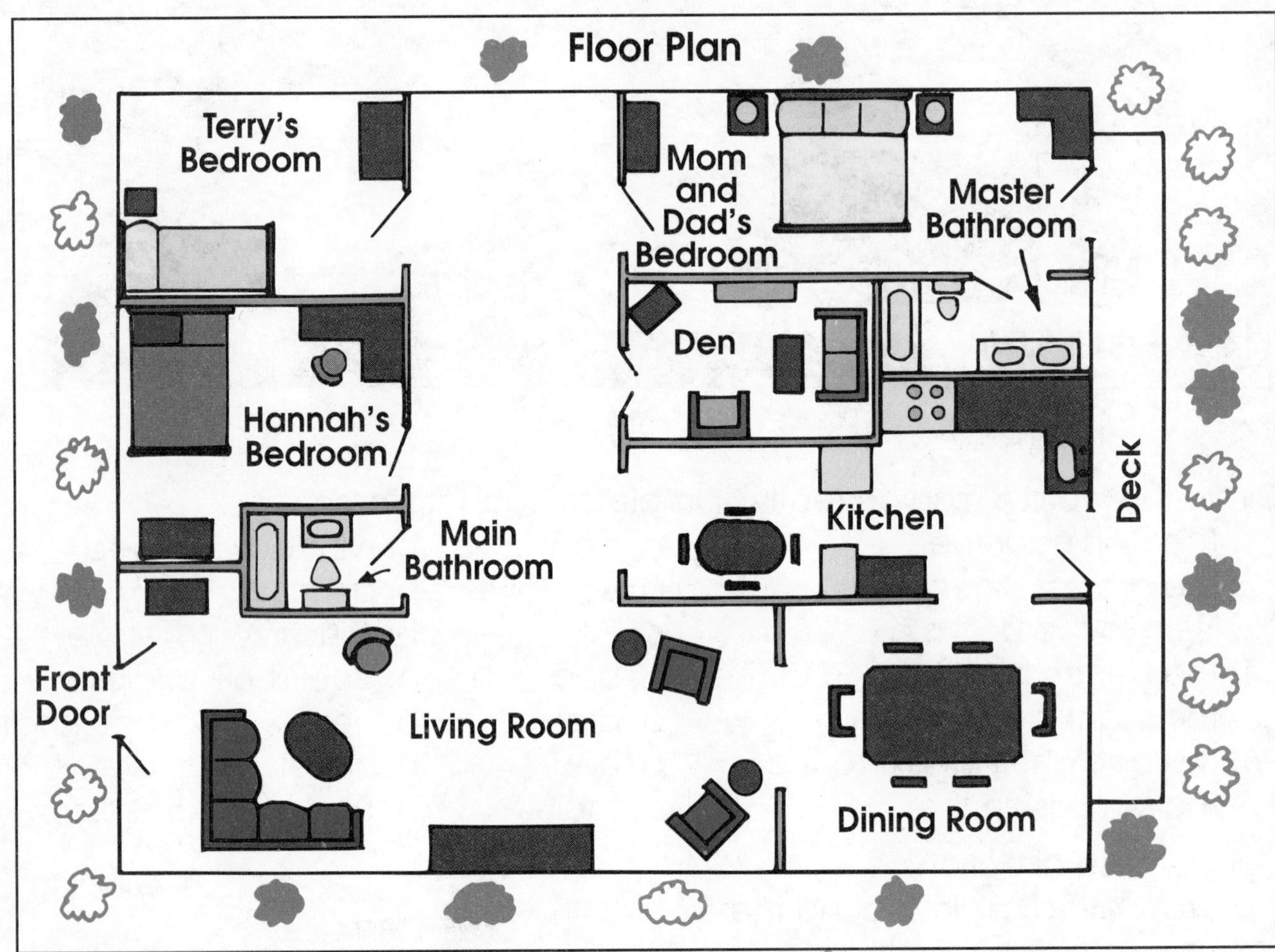

1. How many rooms does the house have? 9
2. Which room is the smallest? Main Bathroom
3. Which room is the largest? living Room

Name ____________________

Hannah's New House

4. Who has a room across from Mom and Dad's bedroom?

____

5. Which rooms does Hannah walk past to go from the living room to her own bedroom?

____

6. How many bedrooms are there? ____________________

7. Which rooms have a door leading onto the deck?

____

8. The front door opens into what room?

____

9. On the floor plan on page 6, use a red crayon to draw the routes Hannah could take from her room to a door leading outside in case of an emergency.

This page has been intentionally left blank.

Name____

Fantastic Seats!

A floor plan can help you find your seat at a sports arena, concert hall or any place where you may go to see a special event.

Read each ticket. Find the seat on the floor plan. Color the seat on the floor plan the correct color.

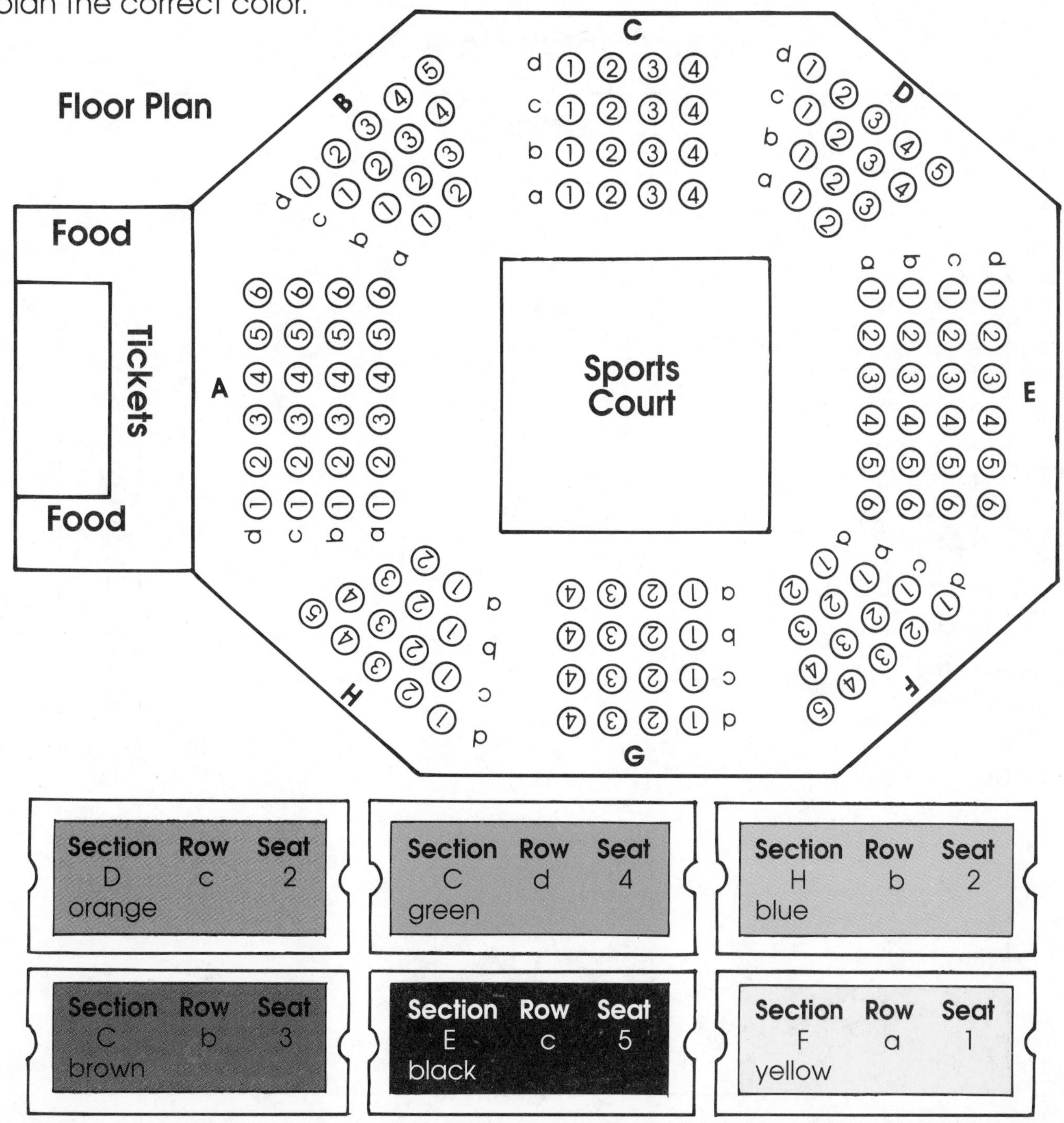

Name____

Prepare for the Show

It's the big event of the year! Old cars from all over the United States are being put on display. The boxes on the floor plan show the spaces where cars will be placed. Follow the directions on page 11 to complete the floor plan.

Car Display Floor Plan

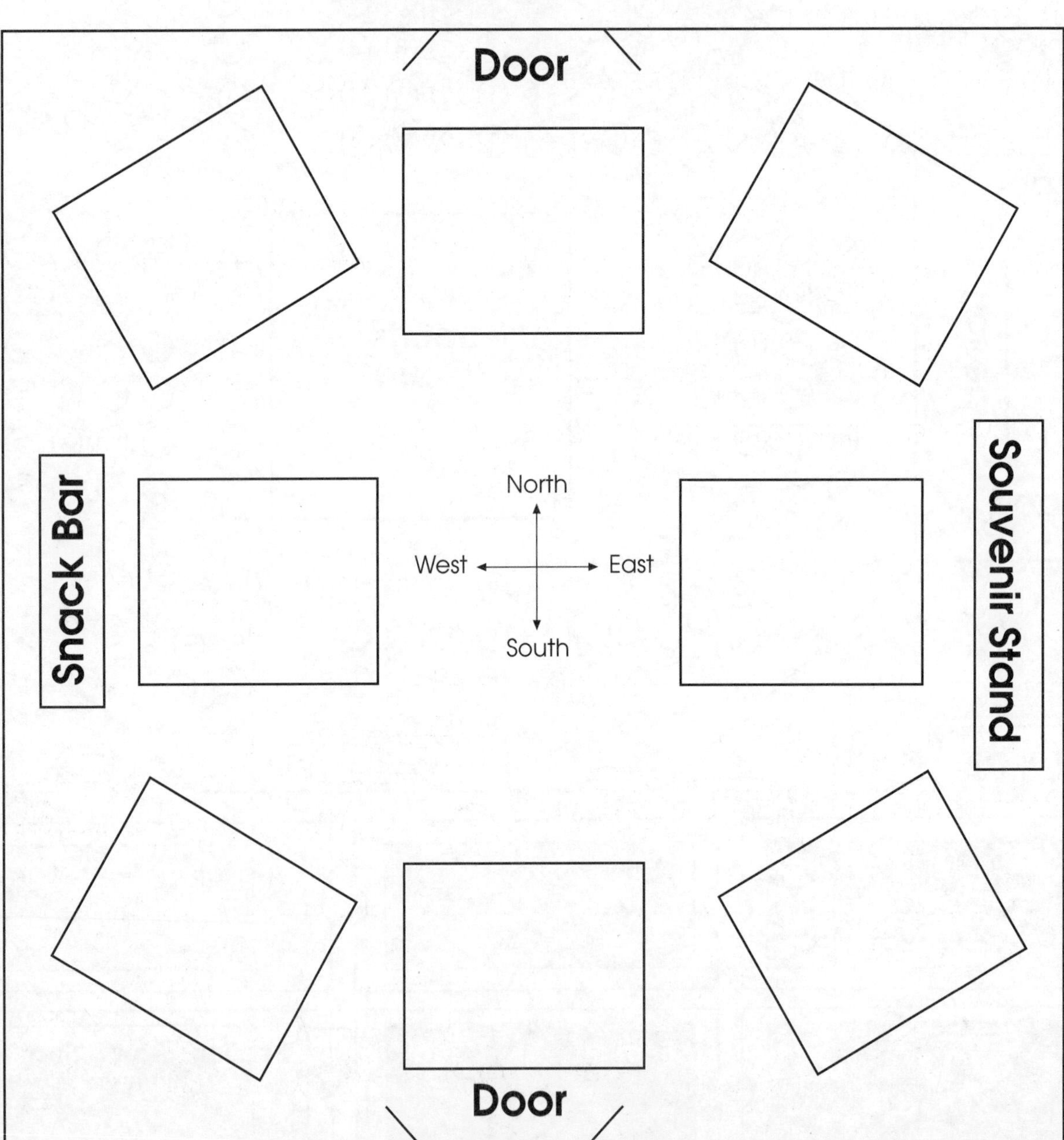

Name ____________________

Prepare for the Show

Color and cut out the pictures of the cars at the bottom of the page. Read the directions below to glue the pictures where they belong on page 10.

Directions:

1. The station wagon is in the space near the north door.
2. The roadster is in the space near the south door.
3. The van is in the space east of the station wagon.
4. The pickup is in the space west of the roadster.
5. The coupe is in the space west of the station wagon.
6. The carriage is in the space east of the roadster and south of the Souvenir Stand.
7. The Model A is east of the Snack Bar.
8. The Model T is east of the Model A.

Page is blank for cutting exercise on previous page.

Name____

Creating a Floor Plan

Pretend you are looking at your classroom or a room in your home from high atop the lighting fixtures. Draw how the room looks.

Name____

Picture This

This is a photograph that shows part of what is left of the town of Bodie, California. It was a mining town long ago. The photo shows a house, a barn and an old wagon. It also shows where a fence once was.

This is a map, or drawing, of the photo. It shows where the things in the photo can be found.

Bodie Map

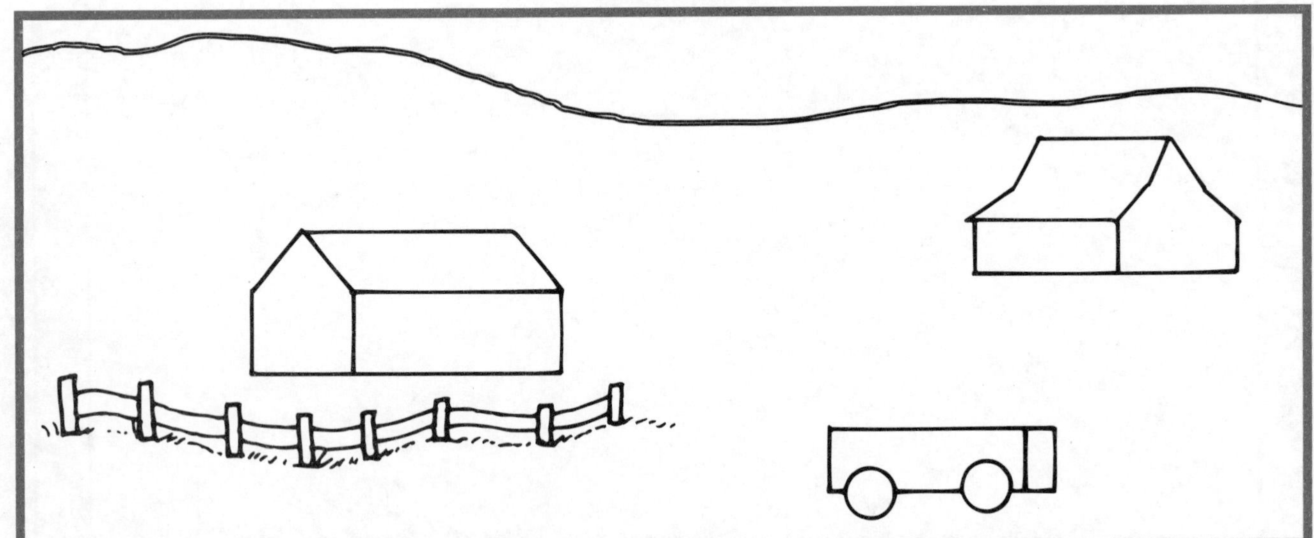

Directions:

1. Color the wagon red.
2. Color the fence brown.
3. Color the house yellow.
4. Color the barn blue.

Name______________________________

Make a Map

Look closely at this photograph of an old pioneer schoolhouse and playground.

Directions:

In the box, draw a map to show what is in the photograph. Use the shapes to help you draw the pictures on your map that stand for things in the photo.

Pioneer Map

Name________________________________

Symbols on Maps

A symbol is a picture that stands for something that is shown on a map. Symbols used in a map are shown in the Map Key. Look at the symbols. Draw a line from each symbol to what it stands for in the drawing below.

Name______________________________

Symbols Replace Words

Symbols on a map show you where things are located.

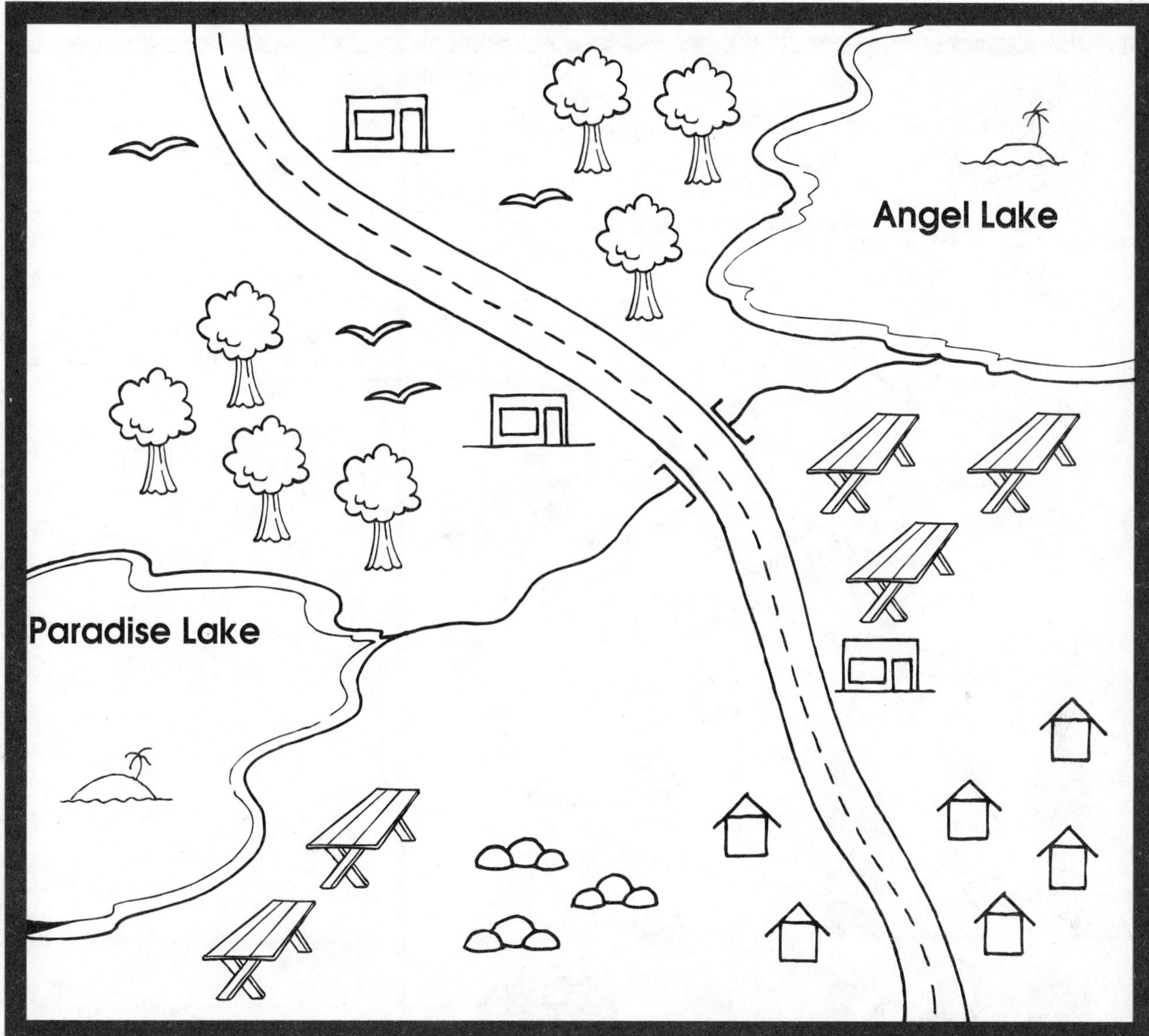

Directions: Use crayons or markers to complete the map.

1. Color the islands brown.
2. Color the trees green.
3. Color the rocks black.
4. Color the houses blue.
5. Color the stores orange.
6. Color the birds purple.
7. Color the picnic tables red.
8. Color the road yellow.

Name ______________________________

The Wild Geese

Twice a day the wild geese fly from the river to a farm. Use this map with page 19.

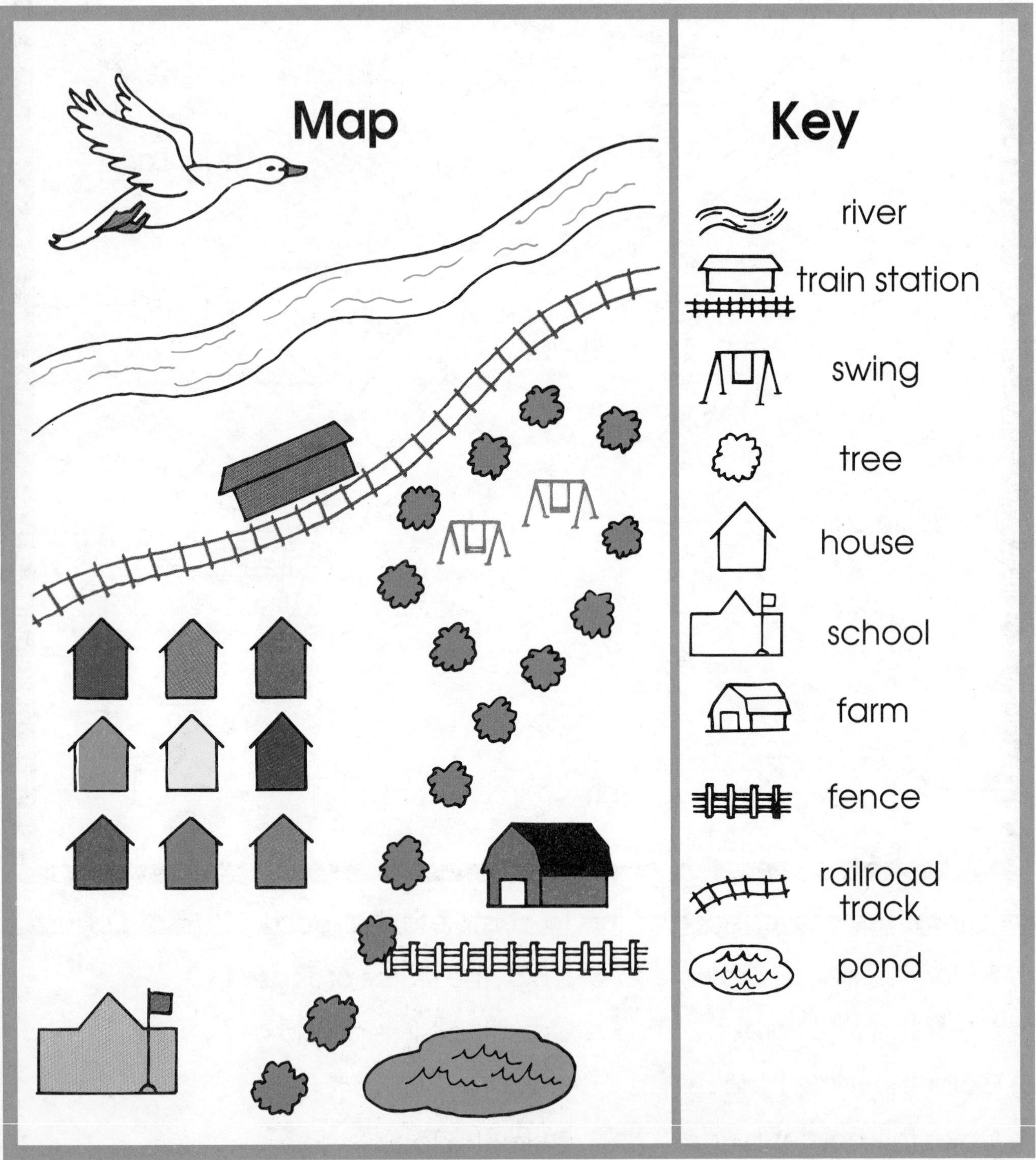

Name ________________________________

The Wild Geese

Directions: Write the word on the lines that tells what each symbol from the map key stands for.

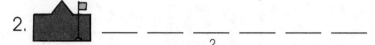

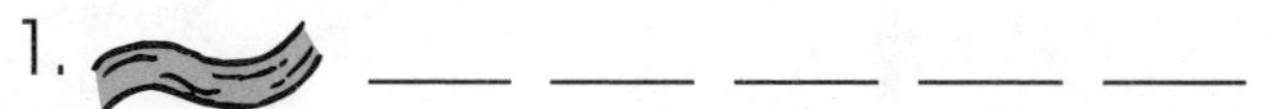

1. ___ ___ ___ ___ ___
   (1 under 4th blank)
2. ___ ___ ___ ___ ___ ___
   (2 under 3rd blank)
3. ___ ___ ___ ___
   (3 under 1st blank, 4 under 4th blank)
4. ___ ___ ___ ___ ___
   (5 under 5th blank)
5. ___ ___ ___ ___
   (6 under 4th blank)
6. ___ ___ ___ ___
   (7 under 4th blank)
7. ___ ___ ___ ___ ___
   (8 under 1st blank)
8. ___ ___ ___ ___ ___   ___ ___ ___ ___ ___ ___ ___
   (9 under 2nd blank, 10 under 8th blank)
9. ___ ___ ___ ___ ___
   (11 under 1st blank, 12 under 2nd blank)
10. ___ ___ ___ ___ ___ ___ ___ ___
    (13 under 2nd blank, 14 under 5th blank)
    ___ ___ ___ ___ ___
    (15 under 1st blank)

Use the numbered letters to solve the puzzling question. Why do the geese fly this path twice a day?

___   ___ ___ ___ ___ ___ ___
10   3 13 9 4 12 14

___ ___ ___ ___ ___   ___ ___ ___ ___.
11 5 6 7 8   15 2 1 4

Name______________________________________

Kool Kids Mall

Mall Map

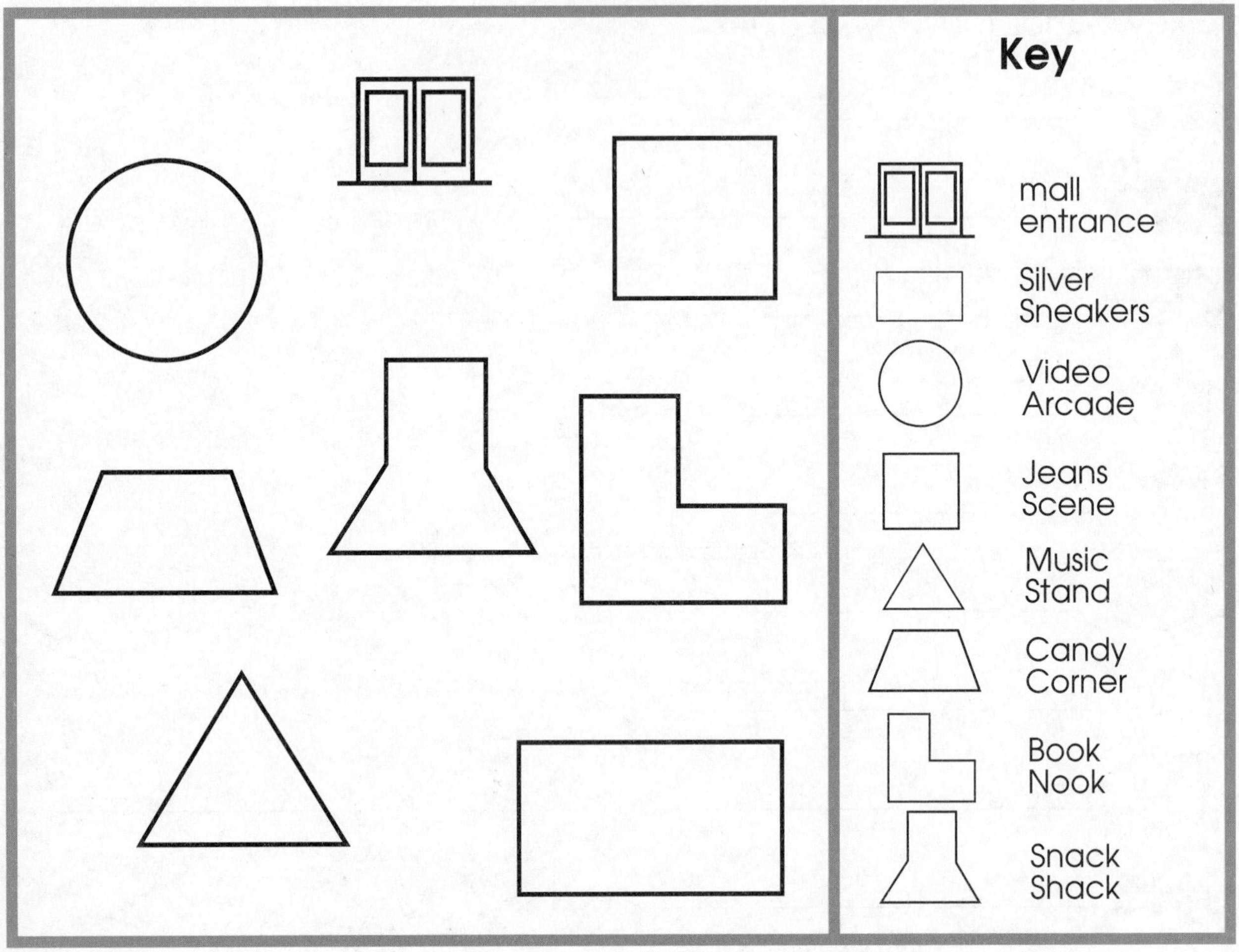

Key	
(double door symbol)	mall entrance
(rectangle)	Silver Sneakers
(circle)	Video Arcade
(square)	Jeans Scene
(triangle)	Music Stand
(trapezoid)	Candy Corner
(L-shape)	Book Nook
(flask shape)	Snack Shack

Directions: Use the key to locate the stores. Draw the following:

1. a red and blue sneaker in Silver Sneakers
2. a black musical note in the Music Stand
3. a pair of blue jeans in the Jeans Scene
4. a green tree on each side of the mall entrance
5. a red piece of pizza in the Snack Shack
6. a pair of eyes in the Video Arcade
7. a yellow book and a blue book in the Book Nook
8. an orange lollipop in the Candy Corner

Name ______________________________

Science Sense

This is a floor plan of the Science Sense Museum. Use the floor plan and key to complete this page.

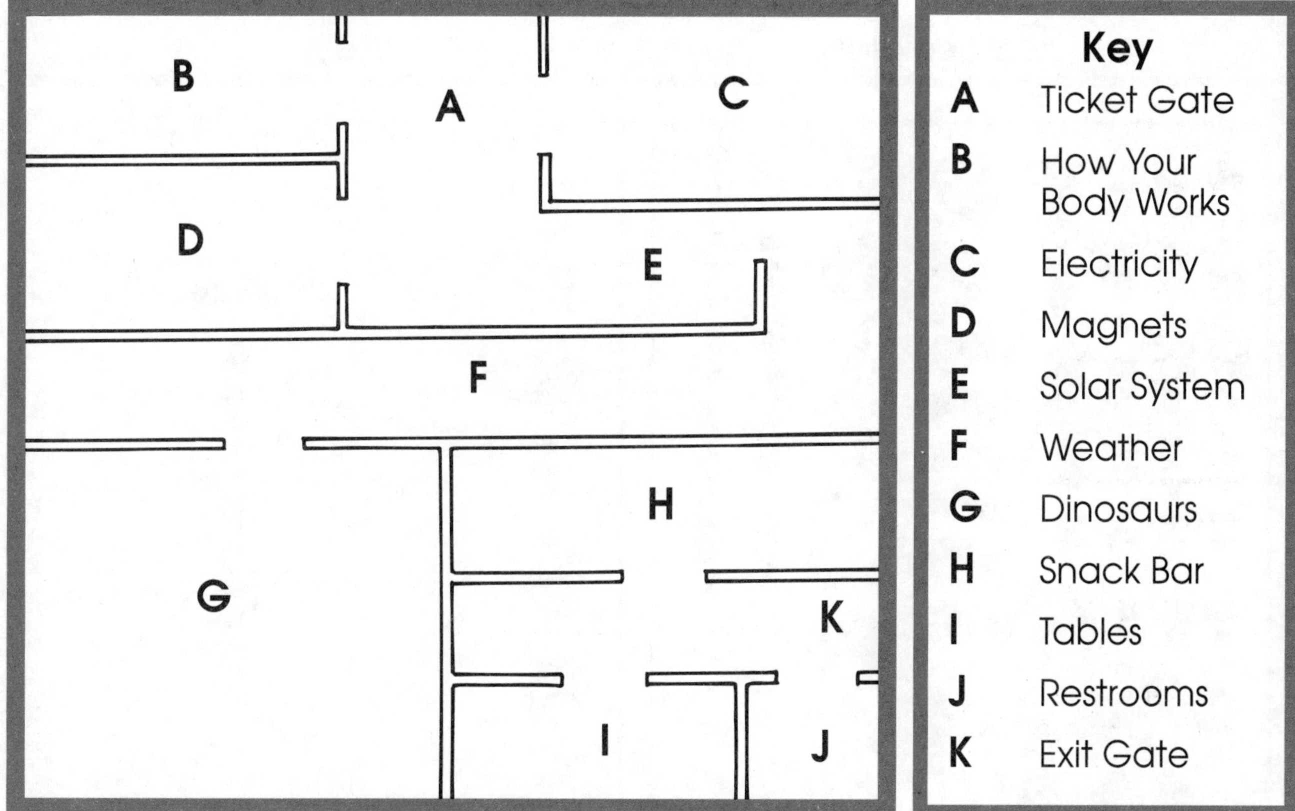

1. In which room would you go to see dinosaurs? ____________________
   Color the room brown.
2. In which room would you go to try using magnets? ______________
   Color the room blue.
3. Draw a hot dog in the snack bar.
4. Draw a table in the area in which tables are located.
5. Draw an **X** where you would buy a ticket to the museum.
6. If you go to room E, what will you learn about? ____________________

Name____

Farmer Fritz

Map symbols can tell us how many of something there are. Each symbol can stand for 1 or any number of that item. This map shows Farmer Fritz's crops. Each vegetable or fruit stands for 1 plant. Use the map and key to answer the questions.

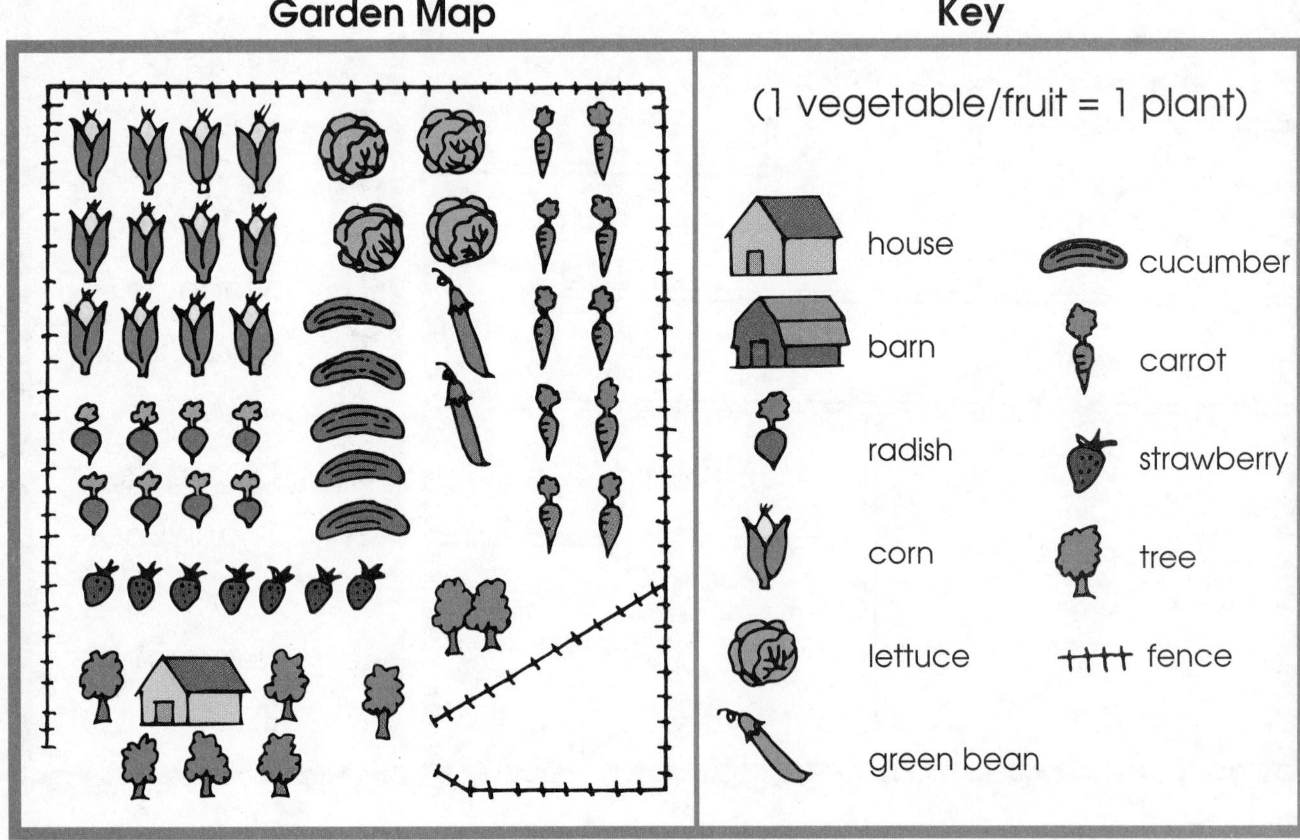

1. How many plants of each vegetable does Farmer Fritz have?

   radish ________ cucumber ________ corn ________

   carrot ________ green bean________ lettuce______

2. What fruit did Farmer Fritz plant? ______________________________

   How many of these plants did he have? ______________________________

3. Farmer Fritz planted the most of which vegetable? ________________

Name ______________________________

Carmella's Candy

Carmella made a map of her candy store so that her customers could easily find their favorite candy. Use the map and key to answer the questions.

Candy Store Map

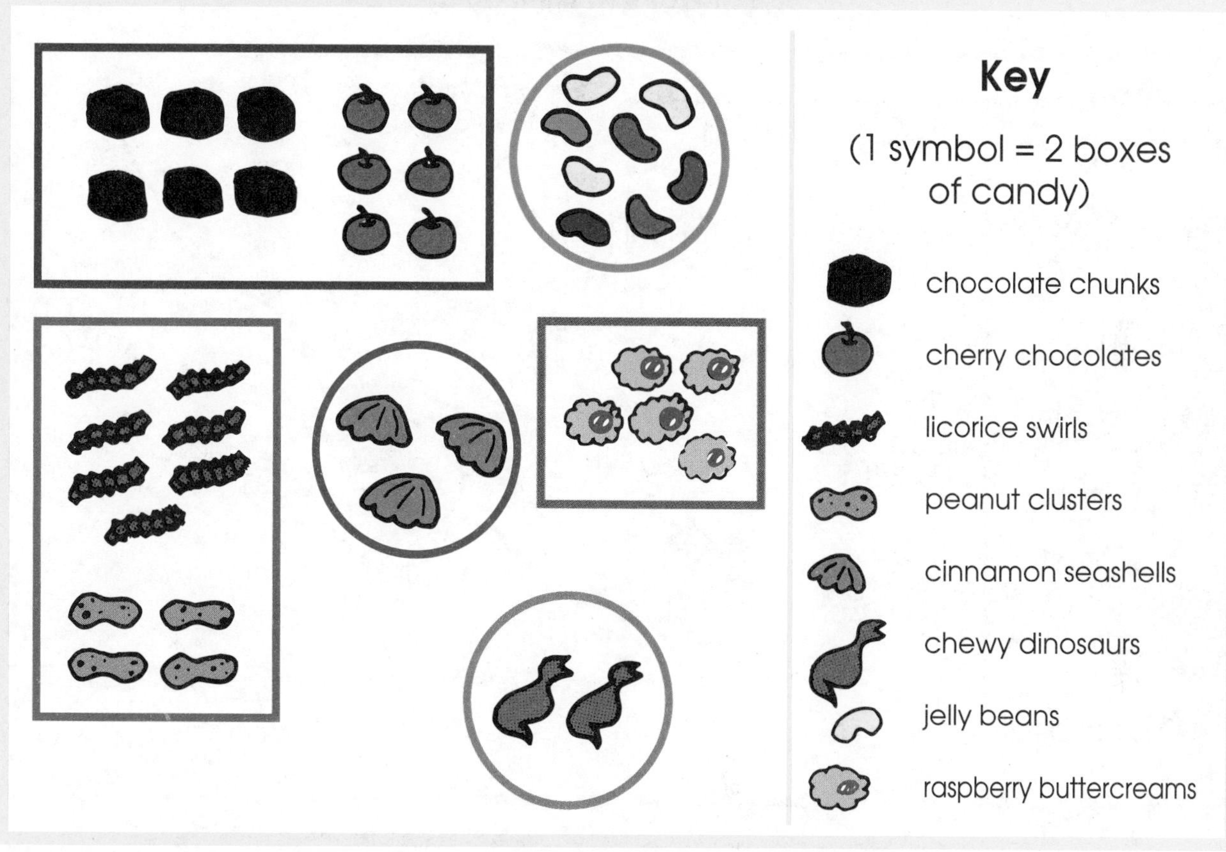

1. Each symbol equals how many boxes of candy? ____________

2. How many boxes of each kind of candy are there?

jelly beans	______	licorice swirls	______
chocolate chunks	______	cherry chocolates	______
peanut clusters	______	chewy dinosaurs	______
raspberry buttercreams	______	cinnamon seashells	______

3. Carmella has the greatest number of boxes of which candy?

____

Name____

Map Keys

Mixed-Up Map Maker

Mattie Map Maker goofed when creating a map of the state of Oopsylvania. Circle her mistakes and put a number by each one. Then, describe each error on the line with the matching number. (Hint: The key shows the correct map symbols.)

Oopsylvania Map

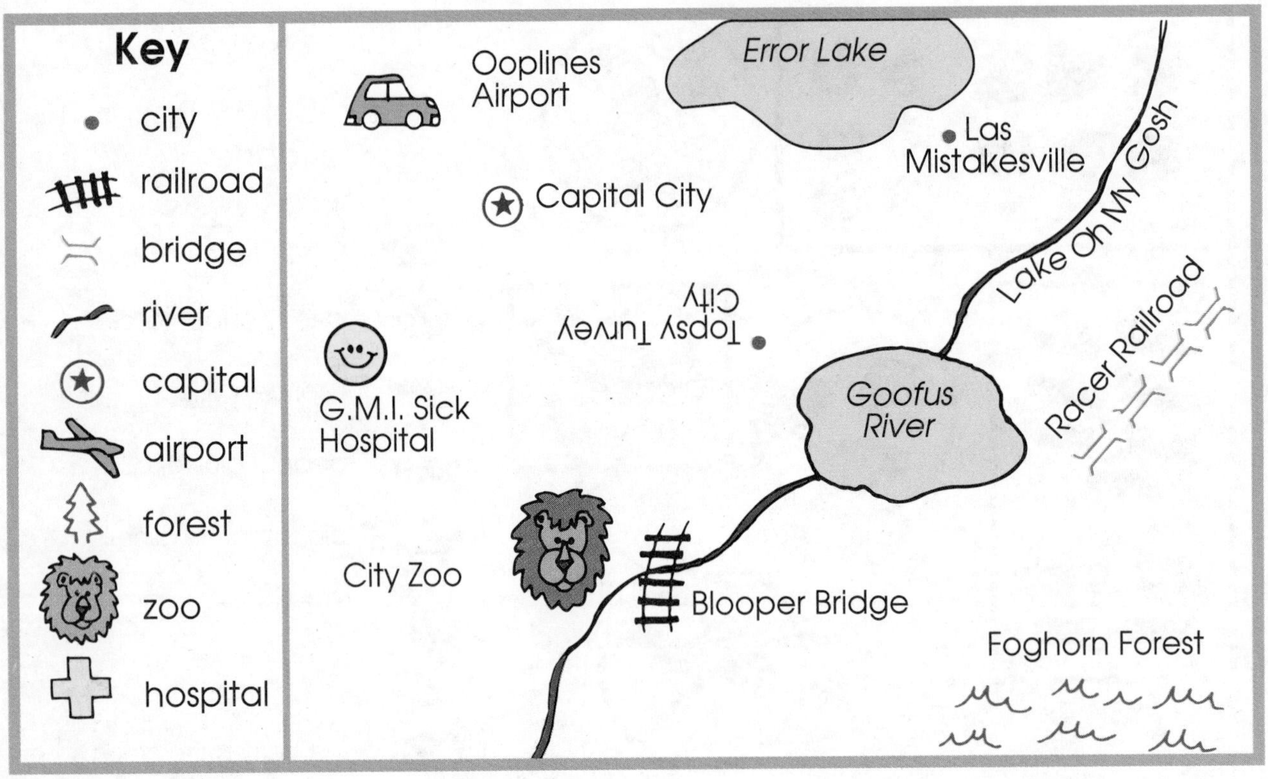

Key

- city
- railroad
- bridge
- river
- capital
- airport
- forest
- zoo
- hospital

Ooplines Airport

Error Lake

Las Mistakesville

Capital City

Lake Oh My Gosh

Topsy Turvey City

Racer Railroad

G.M.I. Sick Hospital

Goofus River

City Zoo

Blooper Bridge

Foghorn Forest

1. ____

2. ____

3. ____

4. ____

5. ____

6. ____

7. ____

8. ____

Name ____________________

Time to Go Home

This map shows routes the dinosaur can take to get to its cave. Use the key to find each symbol on the map. Then, follow the directions.

Dinosaur Cave Map

Directions:

1. Write the word **H O M E** on the dinosaur cave.
2. Color the volcano red.
3. Color the trees green.
4. Draw a blue line to show a route the dinosaur can take home that goes past the volcano.
5. Draw a yellow line to show a route the dinosaur can take home. Make the route go past the rocks.

Name____

Seeing the Wildlife

Martin and Norma are excited about visiting the Wildlife Safari. It is different from a zoo. Here they drive slowly along a road to see the animals run freely in large fenced areas. They stop at the gate to buy tickets and to get a map. They will use the map so that they will be sure to see all the animals.

Safari Map

Directions: Follow Martin and Norma's route. Write the names of the animals in the order they will see them.

1.________________________ 4.________________________

2.________________________ 5.________________________

3.________________________ 6.________________________

Name ____________________

Take a Hike

This is a map showing three hiking trails.

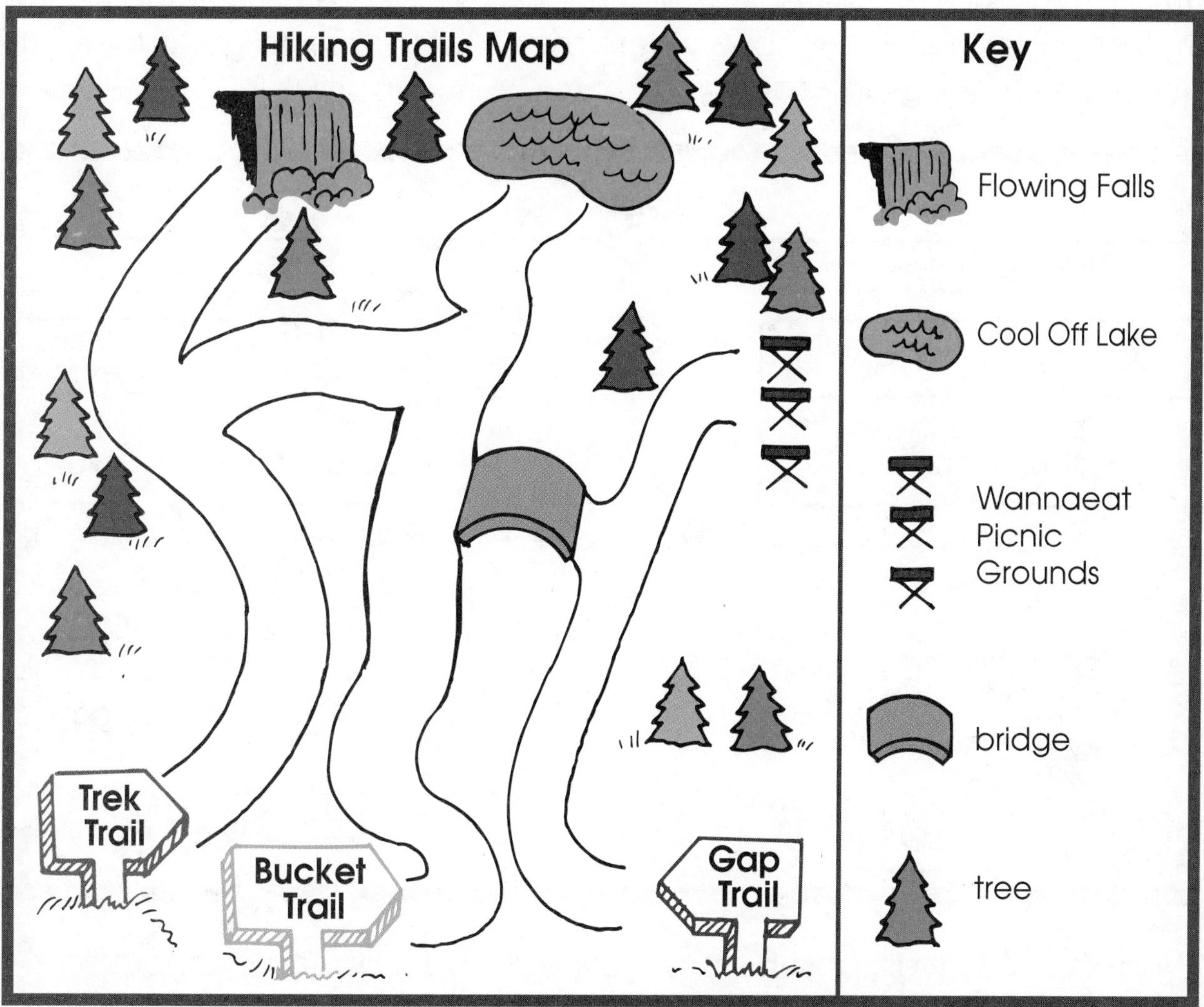

Directions:

1. Draw a red line along the trail that leads to the Wannaeat Picnic Grounds.
2. Draw a yellow line along the trail that leads to Flowing Falls.
3. Draw a green line along the trail that leads to Cool Off Lake.
4. Draw a blue line to show how you can go from Trek Trail to Cool Off Lake.
5. Draw an orange line to show how you can go from Bucket Trail to the Wannaeat Picnic Grounds.

Name____

Waiting at the Airport

Jenny and Carl went to the airport to pick up their grandparents. Dad let Mom and the kids out in front of the airport doors while he went to park the van. The dotted line (- - -) shows where they had to walk to go to the correct gate to meet their grandparents.

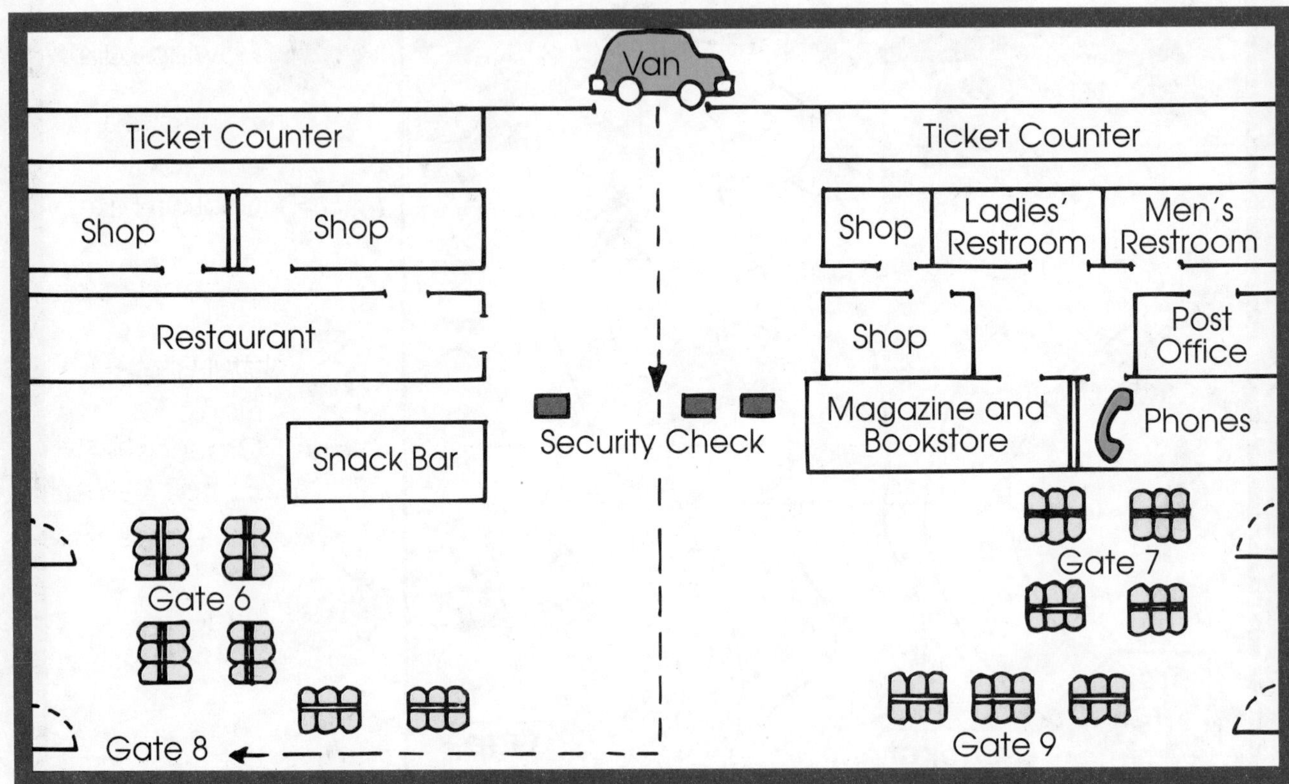

1. What did they walk past before they reached the security check?

____

____

2. Soon Dad joined them at the gate. Mom remembered she had to make a telephone call. Use an orange crayon to show the route she took to go from the gate to the telephones.

3. At what gate number will Jenny and Carl's grandparents arrive? ______

Name________________________________

A Real "Moose-tery"

Horrible Harvey Hunter has disappeared somewhere in the Mysterious Moosehead Mansion. Detective Dimwitt is trying to find him. Use the key to identify rooms in the mansion. Then, use a pencil to trace the route Detective Dimwitt took to locate the hapless Harvey.

Moosehead Mansion Map

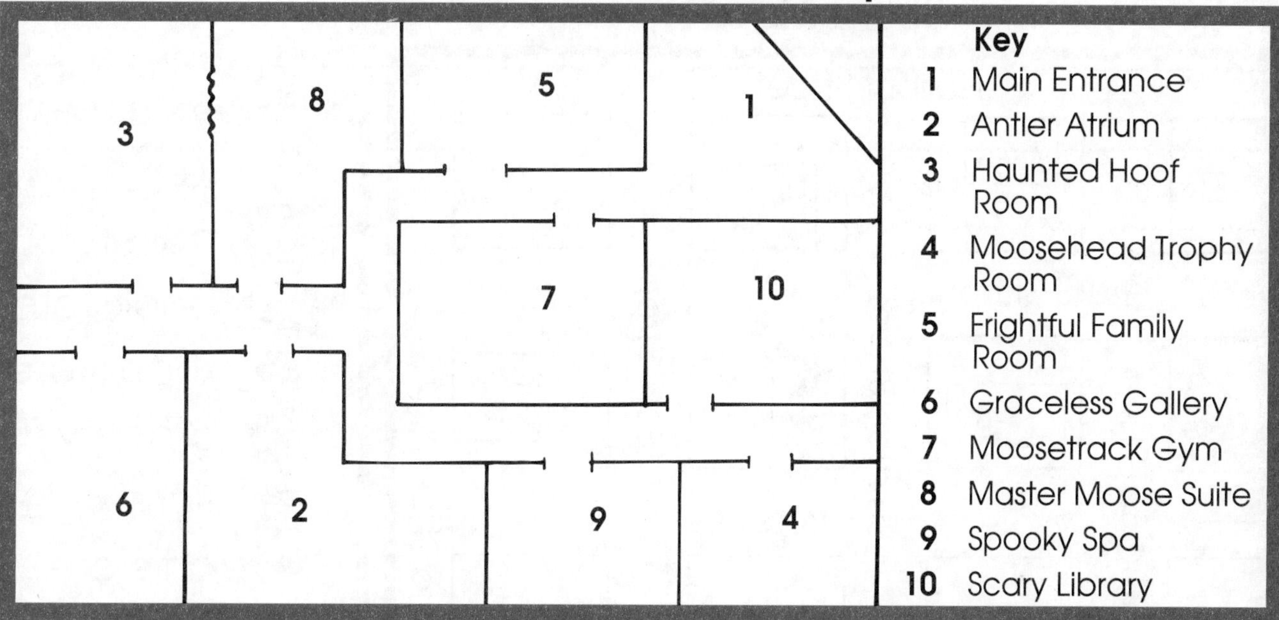

Detective Dimwitt's Route:

1. He enters the mansion at the Main Entrance.
2. Next, he checks out the Moosetrack Gym.
3. Then, he sneaks down the hall to the Antler Atrium.
4. From there he checks the Spooky Spa.
5. No luck, so on to the Scary Library he goes.
6. Next, the detective scans the Moosehead Trophy Room.
7. Then, he walks along the hall to look in the Frightful Family Room.
8. No Harvey there, so he moves on to the Graceless Gallery.
9. Could he be in the Master Moose Suite? He checks there.
10. Then, he looks in the Haunted Hoof Room.
11. There he discovers a secret room. Inside he finds Harvey reading a hunting magazine. The search is over!

Name ____________________________

Find It There

To find your way around a town or city you can use a street map.

Find the bookstore on the key. Now, find it on the map. Look at the name of the street that goes past the bookstore. If you want to go to the bookstore, you will have to go to Smelt Street.

Street Map

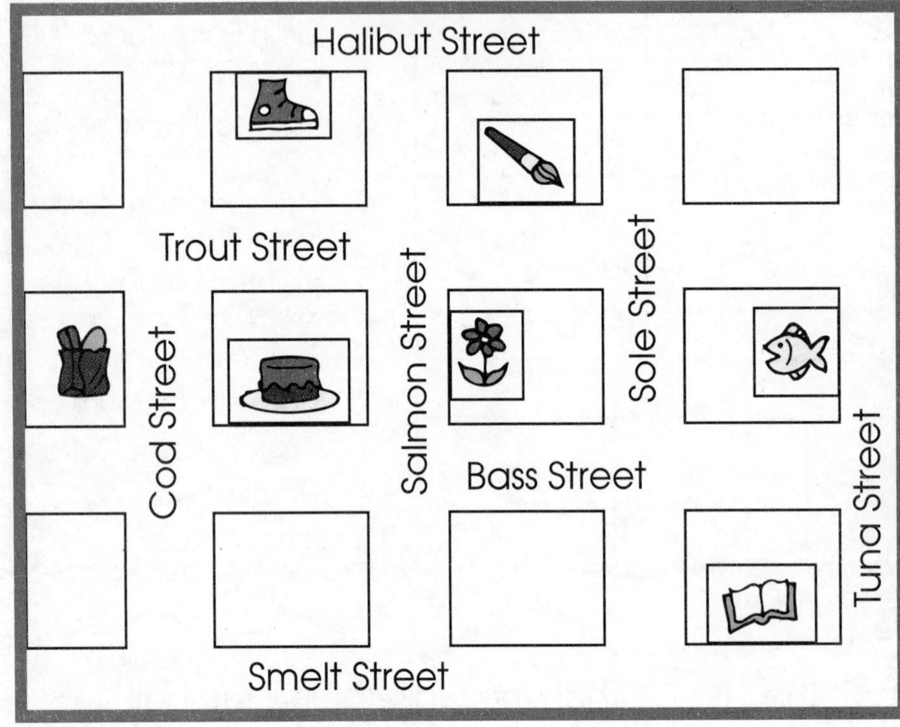

Directions:

Use the street map and map key. Fill in the blanks.

1. You can buy a cake on ____________________________ Street.
2. You can buy new shoes on ____________________________ Street.
3. You can buy a new fish tank on ____________________________ Street.
4. What store is on Salmon Street? ____________________________

Name____________________

Going from Place to Place

Some maps show you where places are located in a town.

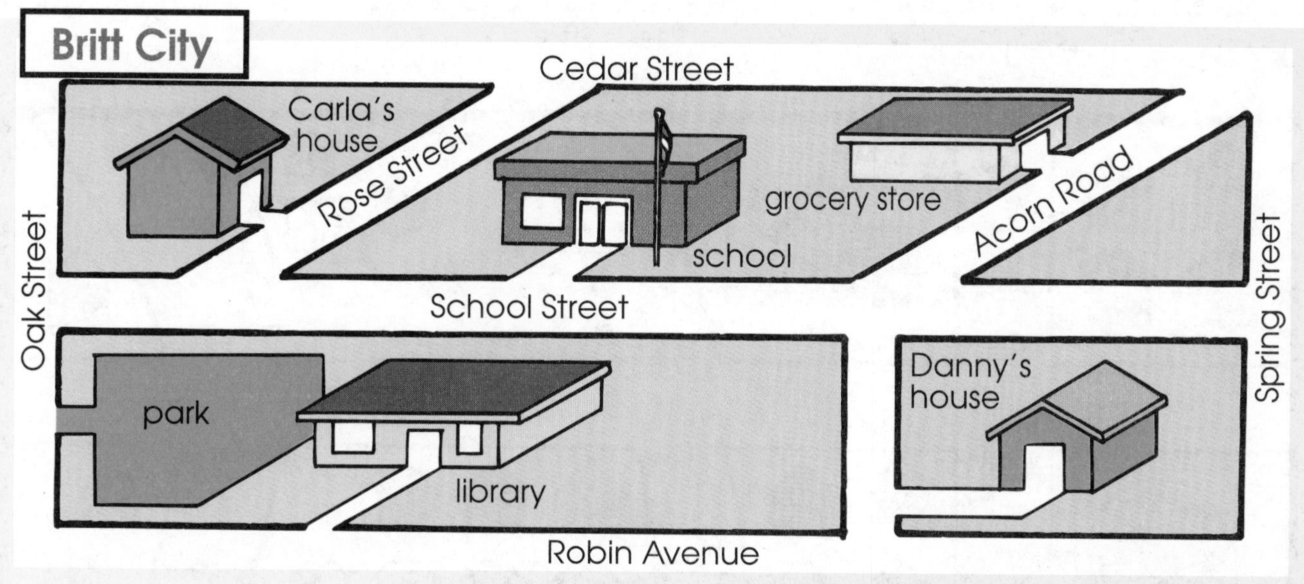

Circle the word that tells which is **closest** to Danny's house.

1. Carla's house	OR	the library
2. Robin Avenue	OR	Oak Street
3. the park	OR	the grocery store
4. Spring Street	OR	Cedar Street

Circle the word that tells which is **farthest** from Carla's house.

1. Spring Street	OR	Rose Street
2. the park	OR	Danny's house
3. the school	OR	the library
4. Oak Street	OR	Acorn Road

Add the following items to the map of Britt City.

1. Draw a flower garden on the corner of Spring Street and Robin Avenue.
2. Draw a swimming pool behind Carla's house.
3. Draw a baseball or football field behind the school.
4. Draw a car in front of Carla's house.
5. Draw a school bus on School Street.
6. Use a red crayon to draw the shortest path from Carla's house to Danny's.

Name________________________________

Victory Celebration

Betsy, Rachel and Pat were so happy! They won their first baseball game. To celebrate, they wanted to have pizza and ice cream. Use this map and key to complete page 33.

Map

Baseline Avenue
Center Street
Second Street
Fielding Street
Oak Street
Pine Road
R
P
B

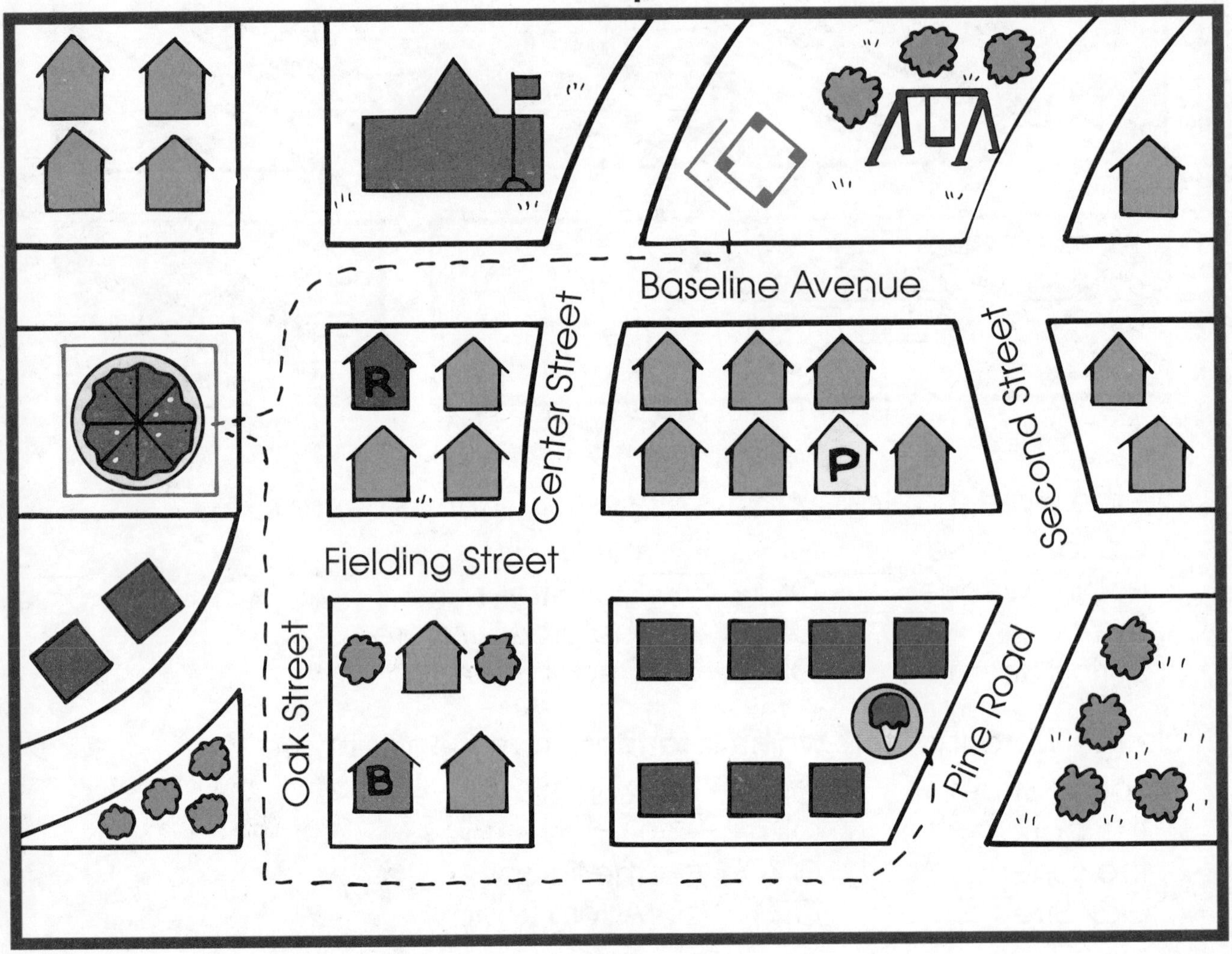

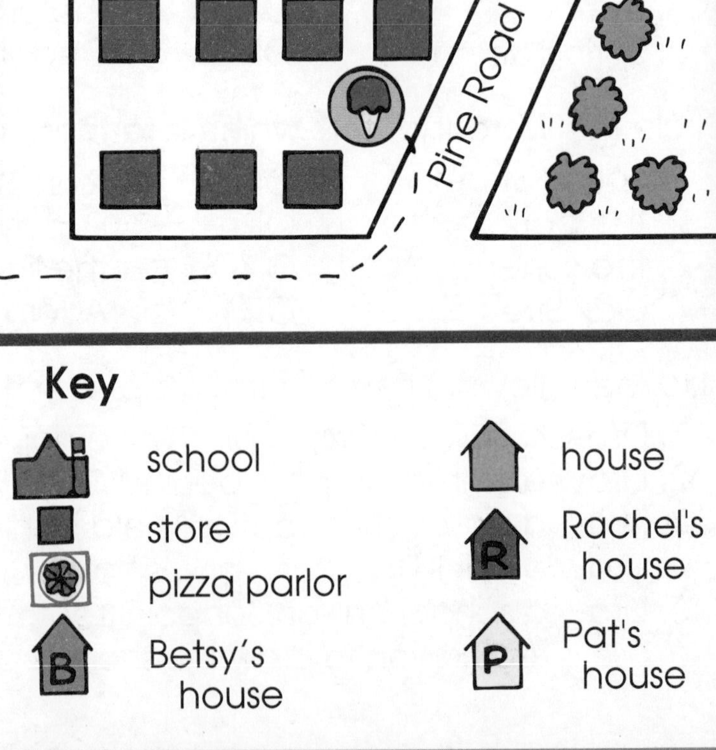

Key

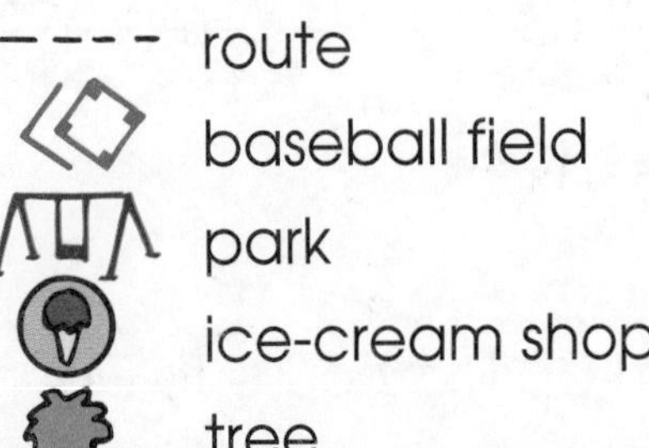

route
baseball field
park
ice-cream shop
tree
school
store
pizza parlor
Betsy's house
house
Rachel's house
Pat's house
R
B
P

Name_______________________________________

Victory Celebration

1. Use your finger to follow the route the girls took from the baseball field to the pizza parlor. On what street did they walk when they first left the baseball field?

   ____

2. Did they walk past the school? ___________________________

3. Did they walk past a park? ___________________________

4. On what street is the pizza parlor? ___________________________

5. Use your finger to trace their route to the ice-cream shop. On what street is the ice-cream shop?

   ____

6. Then, it was time to go home. Use a blue crayon to mark a route Betsy might have taken home.

7. Use a red crayon to mark a route Rachel might have taken home.

8. Use a purple crayon to mark a route Pat might have taken home.

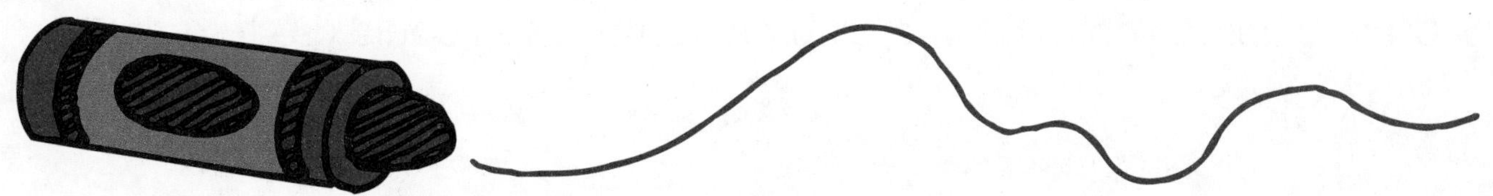

Name ____________________________________

A New Puppy

Mike's dog had puppies. Jason and his parents are going to Mike's house to get one of the puppies. Use the street map and key to help you answer the questions.

Map

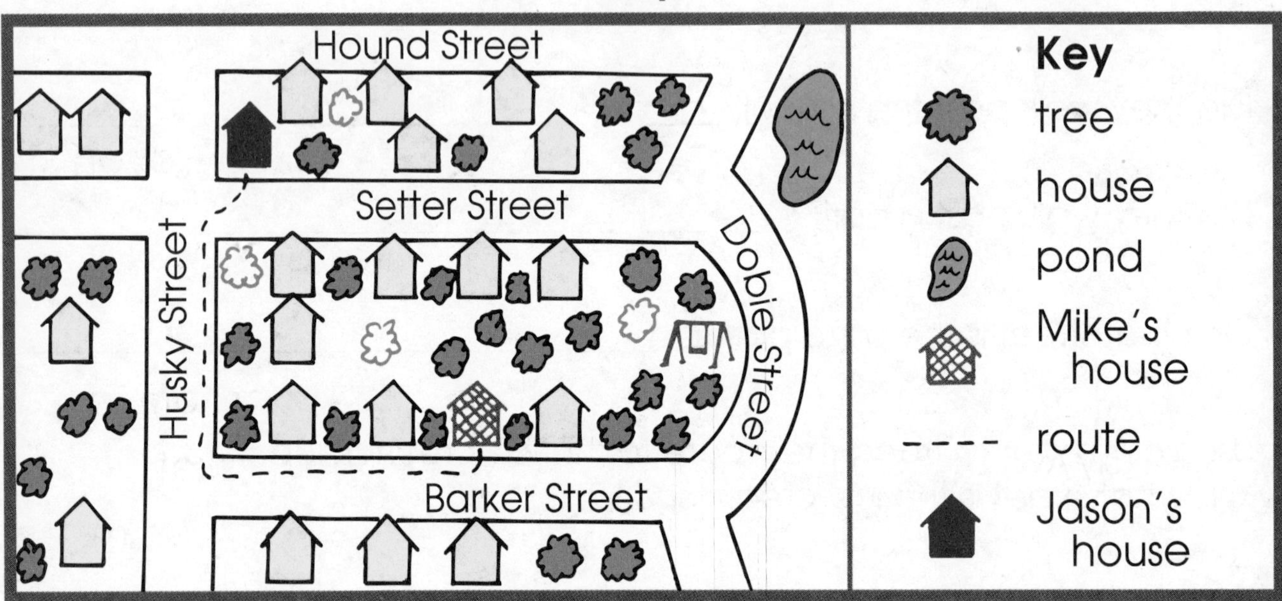

1. Find Jason's house. On what street does he live?

____

2. Find Mike's house. On what street does he live?

____

3. Use a red crayon to trace the route Mike drew for Jason to follow.

4. Which streets will Jason use to get to Mike's house?

____

5. Use a blue crayon to draw a different route Jason could use to get to Mike's house.

Name___________________________________

Places to Go

Mrs. Nelson needs to do many errands this afternoon. She only has a short time in which to do everything. Read Mrs. Nelson's list of things to do. Use the street map and key to answer the questions.

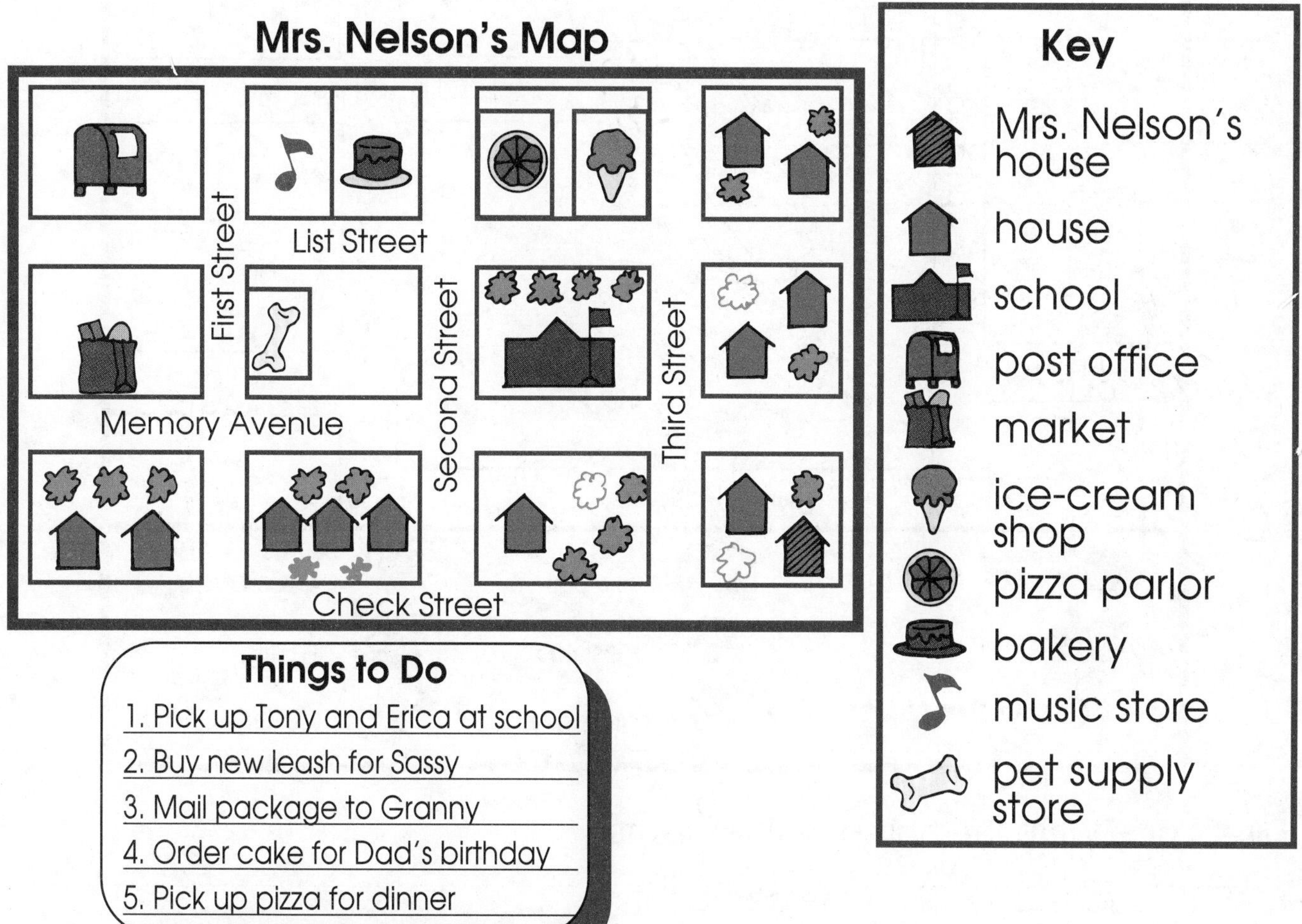

1. On the map, find the places Mrs. Nelson needs to go.
2. Mrs. Nelson will go to these places in the same order as her list of things to do. Write the number on each place on the map to show the order in which she will go to these places.
3. Start at Mrs. Nelson's house. Use a red crayon to draw the route Mrs. Nelson will take to do all of her errands.

Name ________________________________

My Home Town

Complete the map by drawing the symbols from the key by each matching number on the map.

Map

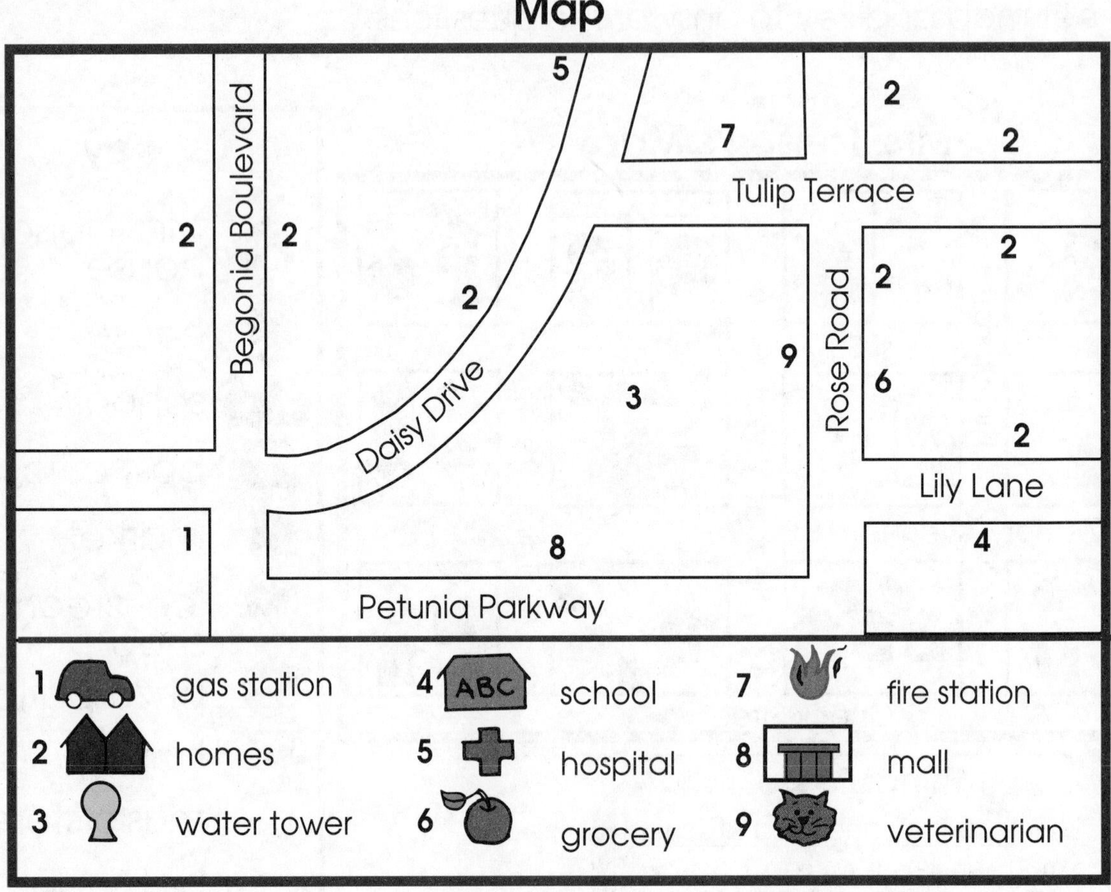

Directions: Write the name of the streets.

1. The gas station is on the corner of ____________________ and ____________________.
2. The vet is on ____________________.
3. The fire station is on ____________________.
4. There are no homes on ____________________.
5. The school is on ____________________.
6. The grocery store is on ____________________.

Name____

The Compass Rose

This is a compass rose. It tells the directions on a map. There are four arrows. Each arrow points in a different direction. These are called **cardinal** directions.

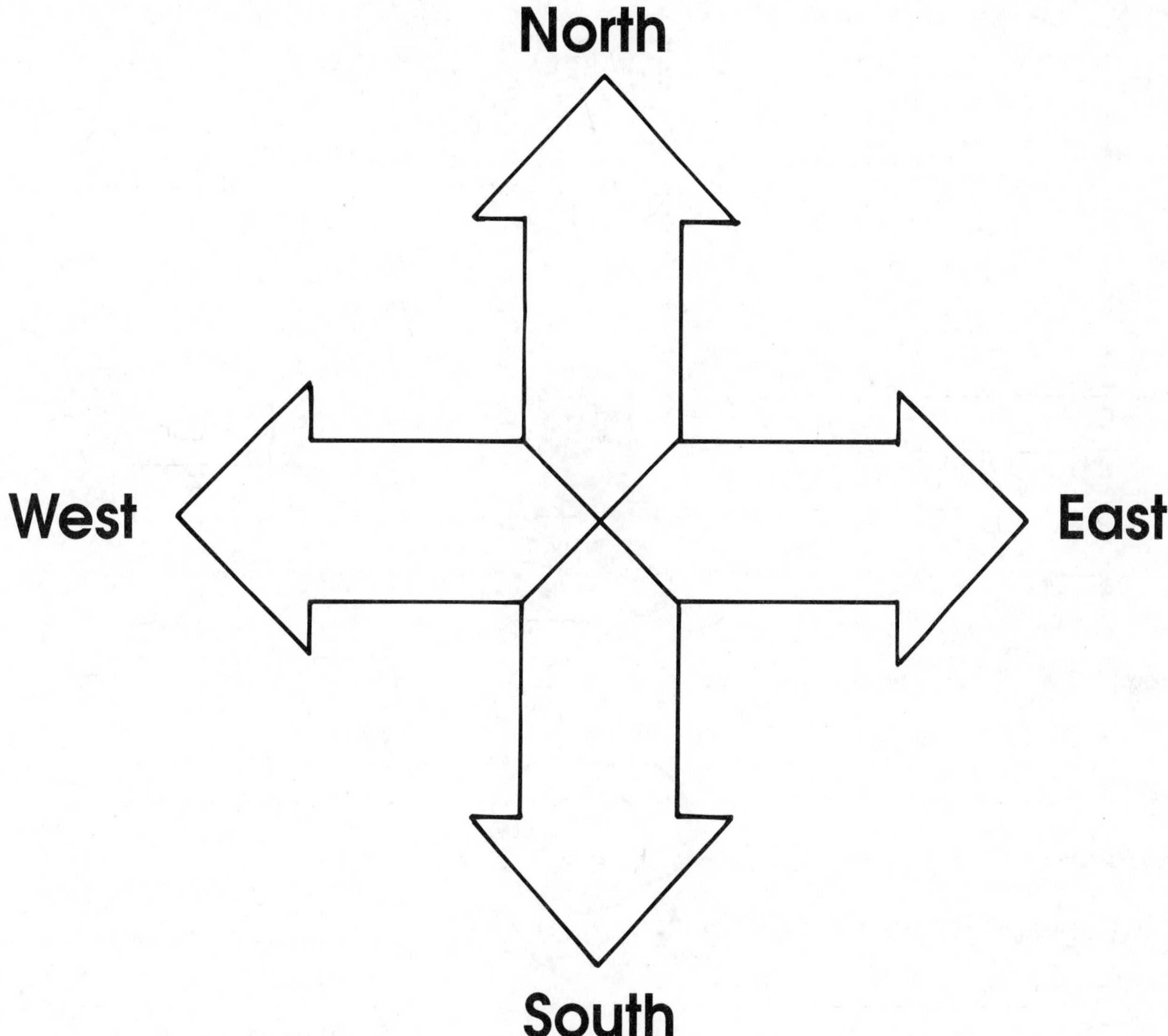

1. The arrow that points up is **north**. Color it blue.
2. The arrow that points down is **south**. Color it red.
3. The arrow that points to the right is **east**. Color it green.
4. The arrow that points to the left is **west**. Color it brown.

Name_______________________________________

Compasses

Finding a Snack

The little bear cub is hungry for a snack. Read the clues. In each bear paw print, draw a picture of the snack he will find if he goes in that direction. Use the compass rose to help you.

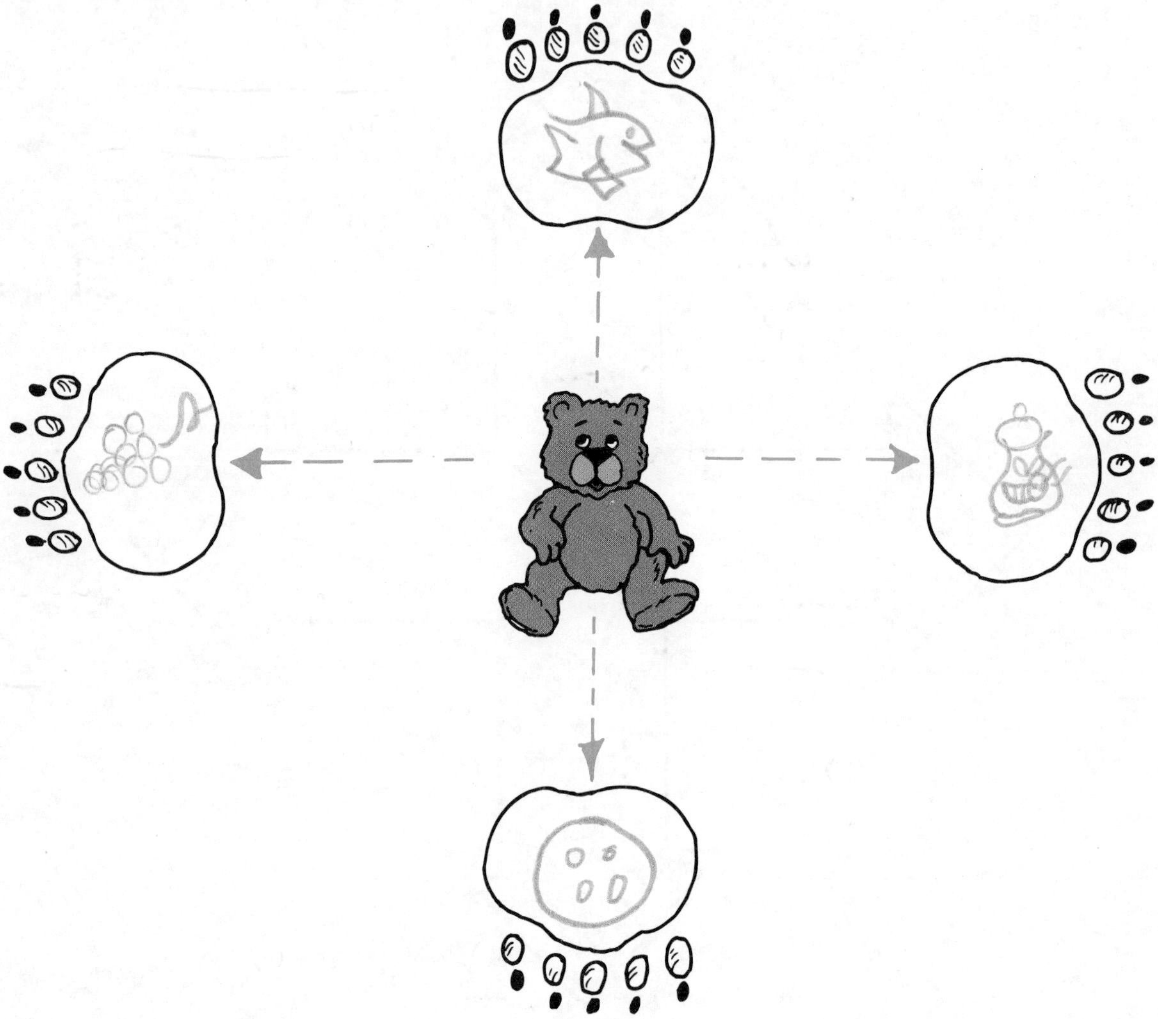

1. He will find [grapes] to the **west**.
2. He will find [cookie] to the **south**.
3. He will find [fish] to the **north**.
4. He will find  to the **east**.

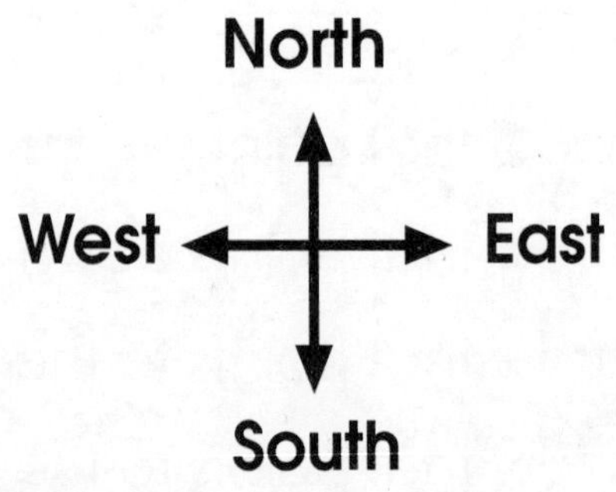

Name ______________________________

Pirate's Booty

Sedgewick the Pirate must be able to find his buried treasure when he returns to the island. Read the sentences. Write the words **north**, **south**, **east** and **west** in the blanks to help Sedgewick locate his treasure. Use the compass rose to help you.

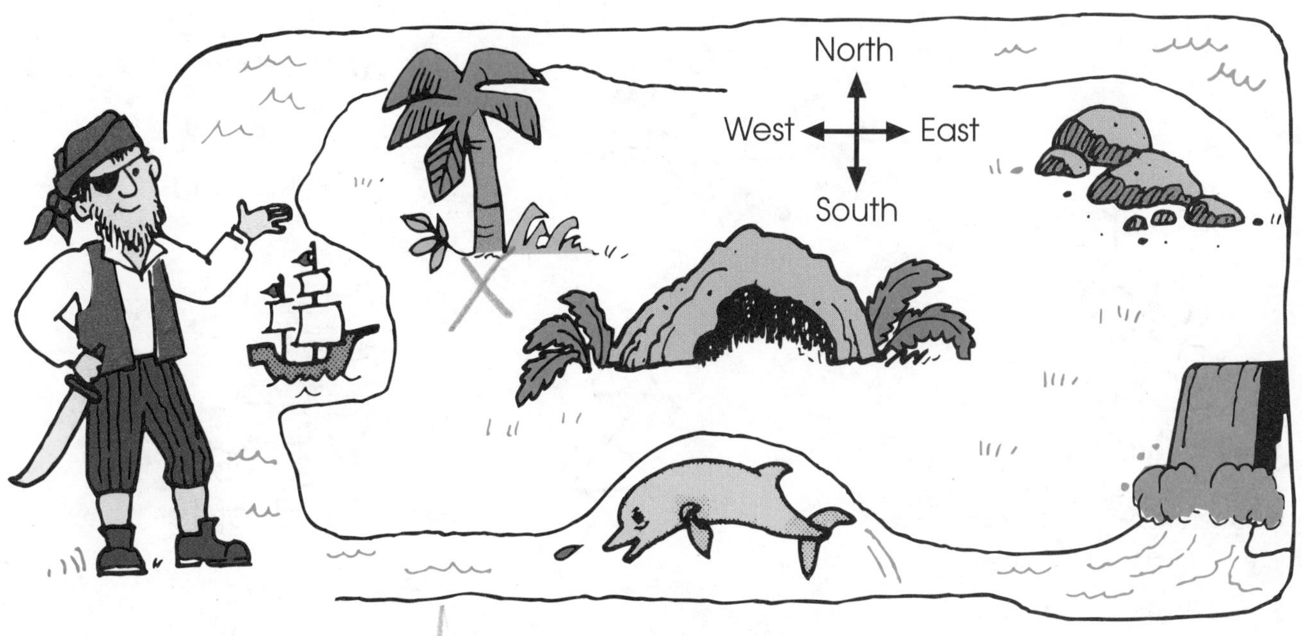

1. Dock the ship on the ___West___ side of the island.
2. Walk ___east___ to the cave.
3. Then, walk ___South___ to Dolphin Cove.
4. Go ___East___ to the waterfall.
5. Go ___North___ to the rocks.
6. Then, go ___West___ to the palm tree.
7. Draw an **X** below the palm tree to show where the treasure is buried.

Name ____________________

Compasses

Look to the Sky

Mr. McGill took his students on a field trip to the airport. A boy in his class drew this map of things they saw.

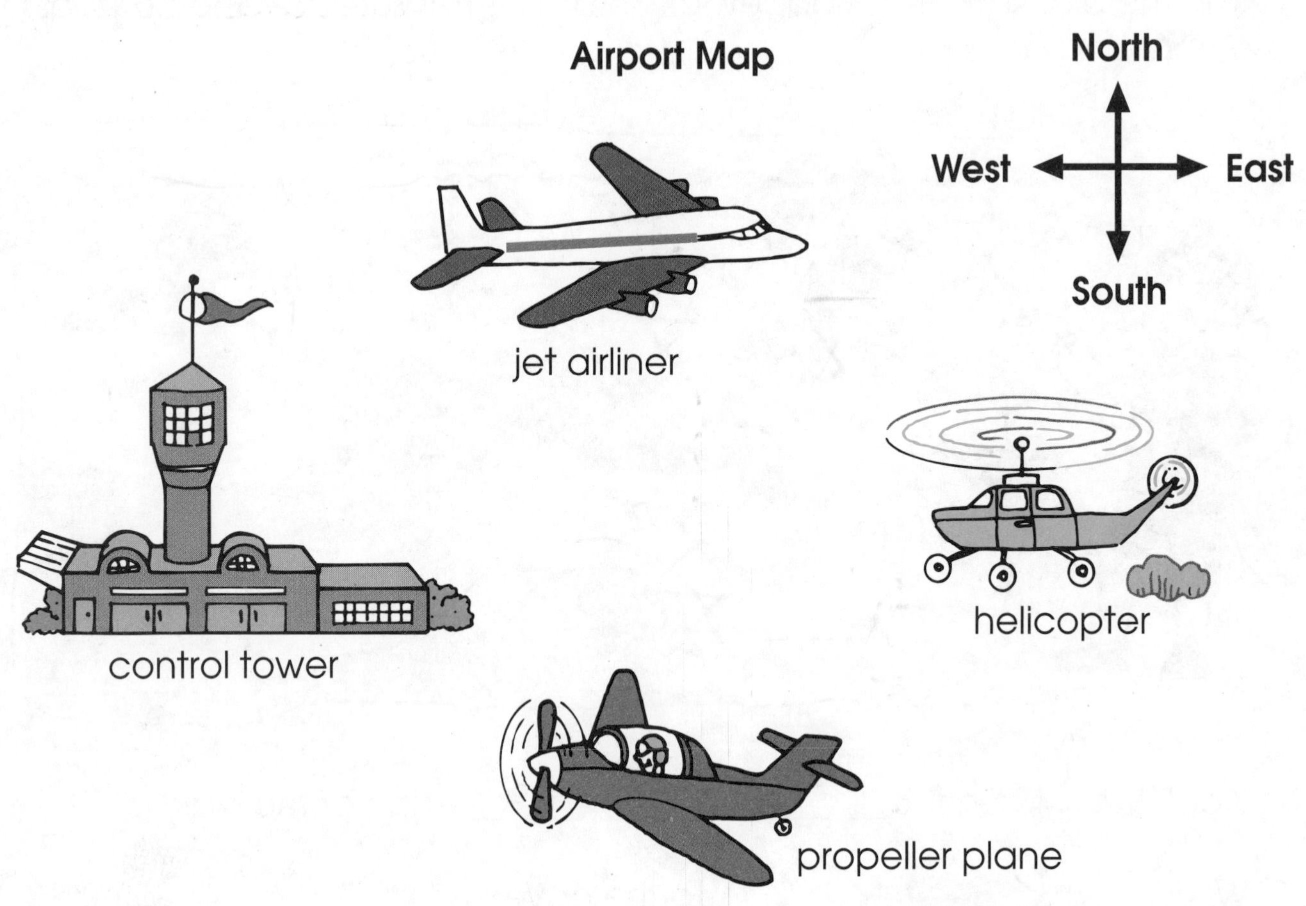

Directions: Write **north, south, west** or **east** to complete each sentence.

1. Look North to see the jet airliner.

2. Look West to see the control tower.

3. Look South to see the propeller plane.

4. Look East to see the helicopter.

Name Stephanie Rocha

Sign Search

Gina went for a hike. She found a piece of paper. There were strange directions written on it. Then, she looked around and saw pictures drawn on the rocks in the area. Aha! The paper she had found was a route to follow. Read the directions and draw the route on the map.

Map

1. Start at the fish.
2. Go north to the corn.
3. Then go east to the hunter.
4. Go south to the river.
5. Go west to the buffalo.
6. Go south to the tree.
7. Go east to the arrowhead.
8. Go north to the cave. Draw a picture on the cave to show the treasure chest Gina finds there.

Name ______________________________

What Do Hikers See?

Follow the directions to complete this area map.

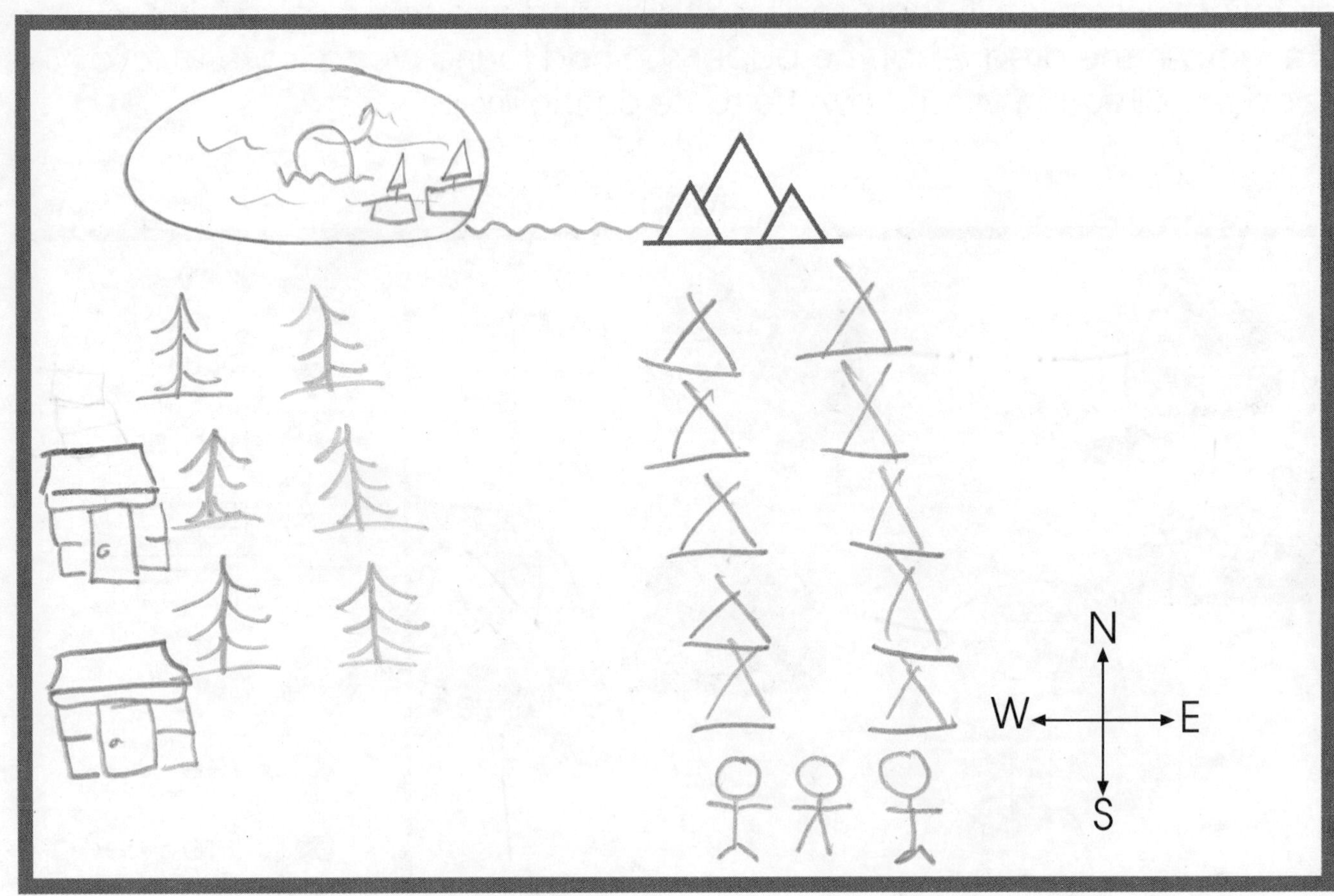

1. Draw a (lake) west of the (mountains).
2. Draw 6 (trees) south of the (lake).
3. Draw an (island) in the middle of the (lake).
4. Draw 10 (tents) south of the (mountains).
5. Draw a (river) between the (mountains) and the (lake).
6. Draw 2 (boats) on the east side of the (lake).
7. Draw 2 (cabins) south of the 6 (trees).
8. Draw 3 (hikers) south of the (tents).

Name Stephanie Rocha #20

You're Invited

Liz sent out invitations to her birthday party. She drew a map to show how to go from school to her house.

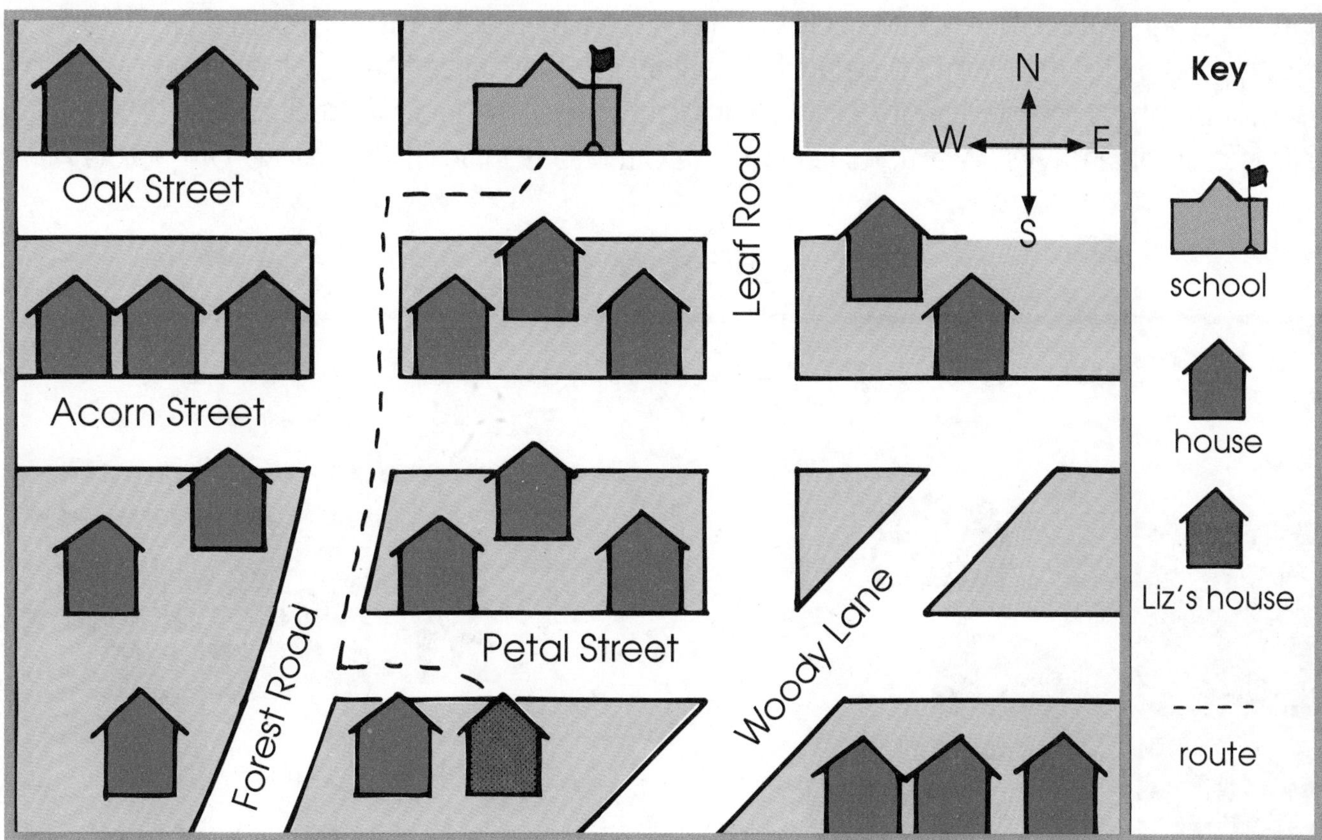

Directions:

Write **north**, **south**, **east** or **west** and the street name to complete the sentences.

1. Leave the school and go West along Oak Street.
2. Turn South onto Forest Road.
3. Then, turn East onto Petal Street.

Name____

Missing Diamonds

Mrs. Wently's diamonds are missing. Seth Sleuth has been hired to find them. He listens to Mrs. Wently's story. She had seen the robber run through the library and out onto the balcony. Then, he jumped to the ground and ran away. Seth Sleuth went to search the library. Perhaps the robber had hidden the diamonds in the library and planned to come back later to get them. This is a map of Mrs. Wently's library. Read more about the case on page 45.

Library Map

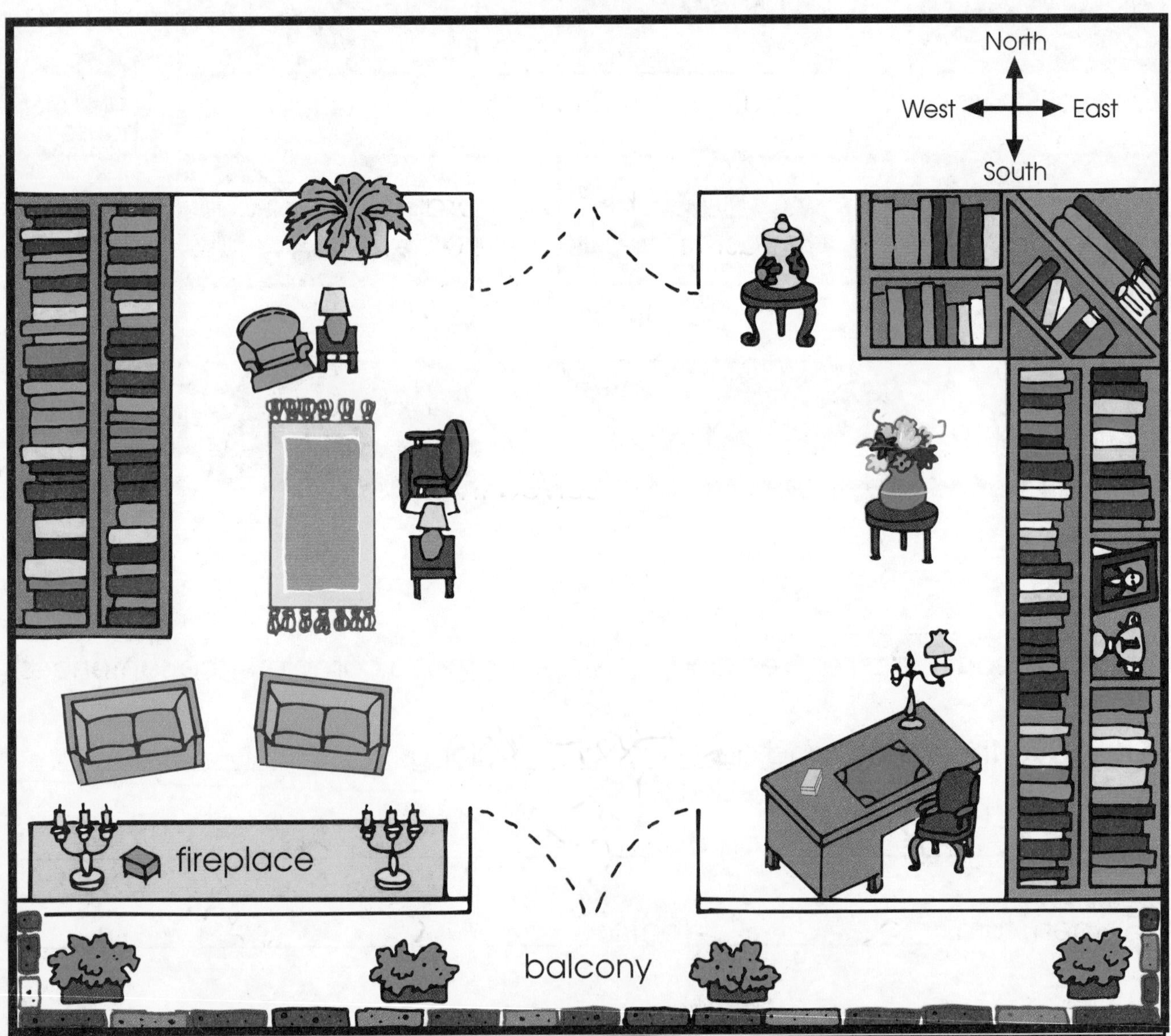

Name____________________________________

Missing Diamonds

Can you find the missing diamonds? Help Seth Sleuth search the library. Read the directions. Use the compass rose to help you. Use a red crayon to draw the route on the library map to show where you search.

1. You walk through the doors at the north end of the library.
2. Walk west to the bookcase and look behind every book.
3. Now, walk south to the fireplace. Look around the things on the mantel.
4. Walk north to the rug. There's a lump! Lift the rug. It is only the cat's toy mouse.
5. Walk east and then south to the balcony doors. Maybe the robber hid the diamonds outside. Look out on the balcony. No diamonds there.
6. Hmmmm. The diamonds must be in the library. Go back inside the balcony doors. Walk east to the desk. No diamonds in sight.
7. Walk north and look behind every book. Look inside the vase on the small table. Nothing there.
8. Head west and then north to look at the beautiful jar. Lift the lid. Inside are the sparkling diamonds. Draw a ◇ where you found the missing diamonds. Congratulations! You solved the case.

Name____

Ice Cream!

Ding. Ding. Ding-a-ling! Here comes the ice-cream truck. On hot summer days, Stan drives his ice-cream truck around the neighborhood. He takes the same route every day. This map shows the neighborhood where Stan drives. Follow the directions on page 47.

Ice-Cream Truck Route Map

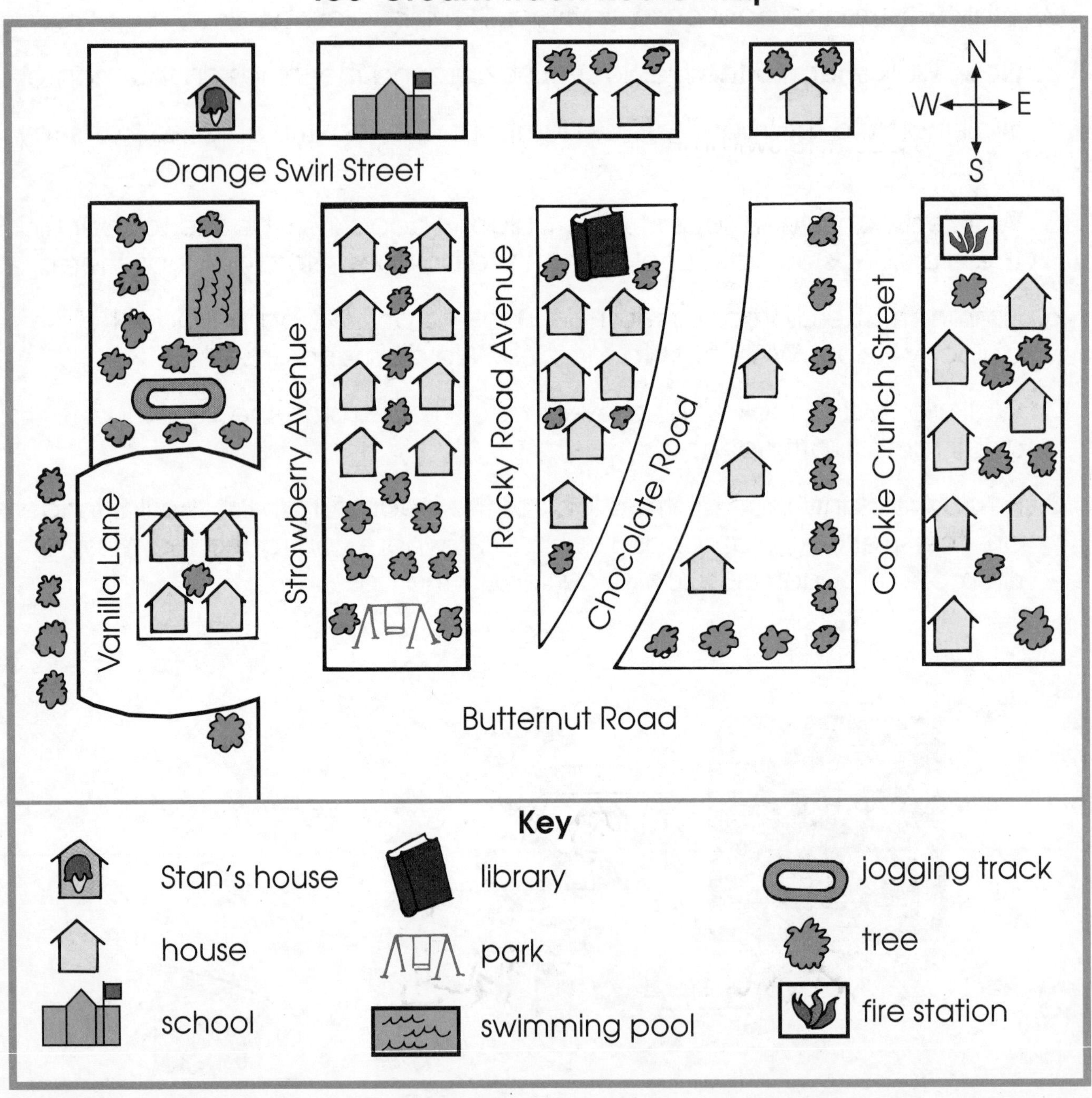

Name____________________________________

Ice Cream!

Draw Stan's route on the map on page 46. To do this, read the information below. Use the map key and compass rose to help you.

1. Stan backs out of his driveway onto Orange Swirl Street.
2. He goes east.
3. Then, he turns south onto Strawberry Avenue.
4. He drives past the swimming pool. After he passes the jogging track, he turns west onto Vanilla Lane.
5. He drives around Vanilla Lane. Then, he drives east on Butternut Road past the park.
6. He turns and drives north along Rocky Road Avenue.
7. At the corner he turns and drives east along Orange Swirl Street.
8. He passes the library and drives south along Chocolate Road.
9. He turns east onto Butternut Road and drives past the row of trees.
10. Then, he turns north and drives along Cookie Crunch Street.
11. He passes the fire station and turns west and drives along Orange Swirl Street until he reaches his home.

Name________________________________

Secret Mission

Sam Super Spy is on a mission. He must get the secret papers and deliver them to his boss as soon as possible. This is a map of where the mission is to take place. Follow the directions on page 49 to help Sam.

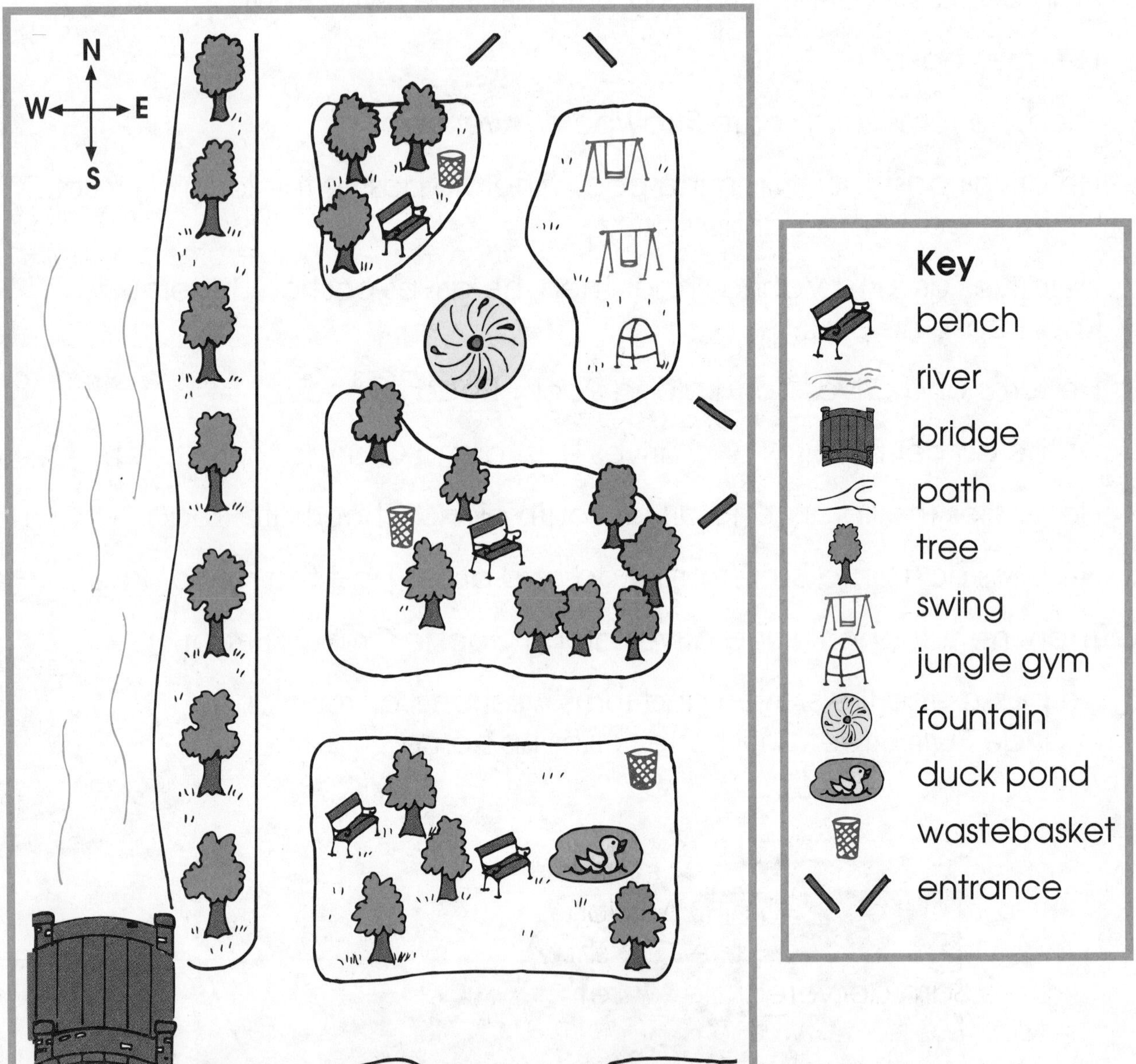

Name________________________________

Secret Mission

Directions: Use a red crayon to mark the route Sam will take.

1. Enter the park through the entrance at the north end of the park.
2. Turn and walk east and then south past the swings and jungle gym.
3. Turn and go west to the fountain.
4. Walk to the south side of the fountain.
5. Walk to the bench south of the fountain.
6. You will find the papers you want under the wastebasket to the west of the bench. Draw a red **X** on where Sam finds the secret papers.

Now, Sam must deliver the secret papers to his boss. Use a blue crayon to mark the route Sam will take. Start at the red **X** you drew.

1. Walk south to the path.
2. Turn and walk east along the path to the wastebasket.
3. Turn and walk south near the duck pond.
4. Walk south to the path.
5. Turn and walk west toward the bridge.
6. There is a man standing under the tree north of the bridge. Sam hands the secret papers to him. Mission completed! Draw a blue **X** to show where Sam delivered the secret papers.

Name ____________________________________

Connect - A - Dot

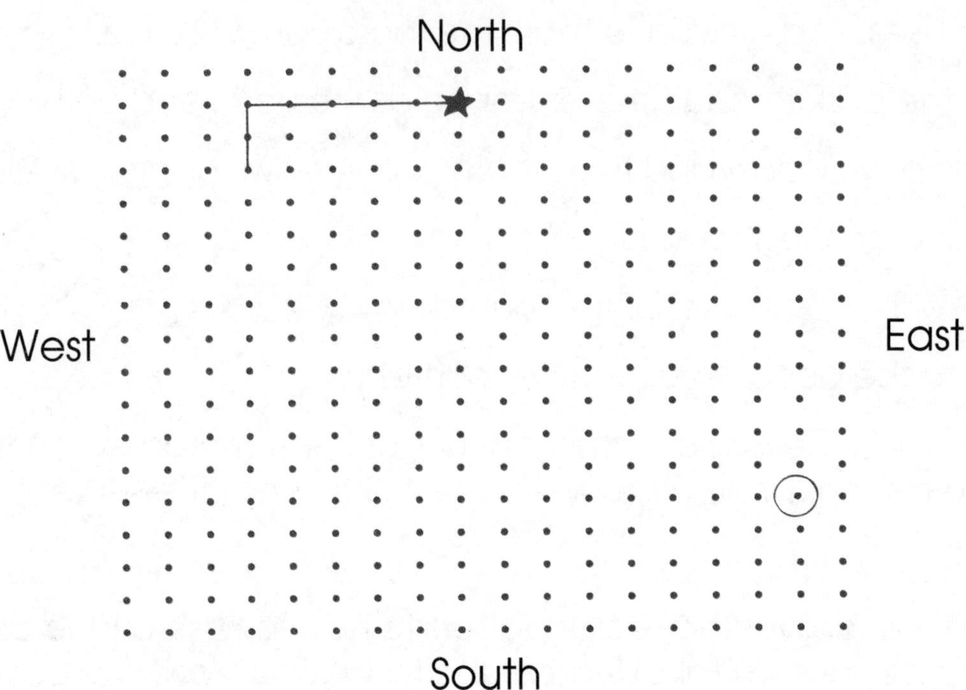

Directions: Follow the instructions below to complete a drawing. Begin at the star. The first two steps are done for you.

Draw a straight line . . .

1. Five spaces west.
2. Two spaces south.
3. Four spaces east.
4. Nine spaces south.
5. Two spaces east.
6. Nine spaces north.
7. Four spaces east.
8. Two spaces north.
9. Five spaces west.

What letter did you draw? ____________

Begin at the circle to complete another drawing.

Draw a straight line . . .

1. Four spaces south.
2. One space west.
3. Three spaces north.
4. One space west.
5. One space north.
6. Two spaces east.

What number did you draw? _________

Name____

Finding Your Way Around Town

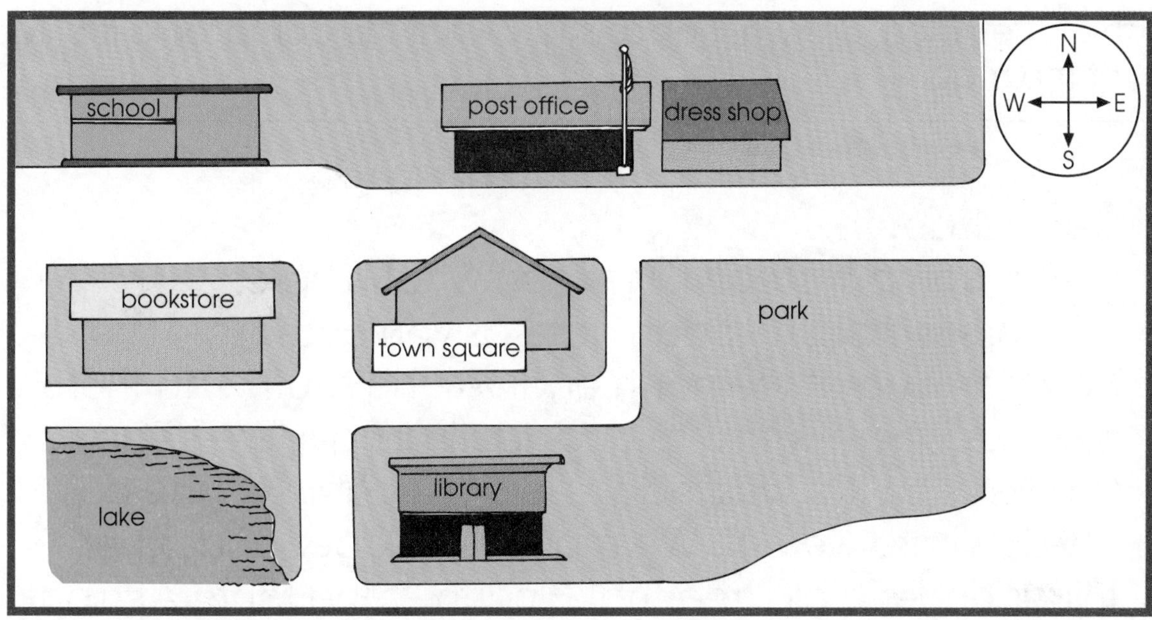

Directions: You are in the middle of the town square. Circle the correct answer to each question.

1. What direction is the library from you?	north	west	south
2. What direction is the bookstore from you?	west	east	south
3. What direction must you go to reach the post office?	east	north	west
4. Which direction must you go to get to the park?	north	west	east

Use crayons or markers to complete the map.

1. Place a red **X** on the first place north of the library.
2. Place a black **X** on the place east of the post office.
3. Draw a red circle on the place west of the dress shop.
4. Draw a blue fish on the place south of the bookstore.
5. Draw three trees east of the library.
6. Draw a movie theater east of the dress shop.
7. Draw a car south of the dress shop.
8. Draw a slide east of the school and west of the post office.
9. Draw doors and windows on the first building north of the lake.
10. Draw a yellow bus south of the place which is west of the post office.

Name____

A Great Camp!

Read the letter. Then, draw a map to show what the camp looks like. Make a key for the map.

June 20, 1998

Dear Elizabeth,

This camp is great! I'll tell you what is here.

There is a big wooden gate as you come into the campground at the north end. At the south end there is a lake where we swim and ride in boats. We sleep in five tents on the west side. A big log cabin on the east side is where we eat. We make necklaces and other things under a big tree that is north of the tents. At night we sing songs and tell stories around a campfire south of the log cabin.

Hope you are having fun at home. See you soon.

Your friend,
Sandy

Camp Map

N
W E
S

Key

Name ______________________________

Making a Compass

A compass is a magnet that can identify geographic direction. It is very easy and a lot of fun to make your own compass!

You will need:
magnet
steel sewing needle
piece of thin plastic foam
(from fast-food packaging)
shallow glass or plastic bowl
masking tape
water

Directions:

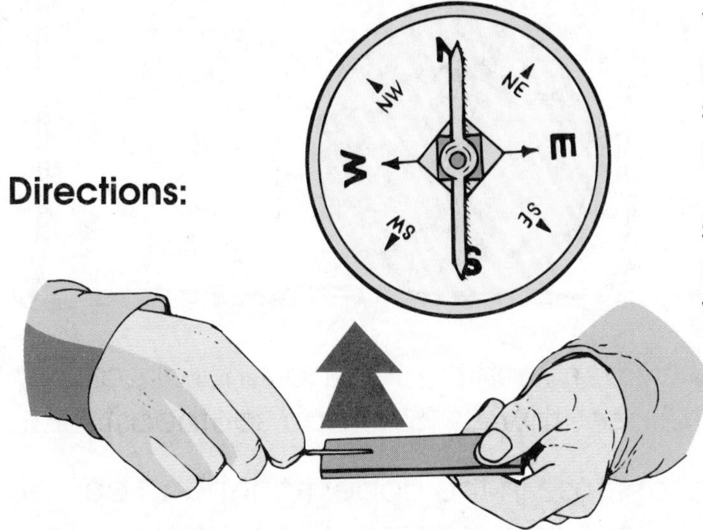

1. Pull the sewing needle toward you across the magnet. Repeat this 20 times. Be sure to always pull in the same direction.

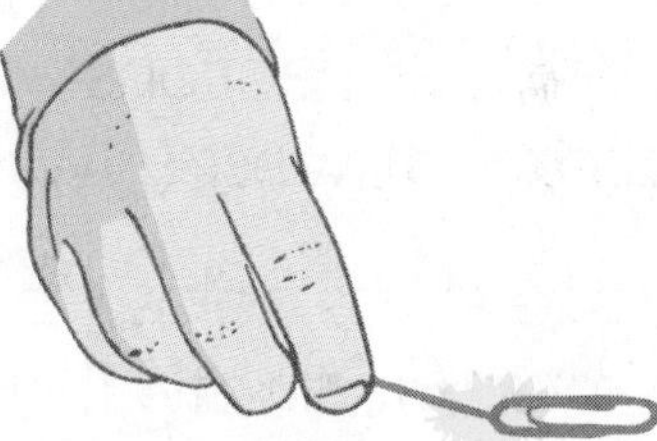

2. Test your needle on a steel object. If it is not yet magnetized, repeat step #1.

3. Tape the needle to a small piece of plastic foam.

4. Float your magnet in a dish of water.

What happened?

Wait for your floating needle to stop spinning. In what direction is it pointing?

____

Try giving the floating needle a little spin. Wait for it to stop spinning.

Now what direction is it pointing? ______________________________

Name____

Drawing a Compass Rose

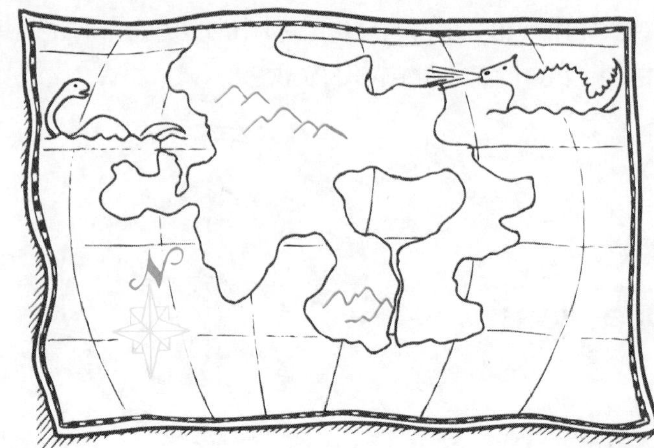

The maps of the early explorers were beautiful pieces of art. Their maps would often have pictures of fire-breathing dragons and sea monsters warning of dangers where they were traveling.

In a corner of their map would be a beautiful compass rose. The compass rose indicated the four cardinal directions—north, south, east and west. The compass rose also indicated four intermediate directions which are halfway between the four cardinal directions. They are northwest (NW), northeast (NE), southwest (SW) and southeast (SE).

Follow the steps below to draw a **compass rose** in the upper right-hand corner of the map. Indicate the cardinal **directions** on your rose. Then, draw a map of your own make-believe land.

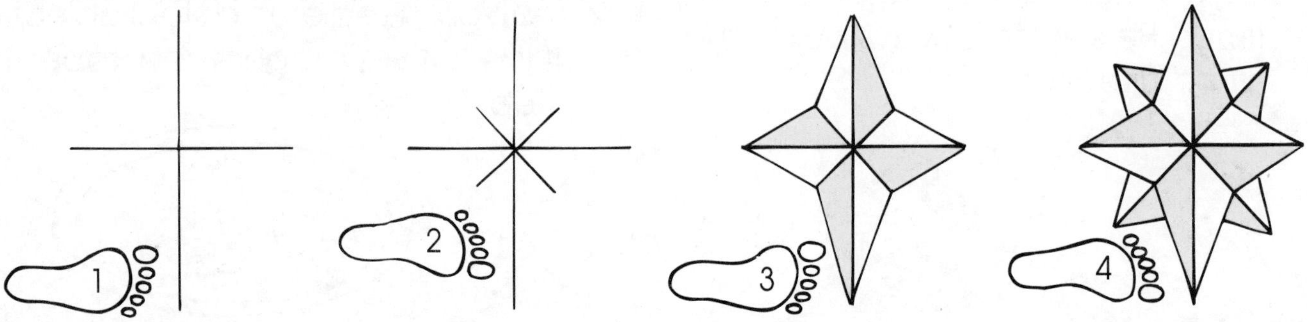

1 2 3 4

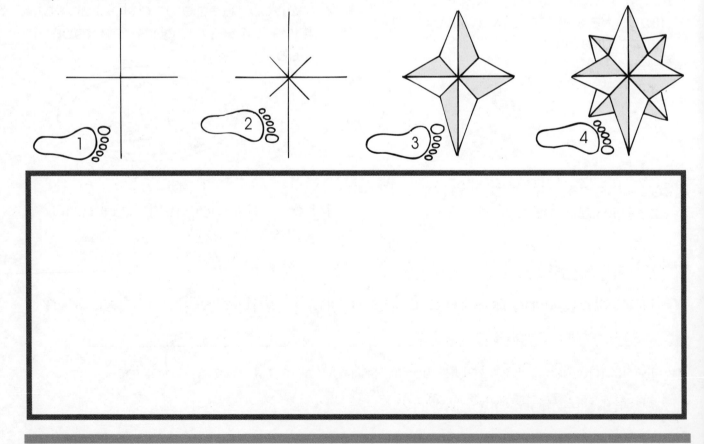

Name____

Dizzy Designers

Decorate the compass rose boxes by following the directions below.

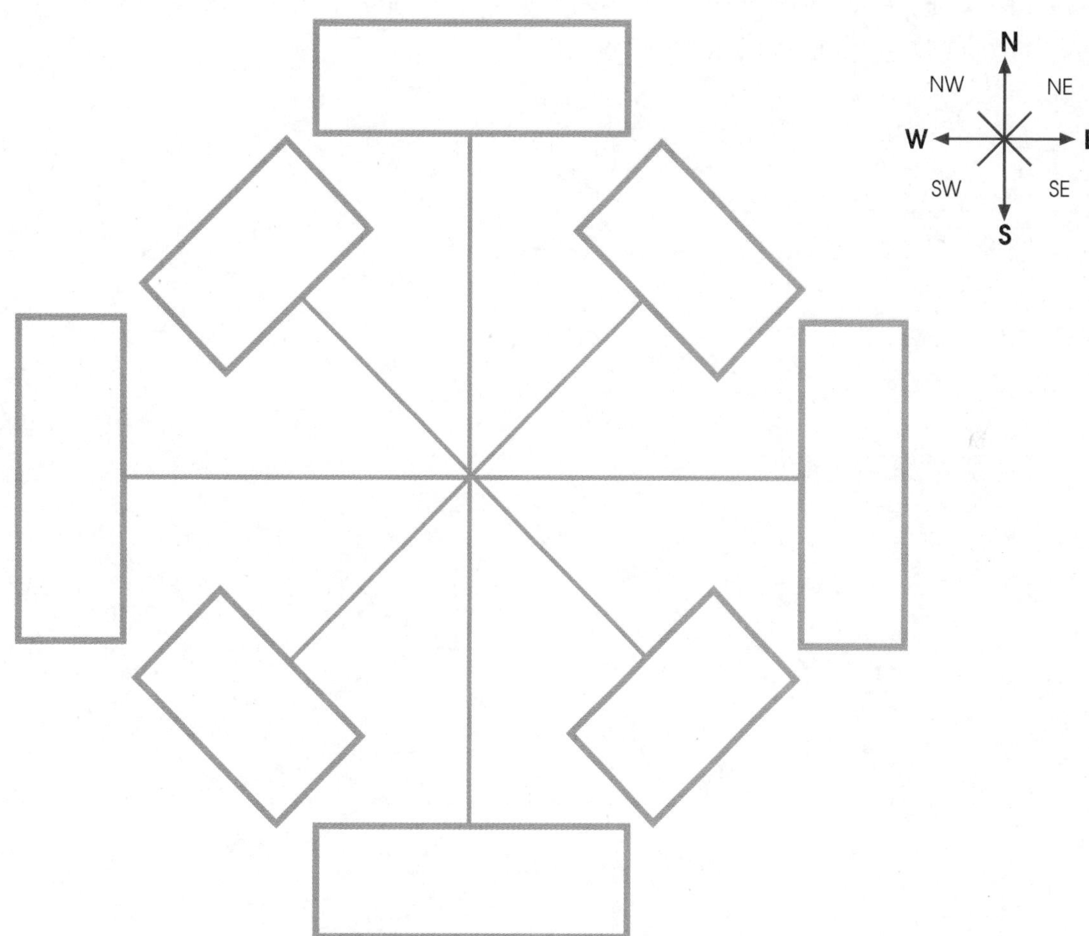

1. Draw red and black stripes in the **SW** box.
2. Draw 3 green triangles in the **N** box.
3. Make the **E** box red and blue plaid.
4. Draw purple polka dots in the **NW** box.
5. Make orange wavy lines in the **SE** box.
6. Draw two red squares in the **S** box.
7. Draw green diagonal lines in the **W** box.
8. Make two yellow smiling faces in the **NE** box.

Name________________________________

Which Way is Up?

Label the direction each arrow is pointing on the matching line. Use N, E, S, W, NE, SE, NW, SW. Then, color the arrows as directed in the Color Code Box.

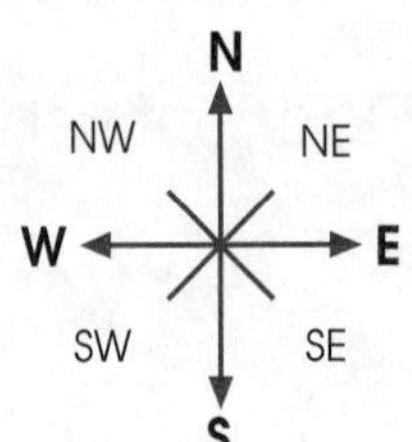

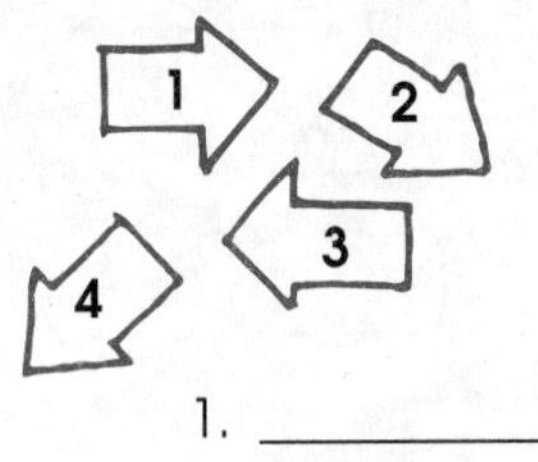

1. ____________
2. ____________
3. ____________
4. ____________

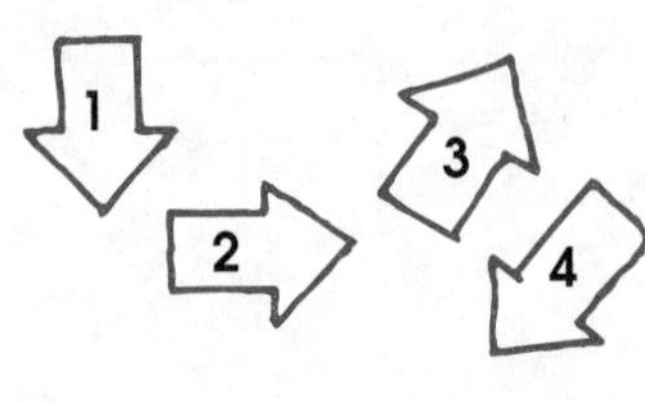

1. ____________
2. ____________
3. ____________
4. ____________

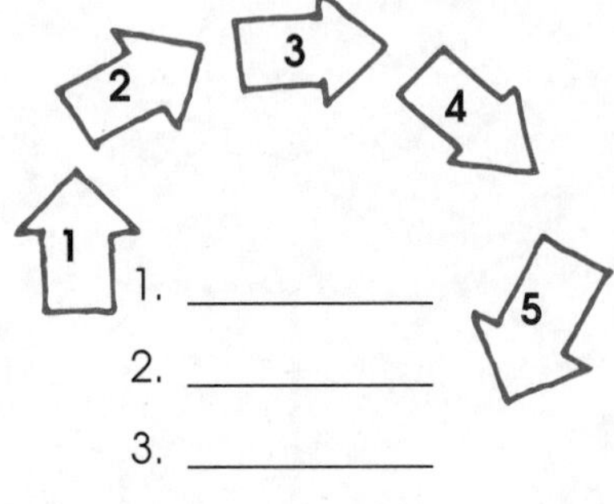

1. ____________
2. ____________
3. ____________
4. ____________
5. ____________

1. ____________
2. ____________
3. ____________
4. ____________
5. ____________

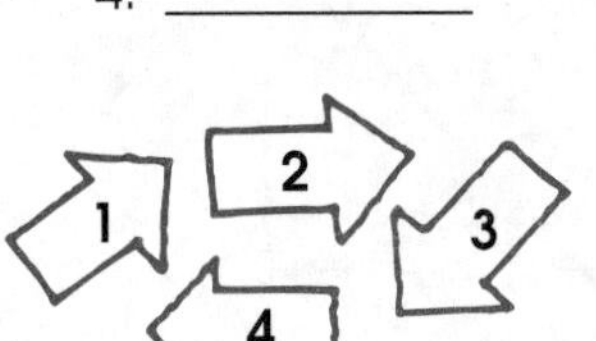

1. ____________
2. ____________
3. ____________
4. ____________
5. ____________

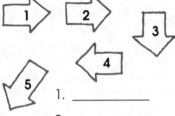

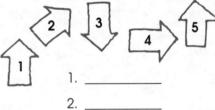

1. ____________
2. ____________
3. ____________
4. ____________
5. ____________

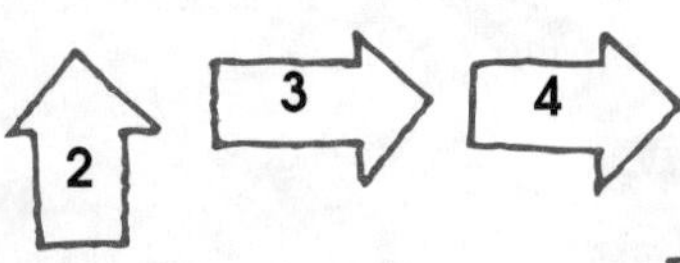

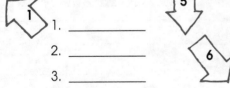

1. ____________
2. ____________
3. ____________
4. ____________
5. ____________
6. ____________

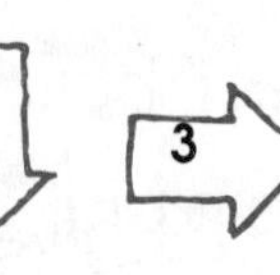

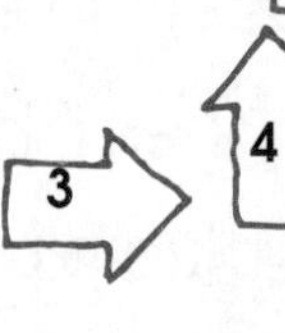

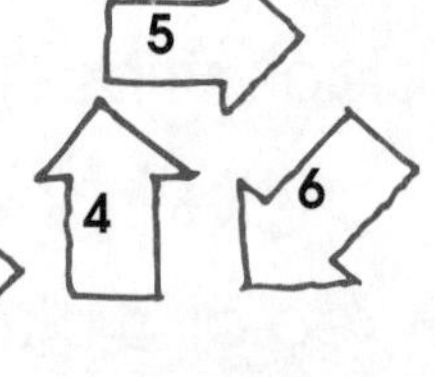

1. ____________
2. ____________
3. ____________
4. ____________
5. ____________
6. ____________

Color Code Box

N	red	**W**	brown
NE	blue	**NW**	orange
S	green	**SW**	yellow
SE	pink	**E**	purple

Name ____________________

Space Ship Search

Gus Galactic needs help in identifying these alien spaceships. Write a ship's letter in each blank to solve these riddles.

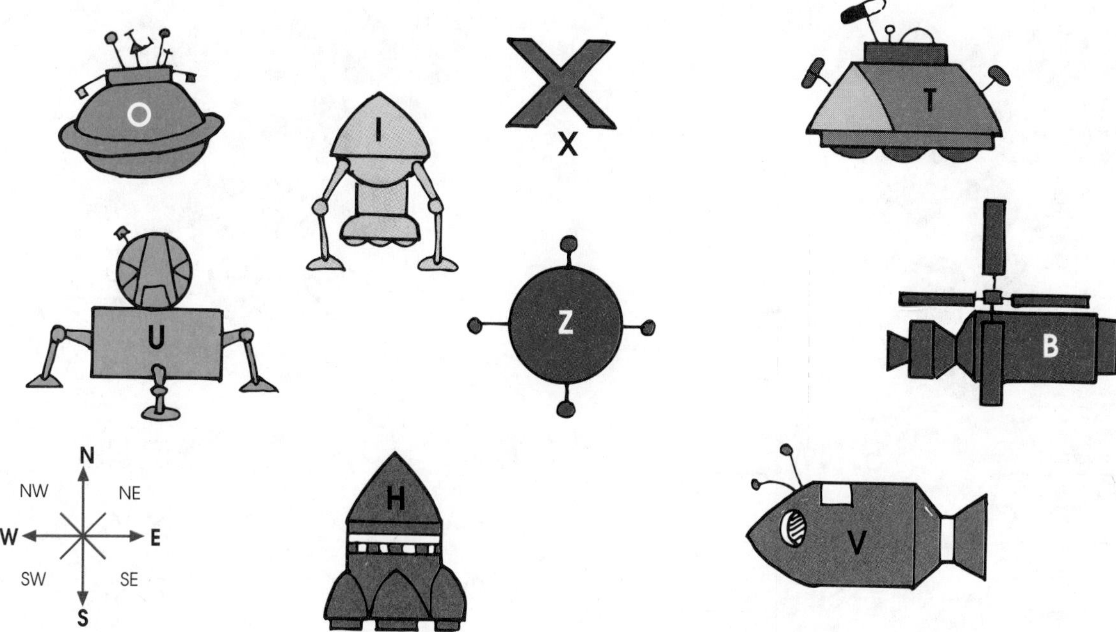

1. I am **N** of Ship **H**. ________
2. I am **E** of Ship **Z**. ________
3. I am **SE** of Ship **Z**. ________
4. I am **S** of Ship **O**. ________
5. I am **NW** of Ship **Z**. ________
6. I am **SW** of Ship **B**. ________
7. I am **NE** of Ship **Z**. ________
8. I am **NE** of Ship **I**. ________
9. I am **SE** of Ship **U**. ________
10. I am **NW** of Ship **B**. ________

Cosmic Challenge

Start at Ship H. Travel in the orbit given. Which ship will you dock with?

1. Go **NW** to Ship ________.
2. Go **NE** to Ship ________.
3. Go **NE** to Ship ________.
4. Go **S** to Ship ________.
5. Go **SE** to Ship ________.
6. Go **NE** to Ship ________.
7. Go **NW** to Ship ________.

This is your docking station. Congratulations!

Name____

Compass Rose Pool

Chalk your cue! Start with the numbered ball given. Follow the directions to find the mystery ball.

Start 3

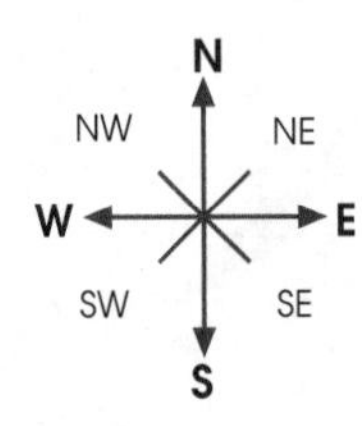

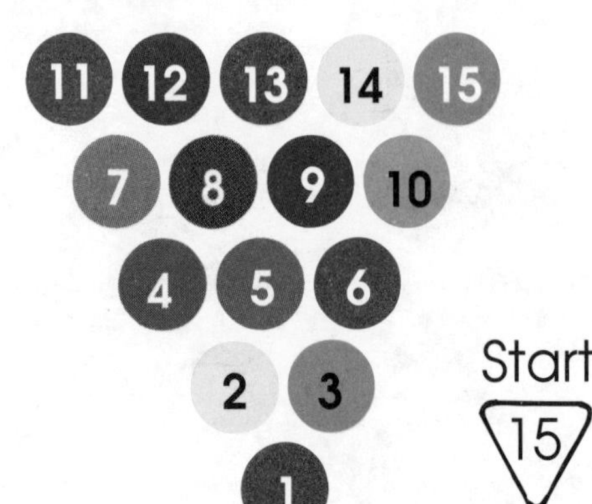

Start 15

1. NW ______
2. NE ______
3. W ______
4. W ______
5. NW ______
6. E ______
7. SE ______
8. NE ______

1. W ______
2. SW ______
3. SW ______
4. E ______
5. NE ______
6. W ______
7. SW ______
8. SW ______

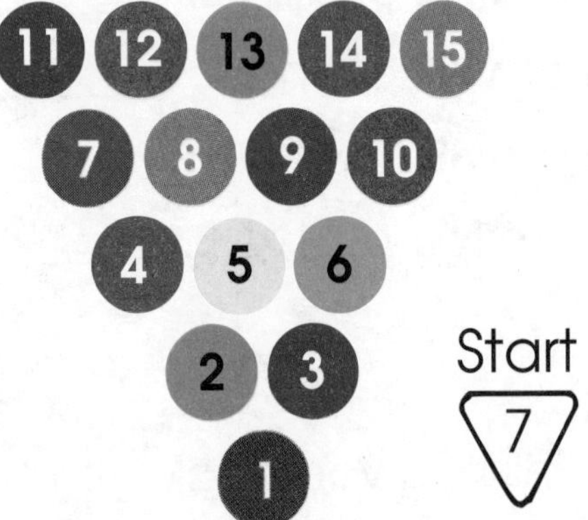

Start 7

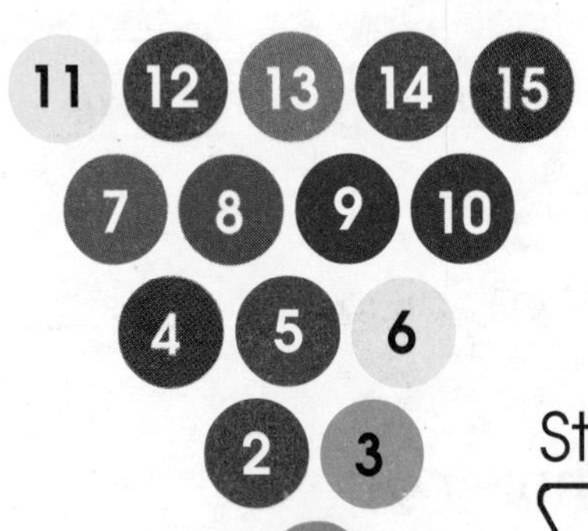

Start 1

1. E ______
2. E ______
3. SW ______
4. SW ______
5. E ______
6. NE ______
7. NW ______
8. NE ______

1. NE ______
2. NE ______
3. W ______
4. NE ______
5. E ______
6. NE ______
7. W ______
8. SW ______

Name________________________________

The Sleuth Pooch

Help the Sleuth Pooch find his missing collar. Trace over only the arrows given in order on his notepad. Then, color the Sleuth Pooch's collar.

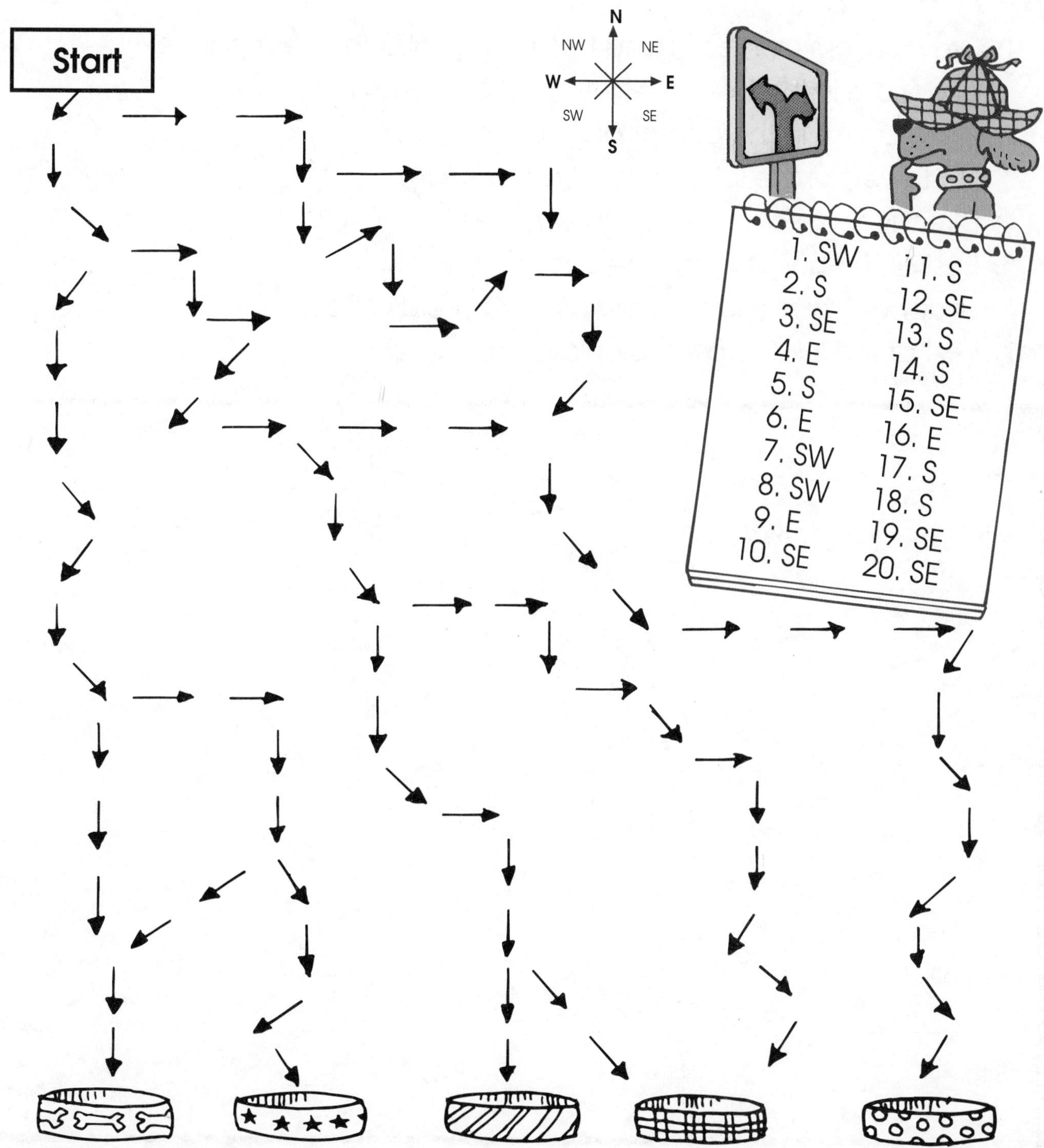

Name______________________________________

Draw Your Own Map

A cartographer makes maps. Try your hand at being a cartographer and make your own map by following these directions. Read all directions before you begin.

1. Draw a compass rose using both cardinal and intermediate directions in the bottom right-hand corner of the map.
2. Draw a lake in the center of the map.
3. Northwest of the lake, draw some ducks in flight.
4. Directly south of the lake, draw six trees.
5. East of the ducks, draw the sun.
6. Southwest of the lake, draw a playground area.
7. East of the lake, draw a picnic area.

Name ____________________

Acorn Park

Write the names of the intermediate directions correctly on the lines below.

NW is ____________________. NE is ____________________.

SW is ____________________. SE is ____________________.

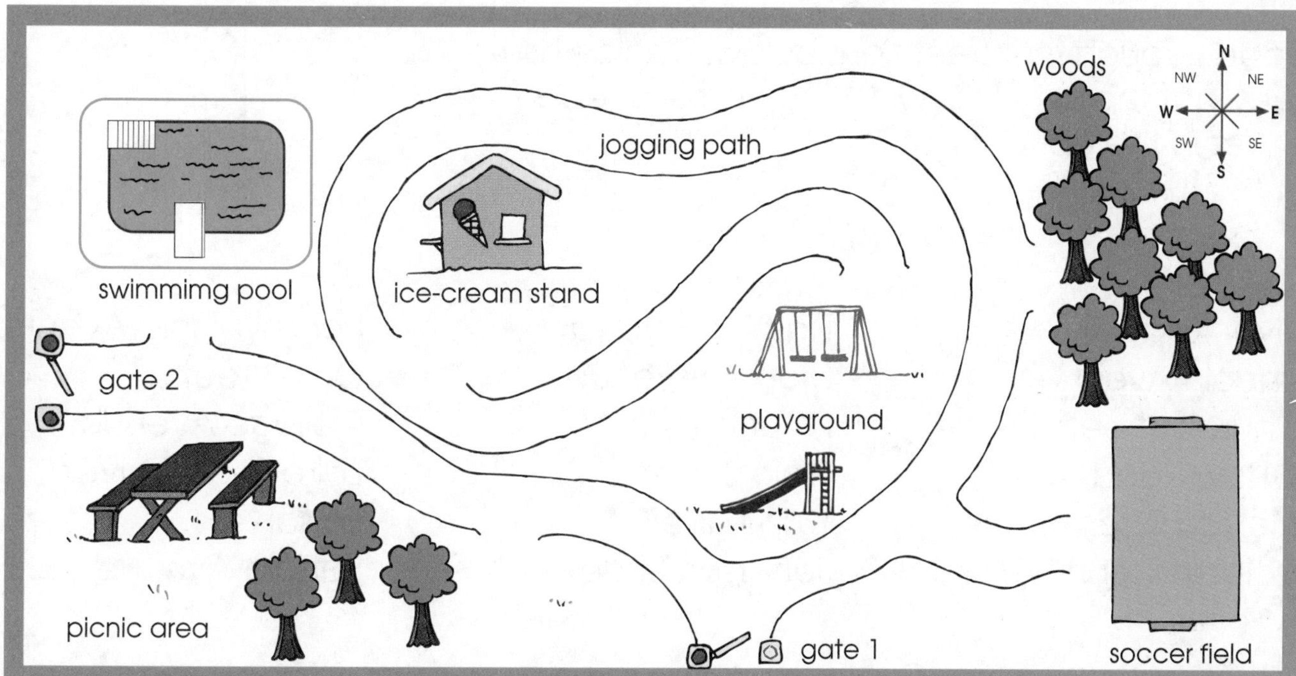

Directions: Use the names of cardinal and intermediate directions to complete these sentences about the map of Acorn Park.

1. The swimming pool is ____________________ of the playground.
2. The ice-cream stand is ____________________ of the picnic area.
3. The soccer field is ____________________ of the swimming pool.
4. The playground is ____________________ of the picnic area.
5. The woods are ____________________ of the playground.
6. Gate 2 is on the ____________________ side of Acorn Park.
7. The swimming pool is ____________________ of the picnic area.
8. Gate 1 is in the ____________________ part of Acorn Park.
9. The woods are ____________________ of gate 1.

Name______________________________________

Street Names

How did your street get its name? Was it named after a famous explorer like Columbus? Maybe it's named after a state, like Michigan Avenue. Perhaps it's named after a tree (Oak Street) or a food (Apple Avenue).

Read through the street signs below. Decide how they got their names. Write the name of each street in the correct category.

River Road	Flamingo Road	Pennsylvania Avenue
Lincoln Avenue	Market Avenue	Oak Street
Church Street	Hill Street	College Avenue
Willow Road	Ohio Street	Lake Shore Drive
Mexico Avenue	Tulip Lane	Edison Court
Dolphin Court	Jefferson Street	Buffalo Avenue

Famous People	Places	Trees and Plants
________________	________________	________________
________________	________________	________________
________________	________________	________________

Land and Water Features	Human Institutions	Animals
________________	________________	________________
________________	________________	________________
________________	________________	________________

Name______________________________

City Streets

Every town has some interesting street names. Streets can get their names in many different ways. They are often named after presidents, states, trees and flowers. What are some of the interesting street names in your town?

People's Names	Places	Funny Names
Human Institutions	Natural Features	Animals
Plants and Trees	Directions	Other

Name________________________________

Near School

Geographers can tell us how places are the same and how they are different. Where you live is different from where your friend lives. Maybe you live southwest of school while your friend lives north of the school.

Directions: Write the names and draw pictures of landmarks that are found near your school. Place each one on the chart in its correct location relative to your school.

Northwest	North	Northeast
West	School 	East
Southwest	South	Southeast

Name____________________

A Walk Around Town

Let's take a walk around the town of Forest Grove. Use a marker or crayon to trace your route.

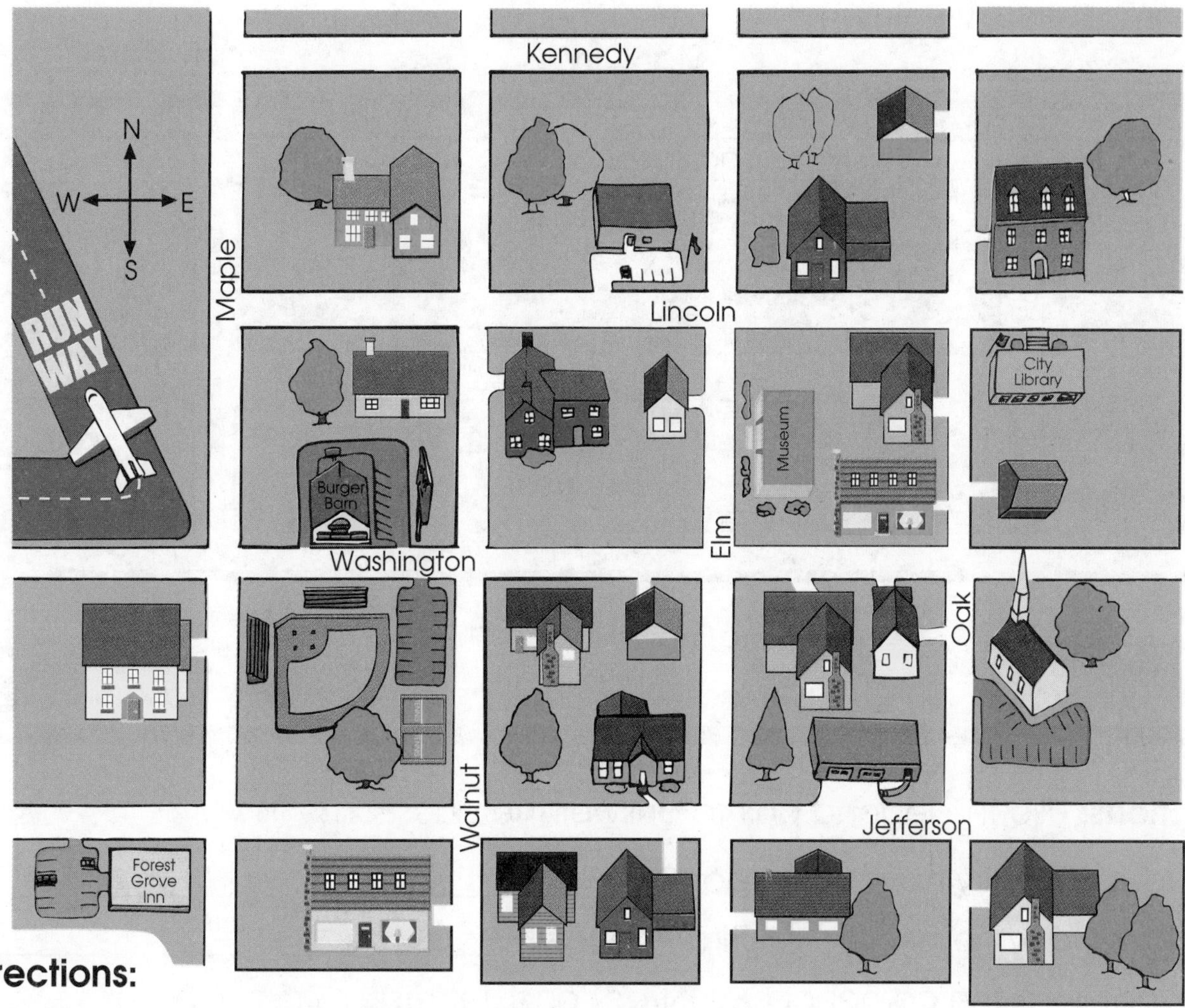

Directions:

1. Begin your walking tour at Forest Grove Inn.
2. Walk two blocks east to Elm Street.
3. Turn north on Elm Street. Walk to the Museum.
4. Go one-half block north to the corner of Elm and Lincoln.
5. Turn east on Lincoln. Walk until you come to the City Library.
6. Go south on Oak Street until you reach Washington Street.
7. Turn west on Washington and walk two and one-half blocks to the Burger Barn.
8. Lunch is over. Take the shortest way back to Forest Grove Inn.

Name ____

Legends Help You Read Maps

A legend is another word for a key. A map legend explains the symbols found in a map.

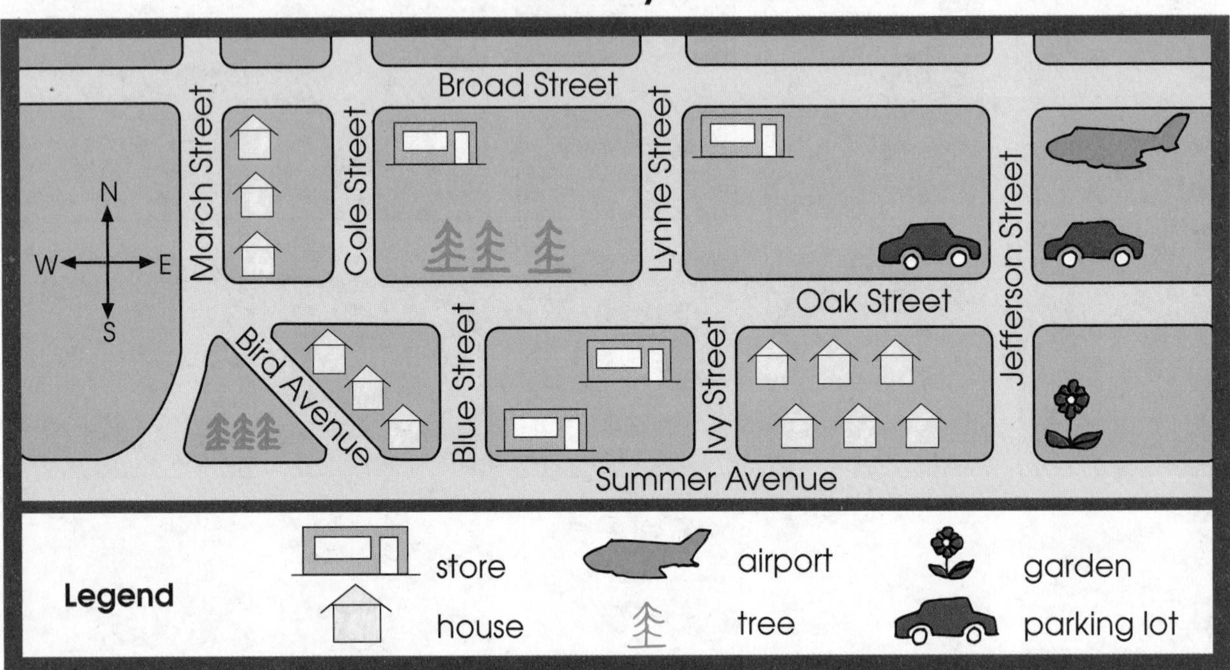

Directions: Use the legend box to answer the questions.

1. Does Star City have an airport? ____________________
2. How many houses are on Bird Avenue? ____________________
3. What is on the corner of Oak Street and Jefferson Street? ____________________
4. The garden is on the corner of Jefferson Street and ____________________.
5. How many stores are in Star City? ____________________
6. What direction is Summer Avenue from Oak Street? ____________________
7. Which street is directly west of Ivy Street? ____________________
8. How many trees are north of Oak Street? ____________________
9. How many houses are between Ivy Street and Jefferson Street? ____________________
10. How many stores are north of Summer Avenue? ____________________

Name ____________________

Cartographers Use Symbols

Directions: On another sheet of paper, draw a map using the symbols and directions given below.

1. Draw a compass rose in the lower right-hand corner of the page.
2. Draw a in the center of your paper from west to east.
3. Draw 6 in the southwest corner of the map.
4. Draw 4 east of the .
5. Draw a north of the .
6. Draw a west of the .
7. Draw a south of the .
8. Draw a north of the .

On another sheet of paper, draw another map using the symbols and directions given below.

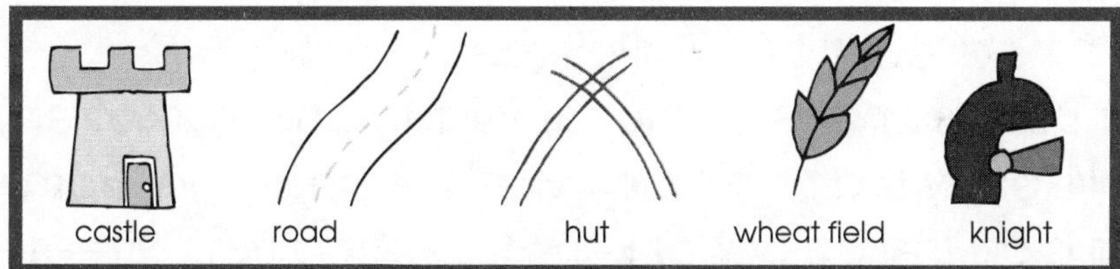

1. Draw a compass rose in the lower right-hand corner of the page.
2. Draw a castle in the center of the page.
3. Draw a road from the castle door southeast to the bottom of the page.
4. Draw 4 huts west of the castle.
5. Draw a knight on the east and west sides of the castle door.
6. Draw a wheat field east of the castle.
7. Draw a road east from the huts to the castle road.

Name____

Welcome to Crystal River

Crystal River is a great small town to live in. It has stores, parks, churches, schools, libraries, etc.

Complete the map of Crystal River on page 69. Use the directions below to draw the buildings and parks, and to write the names of the streets and businesses on the map where they belong.

When you finish your map, share it with a friend. How are your maps alike? How are they different?

Directions:

1. Bridge Street crosses the Crystal River.
2. Diamond Avenue runs east and west. It is south of the Crystal River.
3. North Street is one block north of Park Street.
4. Elm Street runs directly into Park Street.
5. The Burger Barn is on the corner of Bridge and Park Streets.
6. The Crystal Library is a half block west of the Burger Barn.
7. Elm School is on the corner of Elm Street and Park Street.
8. Crystal Church is west of Elm School.
9. There are stores on the remainder of the north side of Park Street.
10. Bob's Bait Shop is on Bridge Street near the river.
11. The only buildings on North Street are houses.
12. The Crystal River flows through the middle of the city park.
13. The Crystal Airport is on the south edge of town.
14. Memorial Hospital is south of the river.
15. The fire station is on Bridge Street.

Name ______________________________

Welcome to Crystal River

Use the directions from page 68 to complete the map of Crystal River.

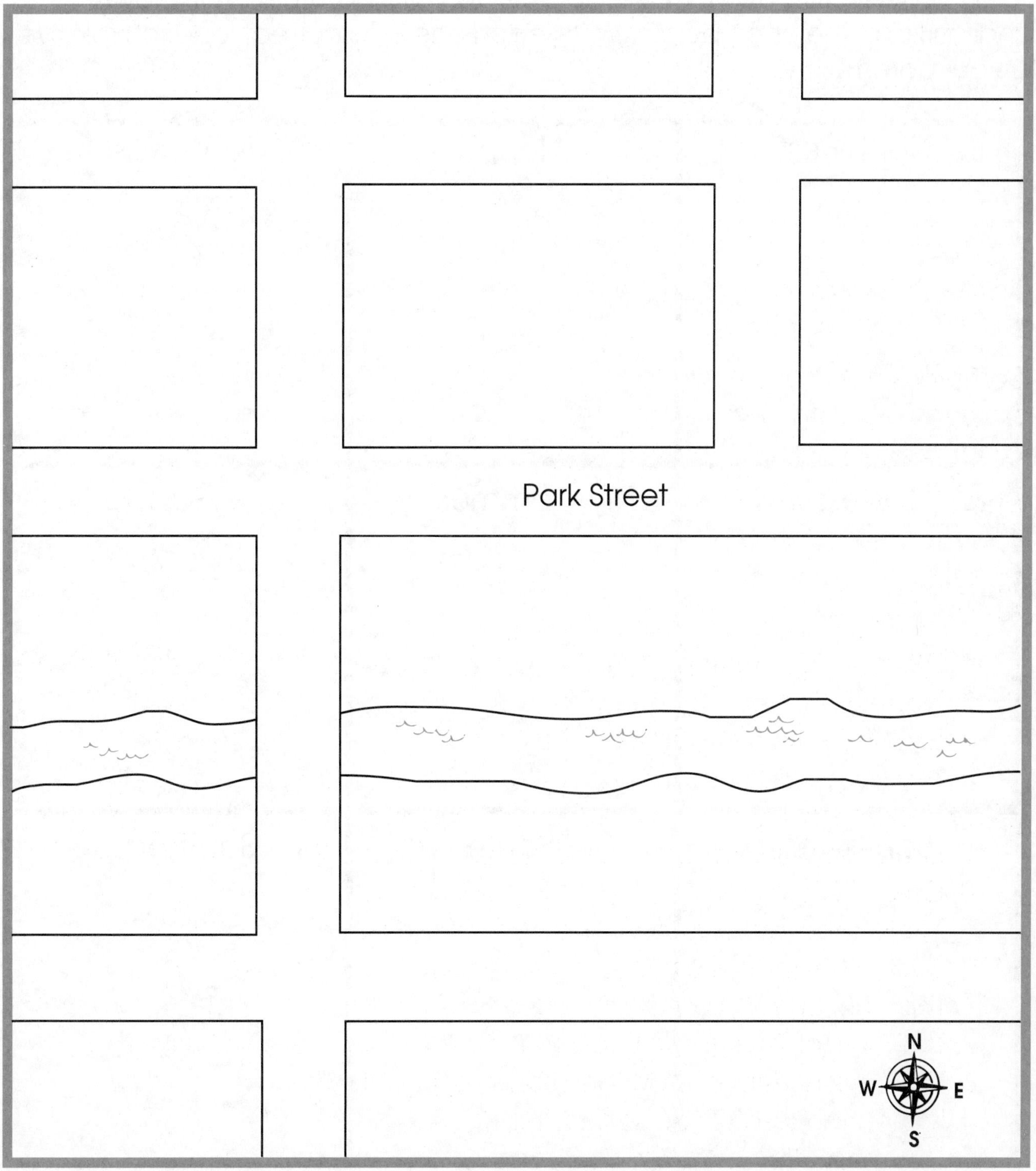

Park Street

N
W E
S

Name____________________________________

Near My Community

Use a state map to locate your community. Then, write the names of other communities, cities, towns, lakes, places to visit and other well-known landmarks on the chart below. Write each one in its correct location relative to your community.

Northwest	North	Northeast
West	My Community	East
Southwest	South	Southeast

Name ______________________________

Tourist Map of Oldtown

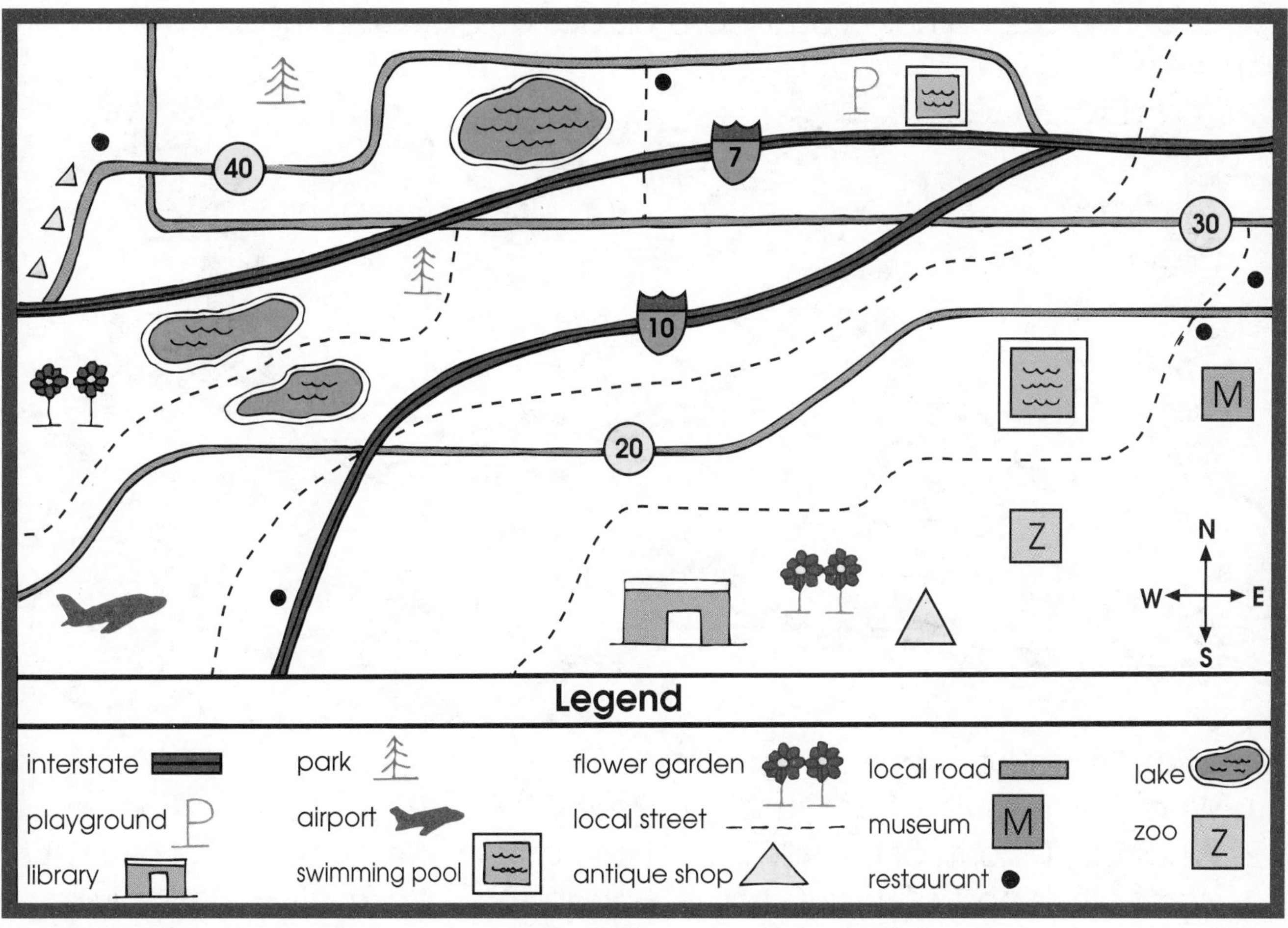

1. The airport is located between interstate ________ and local road ______________.
2. What attractions are north of interstate 7? ______________________________

____

3. Could you take a local street from the airport to the library? ______________
4. How many lakes are in Oldtown? ______________________________
5. On which side of town is the museum located? ______________________________
6. What is located at the point where local road 30 crosses interstate 7? ______________
7. Name the road that runs north of the playground. ______________________________
8. How many swimming pools are in Oldtown? ______________________________
9. How many antique shops are in the town? ______________________________
10. Is there a local street between the zoo and the swimming pool? ______________

Name________________________________

Is It North, South, East or West?

Direction words can help you locate places quickly on a map.

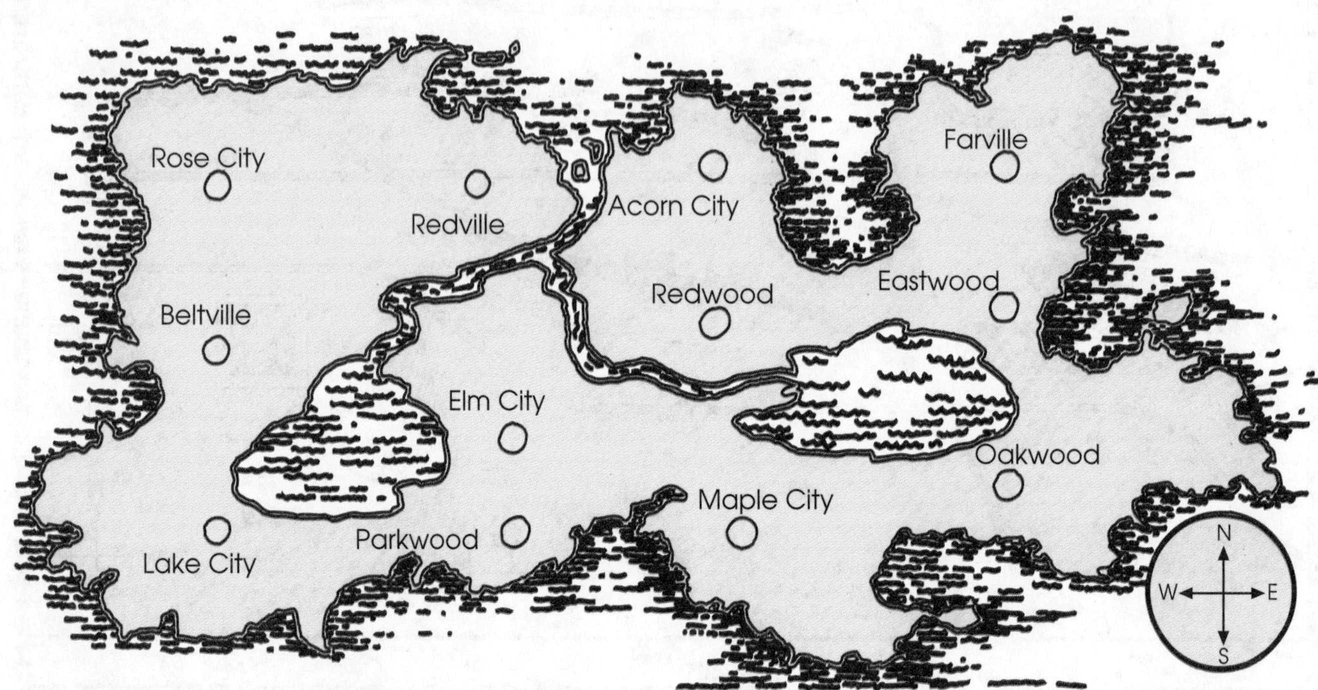

Directions: Circle the correct answer.

1. What city is south of Acorn City?	Rose City	Redwood	Farville
2. What city is north of Beltville?	Rose City	Redwood	Lake City
3. What city is east of Rose City?	Beltville	Lake City	Redville
4. What city is west of Maple City?	Redwood	Acorn City	Parkwood
5. What city is south of Farville?	Acorn City	Eastwood	Redville
6. What city is west of Redwood?	Eastwood	Maple City	Beltville
7. What city is north of Lake City?	Beltville	Maple City	Oakwood
8. What city is west of Farville?	Acorn City	Oakwood	Eastwood

Use crayons or markers to follow these directions.

1. Draw a line south from Farville to Eastwood.
2. Draw a line north from Maple City to Redwood.
3. Draw a line east from Beltville to Redwood.
4. Draw a line west from Redville to Rose City.
5. Place an A on the city directly south of Eastwood.
6. Place a B on the city east of Acorn City.

Name ____________________

North, South, East and West

You are flying in an airplane with the wind blowing sharply in your face. You are flying from Chicago to Nashville. In what direction are you traveling?

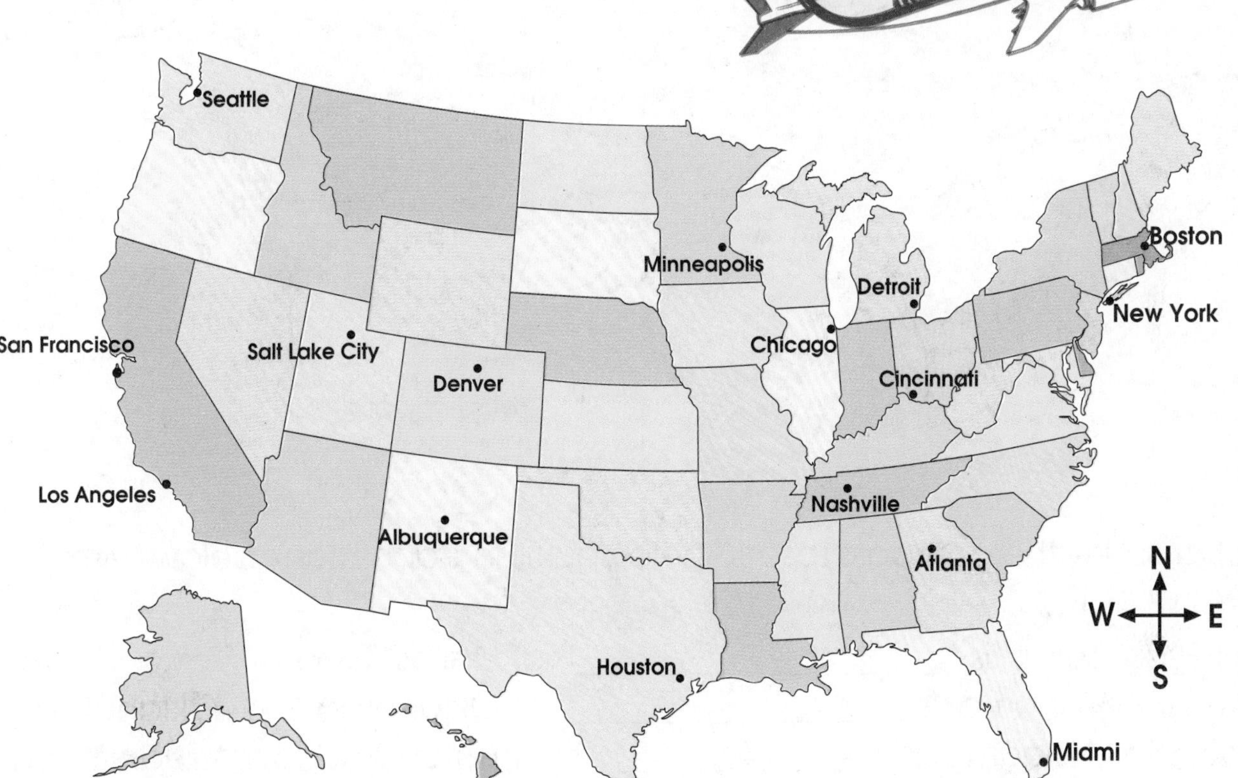

If you said "south" to the above question, you are correct!

Write the direction you would be traveling for each set of cities. Use the four cardinal directions—north, south, east and west.

Atlanta to Los Angeles ______________

Seattle to Los Angeles ______________

San Francisco to Nashville______________

Denver to Salt Lake City______________

Cincinnati to Detroit ______________

Chicago to Boston ______________

Houston to Minneapolis ______________

Miami to New York ______________

Detroit to New York ______________

Boston to Minneapolis ______________

Atlanta to Albuquerque ______________

Nashville to Miami ______________

Name ______________________________

Locating Cities

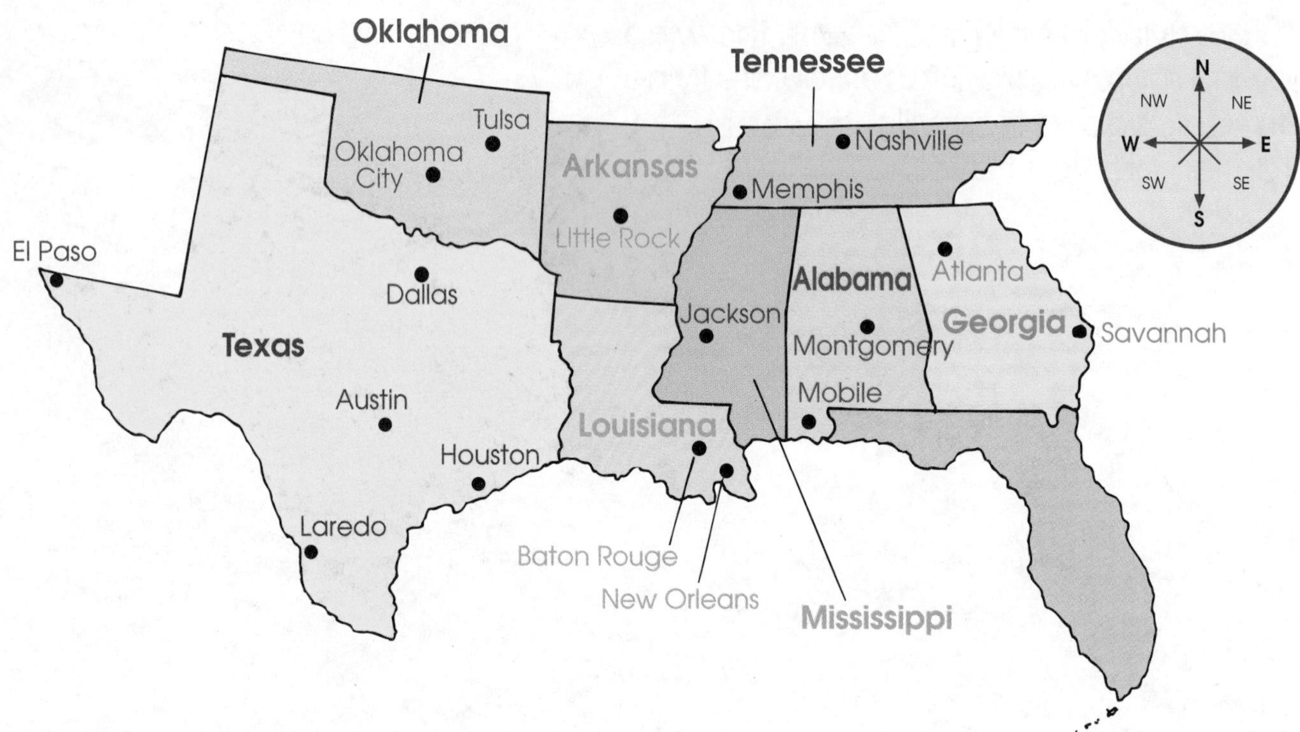

Directions: Use the compass rose to help you fill in each blank below with the correct direction.

1. El Paso, Texas, is ______________________ of Dallas, Texas.
2. Tulsa, Oklahoma, is ______________________ of Oklahoma City, Oklahoma.
3. Mobile, Alabama, is ______________________ of Baton Rouge, Louisiana.
4. Little Rock, Arkansas, is ____________________ of Nashville, Tennessee.
5. Houston, Texas, is ______________________ of New Orleans, Louisiana.
6. Jackson, Mississippi, is ____________________ of Memphis, Tennessee.
7. Dallas, Texas, is ______________________ of Austin, Texas.
8. The state of Louisiana is __________________ of Arkansas.
9. The state of Alabama is __________________ of Texas.
10. The state of Oklahoma is _________________ of Tennessee.
11. The state of Georgia is ___________________ of Texas.
12. Atlanta, Georgia, is ______________________ of Savannah, Georgia.
13. The state of Tennessee is _________________ of Arkansas.
14. Dallas, Texas, is ______________________ of Little Rock, Arkansas.
15. Mobile, Alabama, is ______________________ of Atlanta, Georgia.

Name________________________________

Scale is Fun!

Scale measures distance on a map. Use the scale given to measure distances in this winter wonderland. Cut out the ruler. Use it to measure from ❄ to ❄ to answer the questions below.

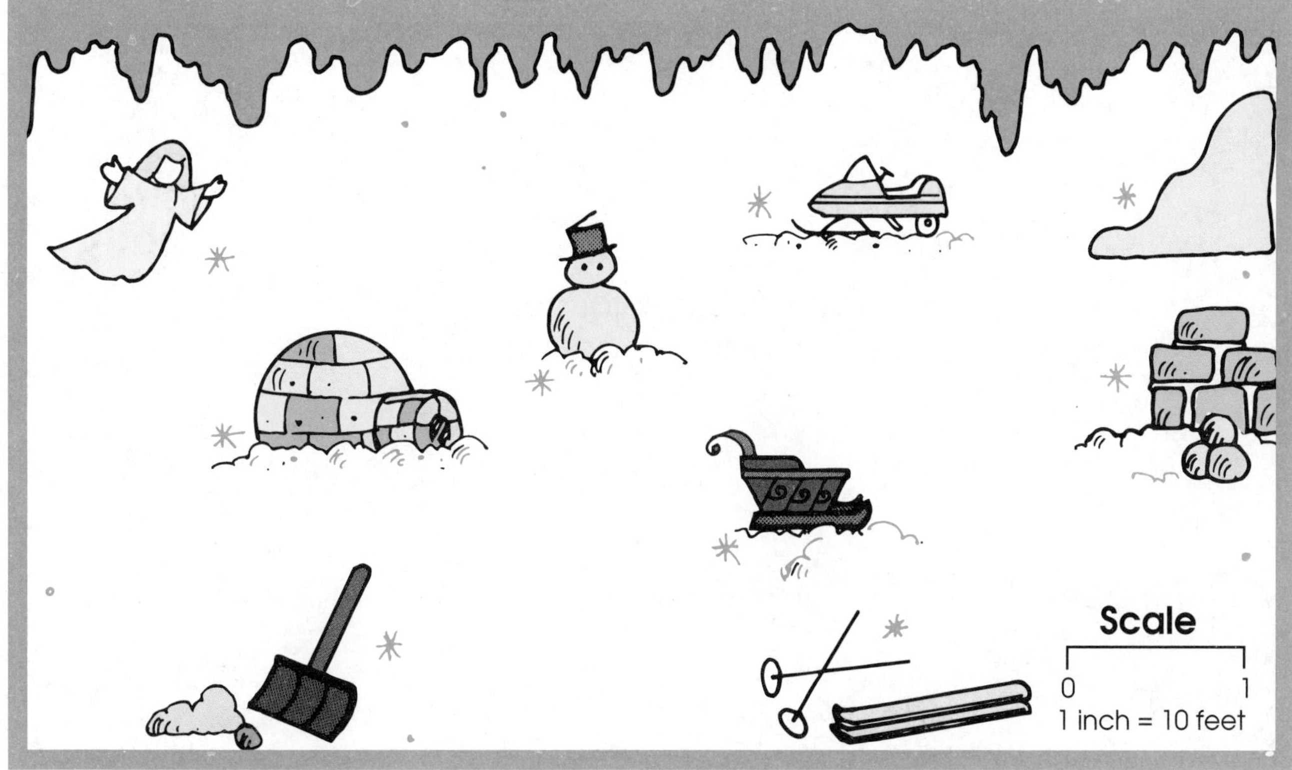

1. On the scale, how many feet equal one inch? __________
2. How far is it from the shovel to the sleigh? __________
3. How many feet is the snow angel from the snowman? __________
4. How far is the igloo from the sleigh? __________
5. How many feet is it from the snowmobile to the skis and poles? ______
6. How many feet is the snow fort from the shovel? __________
7. It is ________feet from the sledding hill to the shovel.
8. It is ________feet from the skis and pole to the sleigh.
9. It is ________feet from the skis and pole to the igloo.

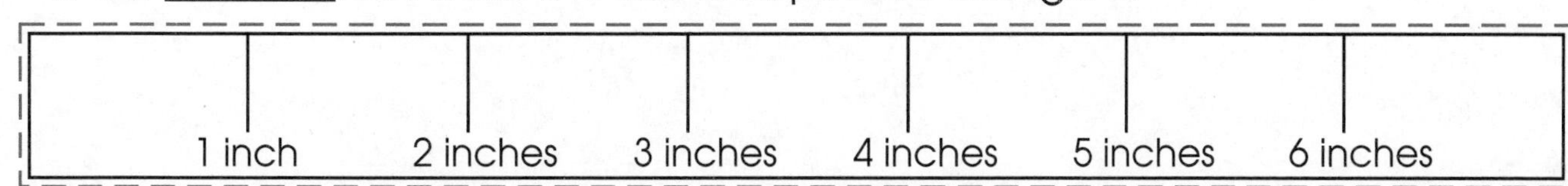

Page is blank for cutting
exercise on previous page.

Name ______________________________

Go the Distance

This map shows the route for the yearly Pedalville Bike-a-thon. At the bottom of the map is a scale.

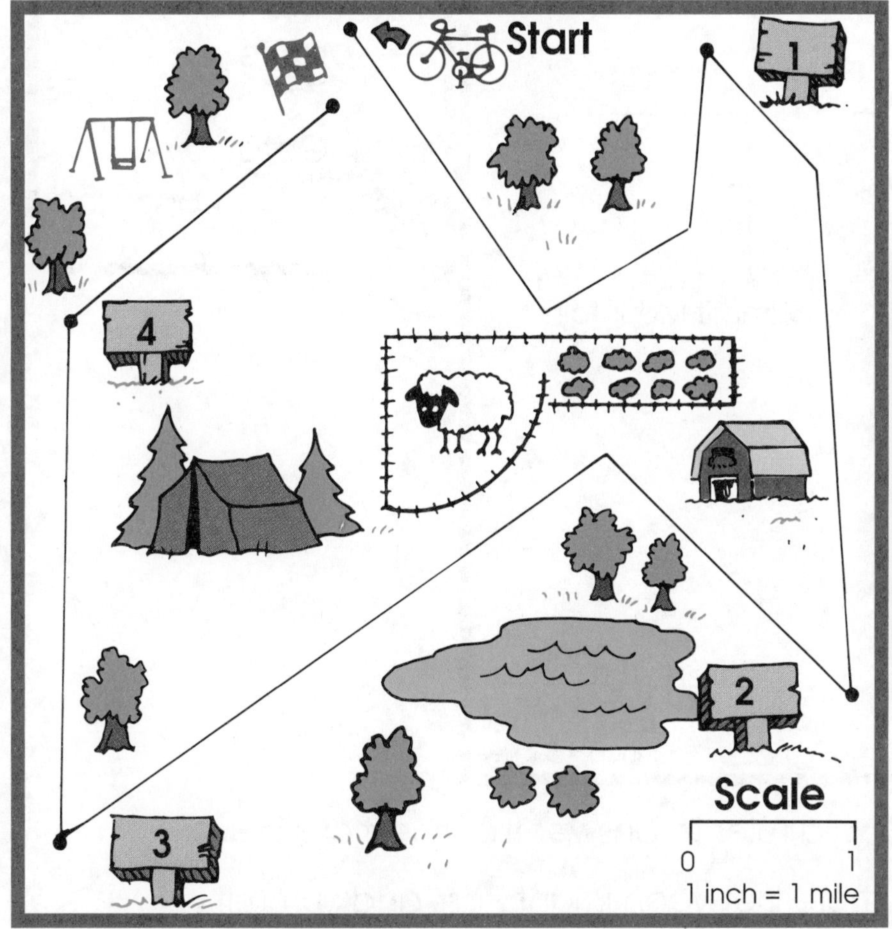

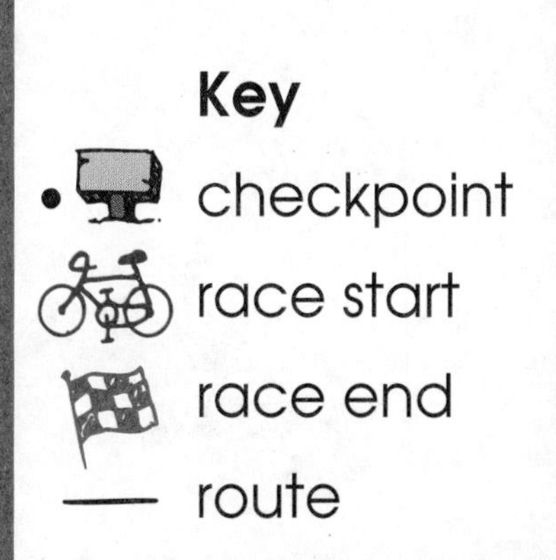

Directions: Use a ruler and the scale to measure the distances on the map.

1. How many miles are between "race start" and checkpoint 1? ______
2. How many miles are between checkpoint 1 and checkpoint 2? ______
3. How many miles are between checkpoint 2 and checkpoint 3? ______
4. How many miles are between checkpoint 3 and checkpoint 4? ______
5. How many miles are between checkpoint 4 and "race end"? ______

Name____

Are We There Yet?

Calvin is going on a vacation to Getaway Campground.

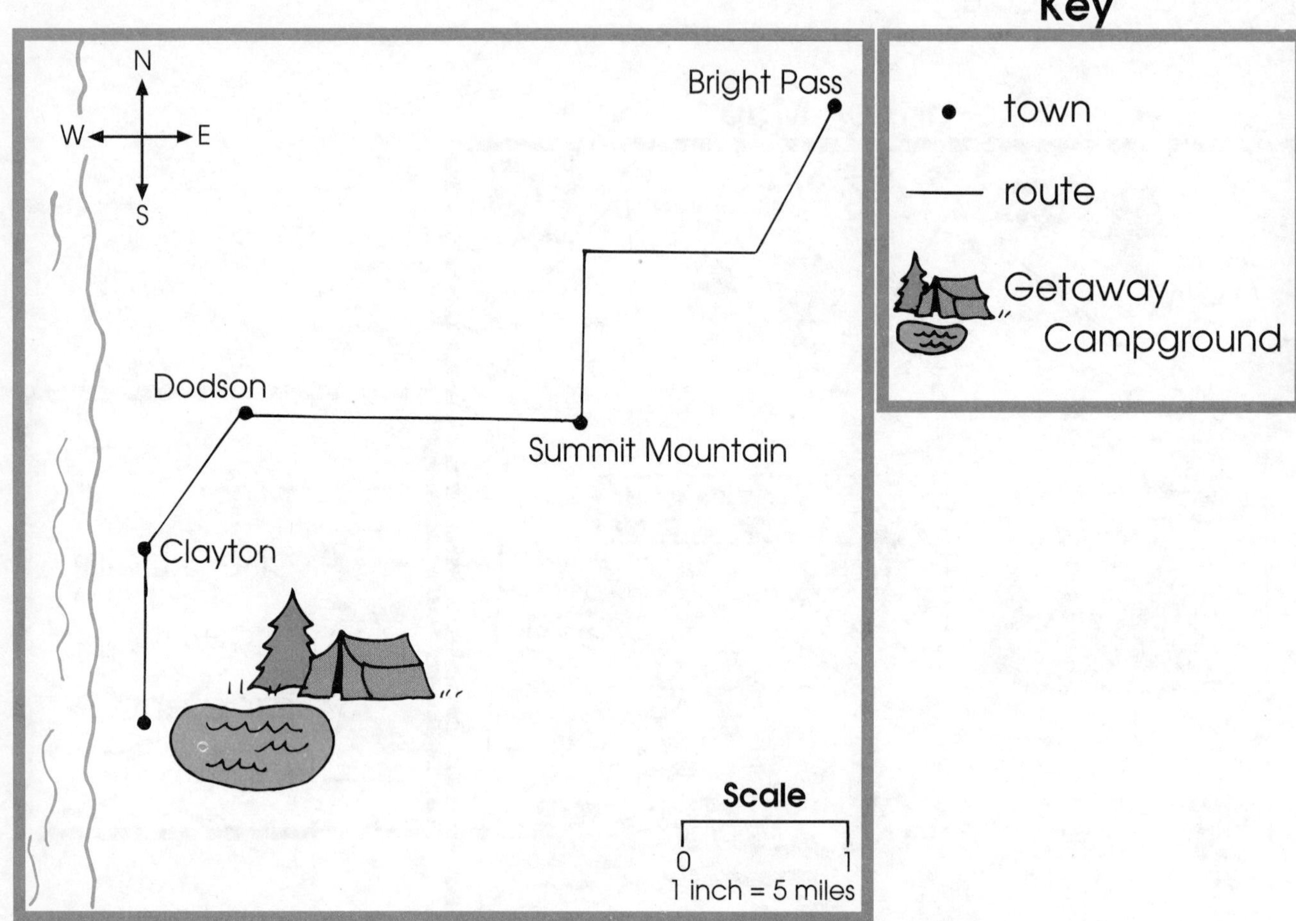

Directions: Use the scale and a ruler to answer the questions below.

1. How many miles are there between Bright Pass and Summit Mountain?____________
2. How far is it from Summit Mountain to Dodson? ____________________
3. How many miles are there between Dodson and Clayton? __________
4. How far is it from Clayton to Getaway Campground? ______________
5. How many miles in all are there between Bright Pass and Getaway Campground?____________

Name ______________________________

How Far Is It?

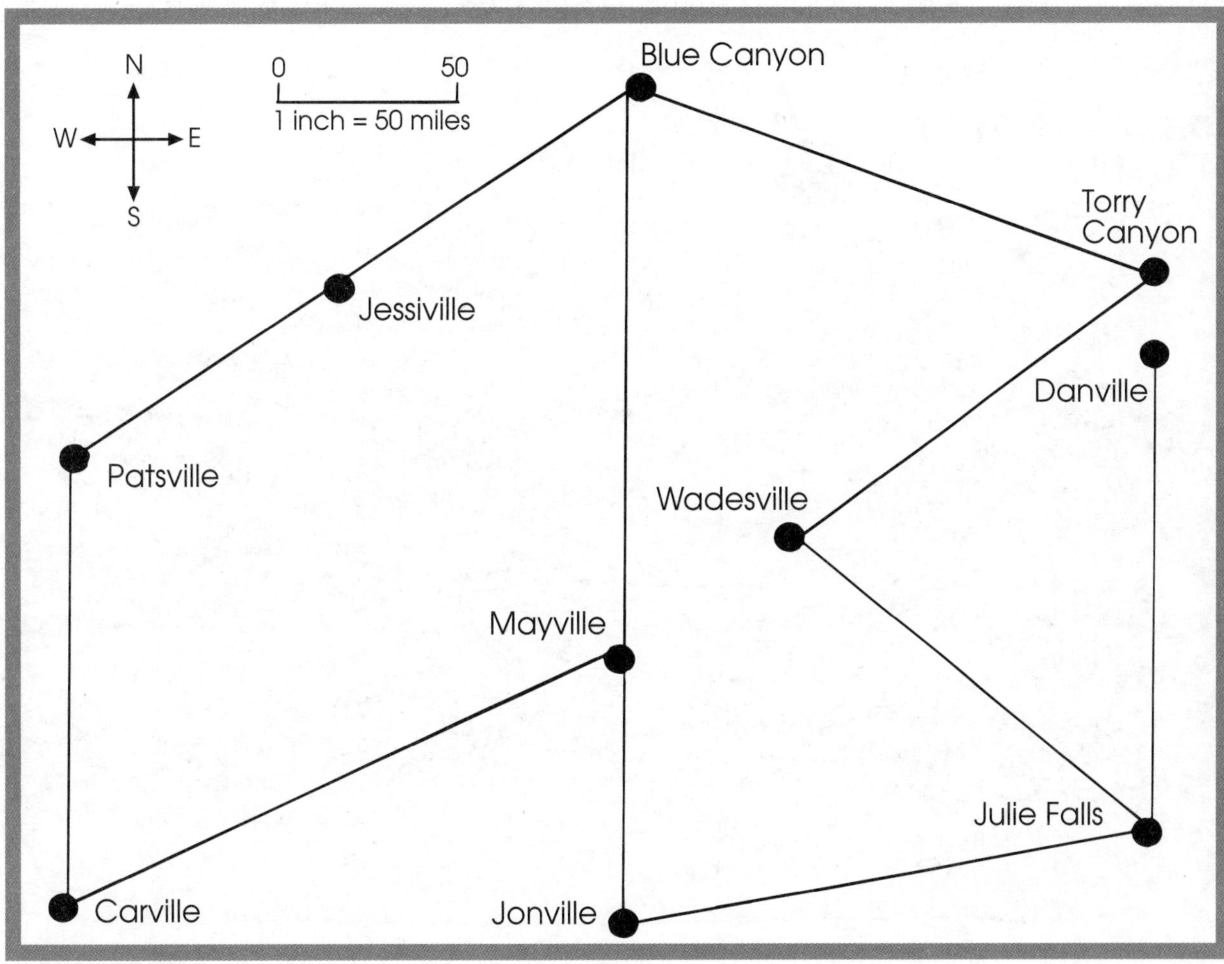

Directions: Measure these distances and answer the questions below.

1. How far is it from Carville to Mayville? ______________________________
2. How far is it from Wadesville to Torry Canyon? ______________________________
3. If you travel from Blue Canyon to Jonville, how far will you travel? ______________
4. What town is between Patsville and Blue Canyon? ______________________________
5. If you go through Wadesville, how far is it from Torry Canyon to Julie Falls? __________
6. Which is longer—going from Carville to Patsville, or Carville to Mayville?

____

Name______________________________________

Map Scales

Welcome to the mouth-watering county of Hamburg Haven! Use a ruler and the map scale to figure approximate distances around this "burg."

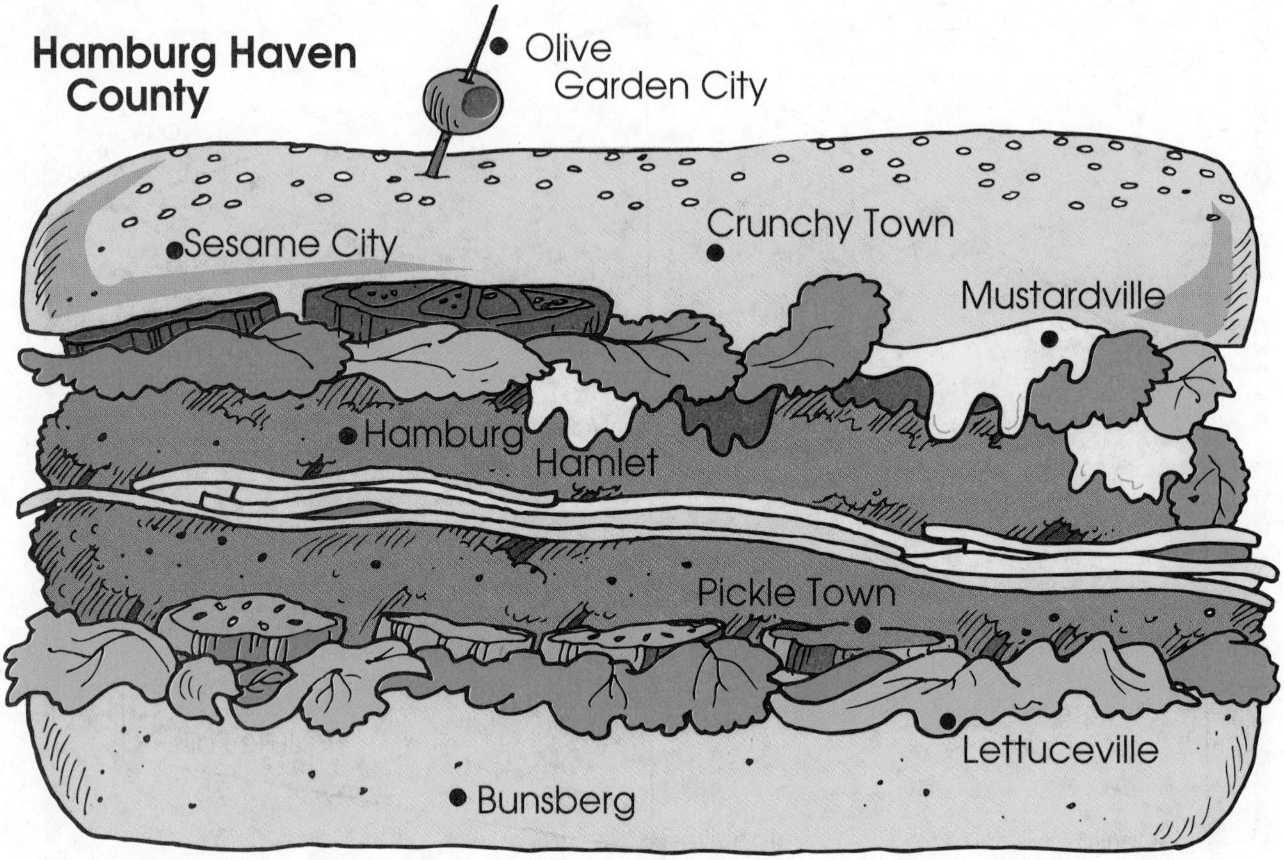

Hamburg Haven County

Olive Garden City

Sesame City

Crunchy Town

Mustardville

Hamburg Hamlet

Pickle Town

Lettuceville

Bunsberg

About how many miles? (Hint: Measure from dot to dot.)

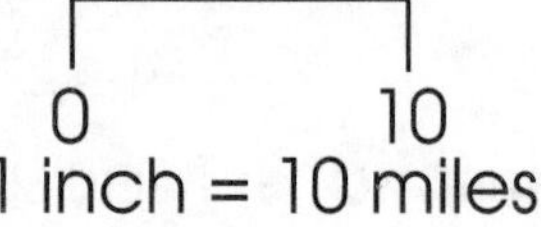

1 inch = 10 miles

1. From Olive Garden City to Pickle Town? __________
2. From Bunsberg to Lettuceville? __________
3. From Crunchy Town to Mustardville? __________
4. From Mustardville to Pickle Town? __________
5. From Bunsberg to Sesame City? __________
6. From Hamburg Hamlet to Lettuceville? __________
7. From Crunchy Town to Bunsberg? __________

Name______________________________

Camping in Nature Park

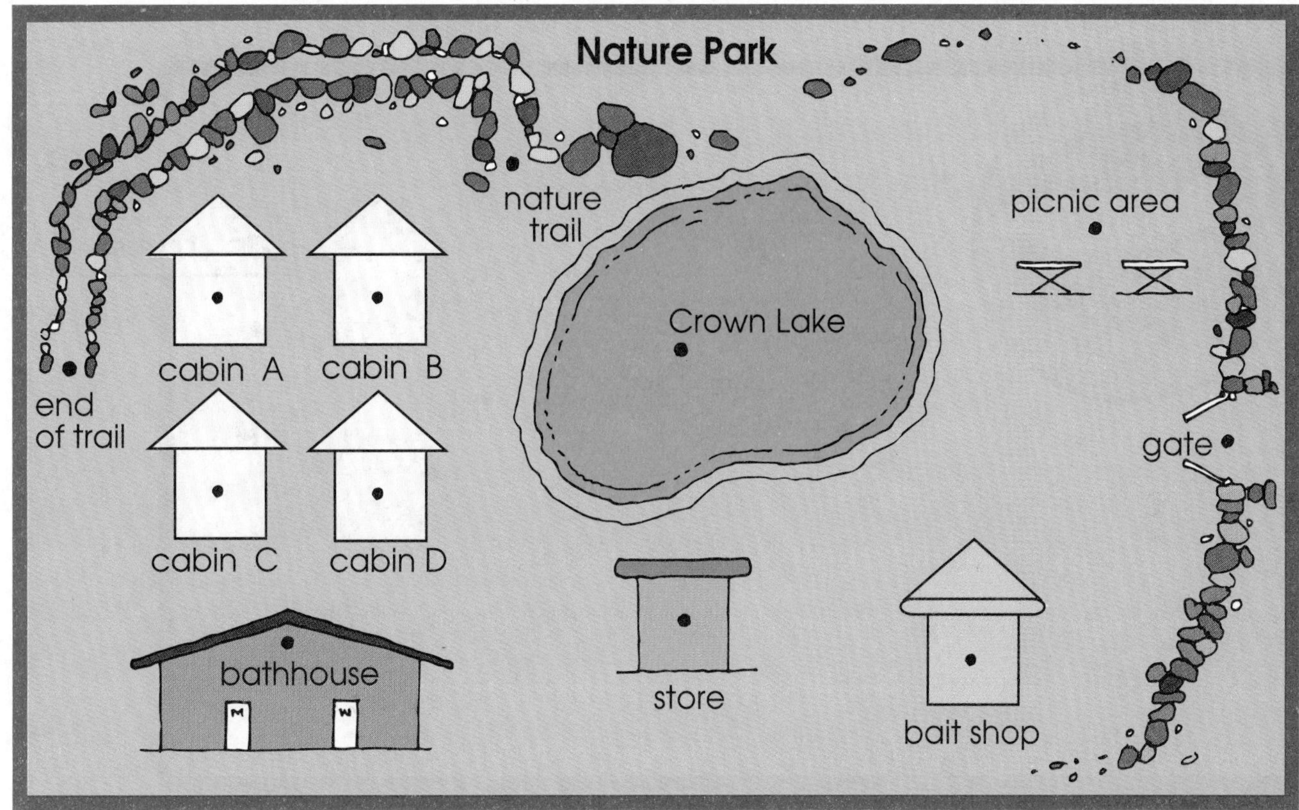

0 1
1 inch = 1 miles

Directions: Use a ruler to help you answer these questions.

1. How far is it from the center of Crown Lake to the bait shop? __________
2. How far is it from the picnic area to Crown Lake? __________
3. How far must you travel from cabin C to the bathhouse? __________
4. What is the distance from the nature trail to Crown Lake? __________
5. Your family is staying in cabin A. How far must you travel from the gate to the cabin? __________
6. What is the approximate distance in miles from the beginning to the end of the nature trail? __________
7. How far must your family travel to the store if you are staying in cabin D?

   ____
8. How far is it from the store to cabin B? __________
9. The end of the nature trail is how far from the picnic area? __________
10. How far is the bathhouse from cabin A? __________

Name ____________________

Flying from Place to Place

You are an airline pilot. You will need a ruler for this activity.

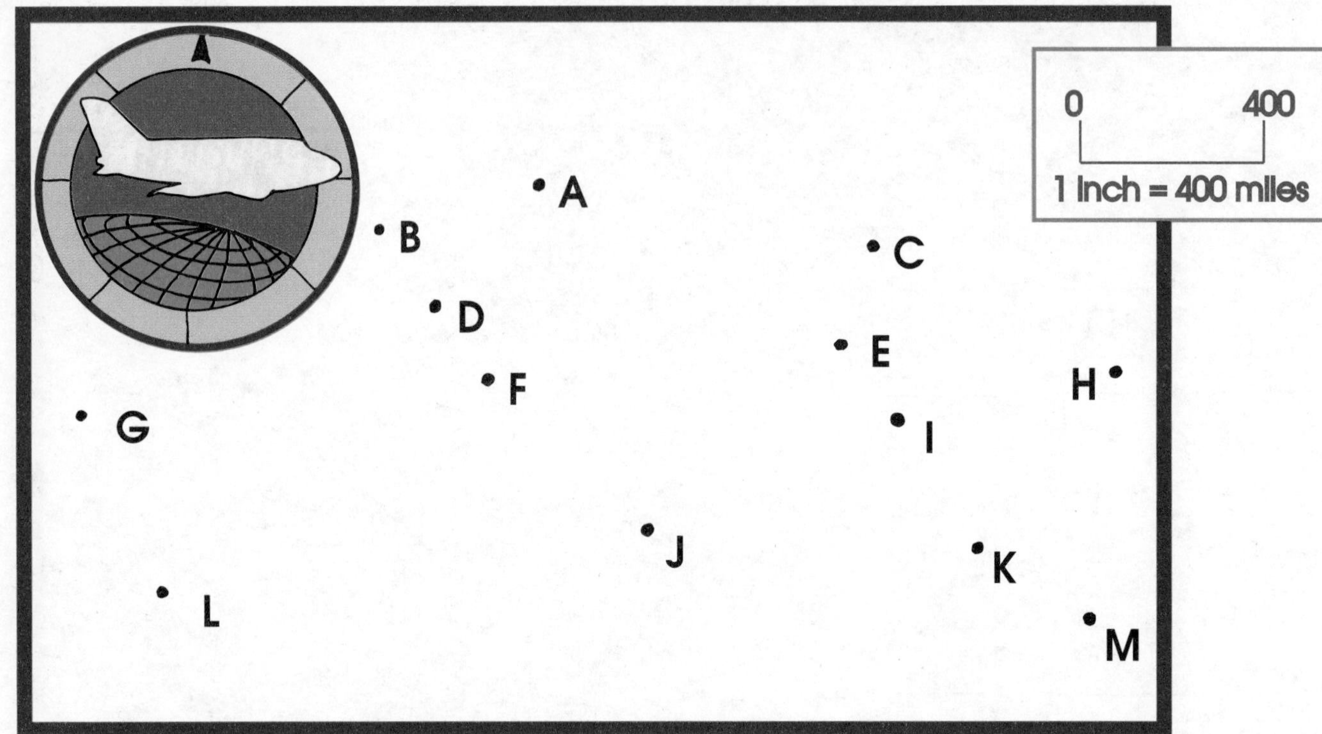

1. You need to file a flight plan from city **J** to city **C**. How far will the plane travel? ____________________
2. You must fly from city **D** to city **F** to city **E**. How many miles will you travel? ____________________
3. How far is it from city **H** to city **C**? ____________________
4. Is it closer to fly from city **I** to city **M** or from city **I** to city **A**? ____________
5. If your plane holds enough fuel to fly 500 miles, can you fly from city **L** to city **G** without refueling? ____________________
6. With fuel for 500 miles, can you fly from city **A** to city **J**? ____________
7. About how many miles is it from city **C** to city **M**? ____________
8. What direction must you fly from city **H** to city **F**? ____________
9. What direction must you fly from city **J** to city **K**? ____________

Name ____________________

Amazing Arizona

Get to know Arizona, the 48th state. Below is a map showing the largest Indian reservations and cities located in or near them in Arizona. Use the scale to answer the questions.

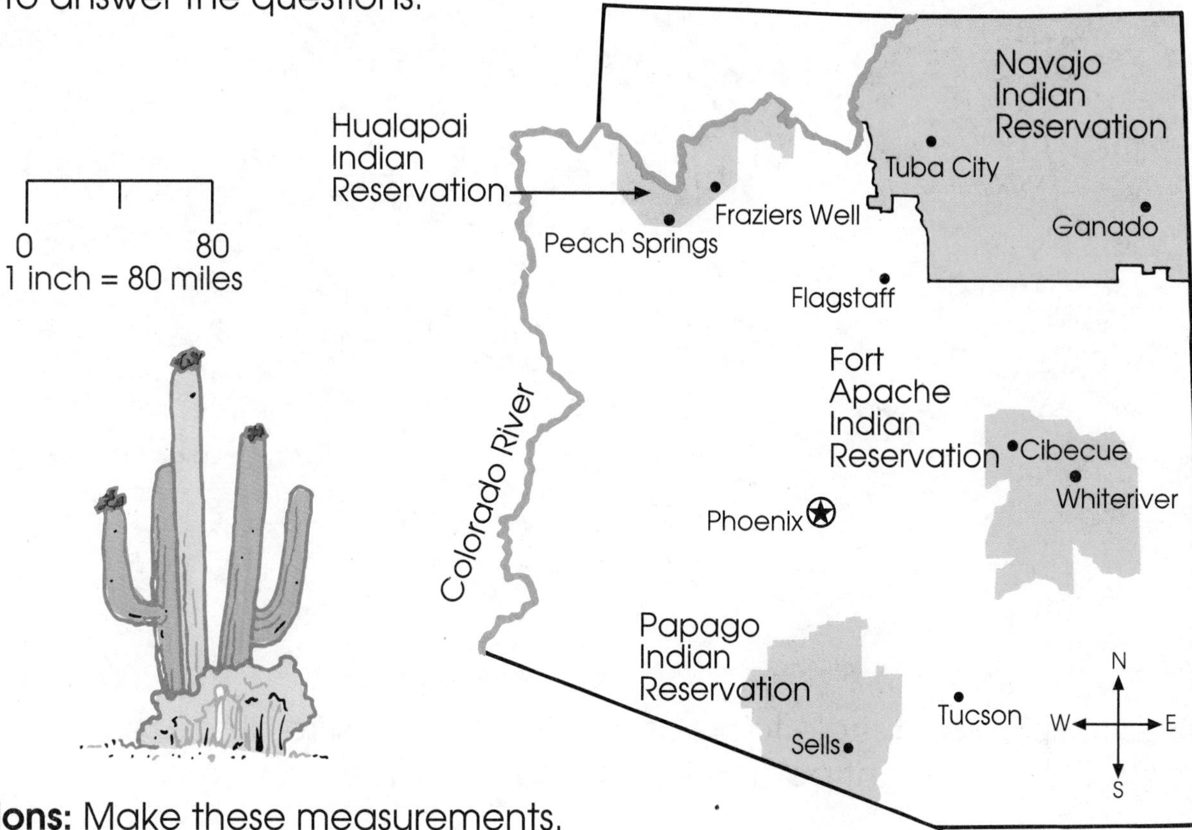

Directions: Make these measurements.

1. About how many miles from Phoenix to Peach Springs? ____________________
2. About how many miles from north to south on its eastern border? ____________________
3. About how many miles from Flagstaff to Ganado? __________
4. From Tucson to Flagstaff? _____
5. From Whiteriver to Ganado? ____________________
6. From Tuba City to Tucson? ____________________
7. From Peach Springs to Sells? ____________________
8. From Cibecue to Sells? __________
9. The Fort Apache Indian Reservation from north to south at its greatest distance. __________
10. The Navajo Indian Reservation from east to west at its greatest distance. ____________________

Name____________________________________

Flight Path Frenzy

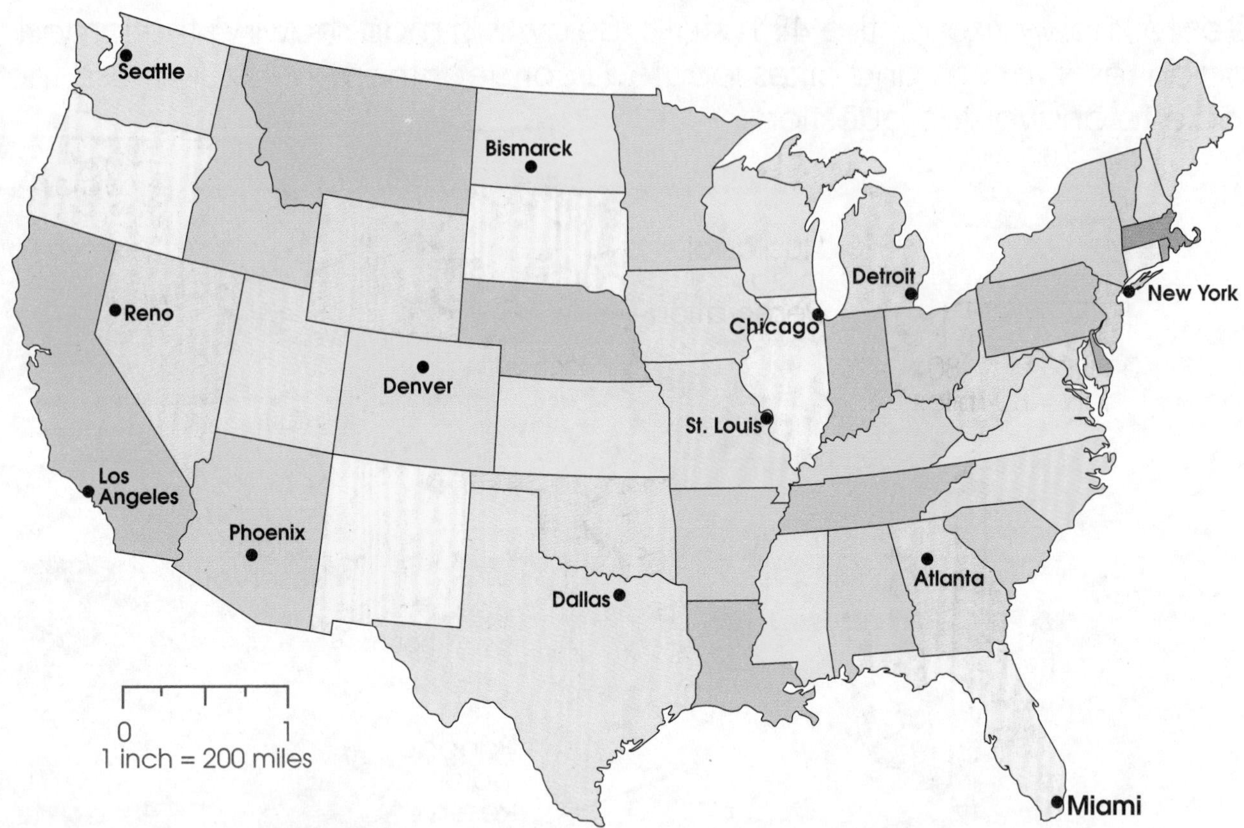

Directions: Use the scale to measure the approximate distance of these flights. Draw the flight paths using the colors stated.

From:

1. Atlanta to Dallas______miles (orange)
2. Denver to Chicago ______miles (purple)
3. Los Angeles to Phoenix______miles (yellow)
4. Seattle to Dallas ______miles (green)
5. St. Louis to New York______miles (brown)
6. Denver to Miami ______miles (red)
7. Reno to Detroit ______miles (dark blue)
8. Los Angeles to New York______miles (pink)
9. Seattle to St. Louis______miles (black)
10. Chicago to Miami______miles (light blue)

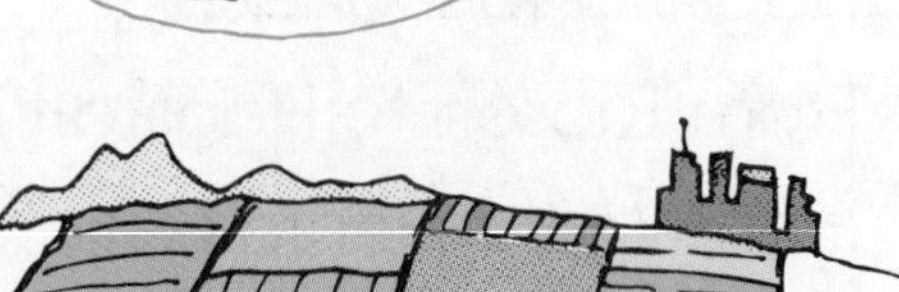

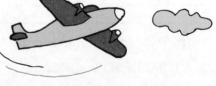

Name ______________________________

Traveling on Different Roads

Use a ruler to measure distances on this map and answer the questions below. Don't forget to use the compass rose and the legend.

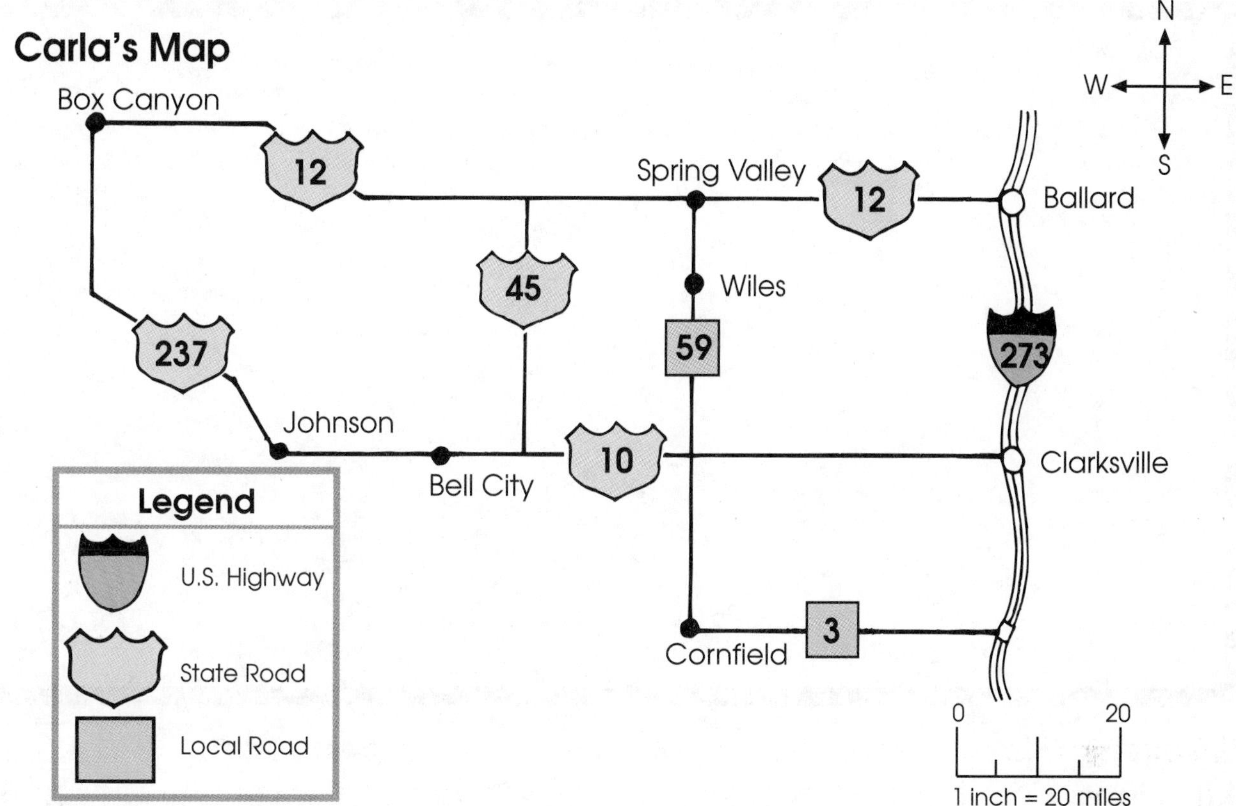

1. What U. S. highway would you travel on from Clarksville to Ballard? ________
2. If Carla travels from Bell City to Clarksville, what state road will she use?
   ____
3. How far is it from Johnson to Bell City? ______________________________
4. Do you take a state or local road to travel from Wiles to Spring Valley? ______
   ____
5. Cornfield is located at the junction of which two local roads? __________
   ____
6. What direction is Johnson from Bell City? ______________________________
7. If you plan a trip from Clarksville to Ballard, what direction will you be traveling? ______________________________

Name ____________________________________

Recreation Location

You are the planner for a new recreation center. Use the map scale to measure and draw its features, following the directions below.

0 20
1 inch = 20 feet

Directions:

1. Draw a 20 ft. square in the SE corner of the map.
2. Draw a rectangle N of the square 25 ft. wide by 45 ft. long.
3. Draw a rectangle in the SW corner, measuring 60 ft. long by 25 ft. wide.
4. Draw a 20 ft. square in the NW corner of the map.
5. Draw another 20 ft. square east of the square you drew in #4.

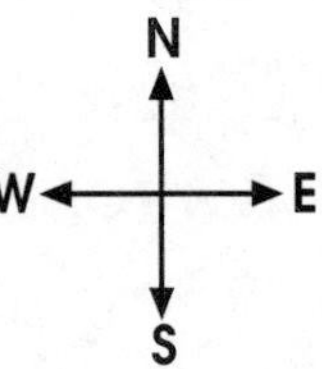

Add details to your shapes to transform the shapes into . . .

1. a racquetball court.
2. a basketball court.
3. a swimming pool.
4. a golf driving range.
5. a baseball batting cage.

Write a name for the recreation center in the middle.

Name ______________________________

How Many People?

This map uses symbols to show how many people live in each town. Use this map and the legend to answer the questions below.

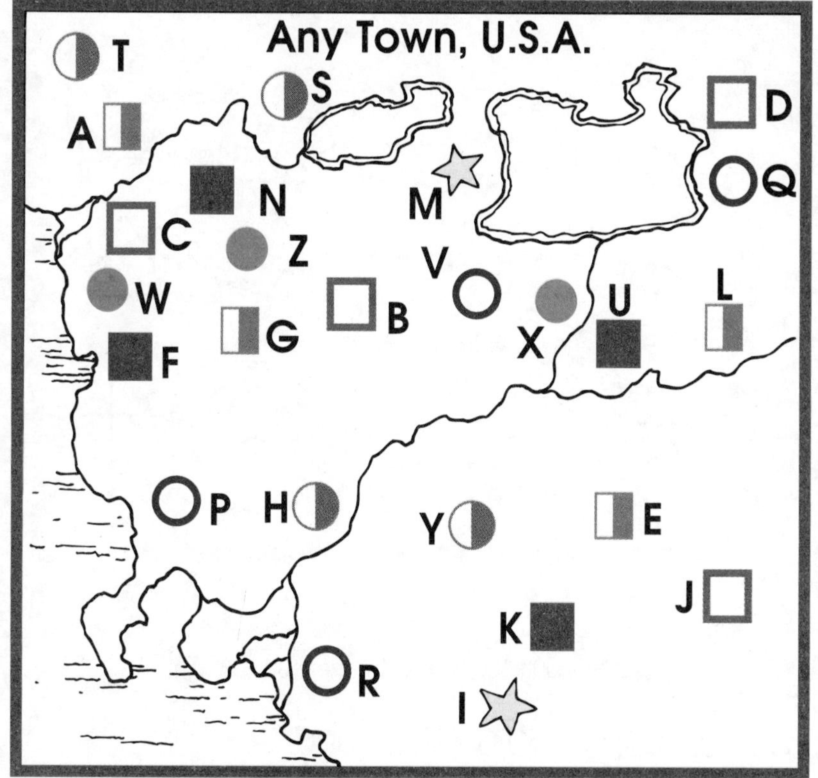

Legend

People

0-500

500-1,000

1,000-5,000

5,000-25,000

25,000-50,000

50,000-100,000

over 100,000

1. How many people live in a town that has this symbol ? __________
2. What does mean on the map? __________
3. Name the four towns with 0-500 people. __________
4. How many towns have 1,000-5,000 people? __________
5. How many people live in town G? __________
6. Circle the town with the most people. A B I
7. Circle the town with the fewest people. L K J
8. Name the towns with 1,000-5,000 people. __________
9. How many towns have over 100,000 people? __________
10. Name the towns with 50,000-100,000 people. __________
11. Draw a circle around the towns with 500-1,000 people.
12. Draw a large **X** on the towns with 25,000-50,000 people.

Name ______________________________

What Is the Population?

Use this map of an imaginary state to answer the following questions.

Population Map

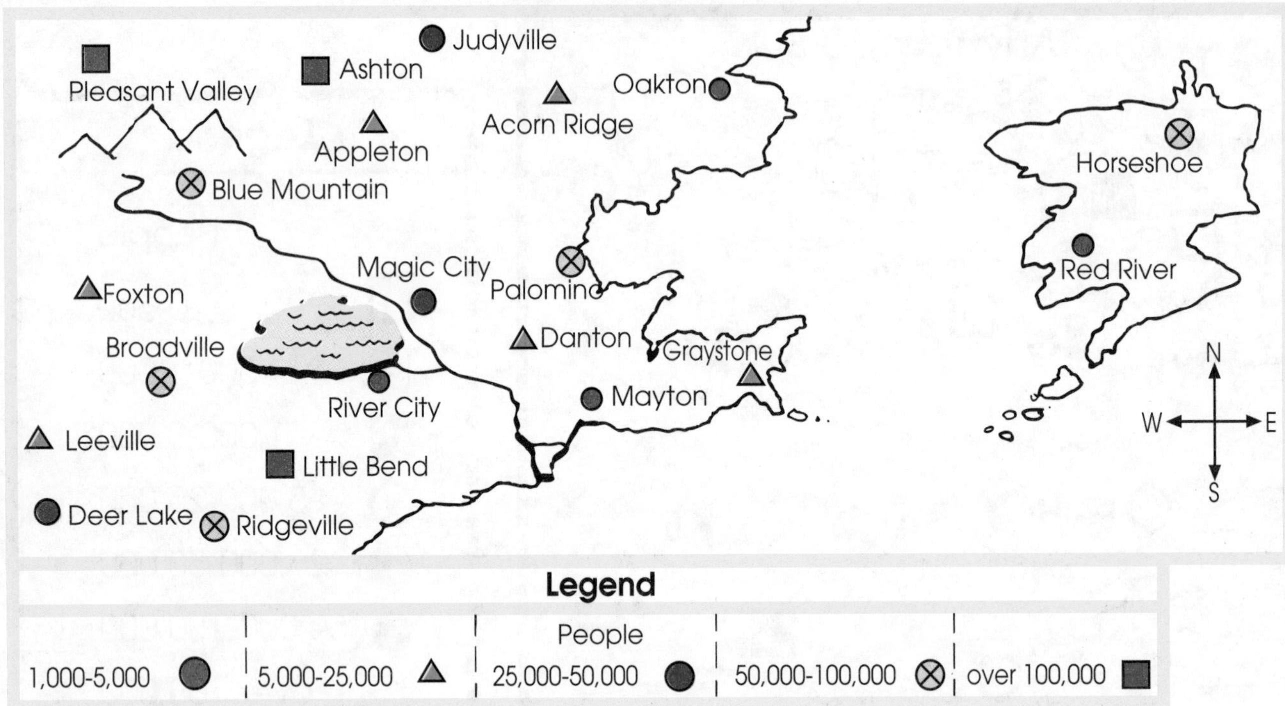

1. Name the five cities with a population of 50,000-100,000.

____

2. Would you choose Foxton or Ashton for a baseball stadium which seats 50,000 people? ______________________________
3. Name the three towns with a population over 100,000. ______________

____

4. Which is bigger—Pleasant Valley or Mayton? ______________
5. Which town has more people—River City or Magic City? ______________
6. Which town has more people—Judyville or Danton? ______________
7. Which is larger—Little Bend or Ridgeville? ______________
8. Which city is smaller—Blue Mountain or Deer Lake? ______________
9. How many towns have 1,000-5,000 people? ______________
10. How many towns have 5,000-25,000 people? ______________

Section 2

United States Geography

This page has been intentionally left blank.

Name Stephanie Rocha

What a Great Country!

The United States is a country. It is made up of many states. Make your own map of the United States. Cut out this page and page 93 along the outer dotted (- - - -) lines. Glue the tab to the back of the map on page 93.

United States Map

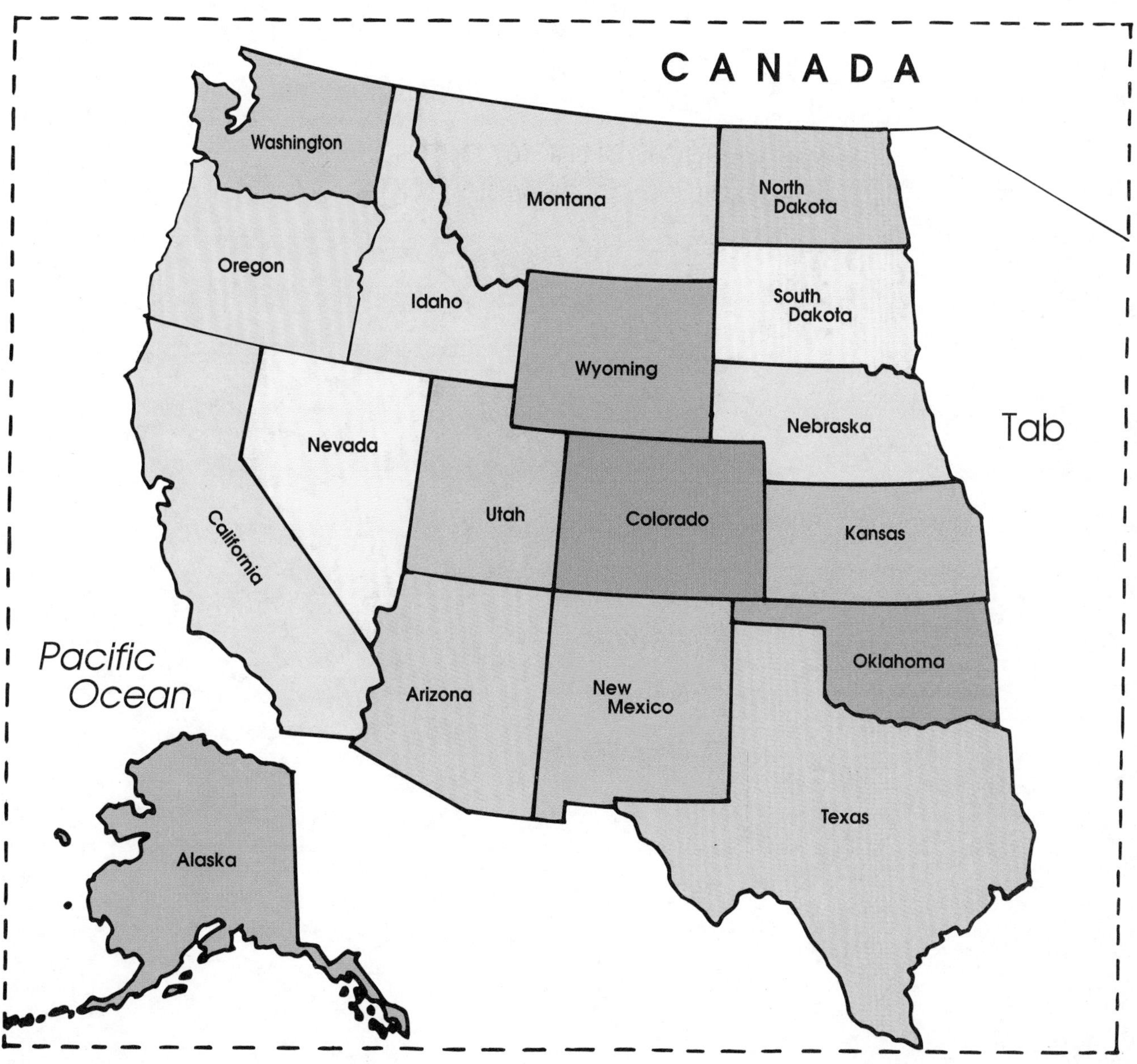

Page is blank for cutting exercise on previous page.

Name____________________

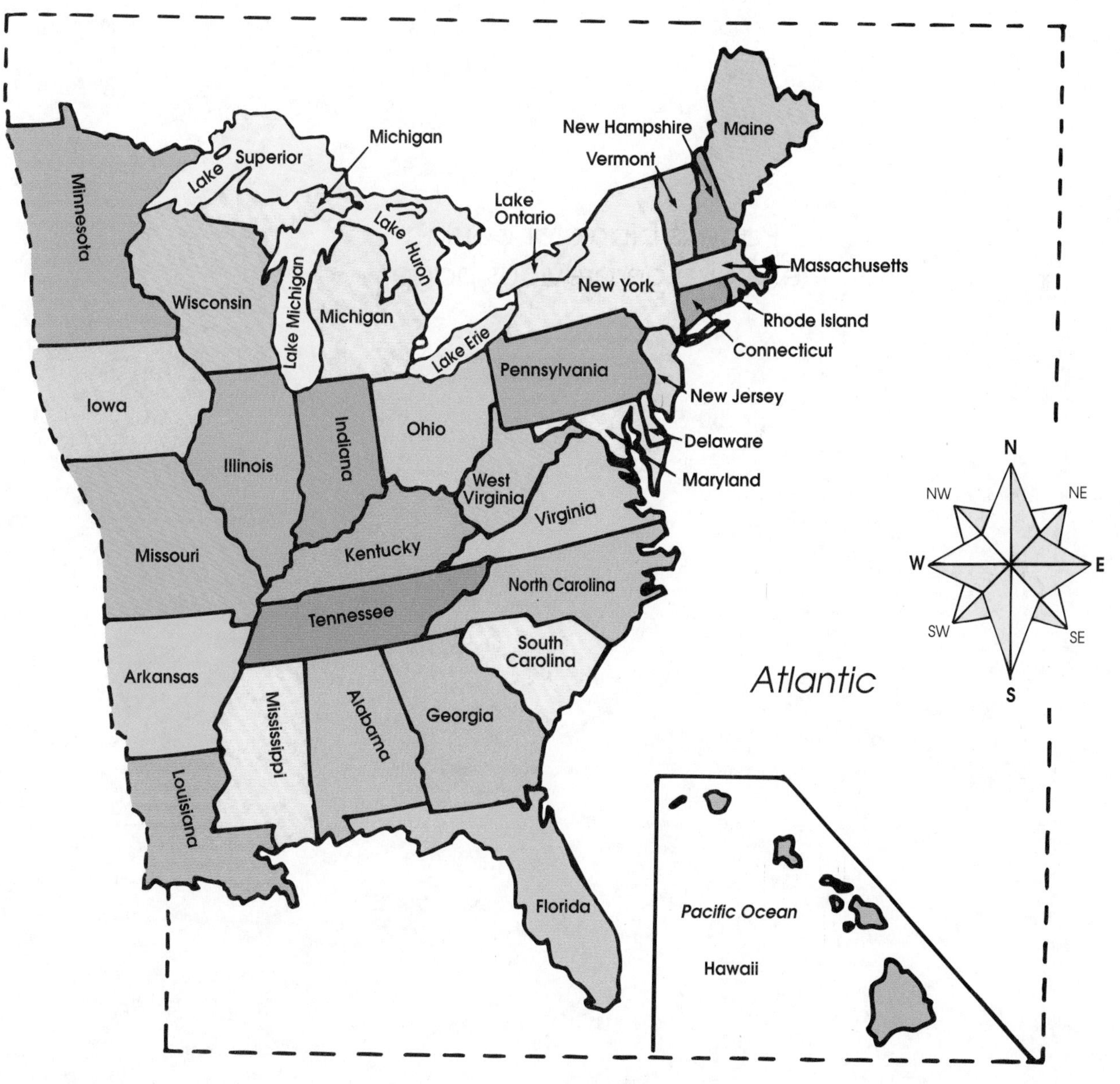
Lake Superior
Michigan
New Hampshire
Maine
Vermont
Minnesota
Lake Huron
Lake Ontario
Massachusetts
Wisconsin
Lake Michigan
Michigan
New York
Rhode Island
Connecticut
Lake Erie
Pennsylvania
Iowa
New Jersey
Ohio
Illinois
Indiana
Delaware
West Virginia
Maryland
Virginia
Missouri
Kentucky
North Carolina
Tennessee
South Carolina
Arkansas
Mississippi
Alabama
Georgia
Louisiana
Atlantic
Florida
Pacific Ocean
Hawaii
N
NW
NE
W
E
SW
SE
S

Page is blank for cutting exercise on previous page.

Name________________________________

Crossing the States

Use the map of the United States on pages 91 and 93 and the compass rose to fill in the puzzle.

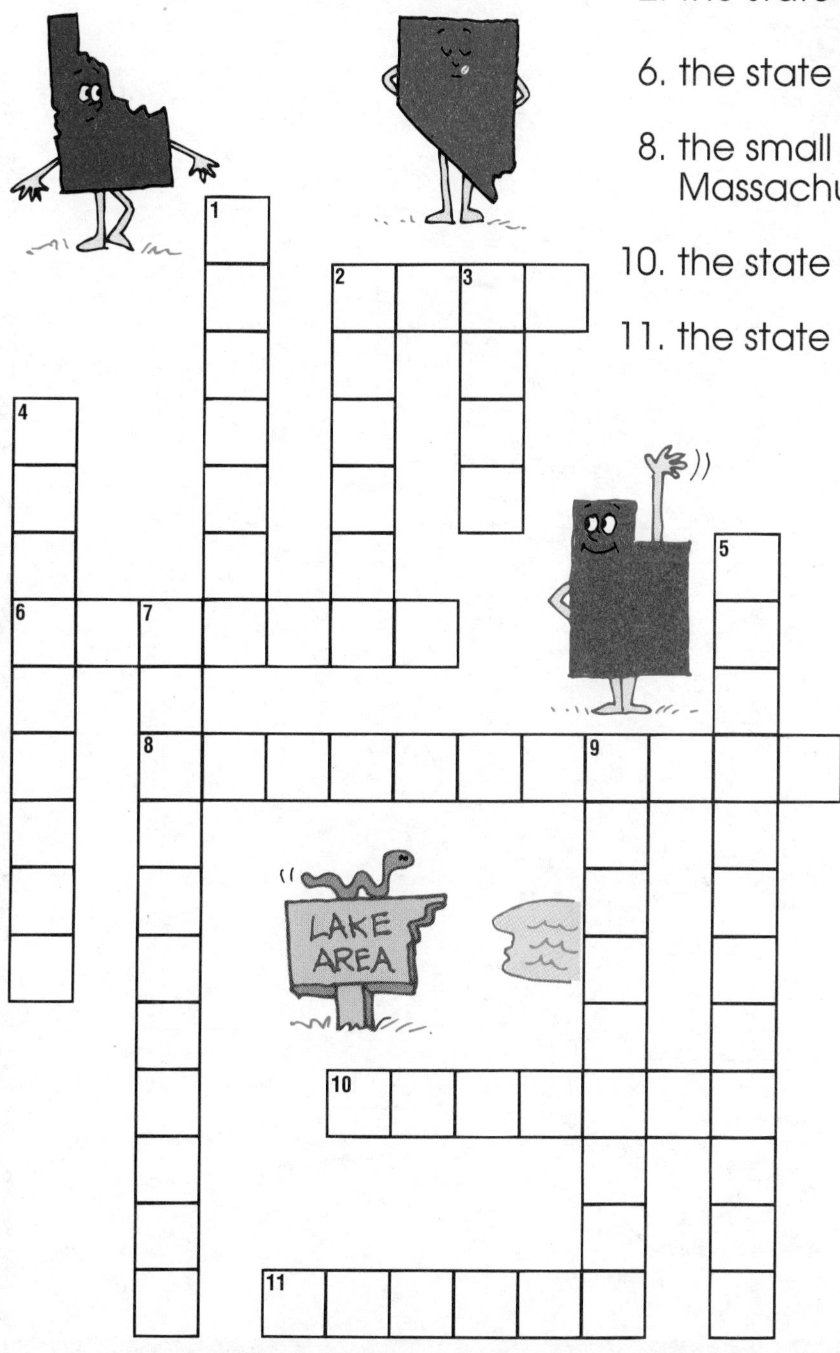

Across:

2. the state east of Indiana
6. the state west of North Dakota
8. the small state south of Massachusetts
10. the state south of Georgia
11. the state west of Utah

Down:

1. the state west of New Hampshire
2. the state south of Washington
3. the state north of Missouri
4. the state east of Arizona
5. the larger state south of New York
7. the state north of South Dakota
9. the state south of Arkansas

Name ______________________________

Postcard Geography

Use this postcard to tell a friend about a place within the states where you are vacationing.
Design your own stamp and write in your friend's address.

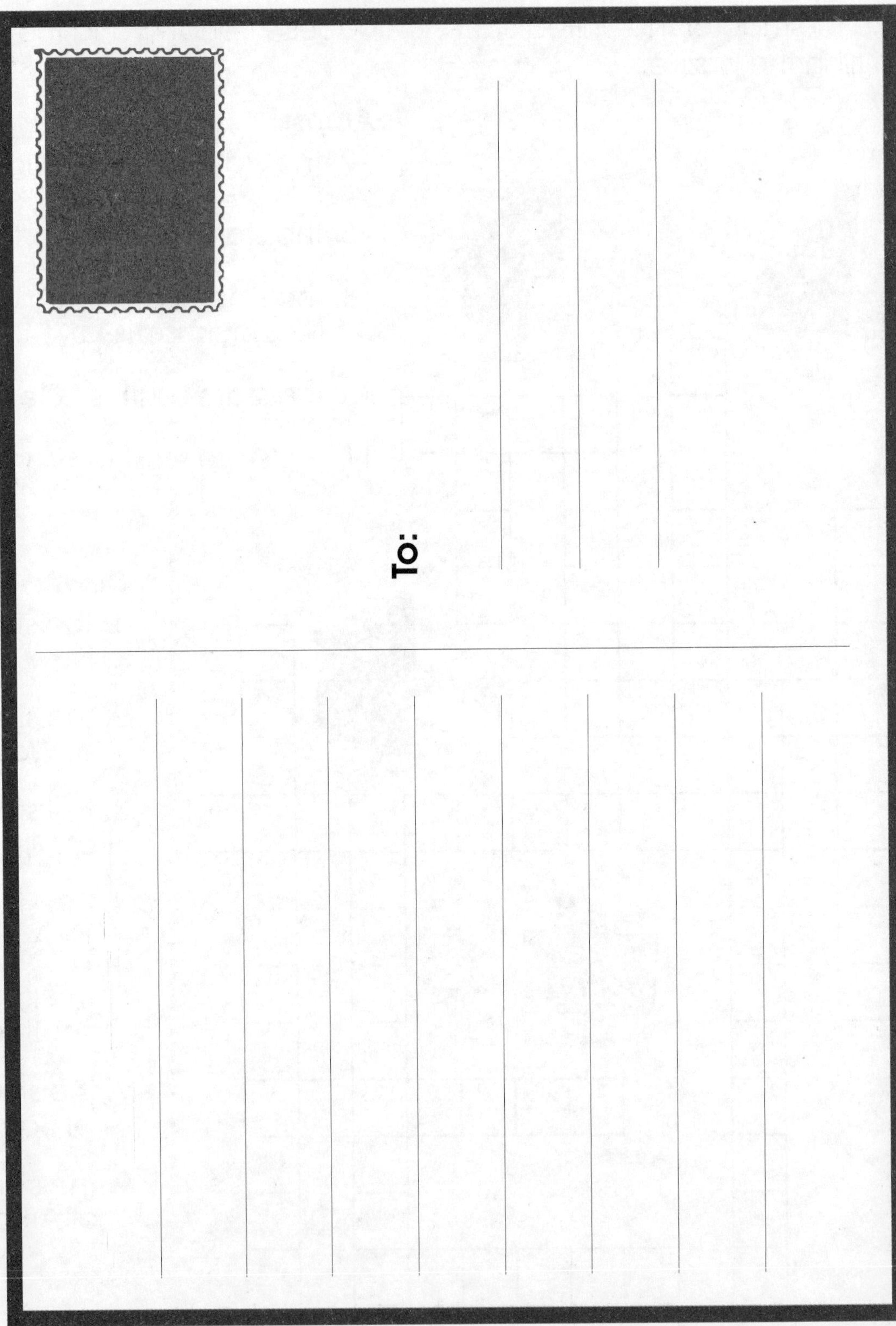

Name ____________________

See the States

Use the map of the United States that you made with pages 91 and 93. Color the van at the bottom of this page. Cut out along the outer line of the oval. Use a piece of tape to attach it to your pencil.

Now your van is packed and you are ready to start your trip. Read the sentences below. Move your pencil where the directions lead you to find answers to the questions below.

Directions:

1. Start in Ohio.
2. Go west to Iowa. Which states did you pass through?

   ____

3. Go south to Louisiana. Which states did you pass through?

   ____

4. Go west to California. Which states did you pass through?

   ____

   ____

5. Turn and go north to Washington. What state did you pass through?

   ____

6. It's time to head home to Ohio. In which direction will you travel?

   ____

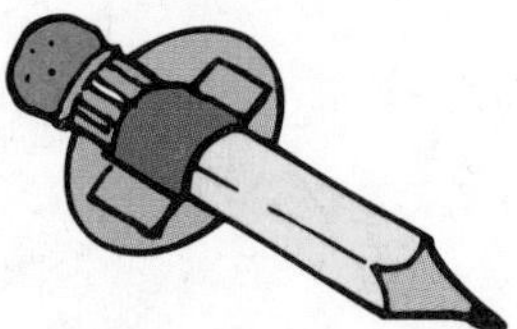

Name________________________________

Introduction: U.S. and States

What a Vacation!

This is a map of the United States. It shows where four children went for a vacation. Use this map and the key on page 99 to find out where each child went.

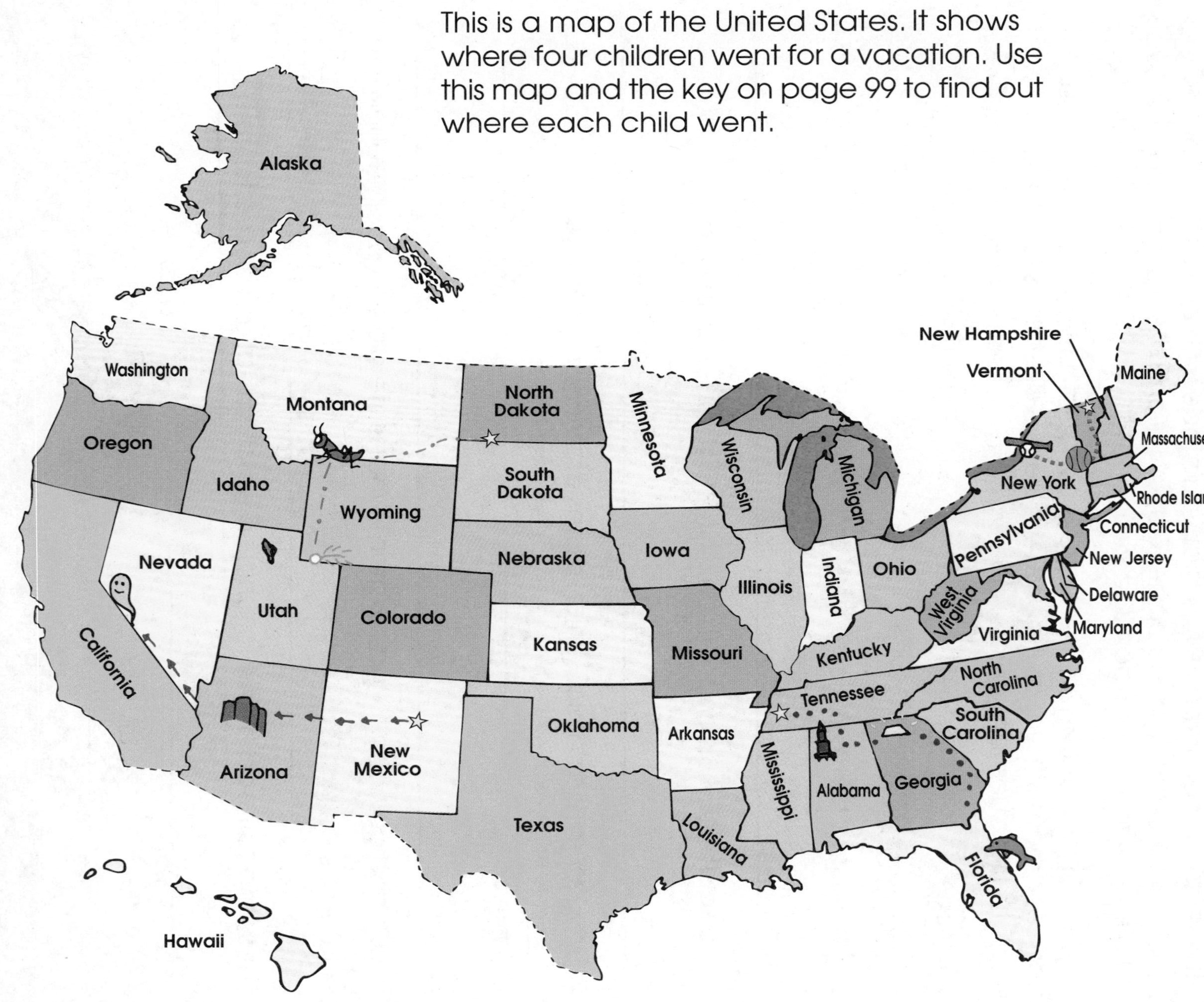

Name____________________________________

What a Vacation!

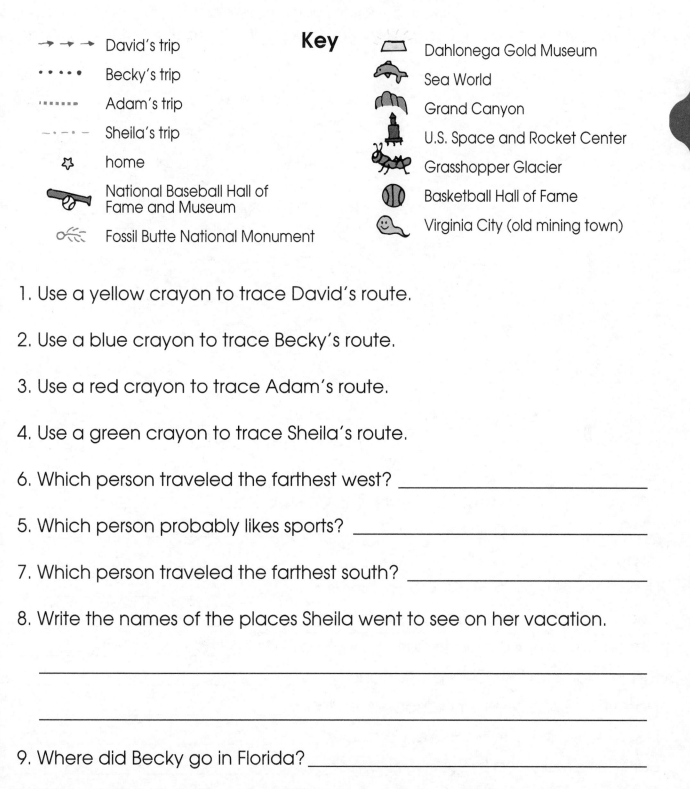

Key

- David's trip
- Becky's trip
- Adam's trip
- Sheila's trip
- home
- National Baseball Hall of Fame and Museum
- Fossil Butte National Monument
- Dahlonega Gold Museum
- Sea World
- Grand Canyon
- U.S. Space and Rocket Center
- Grasshopper Glacier
- Basketball Hall of Fame
- Virginia City (old mining town)

1. Use a yellow crayon to trace David's route.

2. Use a blue crayon to trace Becky's route.

3. Use a red crayon to trace Adam's route.

4. Use a green crayon to trace Sheila's route.

6. Which person traveled the farthest west? ____________________

5. Which person probably likes sports? ____________________

7. Which person traveled the farthest south? ____________________

8. Write the names of the places Sheila went to see on her vacation.

____

____

9. Where did Becky go in Florida? ____________________

Name ____________________

Flying Cross-Country

Pretend you are on an airplane that is flying cross-country. Name the states that you would fly over if you flew in a straight line from the first city to the second.

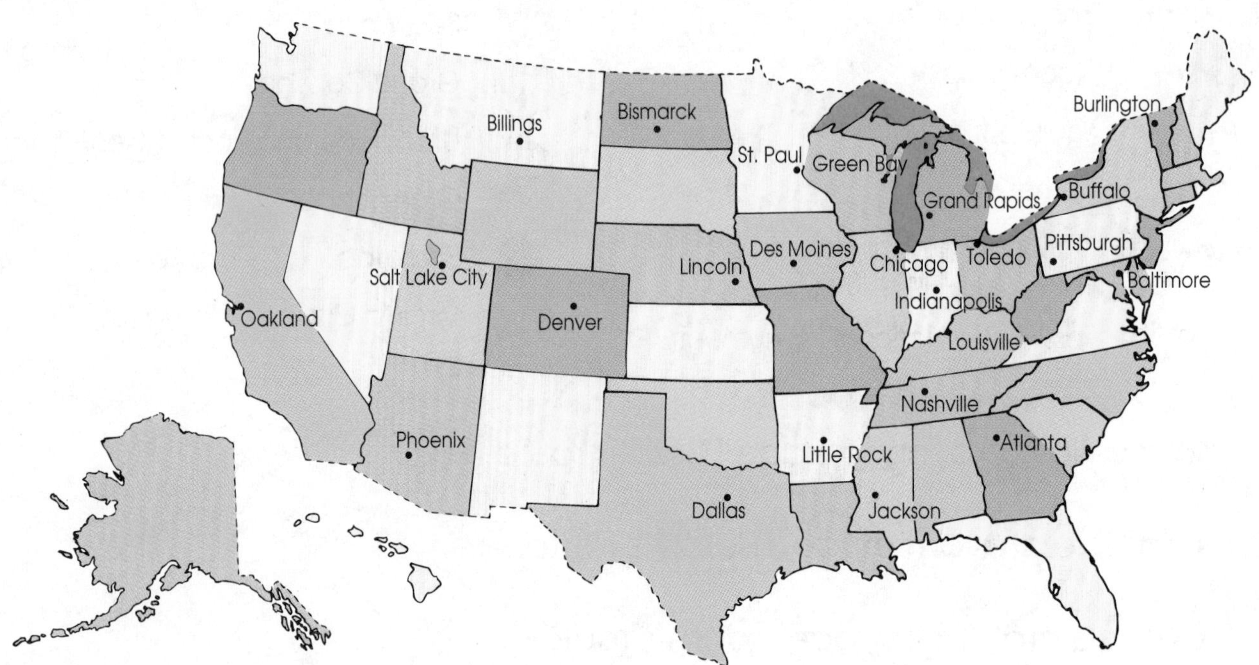

Atlanta, Georgia to Jackson, Mississippi ____________________

Grand Rapids, Michigan to St. Paul, Minnesota ____________________

Bismarck, North Dakota to Lincoln, Nebraska ____________________

Oakland, California to Salt Lake City, Utah ____________________

Phoenix, Arizona to Dallas, Texas ____________________

Little Rock, Arkansas to Chicago, Illinois ____________________

Toledo, Ohio to Green Bay, Wisconsin ____________________

Pittsburgh, Pennsylvania to Burlington, Vermont ____________________

Denver, Colorado to Billings, Montana ____________________

Nashville, Tennessee to Indianapolis, Indiana ____________________

Des Moines, Iowa to Louisville, Kentucky ____________________

Baltimore, Maryland to Buffalo, New York ____________________

Name ____________________

State Snatcher

The State Snatcher has stolen some of the abbreviations of the states. Write in the missing abbreviations. Use another U.S. map to help you.

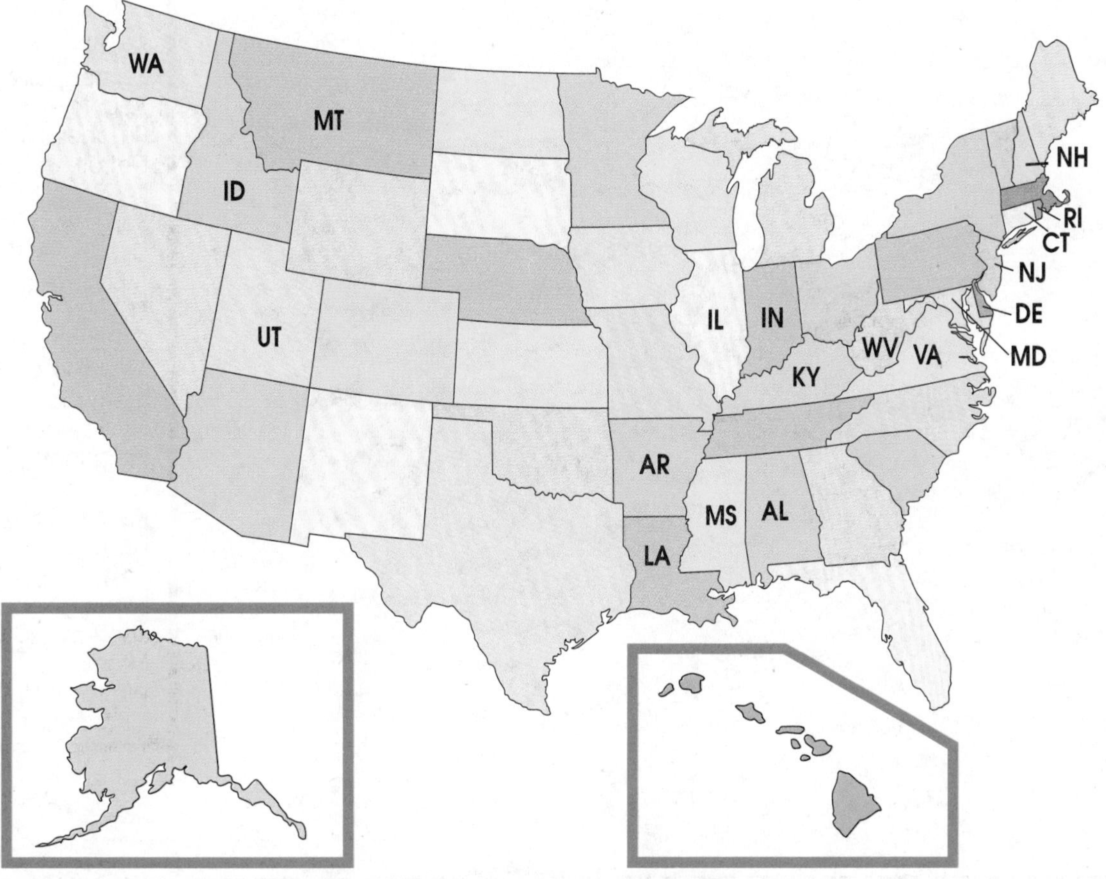

Postal Abbreviations Chart

Alabama	AL	Indiana	IN	Nebraska	NE	South Carolina	SC
Alaska	AK	Iowa	IA	Nevada	NV	South Dakota	SD
Arizona	AZ	Kansas	KS	New Hampshire	NH	Tennessee	TN
Arkansas	AR	Kentucky	KY	New Jersey	NJ	Texas	TX
California	CA	Louisiana	LA	New Mexico	NM	Utah	UT
Colorado	CO	Maine	ME	New York	NY	Vermont	VT
Connecticut	CT	Maryland	MD	North Carolina	NC	Virginia	VA
Delaware	DE	Massachusetts	MA	North Dakota	ND	Washington	WA
Florida	FL	Michigan	MI	Ohio	OH	West Virginia	WV
Georgia	GA	Minnesota	MN	Oklahoma	OK	Wisconsin	WI
Hawaii	HI	Mississippi	MS	Oregon	OR	Wyoming	WY
Idaho	ID	Missouri	MO	Pennsylvania	PA		
Illinois	IL	Montana	MT	Rhode Island	RI		

Name ______________________________

Super Cities

Write the name of each city in the blank by its number. Then, write each state's two-letter state abbreviation.

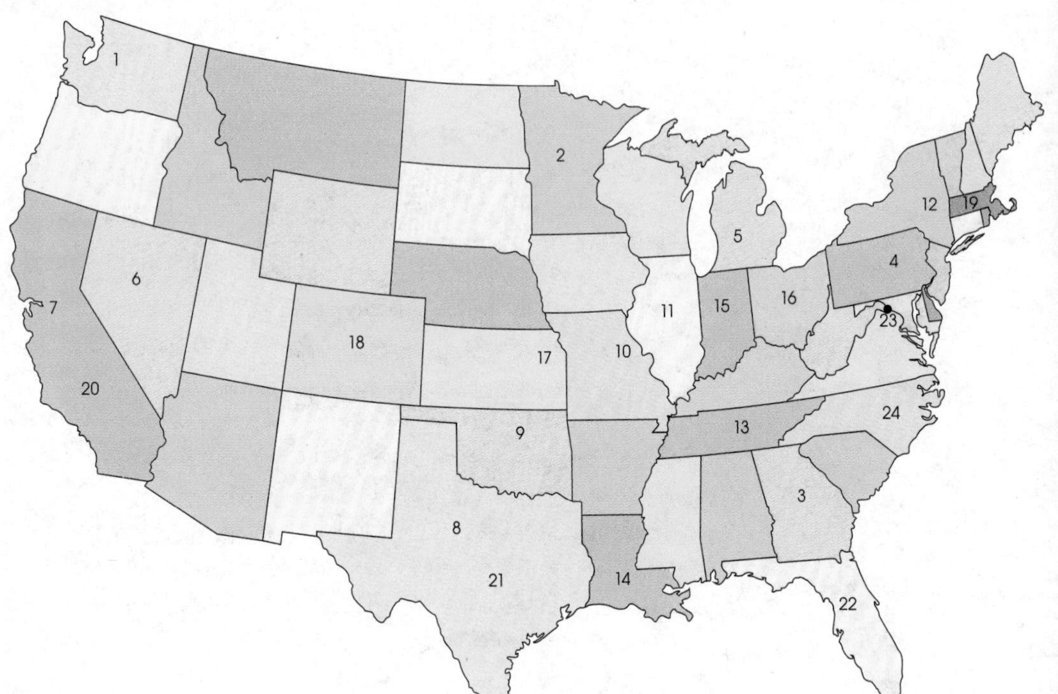

Cities

Seattle
Minneapolis
Atlanta
Philadelphia
Detroit
Las Vegas
San Francisco
Dallas
Tulsa
St. Louis
Chicago
New York City
Memphis
New Orleans
Indianapolis
Columbus
Kansas City
Denver
Boston
Los Angeles
San Antonio
Miami
Washington, D.C.
Charlotte

	City	State		City	State
1.	______	______	13.	______	______
2.	______	______	14.	______	______
3.	______	______	15.	______	______
4.	______	______	16.	______	______
5.	______	______	17.	______	______
6.	______	______	18.	______	______
7.	______	______	19.	______	______
8.	______	______	20.	______	______
9.	______	______	21.	______	______
10.	______	______	22.	______	______
11.	______	______	23.	______	______
12.	______	______	24.	______	______

Name ______________________

Play Ball!

In the spring, you can hear the umpire shout, "Play Ball!" In North America, there are 30 Major League baseball teams. Most of the teams are named after the city in which they play, but four teams are named after their states. Two of the teams are in Canada.

Write the name of the state/province where each team plays. You get bonus points if you can give the team name. Then, complete the map on page 104.

American League

City	State/Province	Team name
Baltimore		
Boston		
Anaheim	California	
Chicago		
Cleveland	Ohio	
Detroit		
Kansas City		
Minneapolis	Minnesota	
New York		
Oakland		
Seattle		
Arlington	Texas	
Tampa Bay		
Toronto		

National League

City	State/Province	Team name
Chicago		
Cincinnati		
Denver	Colorado	
Miami	Florida	
Houston		
Los Angeles		
Milwaukee		
Montreal		
New York		
Philadelphia		
Phoenix	Arizona	
Pittsburgh		
San Diego		
San Francisco		
St. Louis		
Atlanta		

Name____

Play Ball!

Label the cities where the Major League baseball teams play. Label the American League cities red and the National League cities blue.

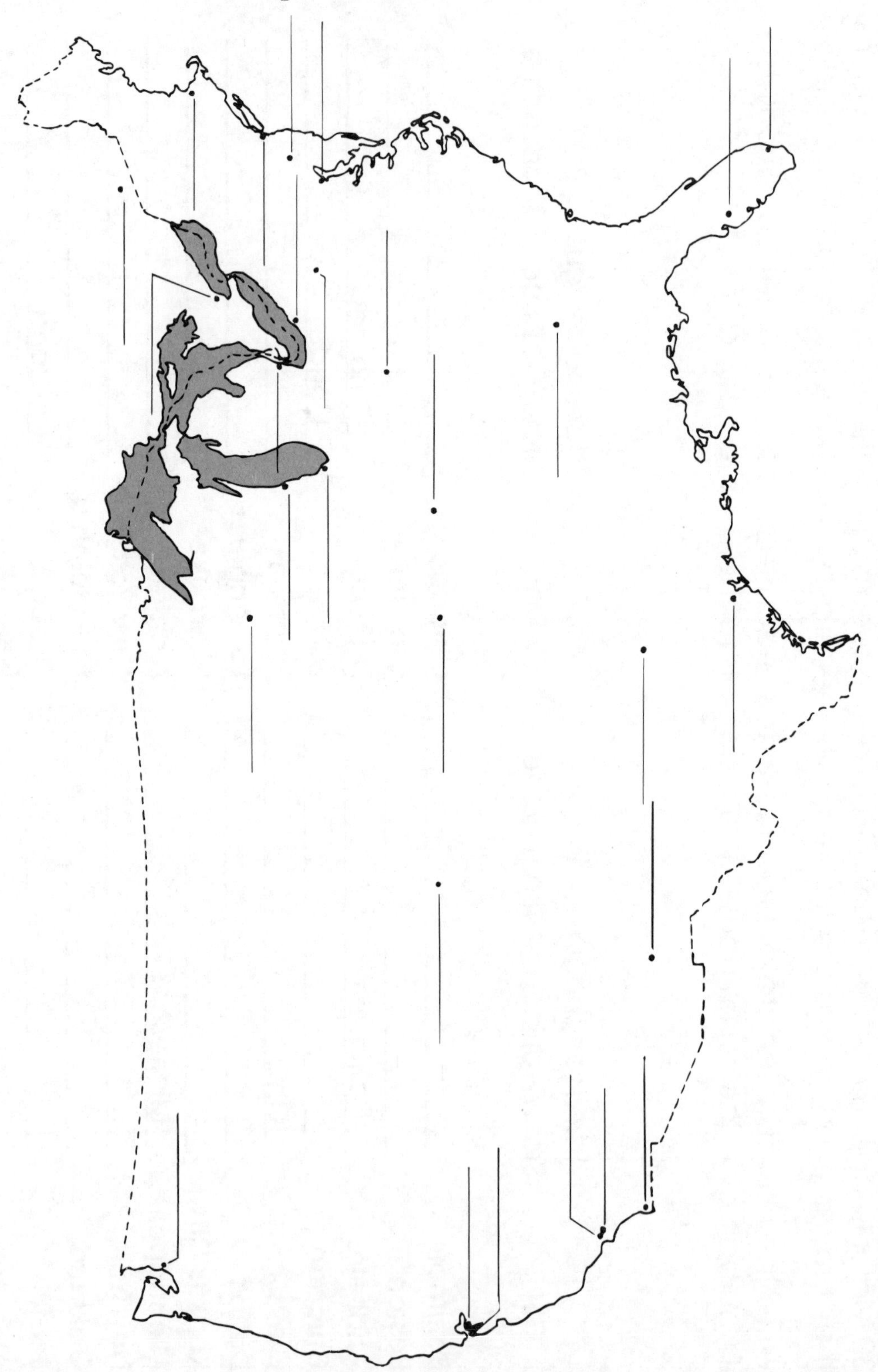

Name ____________________

Mystery States I

Can you identify these state shapes? Use a U.S. map to help you. Write the name of each state and its capital city ☆.

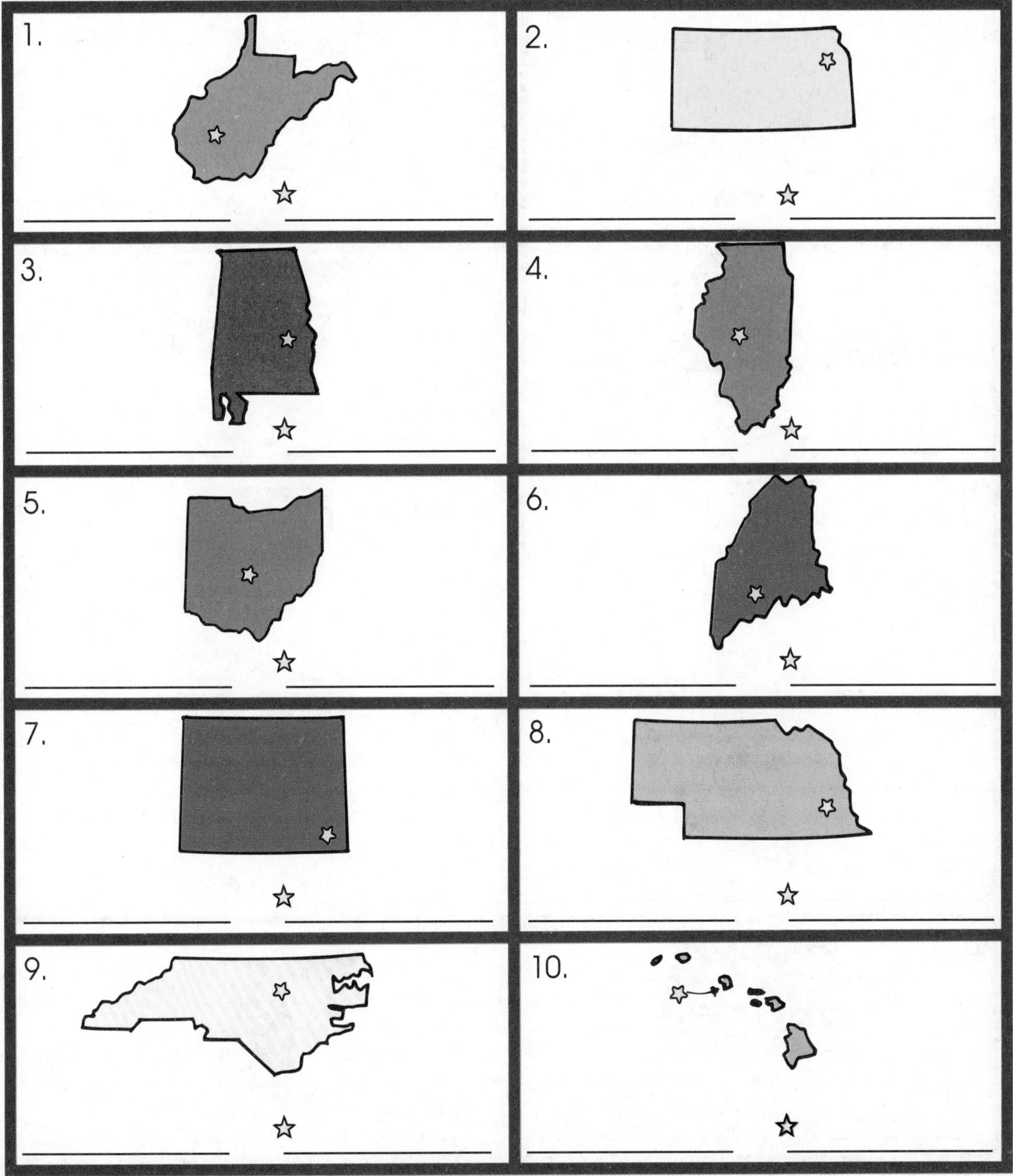

Name________________________________

Mystery States II

Can you identify these state shapes? Use a U.S. map to help you. Write the name of each state and its capital city ☆.

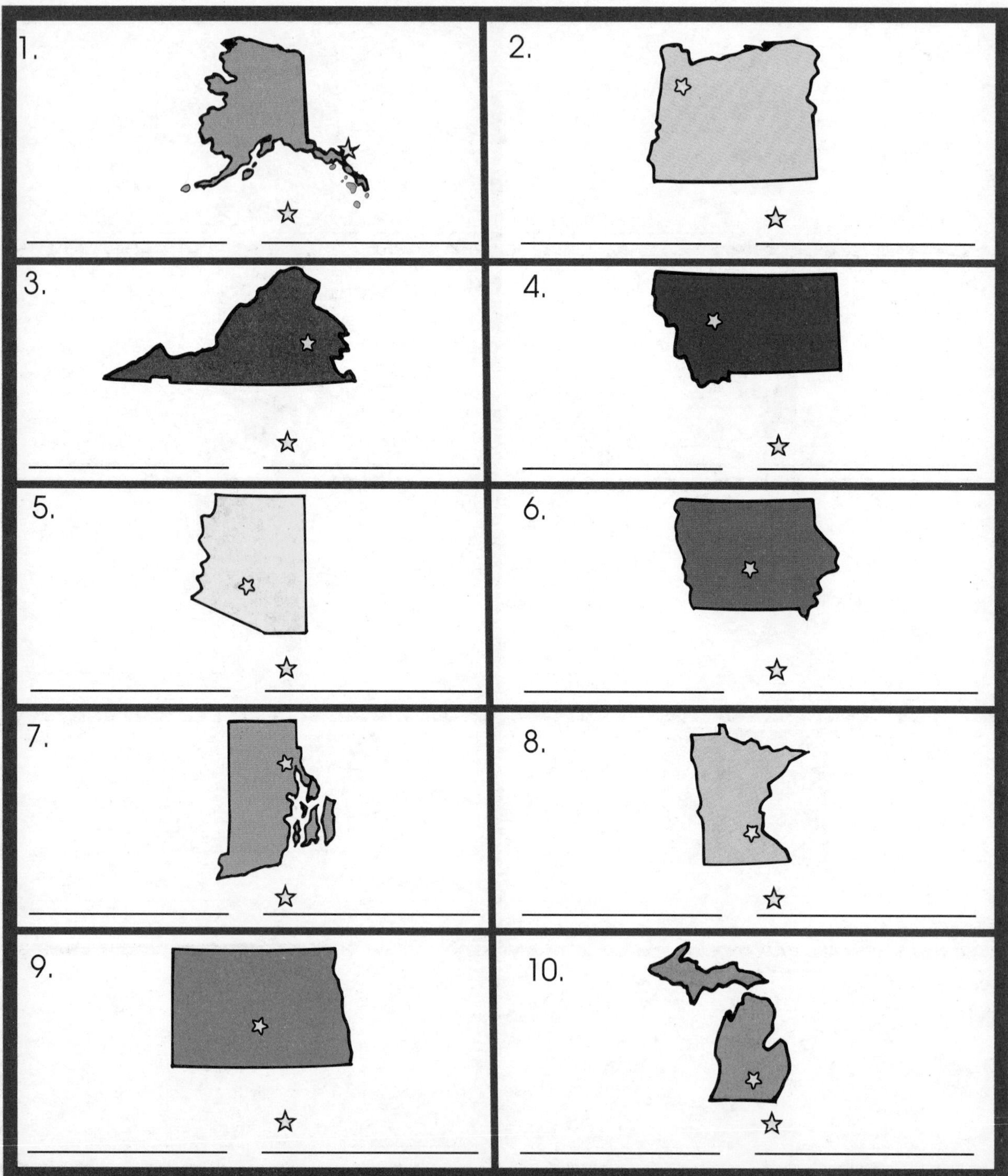

Name ______________________________

Mystery States III

Can you identify these state shapes? Use a U.S. map to help you. Write the name of each state and its capital city ☆.

1. ____________ ☆ ____________ 
2. ____________ ☆ ____________ 
3. ____________ ☆ ____________ 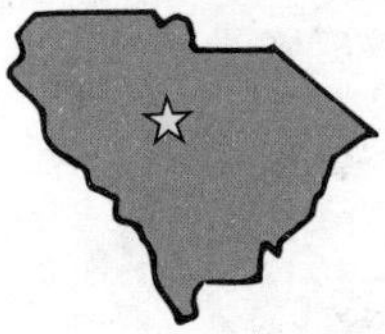
4. ____________ ☆ ____________ 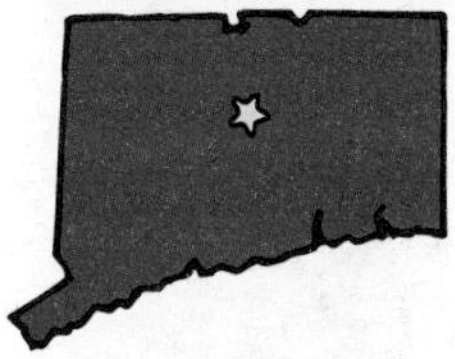
5. ____________ ☆ ____________ 
6. ____________ ☆ ____________ 
7. ____________ ☆ ____________ 
8. ____________ ☆ ____________ 
9. ____________ ☆ ____________ 
10. ____________ ☆ ____________

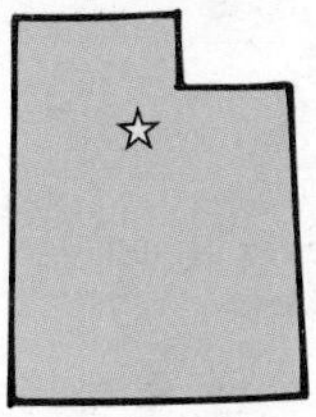

Name___________________________________

Mystery States IV

Can you identify these state shapes? Use a U.S. map to help you. Write the name of each state and its capital city ☆.

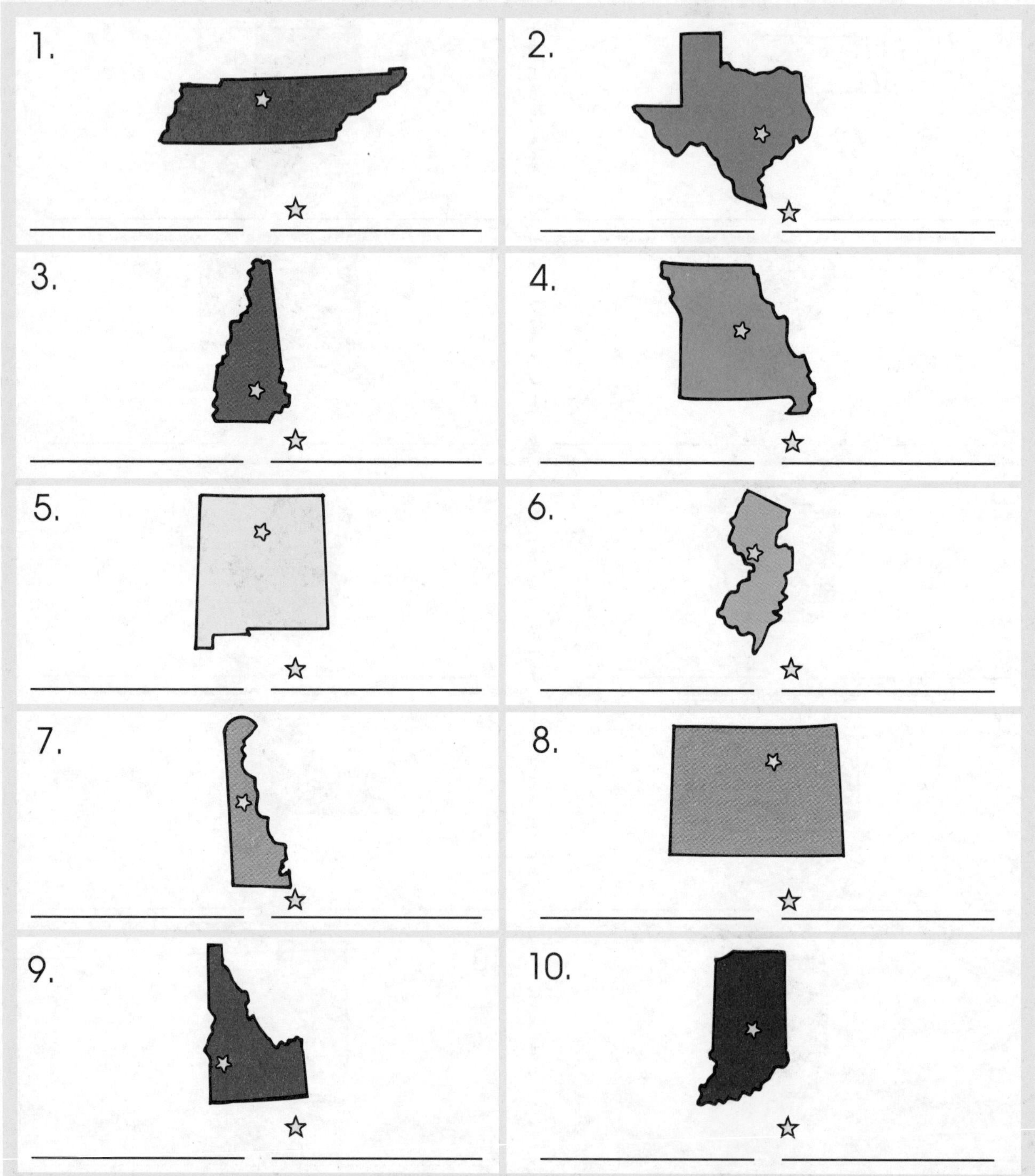

Name ______________________________

Mystery States V

Can you identify these state shapes? Use a U.S. map to help you. Write the name of each state and its capital city ☆.

1. ______________ ☆ ______________

2. ______________ ☆ ______________

3. ______________ ☆ ______________

4. ______________ ☆ ______________

5. ______________ ☆ ______________

6. ______________ ☆ ______________

7. ______________ ☆ ______________

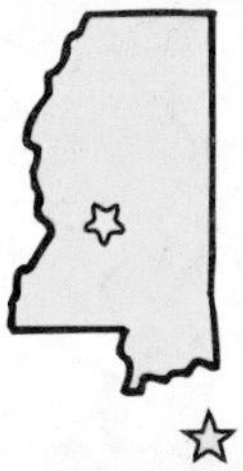

8. ______________ ☆ ______________

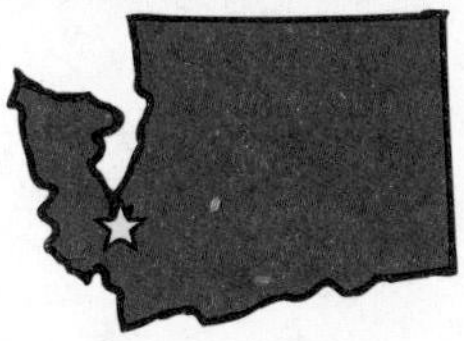

9. ______________ ☆ ______________

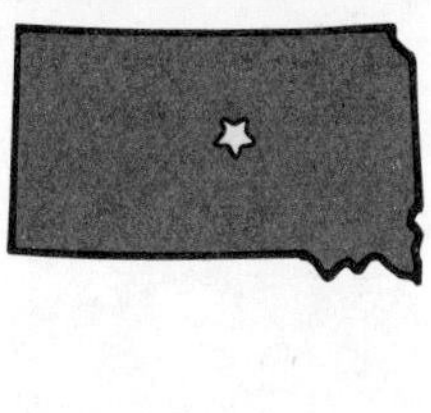

10. ______________ ☆ ______________

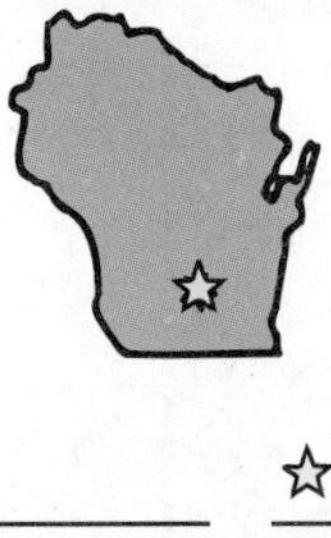

Name ____________________________________

My Hometown

Find and color your state on the United States map. Then, draw an outline map of your state in the space below. Label your hometown, capital and any other important cities, rivers and bodies of water.

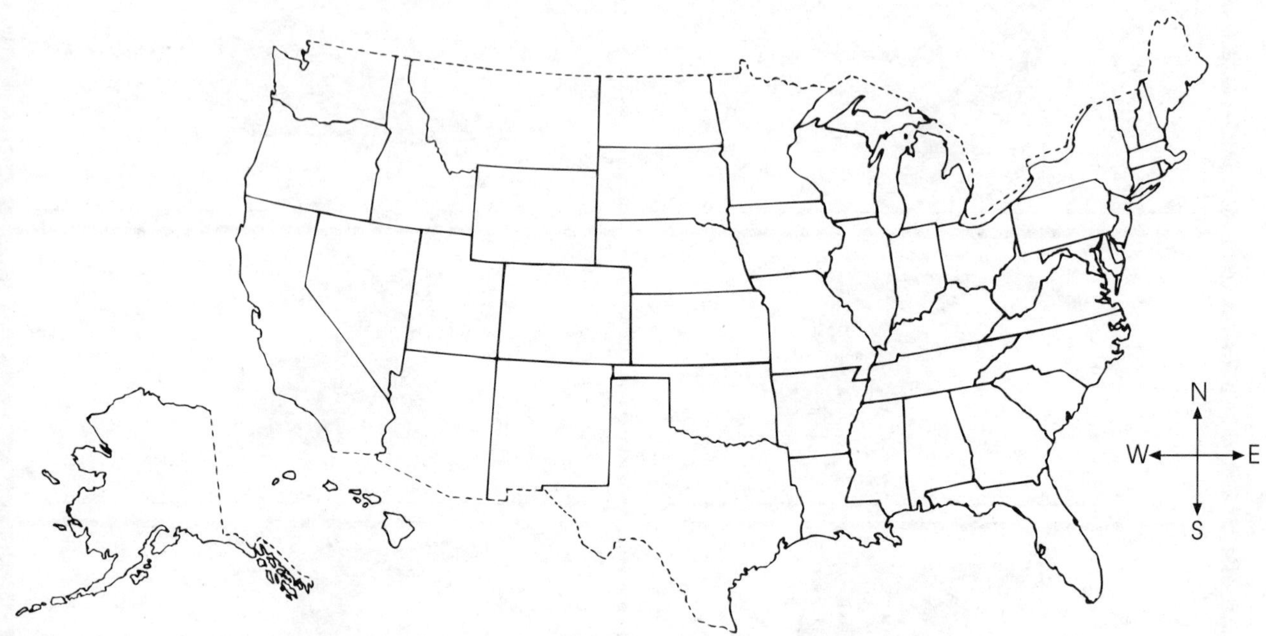

____

My State

Key

Home Town

☆ Capital

● Important Cities

N

W E

S

Name____

Near My State

Use a map of the United States to locate your state. Write the names of the bordering states/countries and/or bodies of water on the chart below. Write each one in its correct location relative to your state.

Northwest	**North**	**Northeast**
West	**My State** Draw an outline of your state.	**East**
Southwest	**South**	**Southeast**

Name____________________________________

"We're Going Places" Mileage Chart

Let's take a trip around your state. On the left side of the chart, fill in the names of five cities in your state. The first one should be your hometown. Then, write the names of five additional cities or places to visit in your state across the top. Use a state highway map or other source to find the number of miles between each place. Complete the chart.

Places to Visit in My State

Beach 21
Big City 14

Your State
AB23

Cities in My State

my hometown					

Name ____________________

Boundary Bonanza

Directions: Use the map on page 114 to answer these questions about boundaries.

1. Which state is made of islands? ____________
2. Which state is S of Utah? ____________
3. Which state is NE of Idaho? ____________
4. Which state is E of Ohio? ____________
5. Which state is W of Arkansas? ____________
6. Which state lies between Colorado and Missouri? ____________
7. Which two states are just S of Michigan? ____________
8. Which states touch New York on its eastern border? ____________

   ____________, ____________.

9. Which state is in the NE corner of the U.S.A.? ____________
10. Which state is S of Oklahoma? ____________
11. Which states border the Gulf of Mexico? ____________, ____________,

    ____________, ____________, ____________ .

12. The only state that borders Maine is ____________.
13. Four states that border Texas are ____________, ____________,

    ____________ and ____________.

14. The state S of North Dakota is ____________.
15. The state SW of Nebraska is ____________.

Name____________________________________

Across the Line

This is a map of the United States. The lines show the boundaries (lines that separate one state from another) of each state. Use this page with pages 113 and 115.

Name ________________________________

Across the Line

Directions: Use the United States map on page 114 to complete the following.

1. What is the name of the state in which you live? ____________________

2. Draw a blue line along the boundary lines of the state where you live.

3. What country is north of the United States? ____________________

4. Draw a green line along the boundary between the United States and Canada.

5. What country is south of the United States? ____________________

6. Draw an orange line along the southern boundary of the United States.

7. Find the state, country or body of water that is the . . .

   a. northern boundary of your state. Color it green.

   b. eastern boundary of your state. Color it blue.

   c. southern boundary of your state. Color it yellow.

   d. western boundary of your state. Color it red.

Name______________________________________

Boundaries and Rivers

Water Watch

Some of the largest lakes are shown on the map. Find and color them blue. Then, go on to page 117.

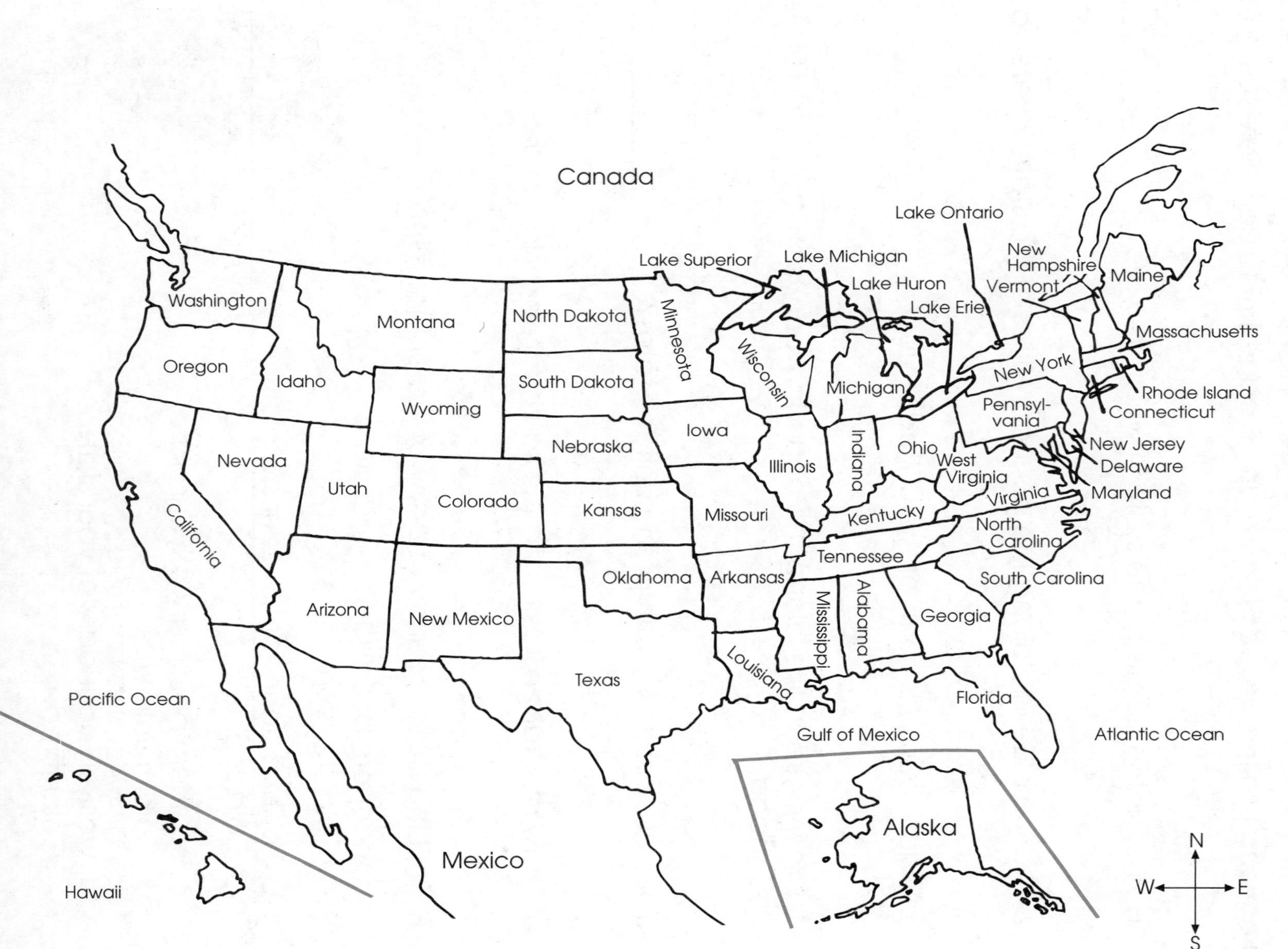

Name____

Water Watch

Directions: Use the maps on page 116 and 118 to find the answers to the questions.

1. The lakes along the northern border of the United States are called the Great Lakes. Write the names of these five lakes.

____

____

2. Which river flows along the border between Canada and Minnesota?

____

3. What is the name of the lake in Utah? ____________________

4. Which river flows along the border between Washington and Oregon?

____

5. Circle the name of the river that flows along the border between Mexico and the United States.

   Mississippi River   Rio Grande River   Yukon River   Missouri River

6. Circle the name of the river that flows through the state of Alaska.

   Mississippi River   Rio Grande River   Yukon River   Missouri River

7. How many states does the Mississippi River flow through or past?

____

Name____

Rivers Run Through It

Trace the contiguous U. S. A.´s major rivers in blue. Then, use the map to answer the river riddles on page 119.

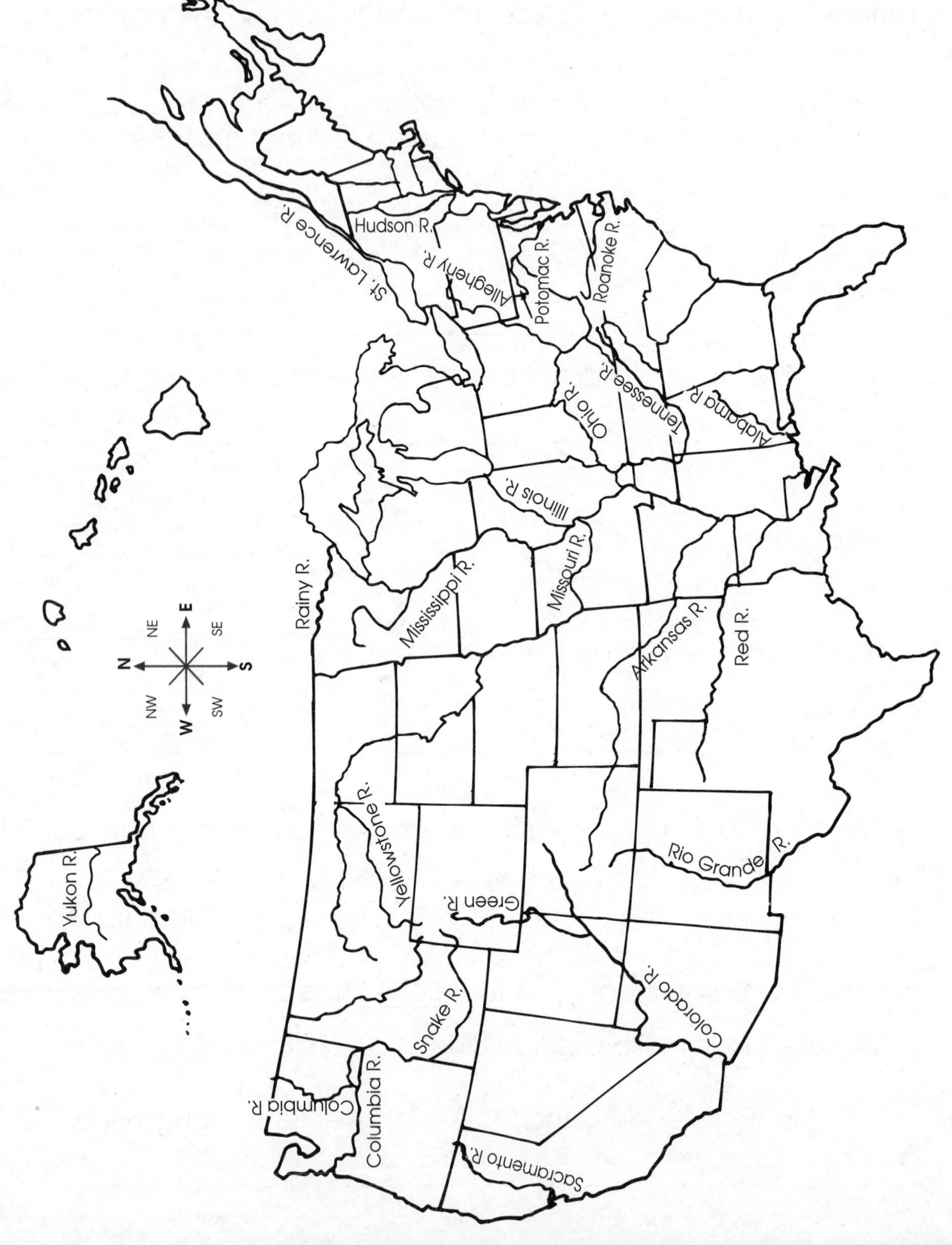

Name____

Rivers Run Through It

Directions: Use with page 118.

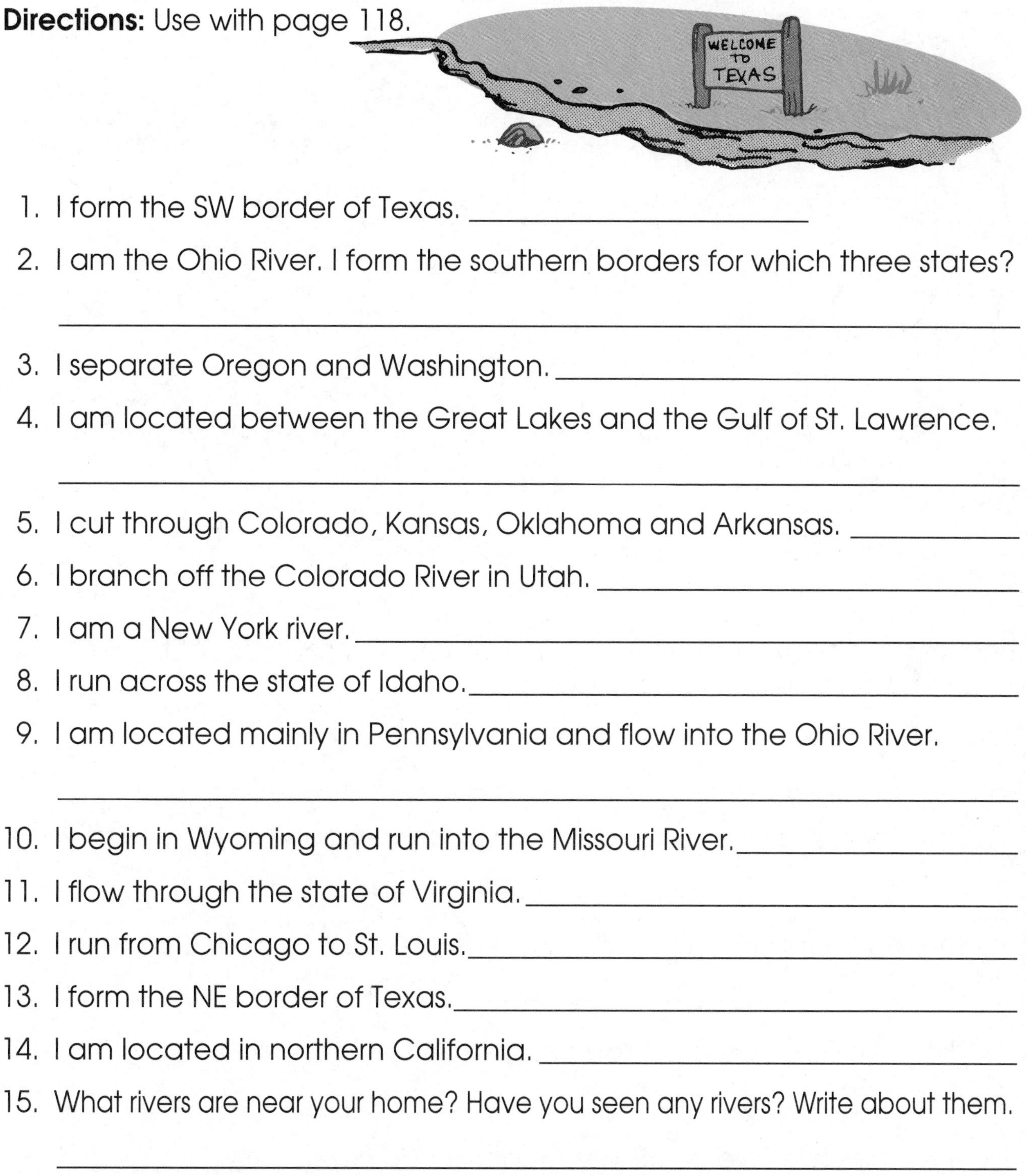

1. I form the SW border of Texas. ____________________
2. I am the Ohio River. I form the southern borders for which three states?

   ____

3. I separate Oregon and Washington. ____________________
4. I am located between the Great Lakes and the Gulf of St. Lawrence.

   ____

5. I cut through Colorado, Kansas, Oklahoma and Arkansas. __________
6. I branch off the Colorado River in Utah. ____________________
7. I am a New York river. ____________________
8. I run across the state of Idaho.____________________
9. I am located mainly in Pennsylvania and flow into the Ohio River.

   ____

10. I begin in Wyoming and run into the Missouri River.____________
11. I flow through the state of Virginia.____________________
12. I run from Chicago to St. Louis.____________________
13. I form the NE border of Texas.____________________
14. I am located in northern California. ____________________
15. What rivers are near your home? Have you seen any rivers? Write about them.

    ____

    ____

Name______________________________________

River Boundaries

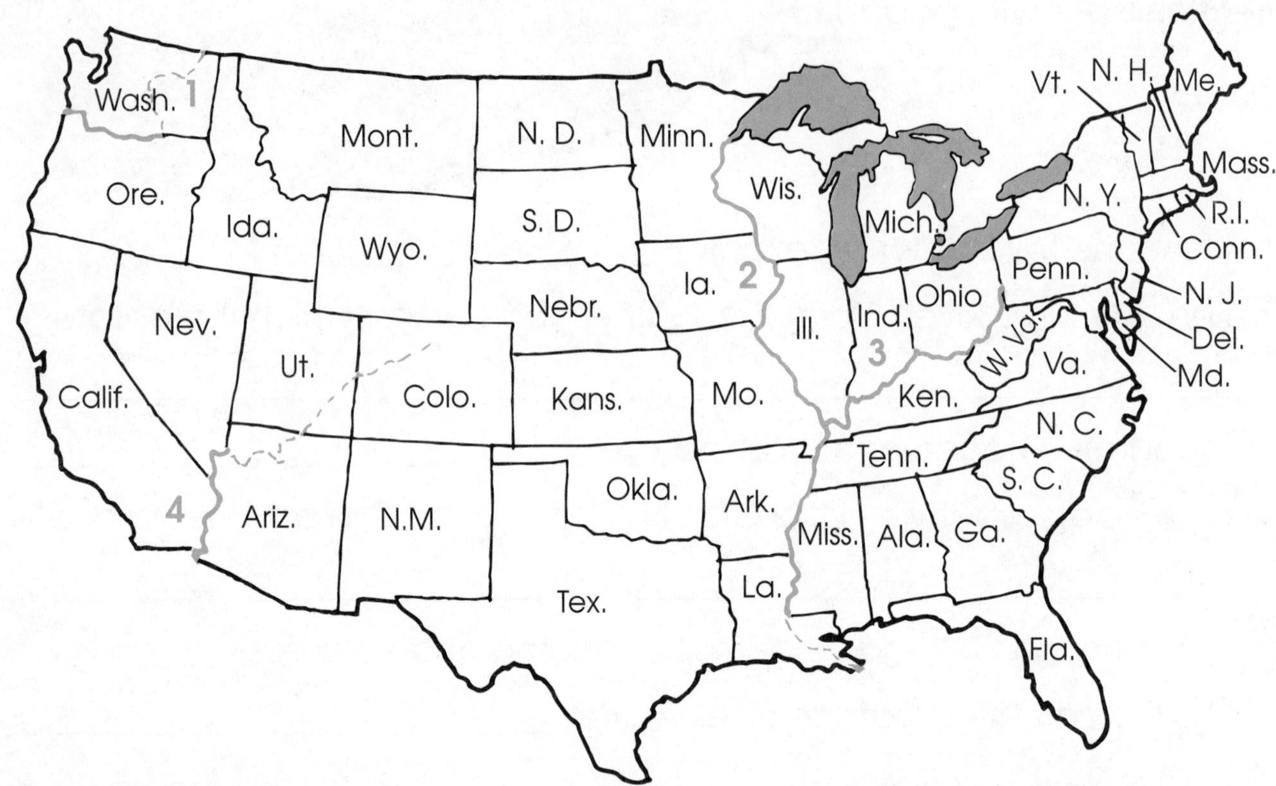

Directions: Write the number from the map by the name of each river. Refer to the map on page 29 to help you.

____ Colorado River ____Mississippi River ____Columbia River ____Ohio River

Use the map above to answer these questions.

1. The Columbia River forms a natural boundary between these states: ________________ and ____________________.

2. The Mississippi River forms all or part of the eastern borders of these states:__________, _________, __________, __________ and ________.

3. The Ohio River forms the southern borders of these states: __________ __________________________________ and____________________.

4. The Colorado River forms a short border between _______________ and____.

Name________________________________

Up the Lazy River

"The steamboat is coming!" was a cry heard in the many small river towns in the 1800s. Steamboats carried people and packages along the waterways before the faster railroads were developed.

The shipping tags below tell where each package is beginning and ending its journey. Use a map, atlas or other reference book to find the river on which the steamboat will be traveling. Some steamboats may have to travel on more than one river.

Directions: Write the name of the river route(s) on each shipping tag.

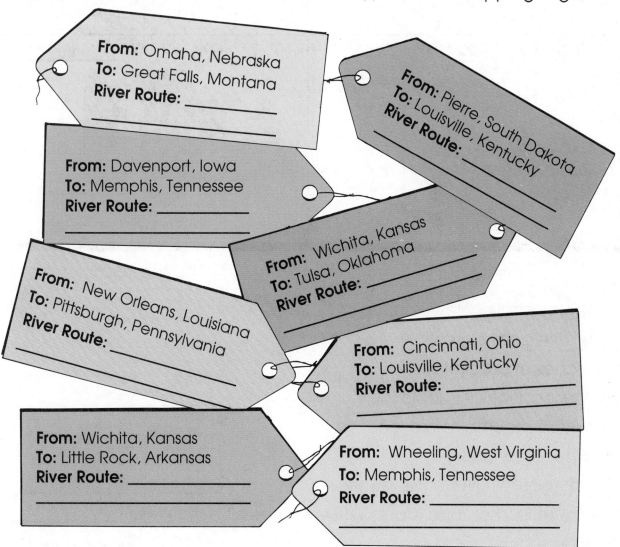

From: Omaha, Nebraska
To: Great Falls, Montana
River Route: ____________
____

From: Pierre, South Dakota
To: Louisville, Kentucky
River Route: ____________
____

From: Davenport, Iowa
To: Memphis, Tennessee
River Route: ____________
____

From: Wichita, Kansas
To: Tulsa, Oklahoma
River Route: ____________
____

From: New Orleans, Louisiana
To: Pittsburgh, Pennsylvania
River Route: ____________
____

From: Cincinnati, Ohio
To: Louisville, Kentucky
River Route: ____________
____

From: Wichita, Kansas
To: Little Rock, Arkansas
River Route: ____________
____

From: Wheeling, West Virginia
To: Memphis, Tennessee
River Route: ____________
____

Name____________________________________

Focusing on Four

Shown are four kinds of maps.

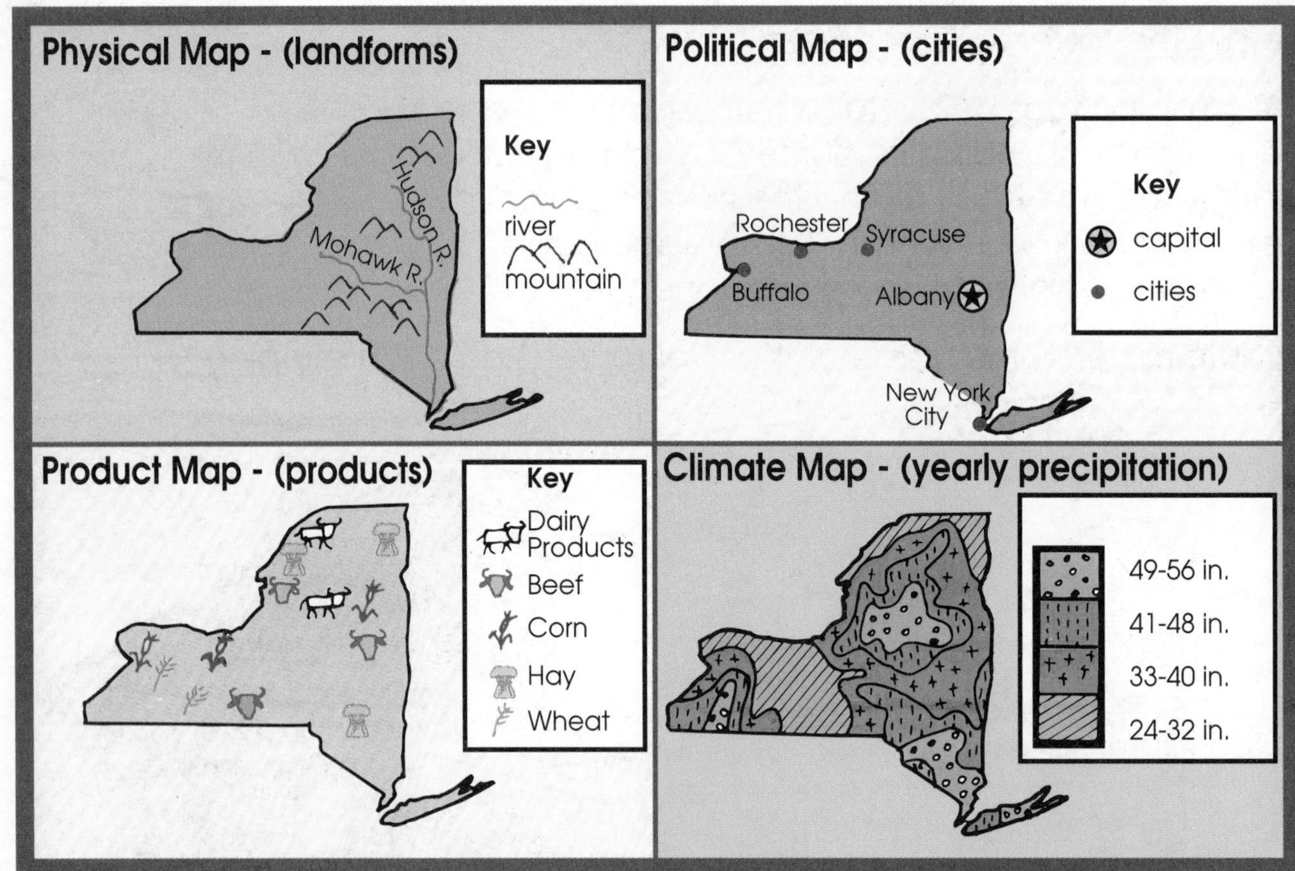

To find out . . .	Use this kind of map . . .
1. the capital of New York	____________
2. where corn is grown	____________
3. inches of precipitation	____________
4. the location of Buffalo	____________
5. where mountains are located	____________
6. where hay grows	____________
7. if Syracuse is NW of New York City	____________
8. where Hudson and Mohawk Rivers meet	____________
9. where dairy cattle are raised	____________

Name________________________________

Political Maps

Political maps not only show where cities are located, they also show boundary lines between states and between countries.

Key

State boundary ____
International boundary - - - -
Cities ●
State Capitals ☆

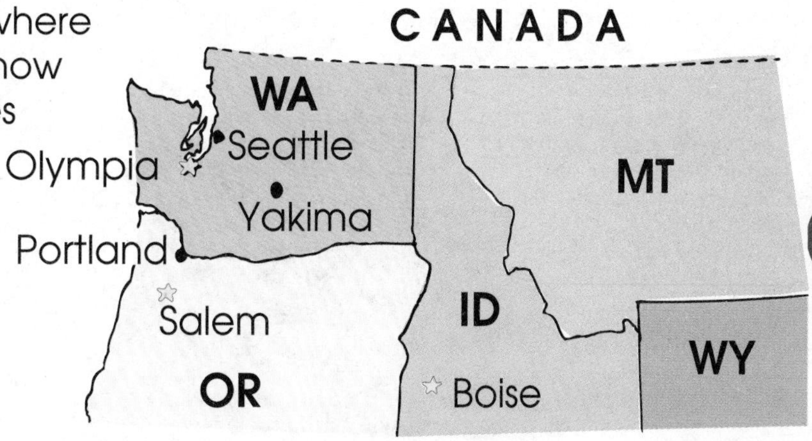

CANADA
WA
Seattle
Olympia
Yakima
Portland
MT
ID
Salem
WY
OR
Boise

Use a map, atlas or other resource to help you label the names of the states and cities on the political map of the United States on page 124. Use the states' postal abbreviations. As you complete the map, cross off each state in the list below.

States

Alabama	AL	Louisiana	LA	Ohio	OH
Alaska	AK	Maine	ME	Oklahoma	OK
Arizona	AZ	Maryland	MD	Oregon	OR
Arkansas	AR	Massachusetts	MA	Pennsylvania	PA
California	CA	Michigan	MI	Rhode Island	RI
Colorado	CO	Minnesota	MN	South Carolina	SC
Connecticut	CT	Mississippi	MS	South Dakota	SD
Delaware	DE	Missouri	MO	Tennessee	TN
Florida	FL	Montana	MT	Texas	TX
Georgia	GA	Nebraska	NE	Utah	UT
Hawaii	HI	Nevada	NV	Vermont	VT
Idaho	ID	New Hampshire	NH	Virginia	VA
Illinois	IL	New Jersey	NJ	Washington	WA
Indiana	IN	New Mexico	NM	West Virginia	WV
Iowa	IA	New York	NY	Wisconsin	WI
Kansas	KS	North Carolina	NC	Wyoming	WY
Kentucky	KY	North Dakota	ND		

Cities

Chicago, Illinois
Los Angeles, California
Atlanta, Georgia
Seattle, Washington
New York, New York
Miami, Florida
Washington D.C.
Boston, Massachusetts
Philadelphia, Pennsylvania
Detroit, Michigan
Denver, Colorado
St. Louis, Missouri

Name________________________________

Kinds of Maps: Political

United States Map

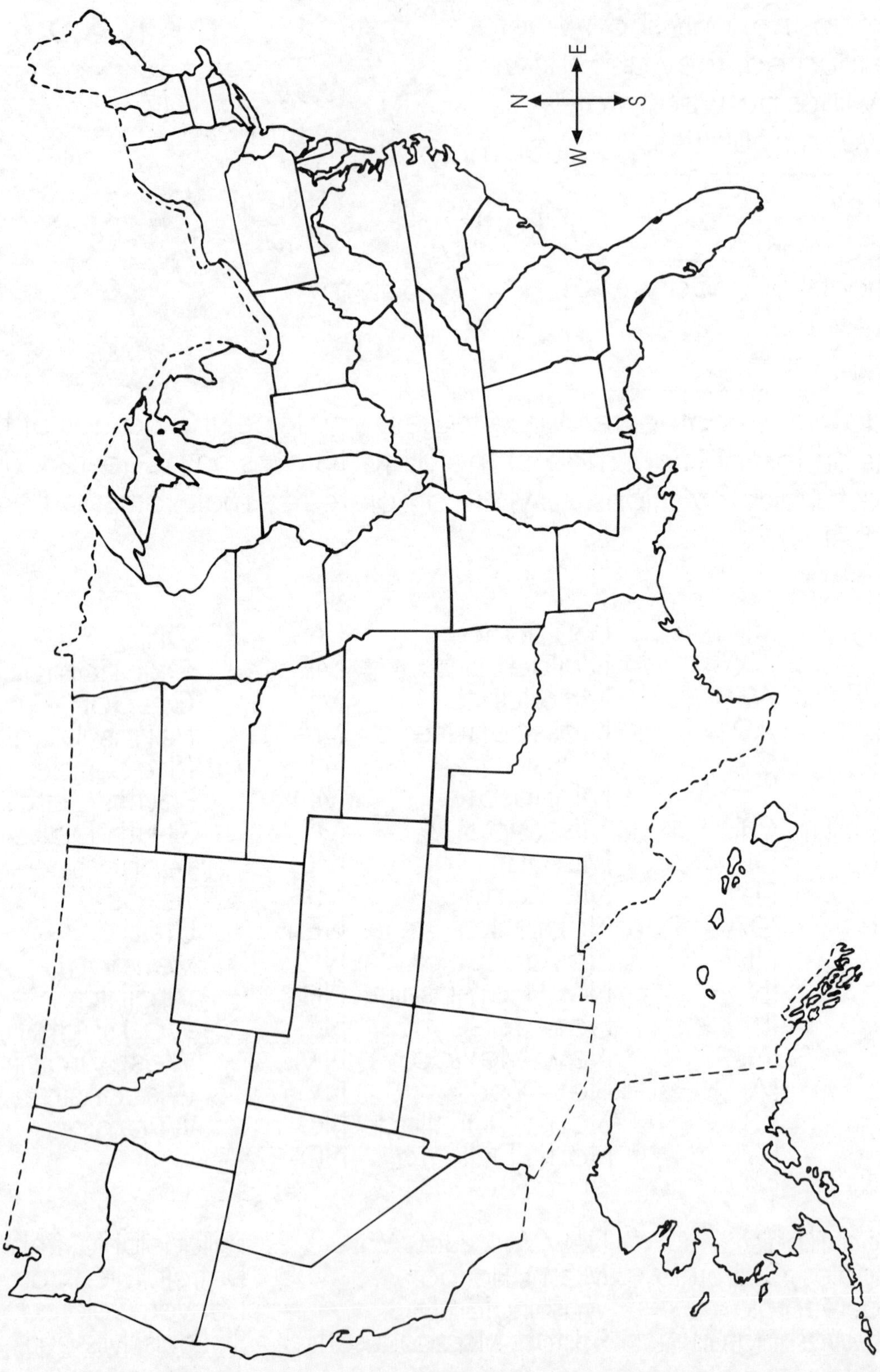

Name ____________________

State Smart

Use this map of some of the states to answer the questions below.

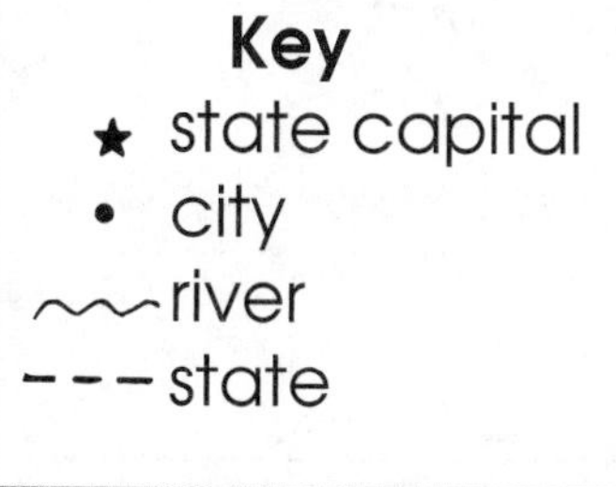

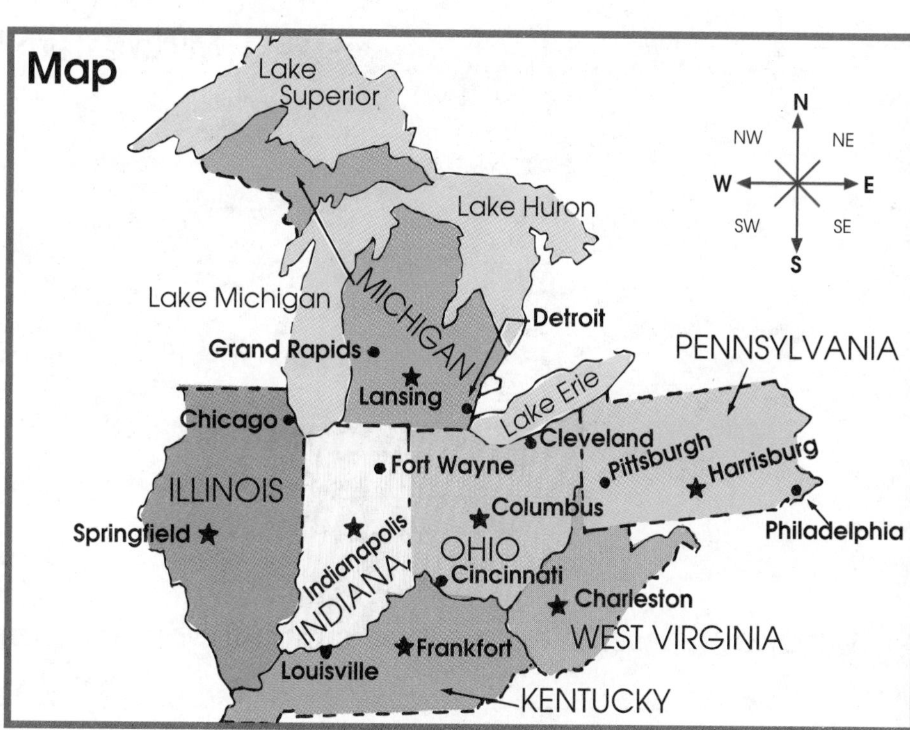

1. What state is west of Ohio? ____________________
2. The capital of West Virginia is ____________________.
3. Pittsburgh is a city in the state of ____________________.
4. What Ohio city is on the Ohio River? ____________________
5. Which state is southwest of Michigan? ____________________
6. What lake is west of Michigan? ____________________
7. Frankfort is the capital of ____________________.
8. What is the capital of Indiana? ____________________
9. Springfield is the capital of ____________________.
10. Chicago is ____________________ of Springfield, Illinois.
11. What Ohio city is northeast of Columbus? ____________________
12. Grand Rapids is ____________________ of Lansing, Michigan.
13. What state is east of Illinois? ____________________
14. What lake forms the northern border of Ohio? ____________________

Name ________________________________

What is a Political Map?

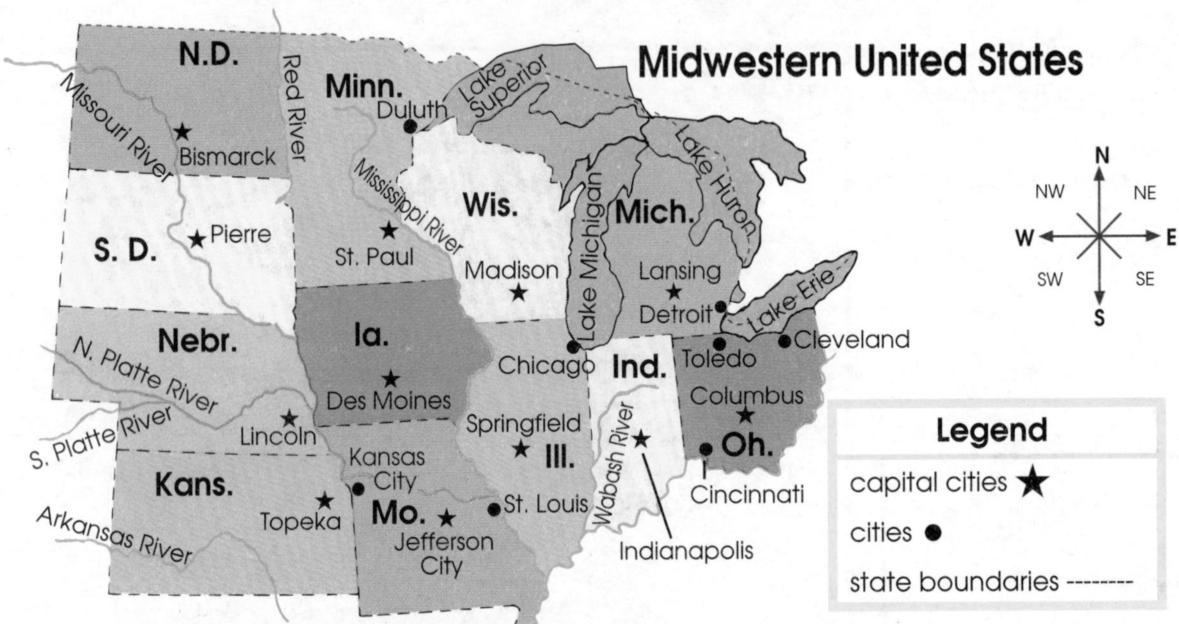

1. What do these three symbols stand for on this map?
   A. ★ ____________________ B ● ____________________
   C. - - - - - ____________________
2. The ____________ forms the boundary between Missouri and Illinois.
3. ____________ forms the boundary between Wisconsin and Michigan.
4. The eastern boundary of North Dakota is formed by the ____________.
5. Ohio's western boundary is formed by the state of ____________.
6. The southern part of Iowa is bordered by the state of ____________.
7. What are the capital cities of these states?
   A. Kansas ____________ D. North Dokota ____________
   B. Indiana ____________ E. Michigan ____________
   C. Wisconsin ____________ F. Illinois ____________
8. The ____________________ River is north of Indianapolis.
9. Name the four lakes shown on this map. ____________________
   ____
10. Name the river which cuts South Dakota in half. ____________
11. The northeastern border of Michigan is formed by Lake ____________.
12. Chicago is on the coast of Lake ____________________.

Name ____________________

Counties in Arizona

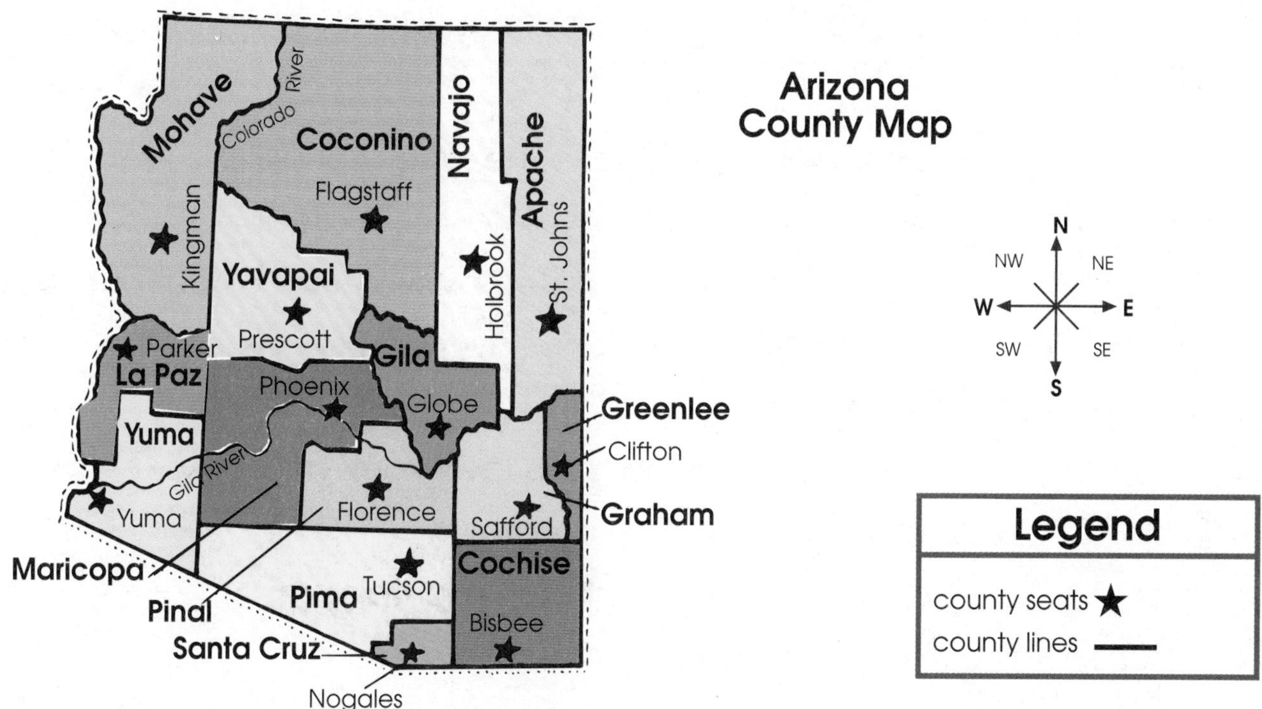

1. What do these symbols stand for on the map?
   A. ★ ____________________ B. ▬ ____________________
2. What county is located in the southwest corner of the state? __________
3. Is Pima in the northern or southern part of Arizona? __________
4. Name the county seat for each county listed.
   A. Cochise __________ D. Yuma __________
   B. Mohave __________ E. Coconino __________
   C. Greenlee __________ F. Navajo __________
5. Is Cochise east or west of Pima County? __________
6. The county directly north of Yuma is __________.
7. What is the county seat for Santa Cruz? __________
8. Name the county which is south of Graham. __________
9. What is the smallest county in Arizona? __________
10. Name the river which flows through Yuma. __________
11. The county seat of Pinal is __________.
12. Which county and county seat have the same name? __________

Name________________________________

Natural Wonders

Earth's physical features are its natural formations. Match each formation with its definition by writing a number in each blank.

______	river	1. land rising high above the land around it
______	bay	2. land surrounded completely by water
______	island	3. piece of land surrounded by water on all but one side
______	gulf	4. inlet of a large water body that extends into the land; smaller than a gulf
______	mountain	5. Earth opening that spills lava, rock and gases
______	plain	6. large inland body of water
______	lake	7. lowland between hills or mountains
______	peninsula	8. long, narrow body of water
______	valley	9. large area of flat grasslands
______	volcano	10. vast body of salt water
______	ocean	11. large area of a sea or ocean partially enclosed by land

Directions: Now, write each feature's number on the map.

Features Map

Name ____________________

Landforms and Physical Features

Notice different landforms and physical features found in the picture.

Label the ten landforms on the picture. Then, write the name of each one next to its definition below.

mountain	lake	peninsula	basin	canyon
plain	plateau	hill	island	river

- a large area of flat or gently sloping land ____________________
- a body of land completely surrounded by water ____________________
- a deep valley with steep sides____________________
- a body of land surrounded by water on three sides____________________
- an area of flat land that is higher than the surrounding land____________________
- a low region surrounded by higher land____________________
- a large stream of water that flows into a larger body of water____________________
- a natural elevation smaller than a mountain ____________________
- a body of water that is completely surrounded by land____________________
- a very high hill ____________________

Name____

Land Regions

Physical maps show natural features of the earth such as water, mountains, deserts and high and low regions. Finish the map as directed.

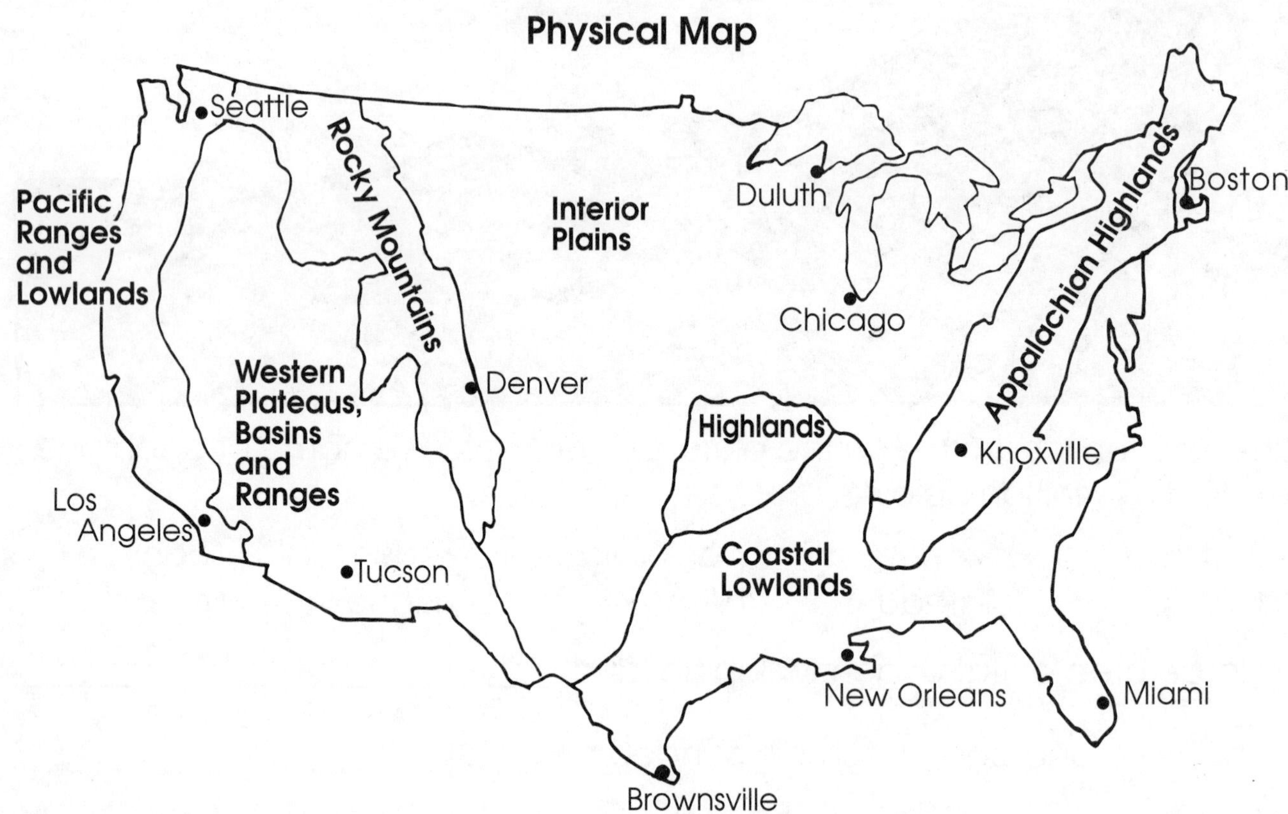

1. Draw brown ⌒⌒ in the mountain and highland regions.
2. Draw orange - - - on the Pacific Ranges and Lowlands.
3. Color the 5 Great Lakes blue.
4. Draw green ~~ on the Coastal Lowlands.
5. Draw red ////////// in the Western Plateaus, Basins and Ranges.
6. Color the Interior Plains yellow.
7. Name one city found in the mountains. ________________________
8. Name one city found in the Coastal Lowlands. ____________________

Name ______________________

Physical Features of the United States

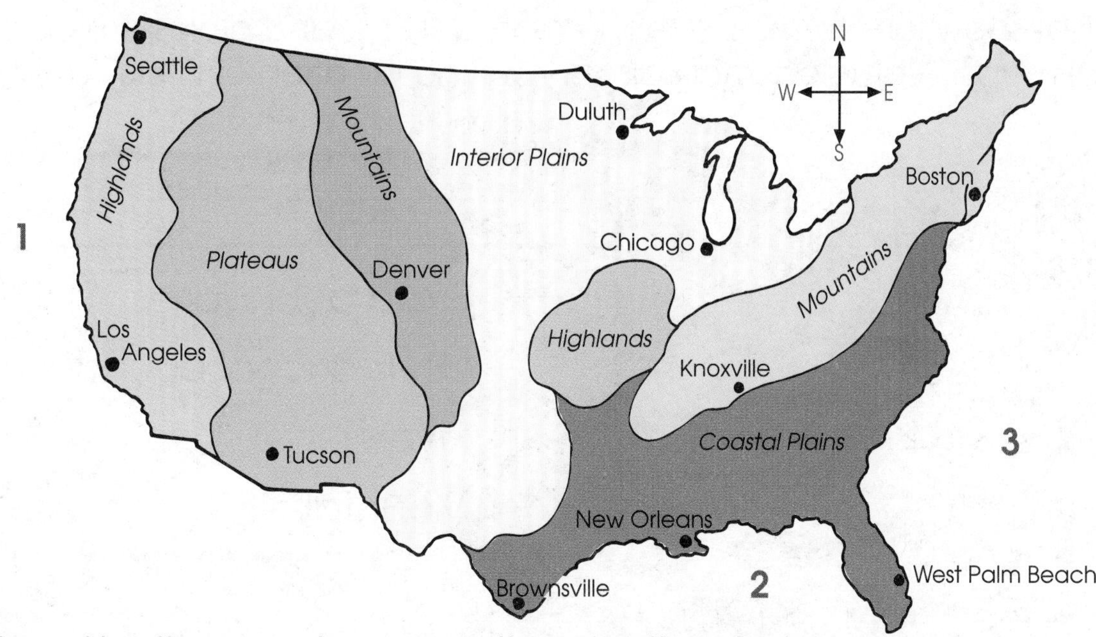

Directions: Use the map to answer the questions below.

1. Name the two cities on the map found in mountain areas.

   ____

2. Name the three cities found on coastal plains.

   ____

3. Seattle and Los Angeles are found on which coast—east or west?_____

   ____

4. Name the two cities located on the interior plains. ________________

   ____

5. Your home state is located on which type of land? ________________

Use a map of North America and the map above to answer these questions.

1. Identify the bodies of water marked with numbers on the map above.

   (1) ________________ (2) ________________ (3) ________________

2. The mountains on the eastern side of the United States are the ________

   ____.

3. The ____________ Mountains are in the western part of the United States.

Name ______________________________

Physical Maps

Maps that show landforms like mountains, deserts, and plains are called physical maps. A physical map also shows the location of rivers, lakes and oceans.

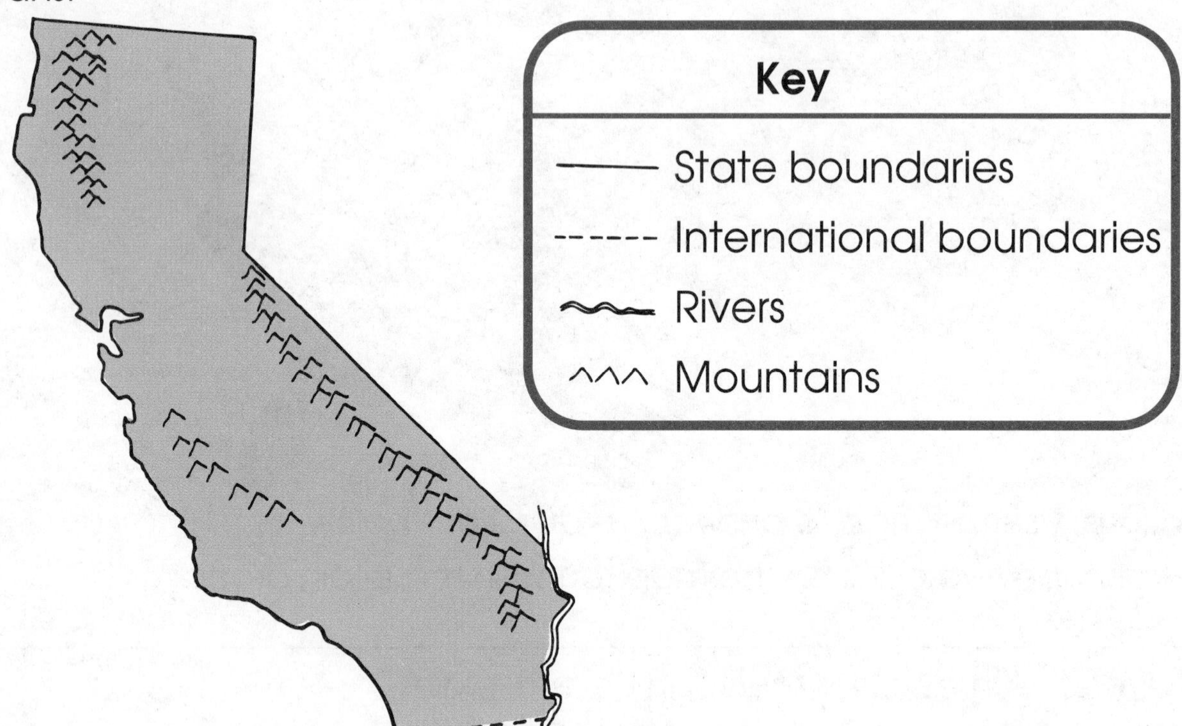

Use a map, atlas or other resource to help you locate the physical features listed below. Label them on the Physical Map of the United States on page 130.

Rivers
Mississippi River
Missouri River
Colorado River
Ohio River
Hudson River
Arkansas River

Mountains
Sierra Nevada Mountains
Cascade Mountains

Lakes
Great Salt Lake
Lake Michigan
Lake Superior
Lake Huron
Lake Erie
Lake Ontario

Land Regions
Great Plains
Mojave Desert
Great Basin

Oceans and Sea
Pacific Ocean
Atlantic Ocean
Gulf of Mexico

Name ____________________

Types of Land

Directions: Use this map of the United States and a large wall map to answer the questions.

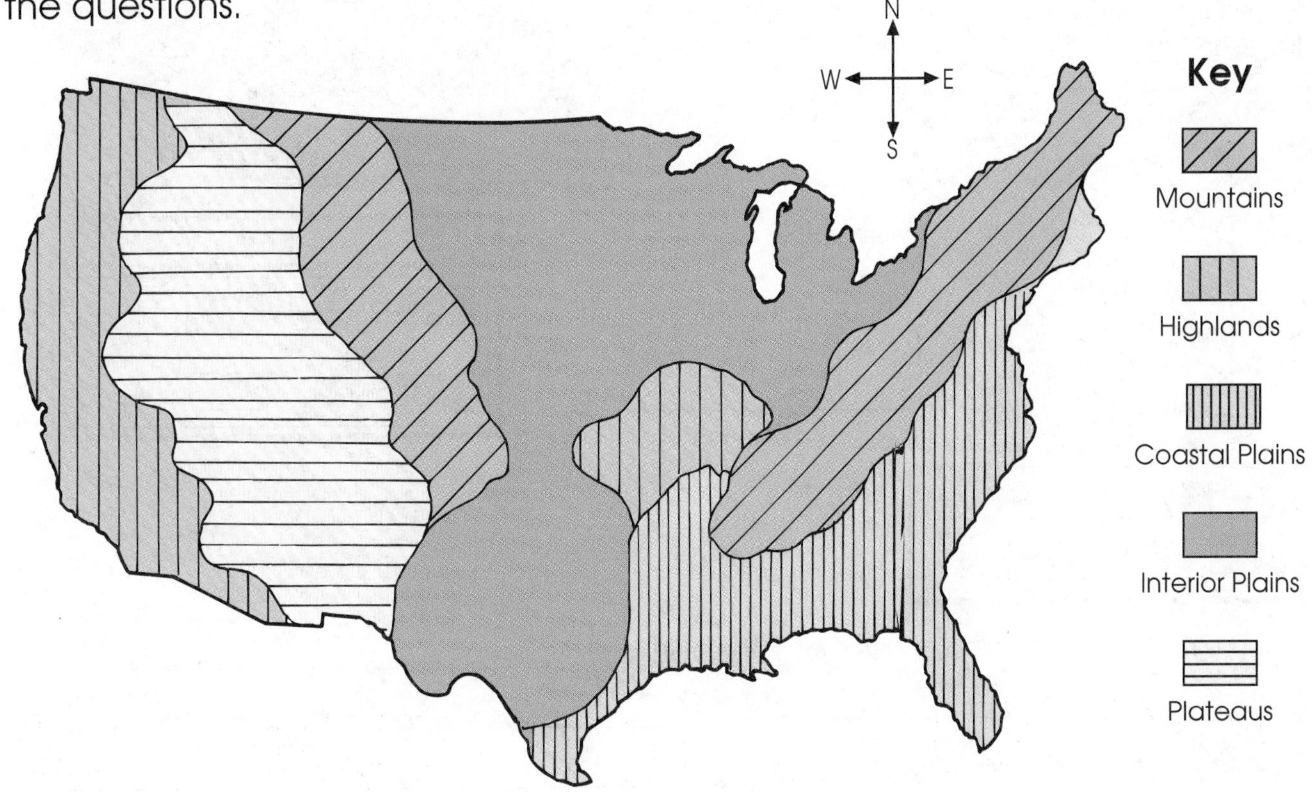

1. The western coast of the United States is composed of ____________.
2. The central part of the United States is ____________.
3. The northeastern part of the United States has____________.
4. What does the symbol [horizontal lines symbol] stand for on the map? ____________
5. In which part of the United States will you find coastal plains?____________
6. The state of California is mostly ____________.
7. Florida is composed of ____________.
8. The southern part of Texas is ____________.
9. What symbol is used to show mountains? ____________

Name ______________________________

Comparing Two States

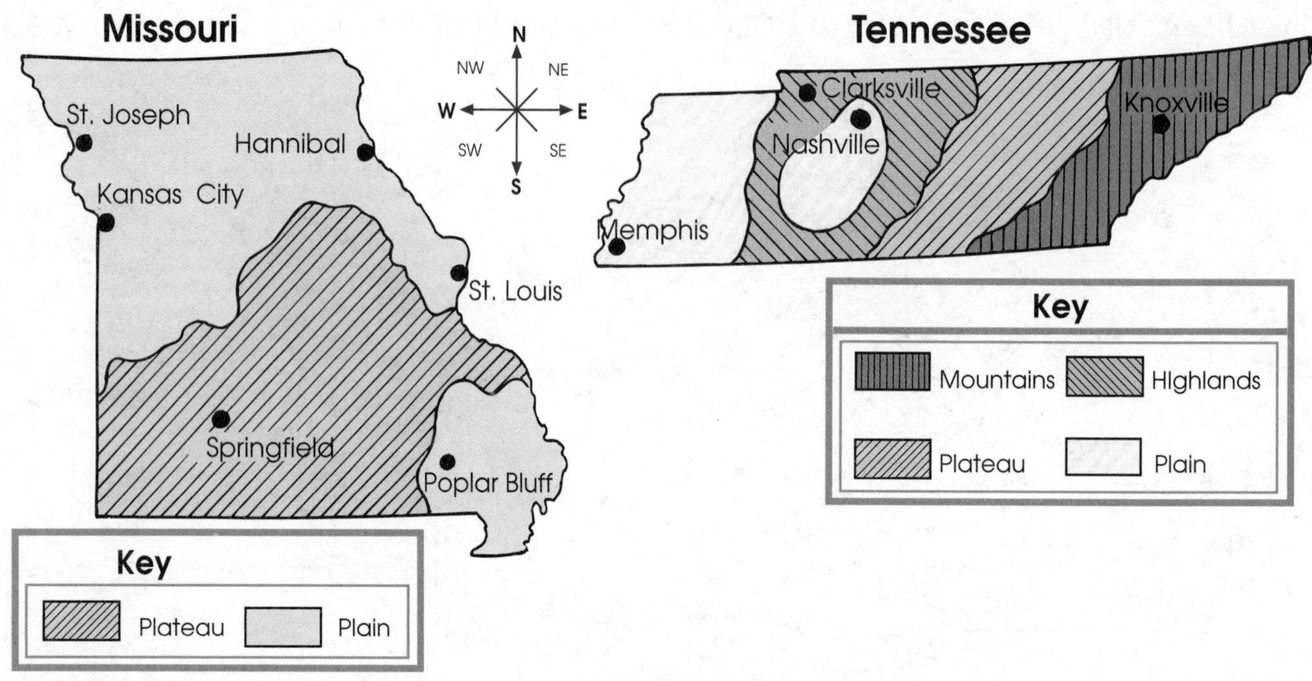

1. The southeastern corner of Missouri is a ______________________.
2. The northern part of Missouri is a ______________________.
3. Most of southern Missouri is a ______________________.
4. What type of land is between Kansas City and Hannibal? ____________
5. On a trip from St. Joseph to Poplar Bluff, what type of land will you travel over? ______________________
6. The eastern half of Tennessee is covered by ______________ and ______________________.
7. Memphis is located on a ______________________.
8. What two features do Tennessee and Missouri share? ____________ and ______________________
9. The central part of Tennessee is mostly ______________________.
10. What types of land will you cross between Memphis and Knoxville?

    ______________________.
11. Which of the states is almost half plateau? ______________

Name ____________________

Alaska and New York

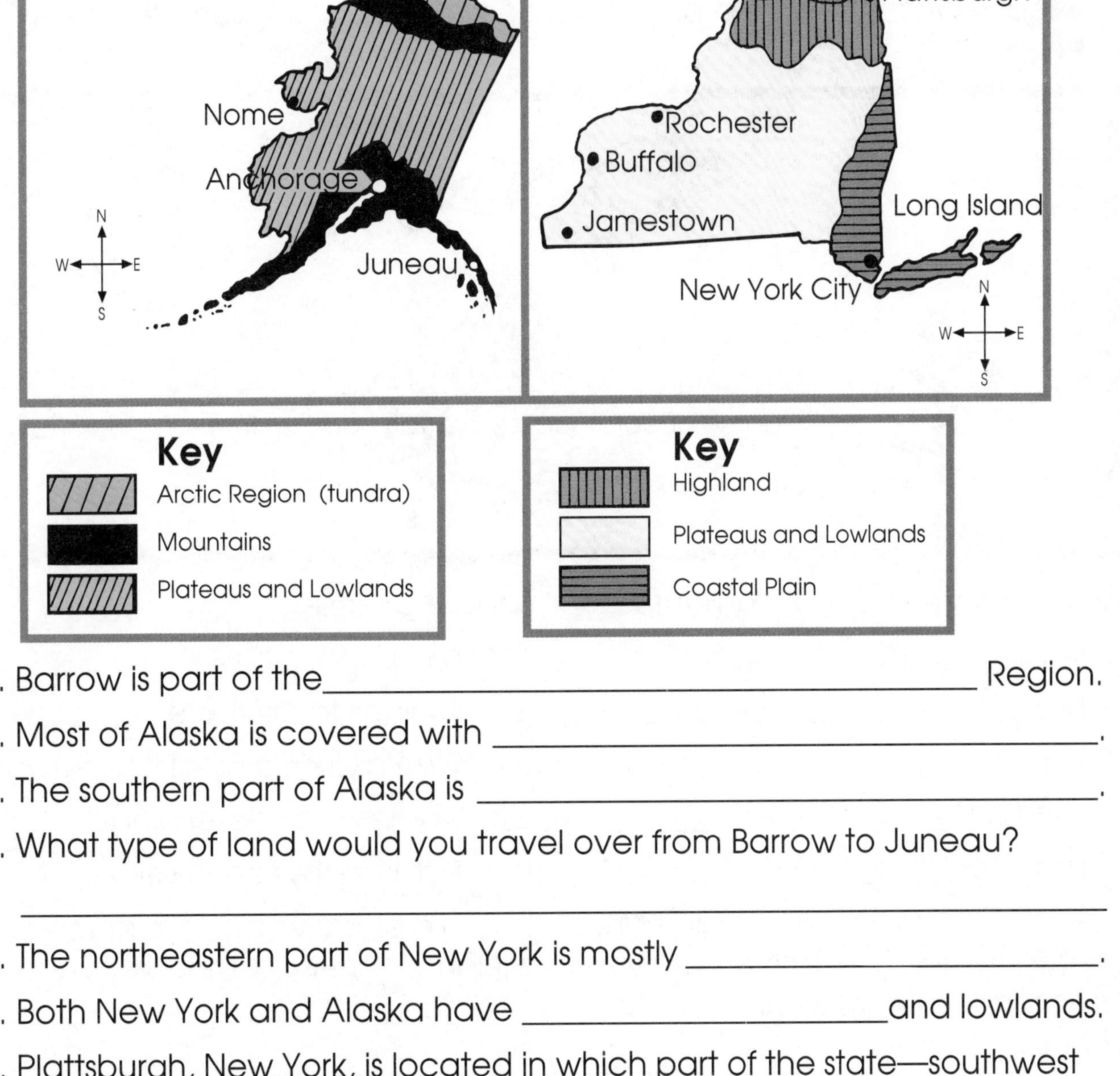

1. Barrow is part of the ____________________ Region.
2. Most of Alaska is covered with ____________________.
3. The southern part of Alaska is ____________________.
4. What type of land would you travel over from Barrow to Juneau?

   ____
5. The northeastern part of New York is mostly ____________________.
6. Both New York and Alaska have ____________________ and lowlands.
7. Plattsburgh, New York, is located in which part of the state—southwest or northeast? ____________________
8. The western half of New York is composed of ____________________.
9. The extreme northern part of New York is a ____________________.
10. Is Nome on the eastern or western coast of Alaska? ____________________

Name_______________________________________

Poetic Forms

Just as there are many kinds of landforms and physical features, there are also many forms of poetry. Let's use what you know about landforms and physical features to write a diamanté poem. Look at the sample below.

Michigan
Swimming, skiing, and sailing
Home of automobiles, cereal, and furniture
Green, sandy, beautiful
Peninsula

This is how you write a diamanté poem about a place:

line one _______________________ place name

line two _______________________ 2 or 3 things to do there

line three _______________________ 3 or 4 words telling what it is known for

line four _______________________ 2 or 3 adjectives describing it

line five _______________________ landform or physical feature

Now it's your turn to write a diamanté. Choose a place with a special landform or physical feature. It might have a cape, island, peninsula, mountain, canyon or desert, among others.

____

____

____

____

____

Name ______________________________

Natural Wonders of the U.S.

Listed below are ten natural physical features found in the United States. Use an encyclopedia, atlas or other source to complete the chart. Write the number of each feature on a copy of the U.S. Products and Natural Resources Map on page 138.

Natural Feature	State	Description
1. Devil's Tower		
2. Grand Canyon		
3. Mount McKinley		
4. Everglades		
5. Mount St. Helens		
6. Kilauea		
7. Carlsbad Caverns		
8. Cape Cod		
9. Badlands National Park		
10. Mojave Desert		

Name________________________________

Kinds of Maps: Product

U.S. Products and Natural Resources

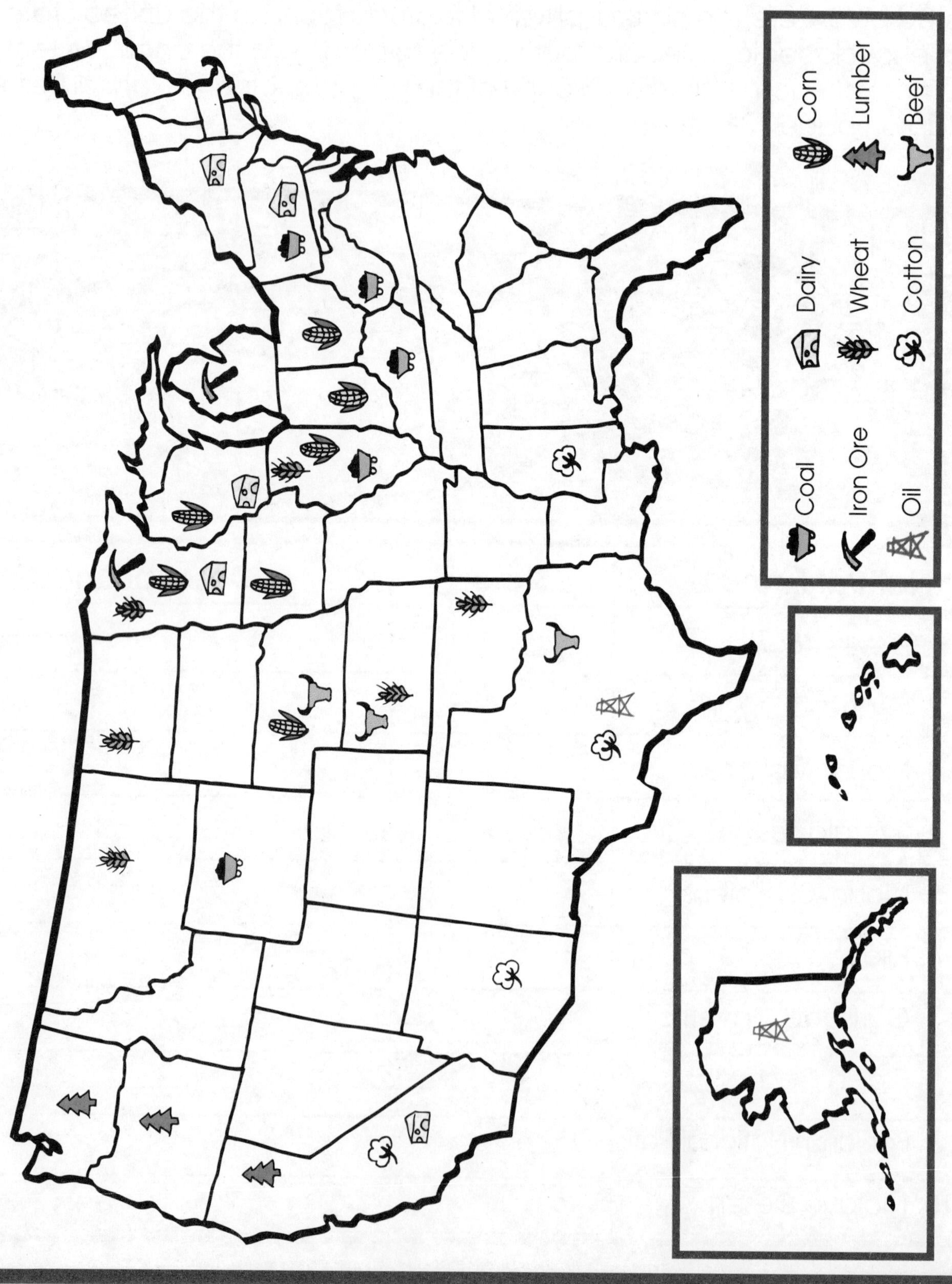

Use with pages 137 and page 139.

Name____

U.S. Products and Natural Resources

The United States is one of the world's largest producers of manufactured goods because it is very rich in natural resources.

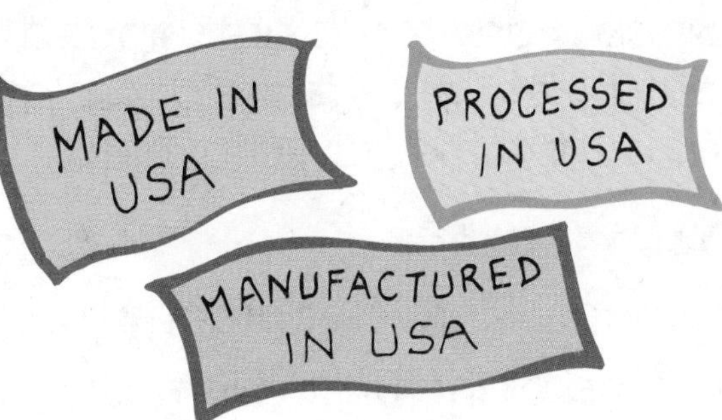

A study of the U.S. Products and Natural Resources map will indicate which states are the chief suppliers of certain products and natural resources.

Directions: For each product and natural resource listed below, use the map on page 138 to name the states that are major suppliers.

Coal

Iron Ore

Oil

Corn

Wheat

Cotton

Dairy

Lumber

Beef

Name________________________________

Grocery Store Geography

Since many foods are shipped long distances, let's create a display showing how far some have traveled.

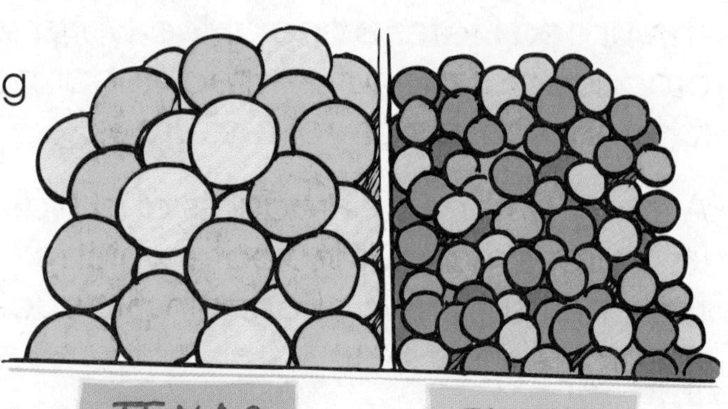

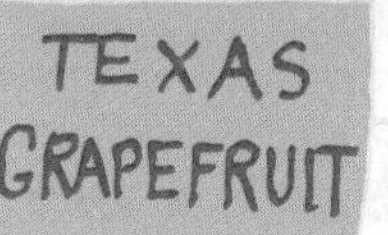

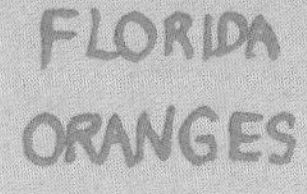

You will need:

Grocery Store Geography (page 141)
a map of the United States
a large piece of posterboard or paper
markers or crayons
glue

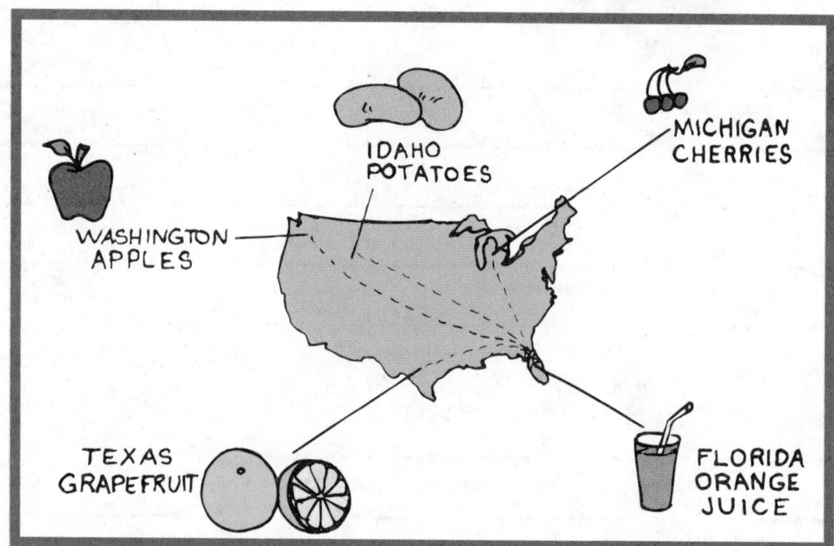

Directions:

1. Glue the outline map of the United States in the middle of your posterboard.
2. Label and color the states where each type of food on your food chart comes from.
3. Draw a picture of each food or cut out pictures from a magazine to glue around the border of the poster. Draw a line from the food to where it is grown.
4. Label your community on the map with a star.
5. Draw a dotted line from the product source to your community.

Name ___________________________

Grocery Store Geography

Many foods that we eat are not grown in our own community. While some foods come from neighboring states, others come from countries halfway around the world.

Check some of the foods in your cupboard and refrigerator at home. Check the labels to find out where they came from. Then, go to a grocery store and look at the labels on some other foods. Where did they come from? Look at the fruits and vegetables in the produce area. Many of them probably came from far away. Ask the grocer or produce manager where some of the fruits and vegetables are from.

Directions: Complete the chart.

Food	Where It Was Grown	Kind of Transportation Used to Ship the Product

On a map, locate where these foods were grown.

Which was shipped the greatest distance? ___________________________

How far did it have to travel to reach your grocery store? ______________

Name________________________________

Tilling the Soil

Use this map to answer the questions on page 143.

Agriculture Map

Legend

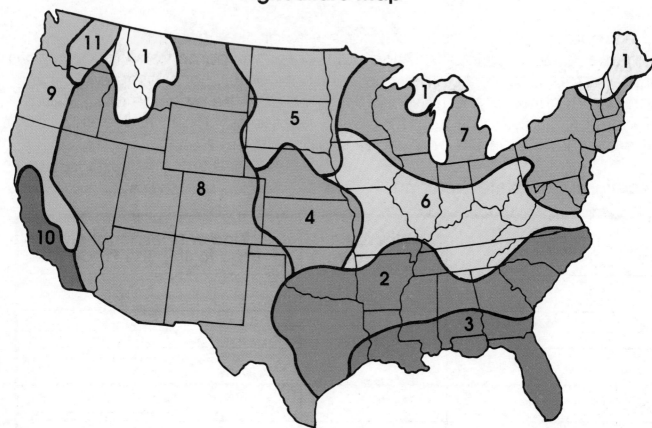

1. Timber
2. Cotton
3. Sub-tropical fruits, vegetables
4. Winter wheat
5. Spring wheat
6. Corn and Livestock
7. Dairy, hardy crops
8. Livestock ranching
9. Pacific hay, pasture and timber
10. Pacific fruits and vegetables
11. Wheat

Name ______________________________

Tilling the Soil

Directions: Use the map on page 142 to answer the questions below.

1. The northeastern corner of the United States has ________________.
2. What types of crops are found on the Pacific coast?

    ____
3. What is a common crop grown in many southern states? ____________
4. What two types of wheat are grown in 4 and 5? ________________

    ____
5. Much of the land in the western part of the United States is used for

    ______________________________.
6. What is most of the land in your state used for? ________________

    ____

Use the map on page 142 and a political map of the United States to help you answer the questions below.

1. What crops are grown in Florida? ______________________

    ____
2. Name the states where cotton is a major crop. ________________

    ____

    ____
3. The major crop in Kansas is ______________________.
4. The eastern part of Washington grows ____________________.
5. Southwestern California grows ______________________.
6. North and South Dakota are major producers of ________________.
7. Which of these states is a major producer of corn—Maine, Illinois or California? ______________________
8. What is done in western Texas? ______________________
9. Michigan and Wisconsin produce ______________________.
10. Most of Nebraska produces winter ______________________.
11. Hay, pasture and timber are produced in ______________California.

Name____

Kinds of Maps: Product

Natural Resource Riddles

U.S. Products and Natural Resources—Leading States

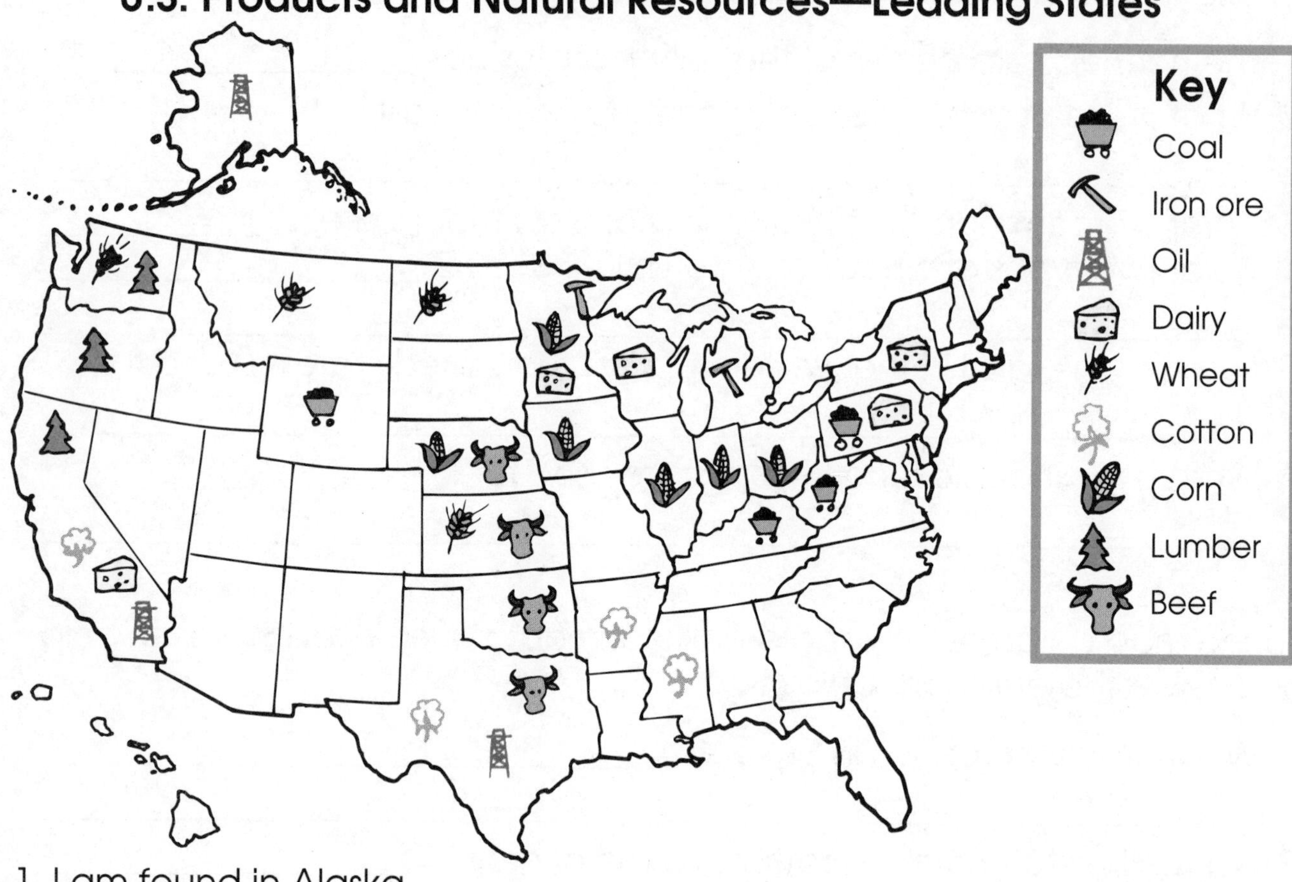

1. I am found in Alaska. ____
2. Montana is a leading producer of me. ________________________________
3. New York produces me. ____
4. Illinois, Indiana and Ohio are all leading producers of me. ____________
5. My name is lumber. Which states are leading suppliers of me?__________

____

6. Michigan is a leading supplier of me. ________________________________
7. I am Texas. Name the products I produce. ____________________________

____

8. I am Nebraska. Name my products.________________________________

Name ____________________

Products in California

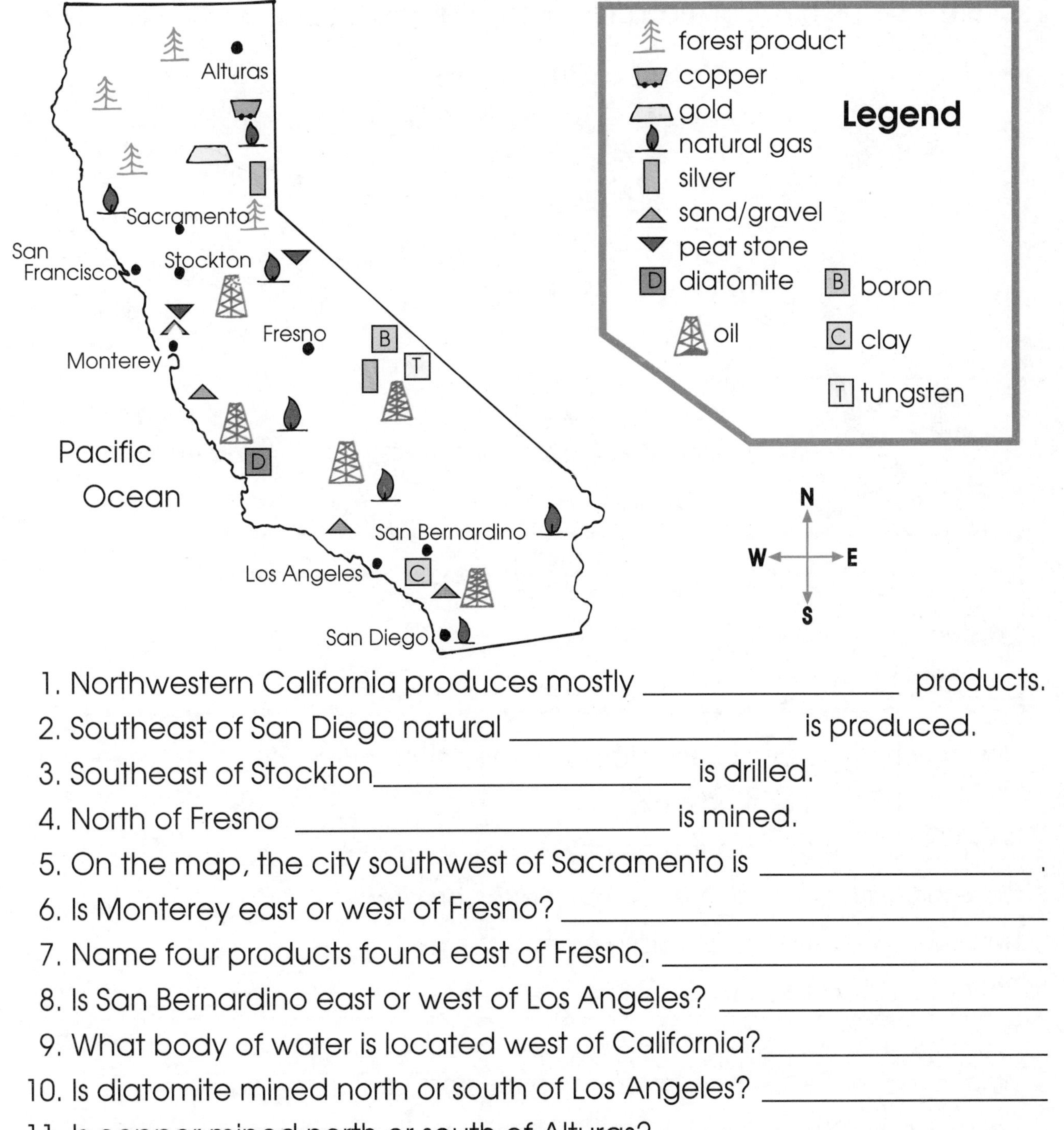

1. Northwestern California produces mostly ____________ products.
2. Southeast of San Diego natural ____________ is produced.
3. Southeast of Stockton ____________ is drilled.
4. North of Fresno ____________ is mined.
5. On the map, the city southwest of Sacramento is ____________.
6. Is Monterey east or west of Fresno? ____________
7. Name four products found east of Fresno. ____________
8. Is San Bernardino east or west of Los Angeles? ____________
9. What body of water is located west of California? ____________
10. Is diatomite mined north or south of Los Angeles? ____________
11. Is copper mined north or south of Alturas? ____________
12. Is San Francisco north or south of Monterey? ____________
13. Does California mine any gold near San Diego? ____________

Name____

How Much Revenue?

Directions: Use the product map of this imaginary state to answer the questions.

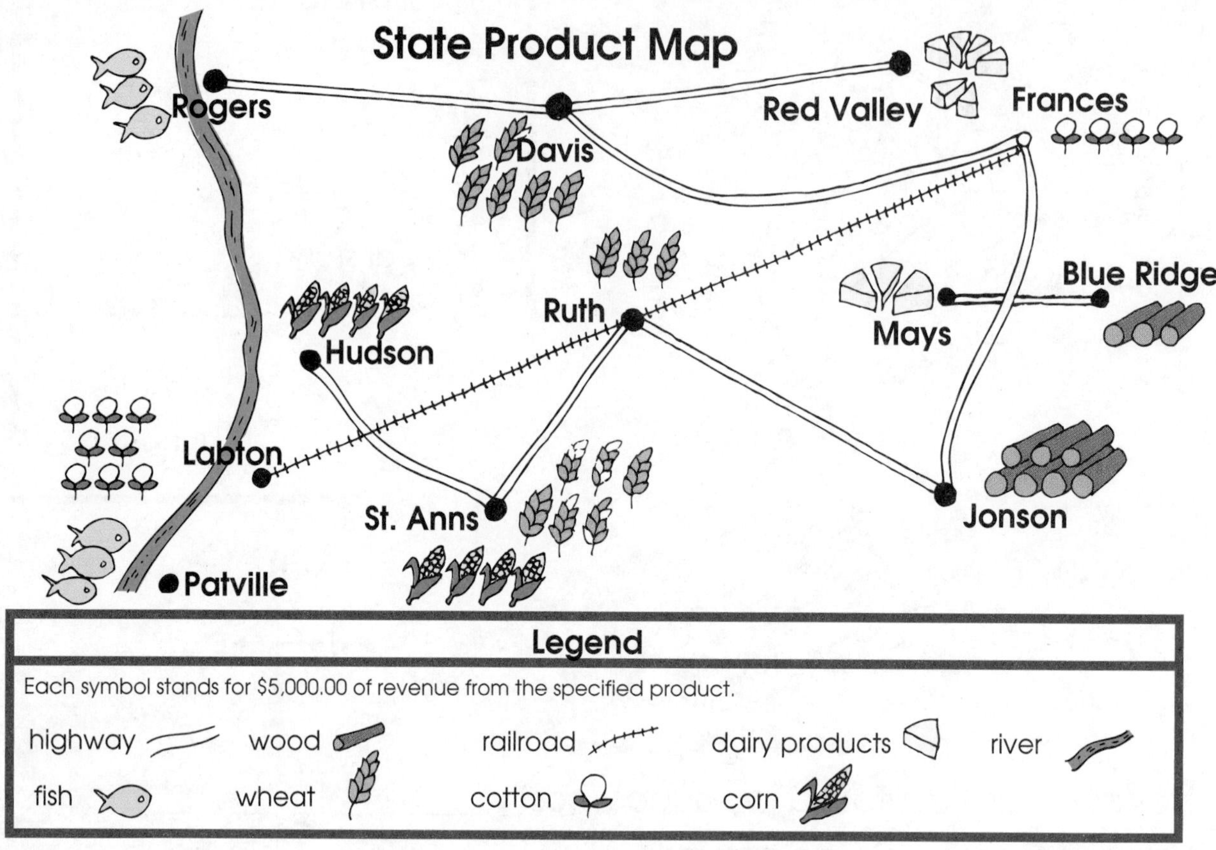

1. How much money, or revenue, does each symbol stand for? ____________
2. How much does the state make from corn?________________________
3. What product is grown near Jonson? ________________________
4. Does this state get more money from cotton or wood? ____________
5. How much money does the state earn from fish?____________________
6. Patville earns money by catching ________________________.
7. The town of Red Valley produces____________________ products.
8. What is the shortest way to transport cotton from Labton to Rogers?__________
9. How much money does the corn grown at Hudson produce for the state?__________
10. How much money does wheat produce for the state?________________
11. What is grown near Ruth? ________________________

Name ______________________________

Products in the United States

Directions: Use the map and the legend to answer the questions below.

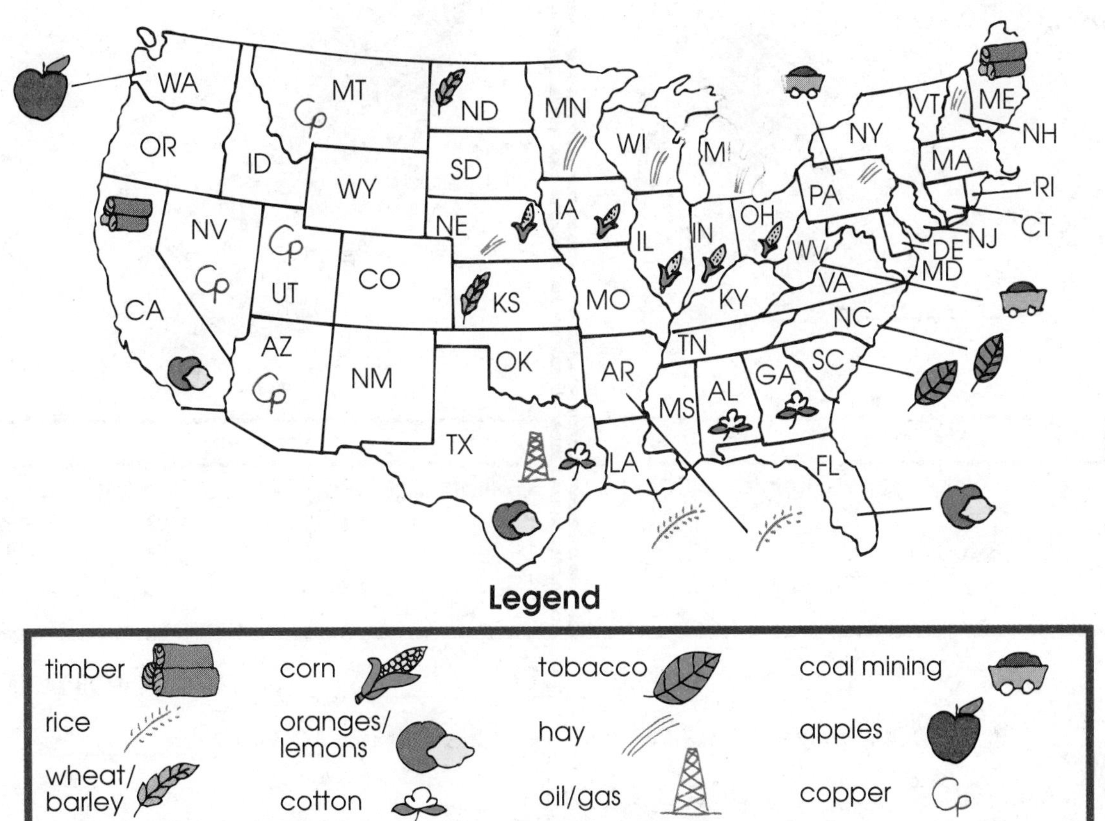

Legend

timber	corn	tobacco	coal mining
rice	oranges/ lemons	hay	apples
wheat/ barley	cotton	oil/gas	copper

1. Which state grows apples? ______________________________
2. How many states on this map grow oranges and lemons? ____________
3. Both Arkansas and Louisiana grow ______________________________.
4. Wheat and barley are grown in ______________________________.
5. North and South Carolina both grow ______________________________.
6. ______________________________ is produced in Maine.
7. Name the product grown in Alabama and Georgia. ____________
8. Coal is mined in the states of ______________________________.
9. Name the states which grow corn. ______________________________

____

10. Name the products produced in California. ______________________

Name____________________________________

Kinds of Maps: Climate

How Much Did It Rain?

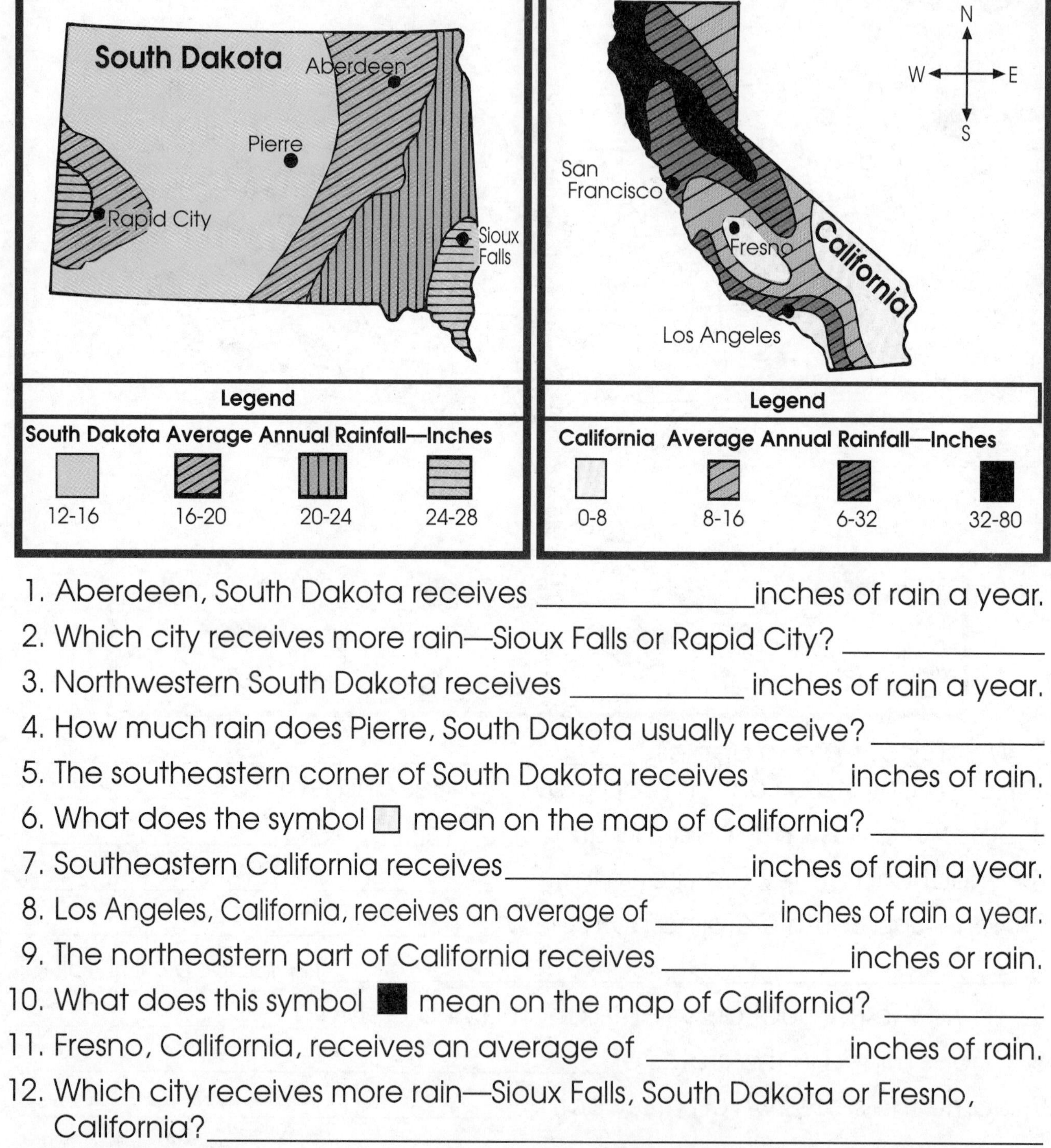

1. Aberdeen, South Dakota receives ______________ inches of rain a year.
2. Which city receives more rain—Sioux Falls or Rapid City? ____________
3. Northwestern South Dakota receives ___________ inches of rain a year.
4. How much rain does Pierre, South Dakota usually receive? ___________
5. The southeastern corner of South Dakota receives ______ inches of rain.
6. What does the symbol ☐ mean on the map of California? ___________
7. Southeastern California receives ________________ inches of rain a year.
8. Los Angeles, California, receives an average of ________ inches of rain a year.
9. The northeastern part of California receives ____________ inches or rain.
10. What does this symbol ■ mean on the map of California? __________
11. Fresno, California, receives an average of ____________ inches of rain.
12. Which city receives more rain—Sioux Falls, South Dakota or Fresno, California?______________________________________
13. The extreme northwestern corner of California receives ________ inches of rain a year.

Name____

Temperature Ranges

What is the average January temperature where you live? The average monthly temperature is figured using the daily temperatures for the whole month. This information can be found in most almanacs and encyclopedias. Why would it be helpful to know the average temperature of a city? __________

____

Directions: Use an almanac or encyclopedia fo find the average high and low temperatures for the cities listed below for January and July.

State	City	Average Monthly Temperatures (F°)			
		January		July	
		High	Low	High	Low
Alaska	Nome				
California	Los Angeles				
Colorado	Denver				
Florida	Tampa				
Iowa	Des Moines				
Michigan	Detroit				
New York	Syracuse				
North Dakota	Fargo				
South Carolina	Columbia				
Texas	Dallas				
Wisconsin	Madison				
State of your choice:					

Circle the highest temperature in each "high" column and the lowest temperature in each "low" column.

Name ___________________________________

U.S. Climate Zones

The word climate is used to describe the weather in a particular place over a long period of time. Because the United States covers such a large area, it has a number of different climate zones. Some areas have long, cold winters and short, cool summers, while other areas are always warm in both the summer and the winter.

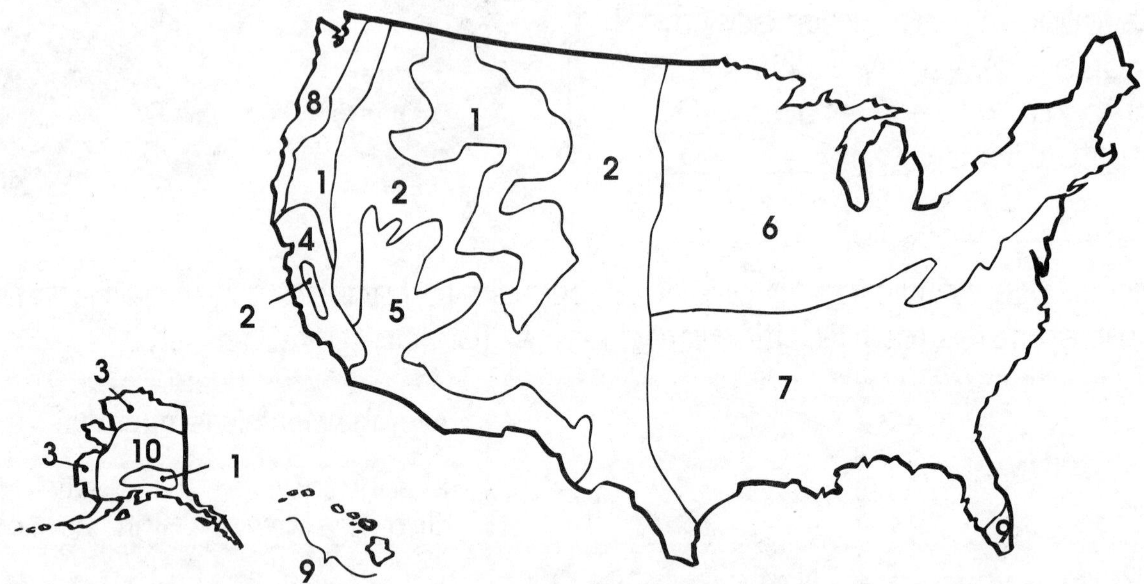

Key

1	☐ alpine	4	☐ mediterranean							
2	☐ steppe	5	☐ desert	7	☐ subtropical	9	☐ tropical
3	☐ tundra	6	☐ continental	8	☐ marine	10	☐ subarctic

Directions: Choose colors to color-code the key and the climate zone map. Then, determine the . . .

- climate zone in which you live ______________________________
- climate zone of the northeast ______________________________
- climate zones of the Rocky Mountains ______________________
- three climate zones found in Alaska ________________________
- climate zones found in Texas ______________________________
- climate zones of Florida __________________________________
- climate zone of Michigan _________________________________

Section 3

United States Regions

PACIFIC STATES

MOUNTAIN STATES

NORTH CENTRAL STATES

SOUTH CENTRAL STATES

MIDWEST STATES

SOUTHEASTERN STATES

NORTHEASTERN STATES

Name_______________________________________

The Pacific States

The Pacific States is a region with majestic mountains, beautiful beaches and coastlines, thick green forests and hot, dry deserts.

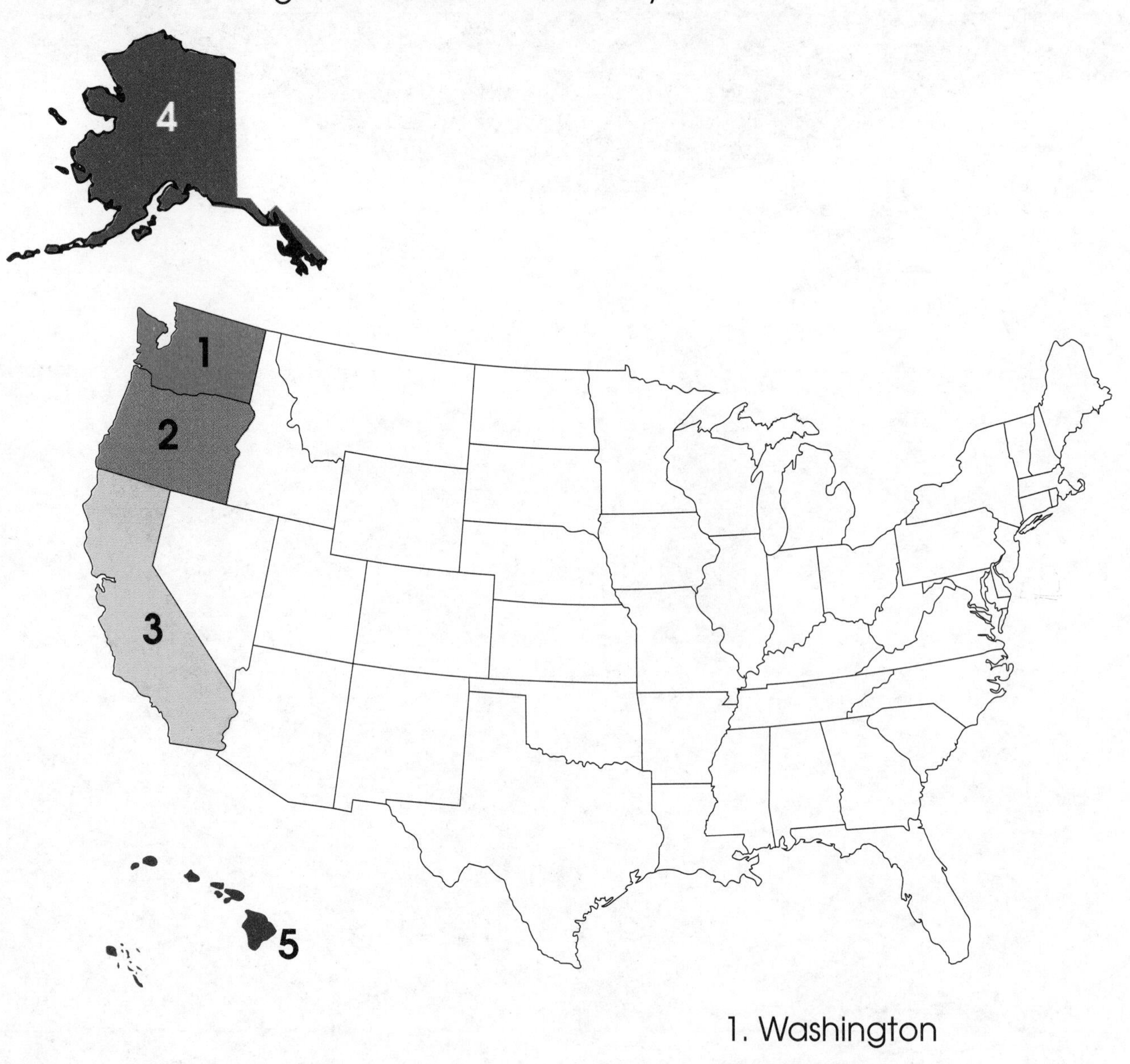

1. Washington
2. Oregon
3. California
4. Alaska
5. Hawaii

Name___________________________

Fill in the "Five Fundamental Themes of Geography" for each state. After "discovering" a state, fill in all the columns of the chart except **Regions**. When you have finished with all of the states in a section, fill in **Regions**.

Five Fundamental Themes of Geography					
Name of State	**Location** (Where is it?)	**Place** (What is it like?)	**People and Environment** (What do the people do?)	**Movement** (How do people, goods and ideas move?)	**Regions** (What are some of the common features?)

Name ______________________________

Washington

The Evergreen State

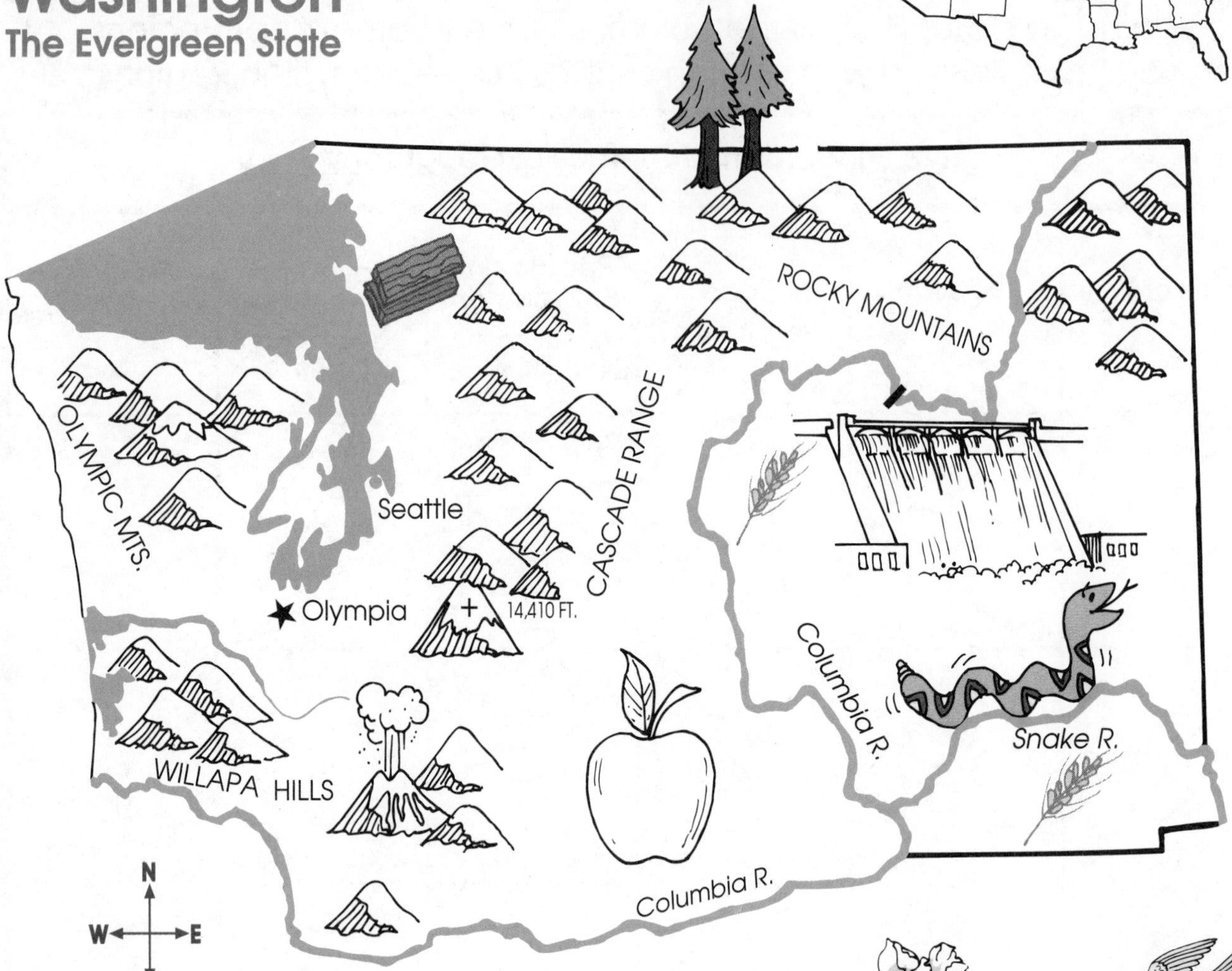

Coast Rhododendron
State Flower

Willow Goldfinch
State Bird

- named for the first president—George Washington
- nicknamed the Evergreen State for the abundance of evergreen trees

Mount Rainier—14,410 ft.

Mt. St. Helens—erupted on May 18, 1980

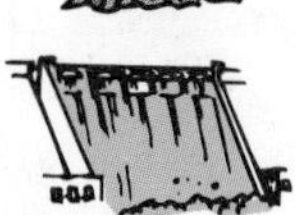

Grand Coulee Dam—largest concrete dam in United States

Apples—leads the states in apple production

Circle the capital city. Locate the landmarks found in the above key. Color them on the map.

Name ______________________________

Oregon
The Beaver State

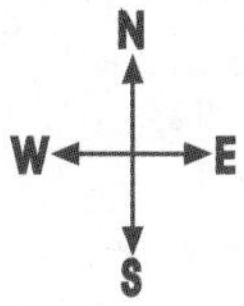

N
W E
S

Columbia R.
Portland
11,239 FT.
★ Salem
Snake R.
Blue Mountains
Willamette R.
Coastal Range
Cascade Range

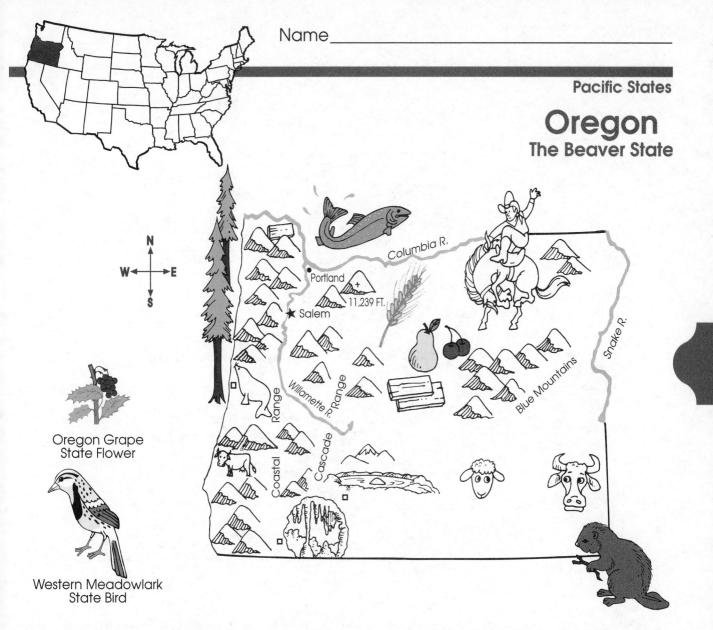

Oregon Grape
State Flower

Western Meadowlark
State Bird

- name originated from the French word *ouragan*, meaning *hurricane*
- nicknamed the Beaver State because the area supplied thousands of beaver skins during early fur trading

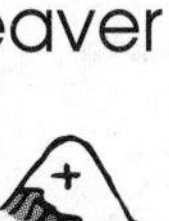

Mount Hood—11,239 ft.

Pendleton Round-Up

Sea Lion Caves

Oregon Caverns

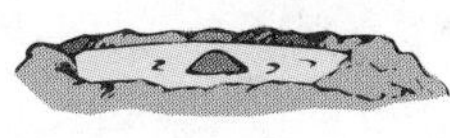

Crater Lake—deepest lake in the United States

Circle the capital city. Locate the landmarks found in the above key. Color them on the map.

Name_______________________________________

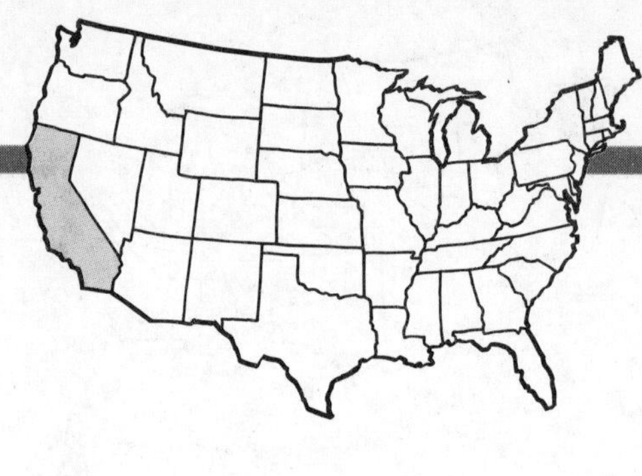

California

The Golden State

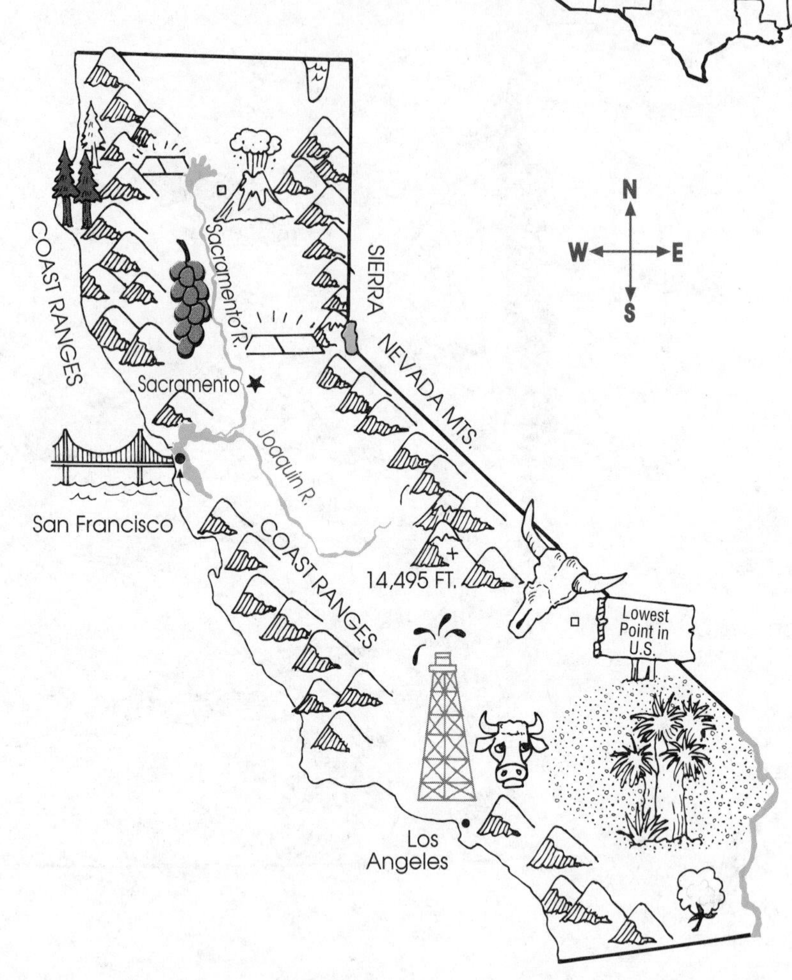

California Valley Quail
State Bird

Golden Poppy
State Flower

- named by early explorers, possibly referring to a treasure island in a Spanish story
- nicknamed the Golden State, possibly for its gold fields, its golden pastures and its sunshine

 Mount Whitney—the highest point in the contiguous United States—14,495 ft.

 Golden Gate Bridge

 Lassen Volcanic Park

 Joshua Tree National Monument

 Death Valley National Monument

Redwood National Park—contains world's tallest known tree

Circle the capital city. Locate the landmarks found in the above key. Color them on the map.

Name____________________

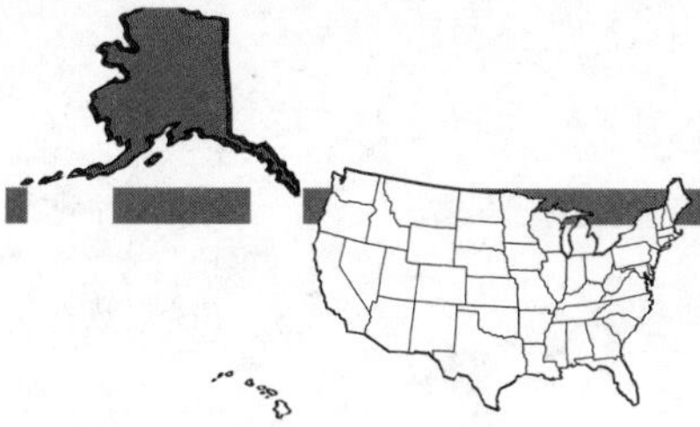

Pacific States

Alaska

The Last Frontier

Forget-Me-Not
State Flower

Willow Ptarmigan
State Bird

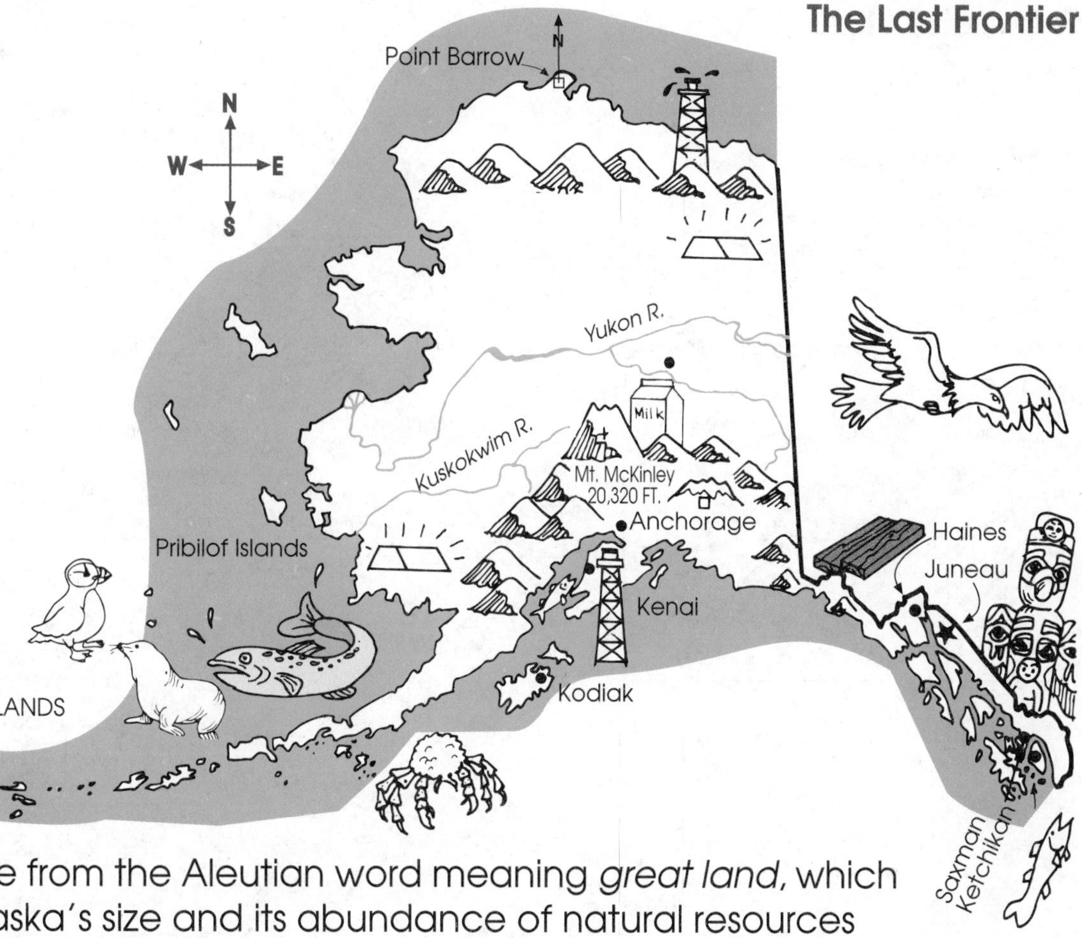

Point Barrow
Yukon R.
Kuskokwim R.
Mt. McKinley 20,320 FT.
Anchorage
Pribilof Islands
Kenai
Kodiak
ALEUTIAN ISLANDS
Haines
Juneau
Saxman
Ketchikan

- name came from the Aleutian word meaning *great land*, which refers to Alaska's size and its abundance of natural resources
- nickname the Last Frontier reflects the fact that much of the region is as yet unsettled

Point Barrow—northernmost point of the United States

Saxman—world's largest collection of totem poles

Malaspina—North America's largest glacier

Kenai and Kodiak—major salmon processing areas

Kodiak and Aleutian Islands—known for their catches of Alaskan King Crab

Pribilof Islands—colonies of puffins and world's largest herd of northern fur seals

Green Creek Mine—largest silver mine in the United States

Mount McKinley—20,320 ft.

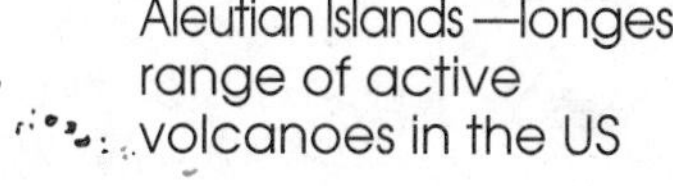
Aleutian Islands—longest range of active volcanoes in the US

Bald Eagles—greater number of bald eagles gather north of Haines than any other place in the world

Circle the capital city. Locate the landmarks found in the above key. Color them on the map.

Name____________________

Pacific States

Hawaii

The Aloha State

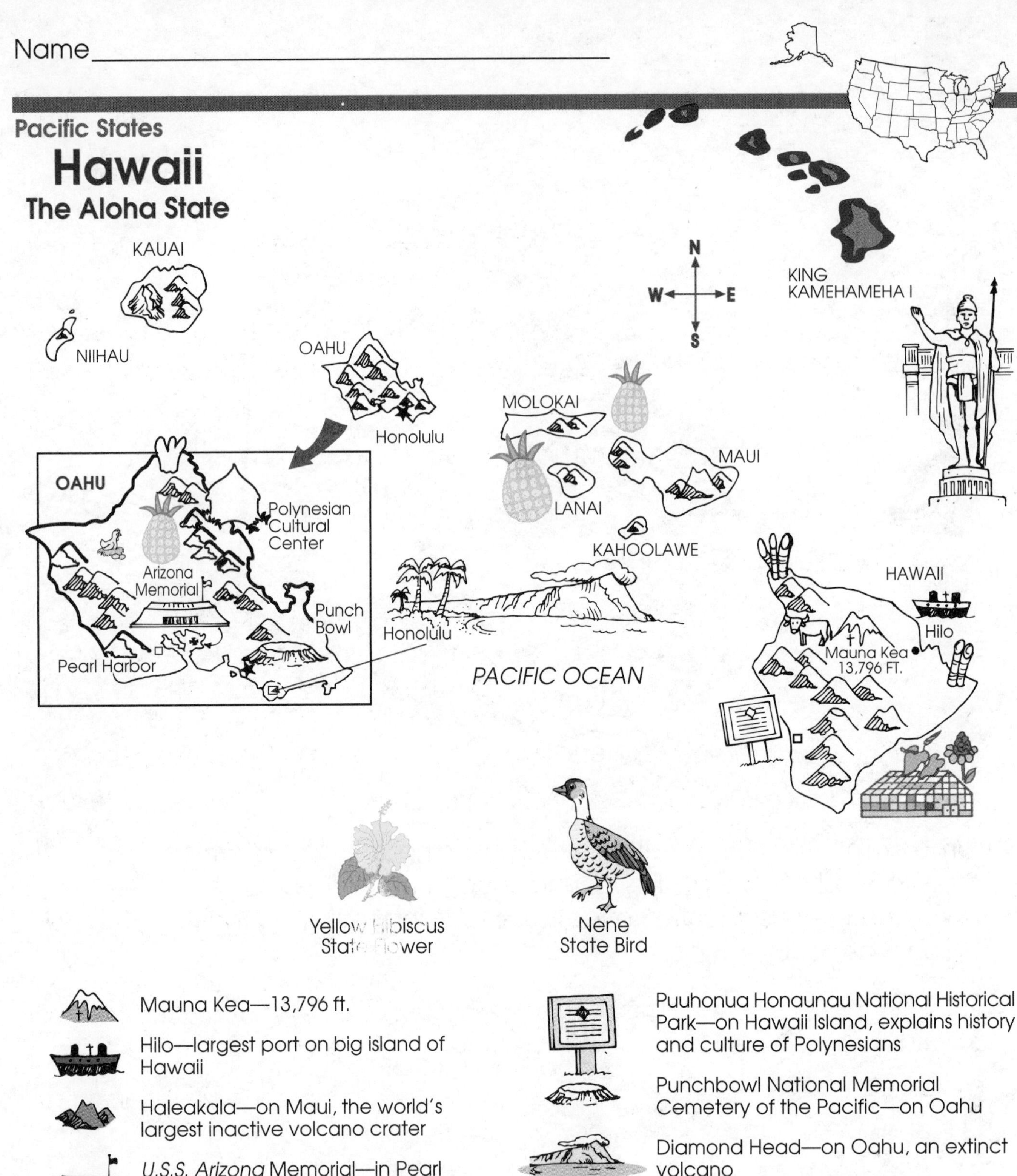

Yellow Hibiscus
State Flower

Nene
State Bird

- Mauna Kea—13,796 ft.
- Hilo—largest port on big island of Hawaii
- Haleakala—on Maui, the world's largest inactive volcano crater
- *U.S.S. Arizona* Memorial—in Pearl Harbor, honors those who died aboard the *U.S.S. Arizona* when Japanese attacked on December 7, 1941
- King Kamehameha—statue of Hawaii's greatest ruler
- Puuhonua Honaunau National Historical Park—on Hawaii Island, explains history and culture of Polynesians
- Punchbowl National Memorial Cemetery of the Pacific—on Oahu
- Diamond Head—on Oahu, an extinct volcano
- Polynesian Cultural Center on Oahu
- Waimea Canyon—on Kauai, gorges of many beautiful colors

Circle the capital city. Locate the landmarks found in the above key. Color them on the map.

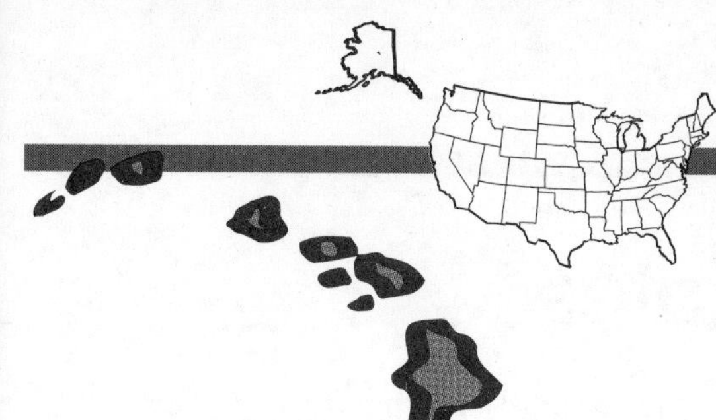

Name____

Hawaii

The Aloha State

- name believed to come from Hawaiian word *Havaiki*, which was the name of a Pacific Island on which the Hawaiian people had resided earlier
- nickname the Aloha State refers to the Hawaiian word *aloha*, which means *love* and is used for greetings of *hello, welcome* or *goodbye*

Islands—Hawaii consists of 132 islands, of which there are 8 main islands

1. Hawaii—nickname the Big Island refers to it being the largest island
2. Lanai—nickname the Pineapple Island refers to the island being one large pineapple plantation
3. Kahoolawe—smallest of the main islands and is uninhabited
4. Molokai—nickname the Friendly Island refers to how graciously the people welcome visitors
5. Kauai—nickname the Garden Island refers to its beautiful gardens and numerous green plants
6. Oahu—nickname the Gathering Place refers to it being the residence of 80% of the population
7. Maui—nickname the Valley Island refers to the canyons cut into the two volcanoes which form the island
8. Niihau—nicknamed the Forbidden Island because no one can visit the island without the owner's permission

Name____

The Mountain States

The Mountain States' major feature is the majestic Rocky Mountains that stretch from north to south in this region. The Mountain States are known for their high plateaus, deep canyons and desert regions.

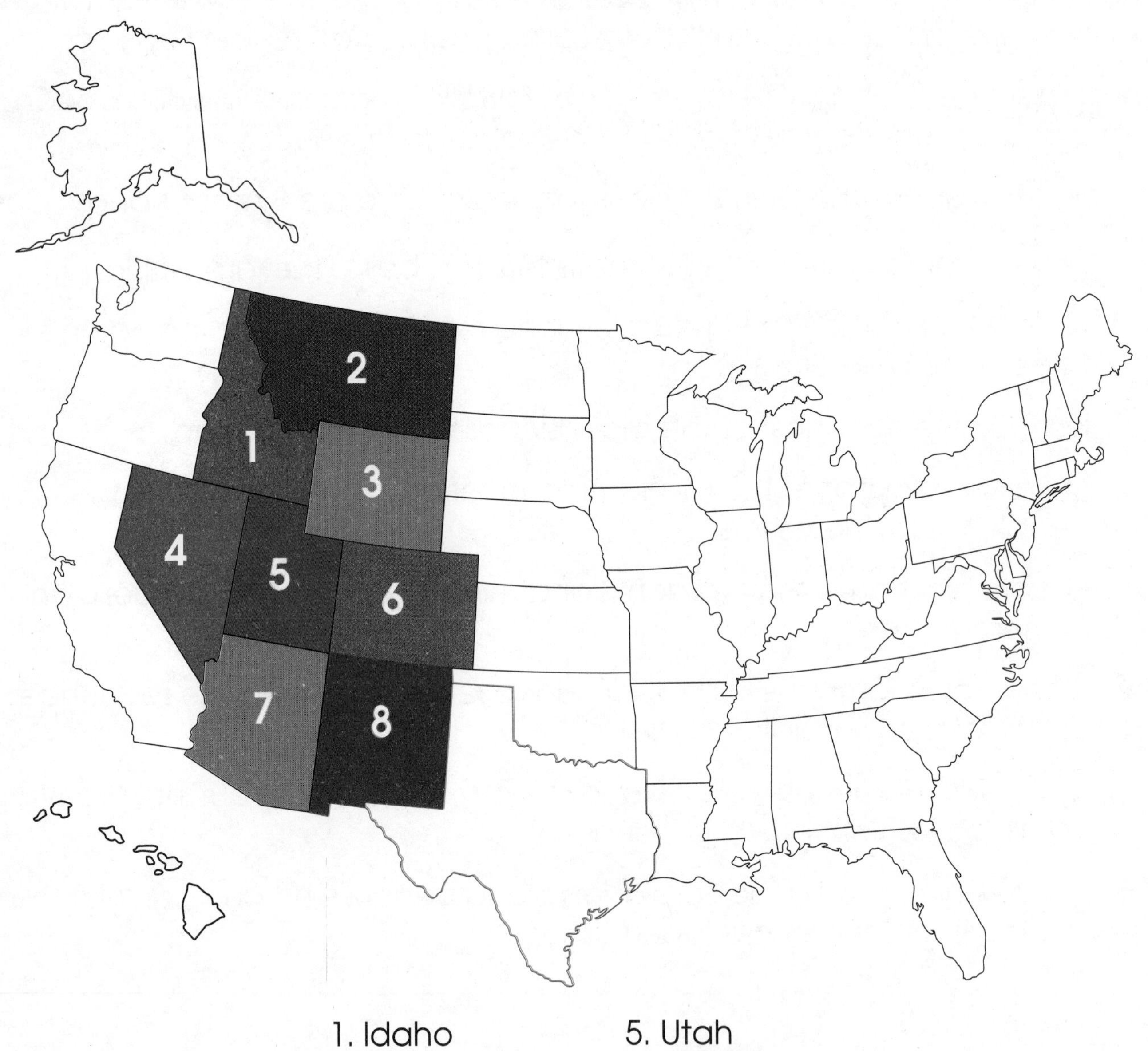

1. Idaho
2. Montana
3. Wyoming
4. Nevada
5. Utah
6. Colorado
7. Arizona
8. New Mexico

Name________________________________

Fill in the "Five Fundamental Themes of Geography" for each state. After "discovering" a state, fill in all the columns of the chart except **Regions**. When you have finished with all of the states in a section, fill in **Regions**.

Five Fundamental Themes of Geography					
Name of State	**Location** (Where is it?)	**Place** (What is it like?)	**People and Environment** (What do the people do?)	**Movement** (How do people, goods and ideas move?)	**Regions** (What are some of the common features?)

Name______________________________

Mountain States

Fill in the "Five Fundamental Themes of Geography" for each state. After "discovering" a state, fill in all the columns of the chart except **Regions**. When you have finished with all of the states in a section, fill in **Regions**.

Five Fundamental Themes of Geography					
Name of State	**Location** (Where is it?)	**Place** (What is it like?)	**People and Environment** (What do the people do?)	**Movement** (How do people, goods and ideas move?)	**Regions** (What are some of the common features?)

Name ______________________________

Mountain States

Idaho

The Gem State

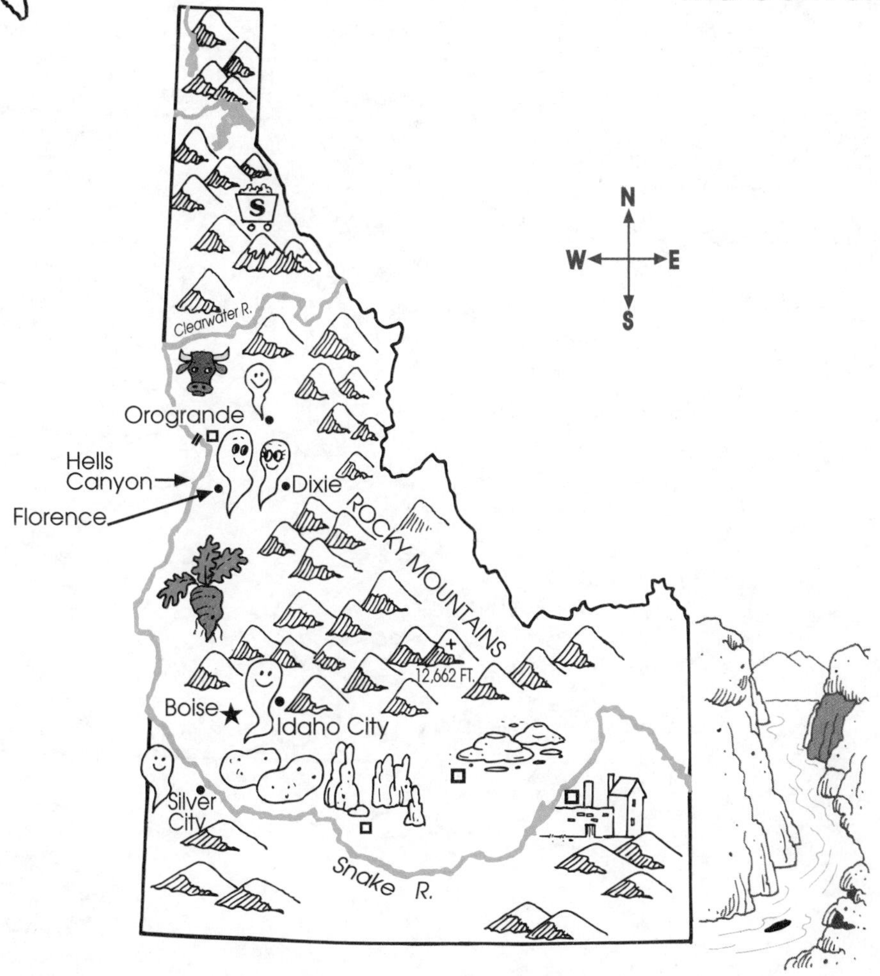

N
W E
S

Clearwater R.
Orogrande
Hells Canyon
Dixie
Florence
ROCKY MOUNTAINS
12,662 FT.
Boise
Idaho City
Silver City
Snake R.

Syringa
State Flower

Mountain Bluebird
State Bird

- name originated from the Shoshone Indian word *ee-dah-how*, which means *sun coming down the mountain* or *daybreak*
- nicknamed the Gem State for the gold, silver and other minerals in the area that brought a mining boom

Borah Peak—12,662 ft.

Craters of the Moon National Monument

Cities of Rock

Ghost Towns—Silver City, Florence, Idaho City, Dixie and Orogrande

Pocatello—contains Old Fort Hall, a reconstruction of a trading post on the Oregon Trail

Hells Canyon—the nation's deepest canyon

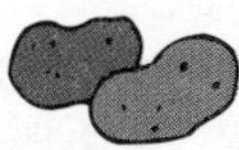
Potatoes—grows more than any other state

Circle the capital city. Locate the landmarks found in the above key. Color them on the map.

Name______________________________

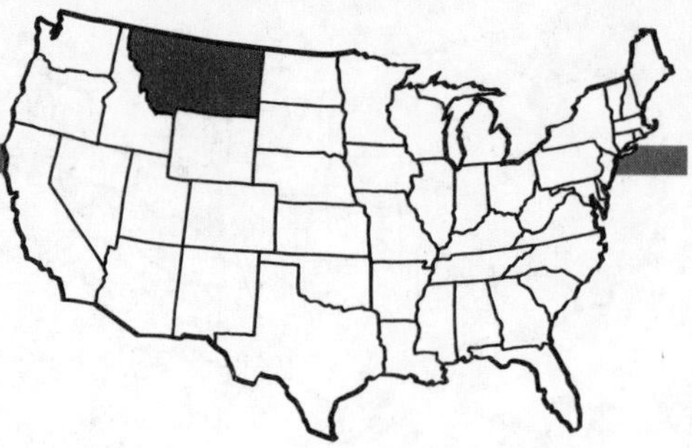

Mountain States

Montana

The Treasure State

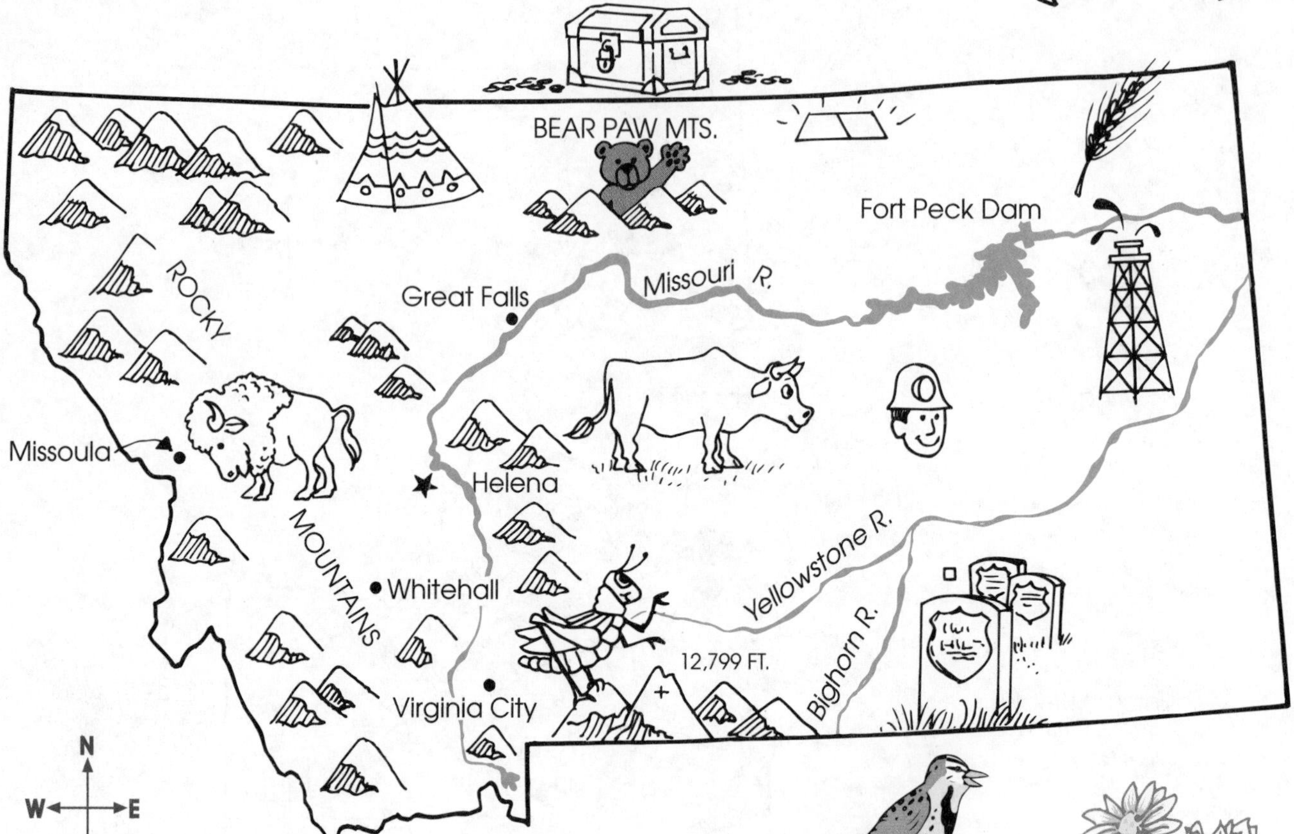

BEAR PAW MTS.
Fort Peck Dam
Missouri R.
ROCKY MOUNTAINS
Great Falls
Missoula
Helena
Whitehall
Virginia City
Yellowstone R.
Bighorn R.
12,799 FT.
N W E S

Western Meadowlark
State Bird

Bitterroot
State Flower

- named from the Spanish word that means *mountainous*
- nicknamed the Treasure State for the vast amounts of gold and silver found in its mountains

Granite Peak—12,799 ft.

Little Bighorn National Monument

Blackfoot Indian Reservation

National Bison Range

Grasshopper Glacier—swarms of grasshoppers trapped in a glacier

● Virginia City—site of one of richest gold deposits in 1862

Circle the capital city. Locate the landmarks found in the above key. Color them on the map.

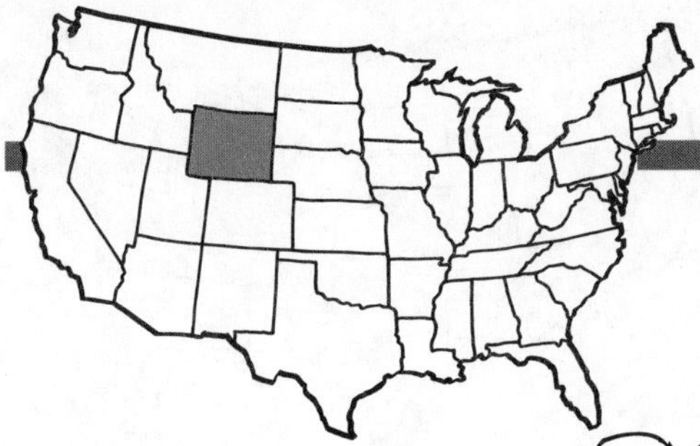

Name ____________________

Mountain States

Wyoming

The Equality State

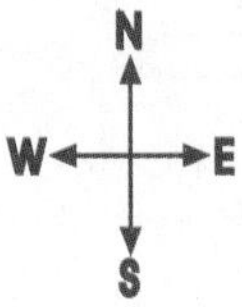

Indian Paintbrush
State Flower

Meadowlark
State Bird

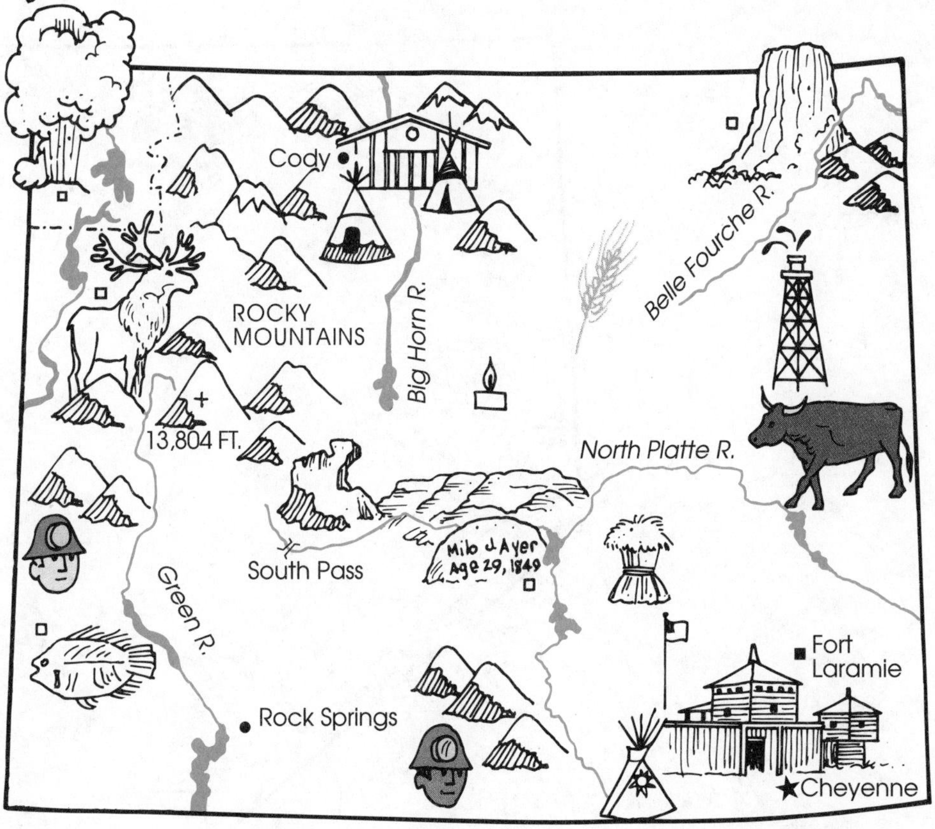

N
W E
S

Cody
ROCKY
MOUNTAINS
Big Horn R.
Belle Fourche R.
13,804 FT.
North Platte R.
South Pass
Milo J Ayer
Age 29, 1849
Green R.
Fort
Laramie
Rock Springs
Cheyenne

- named for the Delaware Indian word which means *upon the great plain*
- nickname the Equality State refers to being the first state in which women could vote, hold a position in public office and serve on a jury

Gannett Peak—13,804 ft.

Old Faithful Geyser in Yellowstone National Park—world's 1st national park

Fossil Butte National Monument

Independence Rock—more than 5,000 pioneers carved their names here

National Elk Refuge

Fort Laramie—restored fur trading center

Buffalo Bill Historical Center

Devil's Tower—United States' first monument

Circle the capital city. Locate the landmarks found in the above key. Color them on the map.

Name ____________________________________

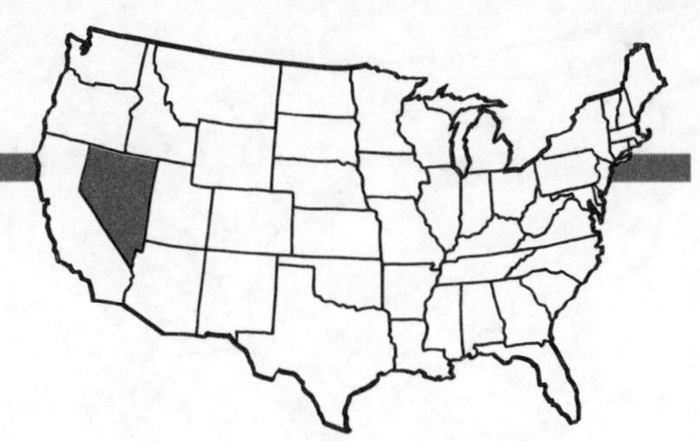

Mountain States

Nevada

The Silver State

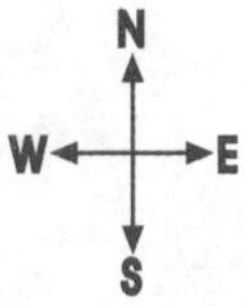

N
W E
S

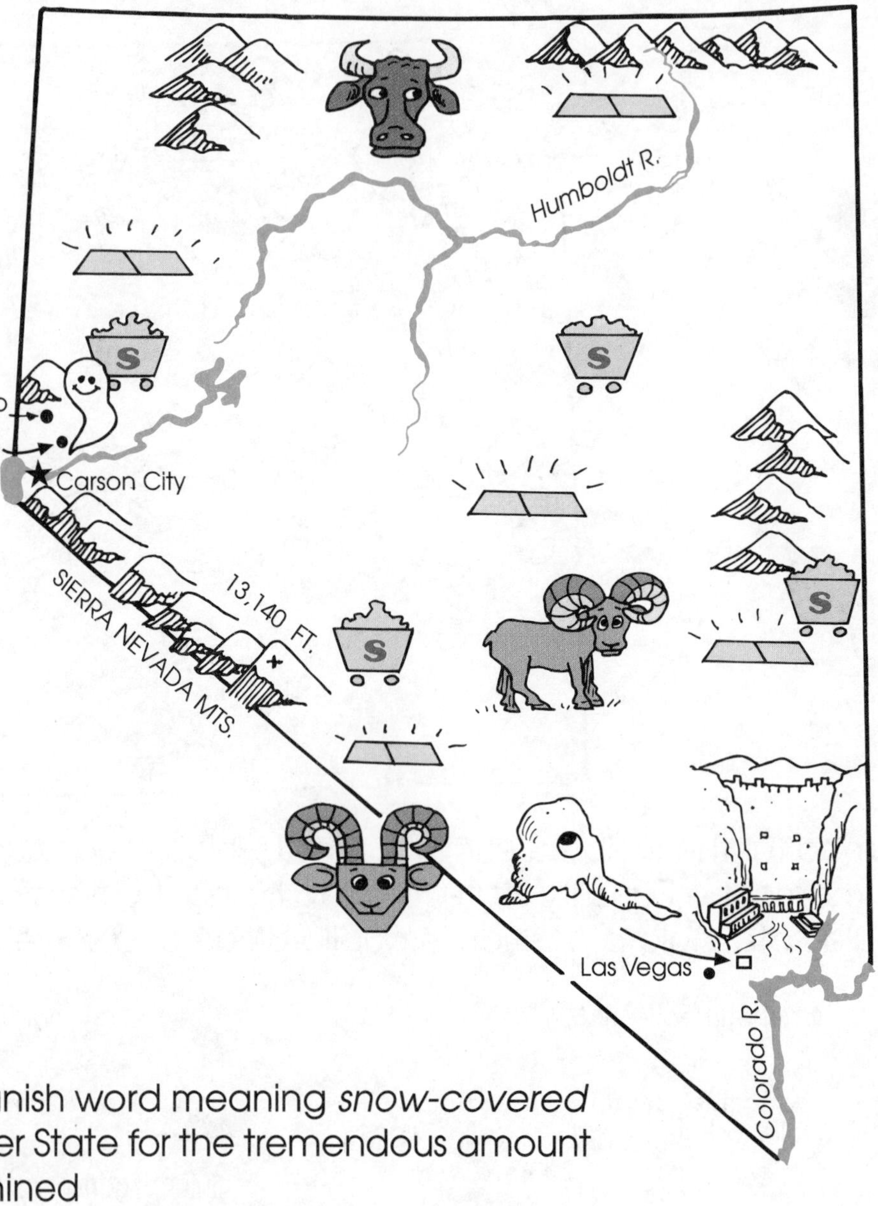

Reno
Virginia City
Lake Tahoe
Carson City
Humboldt R.
SIERRA NEVADA MTS.
13,140 FT.
Las Vegas
Colorado R.

Sagebrush
State Flower

Mountain Bluebird
State Bird

- named for the Spanish word meaning *snow-covered*
- nicknamed the Silver State for the tremendous amount of silver that was mined

Boundary Peak—13,140 ft.

Valley of Fire State Park—contains Elephant Rock, formed by the weather

Hoover Dam—one of the world's largest concrete dams

Lake Tahoe

Circle the capital city. Locate the landmarks found in the above key. Color them on the map.

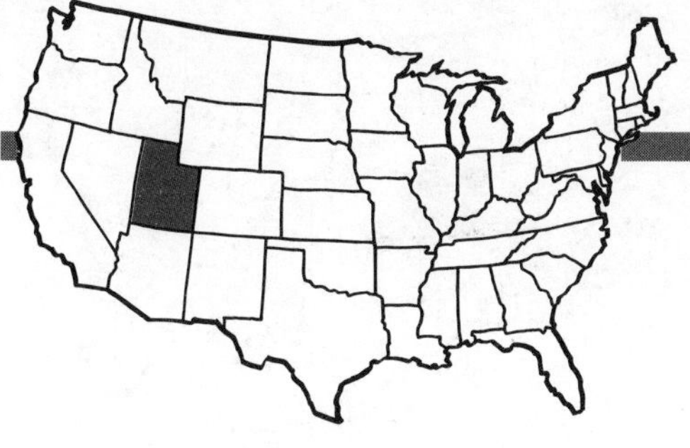

Name ______________________________

Utah

The Beehive State

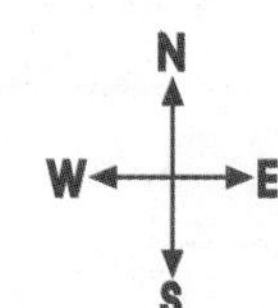

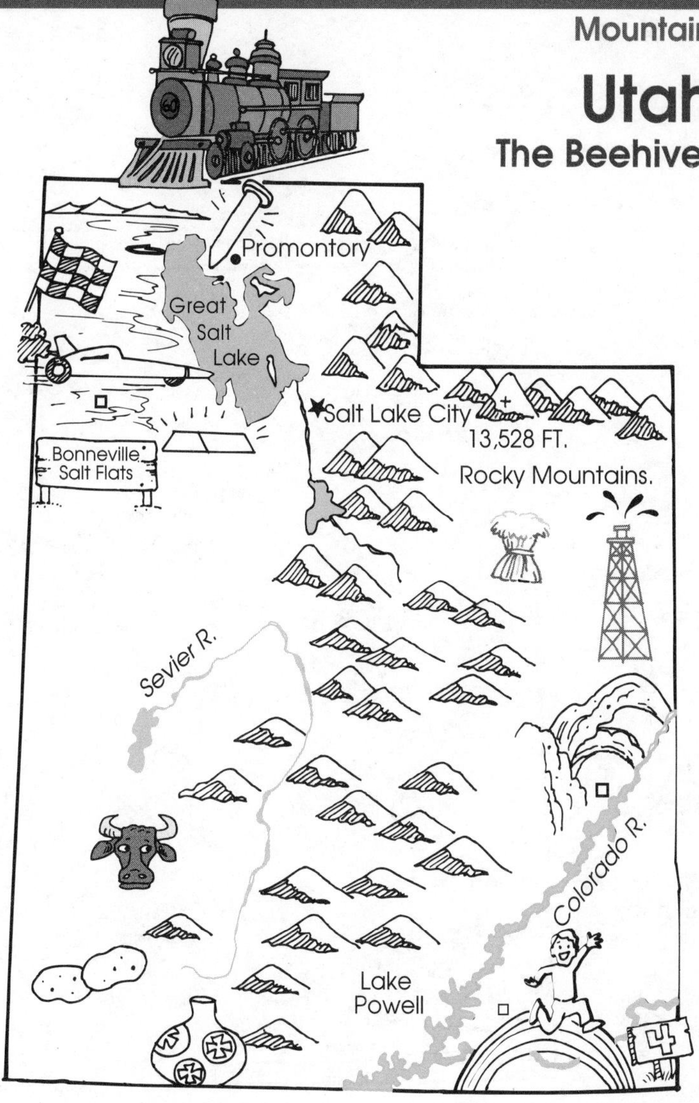

Sego Lily
State Flower

Sea Gull
State Bird

- named for the Ute Indians
- nicknamed the Beehive State because pioneers called the region *Deseret*—Mormon for *honeybee*

 King's Peak—13,528 ft.

 Indian Cliff Dwelling Ruins—housed Anasazi about A.D. 1000-1300

 International Speedway—cars race on flat salt beds

 Promontory—first transcontinental railroad completed in 1869

 Four Corners—where Utah, Arizona, New Mexico and Colorado meet

 Bonneville Salt Flats

 Arches National Park

 Rainbow Bridge National Monument—world's largest natural stone bridge

Circle the capital city. Locate the landmarks found in the above key. Color them on the map.

Name ______________________________

Mountain States

Colorado

The Centennial State

Dinosaur National Park

South Platte R.

Denver

Colorado R.

Rocky Mountain Columbine State Flower

Grand Junction

Aspen

Leadville

14,433 FT.

Gunnison R.

Colorado Springs

Arkansas R.

Lark Bunting State Bird

Rio Grande R.

- named for the Colorado River, whose name is Spanish for *colored red*
- nicknamed the Centennial State for becoming a state in 1876, which was the centennial of the Declaration of Independence

Mount Elbert—14,433 ft.

Mesa Verde National Park—1,000-year-old-cliff dwellings

Four Corners—place where four states meet

Garden of the Gods—giant formations of red sandstone

Royal Gorge Bridge

U.S. Mint—millions of coins made yearly

Circle the capital city. Locate the landmarks found in the above key. Color them on the map.

Name________________________________

Mountain States

Arizona

The Grand Canyon State

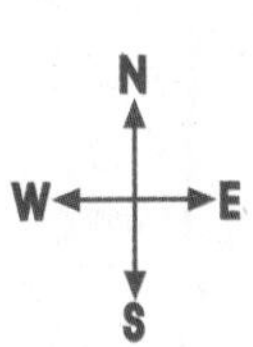

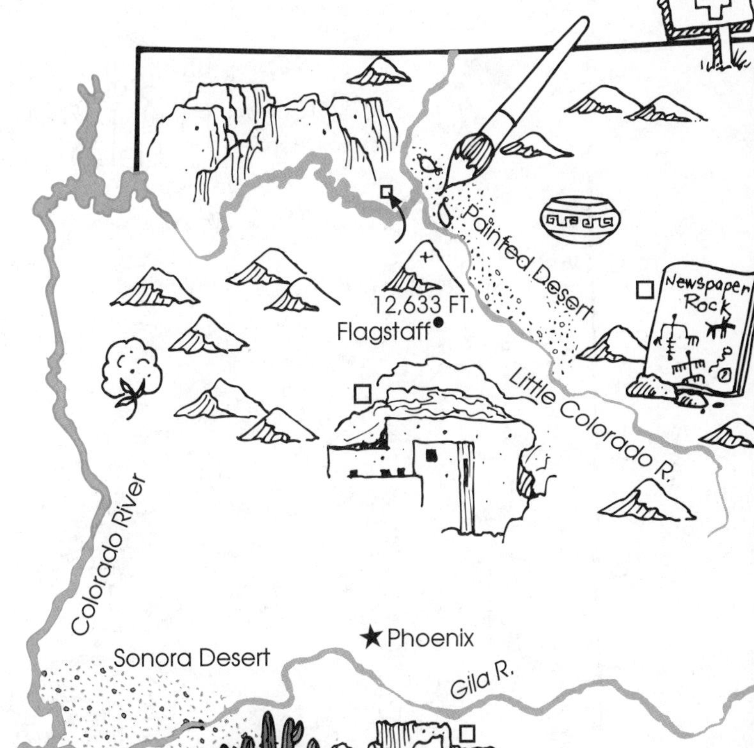

Saguaro
State Flower

Cactus Wren
State Bird

- name derived from the Native American word *arizonac*, which possibly means *small spring*
- nicknamed the Grand Canyon State for the Grand Canyon, which is located in the northwest corner of the state

 Humphreys Peak—12, 633 ft.

 Petrified Forest Park—location of Newspaper Rock

 Four Corners—place where Arizona, Colorado, New Mexico and Utah meet

 Monument Valley Navajo Tribal Park

 Painted Desert—colorful rock and sand

 Montezuma Castle National Monument—five-story cliff-dwelling ruin

 Grand Canyon National Park—one of the U.S.'s most famous scenic wonders

 Casa Grande Tower—built by Hohokum Indians about A.D. 1350

Circle the capital city. Locate the landmarks found in the above key. Color them on the map.

Name____

Mountain States

New Mexico

Land of Enchantment

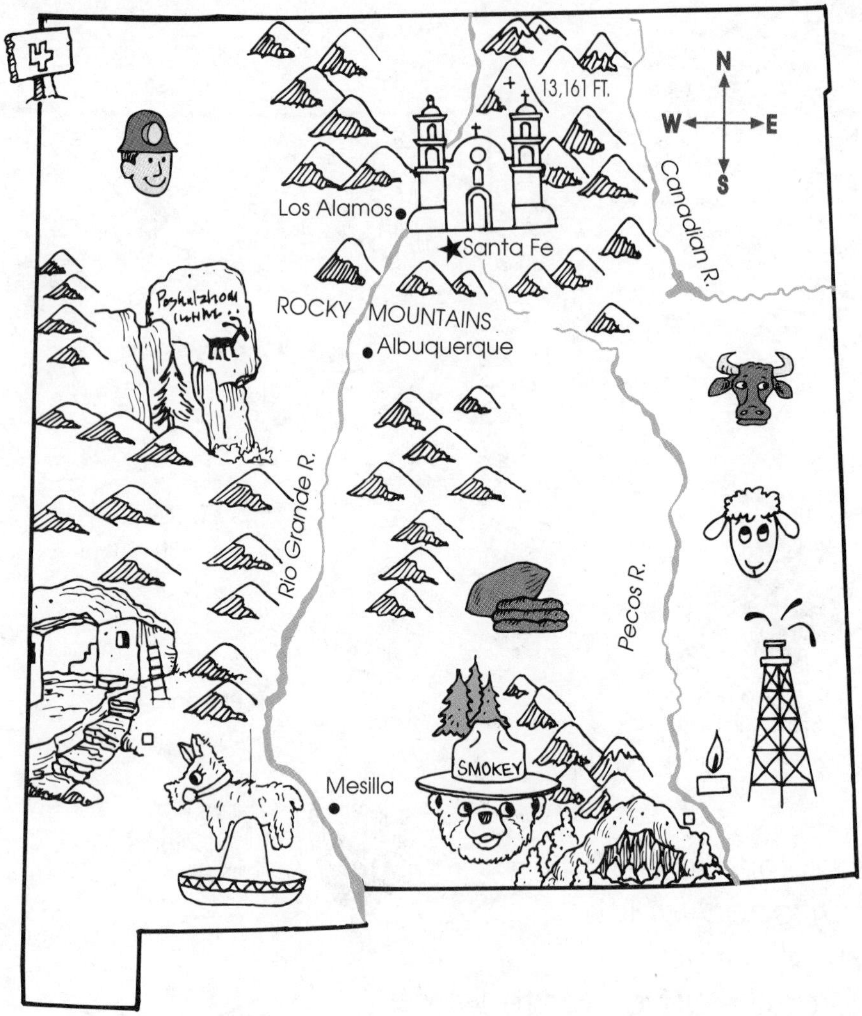

13,161 FT.

N W E S

Los Alamos

Santa Fe

Canadian R.

ROCKY MOUNTAINS

Albuquerque

Rio Grande R.

Pecos R.

Mesilla

SMOKEY

Yucca Flower
State Flower

Roadrunner
State Bird

- named after Mexico, which was named after Mexitli, an Aztec Indian war god
- nicknamed the Land of Enchantment for its beautiful scenery and rich, history

Wheeler Peak—13,161 ft.

Four Corners

San Miguel Mission

Carlsbad Caverns—one of the world's great natural wonders

Gila Cliff Dwellings National Monument

Historic Mesilla

Inscription Rock National Monument—has petroglyphs never deciphered

Smokey the Bear Historical Park

Circle the capital city. Locate the landmarks found in the above key. Color them on the map.

Name____________________

The North Central States

Look around the North Central states and you will see why they are also called the Plains states. The plains have rich soil that makes this area famous for growing wheat and corn.

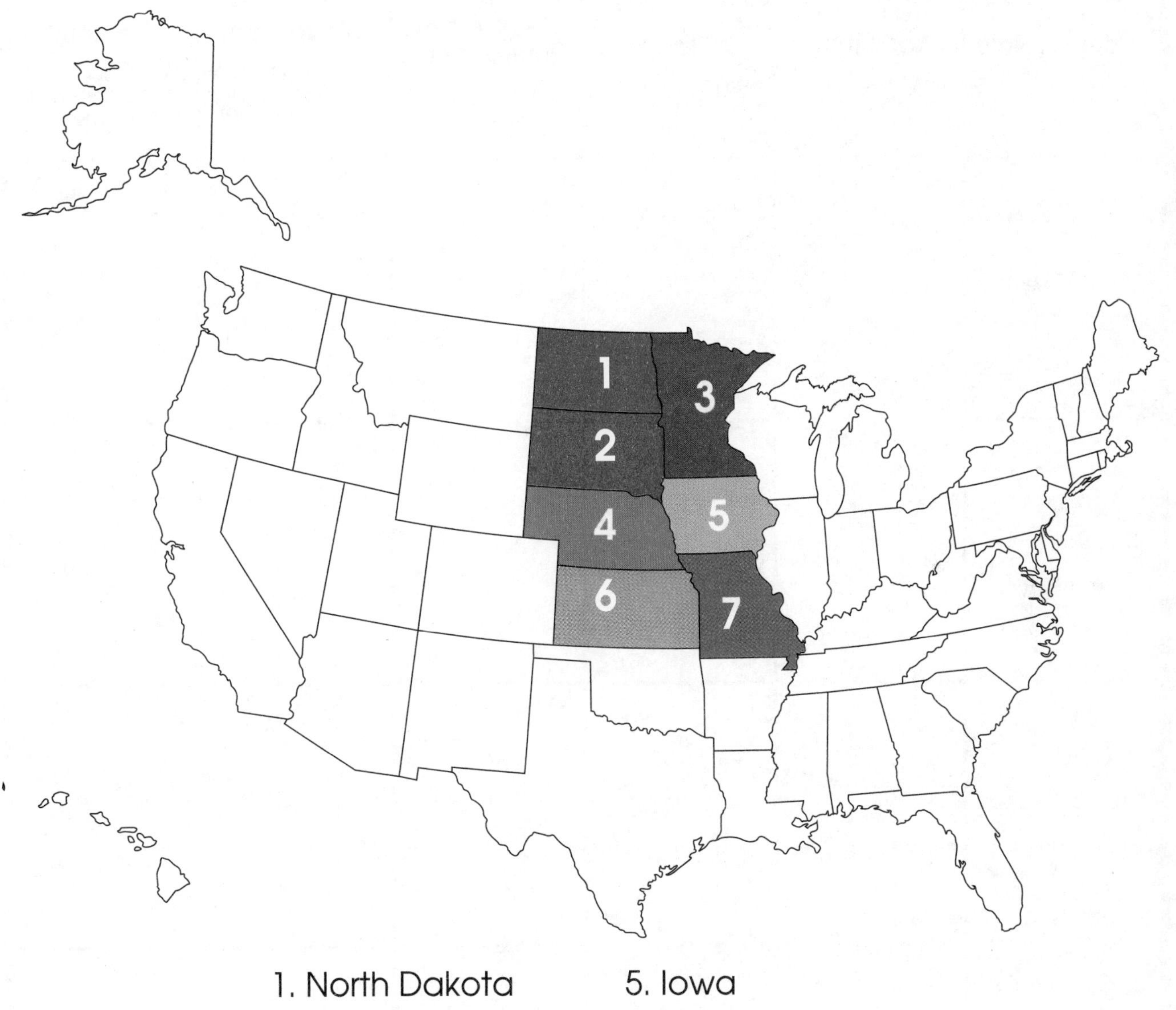

1. North Dakota
2. South Dakota
3. Minnesota
4. Nebraska
5. Iowa
6. Kansas
7. Missouri

Name________________________________

North Central States

Fill in the "Five Fundamental Themes of Geography" for each state. After "discovering" a state, fill in all the columns of the chart except **Regions**. When you have finished with all of the states in a section, fill in **Regions**.

Five Fundamental Themes of Geography					
Name of State	**Location** (Where is it?)	**Place** (What is it like?)	**People and Environment** (What do the people do?)	**Movement** (How do people, goods and ideas move?)	**Regions** (What are some of the common features?)

Name________________________________

Fill in the "Five Fundamental Themes of Geography" for each state. After "discovering" a state, fill in all the columns of the chart except **Regions**. When you have finished with all of the states in a section, fill in **Regions**.

Five Fundamental Themes of Geography

Name of State	Location (Where is it?)	Place (What is it like?)	People and Environment (What do the people do?)	Movement (How do people, goods and ideas move?)	Regions (What are some of the common features?)

Name____

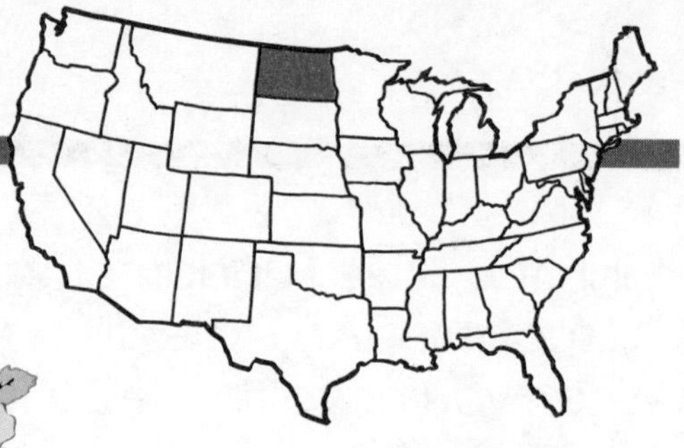

North Dakota

The Flickertail State

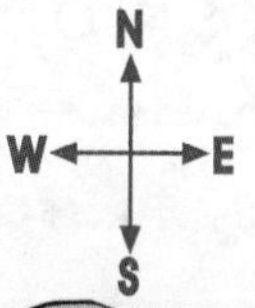

N
W E
S

Wild Prairie Rose
State Flower

Western
Meadowlark
State Bird

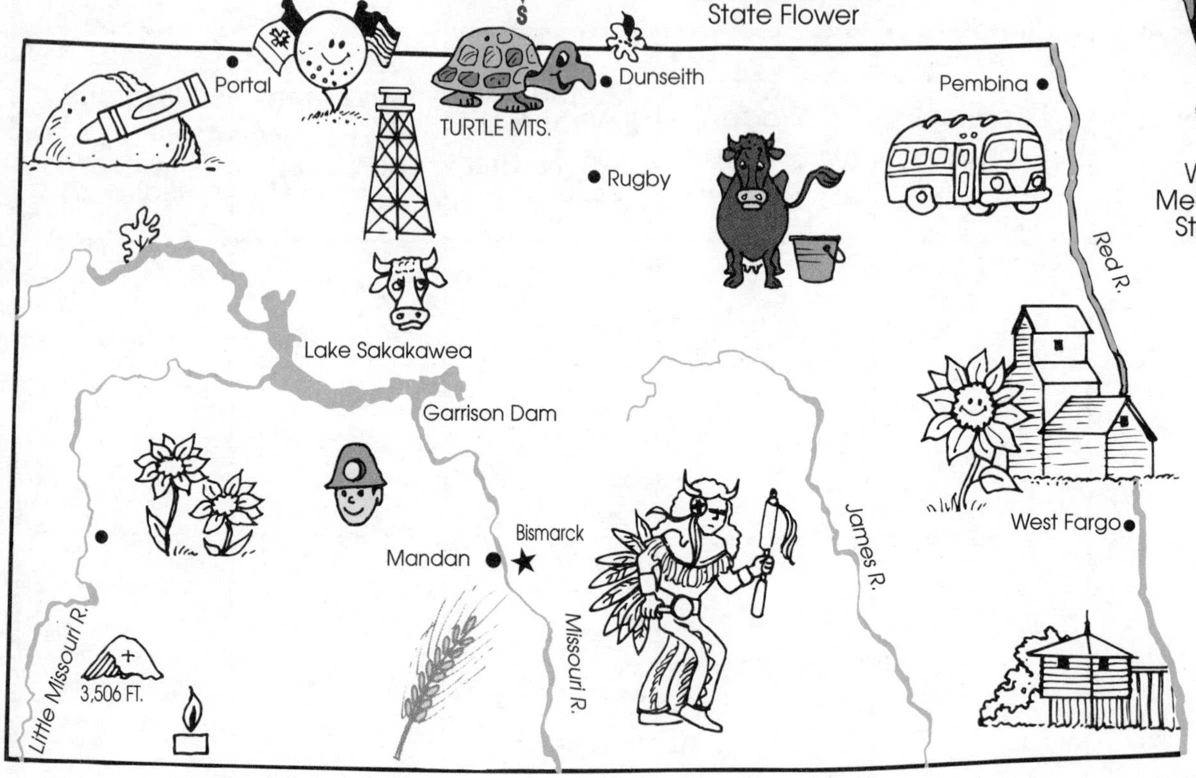

Portal
TURTLE MTS.
Dunseith
Pembina
Rugby
Red R.
Lake Sakakawea
Garrison Dam
Bismarck
Mandan
West Fargo
James R.
Little Missouri R.
Missouri R.
3,506 FT.

- named for Sioux Indians who called themselves Dakota or Lakota, which means *allies* or *friends*
- nicknamed the Flickertail State for the numerous flickertail ground squirrels

White Butte—3,506 ft.

Sunflowers—top producer of seeds

Bonanzaville—preserved pioneer village

United Tribes Powwow

Pembina—nations' largest bus plant

International Peace Garden—symbolizes friendship between U.S. and Canada

Writing Rock—boulder with ancient Indian picture writing

International Golf Course—spans two countries; tee for the 9th hole in Canada and cup in the U.S.

Fort Abercrombie—1st U.S. military post in North Dakota

• Rugby—geographic center of North America

Circle the capital city. Locate the landmarks found in the above key. Color them on the map.

Name ______________________________

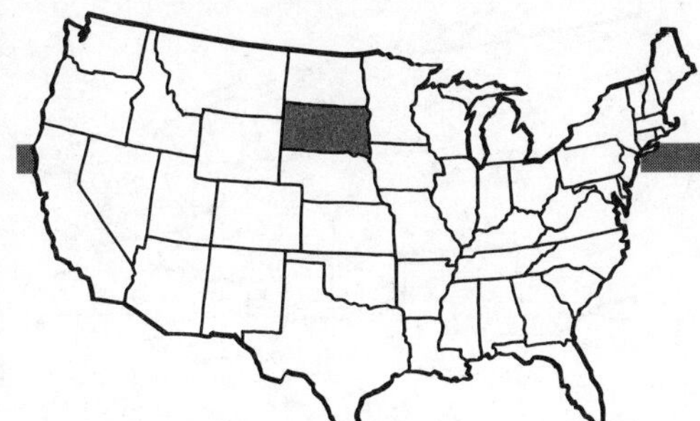

North Central States

South Dakota

The Sunshine State

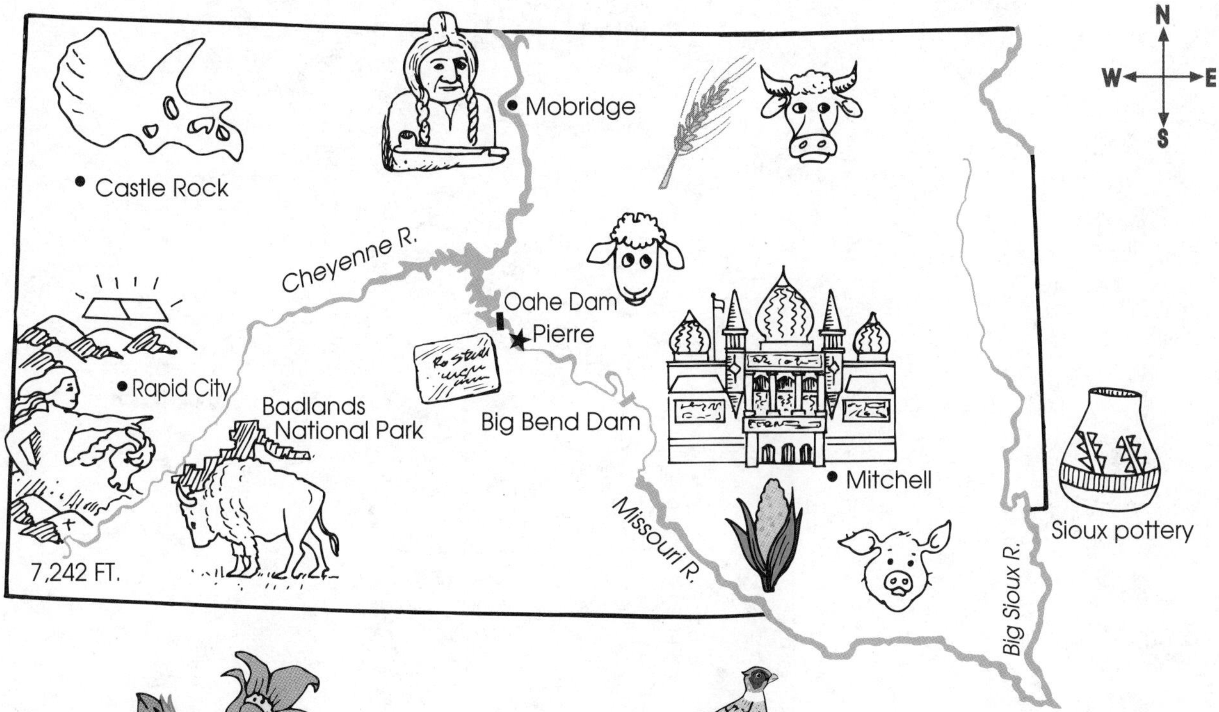

Castle Rock
Mobridge
Cheyenne R.
Oahe Dam
Pierre
Rapid City
Badlands National Park
Big Bend Dam
Mitchell
Missouri R.
Big Sioux R.
Sioux pottery
7,242 FT.
N
W
E
S

American Pasqueflower
State Flower

Ring-Necked Pheasant
State Bird

- named for Sioux Indians who called themselves Dakota or Lakota, which means *allies* or *friends*
- nicknamed the Sunshine State for its many sunny days

Harney Peak—7,242 ft.

Mobridge—sculpture marking the gravesite of Sioux leader Sitting Bull

Triceratops Fossil—found in 1927 in Harding County and now on display

Custer State Park

Castle Rock—geographic center of the 50 United States

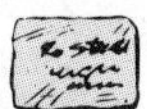

Lead Plate—buried by the La Vérendrye brothers in 1743—discovered in 1913

Circle the capital city. Locate the landmarks found in the above key. Color them on the map.

Name ____________________________________

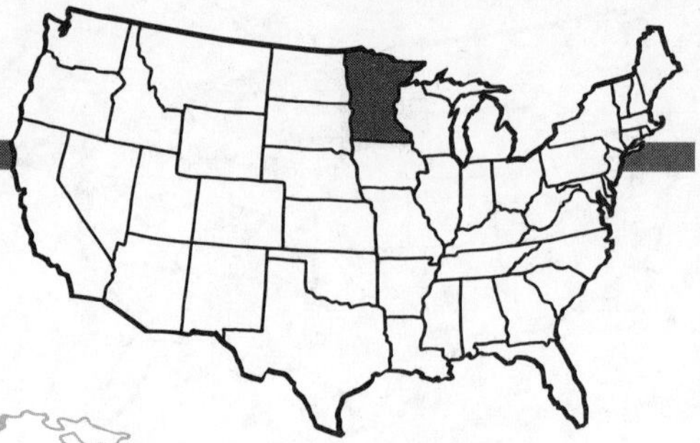

North Central States

Minnesota

The Gopher State

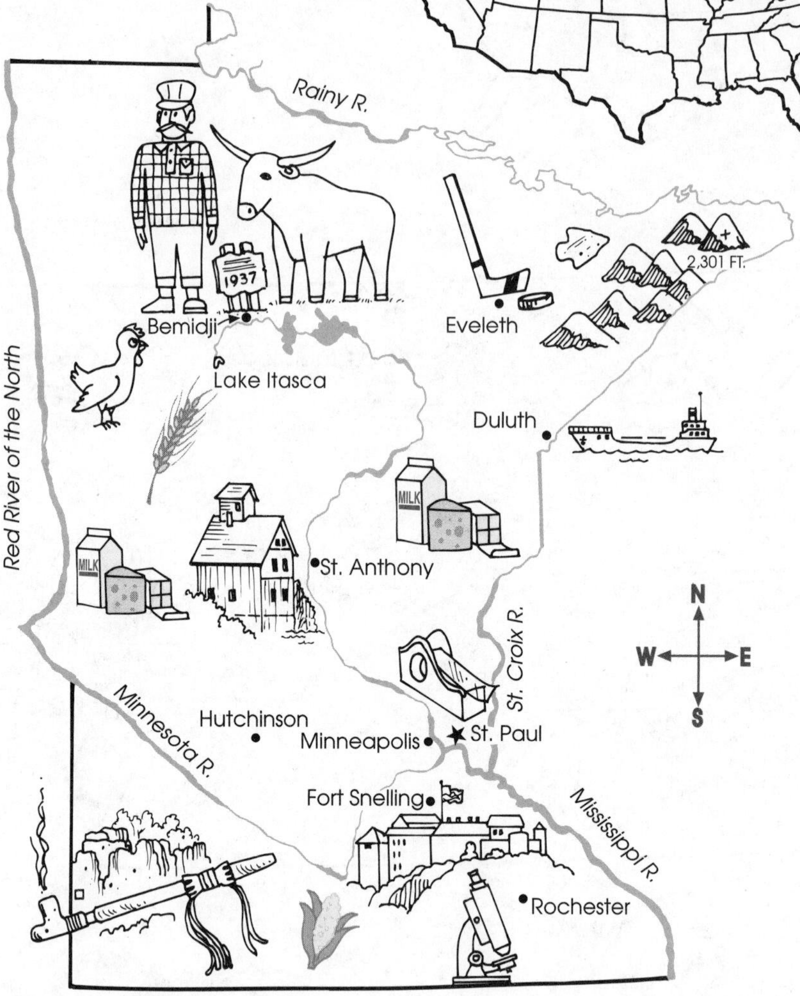

Rainy R.

Bemidji

1937

Eveleth

2,301 FT.

Lake Itasca

Duluth

Red River of the North

MILK

St. Anthony

St. Croix R.

N

W E

S

Minnesota R.

Hutchinson

Minneapolis

St. Paul

Fort Snelling

Mississippi R.

Rochester

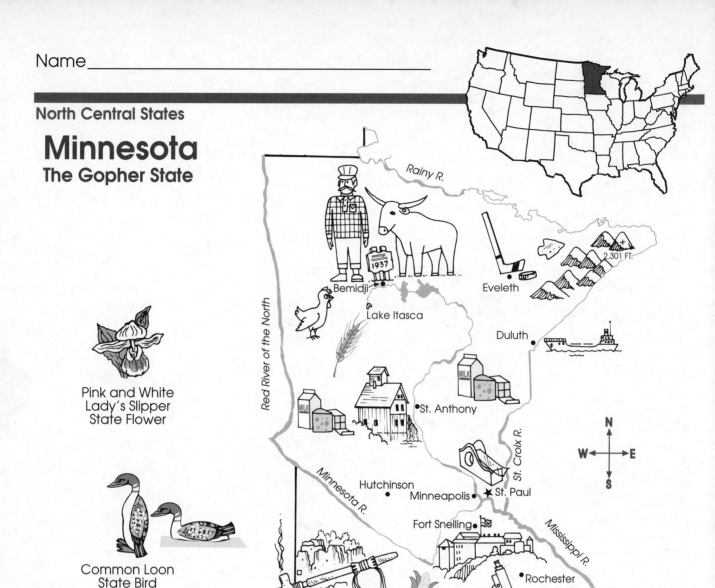

Pink and White Lady's Slipper State Flower

Common Loon State Bird

- name derived from the Sioux Indian words *mini sota*, meaning *sky-tinted water*
- nicknamed the Gopher State for the vast numbers of gophers that inhabited its prairie

Eagle Mountain—2,301 ft.

Arrowhead Country—northeastern tip shaped like an arrowhead

Bemidji—Paul Bunyan and Babe

St. Paul—where cellophane tape was invented

Fort Snelling—1819 restored military post

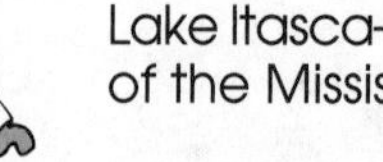
Lake Itasca—beginning of the Mississippi River

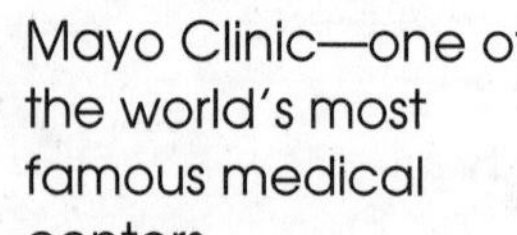
Mayo Clinic—one of the world's most famous medical centers

U.S. Hockey Hall of Fame

Falls of St. Anthony—first flour mill in Minnesota, in 1823

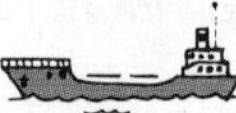
Duluth—farthest inland port in U.S.

Pipestone National Monument—Indians used red pipestone found here to make peace pipes

Circle the capital city. Locate the landmarks found in the above key. Color them on the map.

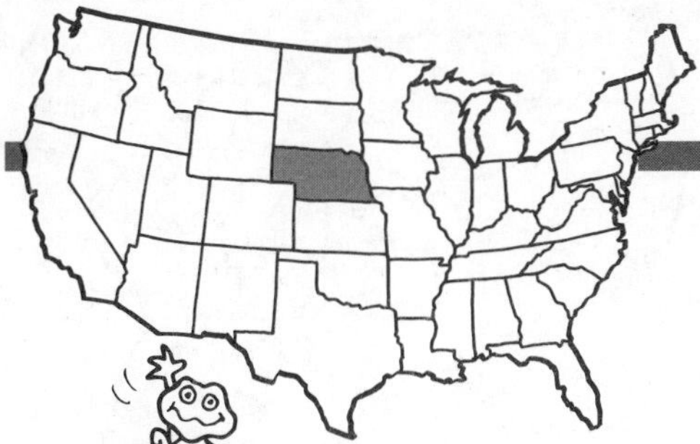

Name ______________________________

Nebraska

The Cornhusker's State

N
W E
S

Niobrara R.

Missouri R.

□Carhenge

SAND HILLS

Platte R.

Omaha

Grand Island

Wellfleet

Kearney

Lincoln

Nebraska City

5,426 FT.

Western Meadowlark
State Bird

Goldenrod
State Flower

- named for the Oto Indian word *nebrathka*, meaning *flat water*, which was the Indian name for the Platte River
- nicknamed the Cornhusker State for the state's leading crop of corn and for the cornhusking contests that used to be held in the fall

Toadstool Park—in the Badlands, has rock formations resembling toadstools

Wellfleet—largest mammoth fossil ever found

National Museum of Roller Skating

Arbor Lodge—home of Julius Sterling Morton, founder of Arbor Day

Chimney Rock National Historic Site

Carhenge—replica of Stonehenge made of cars

Cranes—about 500,000 stop along the Platte River every spring as they migrate north

Buffalo Bill's home

Homestead National Monument of America—site of the first piece of land claimed under the Homestead Act

Circle the capital city. Locate the landmarks found in the above key. Color them on the map.

Name ___________________________

North Central States

Iowa

The Hawkeye State

1,670 FT.

Decorah

Wild Rose
State Flower

N
W E
S

Little Sioux R.

Sioux City

Dubuque

Julien Dubuque Monument

Cedar Rapids

Newton

Des Moines

Indianola

East Peru

Missouri R.

Mississippi R.

Des Moines R.

Skunk R.

Eastern Goldfinch
State Bird

Keokuk Dam

- named after the Sioux Indian tribe Ayuhwa whose name means *beautiful land* or *sleepy ones*
- nicknamed the Hawkeye State in honor of Chief Black Hawk, a Sauk and Fox Indian leader

Vesterheim Museum—Norwegian culture exhibits

Julien Dubuque Monument—gravesite of the first permanent white settler in Iowa

Indianola—National Balloon Museum

Cedar Rapids—one of the largest cereal mills in the U.S.

East Peru—red delicious apple was developed here in the1880s

Newton—washing machine capital of the world

Sioux City—largest popcorn processing plants in U.S.

Effigy Mounds—earthen mounds shaped like animals, built by prehistoric Indians

Circle the capital city. Locate the landmarks found in the above key. Color them on the map.

Name______________________________

Kansas

The Sunflower State

Sunflower
State Flower

Western Meadowlark
State Bird

- named for the Kansa, or Kaw, Indians, whose name means *people of the south wind*
- nicknamed the Sunflower State for the abundance of sunflowers

Mount Sunflower—4,039 ft.

Liberal—home of the original model of Dorothy's house from the 1939 film *The Wizard of Oz*

Old flour mill—represents the many flour mills in Topeka today

Cowboy Capital of the World

Chisholm Trail—used for herding cattle from Texas to Abilene for shipment to the East

Fort Scott—restored 1840's cavalry post

Circle the capital city. Locate the landmarks found in the above key. Color them on the map.

Name ______________________________________

North Central States

Missouri

The Show Me State

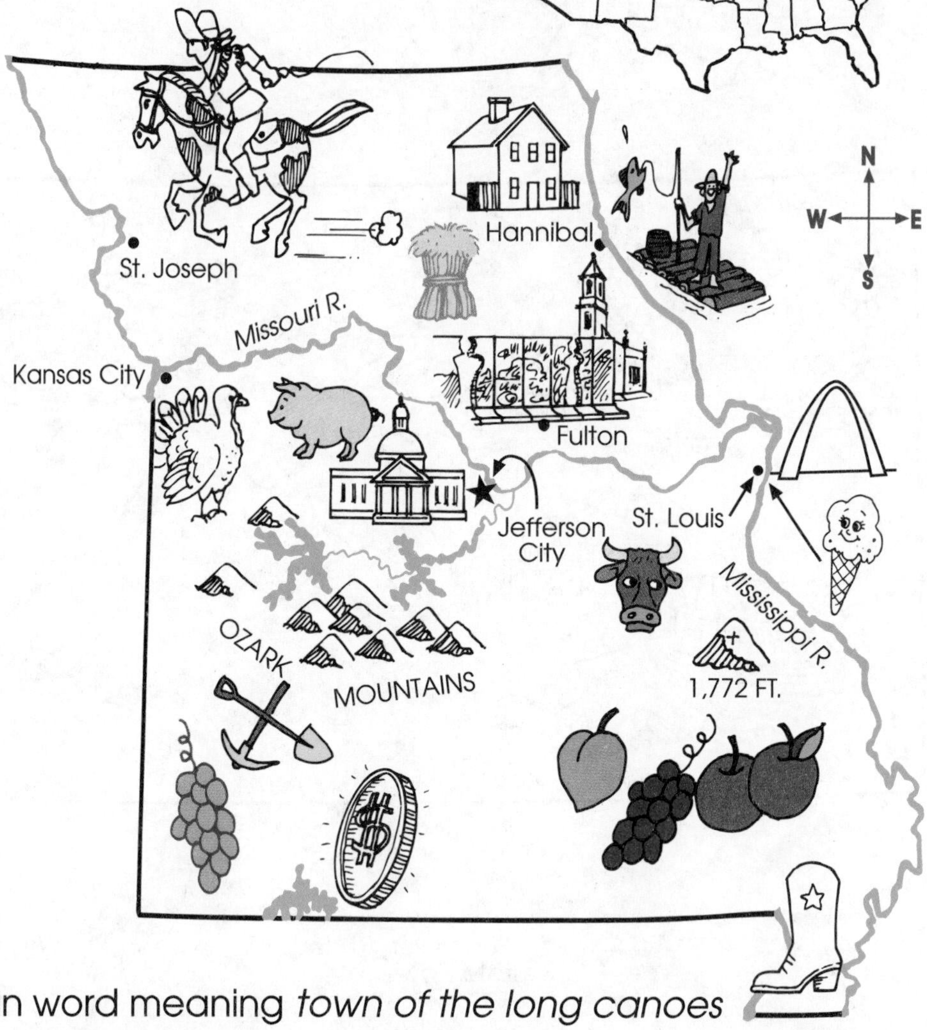

St. Joseph
Hannibal
Missouri R.
Kansas City
Fulton
Jefferson City
St. Louis
Mississippi R.
OZARK MOUNTAINS
1,772 FT.
N
W
E
S

Bluebird
State Bird

Hawthorn
State Flower

- named for an Indian word meaning *town of the long canoes*
- nickname the Show Me State related to an 1899 speech by Congressman Vandiver in which he indicated he was unimpressed with speeches and wanted to be shown results

Taum Sauk Mountain—1,772 ft.

Pony Express—carried mail from St. Joseph, Missouri to Sacramento, California from 1860 to 1861

Hannibal—contains the home and museum of Mark Twain, who wrote *Tom Sawyer*

Fulton—has a 1990 sculpture using eight Berlin Wall sections

Gateway Arch—tallest monument in U.S.

Boot Heel Country—named because the shape resembles a boot heel

Silver Dollar City—reconstructed 1880s mining town

First ice-cream cone—at Louisiana Purchase Centennial Expo in St. Louis in 1904

Circle the capital city. Locate the landmarks found in the above key. Color them on the map.

Name ______________________________

The South Central States

The South Central states is a region with large areas of flat land good for raising cattle and growing cotton. This region is also known for its rich deposits of oil that are found beneath the surface of the land and ocean floor.

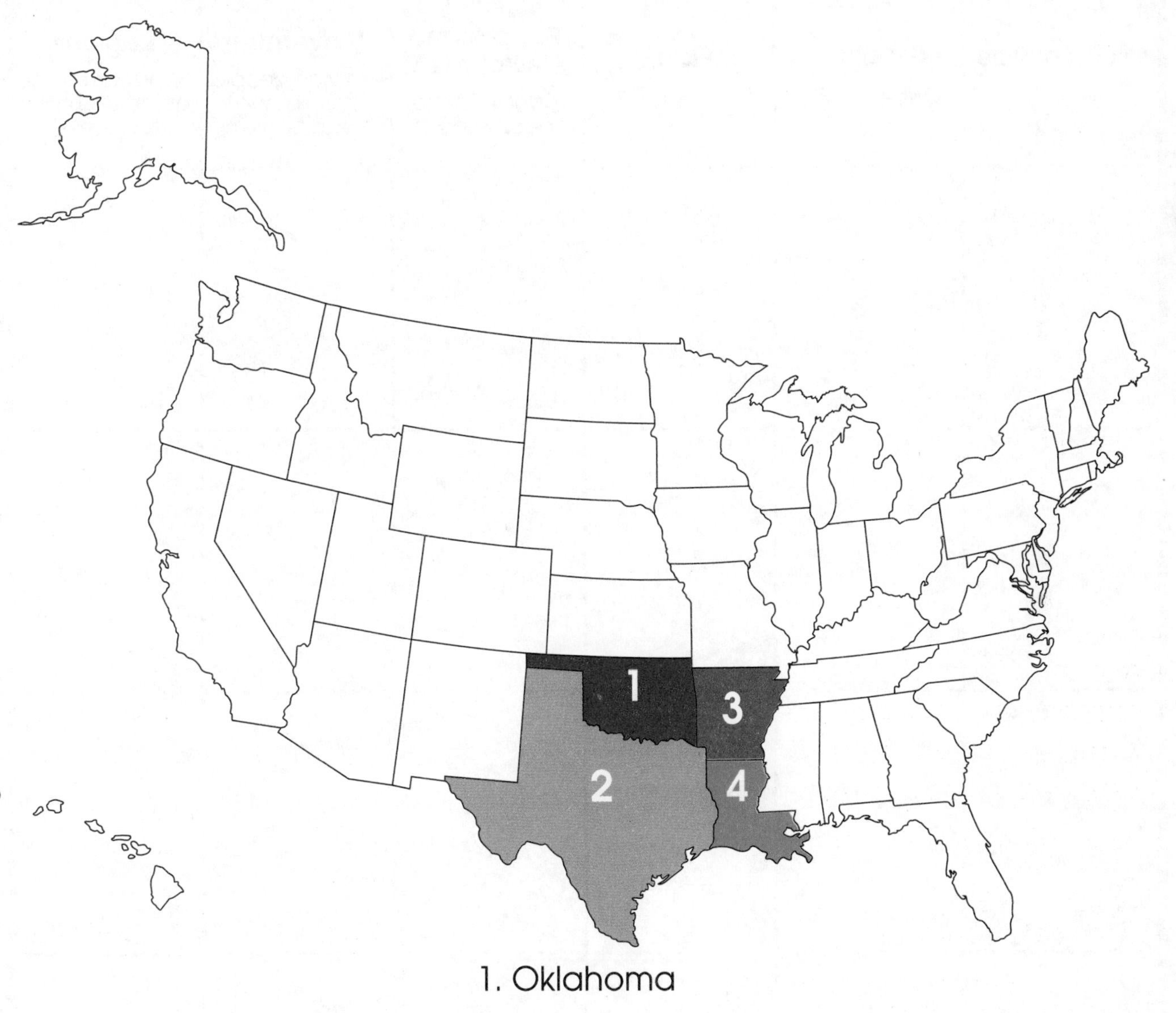

1. Oklahoma

2. Texas

3. Arkansas

4. Louisiana

Name ________________________________

South Central States

Fill in the "Five Fundamental Themes of Geography" for each state. After "discovering" a state, fill in all the columns of the chart except **Regions**. When you have finished with all of the states in a section, fill in **Regions**.

Five Fundamental Themes of Geography					
Name of State	**Location** (Where is it?)	**Place** (What is it like?)	**People and Environment** (What do the people do?)	**Movement** (How do people, goods and ideas move?)	**Regions** (What are some of the common features?)

Name______________________

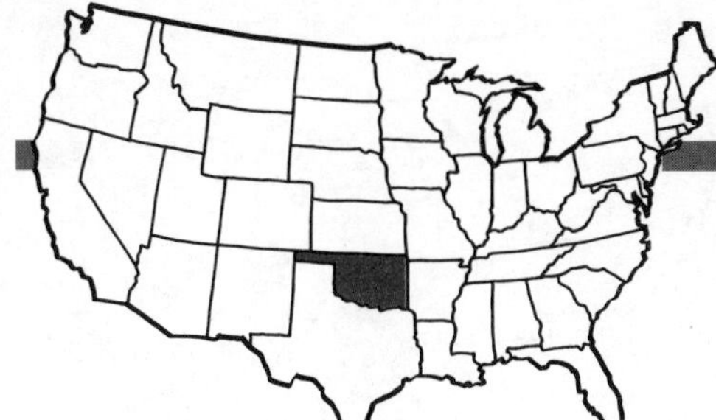

Oklahoma

The Sooner State

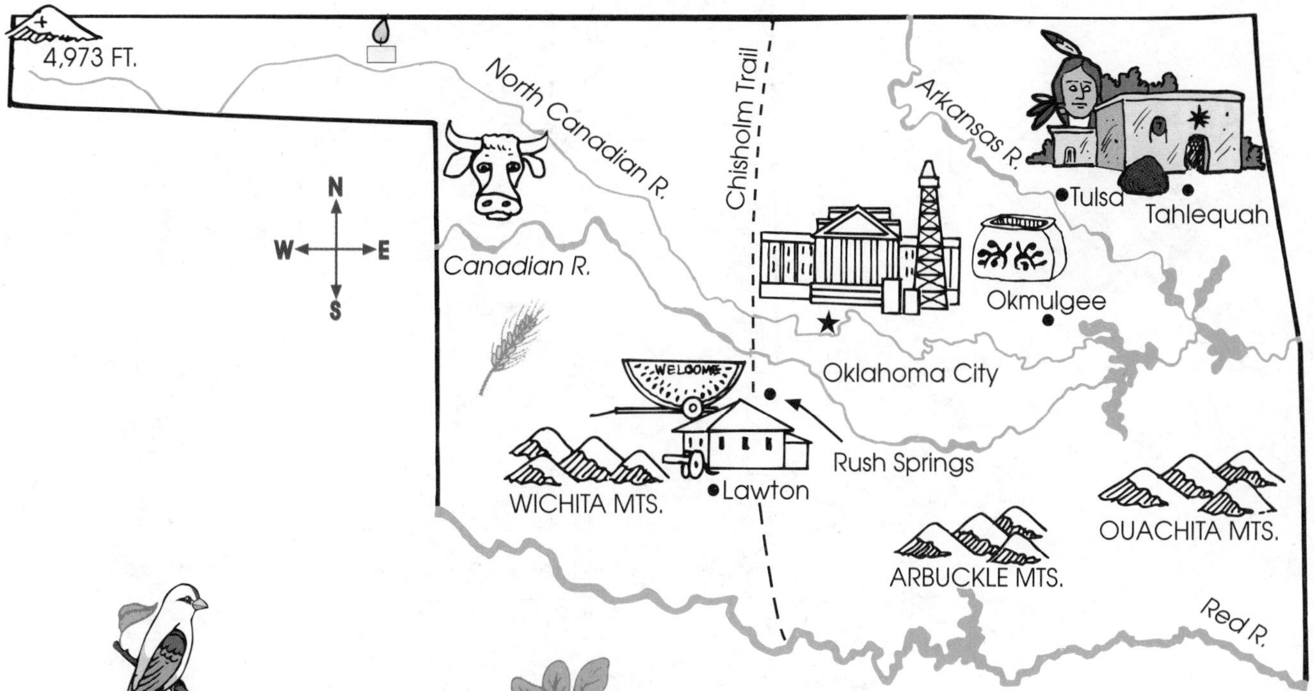

4,973 FT.
North Canadian R.
Chisholm Trail
Arkansas R.
Tulsa
Tahlequah
N
W E
S
Canadian R.
Okmulgee
Oklahoma City
Rush Springs
Lawton
WICHITA MTS.
ARBUCKLE MTS.
OUACHITA MTS.
Red R.

Scissor-Tailed Flycatcher
State Bird

Mistletoe
State Flower

- name derived from the Chocotaw Indian words *okla*, meaning *people*, and *homma*, meaning *red*
- nicknamed the Sooner State for the settlers who arrived before the land was opened for settlement

 Black Mesa—4,973 ft.

 Oklahoma City—only state capital with working oil well on its site

 Fort Sill—historical site built in 1869

 Rush Springs—Watermelon Capital of the World

Circle the capital city. Locate the landmarks found in the above key. Color them on the map.

Name____________________________________

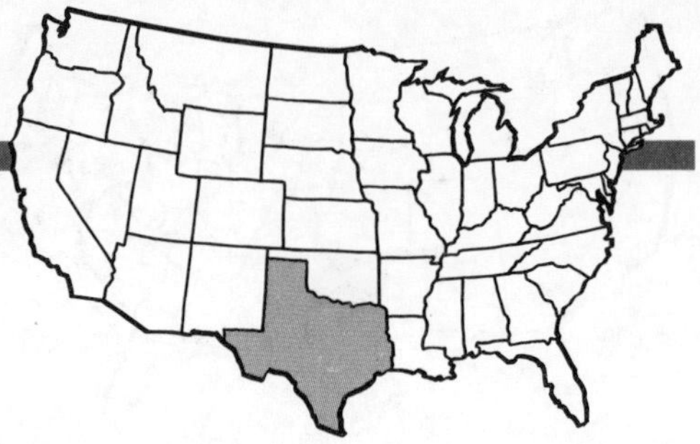

South Central States

Texas

The Lone Star State

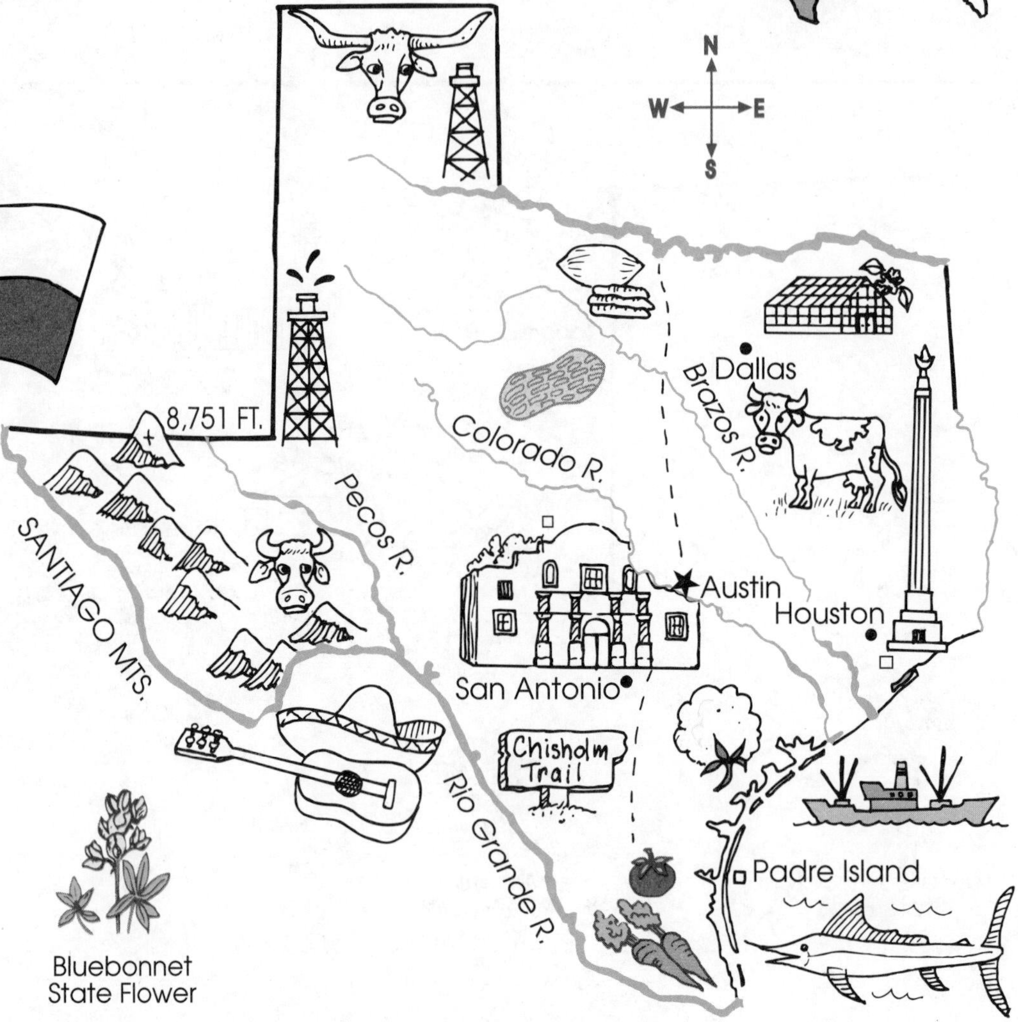

Mockingbird
State Bird

Bluebonnet
State Flower

- name comes from the Spanish pronunciation of the Indian word *Tejas*, which means *allies* or *friends*
- nickname the Lone Star State comes from having only one star on its state flag

Guadalupe Peak—8,751 ft.

San Jacinto Monument—honors Texans who fought and won the battle for independence from Mexico

The Alamo—a famous San Antonio battle site

Chisholm Trail—begins here

Padre Island—national seashore

Mexican culture and influence seen throughout the state

Circle the capital city. Locate the landmarks found in the above key. Color them on the map.

Name____

Arkansas

The Land of Opportunity

Bull Shoals Lake

Eureka Springs

White R.

Mountain View

Arkansas R.

2,753 FT.

Mississippi R.

Little Rock

Hot Springs

OUACHITA MTS.

Murfreesboro

Texarkana

TEXAS STATE LINE ARKANSAS

Red R.

N W E S

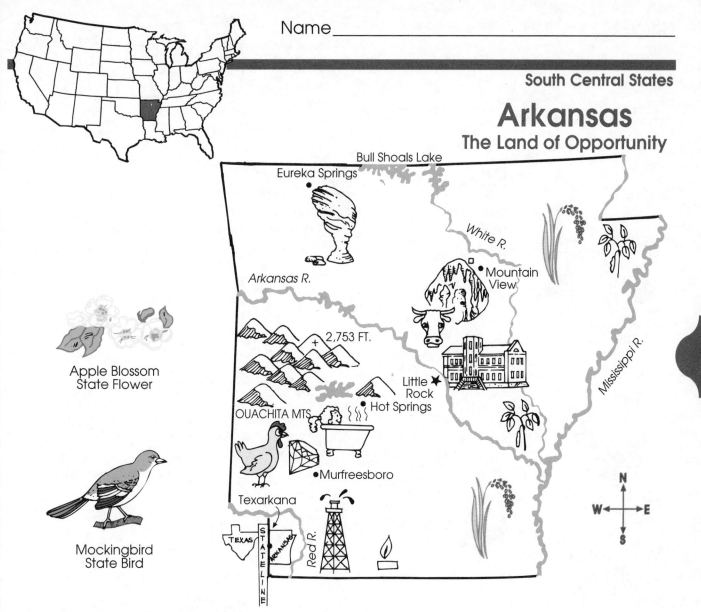

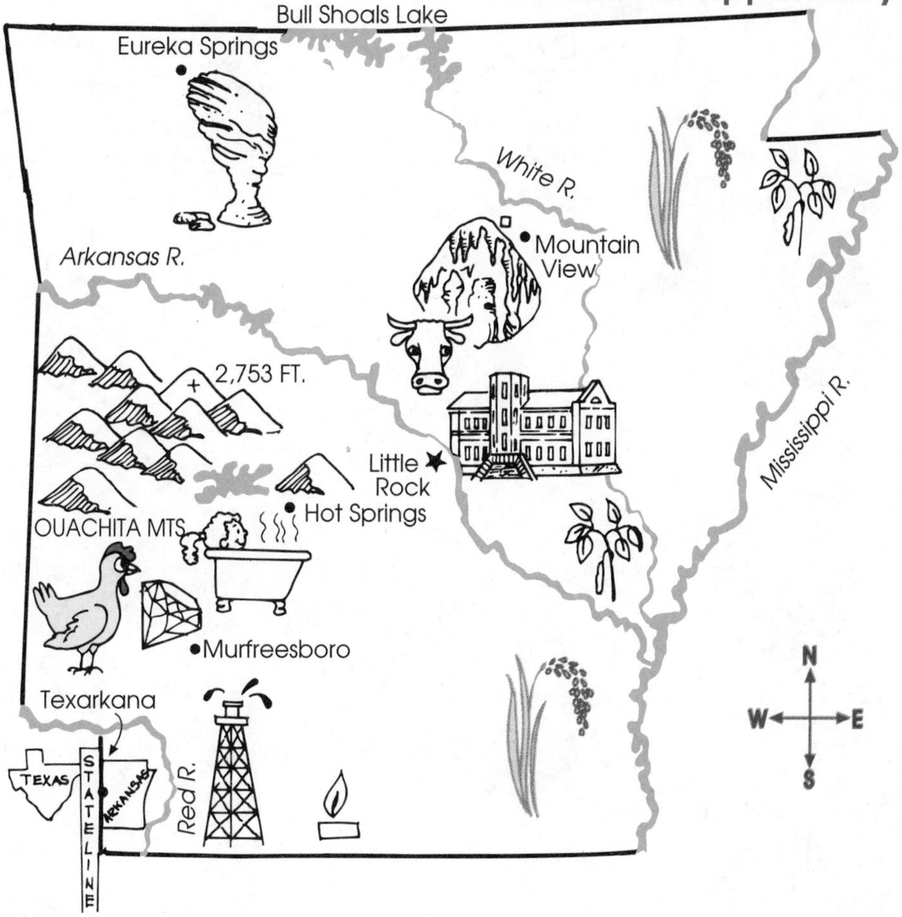

Apple Blossom
State Flower

Mockingbird
State Bird

- named for a Sioux Indian tribe named Arkansa, which means *downstream people*
- nickname the Land of Opportunity relates to the abundance of varied natural resources which provide excellent opportunities for mining, factories and farming

Magazine Mountain—2,753 ft.

Pivot Rock—balances on a small base

MacArthur Park—honors military commander, Douglas MacArthur

Crater of Diamonds State Park—diamond mine which tourists can visit

Hot Springs National Park—minerals and hot springs believed to be helpful for certain illnesses

Blanchard Spring Caverns

Texarkana—town on the border between Texas and Arkansas

Circle the capital city. Locate the landmarks found in the above key. Color them on the map.

Name________________________________

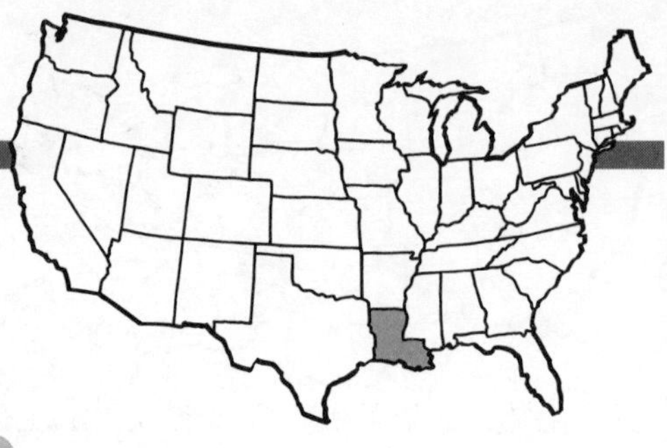

Louisiana

The Heart of Dixie

Magnolia
State Flower

Brown Pelican
State Bird

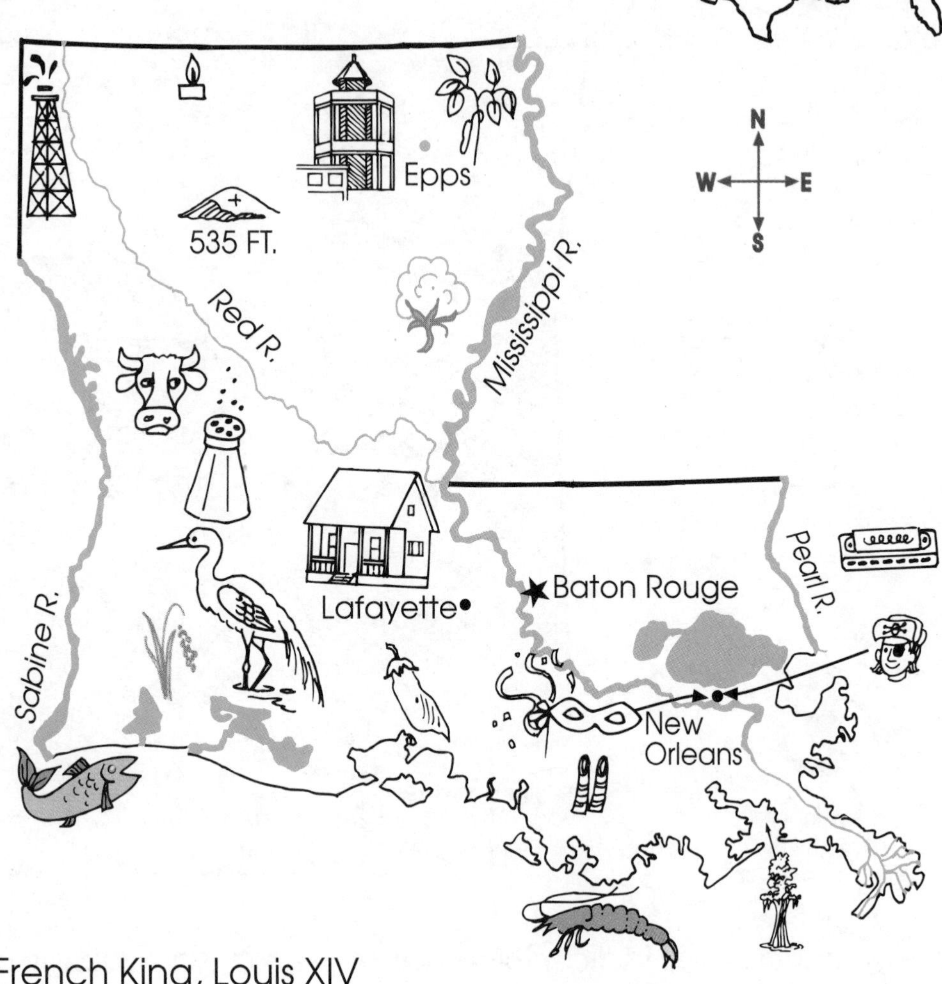

- named for the French King, Louis XIV
- nicknamed the Pelican State for the many brown pelicans that reside along the coast

 Driskill Mountain—535 ft.

 Poverty Point National Monument—ancient Indian ceremonial mounds built between 1700 and 700 B.C.

 Avery Island—chili peppers grown here to make Tabasco sauce

 Egrets—three of the world's largest egret sanctuaries

 Preservation Hall—famous for its jazz bands

 Bald cypress swamps

 Jean Lafitte National Historical Park & Preserve—area where pirate Jean Lafitte fought with Andrew Jackson in the Battle of New Orleans

 Acadian Village—features Cajun food and culture

 Mardi Gras—features dancing, parties and parades

Circle the capital city. Locate the landmarks found in the above key. Color them on the map.

Name________________________________

The Midwest States

The Midwest States is a region with beautiful freshwater lakes, deep green forests and fertile farmland.

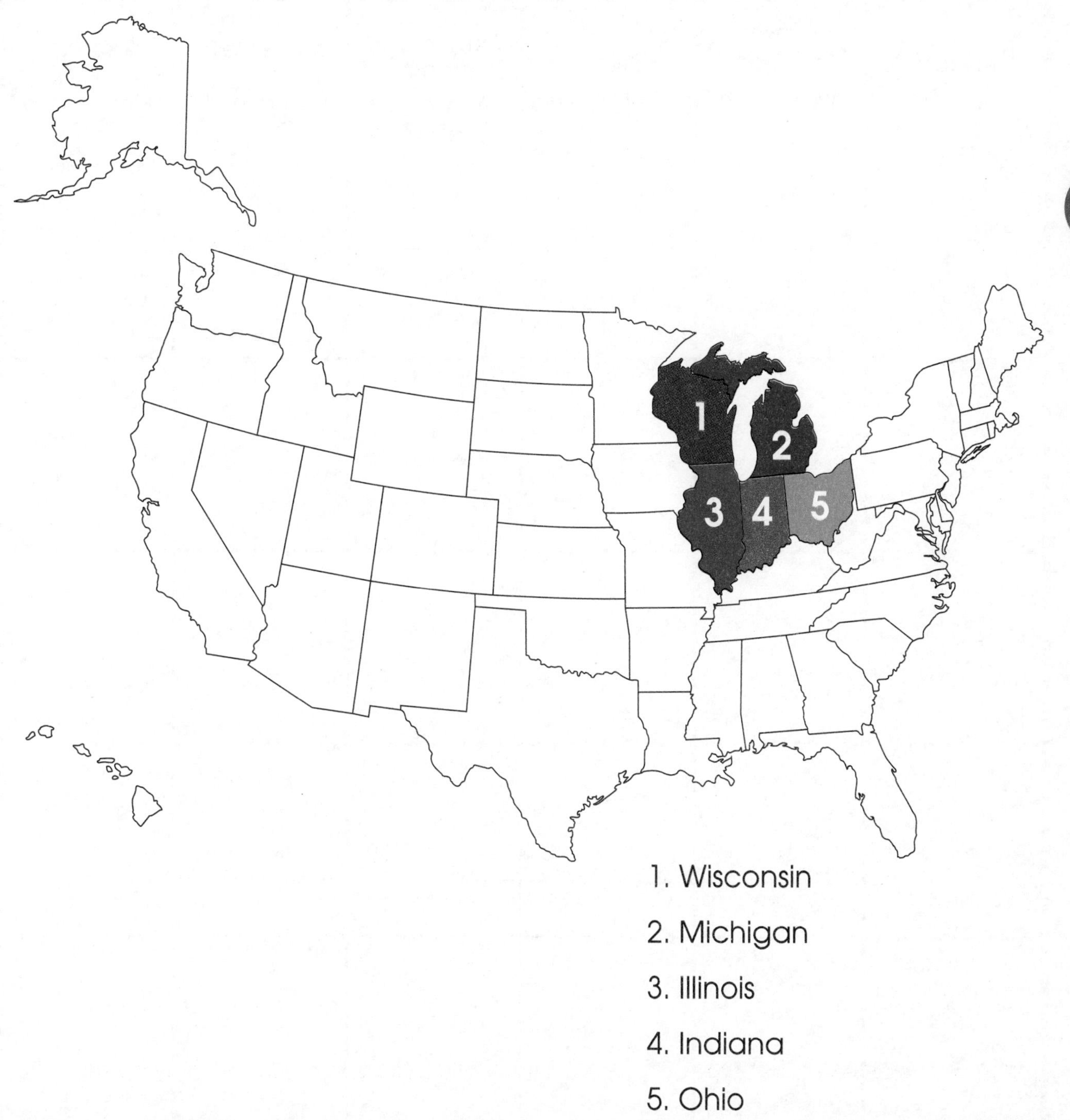

Name________________________________

Midwest States

Fill in the "Five Fundamental Themes of Geography" for each state. After "discovering" a state, fill in all the columns of the chart except **Regions**. When you have finished with all of the states in a section, fill in **Regions**.

Five Fundamental Themes of Geography					
Name of State	**Location** (Where is it?)	**Place** (What is it like?)	**People and Environment** (What do the people do?)	**Movement** (How do people, goods and ideas move?)	**Regions** (What are some of the common features?)

Name______________________________

Wisconsin

The Badger State

N W E S

Hayward
Brule R.
Menominee R.
1,952 FT.
St. Croix R.
MILK
TISSUE
NFL
Green Bay
Mississippi R.
Wisconsin R.
Neenah
Baraboo
Madison
Mt. Horeb
Milwaukee
Racine

Wood Violet
State Flower

Robin
State Bird

- name comes from the Chippewa Indian word *ouisconsin*, meaning *gathering of waters*
- nickname the Badger State used to describe the lead miners of the 1820s who lived in caves dug into the hillsides

Timms Hill—1,952 ft.

Circus World Museum

Racine—malted milk invented here in 1887

Green Bay Packer Hall of Fame

Neenah—facial tissue invented here in the early 1900s

Little Norway—built in 1926, shows Scandinavian pioneer houses

National Freshwater Fishing Hall of Fame

Circle the capital city. Locate the landmarks found in the above key. Color them on the map.

Name ____

Midwest States

Michigan

The Wolverine State

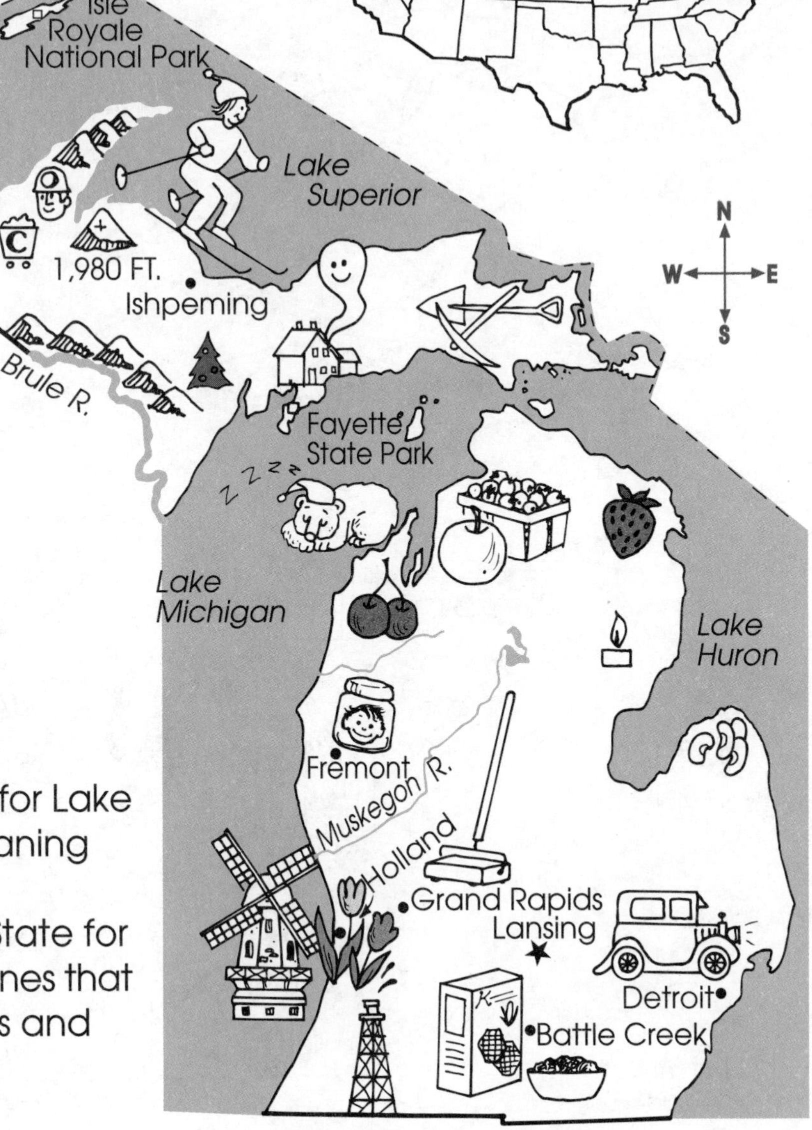

Isle Royale National Park
Lake Superior
1,980 FT.
Ishpeming
Brule R.
Fayette State Park
Lake Michigan
Lake Huron
Fremont
Muskegon R.
Holland
Grand Rapids
Lansing
Detroit
Battle Creek
N
W
E
S

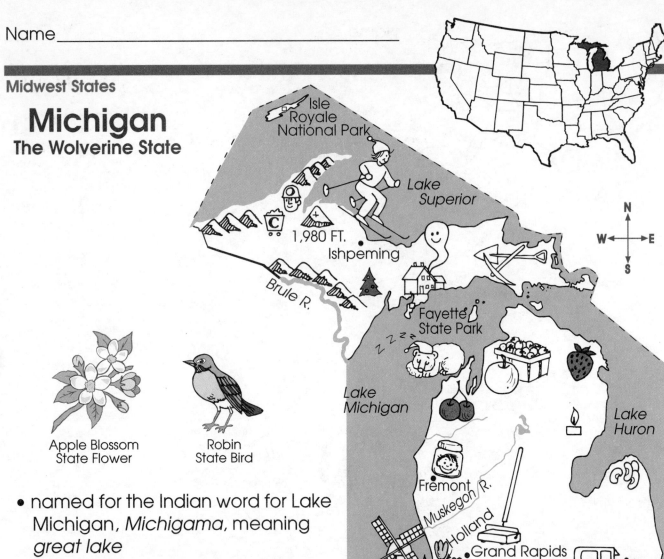

Apple Blossom
State Flower

Robin
State Bird

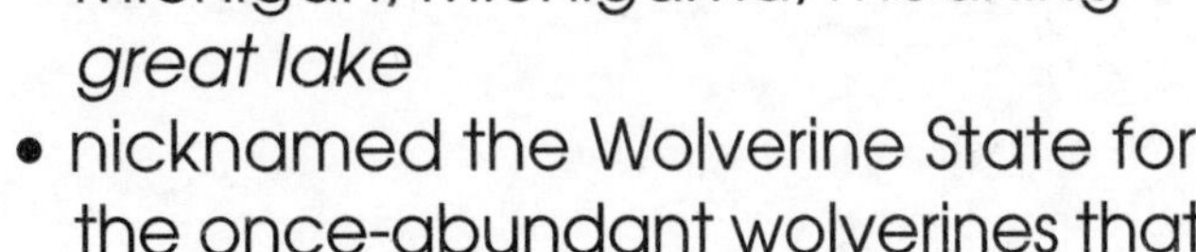

- named for the Indian word for Lake Michigan, *Michigama*, meaning *great lake*
- nicknamed the Wolverine State for the once-abundant wolverines that were trapped by fur traders and sold at trading posts

Mount Curwood—1,980 ft.

United States Ski Hall of Fame

Gerber—largest baby food plant in the U.S.

Fayette State Park—iron-ore smelting village from 1866 to 1890

Isle Royale—has one of the largest herds of moose in the United States

Grand Rapids—first carpet sweeper invented here in 1876 by M.R. Bissel

Battle Creek—produces the most breakfast cereal in the world

Sleeping Bear Dunes National Lakeshore—features sand dune shaped like a sleeping bear

Keweenaw Peninsula—one of the world's few sources of pure copper

Windmill Island Municipal Park—has the only authentic and operational Dutch windmill in the U.S.

Detroit—leads the U.S. in car and truck production (nicknamed Motor City)

Circle the capital city. Locate the landmarks found in the above key. Color them on the map.

Name ____________________

Illinois

The Land of Lincoln

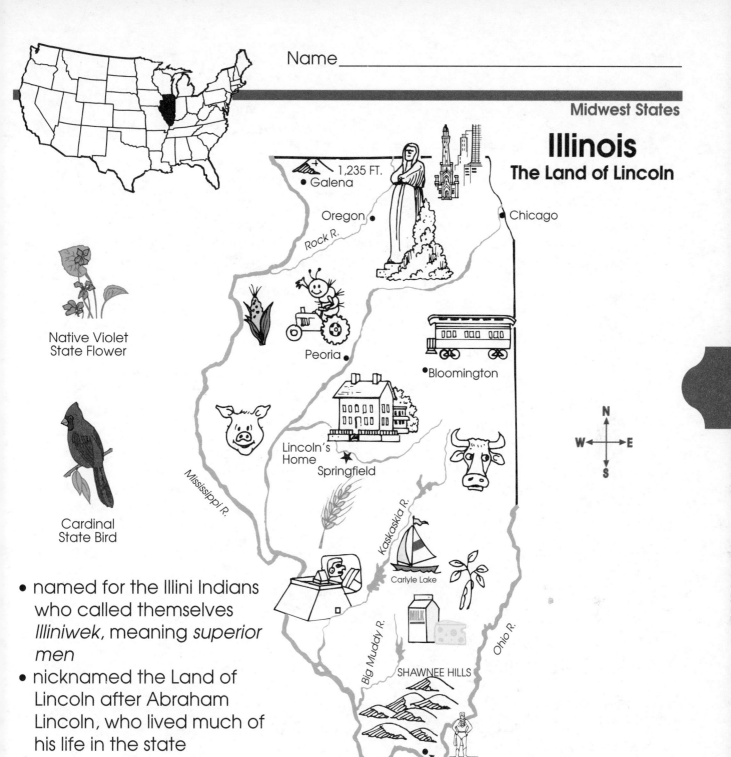

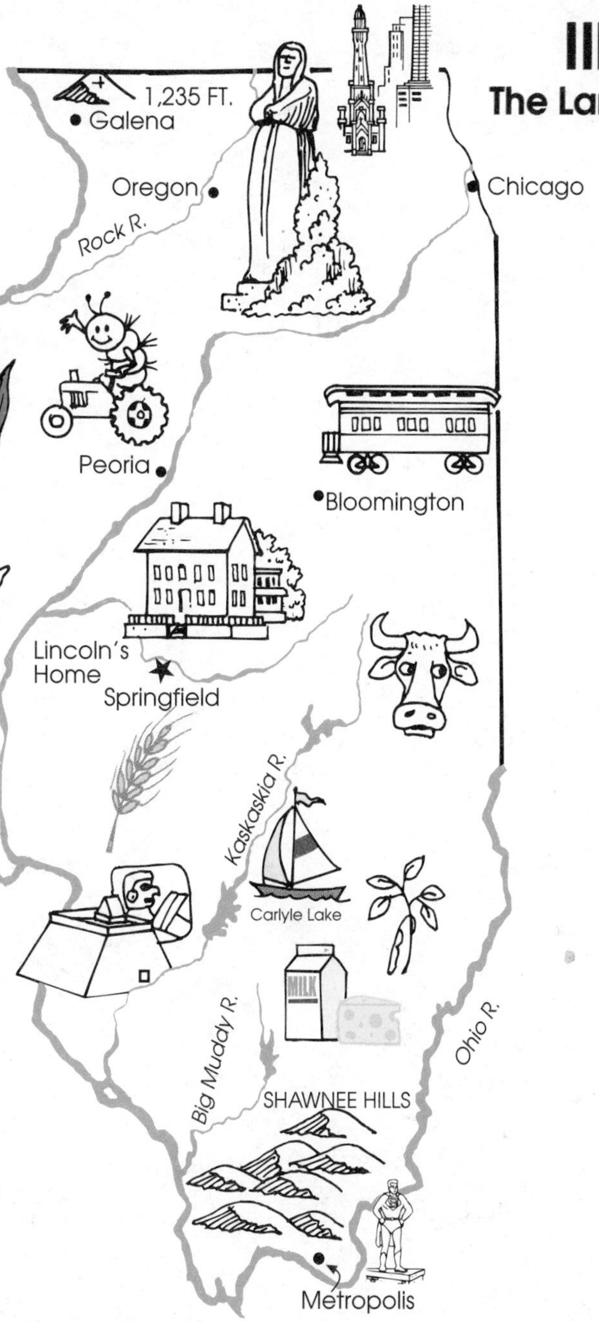

Native Violet
State Flower

Cardinal
State Bird

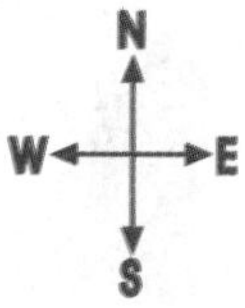

- named for the Illini Indians who called themselves *Illiniwek*, meaning *superior men*
- nicknamed the Land of Lincoln after Abraham Lincoln, who lived much of his life in the state

Charles Mound—1,235 ft.

Cahokia Mounds—65 earthen mounds made by Mississippian Indians

Peoria—headquarters of Caterpillar Co.

Lowden Memorial State Park—statue of Black Hawk honors the area's Indians

Metropolis—town centered around Superman

The Old Water Tower—survived the Great Chicago Fire in 1871

Bloomington—the first pullman sleeping car was made here in 1858

Circle the capital city. Locate the landmarks found in the above key. Color them on the map.

Name____

Midwest States

Indiana

The Hoosier State

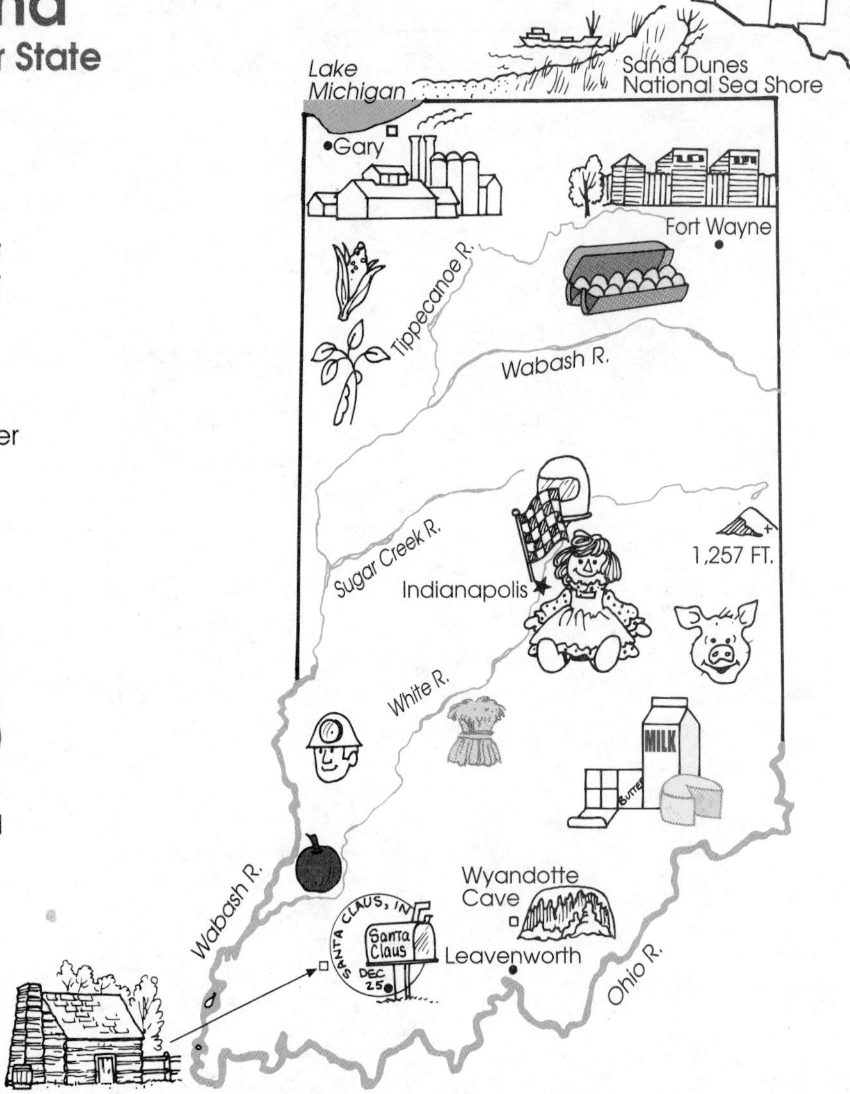

Lake Michigan

Sand Dunes National Sea Shore

Gary

Fort Wayne

Tippecanoe R.

Wabash R.

Sugar Creek R.

Indianapolis

1,257 FT.

White R.

MILK

Wabash R.

Wyandotte Cave

Santa Claus, IN — Santa Claus — DEC 25

Leavenworth

Ohio R.

N W E S

Peony
State Flower

Cardinal
State Bird

- name taken from the Indians living there in the 1700s - 1800s
- nickname the Hoosier State may have come from a pioneer's greeting of "*Who's here?*"

Indianapolis 500—car race

Indianapolis—Raggedy Ann doll created here in 1914

Santa Claus—remails many letters with its postmark at Christmas time

Wyandotte Cave—one of the largest caverns in the U.S.

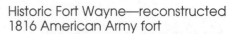

Historic Fort Wayne—reconstructed 1816 American Army fort

Gary—has some of nation's largest steel mills

Lincoln Boyhood National Memorial—original cabin where Abraham Lincoln lived from age 7-21

Circle the capital city. Locate the landmarks found in the above key. Color them on the map.

Name ______________________________

Ohio

The Buckeye State

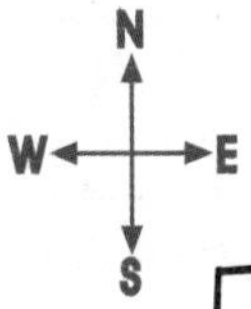

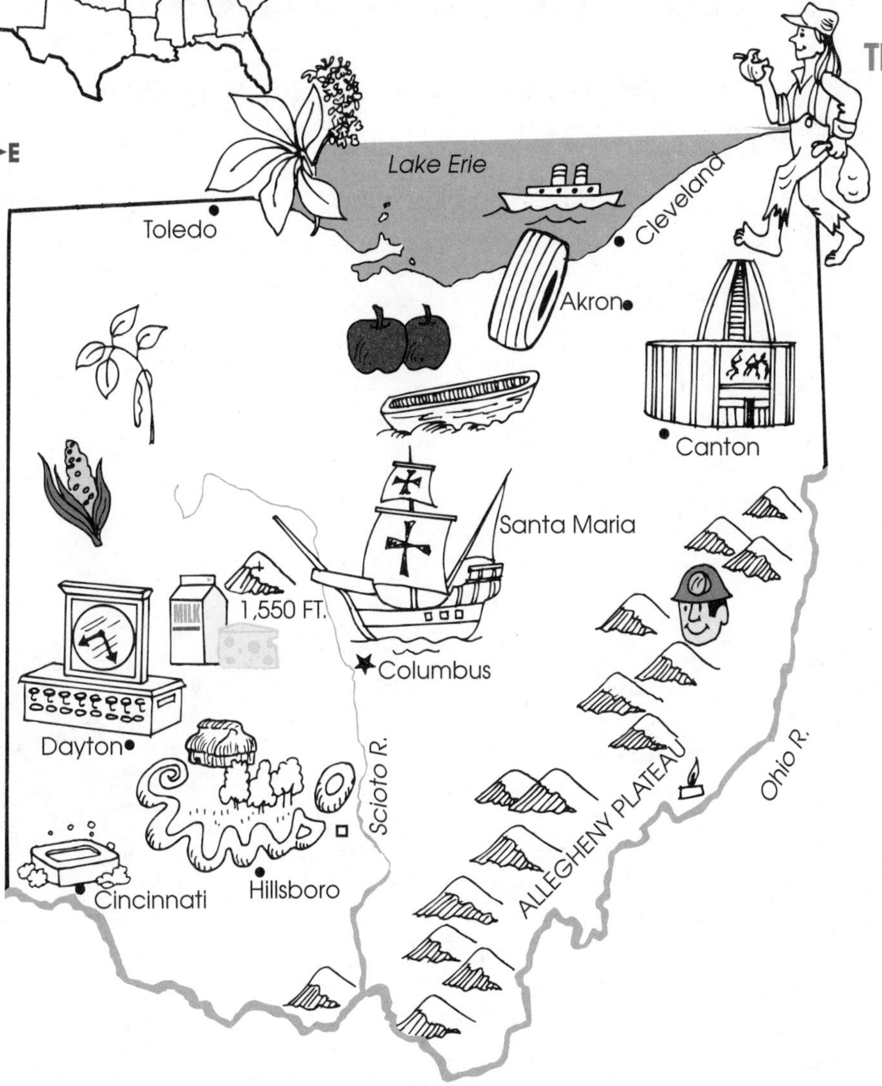

Lake Erie

Toledo

Cleveland

Akron

Canton

Santa Maria

1,550 FT.

Columbus

Dayton

Scioto R.

ALLEGHENY PLATEAU

Ohio R.

Cincinnati

Hillsboro

Cardinal
State Bird

Scarlet Carnation
State Flower

- name derived from Iroquois Indian word meaning *something great*
- nicknamed the Buckeye State for its abundance of buckeye trees

Campbell Hill—1,550 ft.

Dayton—first cash register invented here in 1879

Great Serpent Mound—prehistoric Indian burial mound, resembles a snake

Ancient Dugout Canoe—from about 1600 B.C.; discovered in Ashland County, 1977, oldest known watercraft in North America

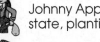

Cincinnati—contains the largest soap factory in the U.S.

Professional Football Hall of Fame

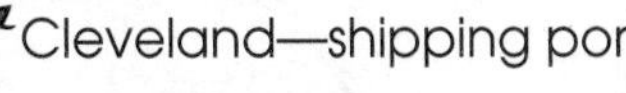

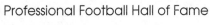

Cleveland—shipping port

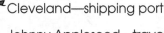

Johnny Appleseed—traveled through state, planting orchards

Akron—for many years, the largest producer of tires

Circle the capital city. Locate the landmarks found in the above key. Color them on the map.

Name______________________________________

The Northeastern States

The Northeastern States is a region with many natural harbors along the Atlantic Ocean. Inland, you will find rugged mountains and dense forests.

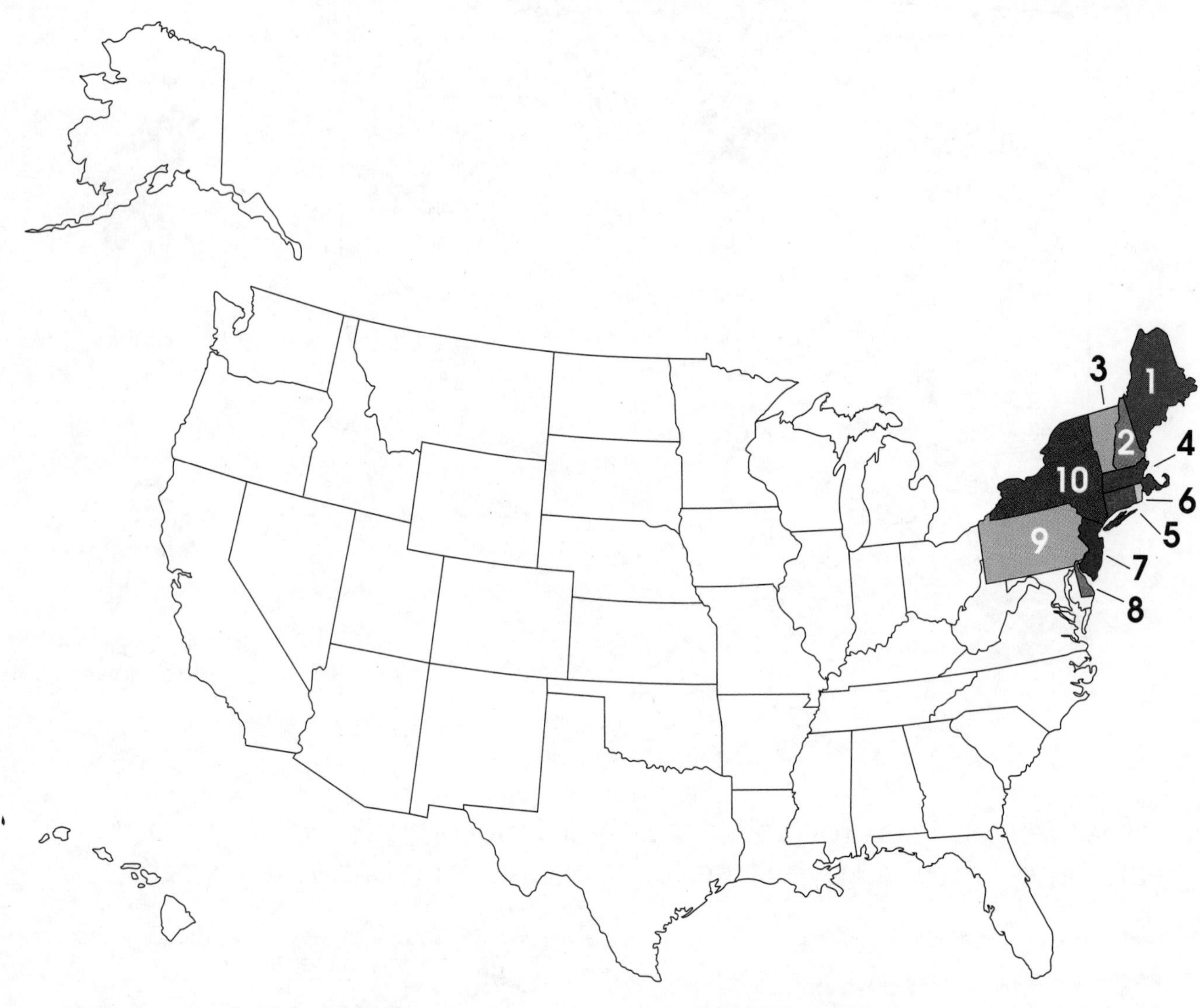

1. Maine
2. New Hampshire
3. Vermont
4. Massachusetts
5. Connecticut
6. Rhode Island
7. New Jersey
8. Delaware
9. Pennsylvania
10. New York

Name____________________

Fill in the "Five Fundamental Themes of Geography" for each state. After "discovering" a state, fill in all the columns of the chart except **Regions**. When you have finished with all of the states in a section, fill in **Regions**.

Five Fundamental Themes of Geography					
Name of State	**Location** (Where is it?)	**Place** (What is it like?)	**People and Environment** (What do the people do?)	**Movement** (How do people, goods and ideas move?)	**Regions** (What are some of the common features?)

Name ____________________________________

Northeastern States

Fill in the "Five Fundamental Themes of Geography" for each state. After "discovering" a state, fill in all the columns of the chart except **Regions**. When you have finished with all of the states in a section, fill in **Regions**.

Five Fundamental Themes of Geography					
Name of State	**Location** (Where is it?)	**Place** (What is it like?)	**People and Environment** (What do the people do?)	**Movement** (How do people, goods and ideas move?)	**Regions** (What are some of the common features?)

Name ____________________

Maine

The Pine Tree State

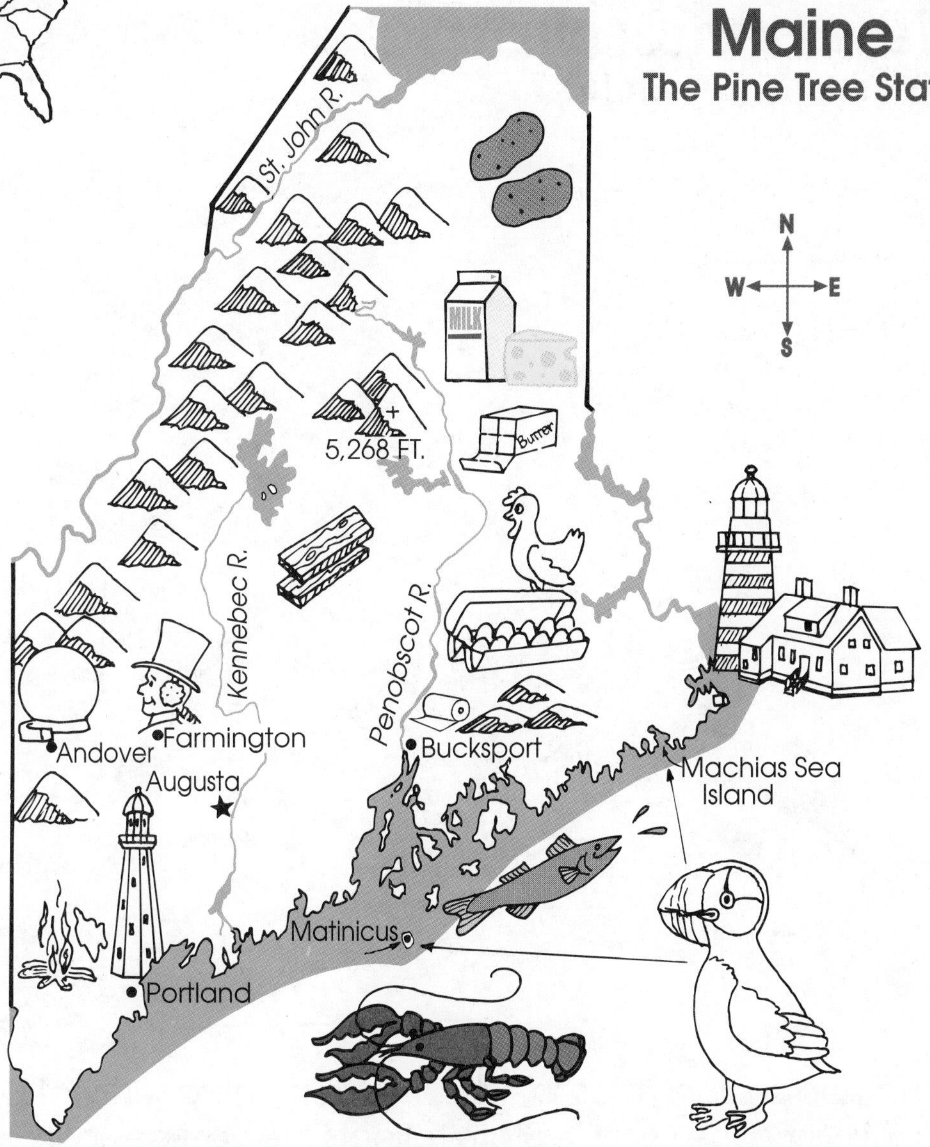

Chickadee
State Bird

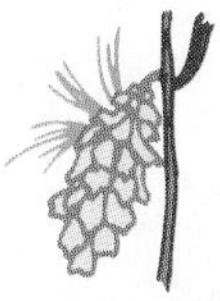

White Pine
cone and tassel
State Flower

- name believed to have originated from the English explorers who used the term *main* to refer to the *mainland*, as opposed to the islands
- nicknamed the Pine Tree State for the abundance of pine tree forests

Mount Katahdin—5,268 ft.

Matinicus—sanctuary for puffins

Satellite Earth Station—sends and receives orbiting satellites' signals

Sebago Lake—Camp Fire Girls originated here in 1910

Farmington—Earmuff Capital of the World—first earmuffs patented here in 1873

West Quoddy Head Light—located on land that is the most easterly point of U.S.

Portland Head Light—among the best known lighthouses in the U.S.

Circle the capital city. Locate the landmarks found in the above key. Color them on the map.

Name ____

Northeastern States

New Hampshire

The Granite State

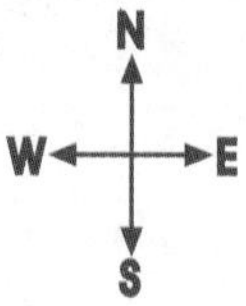

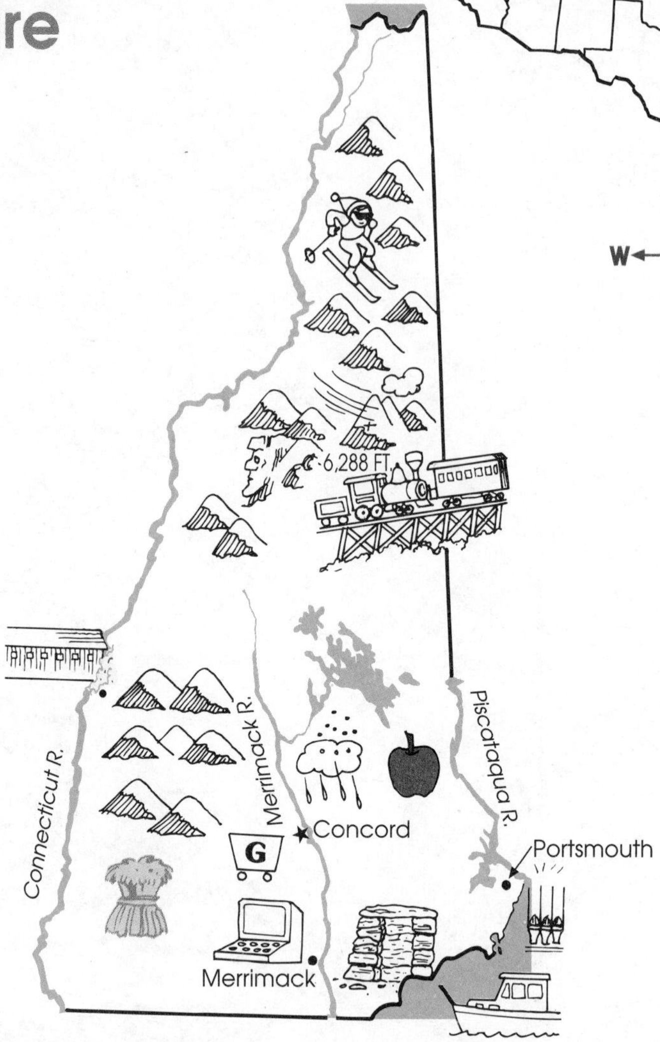

Purple Lilac
State Flower

Purple Finch
State Bird

Connecticut R.

Merrimack R.

Piscataqua R.

6,288 FT.

Concord

Portsmouth

Merrimack

N W E S

- named by John Mason, who was from the county of Hampshire in England
- nickname the Granite State reflects the vast deposits of granite in the state

Mount Washington—6,288 ft.

Waterville Valley—World Cup skiing competitions

Mount Washington—first cog railway in the United States

Merrimack—one of the largest computer companies in the U.S. located here

Concord—first place artificial rain was used to fight a forest fire

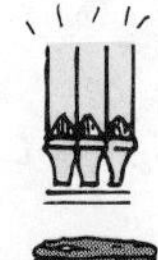

Brattle Organ—in St. John's Episcopal Church, the oldest pipe organ in the U.S.

America's Stonehenge—one of the largest and possibly oldest man-made stone constructions in the U.S.

Windsor-Cornish Covered Bridge—one of the longest covered bridges in the world

Old Man of the Mountain—natural formation of granite

Circle the capital city. Locate the landmarks found in the above key. Color them on the map.

Name______________________________

Vermont

The Green Mountain State

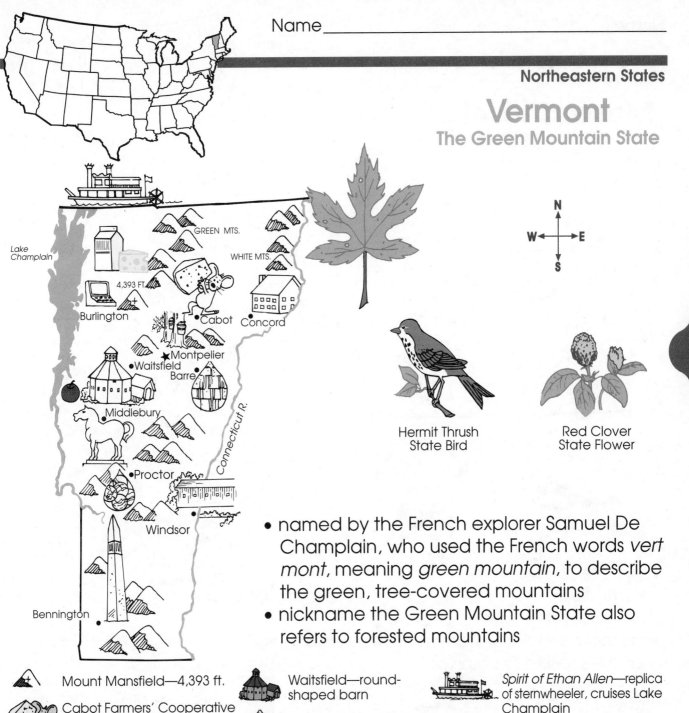

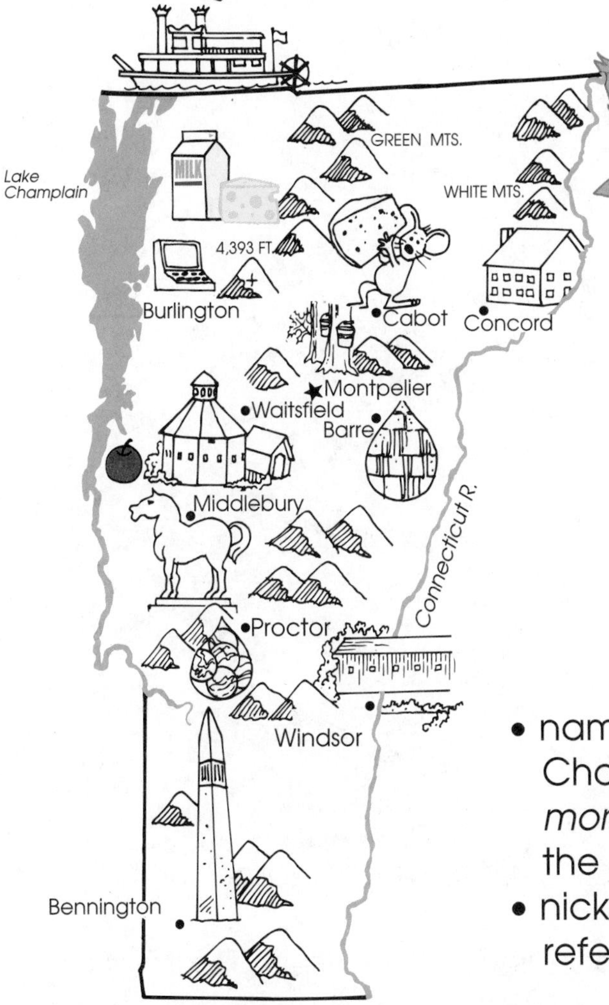

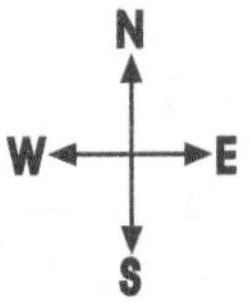

Hermit Thrush
State Bird

Red Clover
State Flower

- named by the French explorer Samuel De Champlain, who used the French words *vert mont*, meaning *green mountain*, to describe the green, tree-covered mountains
- nickname the Green Mountain State also refers to forested mountains

Mount Mansfield—4,393 ft.

Cabot Farmers' Cooperative Creamery—claims to make the best cheddar cheese in the nation

The Concord Academy—first school for training teachers

UVM Morgan Horse Farm—has statue of the first of a breed of Morgan horses

Waitsfield—round-shaped barn

Barre—granite quarry has world's largest stone-finishing plant

Montpelier—largest producer of maple syrup in the U.S.

Proctor—marble quarries there are among the largest in the world

Spirit of Ethan Allen—replica of sternwheeler, cruises Lake Champlain

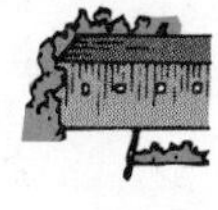

Windsor-Cornish Covered Bridge—one of the longest covered bridges in the world

Bennington Battle Monument—one of the world's tallest monuments, honors colonists who defeated the British

Circle the capital city. Locate the landmarks found in the above key. Color them on the map.

Name ____________________

Northeastern States

Massachusetts

The Bay State

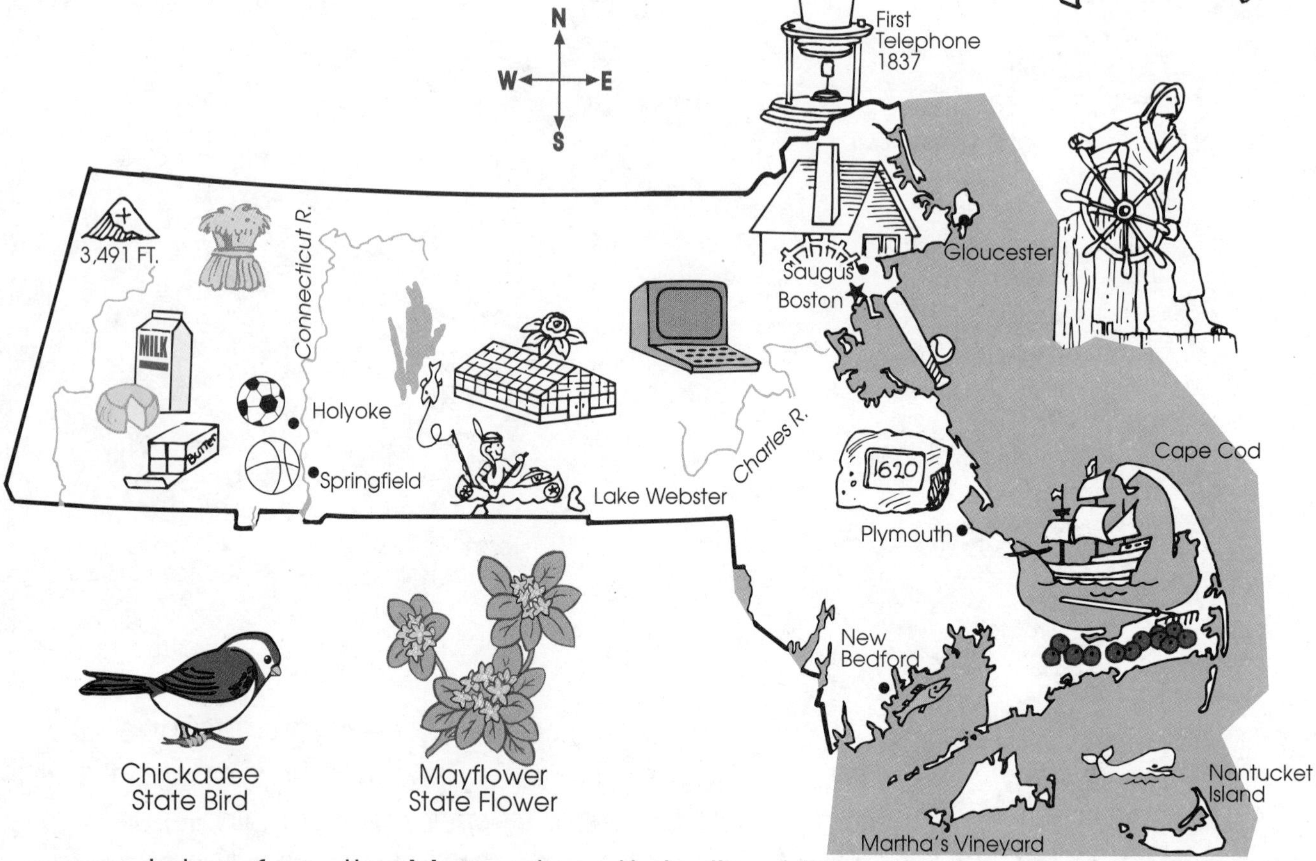

N
W E
S

First Telephone 1837

Saugus
Boston
Gloucester
Connecticut R.
3,491 FT.
Holyoke
Springfield
Lake Webster
Charles R.
Cape Cod
Plymouth
New Bedford
Nantucket Island
Martha's Vineyard

Chickadee
State Bird

Mayflower
State Flower

- name taken from the Massachusetts Indian tribe, whose name means *near the great hill*
- nickname the Bay State refers to Massachusetts Bay, where Puritans established their colony

Mount Greylock—3,491 ft.

Holyoke—volleyball was developed here in 1895

Saugus Iron Works—made and exported iron in the 1600s

Nantucket Island—resort area that was once a whaling port

Springfield—basketball invented here in 1891, contains Basketball Hall Of Fame

Boston—first World Series played here in 1903

Gloucester—statue built to honor all its fishermen who have died at sea

Plymouth Rock—marks where the Pilgrims landed

Cape Cod—Pilgrims landed here before going on to Plymouth

Webster Lake—Algonquian Indians called this lake *Chargoggagoggmanchau-gagoggchaubunagungam-gaug,*which means *You fish on your side, I fish on my side, nobody fish in the middle*

First Telephone—1876 in Boston

Circle the capital city. Locate the landmarks found in the above key. Color them on the map.

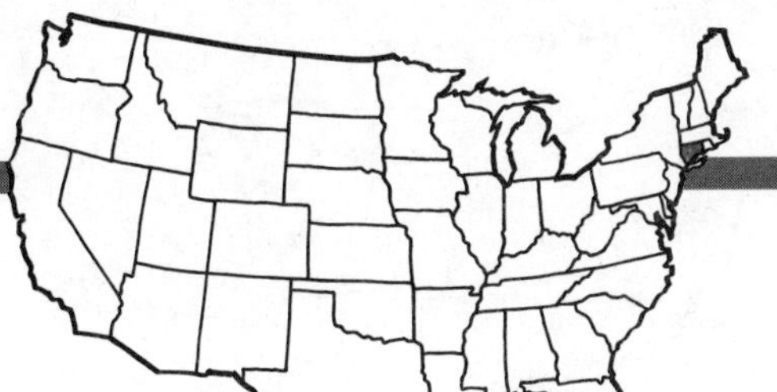

Name ____________________

Connecticut

The Constitution State

Robin
State Bird

Mountain Laurel
State Flower

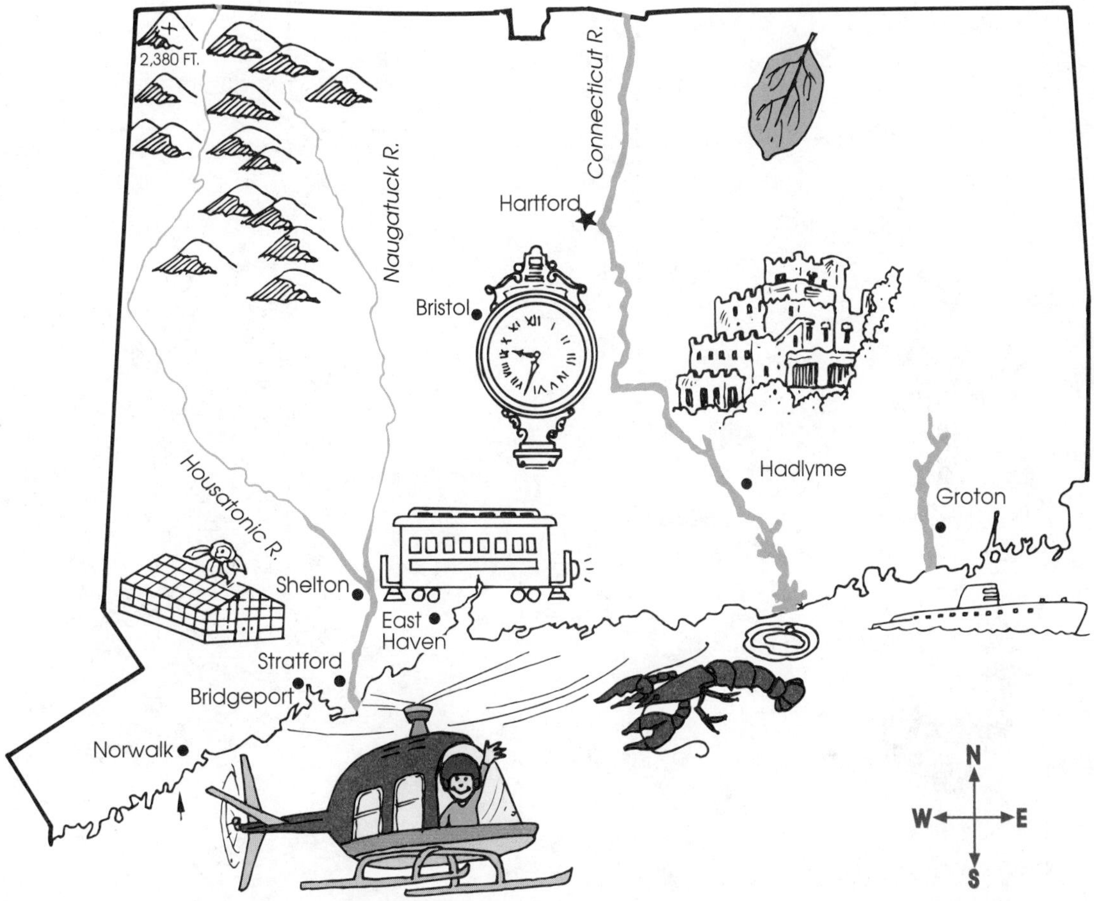

2,380 FT.
Connecticut R.
Naugatuck R.
Hartford
Bristol
Hadlyme
Groton
Housatonic R.
Shelton
East Haven
Stratford
Bridgeport
Norwalk
N
W
E
S

- name came from the Mohican Indian word *Quinnehtukqet*, meaning *on the long tidal river,* which referred to where they lived in relation to the Connecticut River
- nickname the Constitution State refers to Connecticut's colonial laws being used as one of the models for the Constitution of the United States

Mount Frissel—2,380 ft.

Great American Clock and Watch Museum

Gillette Castlle

Groton—United States Naval Submarine Base

Circle the capital city. Locate the landmarks found in the above key. Color them on the map.

Name________________________________

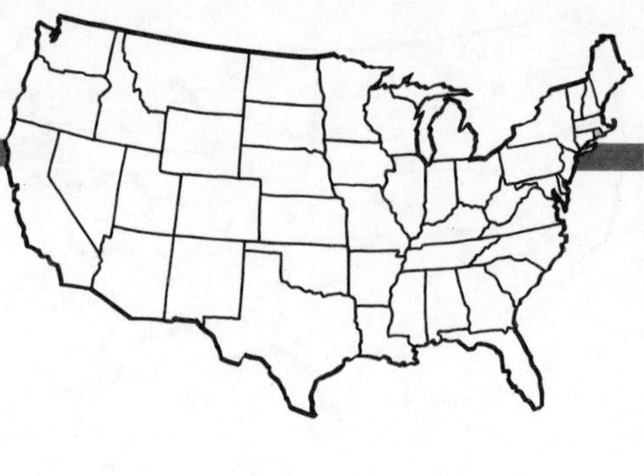

Rhode Island

The Ocean State

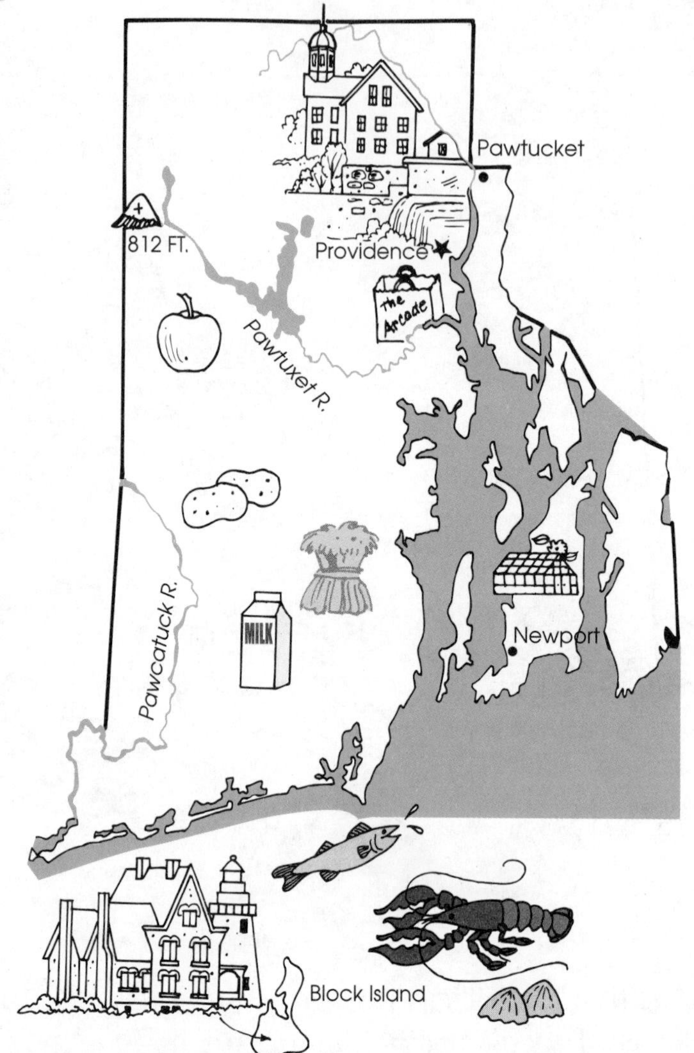

Violet
State Flower

Rhode Island Red
State Bird

- name is officially the State of Rhode Island and Providence Plantations, the largest of the states' islands being called Rhode Island and the towns on the mainland being called Providence Plantations
- nicknamed the Ocean State

Jerimoth Hill—812 ft.

Slater Mill Historic Site—one of the first textile mills in North America

Southeast Lighthouse

The Arcade—oldest indoor shopping mall in the U.S., built in 1828

Circle the capital city. Locate the landmarks found in the above key. Color them on the map.

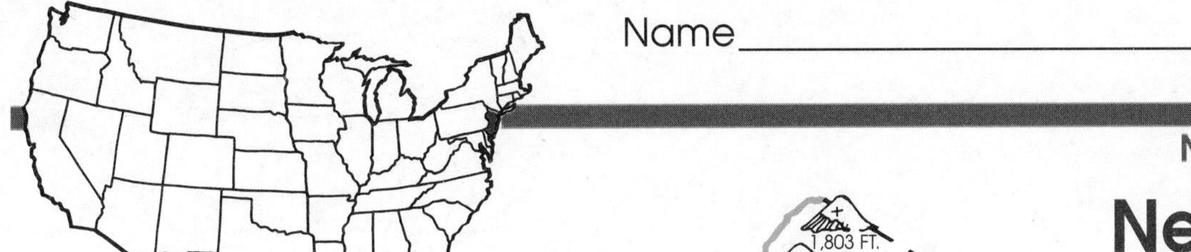

Name ____________________________________

New Jersey

The Garden State

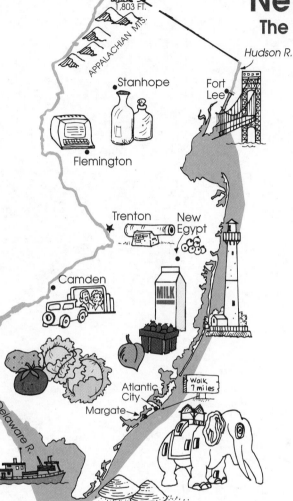

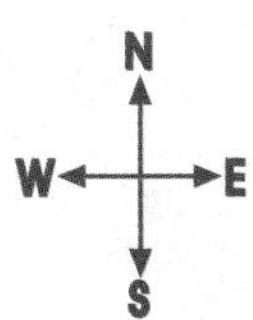

Eastern Goldfinch
State Bird

Purple Violet
State Flower

- named in 1664 by Sir George Carteret after the Isle of Jersey in England
- nicknamed the Garden State for its numerous truck farms, flower gardens and orchards

 High Point—1,803 ft.

 Margate—a 100-year-old house shaped like an elephant, now a museum

 Flemington—leader in machinery and computer assembly

 George Washington Bridge—thousands use this to commute from New Jersey to New York City

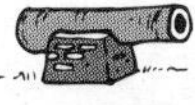 Old Barracks—British soldiers used these barracks during the French and Indian Wars

 Camden—first drive-in theater opened here on June 6, 1933

 New Egypt—Ocean Spray first made

Atlantic City—7-mile boardwalk and casinos make this popular for tourists

 Waterloo Village—a restored town of the 1700s

Circle the capital city. Locate the landmarks found in the above key. Color them on the map.

Name ____

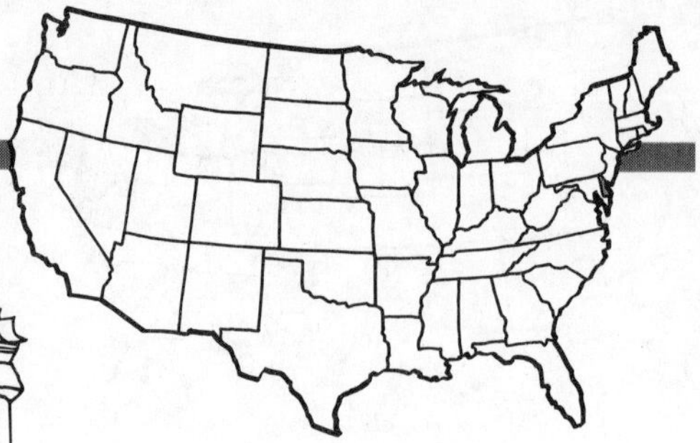

Delaware

The First State

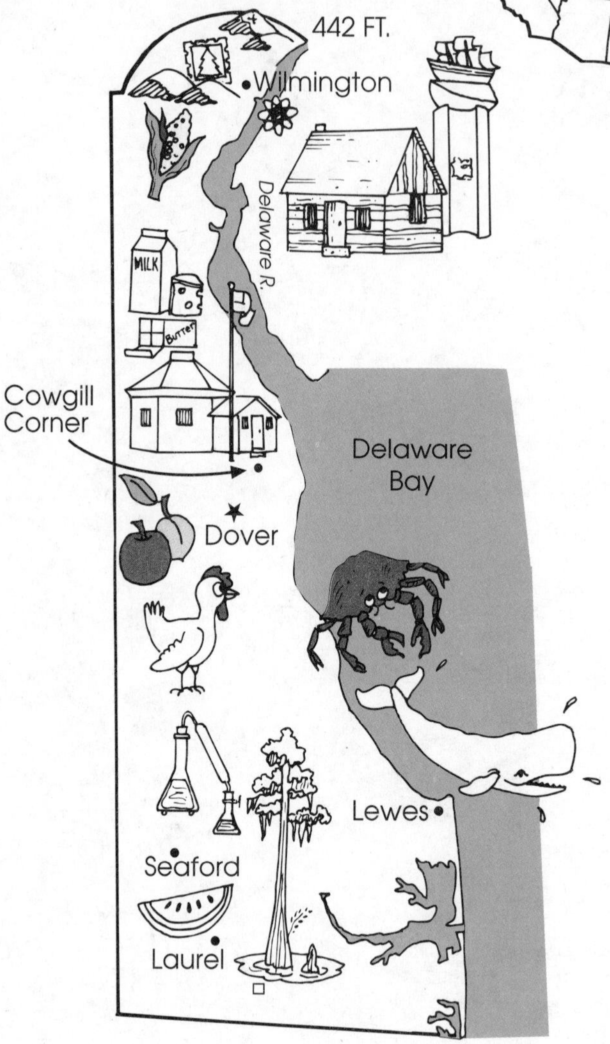

442 FT.

Wilmington

Delaware R.

Cowgill Corner

Delaware Bay

Dover

Lewes

Seaford

Laurel

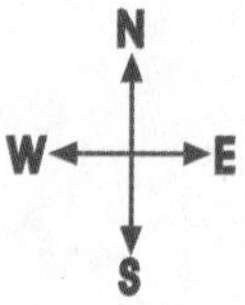

N

W E

S

Peach Blossom
State Flower

Blue Hen Chicken
State Bird

- named for the governor of Virginia, Lord De La Warr
- nickname the First State resulted from being the first state to approve the United States Constitution

Wilmington—Chemical Capital of the World

Great Cypress Swamp—contains the most bald cypress trees found in U.S.

The Octagonal School

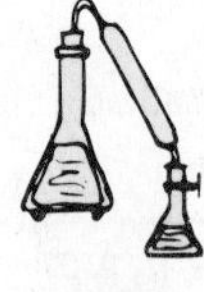

Seaford-Nylon Capital of the World—nylon first made by Du Pont Company in 1939

Annual Watermelon Festival

Lewes—whaling colony settled by the Dutch in 1631

First Christmas Seals—sold in Wilmington Post Office in 1907

Fort Christina—site of the first permanent settlement of Swedes and Finns in Delaware

Circle the capital city. Locate the landmarks found in the above key. Color them on the map.

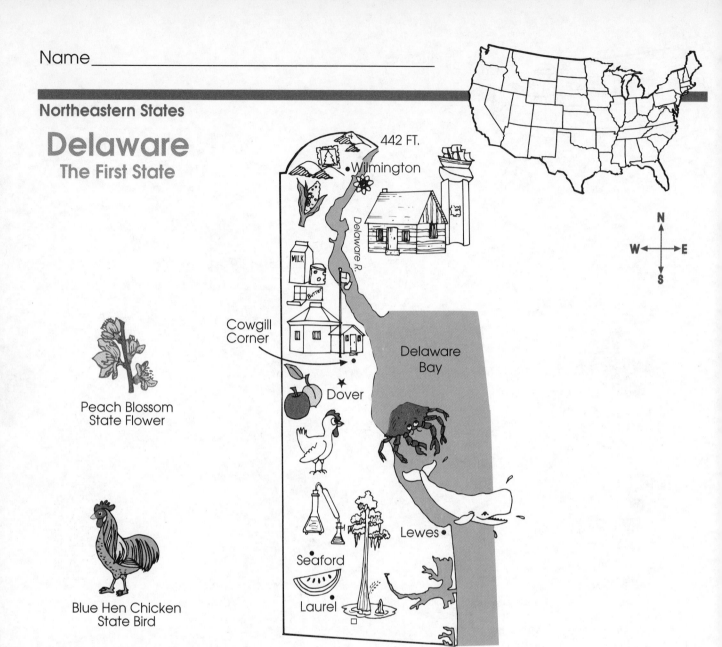

Name______________________________

Pennsylvania

The Keystone State

Mountain Laurel
State Flower

Ruffed Grouse
State Bird

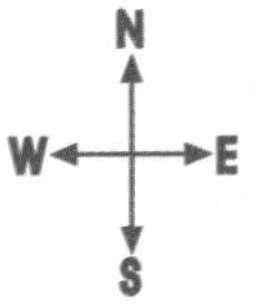

N
W
E
S

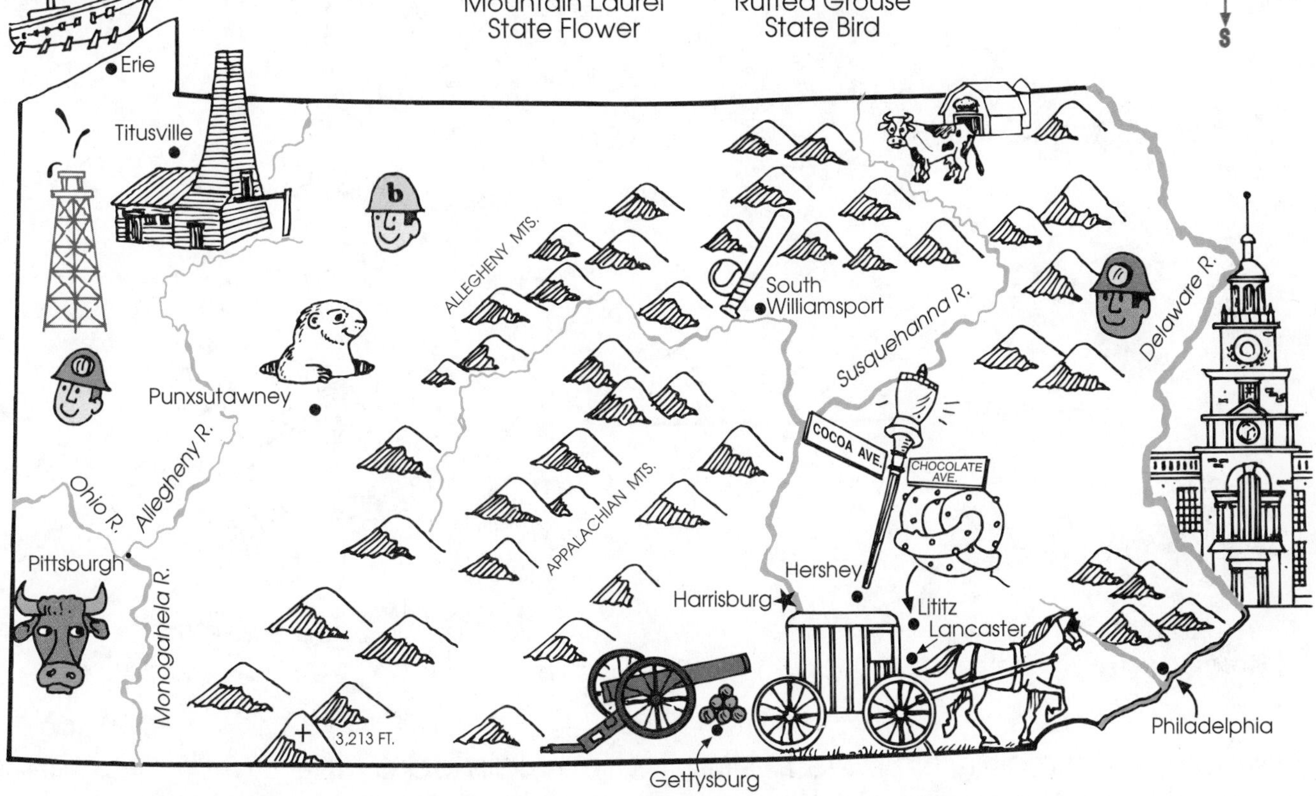

Niagara
Erie
Titusville
ALLEGHENY MTS.
South
Williamsport
Susquehanna R.
Delaware R.
Punxsutawney
Allegheny R.
Ohio R.
COCOA AVE.
CHOCOLATE AVE.
APPALACHIAN MTS.
Pittsburgh
Monogahela R.
Hershey
Harrisburg
Lititz
Lancaster
Philadelphia
3,213 FT.
Gettysburg

- named in 1681 for William Penn, means *Penn's Woods*
- nicknamed the Keystone State because of its location in the center of the thirteen original colonies

Mount Davis—3,213 ft.

Flagship Niagara—used by Oliver Perry to defeat the British in War of 1812

Lititz—first pretzel bakery opened in 1861

Hershey—world's largest chocolate and cocoa factory, established in 1905

Little League Baseball World Series

Drake's Well Museum—site of the first commercial oil well in America

Ground Hog Day Festivities

Pennsylvania Farm Museum of Landis Valley

Independence Hall—Declaration of Independence signed here in 1776

Circle the capital city. Locate the landmarks found in the above key. Color them on the map.

Name____

New York

The Empire State

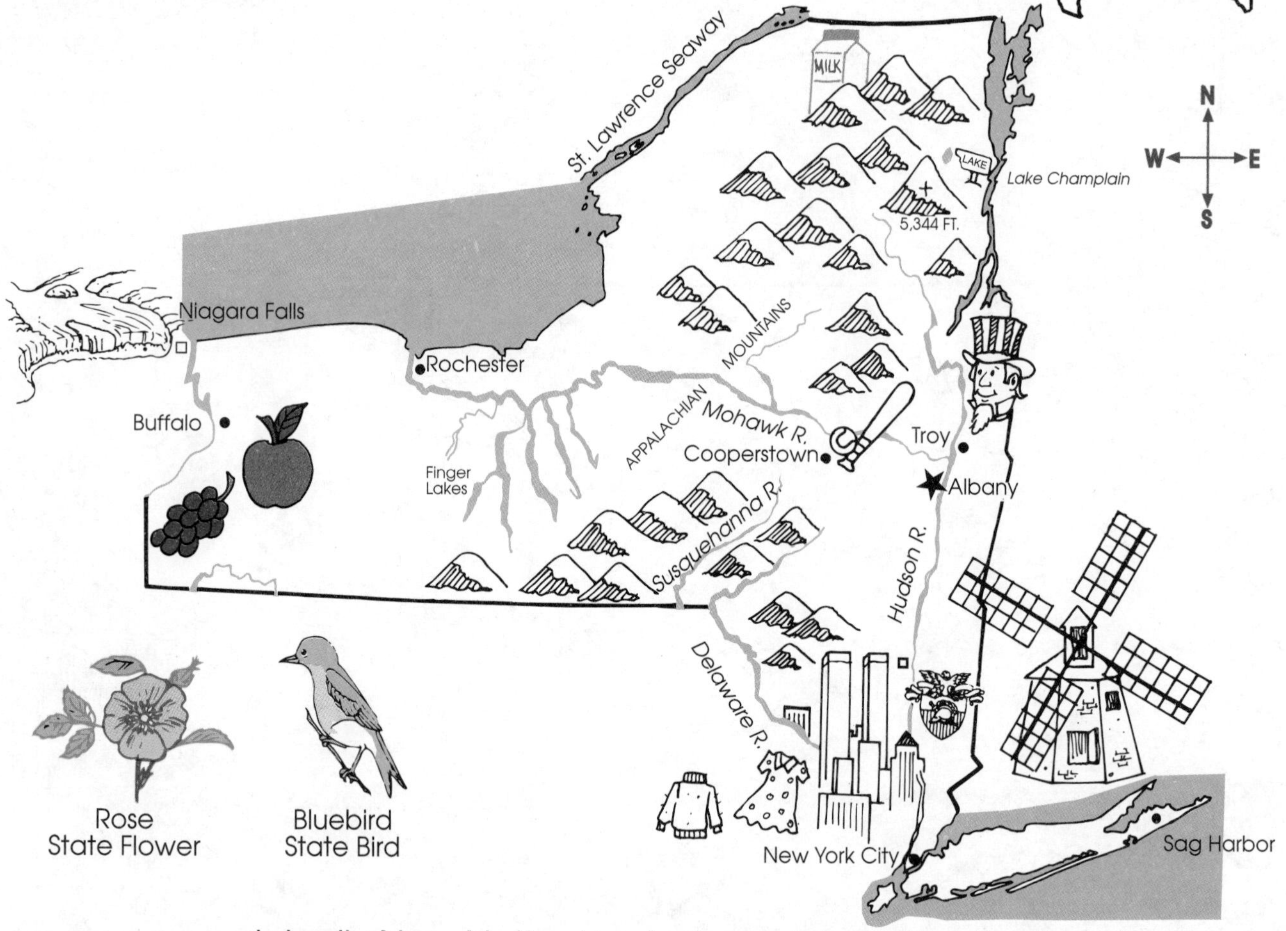

St. Lawrence Seaway
MILK
LAKE
Lake Champlain
5,344 FT.
N
W
E
S
Niagara Falls
Rochester
MOUNTAINS
APPALACHIAN
Mohawk R.
Buffalo
Troy
Cooperstown
Finger Lakes
Albany
Susquehanna R.
Hudson R.
Delaware R.
New York City
Sag Harbor

Rose
State Flower

Bluebird
State Bird

- name was originally New Netherland when claimed by the Dutch; was then claimed by the English and the name was changed to New York to honor the Duke of York
- nickname the Empire State possibly related to a comment made by George Washington in 1783 when he anticipated that New York would become the core of a new empire

Mount Marcy—5,344 ft.

New York City—center of publishing industry and leads women's clothing production in the United States

West Point—U.S. Military Academy

Niagara Falls—most famous waterfall in the world

Lake Placid—world famous resort with a glacial lake

National Baseball Hall of Fame

Sag Harbor—windmill once used here as a major source of energy

Uncle Sam—symbol originated in Troy

Circle the capital city. Locate the landmarks found in the above key. Color them on the map.

Name______________________________

The Southeastern States

The Southeastern States is a region with many different kinds of land formations. It has long jagged coastlines, rugged mountains, deep pine forests, steep valleys and beautiful rivers.

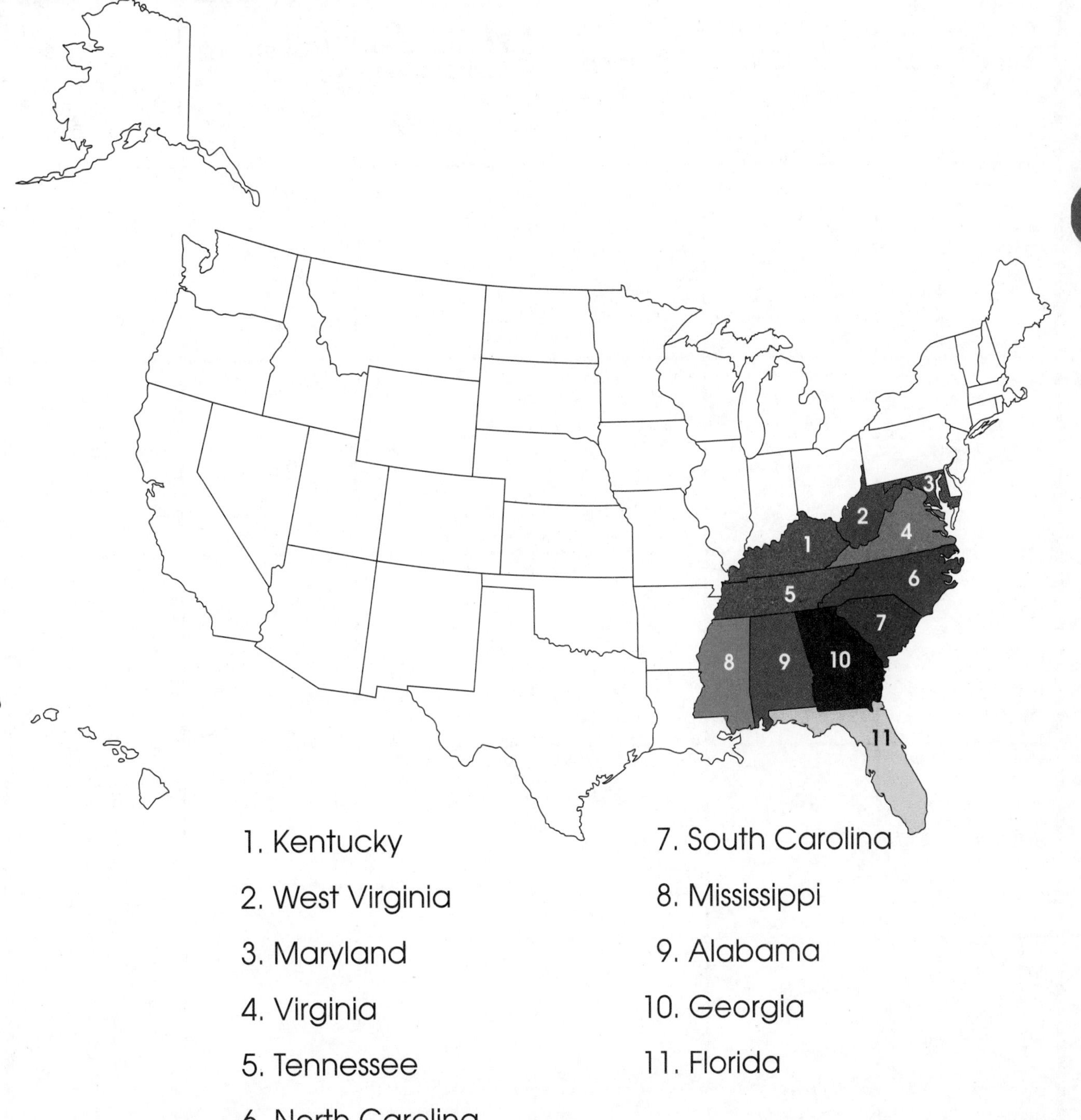

1. Kentucky
2. West Virginia
3. Maryland
4. Virginia
5. Tennessee
6. North Carolina
7. South Carolina
8. Mississippi
9. Alabama
10. Georgia
11. Florida

Name________________________________

Southeastern States

Fill in the "Five Fundamental Themes of Geography" for each state. After "discovering" a state, fill in all the columns of the chart except **Regions**. When you have finished with all of the states in a section, fill in **Regions**.

Five Fundamental Themes of Geography					
Name of State	**Location** (Where is it?)	**Place** (What is it like?)	**People and Environment** (What do the people do?)	**Movement** (How do people, goods and ideas move?)	**Regions** (What are some of the common features?)

Name______________________________

Five Fundamental Themes of Geography

Name of State	Location (Where is it?)	Place (What is it like?)	People and Environment (What do the people do?)	Movement (How do people, goods and ideas move?)	Regions (What are some of the common features?)

Name ______________________________________

Kentucky

The Bluegrass State

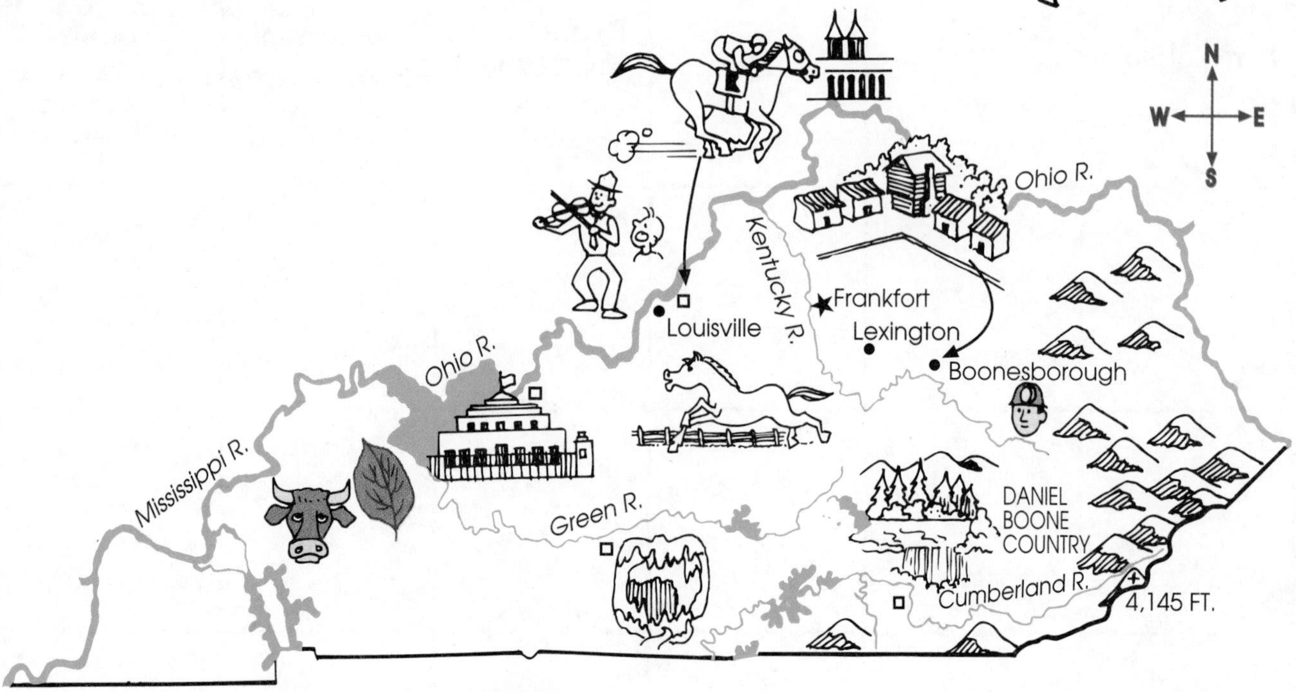

N
W E
S

Ohio R.
Kentucky R.
Frankfort
Louisville
Lexington
Boonesborough
Ohio R.
Mississippi R.
Green R.
DANIEL BOONE COUNTRY
Cumberland R.
4,145 FT.

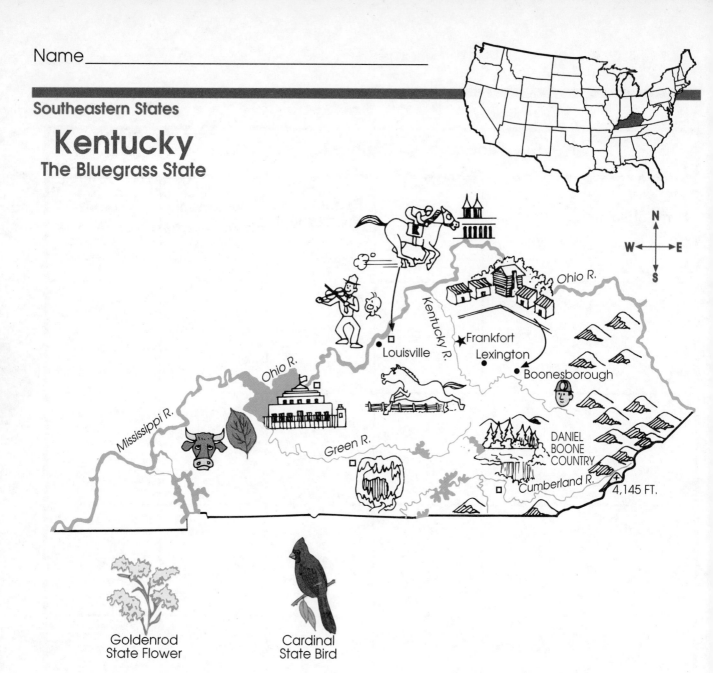

Goldenrod
State Flower

Cardinal
State Bird

- name derived from the Cherokee Indian word *kentake,* which means *meadow* or *pasture*
- nicknamed the Bluegrass State for the blue blossoms on the grass of this region

 Black Mountain—4,145 ft.

 Fort Boonesborough State Park—reconstructed fort founded by Daniel Boone

 Fort Knox Gold Vault—nation's gold depository

 Kentucky Derby—at Churchill Downs Race Track; oldest horse racing event in U.S.

Mammoth Cave National Park—world's longest continuous cave system

Louisville American Bluegrass Music Fest

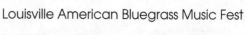

Lexington—thousands of thoroughbred horses raised on horse farms here

Cumberland Falls—nicknamed Niagara of the South

Circle the capital city. Locate the landmarks found in the above key. Color them on the map.

Name ______________________________

West Virginia

The Mountain State

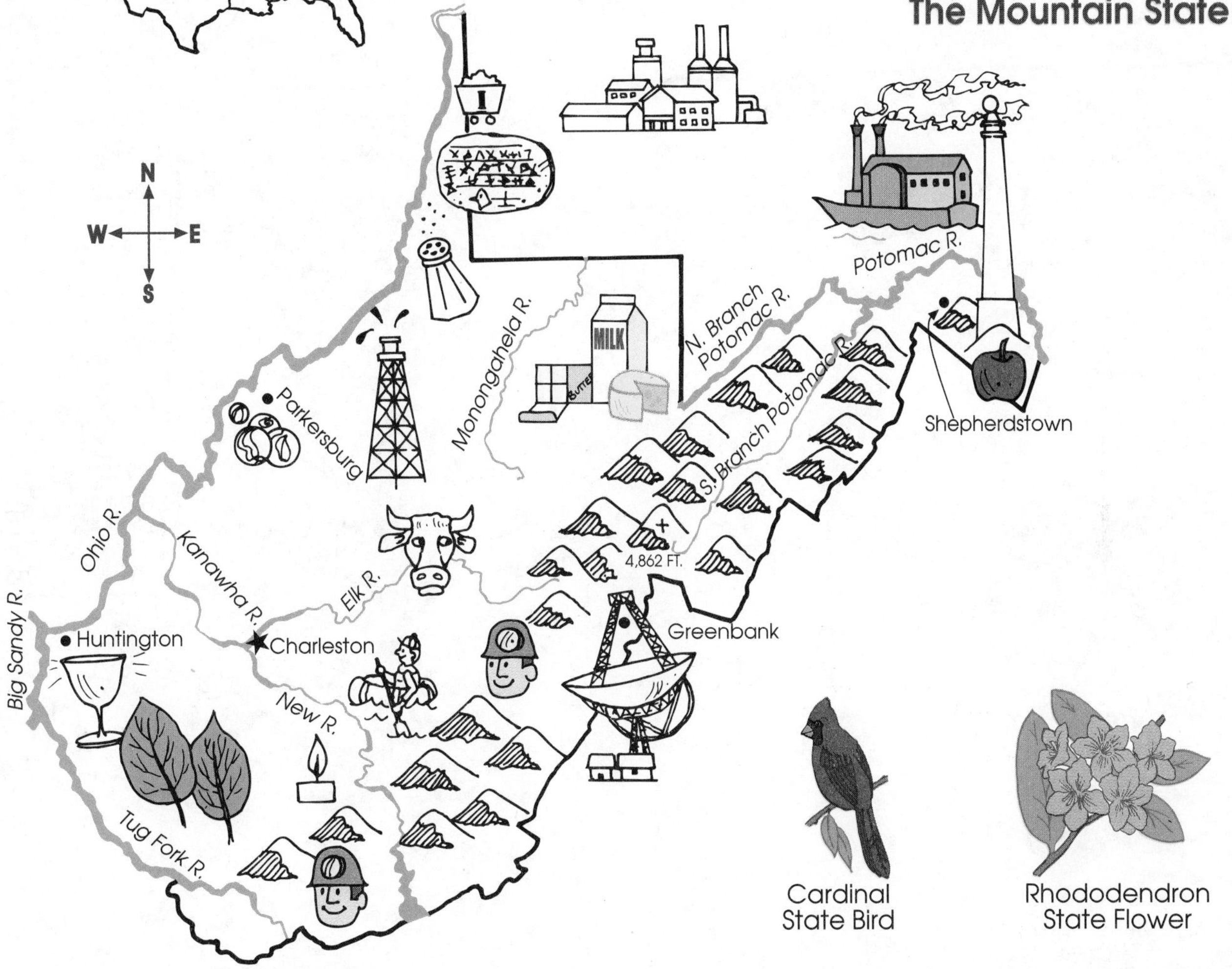

Cardinal
State Bird

Rhododendron
State Flower

- named when northwestern counties separated from Virginia during the Civil War and sided with the North
- nicknamed the Mountain State for its rugged mountains, steep hills and narrow valleys

Spruce Knob—4,862 ft.

Grave Creek Mounds—largest conical burial mound, built 2,000 years ago

Marshall County—underground salt mines

Huntington—famous for its glassware and pottery

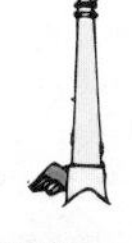

Shepherdstown—monument to James Rumsay, inventor of the steamboat

Parkersburg—glass marble manufacturing center of U.S.

National Radio Astronomy Observatory

Circle the capital city. Locate the landmarks found in the above key. Color them on the map.

Name ____

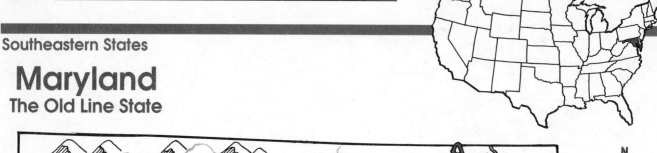

Southeastern States

Maryland

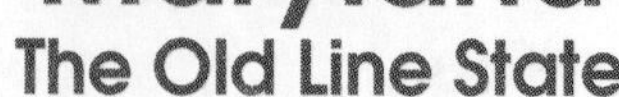

N
W E
S

3,360 FT.

Potomac R.

Monocacy R.

Baltimore

Fort McHenry

Annapolis

Washington, D.C.

Chesapeake Bay

Patuxent R.

U.S. Naval Academy

Potomac R.

Fort McHenry

Black-Eyed Susan
State Flower

Baltimore Oriole
State Bird

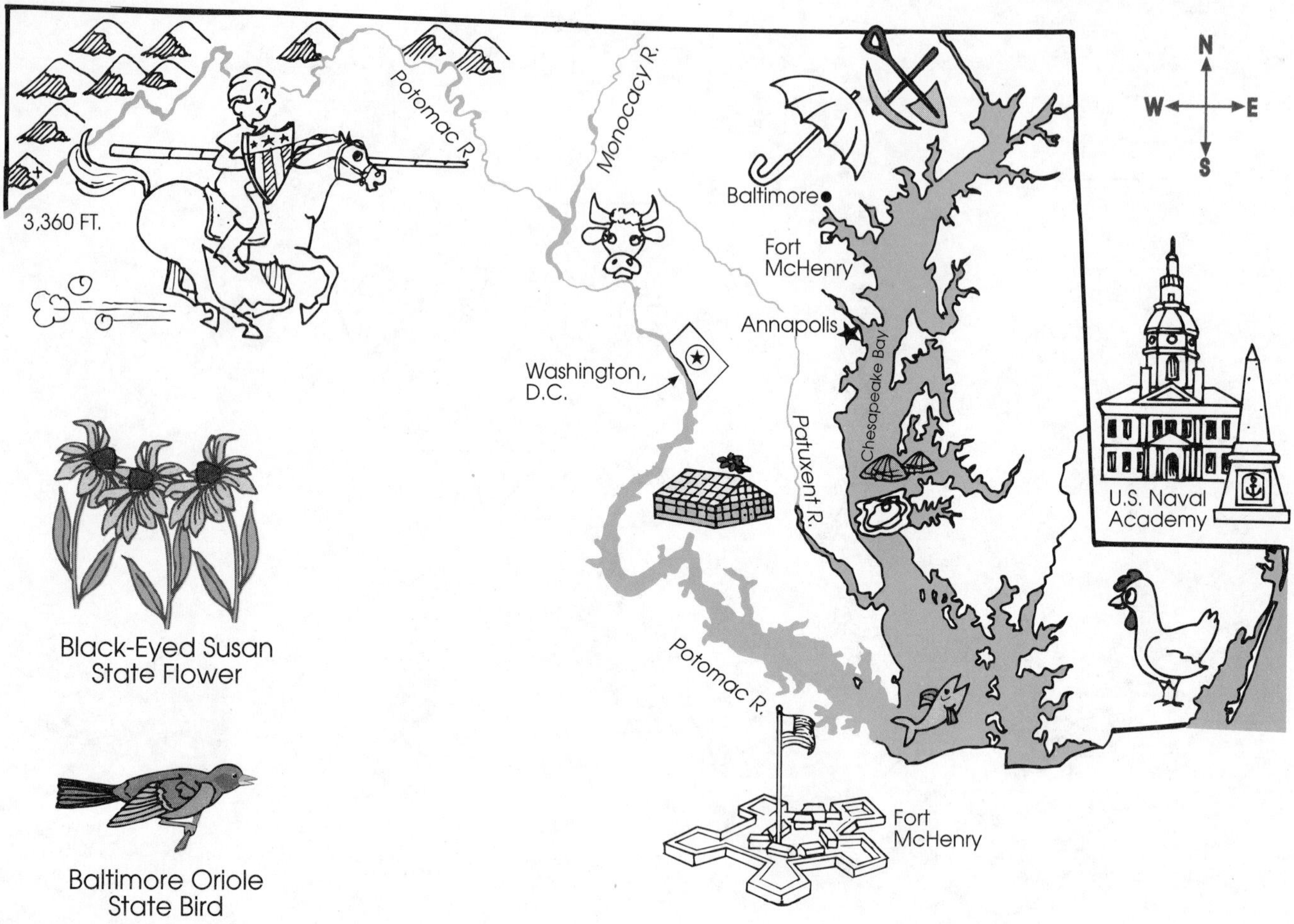

- named in 1632 for Queen Henrietta Maria, the wife of England's King Charles I
- nicknamed the Old Line State in honor of the troops from Maryland who fought so bravely on the line during the Revolutionary War

Backbone Mountain—3,360 ft.

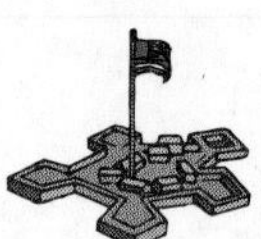

Fort McHenry National Monument and Shrine—Frances Scott Key wrote the "Star-Spangled Banner" here during the War of 1812

State Jousting Championships—held each year

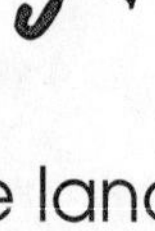

Baltimore—first umbrella factory in the U.S., established in 1828

Washington, D.C.—George Washington chose this spot for the U.S. capital

U.S. Naval Academy

Circle the capital city. Locate the landmarks found in the above key. Color them on the map.

Name____

Virginia
Old Dominion

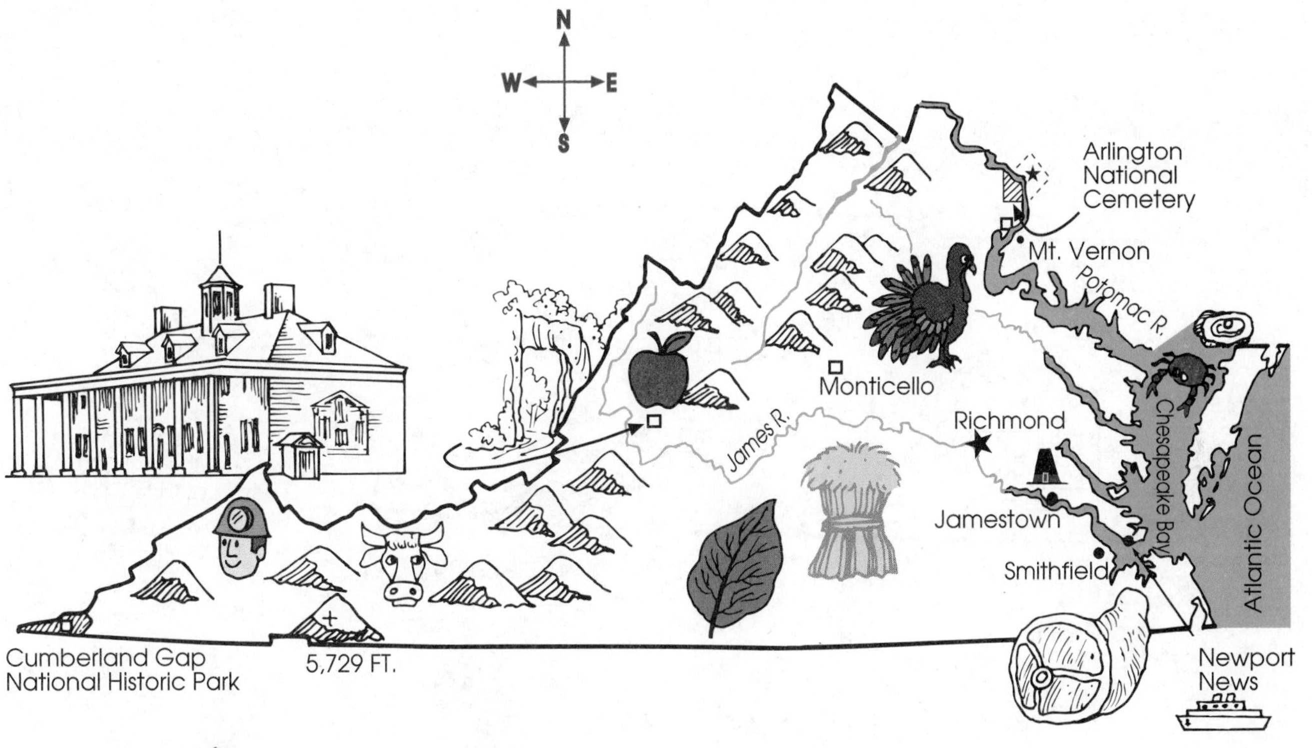

Cardinal
State Bird

American Dogwood
State Flower

- named for England's Queen Elizabeth I, who was called the Virgin Queen because she never married
- nicknamed Old Dominion by Charles II because Virginia was loyal to the crown during the English Civil War

Mount Rogers—5,729 ft.

Washington, D.C.—nation's capital

Arlington National Cemetery—Tomb of the Unknown Soldier

Smithfield—famous for its hams

Circle the capital city. Locate the landmarks found in the above key. Color them on the map.

Name ____

Southeastern States

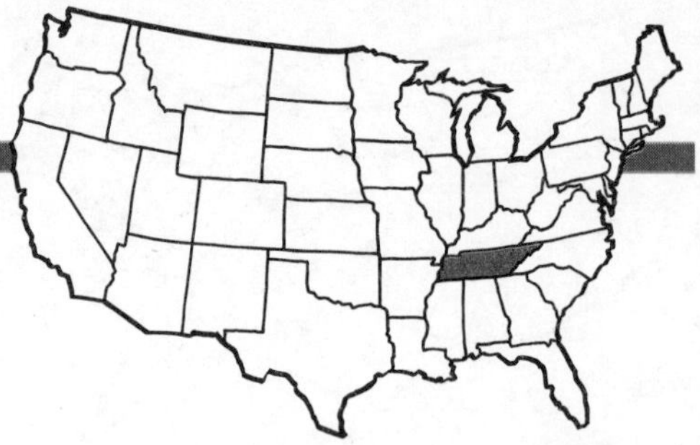

Tennessee

The Volunteer State

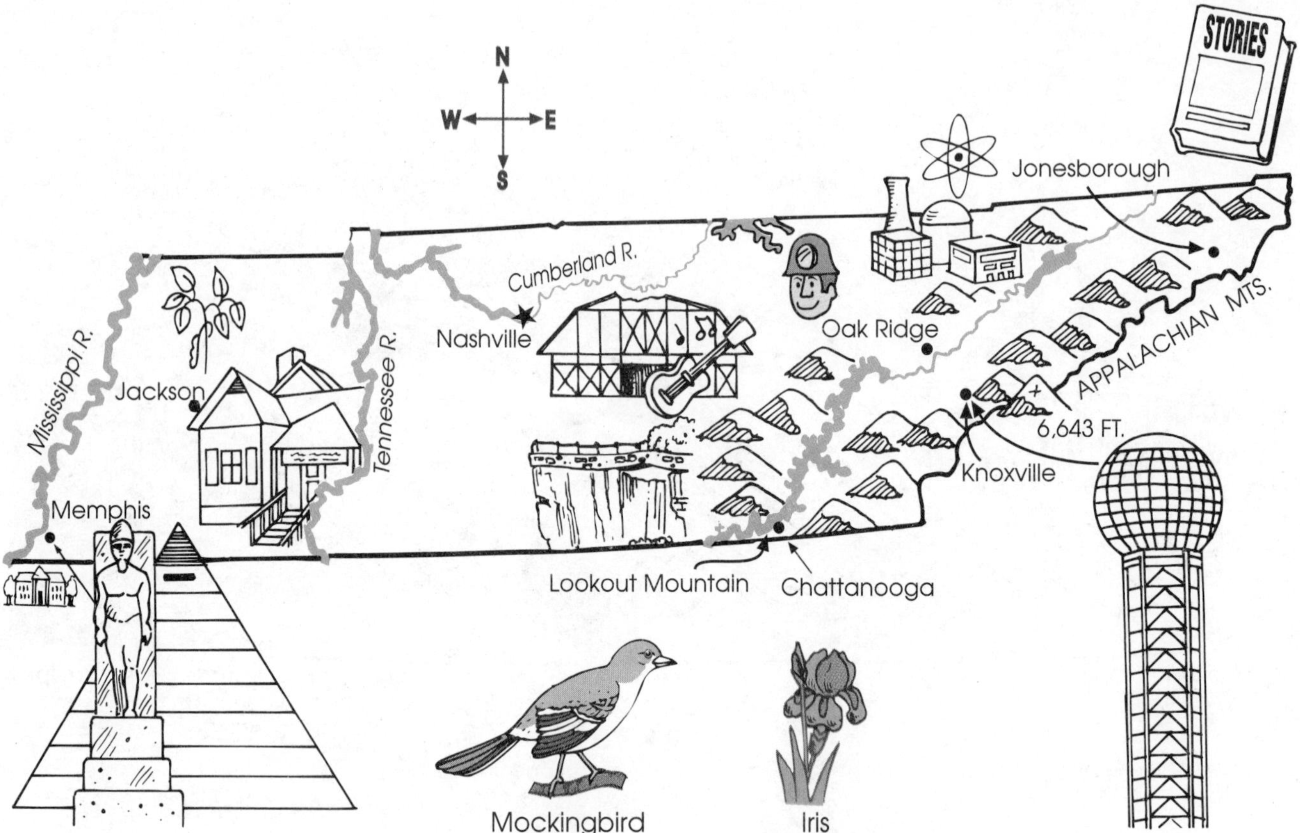

N
W
E
S
STORIES
Jonesborough
Cumberland R.
Nashville
Oak Ridge
APPALACHIAN MTS.
Mississippi R.
Jackson
Tennessee R.
6,643 FT.
Knoxville
Memphis
Lookout Mountain
Chattanooga

Mockingbird
State Bird

Iris
State Flower

- named for a Cherokee village, *Tanasie*
- nickname the Volunteer State refers to the large number of men who unhesitatingly volunteered for military service during the War of 1812 and the Mexican War

 Clingmans Dome—6,643 ft.

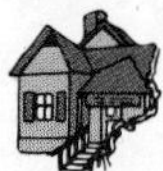

 Casey Jones Home and Railroad Museum

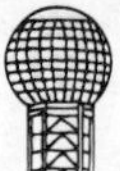

 Sunsphere—266-foot tower built for 1982 World's Fair

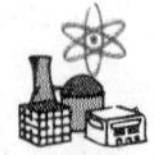

 American Museum of Science and Energy

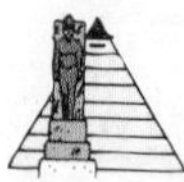

 The Pyramid—32-story stainless steel sports and entertainment facility

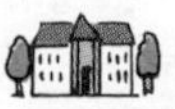

 Graceland—estate of Elvis Presley

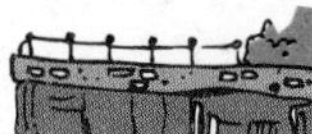

 Lookout Mountain

STORIES

National Storytelling Festival

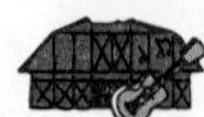

 Grand Ole Opry

Circle the capital city. Locate the landmarks found in the above key. Color them on the map.

Name ____________________________________

North Carolina

The Tarheel State

N
W E
S

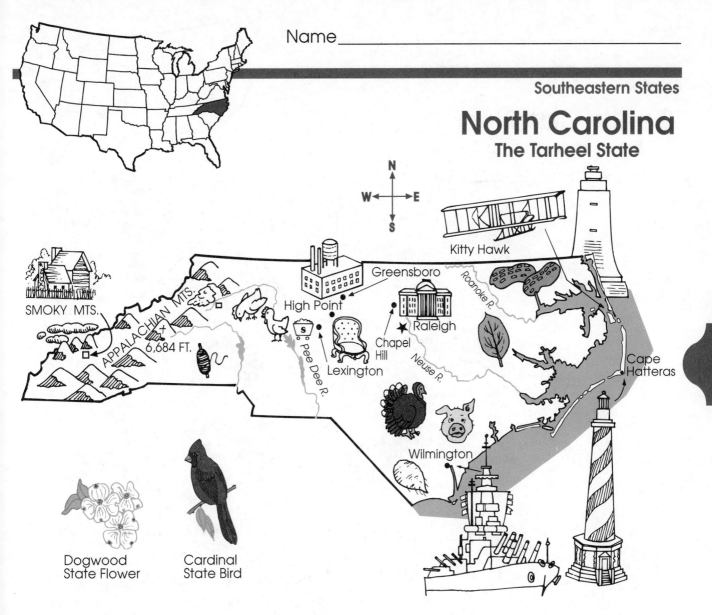

Kitty Hawk
Greensboro
High Point
SMOKY MTS.
APPALACHIAN MTS.
6,684 FT.
Roanoke R.
Raleigh
Chapel Hill
Lexington
Pee Dee R.
Neuse R.
Cape Hatteras
Wilmington

Dogwood
State Flower

Cardinal
State Bird

- named for King Charles I of England
- nickname the Tarheel State refers to the large amount of tar produced which made North Carolina the leading colony in the naval store industry

Mount Mitchell—6,684 ft.

Morehead Planetarium

High Point—often called the Furniture Capital of America

Lexington—location of first silver mine in the U.S.

Gaston County—spins more yarn than any other U.S. county

Greensboro—largest denim-weaving mill in the world

Cape Hatteras Lighthouse—guards the Graveyard of the Atlantic

Wright Brothers National Memorial

Cherokee Indian Reservation—has replica of a 1700 Indian village

Grandfather Mountain—resembles an old man sleeping

U.S.S. North Carolina—took part in every major Pacific Ocean battle in WWII

Circle the capital city. Locate the landmarks found in the above key. Color them on the map.

Name ____

South Carolina

The Palmetto State

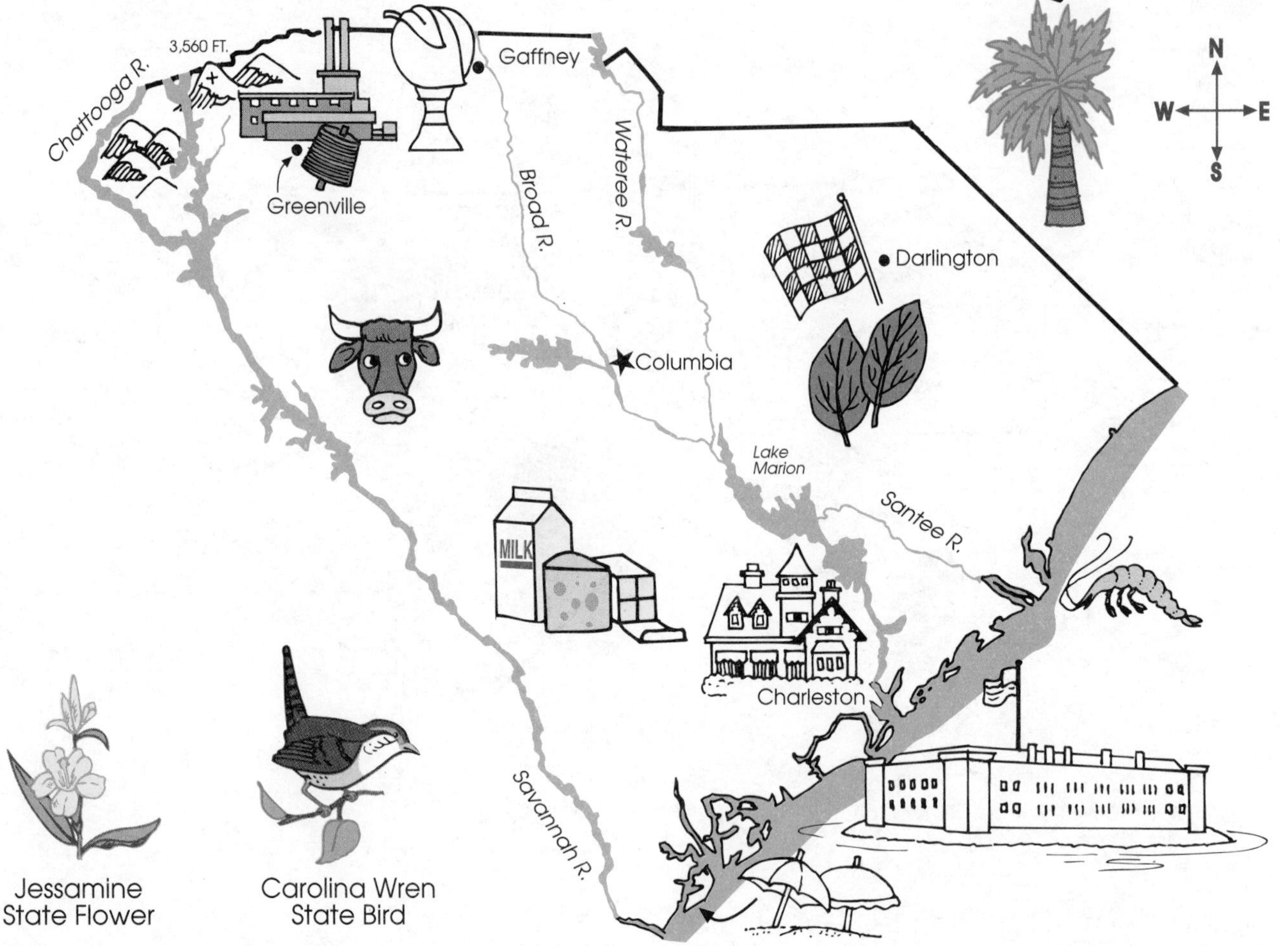

3,560 FT.
Chattooga R.
Greenville
Gaffney
Broad R.
Wateree R.
Darlington
Columbia
Lake Marion
Santee R.
MILK
Charleston
Savannah R.
N
W
E
S

Jessamine
State Flower

Carolina Wren
State Bird

- named for King Charles I of England; "South" was added when the Carolinas separated
- nickname the Palmetto State may be the result of an incident during the Revolutionary War where smoke from a burning British ship resembled the state's palmetto tree

Sassafras Mountain—3,560 ft.

The Peachoid—a tank holding one million gallons of water

Fort Sumter National Monument—site of the beginning of the Civil War

Southern 500—stock car race

Middleton Place—one of Charleston's finest plantations

Hilton Head Island—popular vacation resort

Circle the capital city. Locate the landmarks found in the above key. Color them on the map.

Name ____________________

Mississippi

The Magnolia State

N
W E
S

806 FT.
Clarksdale
Tupelo
DELTA BLUES
Mississippi R.
Yazoo R.
Vicksburg
Jackson
Coke
Natchez
Pearl R.
Biloxi

Mockingbird
State Bird

Magnolia
State Flower

- name taken from two Indian words, *misi* and *sipi* meaning *big river* or *great water*
- nickname the Magnolia State refers to the many magnolia trees that grow in the state

Woodall Mountain—806 ft.

Delta Blues Museum—dedicated to blues musicians and music

Shrimp Festival—chief shrimp-packing port

Elvis Presley Park—site of famous rock 'n' roll singer's birthplace

Vicksburg—site where Coca-Cola was first bottled in 1894

Delta Queen—built in 1926, tours the Mississippi River

Natchez—oldest town on the Mississippi River

Circle the capital city. Locate the landmarks found in the above key. Color them on the map.

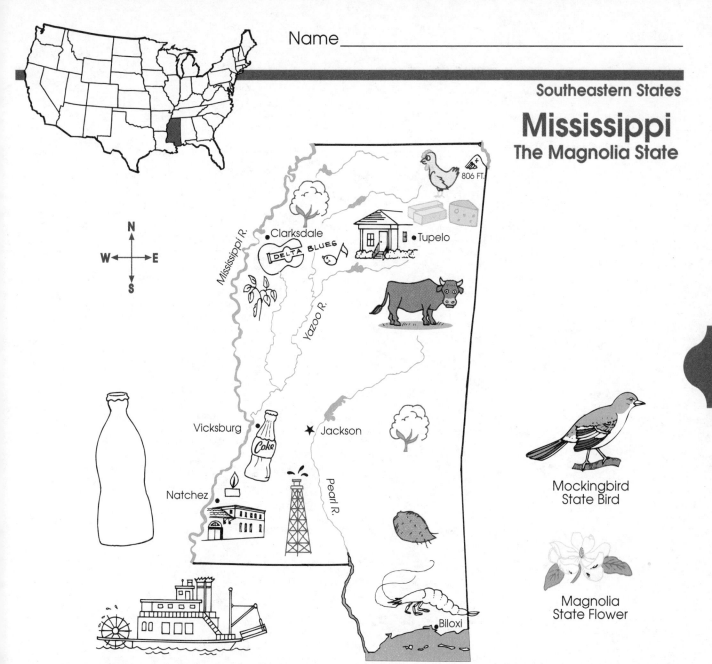

Name ____________________________________

Alabama

The Heart of Dixie

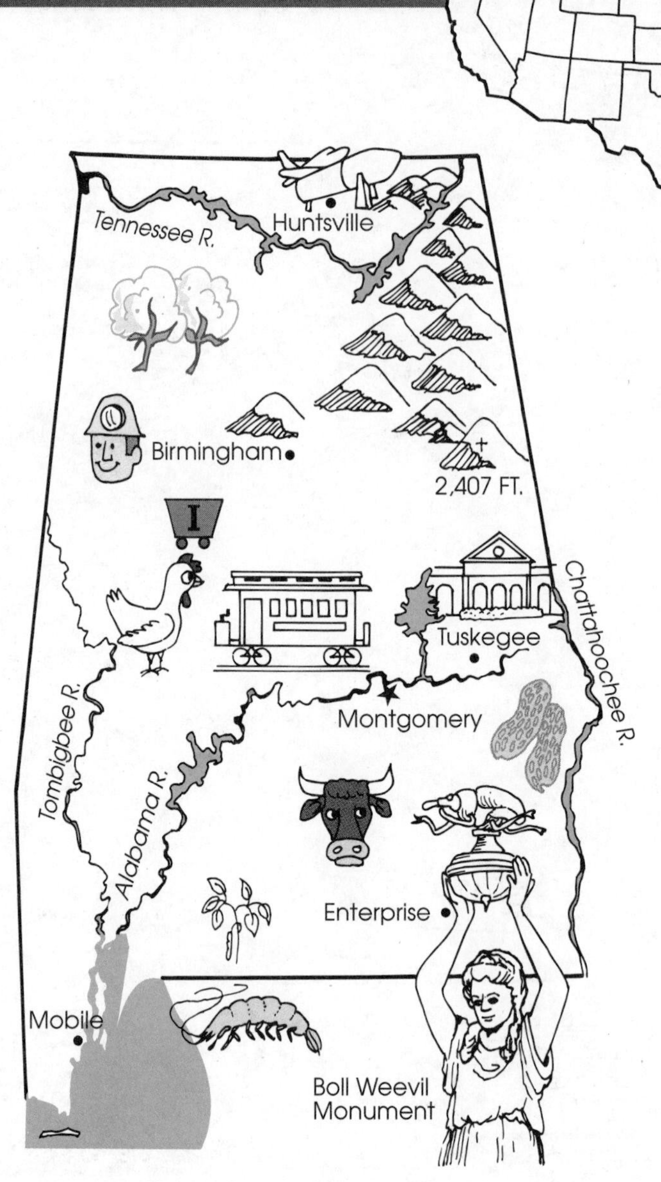

Yellow Hammer
State Bird

Camellia
State Flower

- named for a Creek Indian tribe, the Alibamu, whose name means *clearers of the thickets*
- nickname the Heart of Dixie refers to the importance the state had during the Civil War

 Cheaha Mountain—2,407 ft.

 U.S. Space and Rocket Center

 Boll Weevil Monument

 Montgomery—first electric trolley car in the U.S. began operating here in 1866

 George Washington Carver Museum—honors Carver's discovery of over 300 uses for peanuts and over 100 uses for sweet potatoes

Circle the capital city. Locate the landmarks found in the above key. Color them on the map.

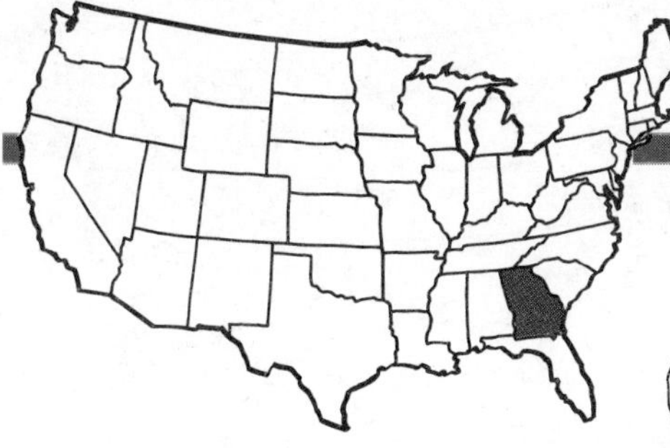

Name____________________

Georgia

The Empire State of the South

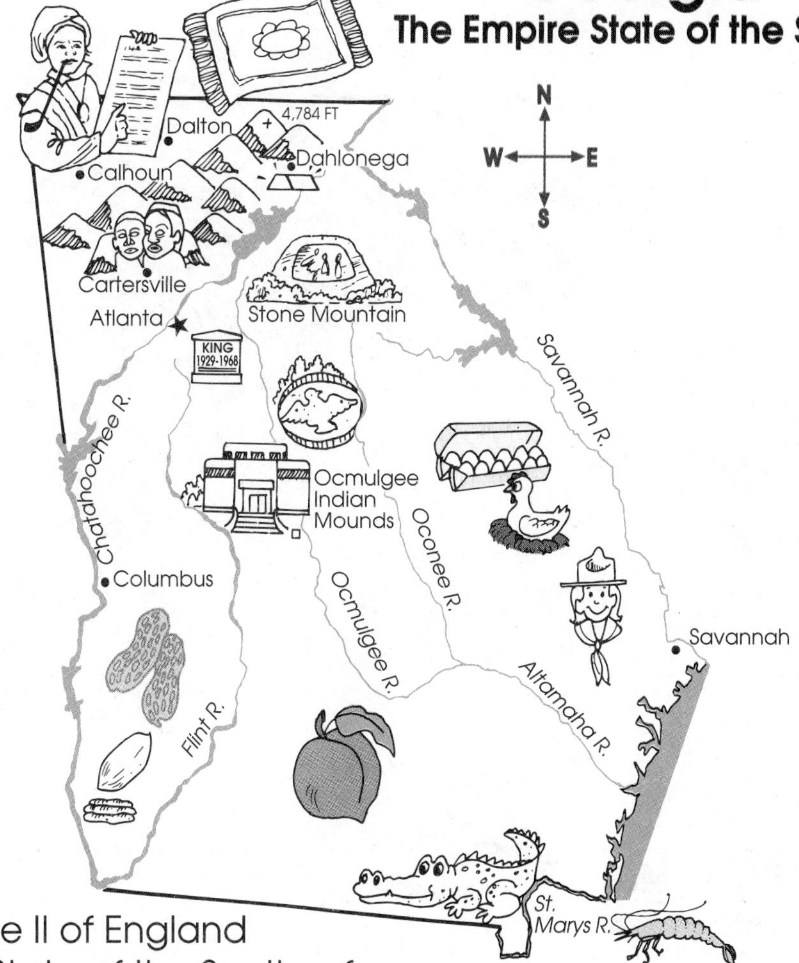

Cherokee Rose
State Flower

Brown Thrasher
State Bird

- named for King George II of England
- nickname the Empire State of the South refers to the state's size and many successful industries

 Brasstown Bald Mountain—4,784 ft.

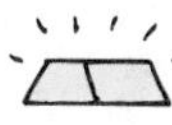 Dahlonega Gold Museum—located at the site of the first gold rush in the U.S.

 Etowah Mounds—built by prehistoric Indians

 Savannah—Juliet Gordon Lowe, founder of the Girl Scouts of the U.S.A., lived here

 Calhoun—statue honors Sequoya, who developed Cherokee alphabet

 Ocmulgee National Monument—contains remains of Indian mounds

 Dalton—produces more carpeting than any other place in the U.S.

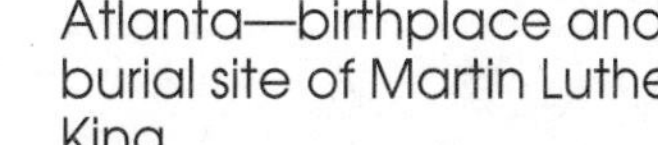 Atlanta—birthplace and burial site of Martin Luther King

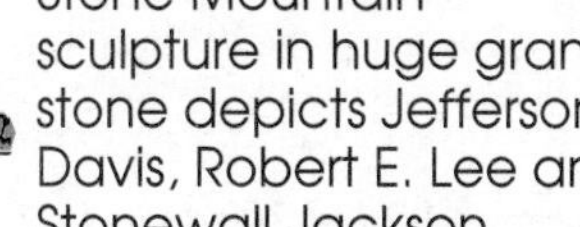 Okefenokee Swamp—national wildlife refuge, which is known as America's greatest botanical garden

 Stone Mountain—sculpture in huge granite stone depicts Jefferson Davis, Robert E. Lee and Stonewall Jackson

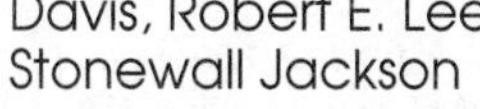

 Rock Eagle Effigy—6,000-year-old monument made by ancient Indians

Circle the capital city. Locate the landmarks found in the above key. Color them on the map.

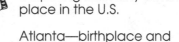

Name ____________________________________

Florida

The Sunshine State

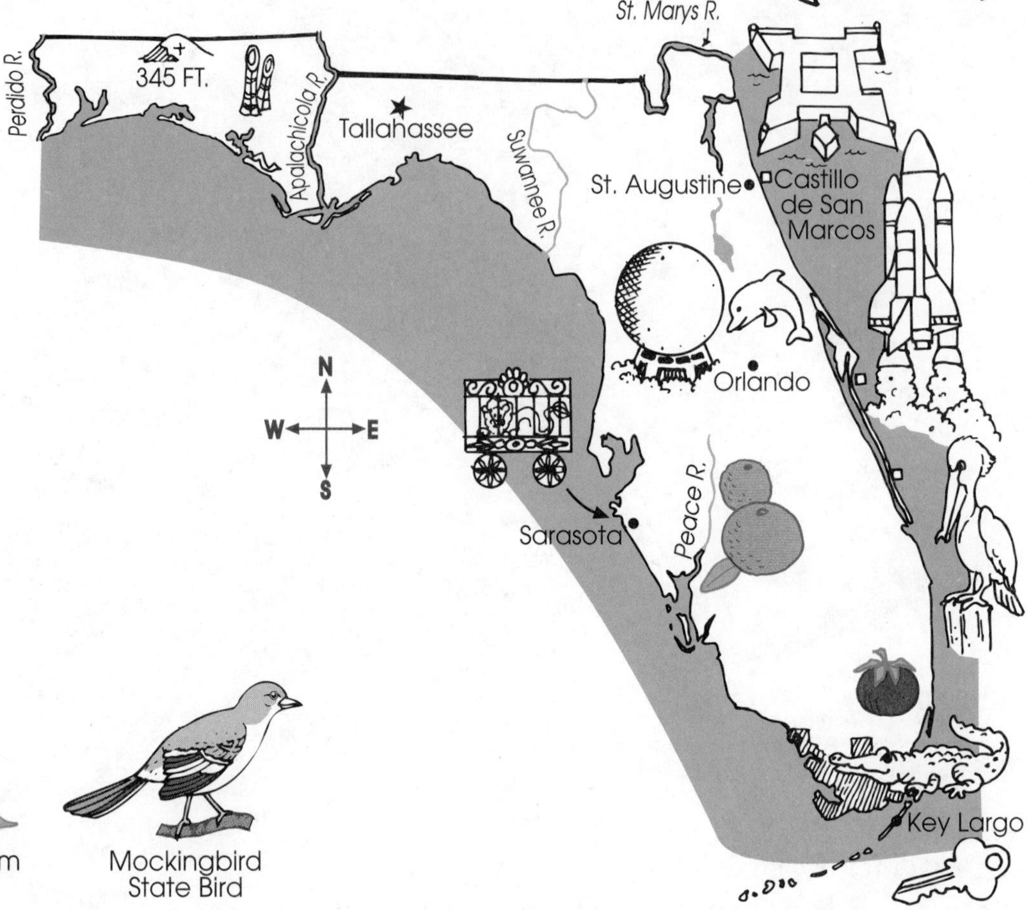

St. Marys R.
Perdido R.
345 FT.
Apalachicola R.
Tallahassee
Suwannee R.
St. Augustine
Castillo de San Marcos
Orlando
N W E S
Sarasota
Peace R.
Key Largo

Orange Blossom
State Flower

Mockingbird
State Bird

- name comes from the Spanish word *florida,* meaning *flowery,* which may refer to the many flowers given by Spanish explorer Juan Ponce de León
- nicknamed the Sunshine State for its warm and sunny climate

Sea World—a popular tourist attraction featuring killer whales and dolphins

Pelican Island National Wildlife Refuge—first federal wildlife refuge

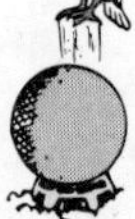

EPCOT Center—displays future technology

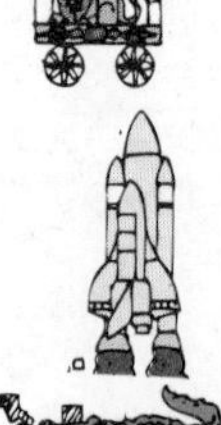

John and Mable Ringling Museum—Museum of Art and Circus Galleries

Cape Canaveral—space and rocket center

Everglades National Park—largest subtropical wilderness in U.S.

Castillo de San Marcos National Monument—oldest permanent European settlement in the United States

John Pennekamp Coral Reef State Park—first underseas park in the continental United States

Circle the capital city. Locate the landmarks found in the above key. Color them on the map.

Section 4

North & South America

Name________________________________

Introduction: North and South America

What Is Where in North and South America?

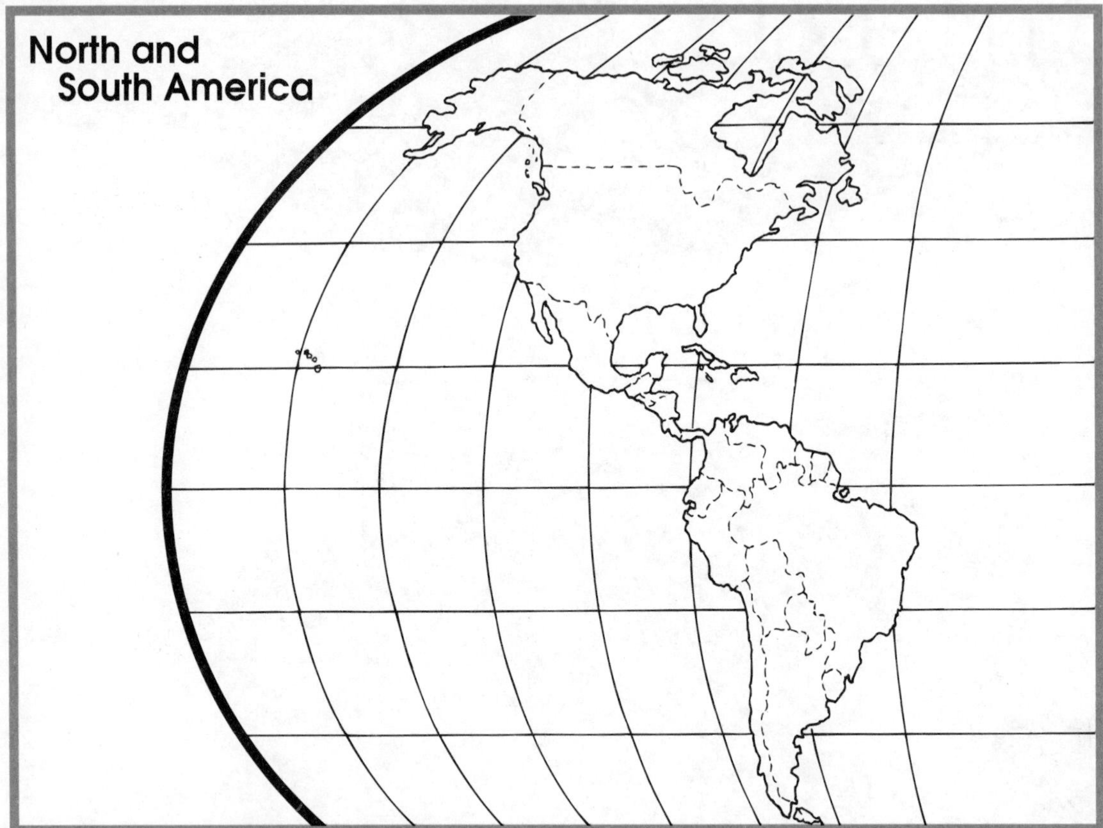

Directions: Follow these directions to complete the map. You may also use a political map of North and South America.

1. Outline Canada in red.
2. Outline the United States in black. (Remember Alaska and Hawaii.)
3. Outline Mexico in orange.
4. Outline Brazil in brown.
5. Outline Chile in red.
6. Outline Argentina in orange.
7. Outline Paraguay in yellow.
8. Outline Colombia in black.
9. Outline Bolivia in red.
10. Color Peru yellow.
11. Color Ecuador orange.
12. Color Uruguay brown.
13. Color Venezuela purple.
14. Color Guyana pink.
15. Color Suriname orange.
16. Color French Guiana yellow.
17. Color the Gulf of Mexico green.
18. Color the Arctic Ocean blue.
19. Color the Pacific Ocean grey.
20. Color the Atlantic Ocean purple.

Name________________________________

Neighboring Countries

Use a map of North America to locate your country. In the direction boxes write the names of all the countries and/or bodies of water surrounding your country.

Northwest	North	Northeast
West	My Country Draw an outline map of your country.	East
Southwest	South	Southeast

Name___________________________________

Within Continents

A continent is a large area of land.

This map shows two continents, North America and South America, and two oceans, the Atlantic Ocean and Pacific Ocean. It also shows the countries that are on each continent. A solid line (——) shows the boundaries of each country. Use this map to answer the questions on page 225.

Name____

Within Continents

1. Write the names of the continents shown on the map.

____

____

2. Find the United States on the map. Color it green.
3. Find Alaska and Hawaii. They are part of the country of the United States. Color them green.
4. What country is north of the United States? Color it orange.

____

5. What large country is south of the United States? Color it red.

____

6. Which South American country is the biggest? ________________________
7. What long, skinny country is on the west coast of South America?

____

8. Which ocean is to the west of the continents of North America and South America? ____
9. In which direction would you go to travel from Canada to Chile?

____

Name____________________________

O Canada!

Canada, the largest country in area in the Western Hemisphere, stretches across the North American Continent with its shores touching three oceans.

Canada has 10 provinces and 2 territories. A province is a political area that is very similar to a state.

You will need:

copy of Political Map of Canada (page 227)
physical Canada map, atlas or encyclopedia,
colored pencils, crayons or markers

Directions:

1. Complete a key with symbols for the national capital, province/territory capitals and cities.
2. Label each of the ten provinces and two territories using upper-case letters.
3. Label the national capital and the capitals of each province and territory.
4. Label these major cities:
   Calgary Saskatoon Windsor Montreal Vancouver
5. Label these bodies of water:
   Atlantic Ocean Pacific Ocean Arctic Ocean Hudson Bay
   Labrador Sea Baffin Bay
6. Color each province and territory a different color.
7. Color the bodies of water blue.
8. Color the United States one color.

Name ____________________

Political Map of Canada

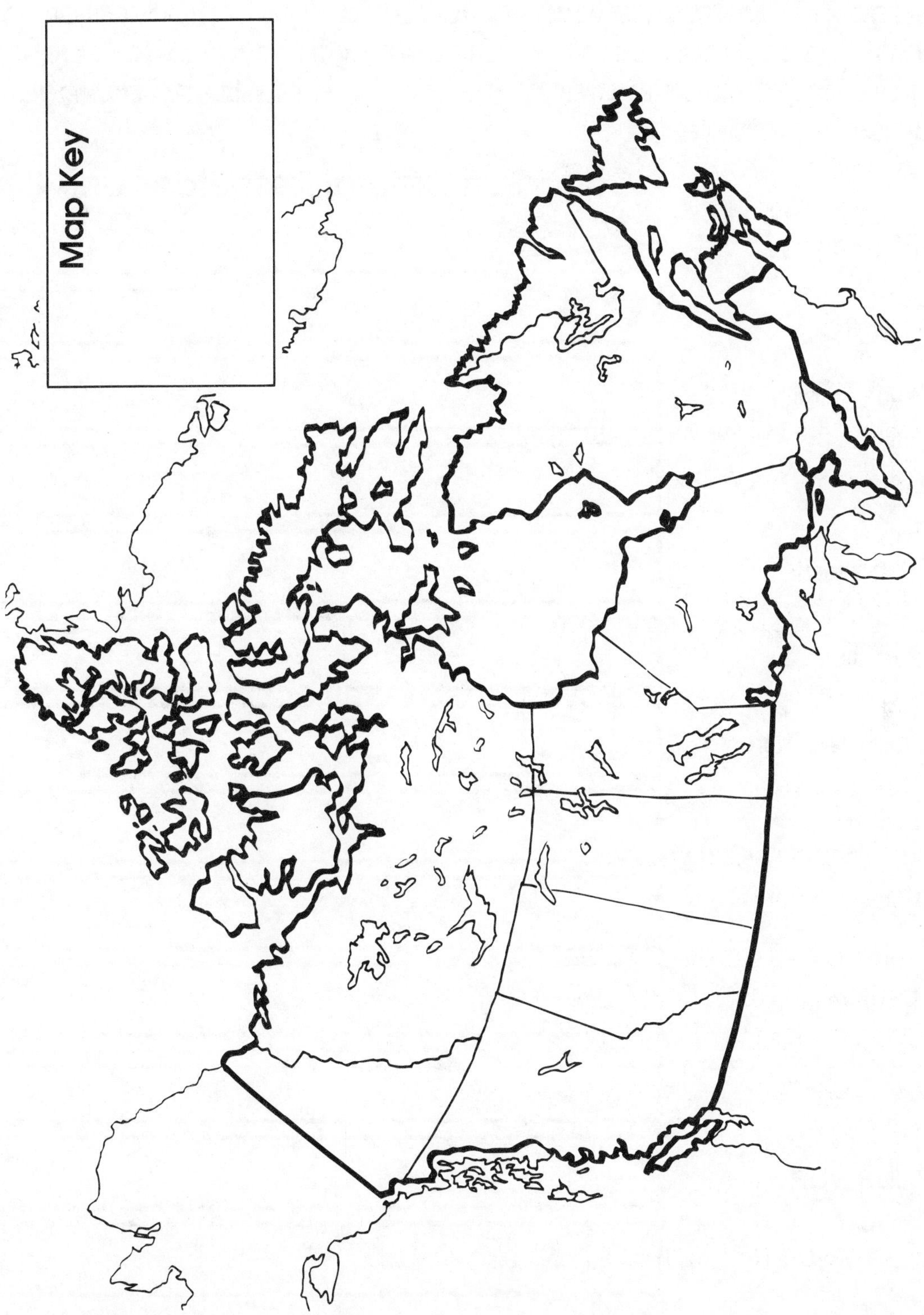

Use with page 226.

Name____

Products and Natural Resources

Canada is rich in natural resources. Study the Products and Natural Resources map (page 229). Determine which natural resources or products are available in each of the provinces and territories. Draw the symbol for each product or natural resource on the graph. The Province of Alberta has been done for you as an example.

Canadian Natural Resources and Products

	Moderate Producer	Major Producer
Alberta		
British Columbia		
Manitoba		
New Brunswick		
Newfoundland		
Northwest Territory		
Nova Scotia		
Ontario		
Prince Edward Island		
Quebec		
Saskatchewan		
Yukon Territory		

Name____________________

Products and Natural Resources

Use with page 228.

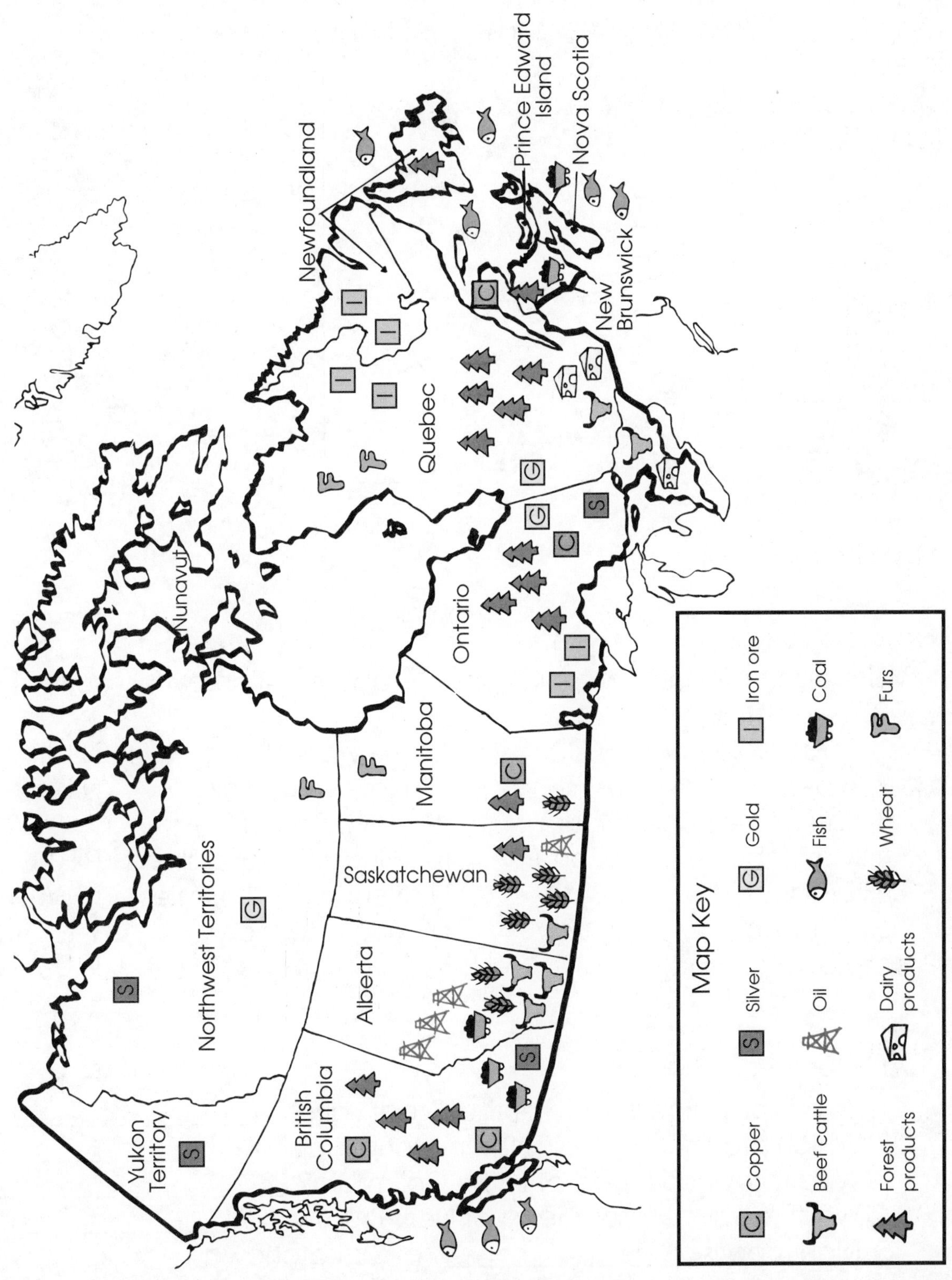

Name ____________________

Northern Neighbors

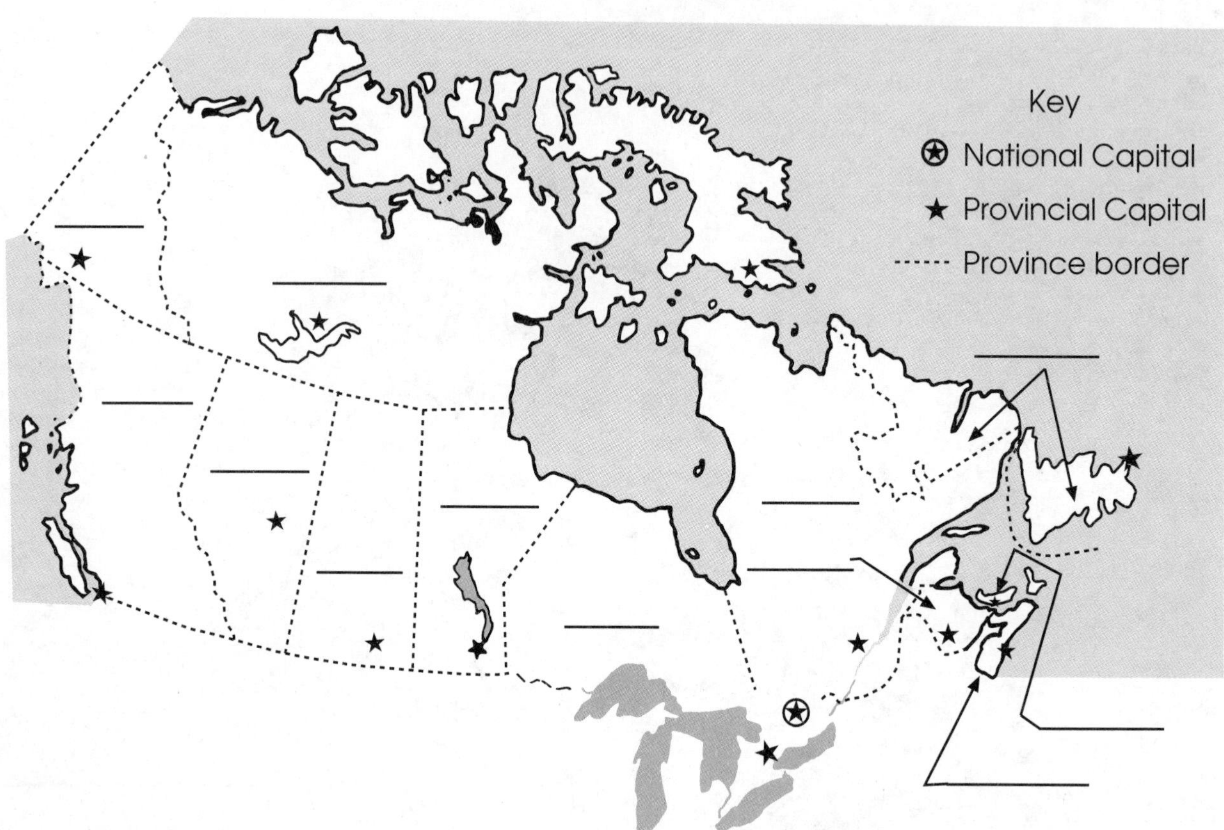

Write each province or territory name abbreviation by the correct number on the map.

1. British Columbia	(B.C.)	7. Newfoundland	(Nfld.)
2. Alberta	(Alta.)	8. New Brunswick	(N.B.)
3. Saskatchewan	(Sask.)	9. Nova Scotia	(N.S.)
4. Manitoba	(Man.)	10. Prince Edward Island	(P.E.I.)
5. Ontario	(Ont.)	11. Northwest Territories	(N.W.T.)
6. Quebec	(Que.)	12. Yukon Territory	(Y.T.)
		13. Nunavut	(N.U.)

Answer these questions.

1. Which province is north of the Great Lakes? ____________________
2. Which province contains the national capital? ____________________
3. What province is east of British Columbia? ____________________
4. What province is southeast of New Brunswick? ____________________
5. Manitoba is ____________________ of Saskatchewan.

Name ____________________________________

Mexico

Mexico is the United States' neighbor to the south. The two countries share a 2,000-mile long border. Mexico is the third most populated country in the Western Hemisphere; only the United States and Brazil have more people.

Mexico is home to the largest city in the world, Mexico City.

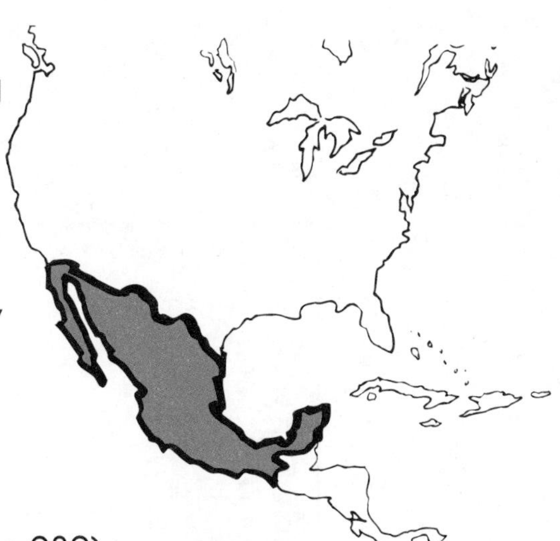

You will need:

copy of Mexico Physical-Political Map (page 232)
physical map of Mexico, atlas or encyclopedia
colored pencils, markers or crayons

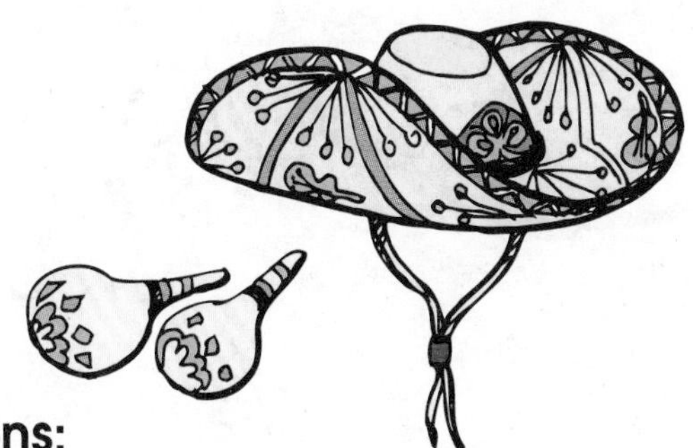

Directions:

1. Label and color-code the map key, and color Mexico's six main land regions:

Pacific Northwest	Plateau of Mexico	Gulf Coastal Plain
Southern Uplands	Chiapas Highlands	Yucatan Peninsula

2. Draw and label the following mountain ranges. Use ΛΛΛ as symbols for mountains.

Sierra Madre Oriental	Sierra Madre del Sur	Sierra Madre Occidental

3. Label these large cities:

Mexico City	Monterrery	Guadalajara
Puebla	Chihuahua	Juarez
Tijuana	Acapulco	Tampico

4. Label these bodies of water:

Gulf of Mexico	Pacific Ocean	Gulf of California

Name____________________________________

Mexico

Physical/Political Map

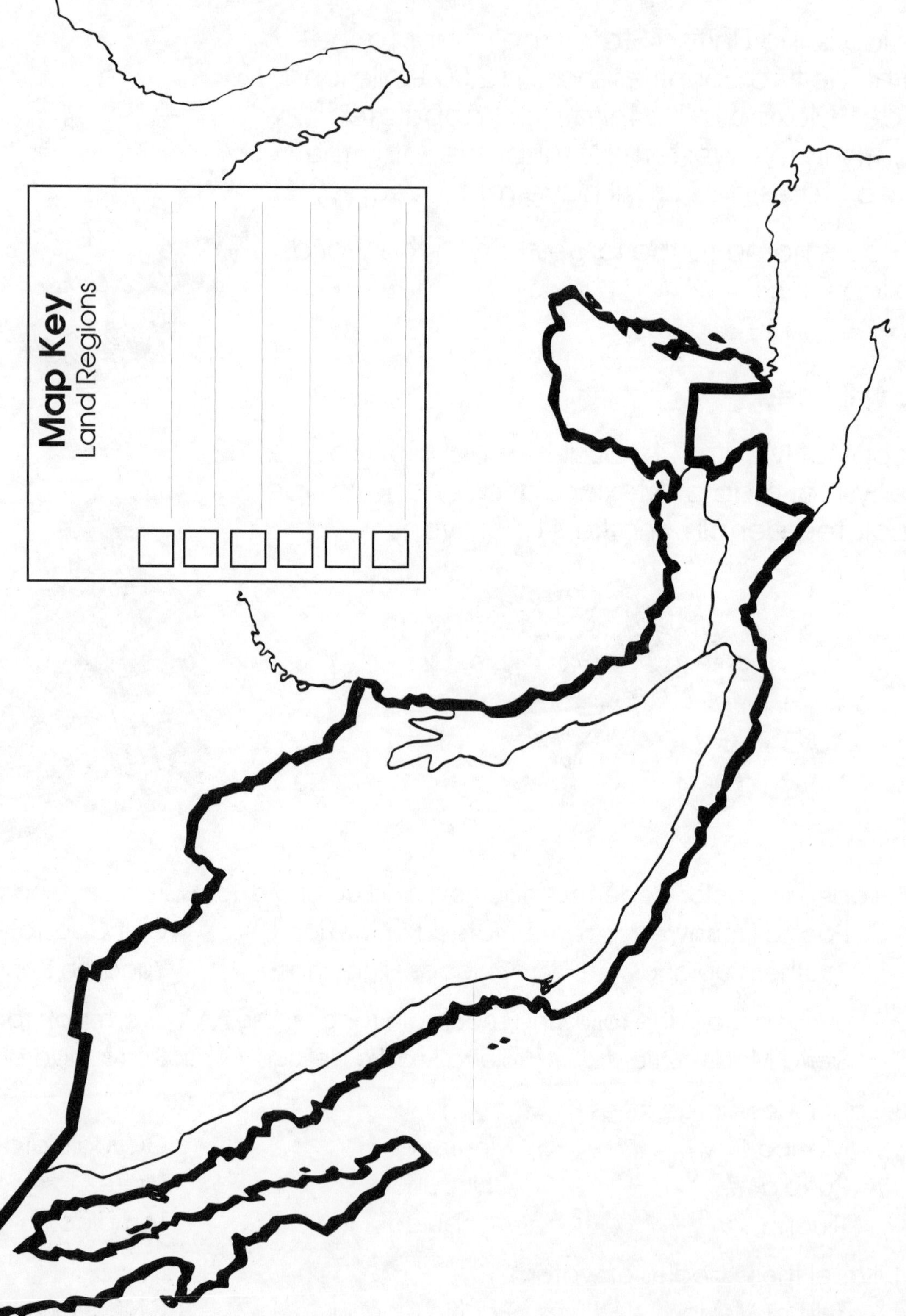

Use with page 231.

Name________________________________

Mexico

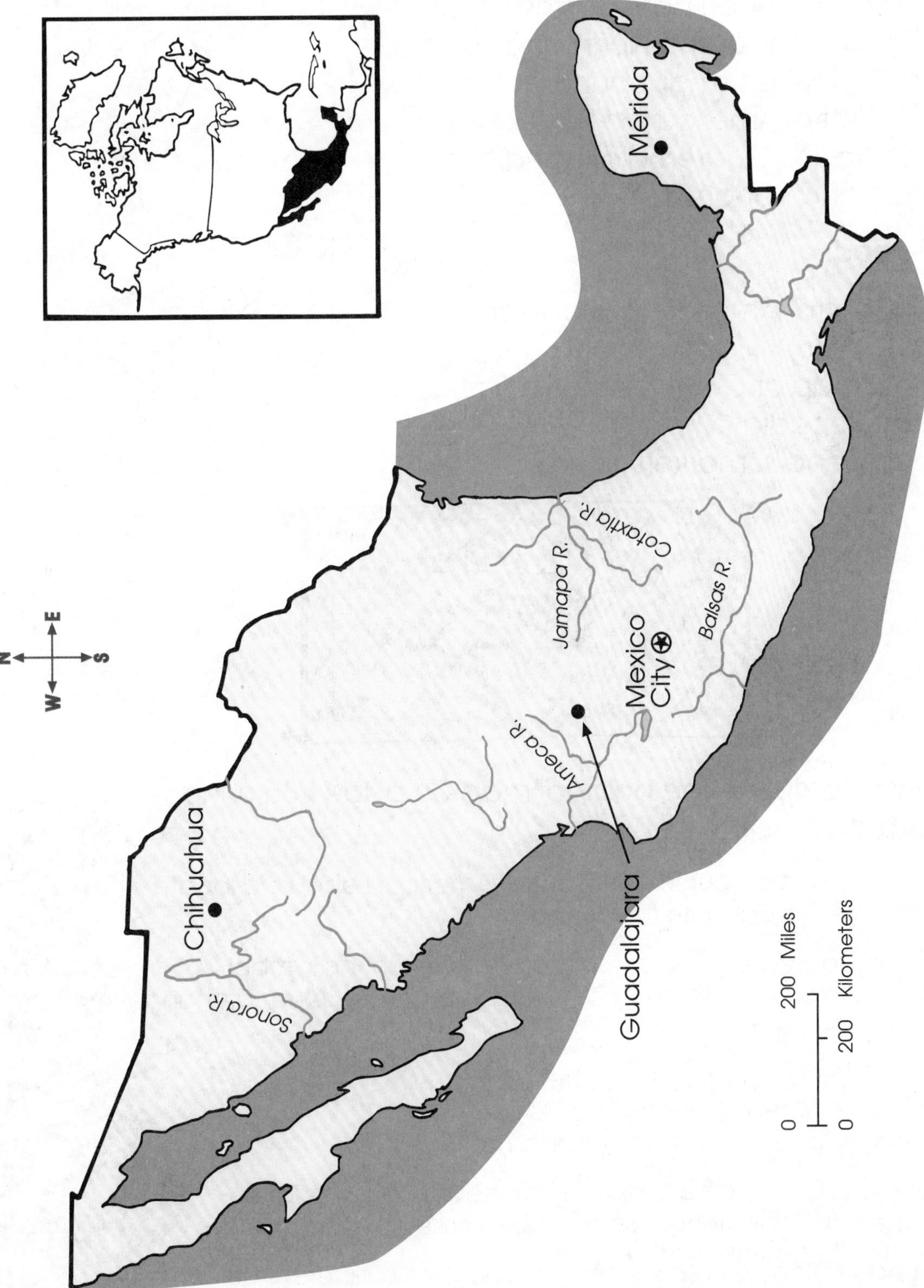

Area: 756,067 sq. mi.

Name____

Central America

Central America is the narrow isthmus, or ridge of land, connecting North and South America. The seven small countries that make up Central America are Belize, Costa Rica, El Salvador, Guatemala, Honduras, Nicaragua and Panama.

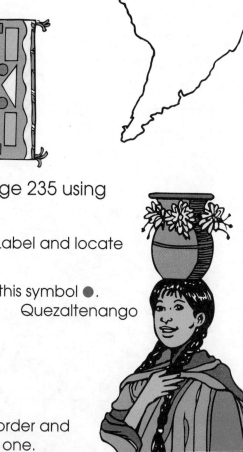

You will need:

blank Central America Political map (page 235)
physical map of Central America, atlas or encyclopedia
colored pencils, markers or crayons

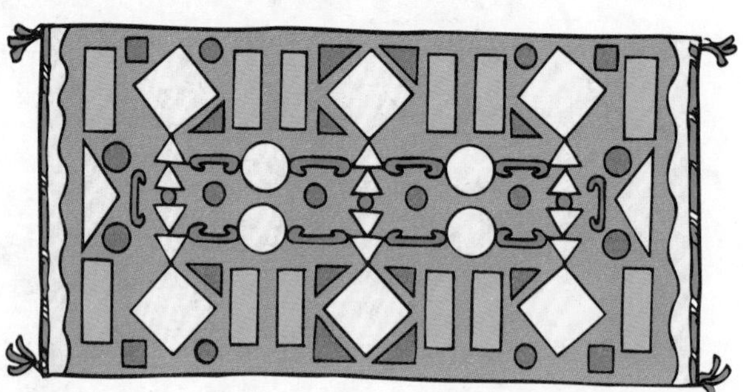

Directions: Complete the political map on page 235 using the information below.

1. Label each of the countries of Central America. Label and locate each of the capitals with this symbol ✪.
2. Label and locate each of these major cities with this symbol ●.
   San Pedro Sula, Santa Ana, Belize City, Quezaltenango, Colon, Limón, León
3. Label the following bodies of water:
   Pacific Ocean, Panama Canal, Caribbean Sea, Gulf of Panama
4. On the Key, list all of the capitals in alphabetical order and write the letter-number coordinates behind each one.
5. Color each of the Central American countries a different color.

Name____

Political Map

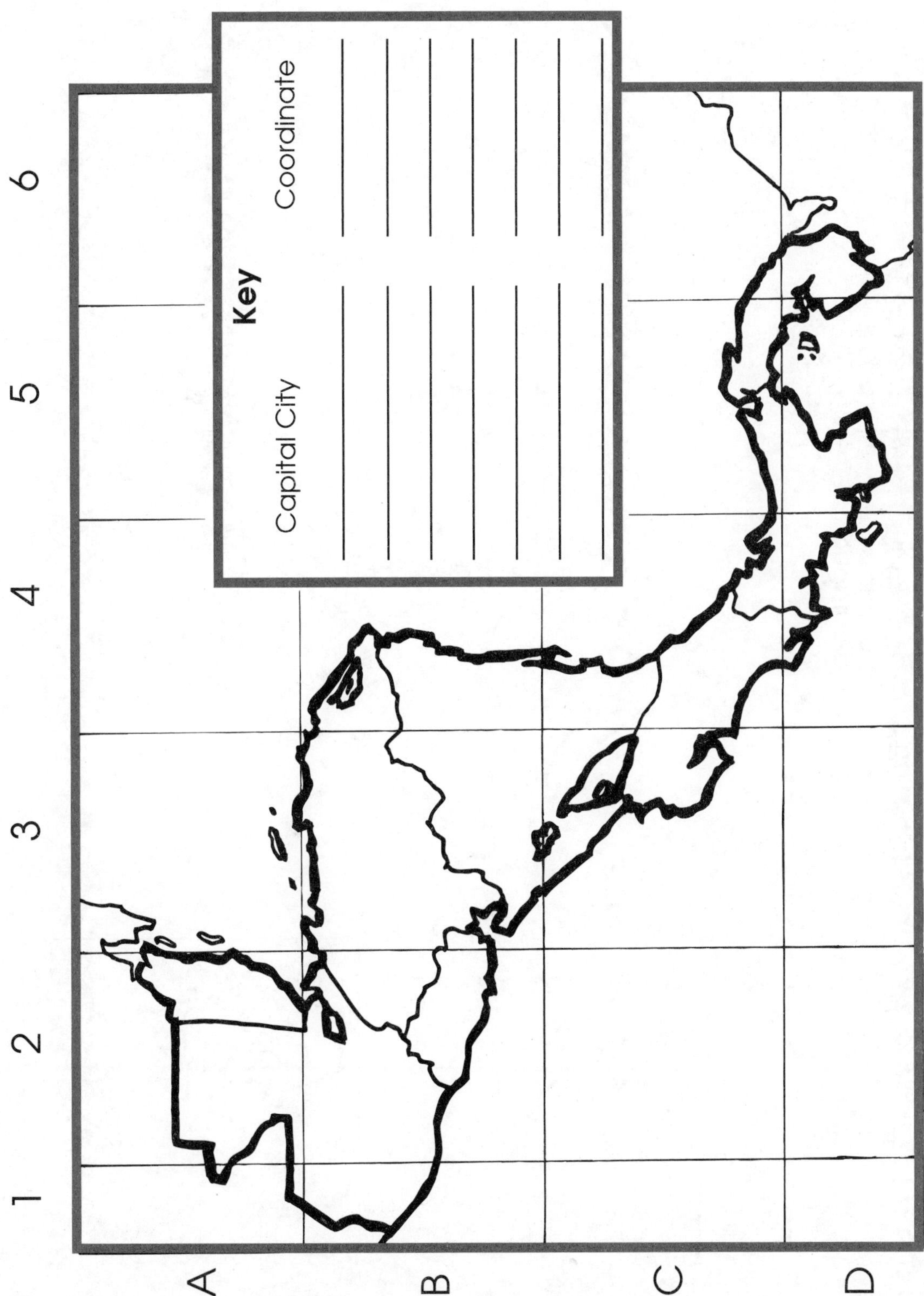

Use with page 234.

Name______________________________________

Central America

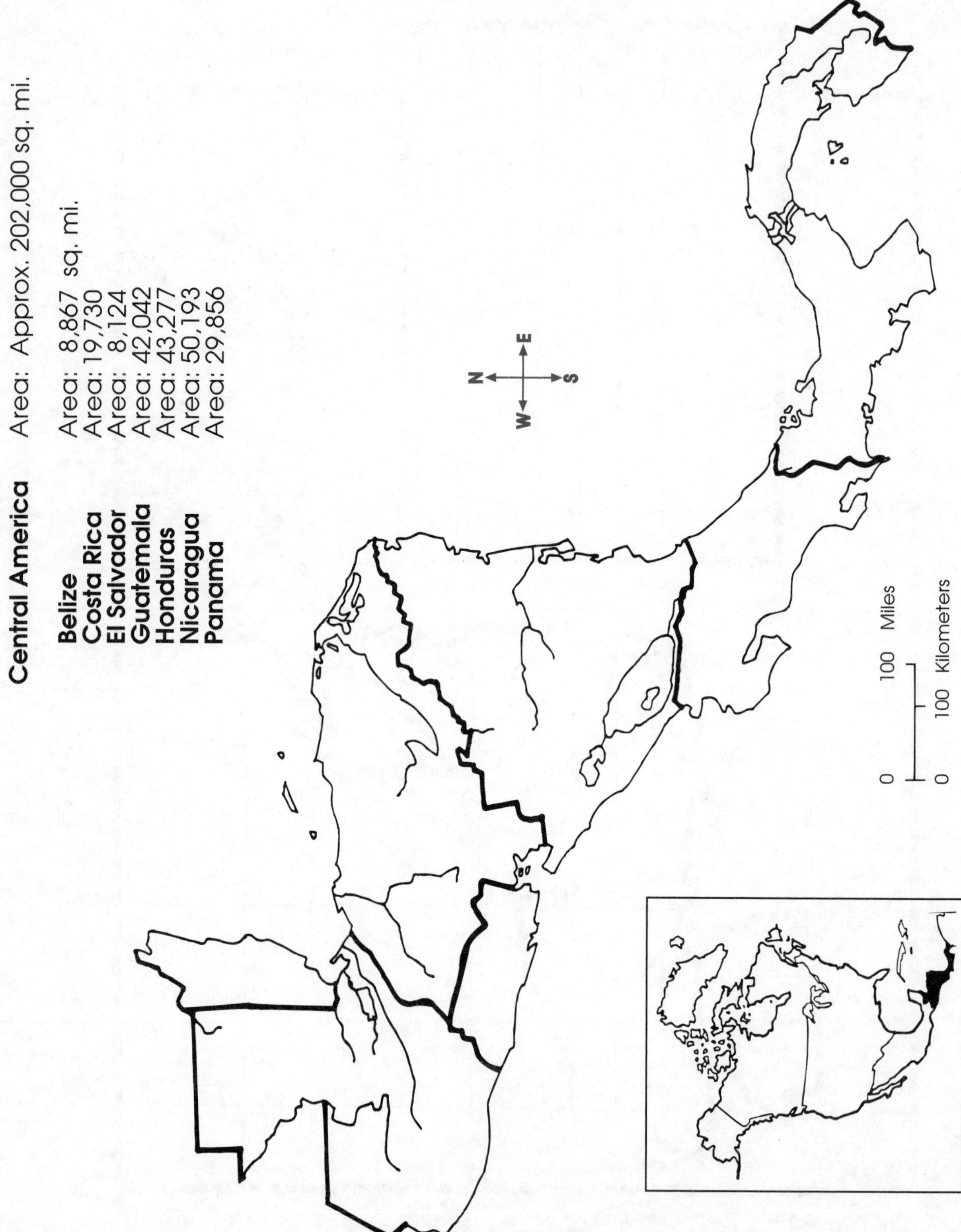
Central America Area: Approx. 202,000 sq. mi.
Belize Area: 8,867 sq. mi.
Costa Rica Area: 19,730
El Salvador Area: 8,124
Guatemala Area: 42,042
Honduras Area: 43,277
Nicaragua Area: 50,193
Panama Area: 29,856
N
E
S
W
0 100 Miles
0 100 Kilometers

Name________________________________

South America

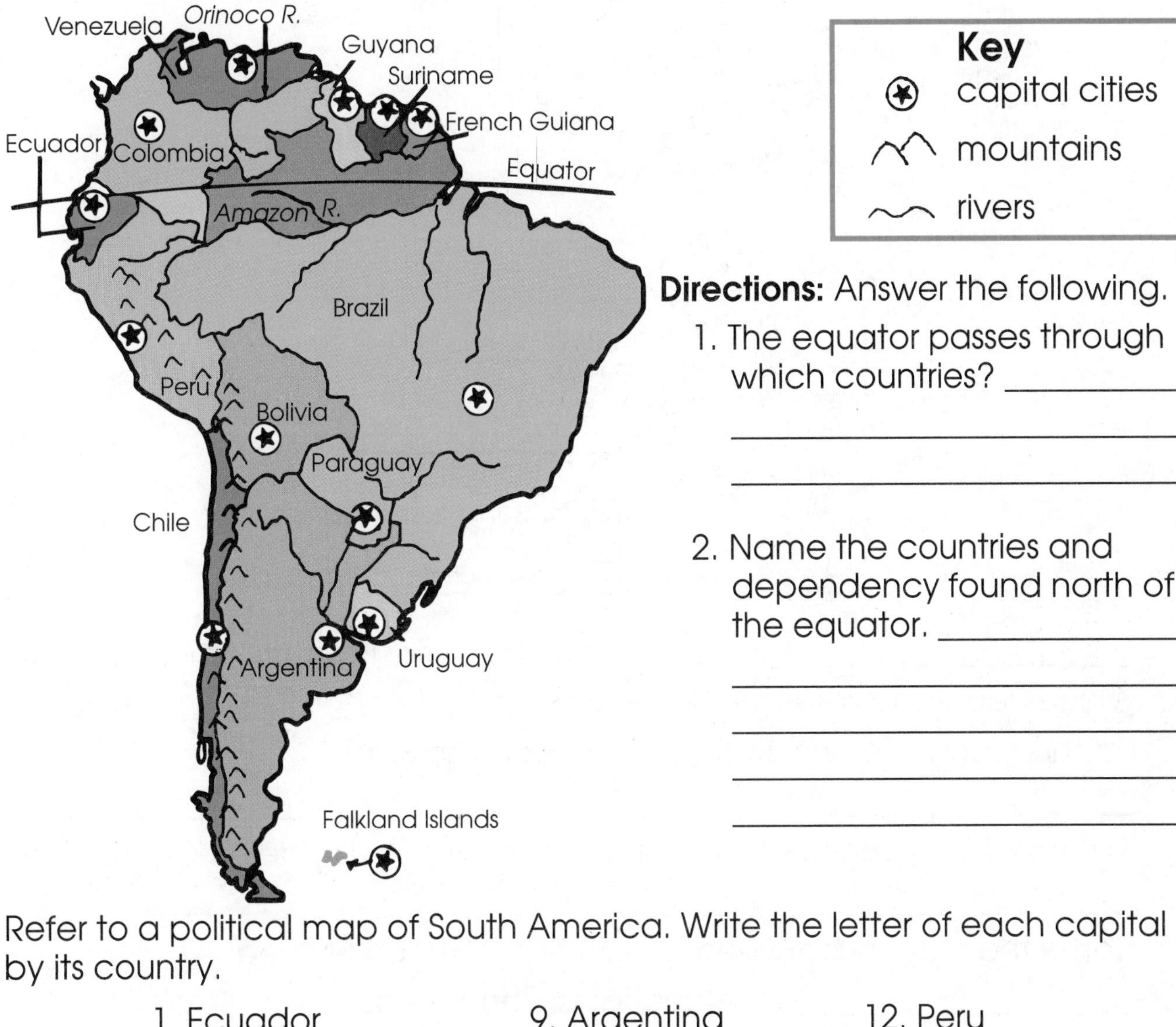

Directions: Answer the following.

1. The equator passes through which countries? ____________
____
____

2. Name the countries and dependency found north of the equator. ____________
____
____
____
____

Refer to a political map of South America. Write the letter of each capital by its country.

______	1. Ecuador	______	9. Argentina	______	12. Peru
______	2. Colombia	______	10. Chile	______	13. Paraguay
______	3. Venezuela	______	11. Bolivia	______	14. Falkland Islands
______	4. Guyana				
______	5. Suriname				
______	6. French Guiana				
______	7. Brazil				
______	8. Uruguay				

A. Buenos Aires	H. Lima
B. Sucre	I. Paramaribo
C. Brasília	J. Montevideo
D. Bogotá	K. Caracas
E. Quito	L. Santiago
F. Georgetown	M. Cayenne
G. Asunción	N. Stanley

Name____

Countries and Cities in South America

1. ____________________ is the largest country in South America.
2. Which country forms Argentina's western border? ____________________
3. List three countries which share a border with Brazil.

   ________________ ________________ ________________

4. Name the two countries which form the southern border of Colombia.

   ____________________ ____________________

5. Name the country between Guyana and French Guiana. __________
6. ________________ is the capital of Venezuela.
7. Uruguay is between the countries of Argentina and ________________.
8. The capital of Bolivia is ____________________.
9. ____________________ forms Peru's northwest border.
10. The capital of Paraguay is ____________________.
11. Cayenne is the capital of ____________________.
12. Name the country west of Guyana. ____________________
13. Name the three countries which share a border with Chile.

    ________________ ________________ ________________

Name ______________________________

Where Is It Raining?

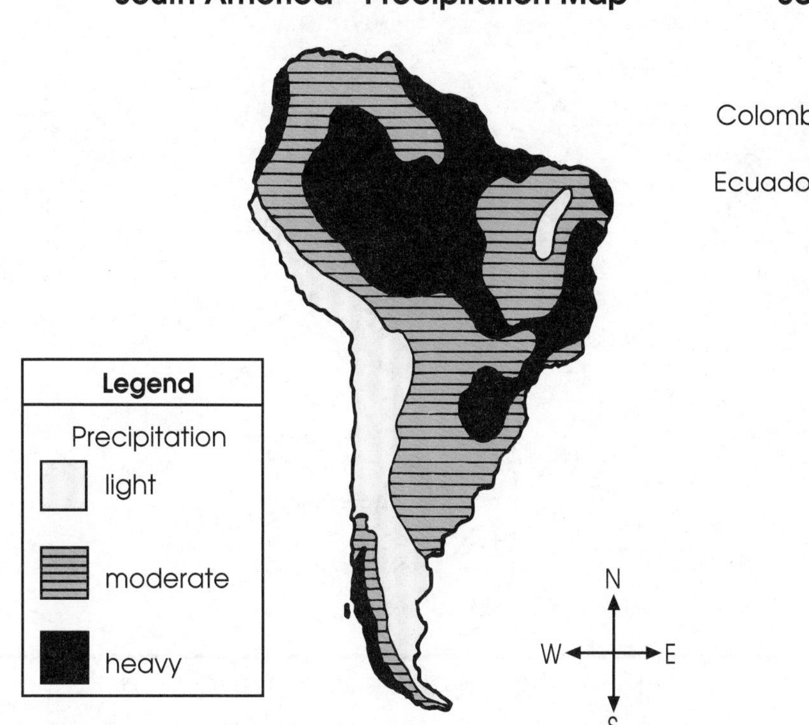

Directions: Use both maps to answer these questions about South America.

1. What do these symbols stand for on the precipitation map?

   A. ______________ B. ______________ C. ______________

2. The lightest precipitation falls mainly on the ______________ part of South America.
3. The heaviest precipitation falls mainly in the ______________ part of South America.
4. The majority of Argentina receives ______________ precipitation.
5. The majority of South America receives ______________ precipitation.
6. Most of Chile receives ______________ precipitation.
7. The northwestern tip of Colombia receives ______________ precipitation.
8. The western half of Ecuador receives ______________ precipitation.
9. Most of Brazil receives ______________ precipitation.

Name ________________________________

Land in South America

Key

Brazilian Highlands	Guiana Highlands	Andes Mountains	Pampas

1. Over half of the continent is covered by ____________________.
2. The ____________________ Mountains run from north to south on the western half of the continent.
3. In what part of the country are the Guiana Highlands located? ________
4. In the eastern part of South America is an area called the __________ ______________________________ Highlands.
5. Most of Argentina is covered by ____________________.
6. The eastern part of Brazil is the ____________________ Highlands.
7. Which country is covered completely by pampas—Uruguay or Venezuela? ____________________
8. Colombia's northeast border is formed by the country of __________.
9. Name the country which borders Argentina to the west. __________
10. Which country does not contain the Andes Mountains within its borders—Chile, Peru or Uruguay? ____________________

Section 5

Grid Maps

Name ____________________________________

Numbers and Letters on a Map

This is a map of Red Falls.

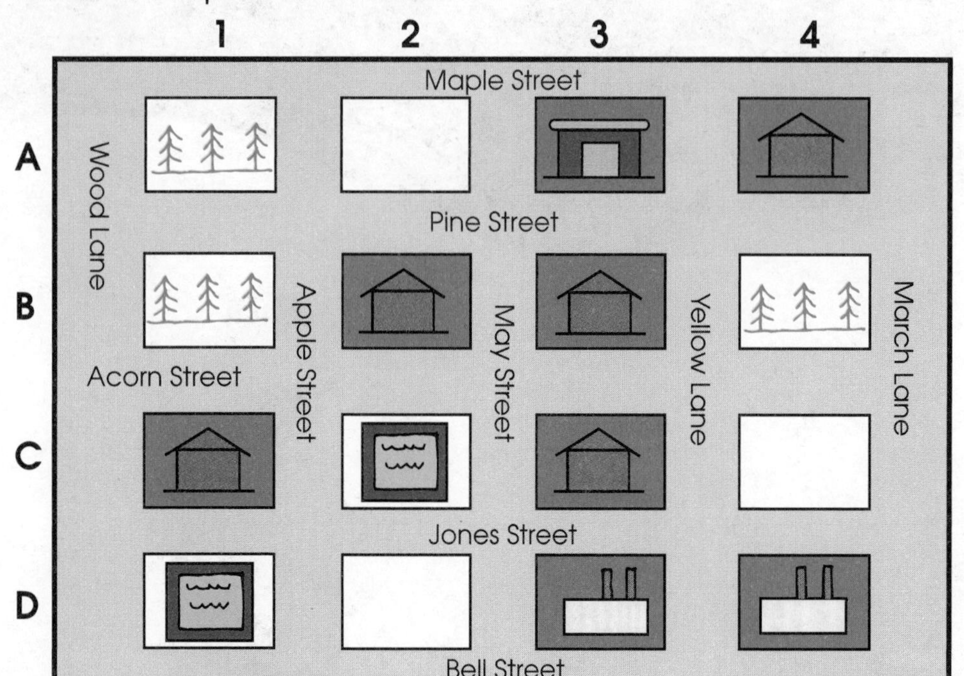

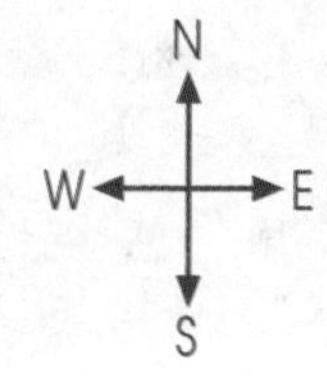

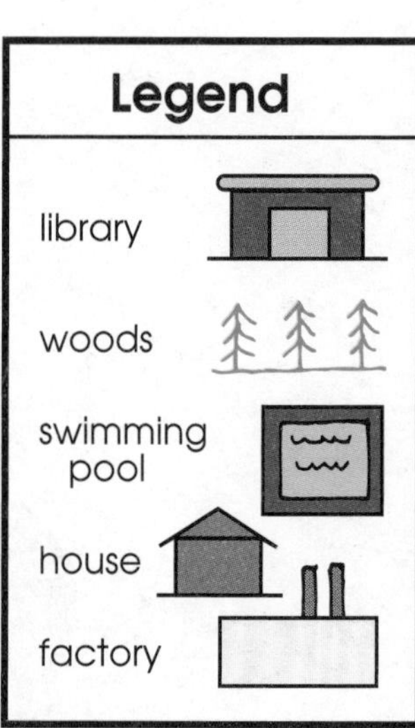

Directions: Use the numbers and letters to help you answer the questions below.

1. Locate the blocks. Write down what you see in each block.
   "A 1" ____________________ "C 1" ____________________
   "D 4" ____________________ "D 1" ____________________
2. Name the blocks with swimming pools. ____________________
3. Name the blocks with houses. ____________________
4. Name the blocks with woods. ____________________
5. Tell what is located in the first block south of "A 3." ____________________
6. What is in the block south of "C 1"? ____________________
7. How many houses are in "B 2"? ____________________
8. What is in the block east of "B 3"? ____________________
9. What is in the block west of "D 4"? ____________________
10. Draw a swimming pool in "A 2."
11. Draw a house in "D 2."
12. Draw a factory in "C 4."

Name ______________________________

Using a Grid

A map grid helps people locate places easily.

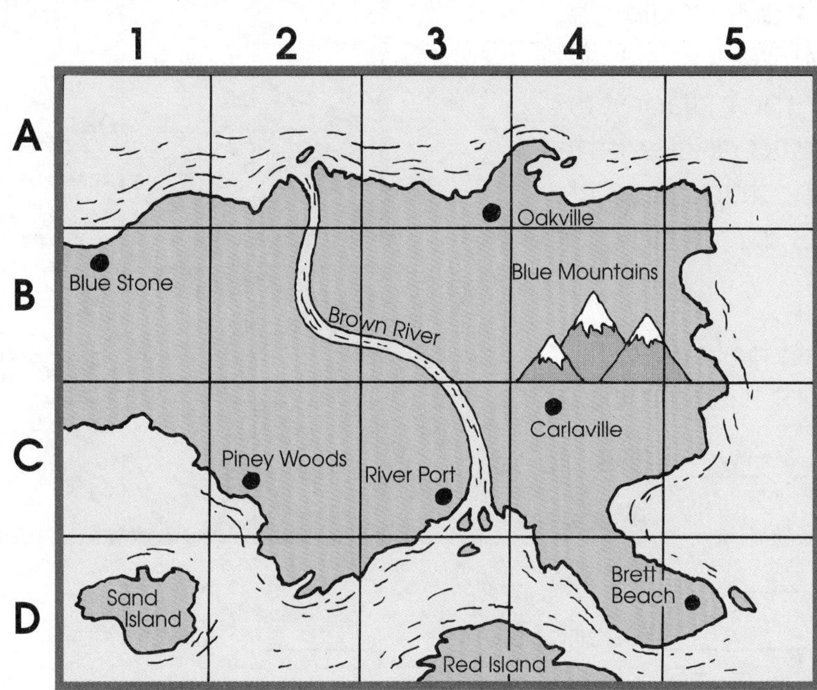

Directions: Use the numbers and letters to help you answer the questions bel

1. In which block is Brett Beach? ______________________
2. In which block is Blue Stone? ______________________
3. In which block is Piney Woods? ______________________
4. In which two blocks is Red Island? ______________________
5. In which four blocks is the Brown River? ______________________
6. In which block is Carlaville? ______________________
7. In which two blocks are the Blue Mountains? ______________________
8. Name the town located in "A 3." ______________________
9. Name the two islands found on the map. ______________________
10. In "C 5," add a town to the map.
11. In "B 2," add some trees.
12. In "A 5," add an island and name the island.

Name____________________________________

A Little Gridwork

A grid makes it easier to find places on a map. The lines of a grid divide the map into imaginary squares. Each square has a number that appears along the side of the grid and a letter that appears along the top. The city of Detroit is found at "D 4" on the map at the right.

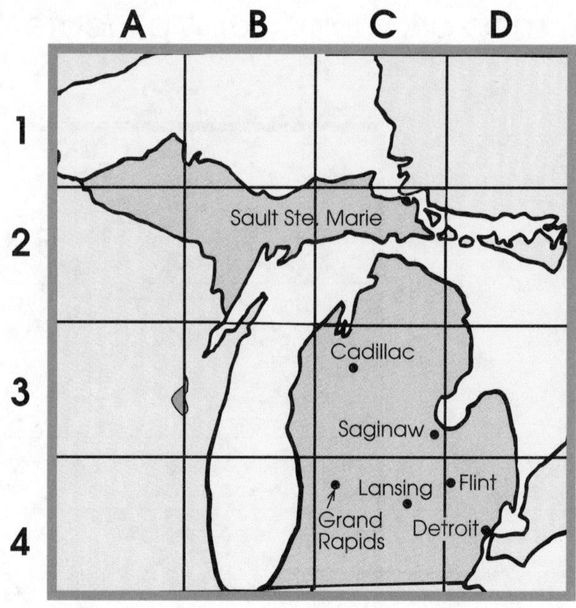

Directions: Use the grid below to find the location of each of these places.

________ Sioux City ________ Des Moines

________ Davenport ________ Ames

________ Dubuque ________ Mason City

________ Waterloo ________ Council Bluffs ________ Cedar Rapids

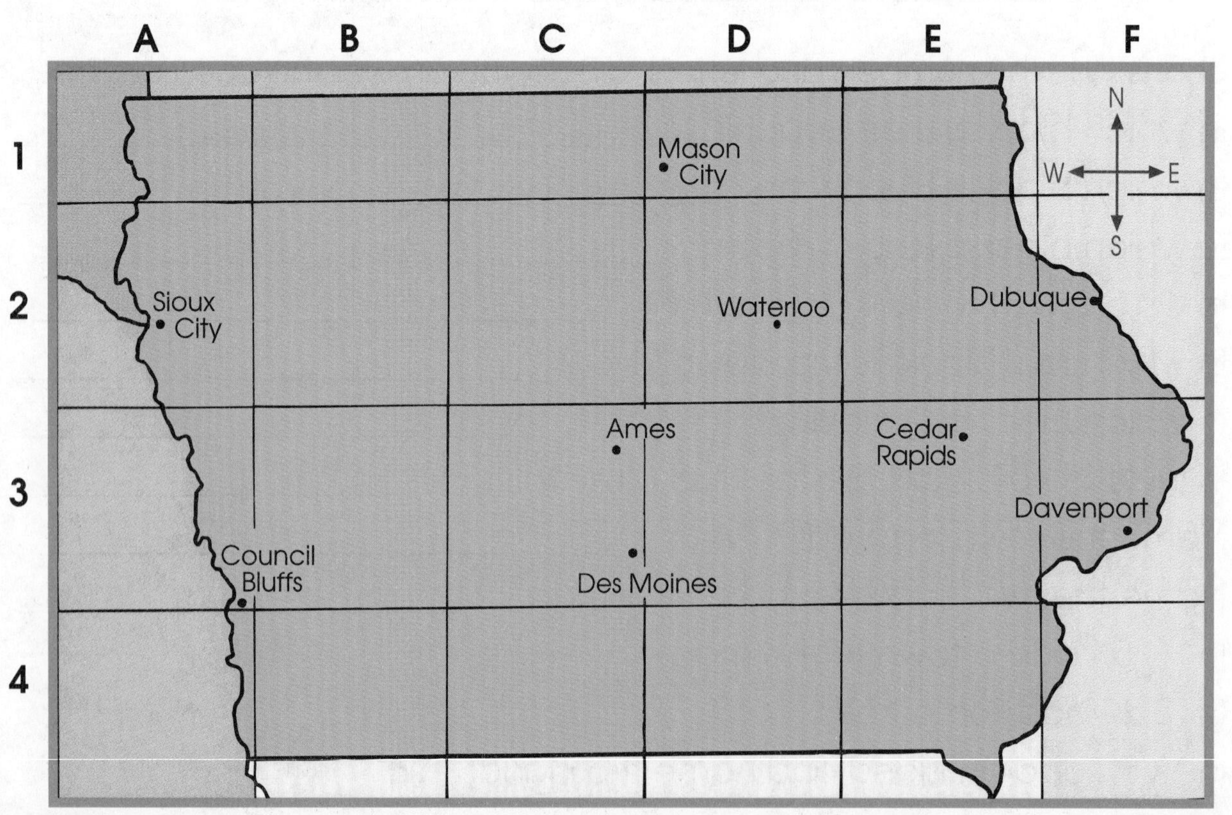

Name_______________________________

Getting to Pirates' Island

You are a pirate captain on your way home to Pirates' Island.

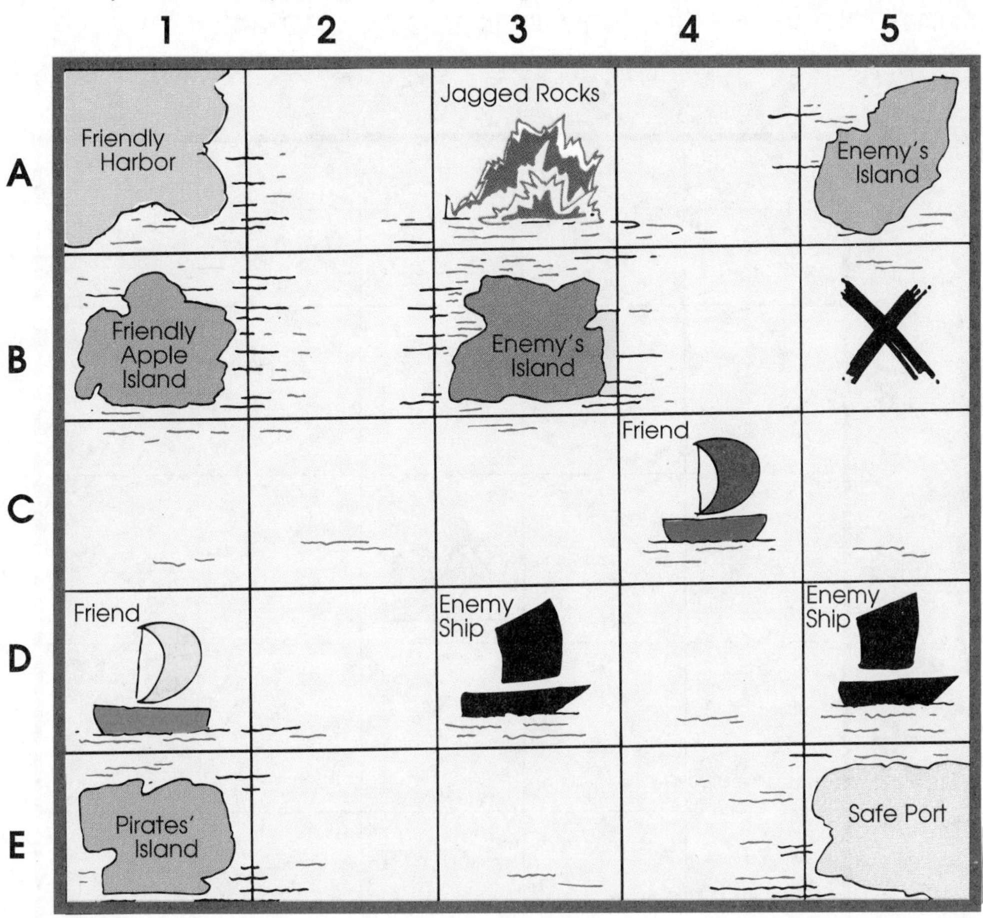

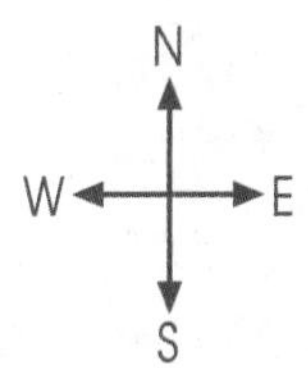

Your Ship

Directions: Draw a picture of your ship in the box and cut it out. Place the ship on the large **X**.

1. In which space is your ship located? _______________
2. If you move your ship west two spaces, will you be safe? _______________
3. Name another space where your ship will not be safe. _______________
4. Move your ship from "B 5" to "B 2." Are you in a safe place? _______________
5. Move your ship south three spaces from "B 2." What is your location?

   ____

6. If you move your ship from "E 2" to "E 1," where will you be? _______________
7. Give the location for both enemy ships. _______________
8. Can you safely move two spaces east of Friendly Apple Island? _______________

Name____________________________________

Creating Your Own Grid Map

Create your own symbols for each object listed in the legend below. Then, follow the directions below. The first one is already done for you.

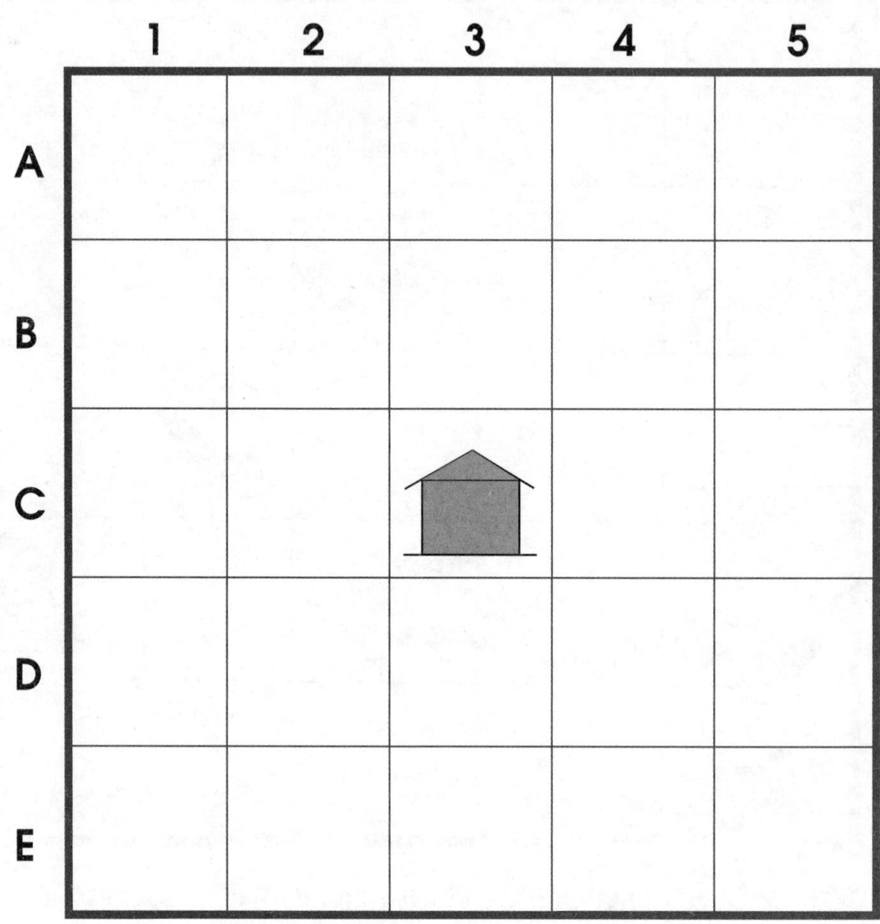

Legend

house	tree	flower
pond	bird	swing set

1. Draw a house in "C 3."
2. Draw a pond in "D 5" and "E 5."
3. Draw two birds in "A 2."
4. Draw one bird in "A 4."
5. Draw a tree in "C 1" and "B 1."
6. Draw a swing set in "E 3" and "E 4."
7. Draw two flowers in "D 2."
8. Draw a tree in "B 5" and "C 5."

Name____

Jumbo Gym

A new gym has been built in your city. Use the coordinates to name the location of the fitness features. The first one has been done for you.

Gym Grid Map

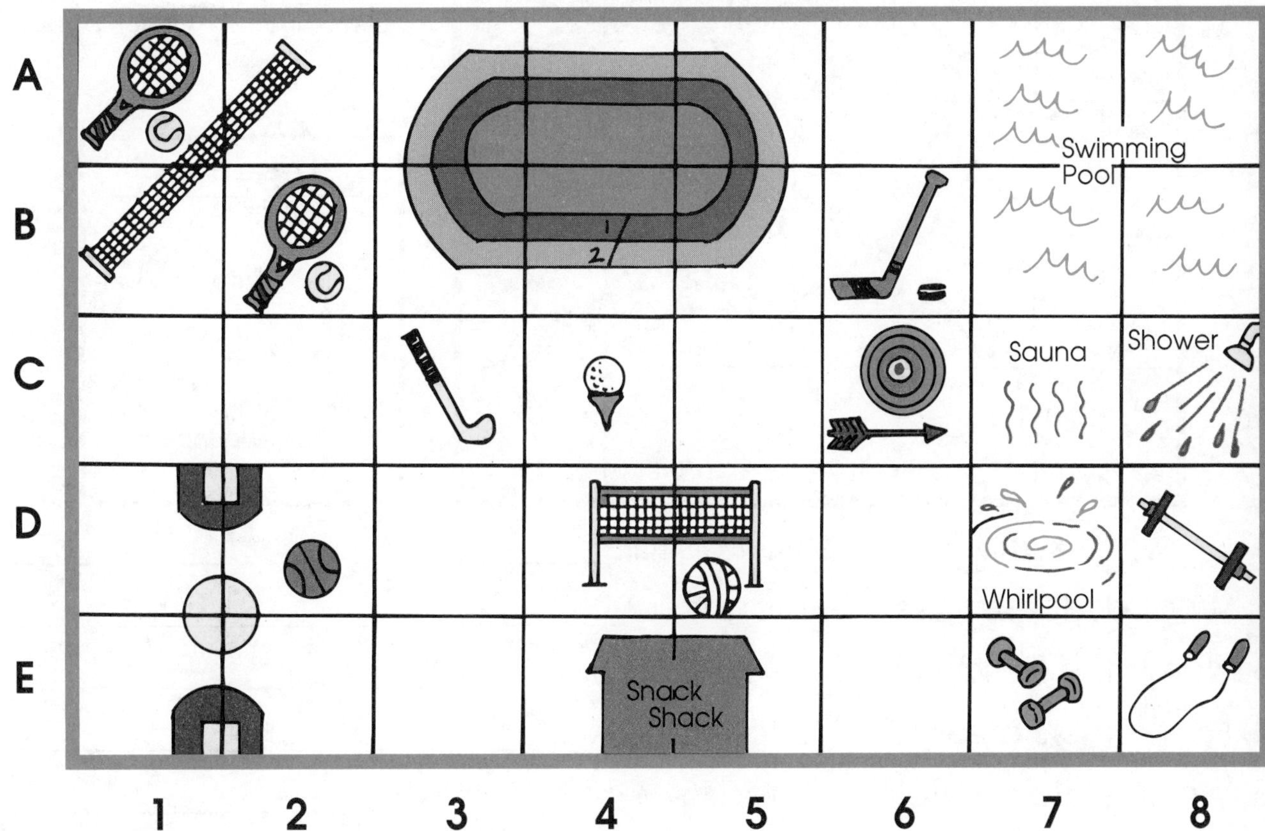

1. Archery ___C6___
2. Whirlpool________
3. Swimming pool________, ________, ________, ________
4. Golf driving range ________, ________
5. Floor hockey________
6. Small weights room ________
7. Basketball court ________, ________, ________, ________
8. Track ________, ________, ________, ________, ________, ________
9. Snack Shack ________, ________
10. Volleyball court ________, ________
11. Weightlifting ________
12. Shower ________
13. Sauna________
14. Rope jumping ________
15. Tennis courts ________, ________, ________, ________

Name____________________________________

Grid Maps

The Southern States

Directions: Use the grid to help you locate places of the southern United States on this map.

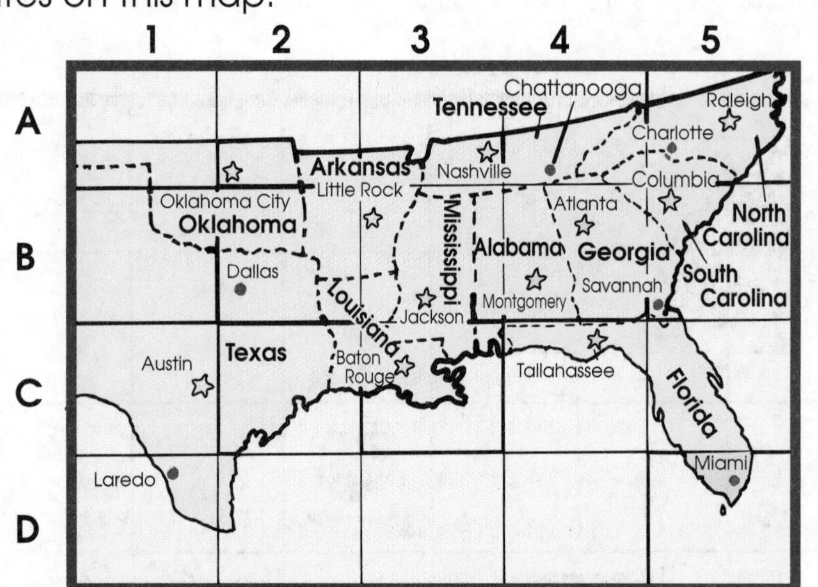

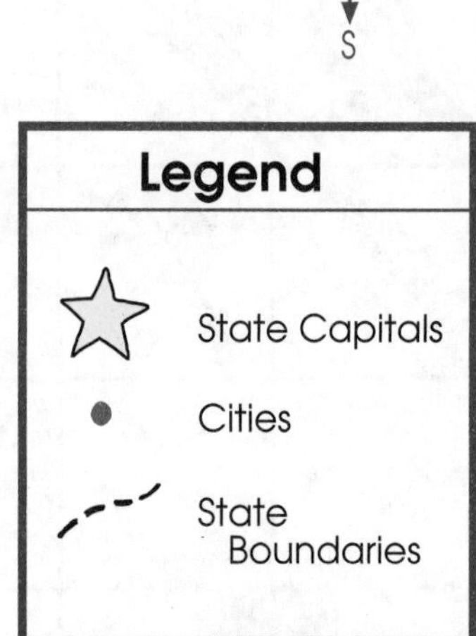

1. Draw the symbol for a state capital. ____________________
2. What do these lines - - - - stand for?____________________
3. Name the Florida city located in "D 5." ____________________
4. Name the state capital located in "A 3." ____________________
5. Which state capital is located in "A 5"?____________________
6. What is the location of Atlanta, Georgia?____________________
7. Name the state capital located in "C 3." ____________________
8. Give the location of Jackson, Mississippi. ____________________
9. What state capital is located in "A 2"?____________________
10. Give the location of Austin, Texas. ____________________
11. Name the cities located in "B 4." ____________________
12. Name the state located in "A 4" and "A 5."____________________
13. Name the Tennessee city found in "A 4."____________________
14. Name the two North Carolina cities located in "A 5." ____________________

Name____________________

We're Going Places

Directions: Draw an outline map of your state on the grid below. Label places or cities that are familiar to you. List them at the bottom of the page using the number and letter coordinates.

	A	B	C	D
1				
2				
3				
4				
5				

City or Place	Location	City or Place	Location
____________	______	____________	______
____________	______	____________	______
____________	______	____________	______
____________	______	____________	______
____________	______	____________	______

Name___________________________________

Grid Maps

Picture This!

Directions: Make a dot at each coordinate on the graph. Draw lines to connect the dots in order to make a picture. Add details and color the fuzzy fellow you drew on the graph.

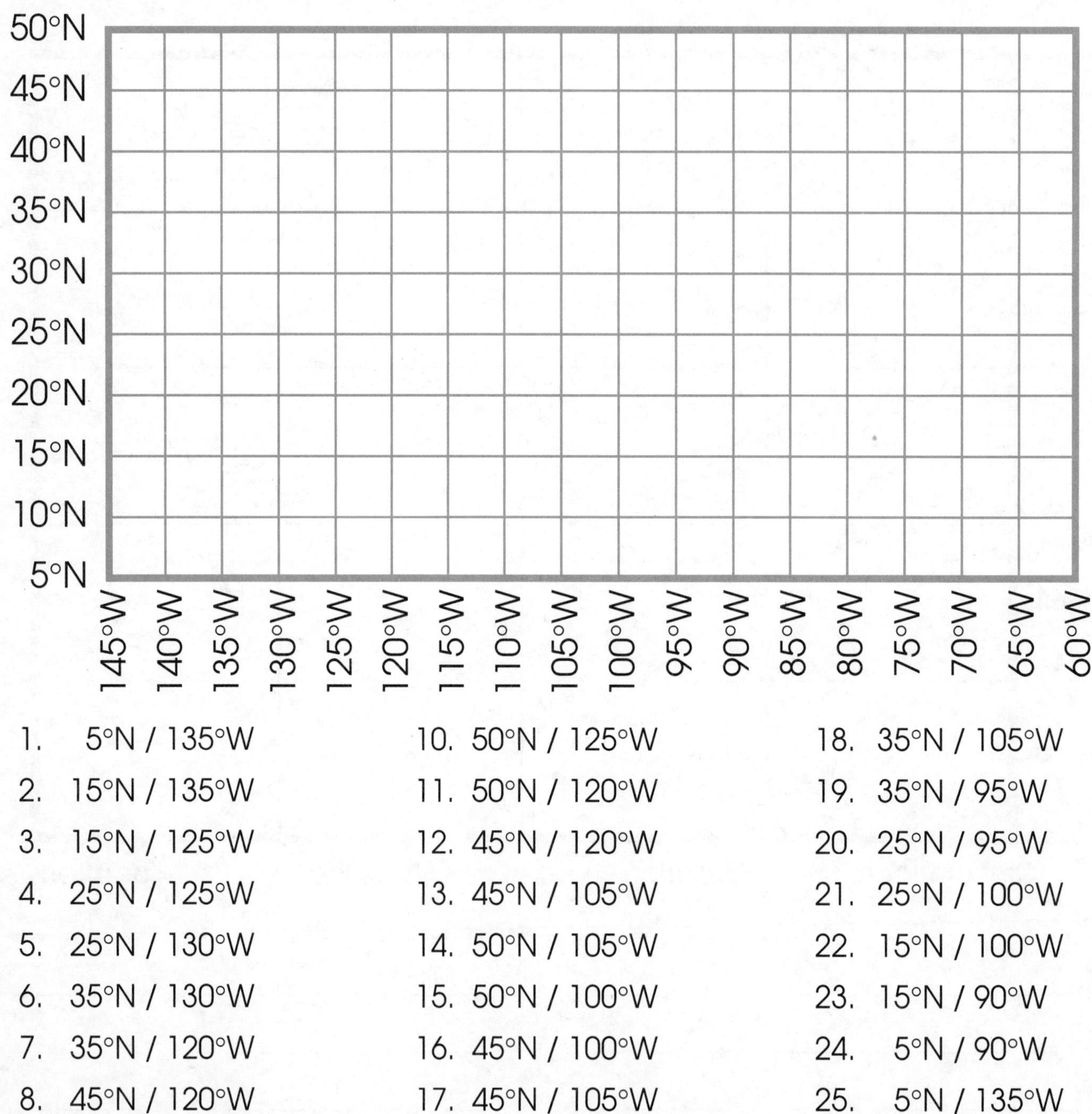

1. 5°N / 135°W
2. 15°N / 135°W
3. 15°N / 125°W
4. 25°N / 125°W
5. 25°N / 130°W
6. 35°N / 130°W
7. 35°N / 120°W
8. 45°N / 120°W
9. 45°N / 125°W
10. 50°N / 125°W
11. 50°N / 120°W
12. 45°N / 120°W
13. 45°N / 105°W
14. 50°N / 105°W
15. 50°N / 100°W
16. 45°N / 100°W
17. 45°N / 105°W
18. 35°N / 105°W
19. 35°N / 95°W
20. 25°N / 95°W
21. 25°N / 100°W
22. 15°N / 100°W
23. 15°N / 90°W
24. 5°N / 90°W
25. 5°N / 135°W

Section 6

Global Geography

Name____

The Globe

Imagine you are flying around in space. You look down and see a big round ball. It is the earth.

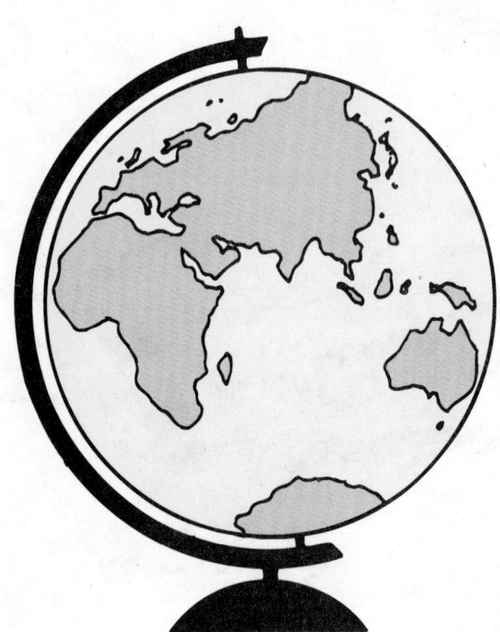

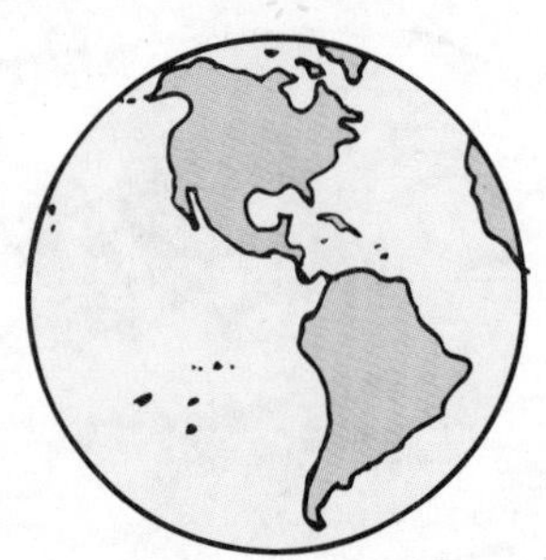

A model of the earth is called a globe. It is a round map that shows land and water. It uses colors to show which is the land and which is the water.

Directions: Unscramble the letters below to find out the colors that are used on the globe.

Land is ____________________. e r g e n

Water is____________________. l u b e

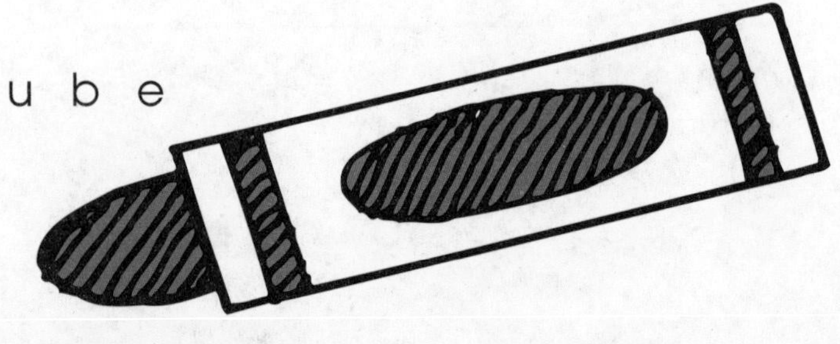

Color the land on the globe green.

Color the water on the globe blue.

Name____________________

It's a Round World

Use these maps with pages 254 and 255.

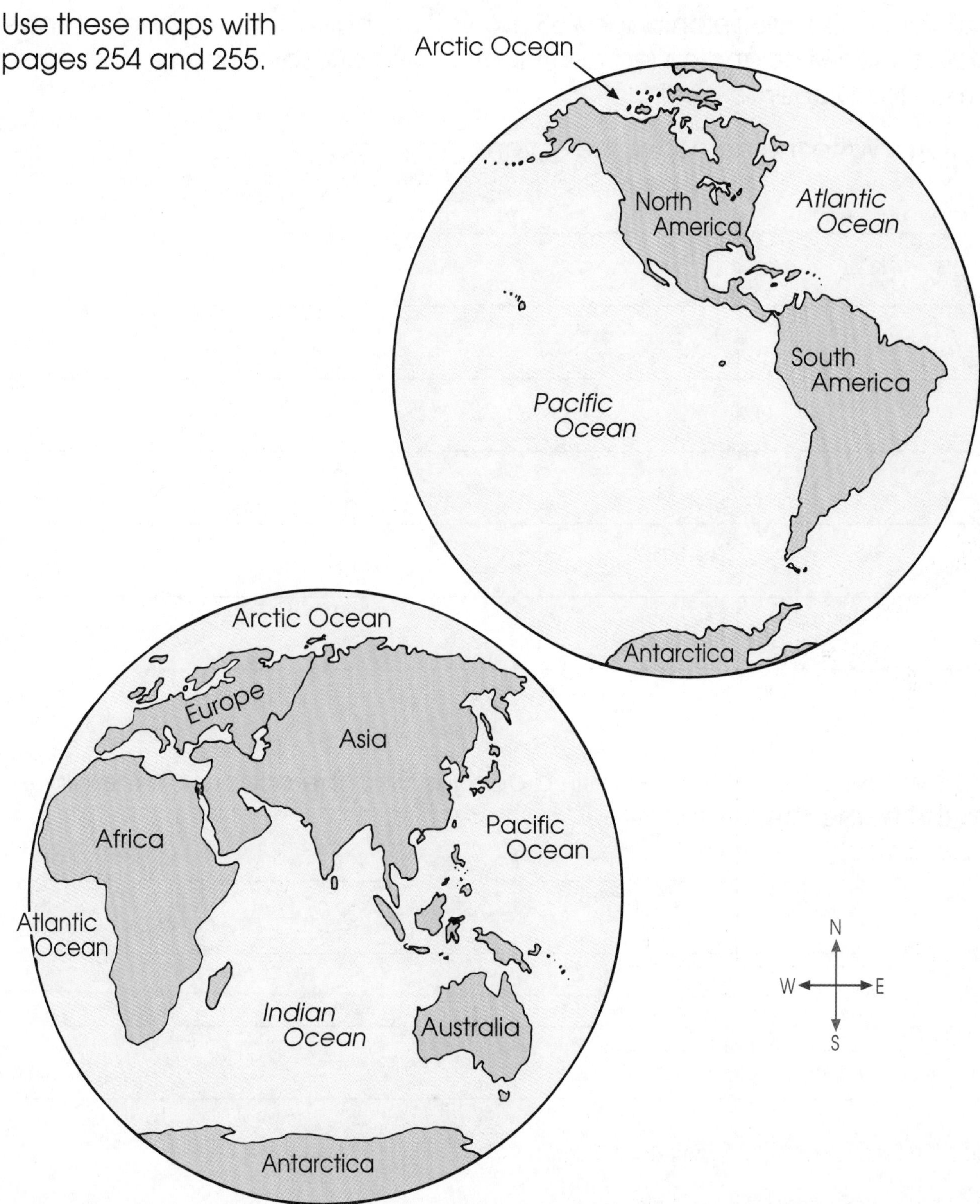

Name______________________________

It's a Round World

The picture of the globe on page 253 shows both halves of the world. It shows the large pieces of land called continents. There are seven continents. Find them on the globe.

Directions: Write the names of the seven continents.

1. ______________________________

2. ______________________________

3. ______________________________

4. ______________________________

5. ______________________________

6. ______________________________

7. ______________________________

There are four bodies of water called oceans. Find the oceans on the globe. Write the names below.

1. ______________________________

2. ______________________________

3. ______________________________

4. ______________________________

Name______________________________

A Global Guide

Use the globe on page 253. Read the clues below. Write the answers on the lines. Then, use the numbered letters to solve the riddle at the bottom of the page.

1. This direction points up. ____ ____ ____ ____ ____
   1 2 22 3

2. This direction points down. ____ ____ ____ ____ ____
   4 5 6

3. This direction points right. ____ ____ ____ ____
   7 8

4. This direction points left. ____ ____ ____ ____
   9 10

5. This ocean is west of North America. ____ ____ ____ ____ ____ ____ ____
   11 12
   ____ ____ ____ ____ ____
   13 14

6. This ocean is south of Asia.

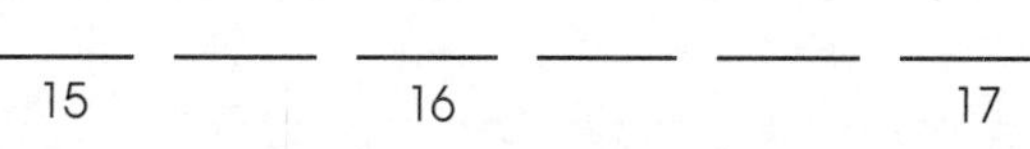

____ ____ ____ ____ ____

7. This ocean is east of South America.

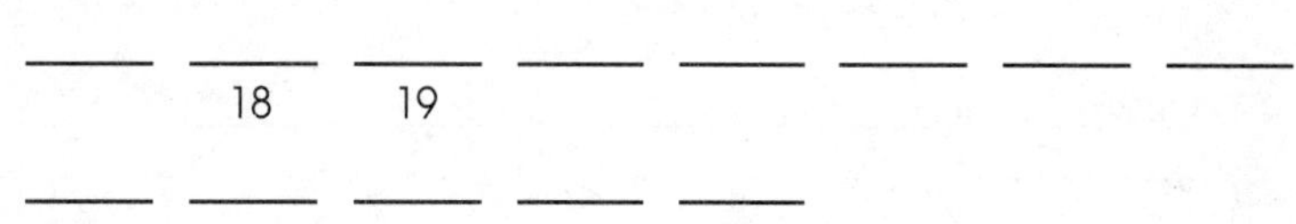

Riddle: What does a globe do?

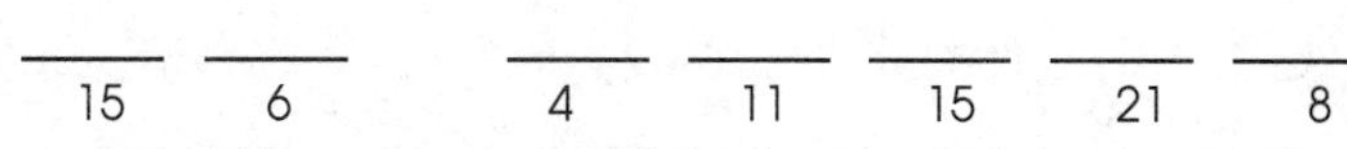

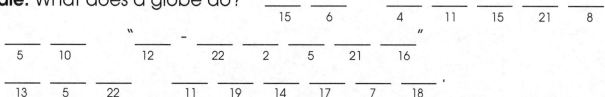

____ ____ "____ - ____ ____ ____ ____ ____"
5 10 12 22 2 5 21 16

____ ____ ____ ____ ____ ____ ____ ____ ____.
13 5 22 11 19 14 17 7 18

Name____

Land and Water

Directions: Use the map below plus a wall map to do this activity.

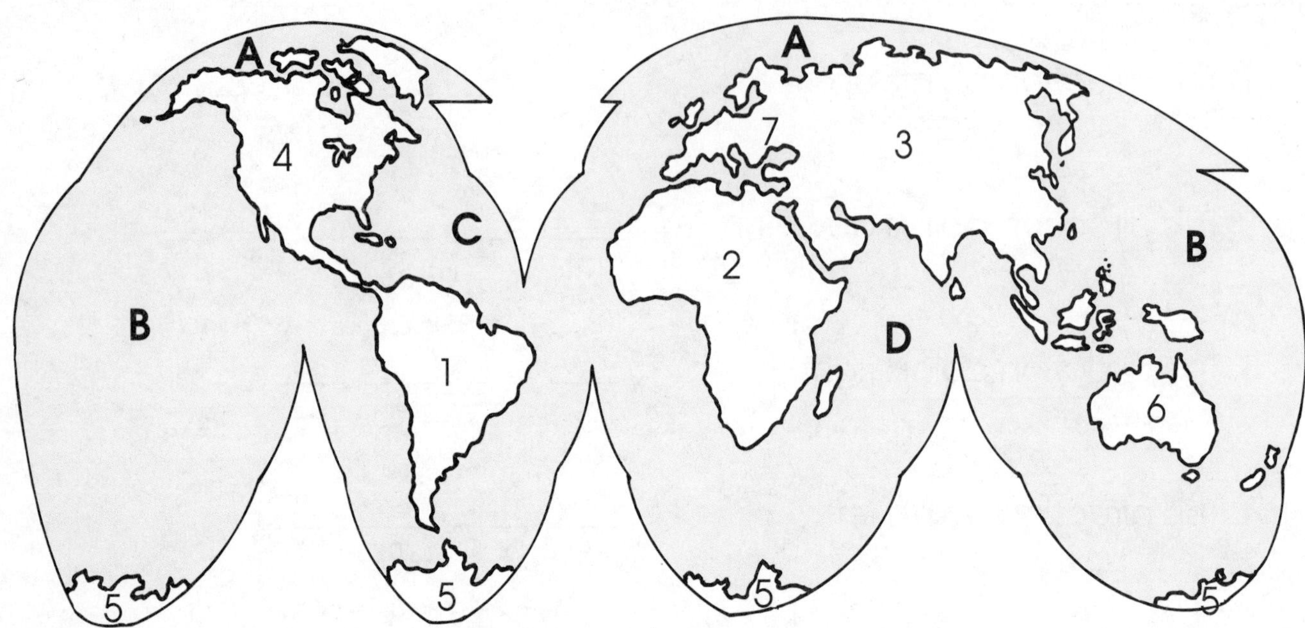

Write the name of each continent in the correct blank.

1. ______________________ 5. ______________________
2. ______________________ 6. ______________________
3. ______________________ 7. ______________________
4. ______________________

Write the name of each ocean in the correct blank.

A. ______________________ C. ______________________

B. ______________________ D. ______________________

Use crayons or markers to follow these directions.

1. Color Australia green.
2. Color Europe yellow.
3. Color Africa orange.
4. Color Antarctica blue.
5. Color North America red.
6. Color South America brown.
7. Color Asia purple.

Name ____________________

Color My World

Is it a city, state, country, continent or body of water? Color each box according to the Color Key. Use an atlas for help.

Color Key

city—orange state—green country—yellow
water—blue continent—purple

Atlantic Ocean	India	Colorado	Miami
Peru	Antarctica	Lake Michigan	Hawaii
New Orleans	Spain	Europe	Gulf of Mexico
Vermont	Phoenix	Japan	Paris
East China Sea	Egypt	Wyoming	Sweden
Africa	London	Hudson Bay	Connecticut
Greece	Minnesota	South America	Dallas
Oakland	Great Salt Lake	Argentina	Arctic Ocean
North America	Canada	Chicago	Arkansas
Lake Victoria	Iowa	Asia	Venezuela
Lima	Persian Gulf	Mexico	Moscow
Pacific Ocean	Maryland	Cincinnati	Brazil

Name____

Where in the World Is. . .

What is your global address? It's more than your street, city, state and ZIP code.

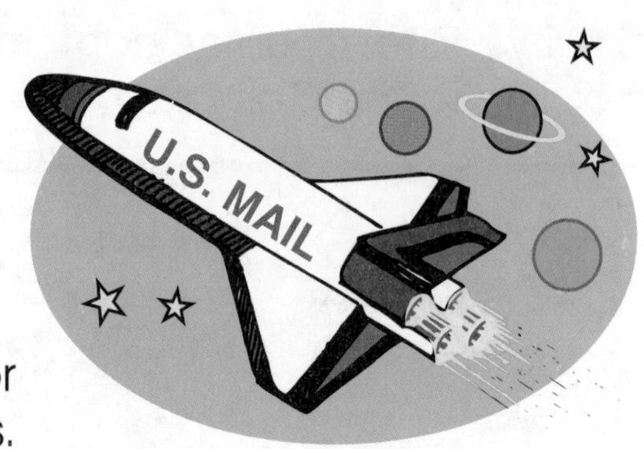

What would your address be if you wanted to get a letter from a friend living in outer space?

Use an atlas, encyclopedia, science book or other source to complete your global address.

Inter-Galactic Address Book

Name ______________________________

Street ______________________________

County or Parish ________________________

State or Province ________________________

Country ______________________________

Continent _____________________________

Hemisphere ____________________________

Planet ______________________________

Galaxy ______________________________

Draw an **X** to mark the approximate place where you live.

Name________________________________

Where in the World?

Refer to the globe on page 253, a real globe or a world map. Find the seven continents and four oceans. Now, you are ready to make your own globe using this page and pages 261 and 263.

Directions:

1. Cut out all the continent and ocean labels.
2. Glue them where they belong in the boxes on the maps on pages 261 and 263.
3. Cut out all of the map circles along the outer lines.
4. Fold each circle in half along the dotted line. Keep the map side on the inside.

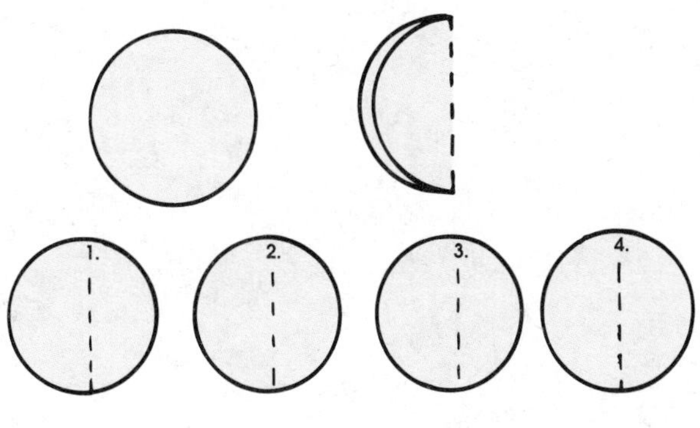

5. Be sure to keep the numbers on the circles at the top. Glue the back of the right half of circle **1** to the back of the left half of circle **2**.
6. Glue the back of the right half of circle **2** to the back of the left half of circle **3**.
7. Glue the back of the right half of circle **3** to the back of the left half of circle **4**.
8. Complete the globe by gluing the back of the right half of circle **4** to the back of the left half of circle **1**.

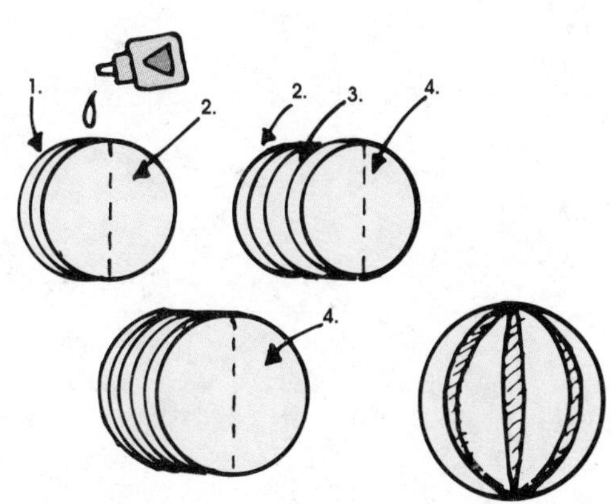

This page has been intentionally left blank.

Name_______________________________________

Where in the World?

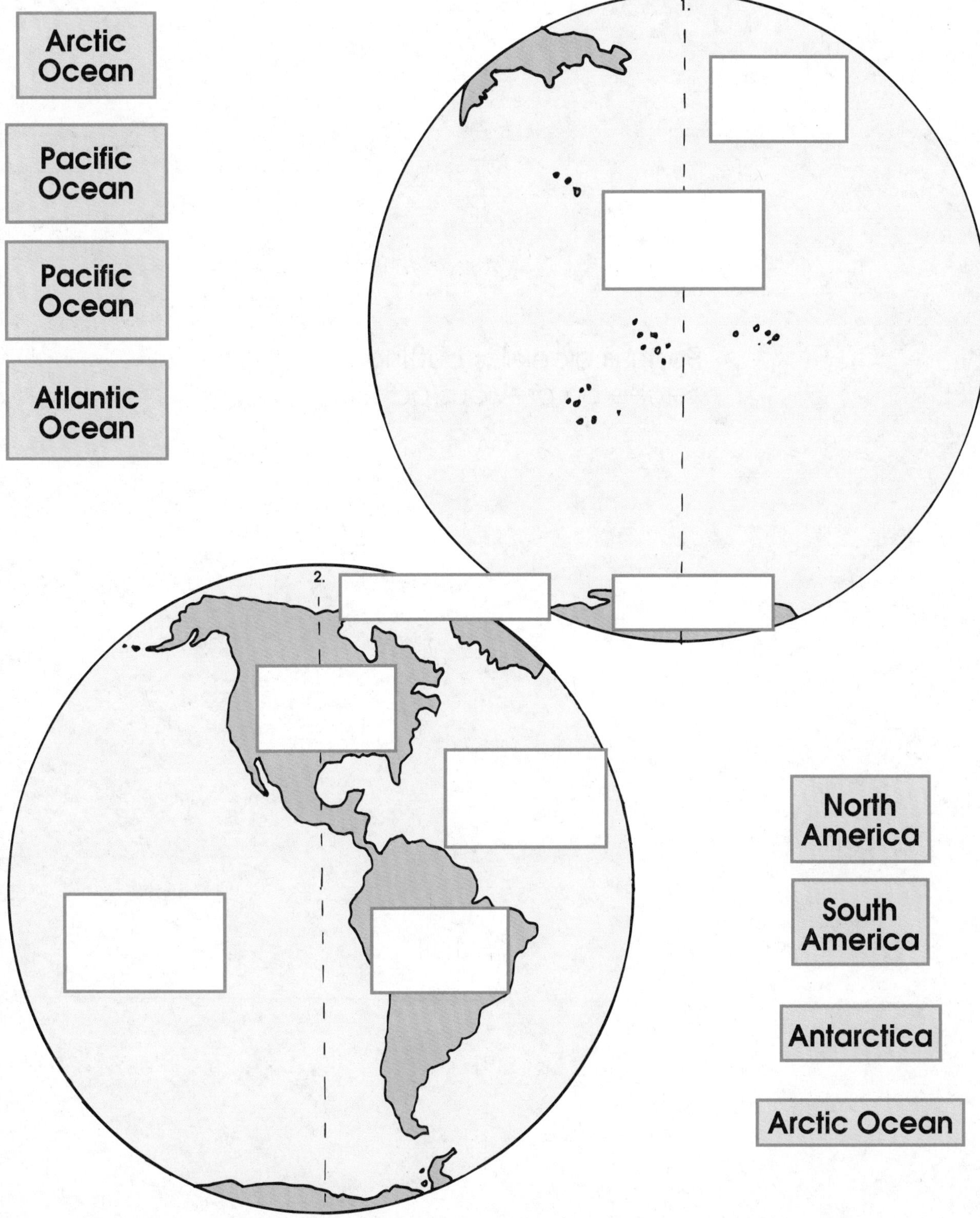

Page is blank for cutting exercise on previous page.

Name____

Where in the World

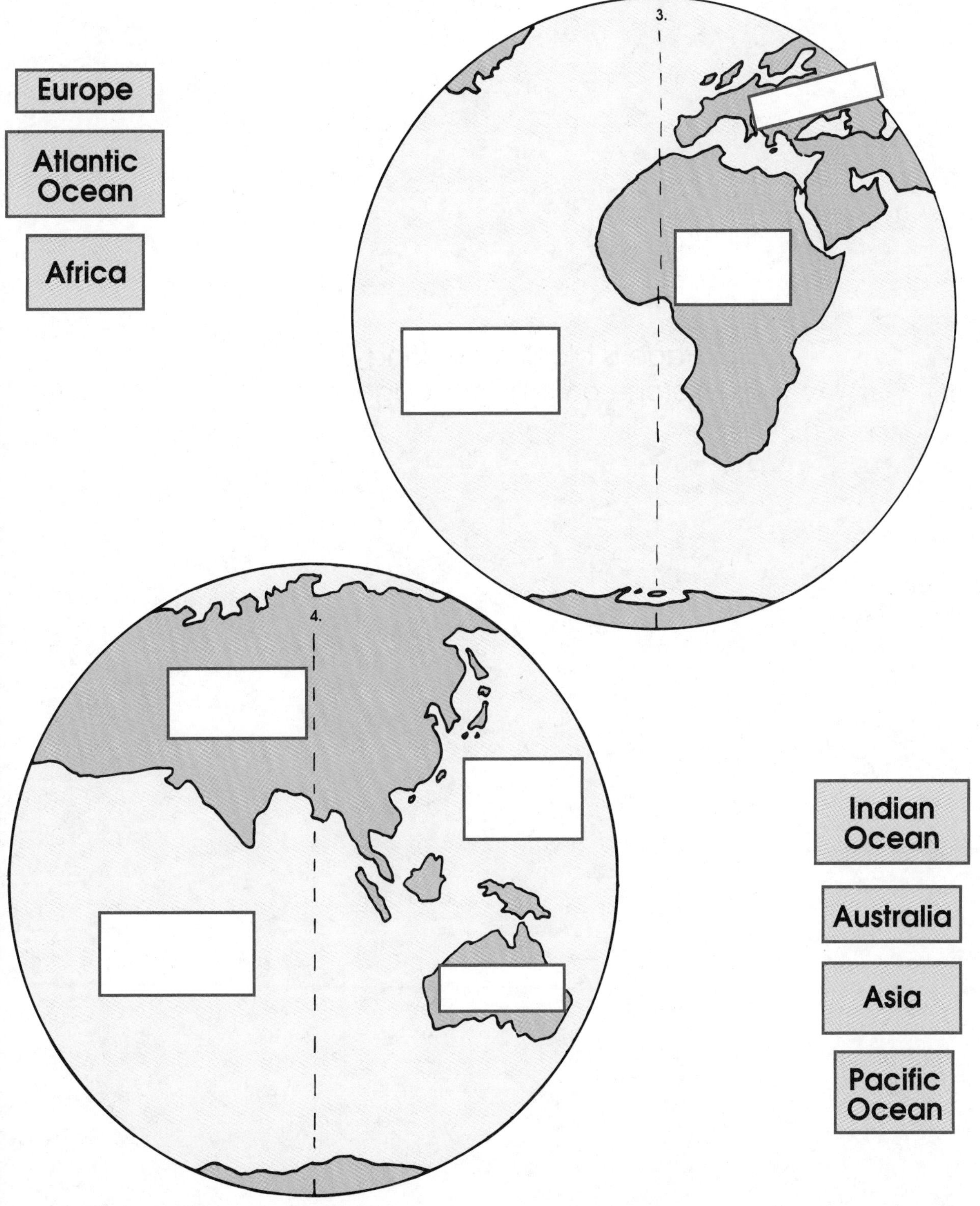

Page is blank for cutting
exercise on previous page.

Name________________________________

Near and Far

Below is a map of the world. It shows the seven continents. Around the map are pictures of animals that are native to the continents. The continent on which each animal can be found is written below the name of the animal.

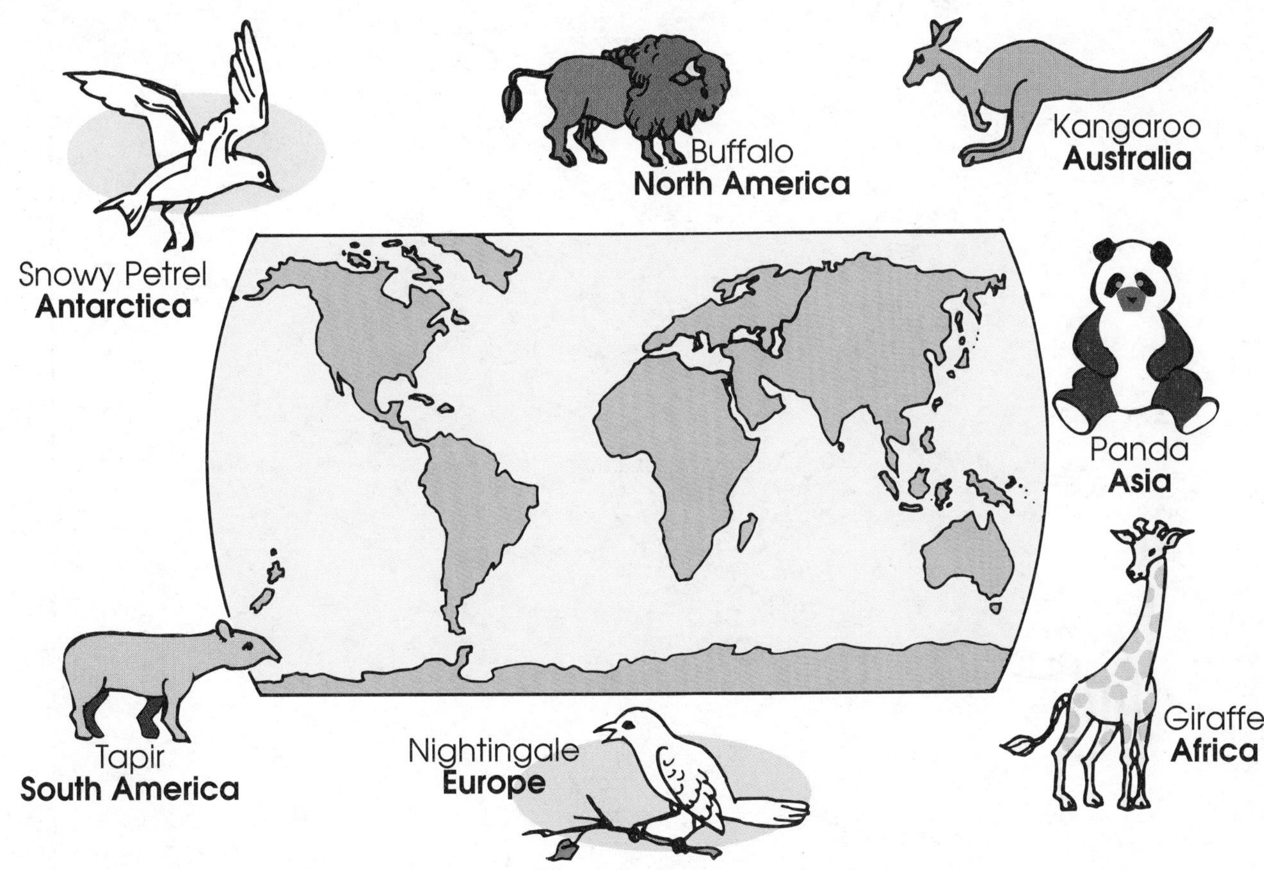

Directions: Use a globe or world map to locate each continent. Draw a line from the picture of the animal to the continent where it is found.

1. Find the continent where you live. Color it green.

2. Which animal lives on your continent? ______________________

3. Which animal lives on a continent far from you? ________________

Name____

Let's Travel the Earth

Use with page 267.

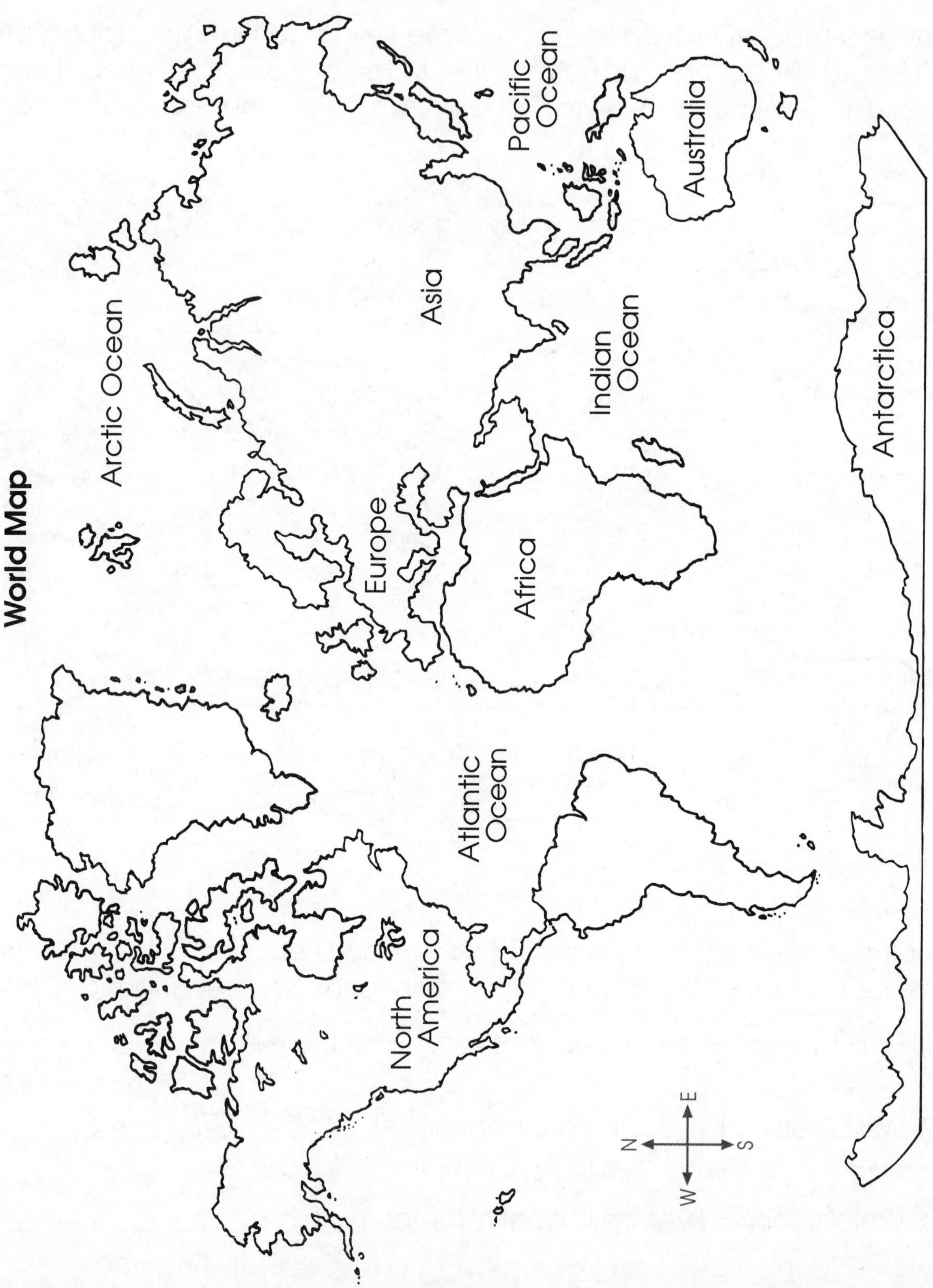

Name____

Let's Travel the Earth

Directions: Use the map on page 266 to answer the questions below.

Circle the word that correctly completes each statement.

1. If you sail from North America to Antarctica, you will be on the . . .
   Arctic Ocean   Atlantic Ocean   Indian Ocean
2. If you fly from Africa to Australia, you will fly over the . . .
   Indian Ocean   Pacific Ocean   Atlantic Ocean
3. To sail from Europe to South America, you will sail on the . . .
   Pacific Ocean   Arctic Ocean   Atlantic Ocean
4. To sail from North America to Europe, you will sail on the . . .
   Indian Ocean   Atlantic Ocean   Pacific Ocean
5. To travel from Europe to Asia, you must cross . . .
   the Pacific Ocean   the Indian Ocean   land

Fill in the blanks with the correct word.

1. The continent north of South America is ____________________.
2. The ocean directly south of Asia is the ____________________.
3. The ocean directly north of Asia is the ____________________.
4. The continent directly south of Europe is ____________________.
5. The continent directly south of Australia is ____________________.

Use a crayon or marker to follow these directions.

1. Draw a red line from North America to Africa.
2. Draw a green line from Asia to Antarctica.
3. Draw an orange line from Australia to Africa.
4. Draw a black line from Europe to South America.
5. Circle the names of all four oceans with blue.
6. Color North America green.
7. Draw a black dotted line (- - - - - -) around South America.

Name____

Hemispheres

The earth is a sphere. When the earth is cut in half horizontally along an imaginary line called the **equator**, the **Northern** and **Southern Hemispheres** of the earth are created.

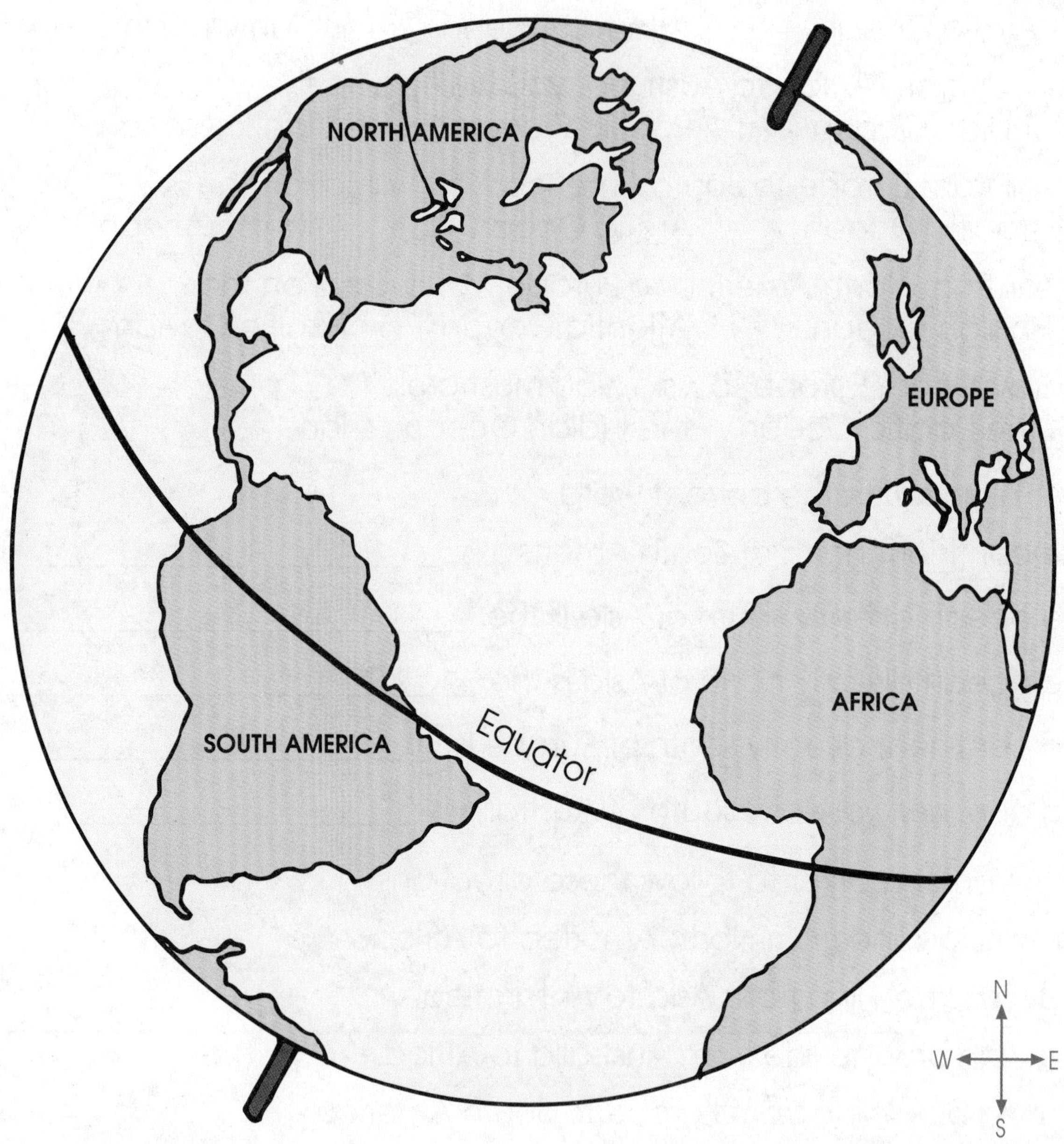

Trace the equator in orange.

Label the two hemispheres on the globe above.

Name ____________________

Hemispheres

When the earth is cut in half vertically along an imaginary line called the **prime meridian**, the **Eastern** and **Western Hemispheres** of the earth are created.

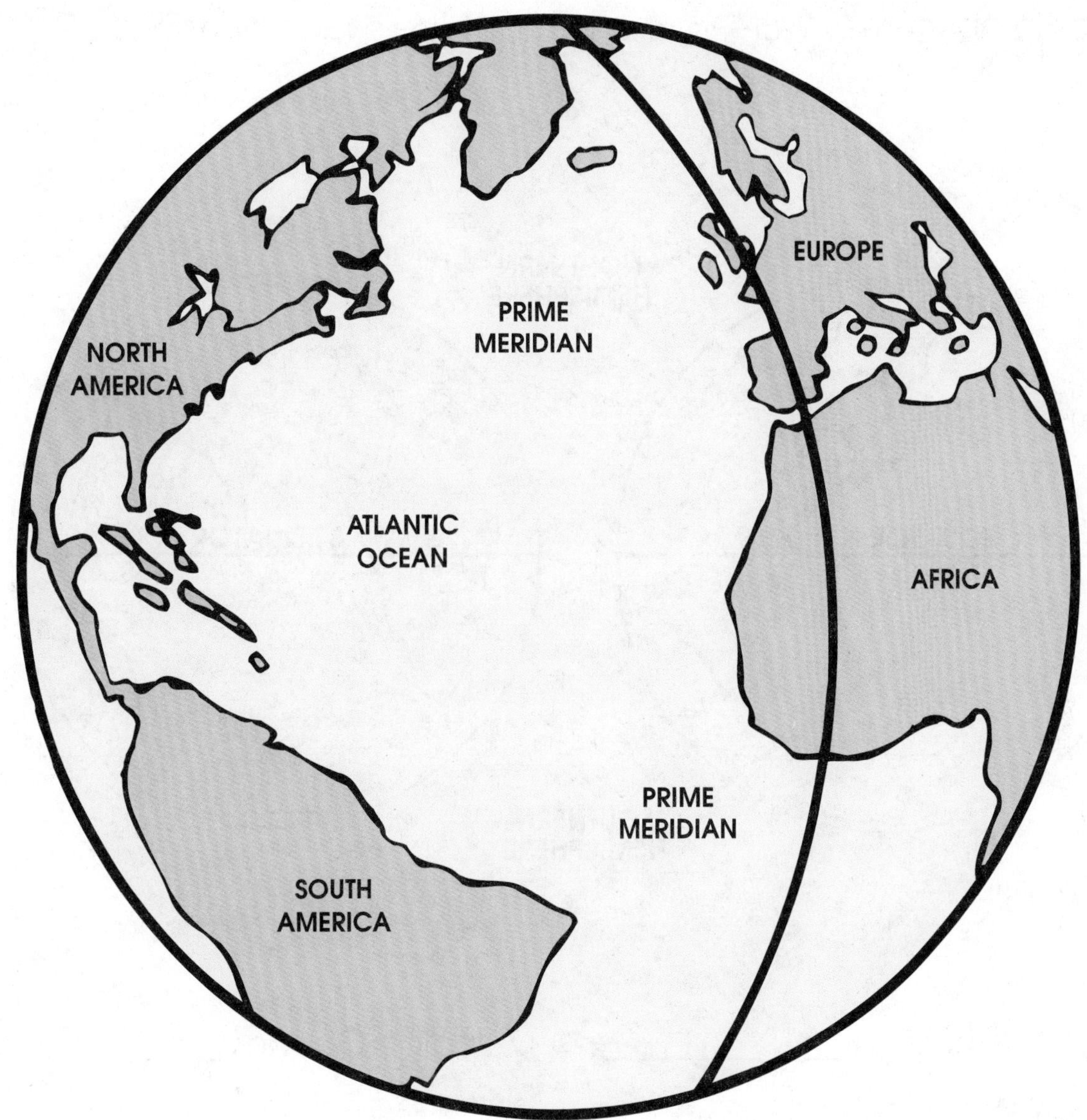

Trace the prime meridian in blue.

Label the two hemispheres on the globe above.

Color the axis, or poles, red.

Name________________________________

Hemispheres

Directions: Examine the illustration below. Decide in which two hemispheres (Eastern or Western and Northern or Southern) each of the following continents or oceans is located. (Example: The United States is in the Northern and Western Hemispheres.) Write your answers in the space provided.

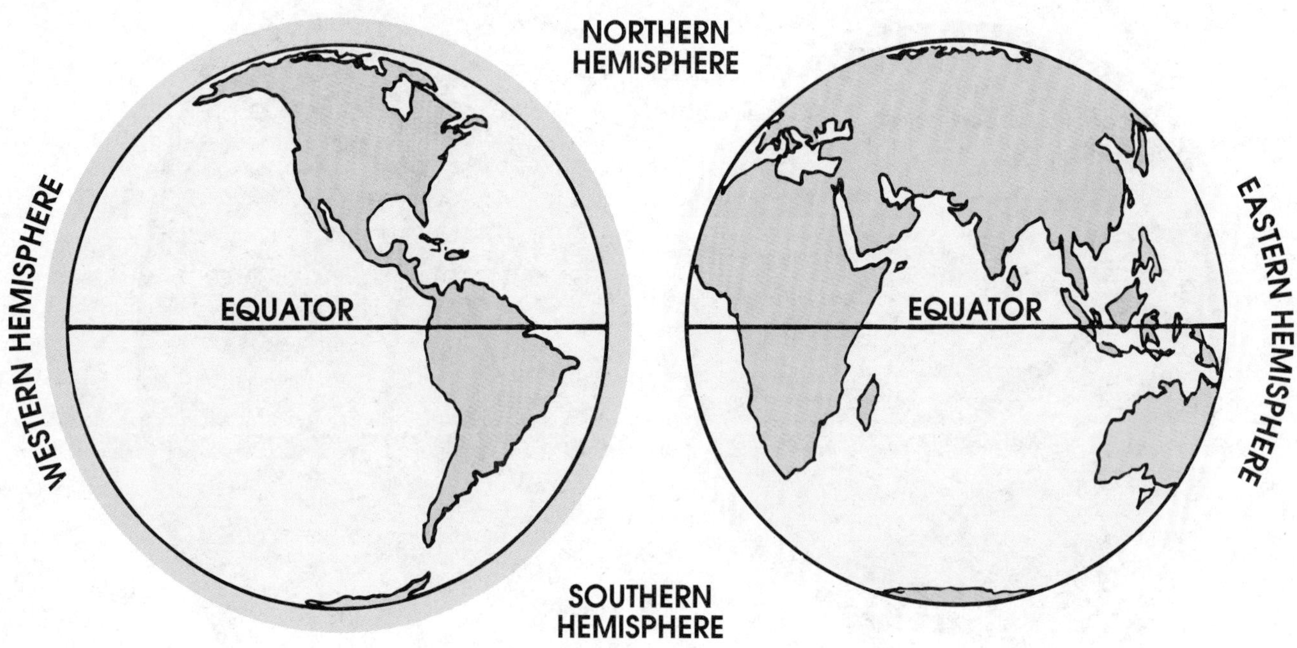

1. North America ______________
2. Europe ______________
3. South America ______________
4. Pacific Ocean ______________
5. Australia ______________
6. Atlantic Ocean ______________
7. Indian Ocean ______________
8. Asia ______________
9. Africa ______________
10. Antarctica ______________
11. Arctic Ocean ______________

Name ______________________________

Locating the Continents and Oceans

Directions: Use these maps plus wall maps to complete this page. **Note**: Some continents belong to more than one hemisphere.

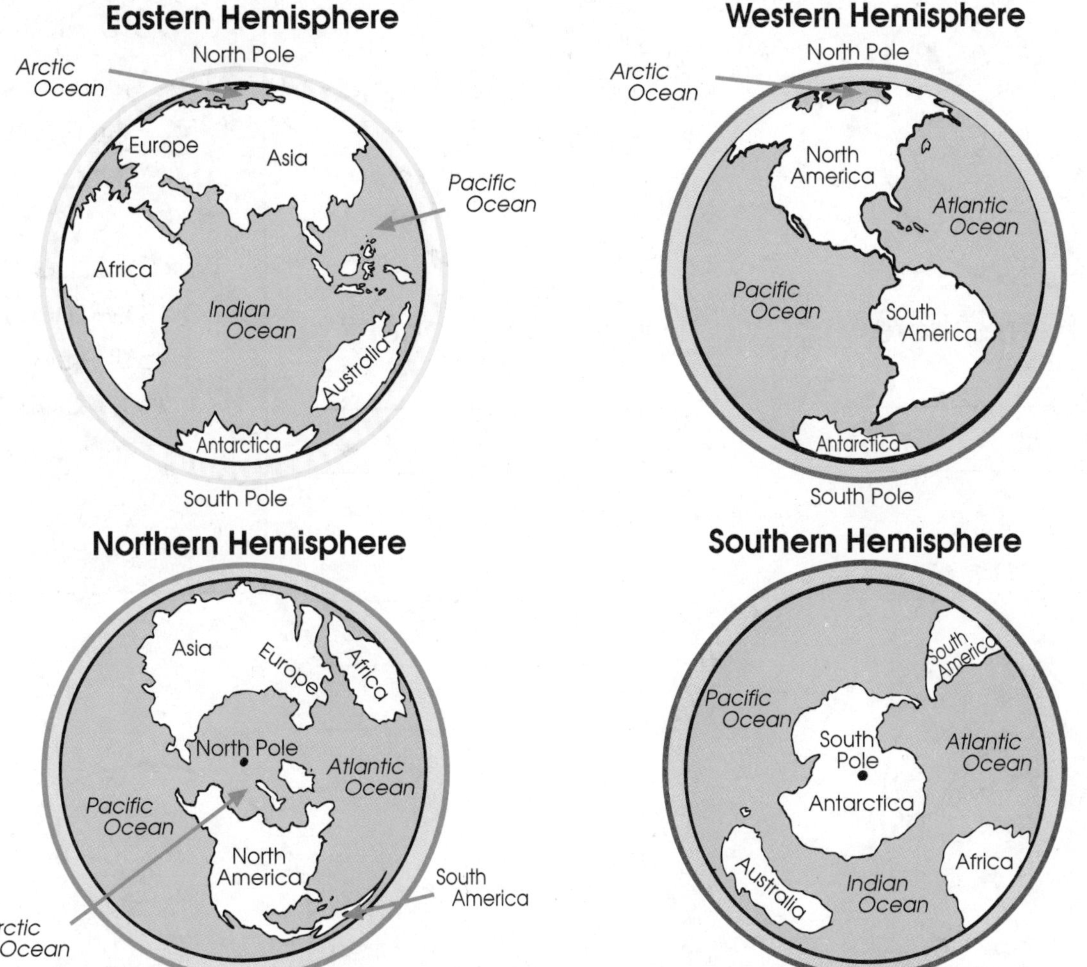

1. Which continent is found in both the Eastern and Western Hemispheres?

____

2. Which map does not show any part of Antarctica?

____

3. Which hemisphere does not include any part of Africa?

____

4. Color the continent located entirely in the Western and Northern Hemispheres red.
5. Color the continent located entirely in the Eastern and Southern Hemispheres green.

Name ______________________________

Happy Hemispheres

Write the name of each continent and ocean next to its number.

Western Hemisphere

1. ______________________
2. ______________________
3. ______________________
4. ______________________

Eastern Hemisphere

1. ______________________
2. ______________________
3. ______________________
4. ______________________
5. ______________________
6. ______________________

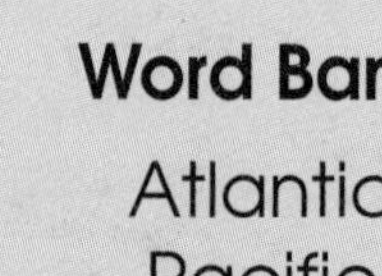

Word Bank

Atlantic
Pacific
Indian
Arctic
North America
South America
Europe
Australia
Asia
Africa
Antarctica

Northern Hemisphere

1. ______________________
2. ______________________
3. ______________________
4. ______________________
5. ______________________
6. ______________________

Southern Hemisphere

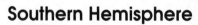

1. ______________________
2. ______________________
3. ______________________
4. ______________________
5. ______________________
6. ______________________
7. ______________________

Name______________________________

North to South

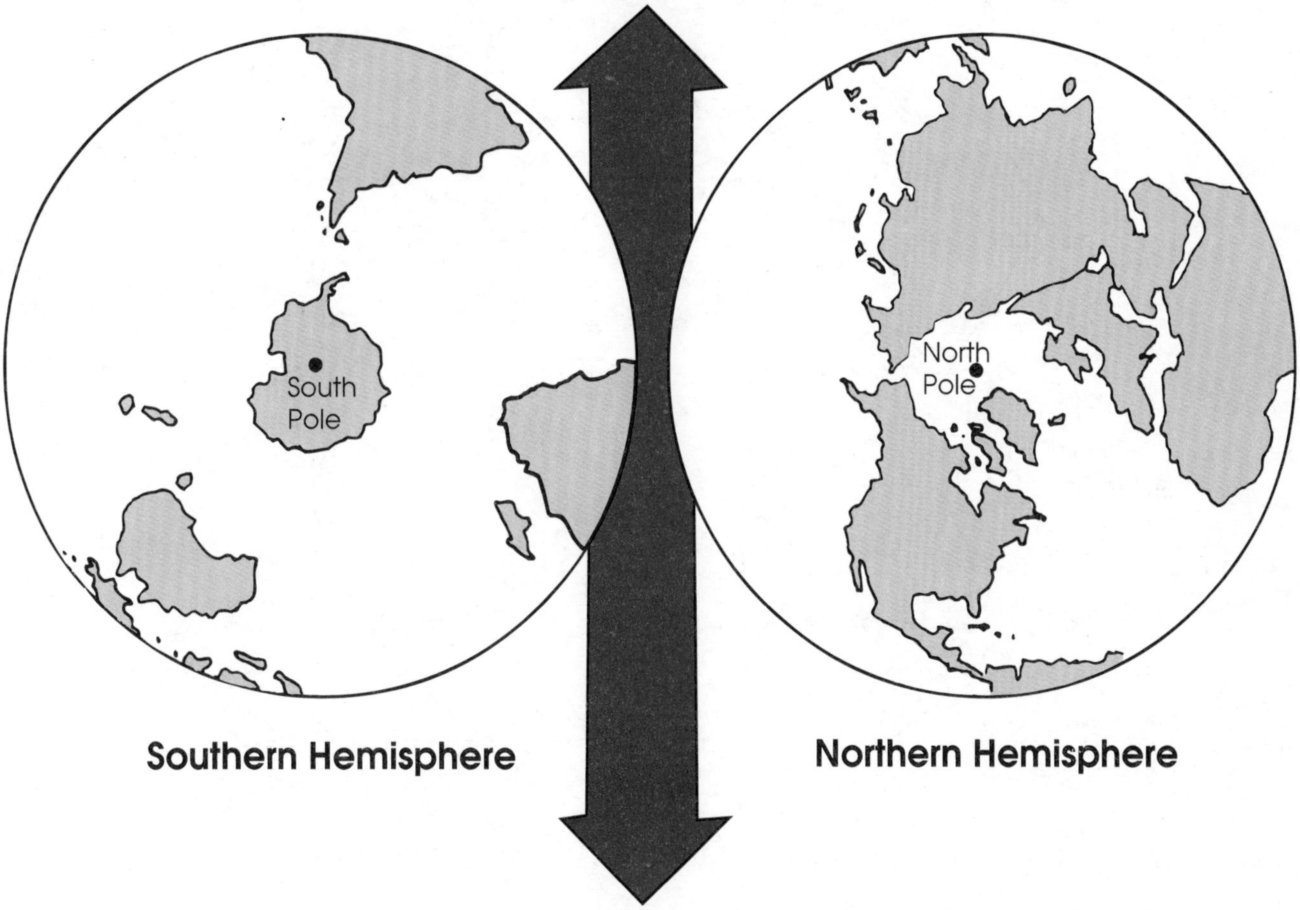

Southern Hemisphere

Northern Hemisphere

Directions: Label the continents on each hemisphere. Use the abbreviations below.

N.A.	=	North America	**Ant.**	=	Antarctica
S.A.	=	South America	**Aust.**	=	Australia
Eur.	=	Europe	**Afr.**	=	Africa
As.	=	Asia			

Color the oceans in each hemisphere using the colors and designs below.

(purple) Indian Ocean

(blue) Pacific Ocean

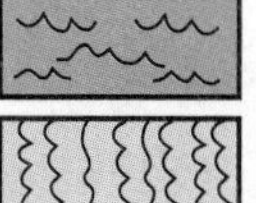

(green) Atlantic Ocean

(lt. green) Arctic Ocean

Name____

Global Fun

Directions: Complete the globe by following the directions below.

1. Draw a whale in the Southern Hemisphere of the Pacific Ocean.
2. Trace the equator in orange.
3. Draw a shark in the Arctic Ocean.
4. Draw a smiling face near Antarctica.
5. Draw an ocean liner in the Northern Hemisphere of the Atlantic Ocean.
6. Color the axis poles red.
7. In North America, color Mexico yellow, Canada green and the U.S.A. red.
8. Draw a yellow **X** in the Northern Hemisphere of Africa.
9. Color Europe purple.
10. Draw rainbow-colored diagonal stripes on South America.
11. Draw an orange circle on the Southern Hemisphere of Africa.

Name________________________________

From East to West

Directions: Label the continents using the abbreviations below. Cut out the continents. Glue them onto the correct hemisphere in the proper places. Include Antarctica on each hemisphere.

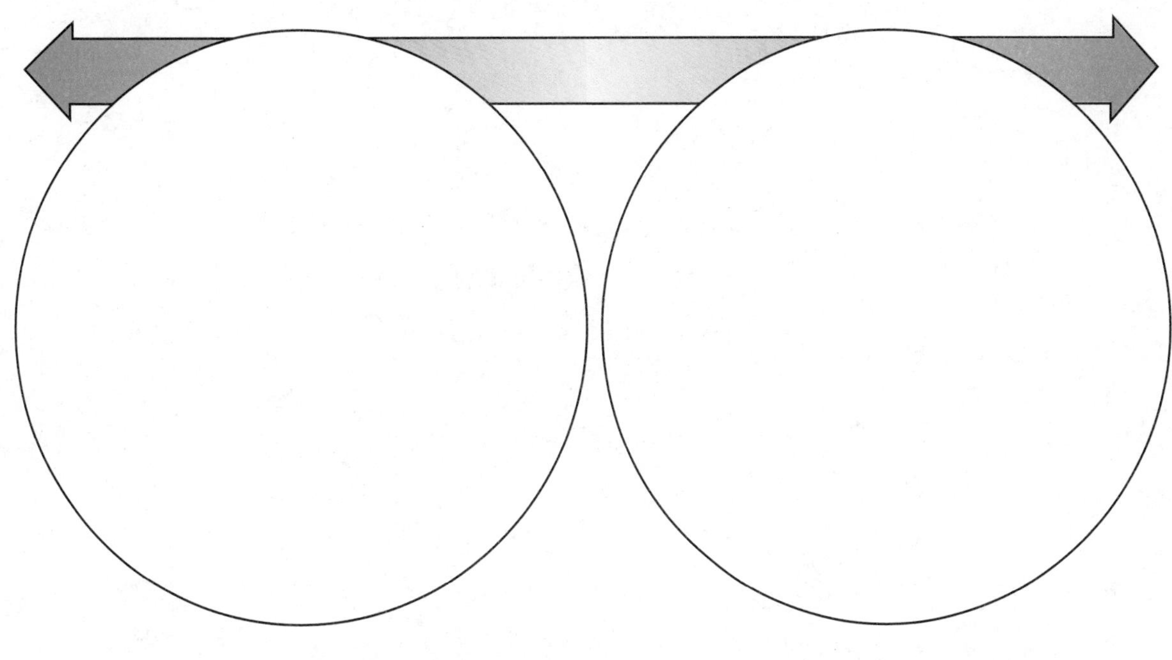

Western Hemisphere | **Eastern Hemisphere**

Abbreviations

N.A. = North America
Eur. = Europe
Aust. = Australia
S.A. = South America
As. = Asia
Afr. = Africa
Ant. = Antarctica

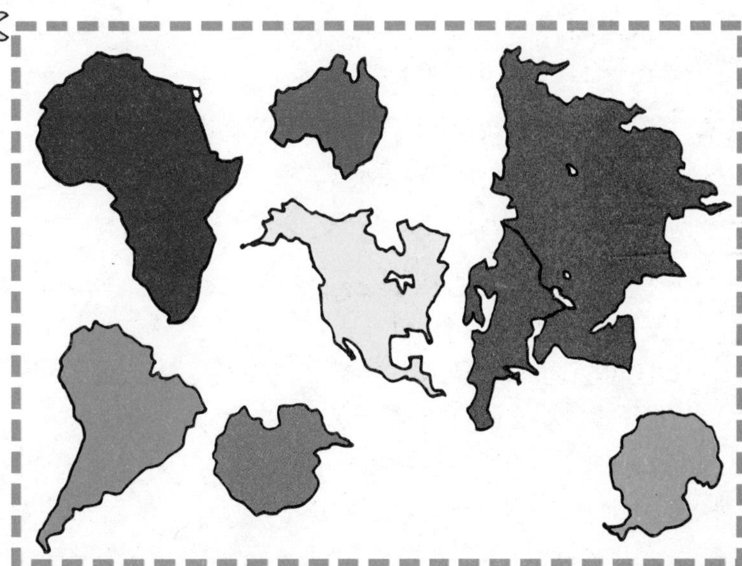

Page is blank for cutting
exercise on previous page.

Name ____________________

The Long Lines

Lines of longitude on a globe run north and south. They are sometimes called **meridians**. Zero degrees longitude (0°) is an imaginary line called the **prime meridian**. It passes through Greenwich, England. Half of the lines of longitude are west of the prime meridian, and half are east of it.

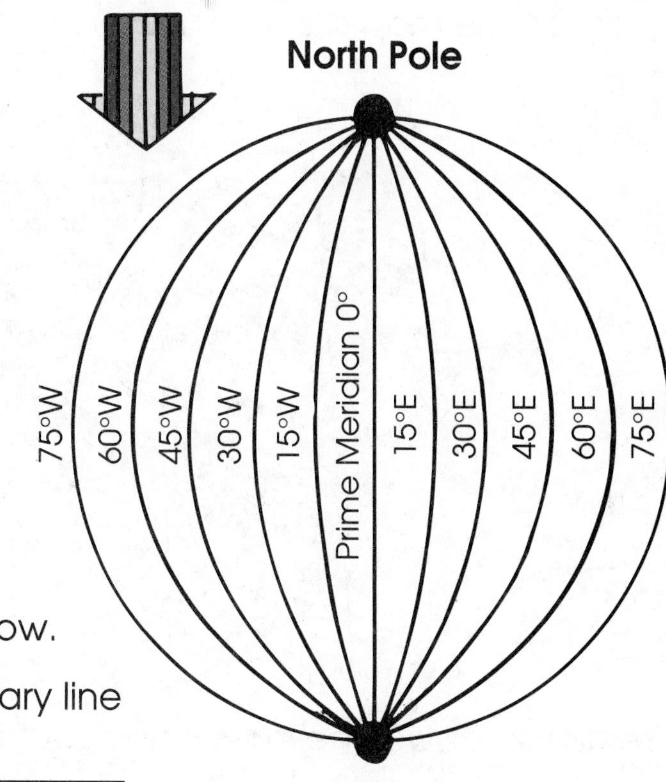

Directions: Answer the questions below.

1. What is the name for the imaginary line at 0° longitude? ____________________
2. Lines to the left of the prime meridian are which direction? ____________________
3. Lines to the right of the prime meridian are which direction? __________
4. Where do lines of longitude come together?
   ____________________ and ____________________
5. Where does the prime meridian pass through?
   ____
6. Lines of longitude run in which directions?
   ____________________ and ____________________
7. Color the prime meridian red.
8. Color the other meridians blue.

Name ____________________

Merry Meridians

Shown on the map are the lines of longitude west of the prime meridian.

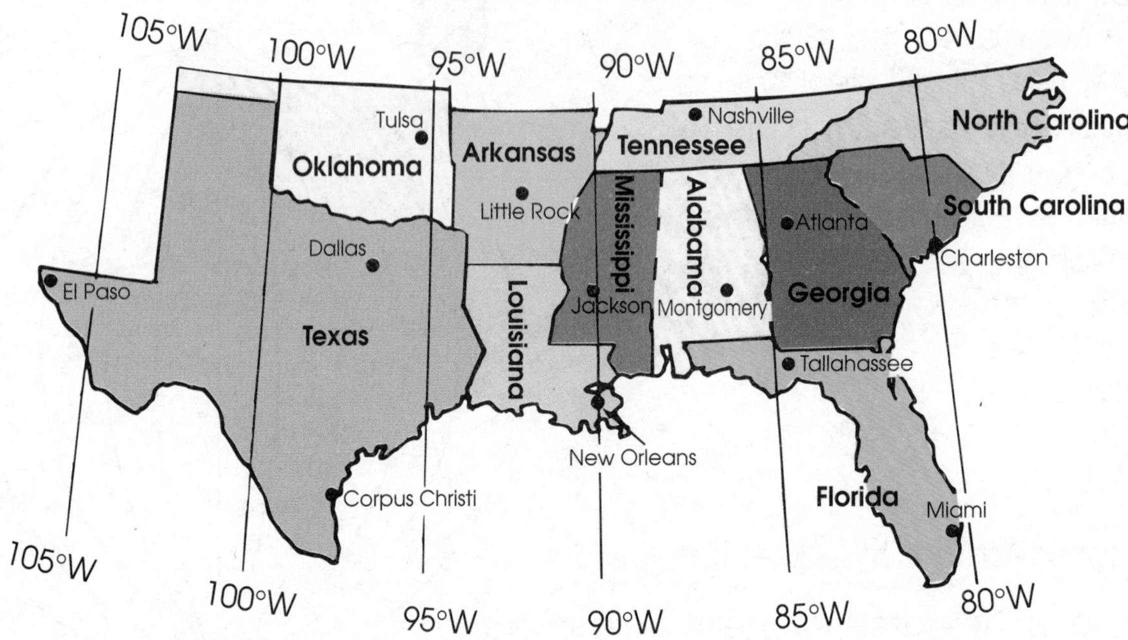

Directions: Answer the questions about these southeastern states.

1. Which two cities lie closest to 90°W?

   ____________, ____________,

2. To which longitude line is Miami, Florida, closest? ____________
3. Which cities lie between 80°W and 85°W? ____________,

   ____________, ____________, ____________,

4. Which city is closest to 95°W? ____________
5. El Paso, Texas, is closest to which meridian? ____________
6. Which two cities are closest to 85°W?____________, ____________
7. Little Rock is between which two meridians? ____________and

   ____

8. Parts of which states lie between 85°W and 90°W?____________,

   ____________, ____________, ____________,

   ____________, ____________, ____________,

9. Most of Florida lies between which meridians? ____________
10. Corpus Christi lies between which meridians? ____________

    and ____________

Name______________________________

Where Is the Prime Meridian?

Meridians of longitude help people locate places east and west of the prime meridian and are measured in units called degrees (°).

Directions: Complete this page and page 280.

1. What do the letters N, S, E and W stand for?

   ____

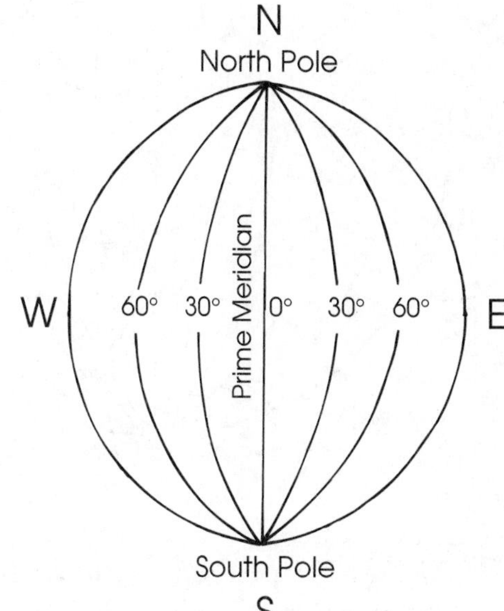

2. The ______________________ is 0° longitude.

3. Meridians of longitude are measured _______________ and _________________ of the prime meridian.

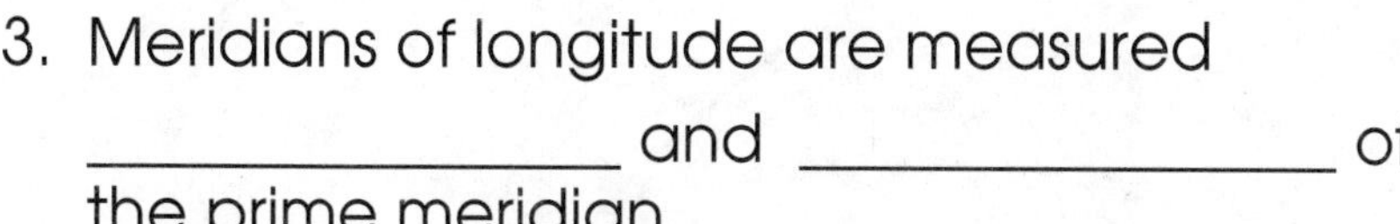

4. Where do all the meridians meet?________

   ____

5. Meridians of longitude are measured in units called

   ____.

Do the following to complete this map.
Hint: The map above will help you.

A. Label the four cardinal directions.

B. Draw a meridian at 30°E and 30°W.

C. Draw a meridian at 60°E and 60°W.

D. Label the North and South Poles.

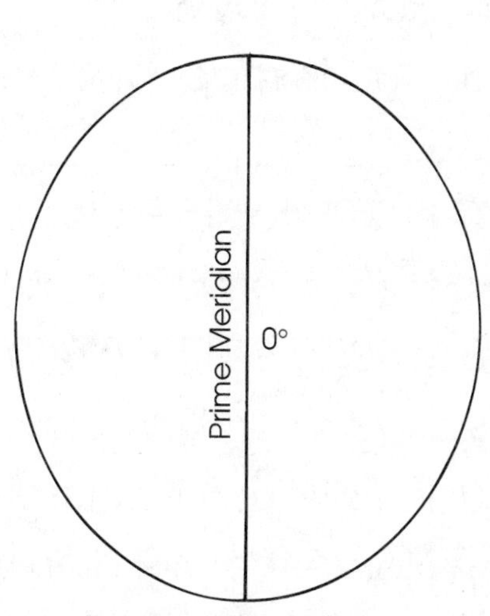

Name ____________________________________

Where Is the Prime Meridian?

Use with page 279.

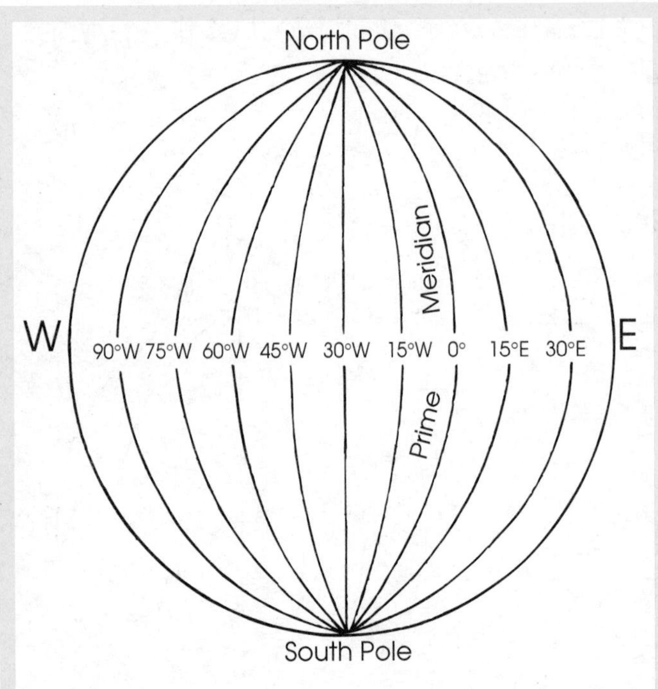

1. Is 15°E or 30°W farther from the prime meridian? ____________
2. Is 60°W or 15°E closer to the prime meridian? ____________
3. Name the two meridians east of the prime meridian on this map.

   ____
4. How many meridians are west of the prime meridian on this map? ____
5. On this map, what meridian is located between 15°W and 15°E?

   ____
6. Is 30°W or 15°E closer to the prime meridian? ____________
7. Is 75°W or 90°W closer to the prime meridian? ____________
8. Is 90°W or 15°E closer to 15°W? ____________
9. Is 90°W or 75°W closer to the prime meridian? ____________
10. Is 45°W or 30°E closer to the prime meridian? ____________
11. Name the meridian west of 75°W. ____________
12. Name the meridian east of 15°E. ____________

Name ____________________

Lines of Longitude

Directions: Use the meridians shown in the globe below to answer the questions.

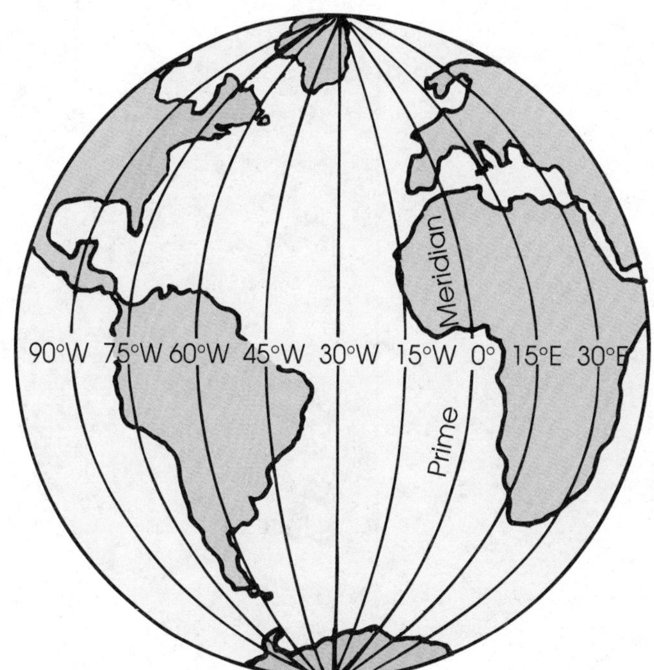

1. Lines of longitude are called ____________________.
2. They run in which directions? __________ and __________
3. 0° longitude passes through ____________________.
4. 0° longitude is called the ____________________.
5. Degrees to the right of the prime meridian are which direction? ____________________
6. What meridian is west of 75°W? ____________________
7. Degrees to the left of the prime meridian are which direction? __________
8. Name the meridians east of 0° on this globe. __________ __________
9. What meridian is east of 15°W? __________
10. Which meridians shown on this map pass through the continent of Africa? ____________________
11. What meridian is west of 45°W? __________
12. Trace the prime meridian orange.
13. Trace the other meridians yellow.

Name ____________________

Locating Cities

This map shows part of the northeastern United States. All longitude meridians on this map are west.

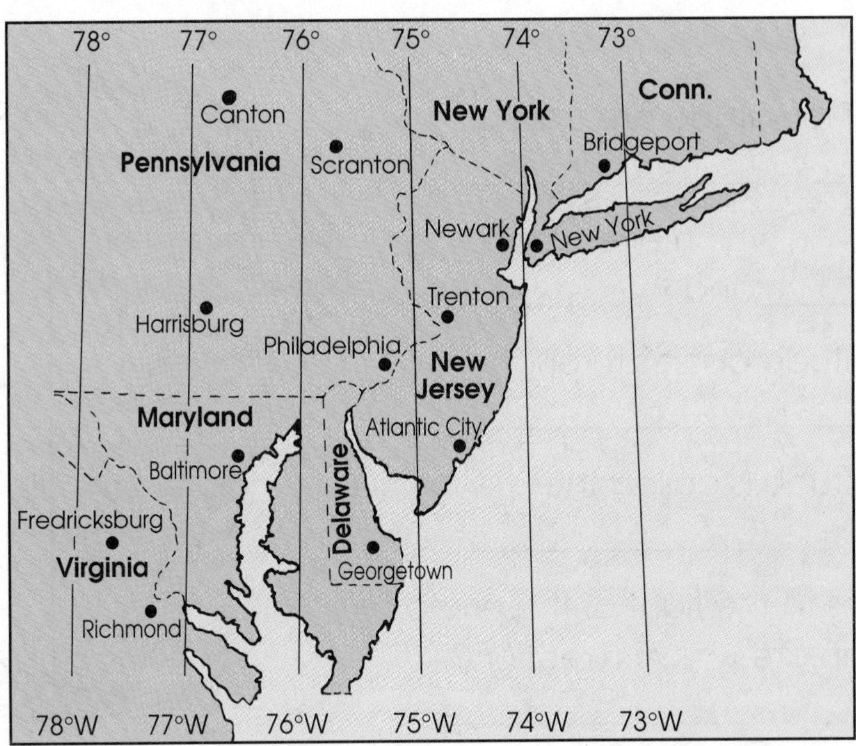

Directions: Use the longitude meridians above to answer the questions below.

1. Bridgeport, Connecticut, is closest to which meridian? ____________
2. Trenton, New Jersey is closest to which meridian? ____________
3. Name the meridians closest to these cities:
   Philadelphia ________ Georgetown ________
   Scranton ________ Newark ________
4. Name the seven states shown on this map. ____________
   ____________ ____________ ____________
   ____________ ____________ ____________
5. Atlantic City is between ________ and ________ longitude.
6. Harrisburg is closest to which meridian? ____________
7. Which is farther west—Harrisburg or Philadelphia? ____________
8. Richmond is closest to ____________longitude.

Name ____________________

North and South Dakota

Directions: Use this map to answer the questions. All longitude meridians will be west.

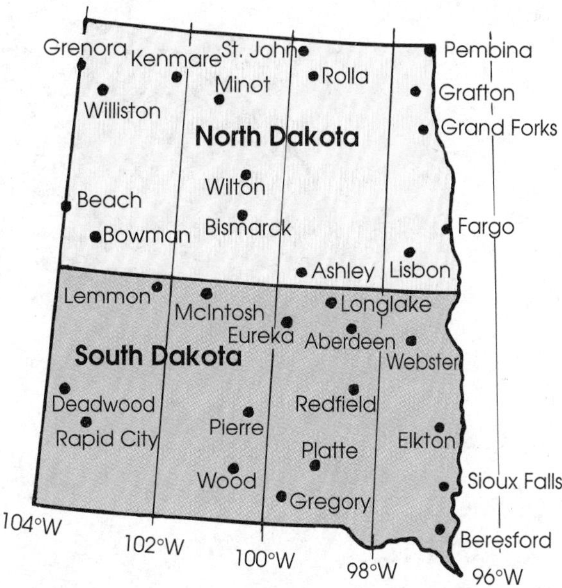

1. Which meridian is closest to Eureka, South Dakota? ____________
2. Which town is closer to 98°W—Platte, South Dakota or Lisbon, North Dakota? ____________
3. Grenora, North Dakota is located almost exactly on the ______ meridian.
4. Is Deadwood, South Dakota north or south of Rapid City? ____________
5. Which town is closer to 104°W—Bowman, North Dakota or Lemmon, South Dakota? ____________
6. If you were traveling east from Rapid City, which meridian would you arrive at first? ____________
7. Which meridian would you reach first when traveling east from Sioux Falls, South Dakota? ____________
8. Bismarck is in the state of ____________.
9. Lemmon, South Dakota is closest to the ____________ meridian.
10. Name the North Dakota cities located east of 98°W longitude.

____

____

____

Name________________________________

Lines of Longitude

Remember... The lines of longitude tell how far east or west of the **prime meridian** (0°) you are.

All lines of longitude are measured from the prime meridian in degrees. Everything west of the prime meridian is labeled **W** for **west**, and everything east of the prime meridian is labeled **E** for **east**.

Directions: Use a globe or map to find the longitude for each of the following cities. Remember to indicate both the number of degrees and whether it is east or west of the prime meridian.

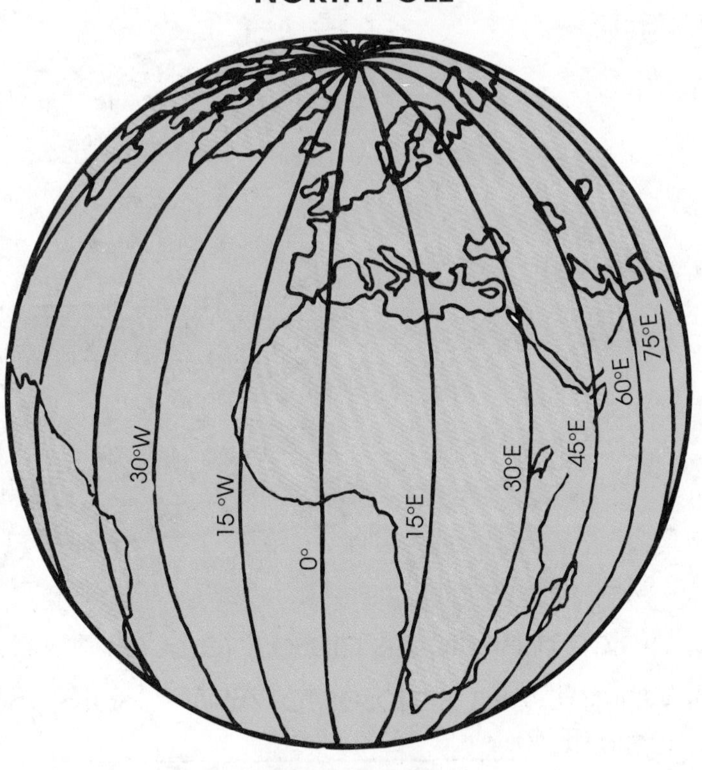

1. Los Angeles, U.S.A. ____________
2. London, England ____________
3. Wellington, New Zealand ____________
4. Tokyo, Japan ____________
5. Bangkok, Thailand ____________
6. Santiago, Chile ____________
7. Nairobi, Kenya ____________
8. Tehran, Iran ____________
9. Paris, France ____________
10. Glasgow, Scotland ____________
11. Rome, Italy ____________
12. Buenos Aires, Argentina ____________
13. Anchorage, Alaska ____________
14. Calcutta, India ____________
15. Cairo, Egypt ____________
16. Shanghai, China ____________

Name____________________________________

Locating Cities in Europe

Directions: Use this map to answer the questions. Pay particular attention to the location of the prime meridian.

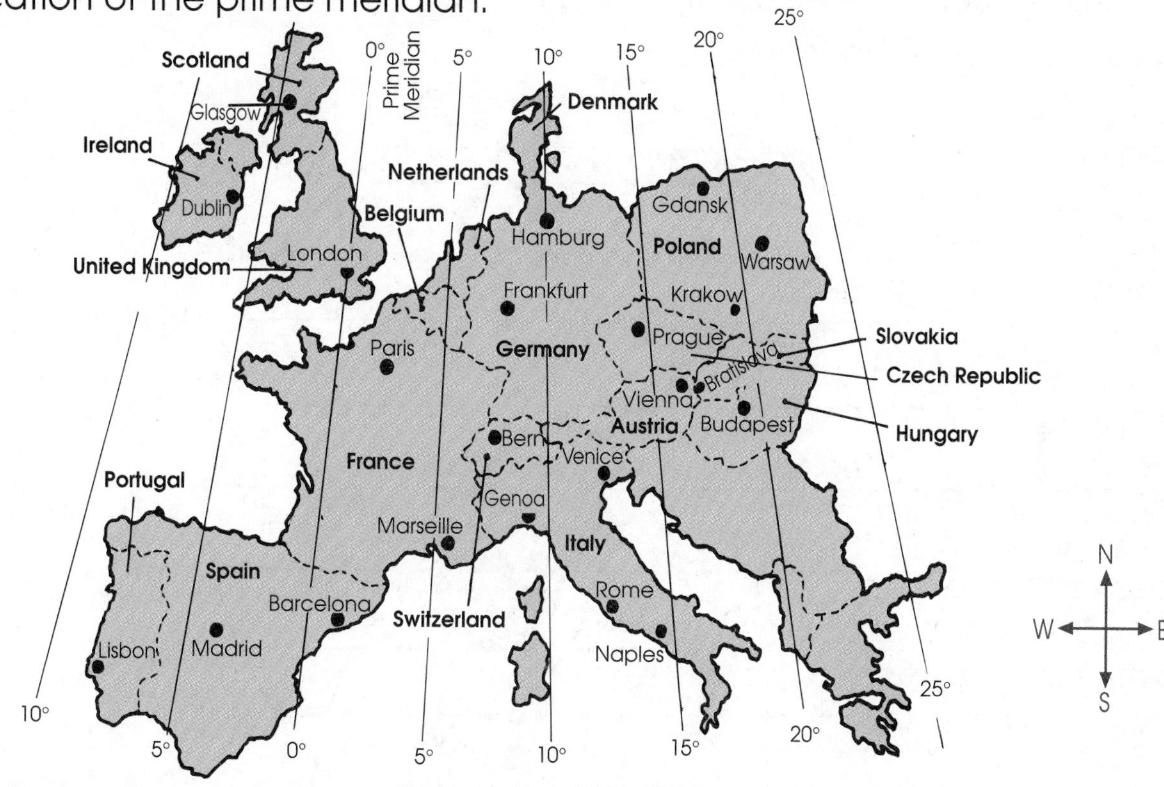

1. On the map label each longitude meridian either east or west.
2. Rome, Italy, is located between the __________ and __________ meridians.
3. Which meridian passes through the western edge of Ireland? __________
4. Portugal is located between the __________ and __________ meridians.
5. Between which two meridians is Switzerland located? __________
6. Explain how you would decide which of the 5° meridians is east and which is west. ____________________
7. Warsaw is closest to the ____________________ meridian.
8. Marseille, France, is which direction from the 5°E meridian? __________
9. Gdansk is in the country of ____________________.
10. Prague is ____________________ of 15°E longitude.
11. Hamburg is on the ____________________ meridian.
12. Marseille is almost on the ____________________ meridian of longitude.

Name____

Lines of Latitude

Lines of latitude on a globe are called parallels. They run east and west. The equator is at 0° latitude. Use the map below to answer the questions.

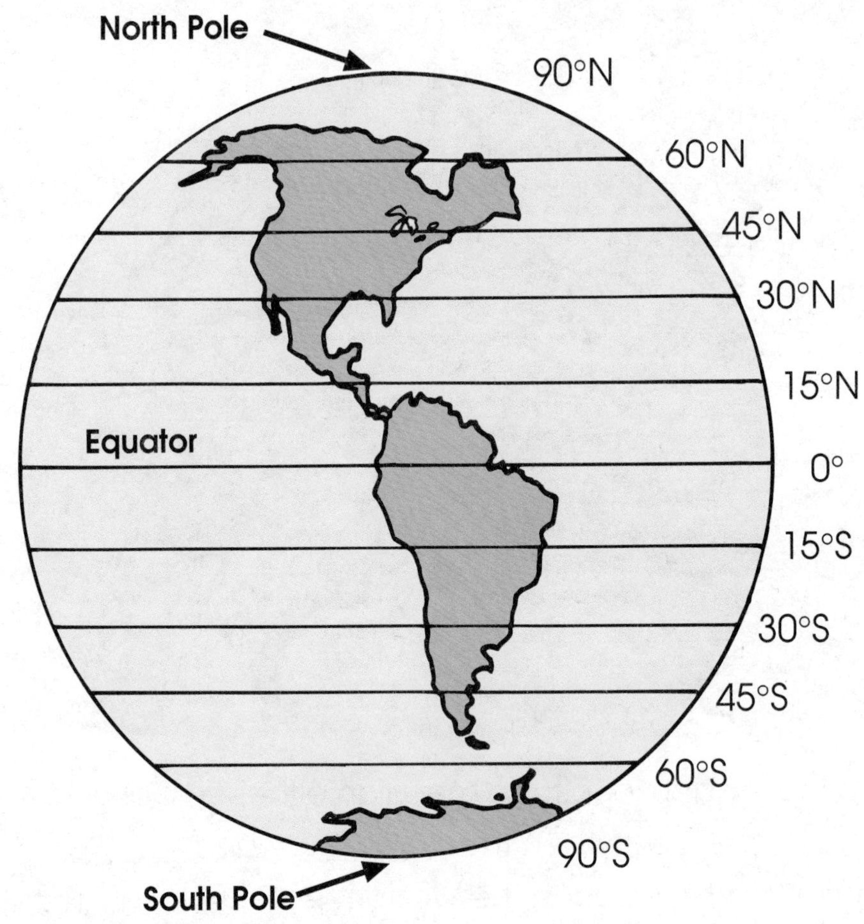

1. 0° latitude is called the ______________________________.
2. Lines of latitude are called ______________________________.
3. Parallels run which directions? ____________________ and ____________________
4. The latitude of the North Pole is ______________________________.
5. Which parallel runs through Florida? ______________________________
6. What is located at 90°S latitude? ______________________________
7. Which parallel runs through Canada? ______________________________
8. Lines of latitude above the equator are which direction?______________
9. Below the equator, the parallels are which direction? ____________________

Name ____________________

Lateral Movement

Parallels measure the distance north or south from the equator. Zero degrees latitude (0°) is at the equator. Half of the parallels are north of the equator and half are south of it. The lines do not meet.

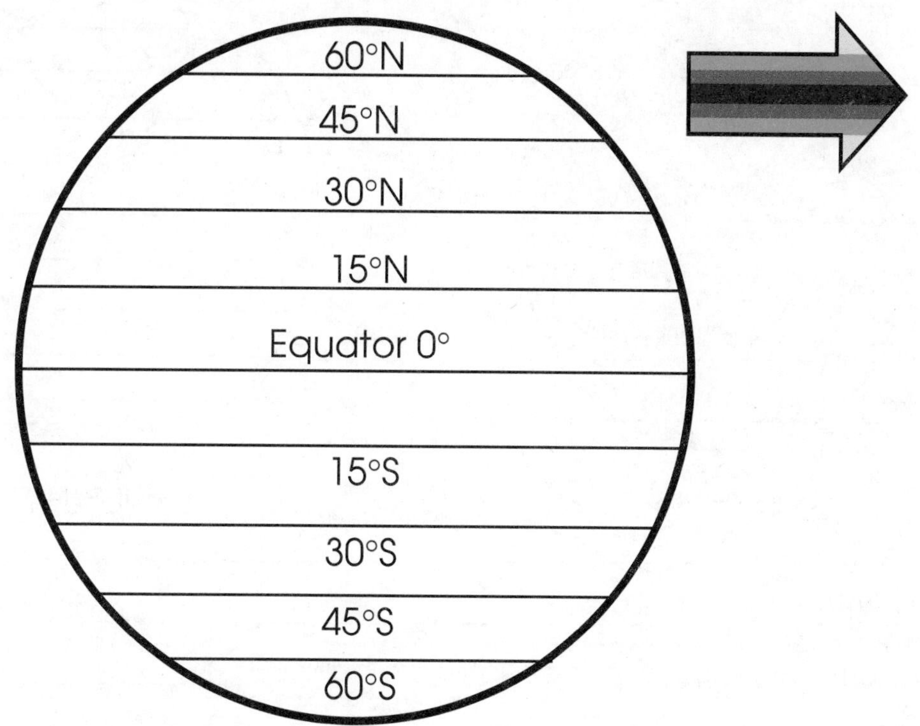

1. What is the symbol for degrees? __________
2. Latitude lines run __________ and __________.
3. Latitude lines are called ______________.
4. Give the latitude of the equator. ______________
5. The parallels above the equator are which direction? ____________
6. The parallels below the equator are which direction? ____________
7. Color the equator parallel orange.
8. Color 15°N and 15°S green.
9. Color 30°N and 30°S blue.
10. Color 45°N and 45°S red.
11. Color 60°N and 60°S purple.

Name______________________________________

Imaginary Lines

Directions: Answer the questions below using these maps.

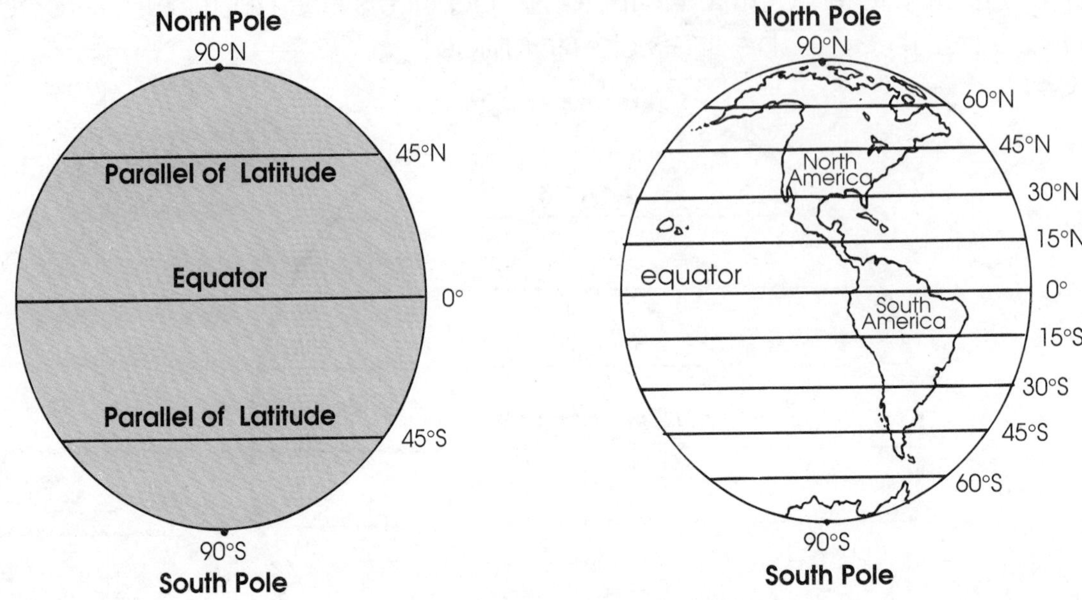

1. The ______________________________________ is 0° latitude.
2. The North Pole is ______________________________ degrees north latitude.
4. Lines north and south of the equator are called ______________________.
5. The ______________________________________ is 90°S latitude.
6. Which line is closer to the equator—30°N or 15°S? ____________________
7. Which is closer to the South Pole—45°S or 30°S? ____________________
8. At what degree is the South Pole? ____________________________
9. If you wanted to find a city located at 45°N, would you look above or below the equator? ____________________
10. Which continent on the map is entirely north of the equator? ______________
11. South America lies between the parallels of latitude ____________°N and 60°S.
12. The equator runs through the northern part of the continent of ______________.
13. Color all the land north of the equator red.
14. Color all of the land south of the equator green.

Name ________________________________

What's My Line?

There are several important lines of latitude on the globe which have special names.

Directions: Use a map, globe or other resource to identify the special lines on the illustration of the globe below.

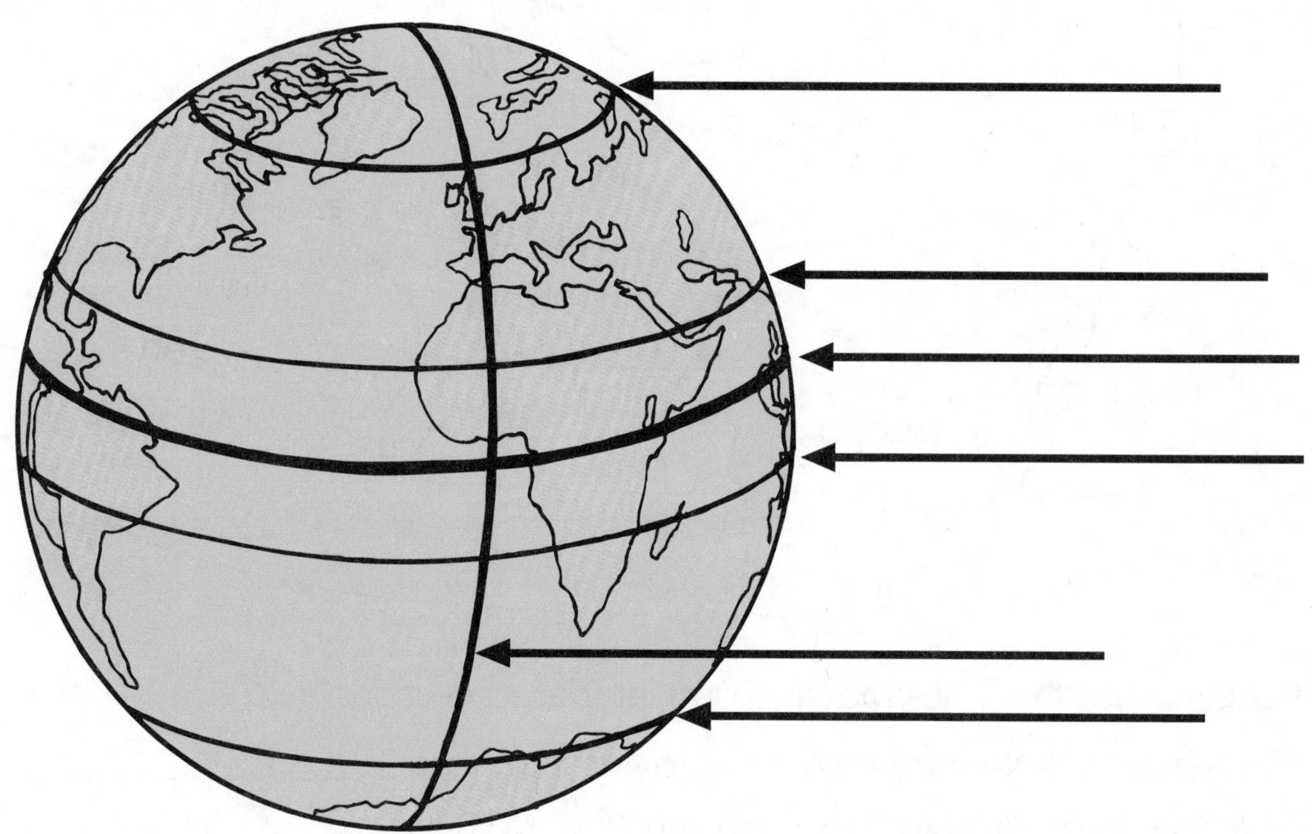

Name the imaginary line that . . .

passes through Mexico. ____________________

is 0° latitude. ____________________

passes through Alaska. ____________________

is 0° longitude. ____________________

divides the Northern and Southern hemispheres. ____________________

passes through Botswana. ____________________

Name ____________________________________

Across the U.S.A.

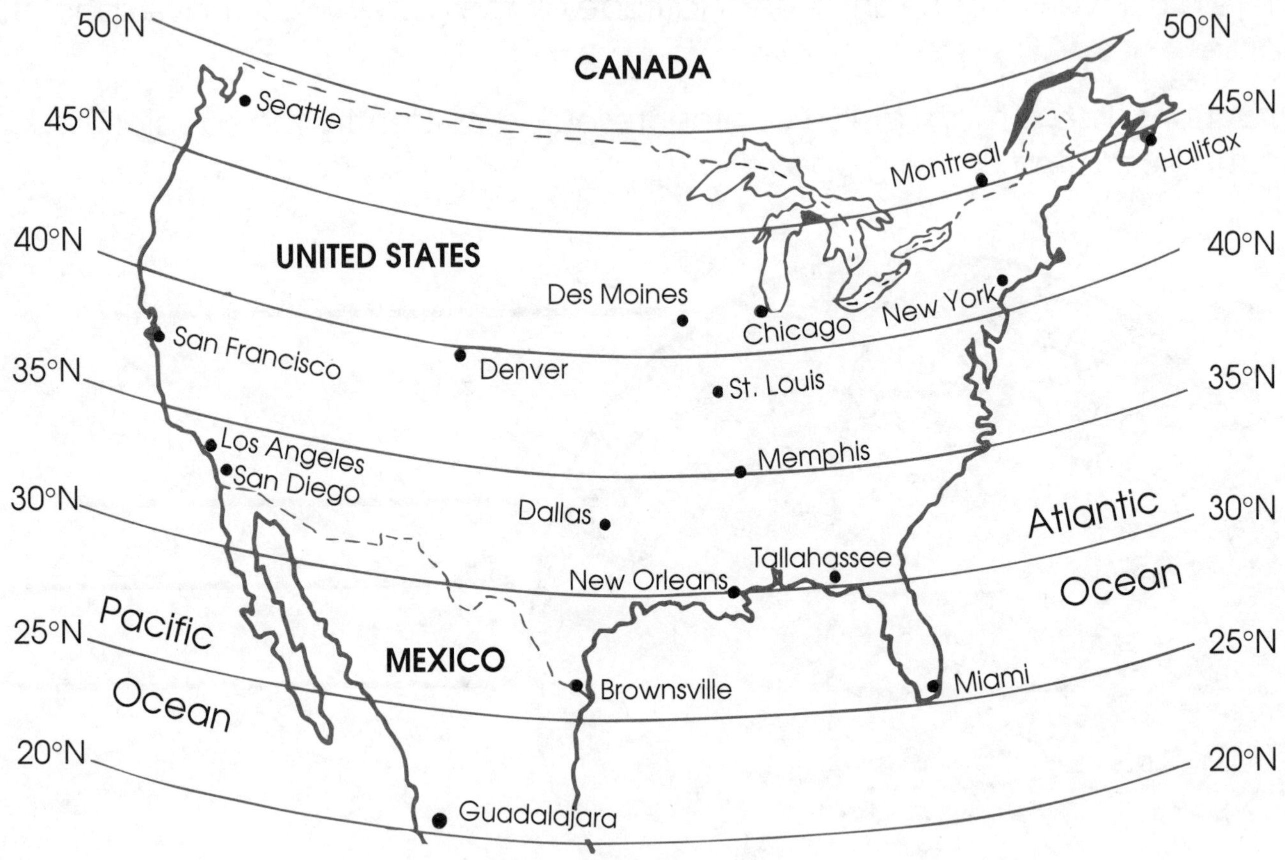

Directions: Use the map above to answer these questions.

1. Denver and New York are close to which parallel? ______________
2. Which two cities are between 45°N and 50°N? ______________
3. Los Angeles and Memphis are near which parallel? ______________
4. Tallahassee is closest to which parallel? ______________
5. St. Louis is between which parallels? ______________ and ______________
6. Which city is farthest north? ______________ It is between which parallels? ______________ and ______________
7. Which city is farthest south? ______________ It is between which parallels? ______________ and ______________
8. San Francisco is halfway between ______________ and ______________.

Name______________________________

Latitude in North America.

Use with page 292.

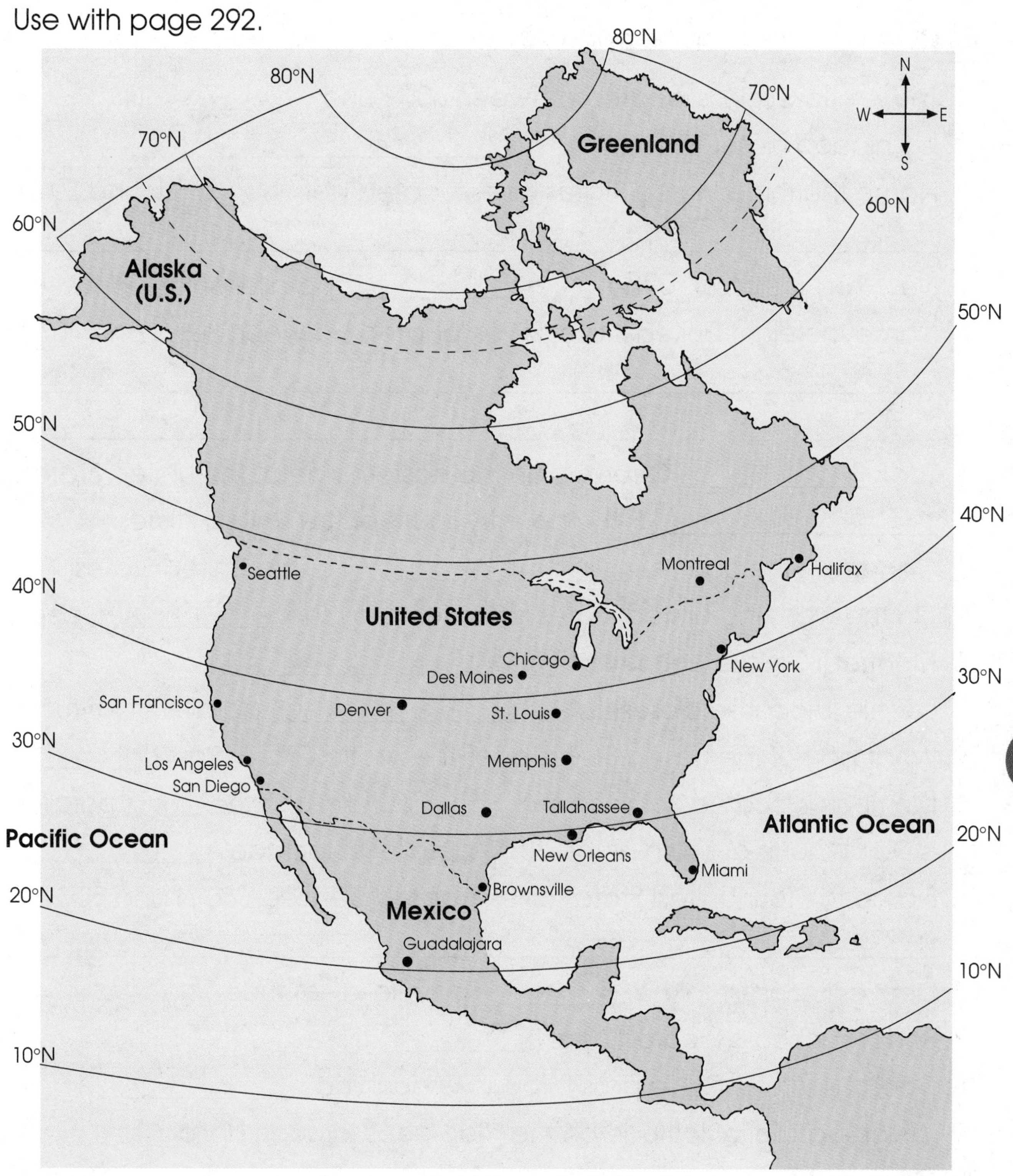

Name____

Latitude in North America

Directions: Use the map on page 291 to answer the questions below.

1. The Arctic Circle is located between 60°N and __________ °N.
2. Is Chicago closer to 40°N or 50°N?________________________
3. Name the three United States cities located between 20°N and 30°N.

    ____________________ ____________________ ____________________

4. New York is closest to the ________________ parallel of latitude.
5. Name the eight United States cities located between 30° N and 40°N.

    _______________ _______________ _______________ _______________

    _______________ _______________ _______________ _______________

6. The ______________ Ocean is on the eastern side of the United States.
7. ____________________ is the country south of the United States.
8. Canada is the country ____________________ of the United States.
9. On the west, the United States is bordered by the ___________ Ocean.
10. Montreal is in the country of ______________________.
11. Seattle is located closest to the ________________ parallel of latitude.
12. What part of the United States does the Arctic Circle cross?_________
13. Memphis is located between the ______ parallel and the _____ parallel.
14. Is Dallas north or south of the 30°N parallel of latitude? ____________
15. Name the four United States cities located between 40°N and 50°N.

    _______________ _______________ _______________ _______________

16. Denver is closest to the __________ parallel of latitude.
17. San Francisco is located near __________ °N.
18. Does the Arctic Circle pass through Greenland? _____________
19. Which parallel of latitude on the map goes through Florida? ________
20. Guadalajara is located in what country? ______________________

Name____________________________________

Parallels Help With Location

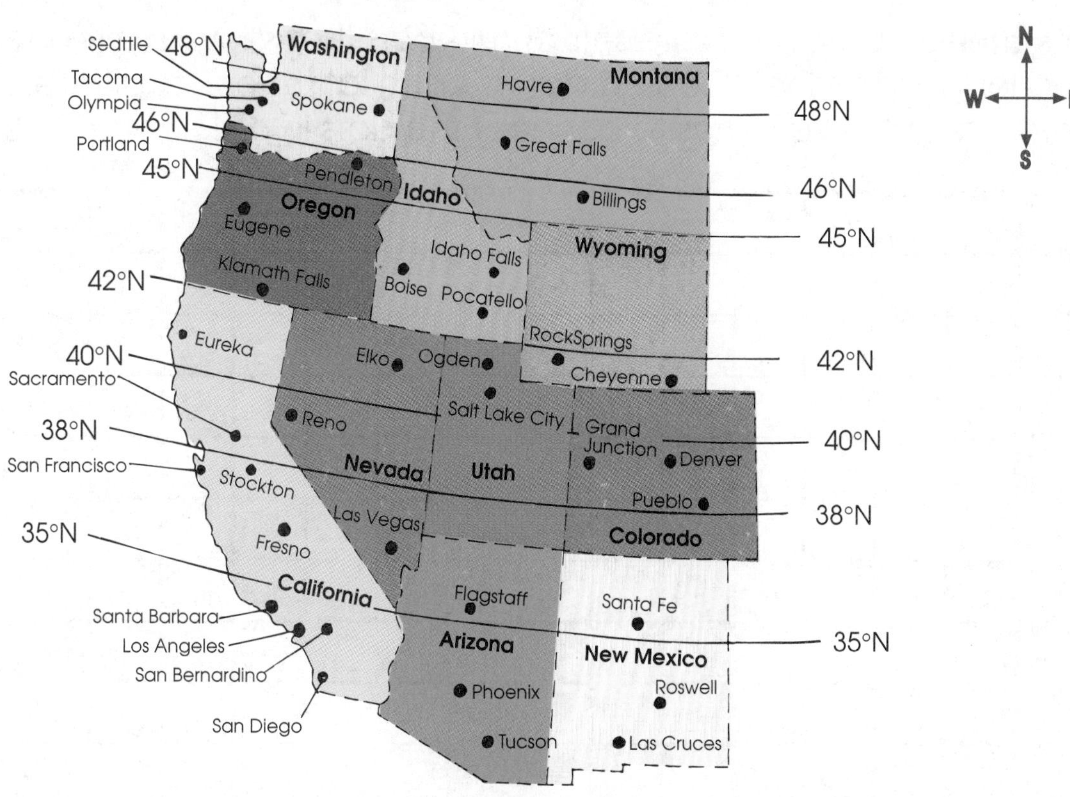

1. Billings, Montana is which direction from the 46°N parallel? ______________
2. Pueblo, Colorado is almost directly on the ____________ parallel of latitude.
3. The boundary between Oregon and California is formed by the ____ parallel.
4. The state of Wyoming is located between 41°N parallel and _______ parallel.
5. Name three cities in Idaho south of the 45°N parallel of latitude.

   ______________________ ______________________ ______________________

6. Which of these cities is south of the 35°N parallel—Flagstaff, Arizona or Roswell, New Mexico? ____
7. Name the three California cities located between the 35°N and 38°N parallels.

   ______________________ ______________________ ______________________

8. All of the cities shown in Washington are between the parallels of ____________ and ____________.
9. Which two Nevada cities are north of the 38°N parallel? ________________ and __________________
10. Klamath Falls, Oregon is almost directly on the ___________ parallel.

Name______________________________

Picture It!

Directions: Coordinates are sets of numbers that show where lines of latitude and longitude meet. Place a dot at each latitude / longitude coordinate on the graph. Draw lines to connect the dots in order.

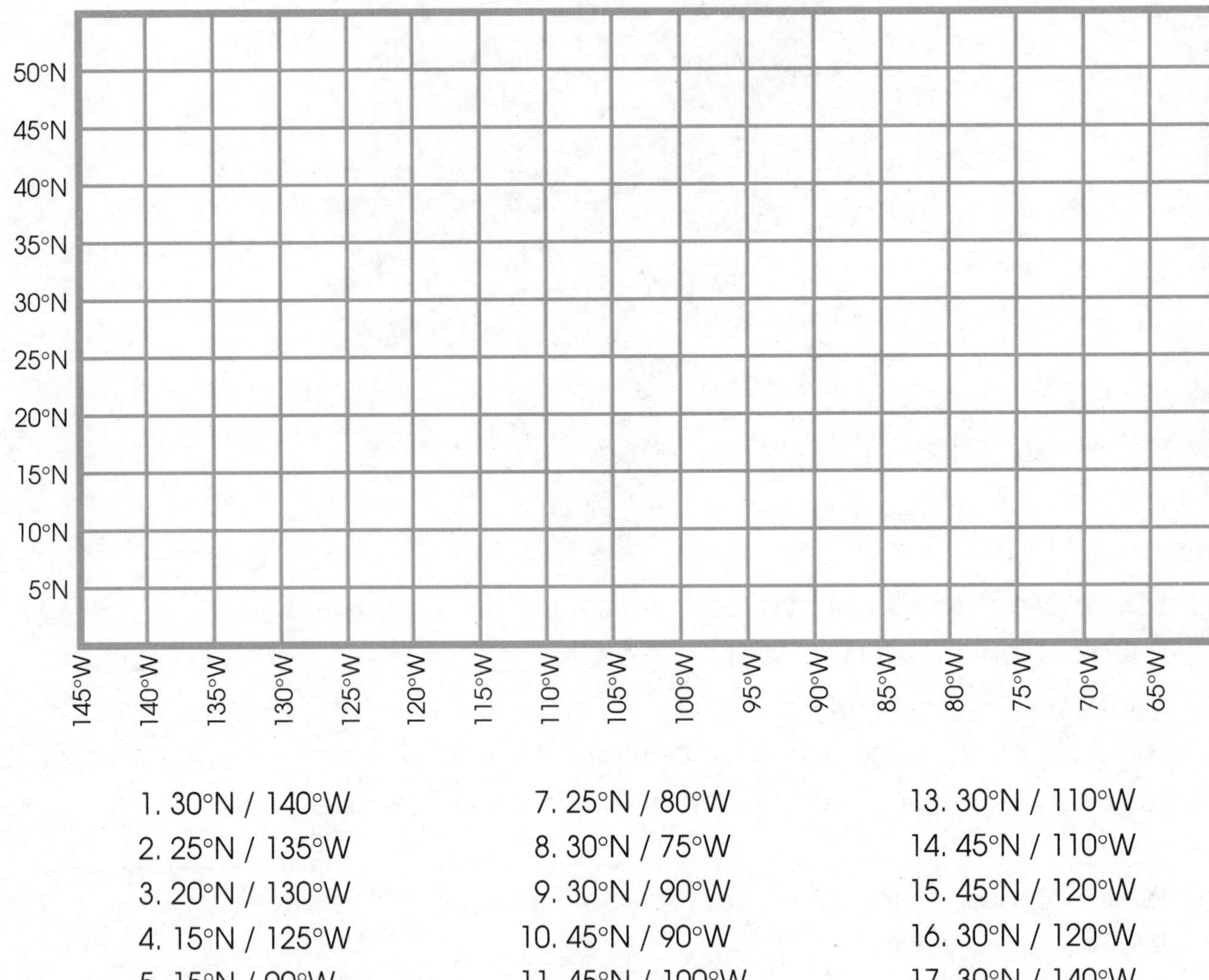

1. 30°N / 140°W
2. 25°N / 135°W
3. 20°N / 130°W
4. 15°N / 125°W
5. 15°N / 90°W
6. 20°N / 85°W
7. 25°N / 80°W
8. 30°N / 75°W
9. 30°N / 90°W
10. 45°N / 90°W
11. 45°N / 100°W
12. 30°N / 100°W
13. 30°N / 110°W
14. 45°N / 110°W
15. 45°N / 120°W
16. 30°N / 120°W
17. 30°N / 140°W

Now place a yellow **X** at each coordinate below. Do not connect the **X**s.

1. 45°N / 140°W
2. 35°N / 135°W
3. 45°N / 130°W
4. 40°N / 80°W
5. 45°N / 70°W
6. 35°N / 65°W

Color the rest of the picture.

Name____________________________________

What Will They Be?

Directions: Place a dot at each of these latitude and longitude points on the graph.

1. 45°N / 105°W
2. 40°N / 110°W
3. 35°N / 115°W
4. 30°N / 120°W
5. 25°N / 125°W
6. 20°N / 120°N
7. 15°N / 115°W
8. 10°N / 110°W
9. 5°N / 105°W
10. 10°N / 100°W
11. 15°N / 95°W
12. 20°N / 90°W
13. 25°N / 85°W
14. 30°N / 90°W
15. 35°N / 95°W
16. 40°N / 100°W

Draw a line to connect the dots in order. What have you drawn?__________

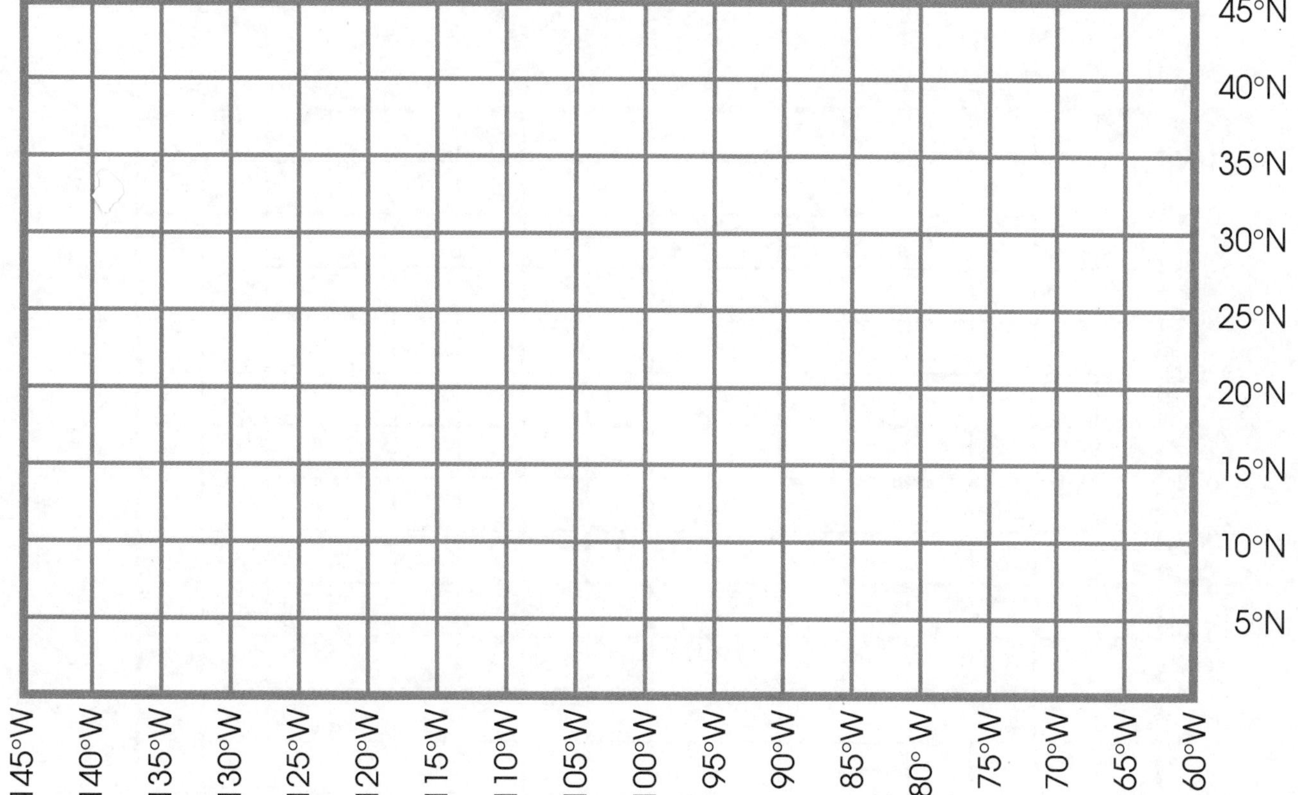

Now with a different color, place a dot at each of these latitude and longitude points.

1. 45°N / 85°W
2. 35°N / 85°W
3. 35°N / 65°W
4. 45°N / 65°W

Connect the dots. What have you drawn? ____________________

Name________________________________

Using Lines to Draw a State

Directions: Place a dot on the grid for each point given. The first two have been done for you.

1. 38°N / 99°W
2. 38° N / 102°W
3. 36°N / 102°W
4. 34°N / 102°W
5. 34°N / 104°W
6. 34°N / 106°W
7. 33°N / 105 1/2°W
8. 32 1/2°N / 105°W
9. 32°N / 104 1/2°W
10. 31°N / 104°W
11. 30°N / 104°W
12. 29 1/2°N / 103°W
13. 30°N / 102°W
14. 30°N / 101°W
15. 29°N / 101°W
16. 28°N / 100°W
17. 27 1/2°N / 99°W
18. 26 1/2°N / 97 1/2°W
19. 28°N / 97 1/2°W
20. 29°N / 96 1/2°W
21. 30°N / 95°W
22. 31°N / 94°W
23. 33°N / 94°W
24. 35°N / 94°W
25. 35°N / 96°W
26. 35°N / 99°W
27. 37°N / 99°W

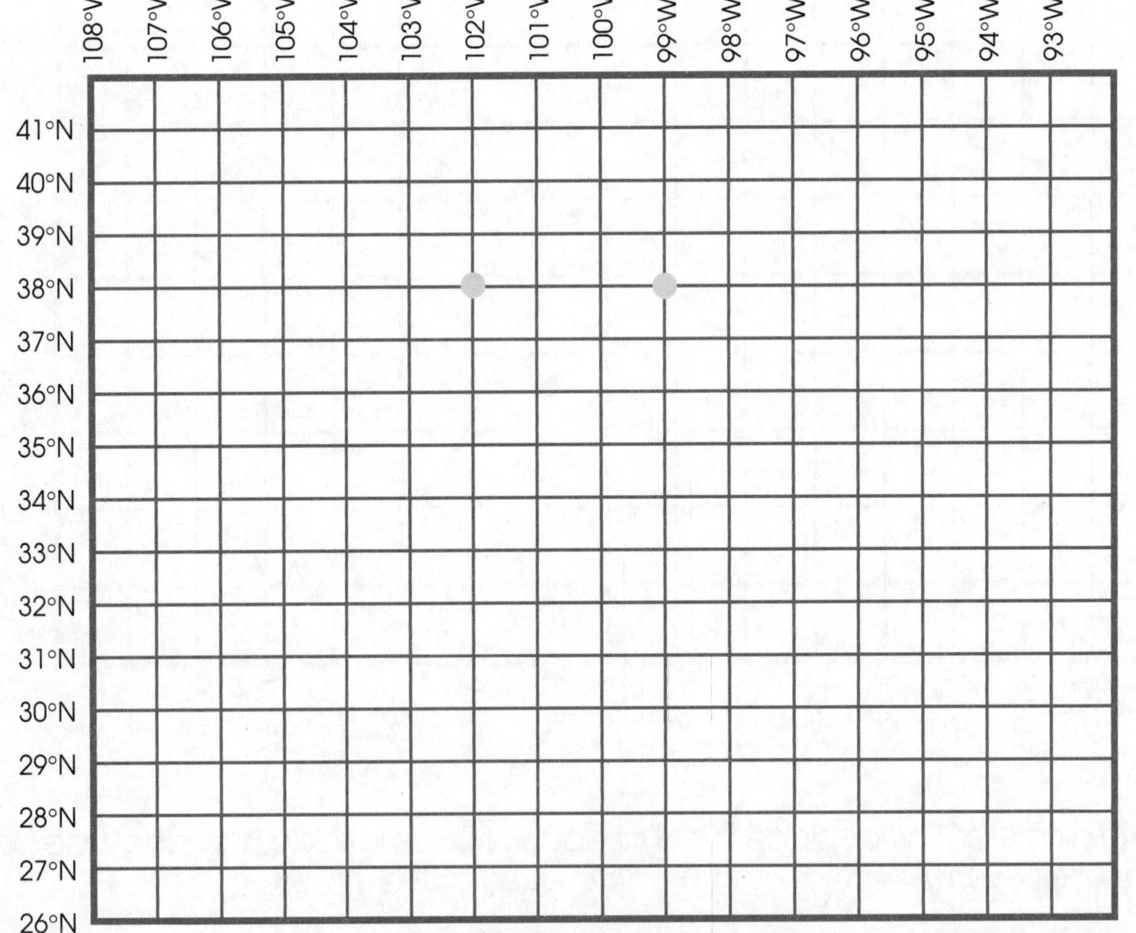

Draw a line to connect all of the dots in order. What state did you draw?

Name ________________________________

Casey's Island

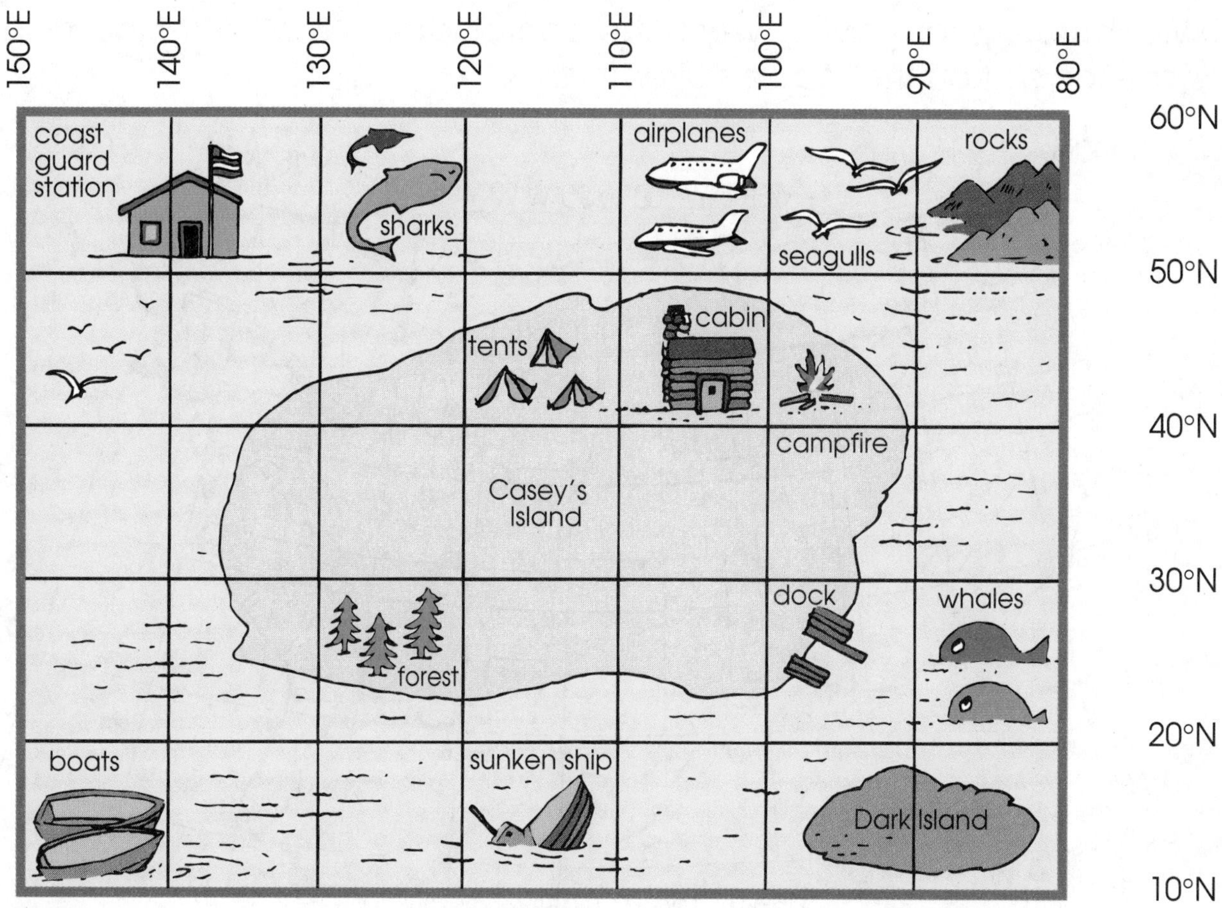

Directions: Use the map above to answer the questions below.

1. The whales are between which two latitude lines? ____________
2. The coast guard station is located between which longitude lines? ______
3. If the whales go north to 55°N latitude, what will they hit? __________
4. The boats must cross what longitude lines to get to the sunken ship? _____

 ____
5. If you draw a latitude line at 35°N, what will you cross? __________
6. If the whales cross 90°E longitude, what will they reach? __________
7. Name the items crossed by the 55°N latitude line. ______________

 ____
8. Which longitude lines cross Casey's Island? ______________

Name______________________________

State Search

Which state is roughly between the coordinates given? After locating the state, color it on the map as directed.

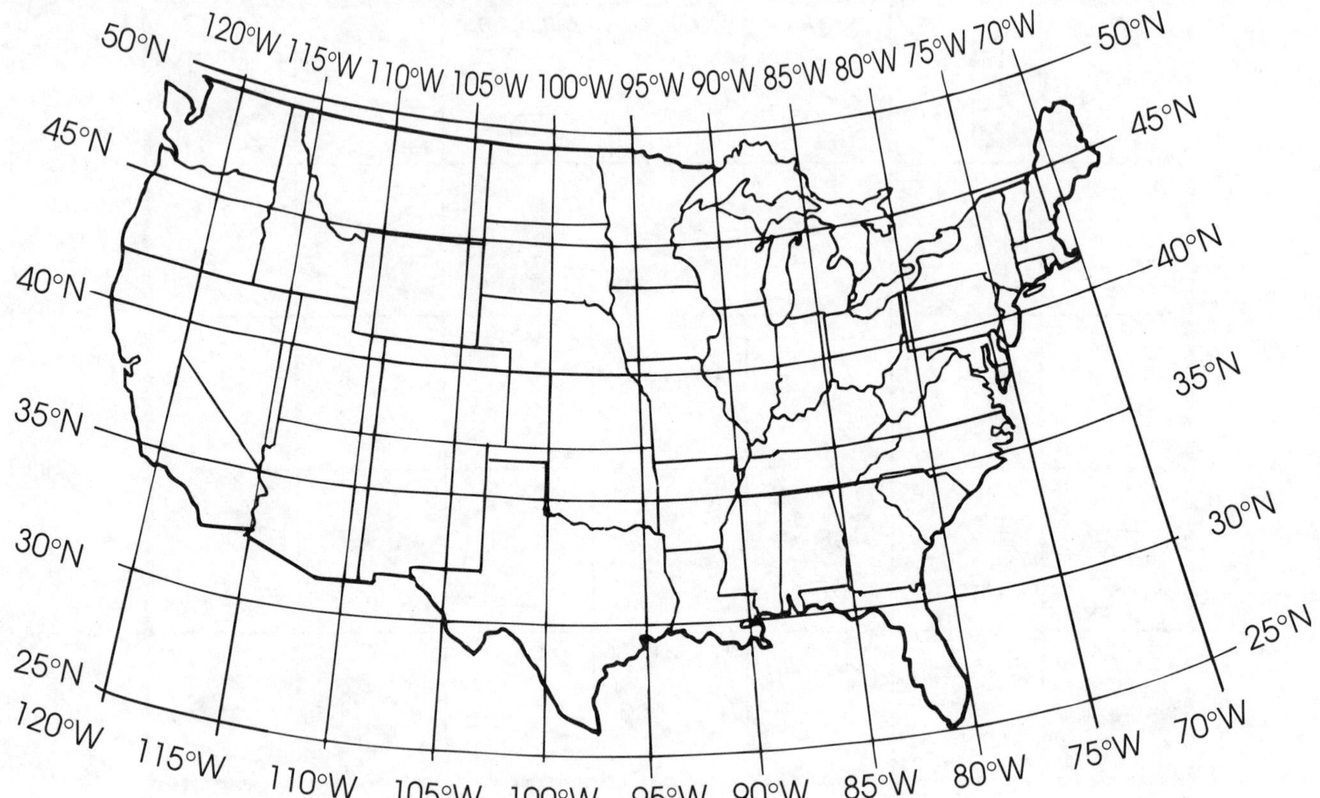

	Latitude	Longitude	State	Color
1.	45°N / 50°N	105°W / 115°W	____________	orange
2.	40°N / 45°N	75°W / 80°W	____________	tan
3.	44°N / 50°N	67°W / 70°W	____________	red
4.	25°N / 30°N	80°W / 85°W	____________	yellow
5.	40°N / 45°N	90°W / 95°W	____________	gray
6.	30°N / 35°N	85°W / 90°W	____________	green
7.	43°N / 47°N	87°W / 93°W	____________	blue
8.	31°N / 36°N	104°W / 109°W	____________	pink
9.	36°N / 38°N	82°W / 89°W	____________	lt. green
10.	36°N / 39°N	76°W / 84°W	____________	gold
11.	26°N / 34°N	94°W / 107°W	____________	purple
12.	41°N / 45°N	104°W / 111°W	____________	lt. blue
13.	36°N / 41°N	90°W / 95°W	____________	brown

Name ____________________

See the U.S.A.

Use the coordinates to plan a trip across the U.S.A.

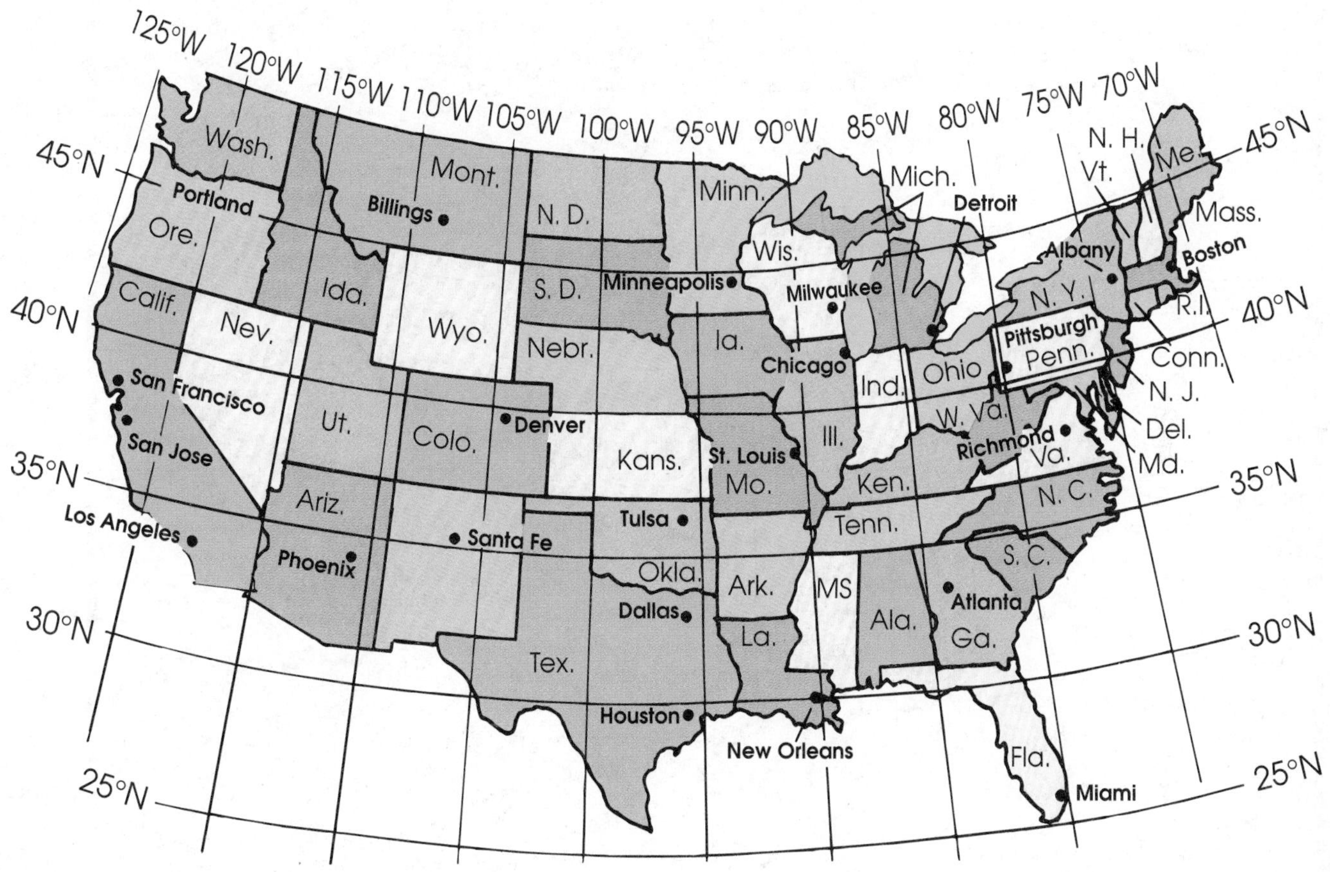

Directions: Write the name of the city closest to the intersection.

1. Your trip begins at 40°N / 105°W, the Mile-High City. ____________
2. You fly over the Rocky Mountains to 45°N / 125°W. ____________
3. Now, to 35°N / 105°W in New Mexico. ____________
4. Next, stop is Texas, the city of . . . 30°N / 95°W. ____________
5. It's Mardi Gras time at 30°N / 90°W. ____________
6. Then, fun in the sun and the Atlantic Ocean 25°N / 80°W. ____________
7. To the Gateway Arch in the city of . . 40°N / 90°W. ____________
8. The Steelers play football here—40°N / 80°W. ____________
9. Next, to the capital of New York—40°N / 75°W. ____________

Name ____________________

Plotting North American Cities

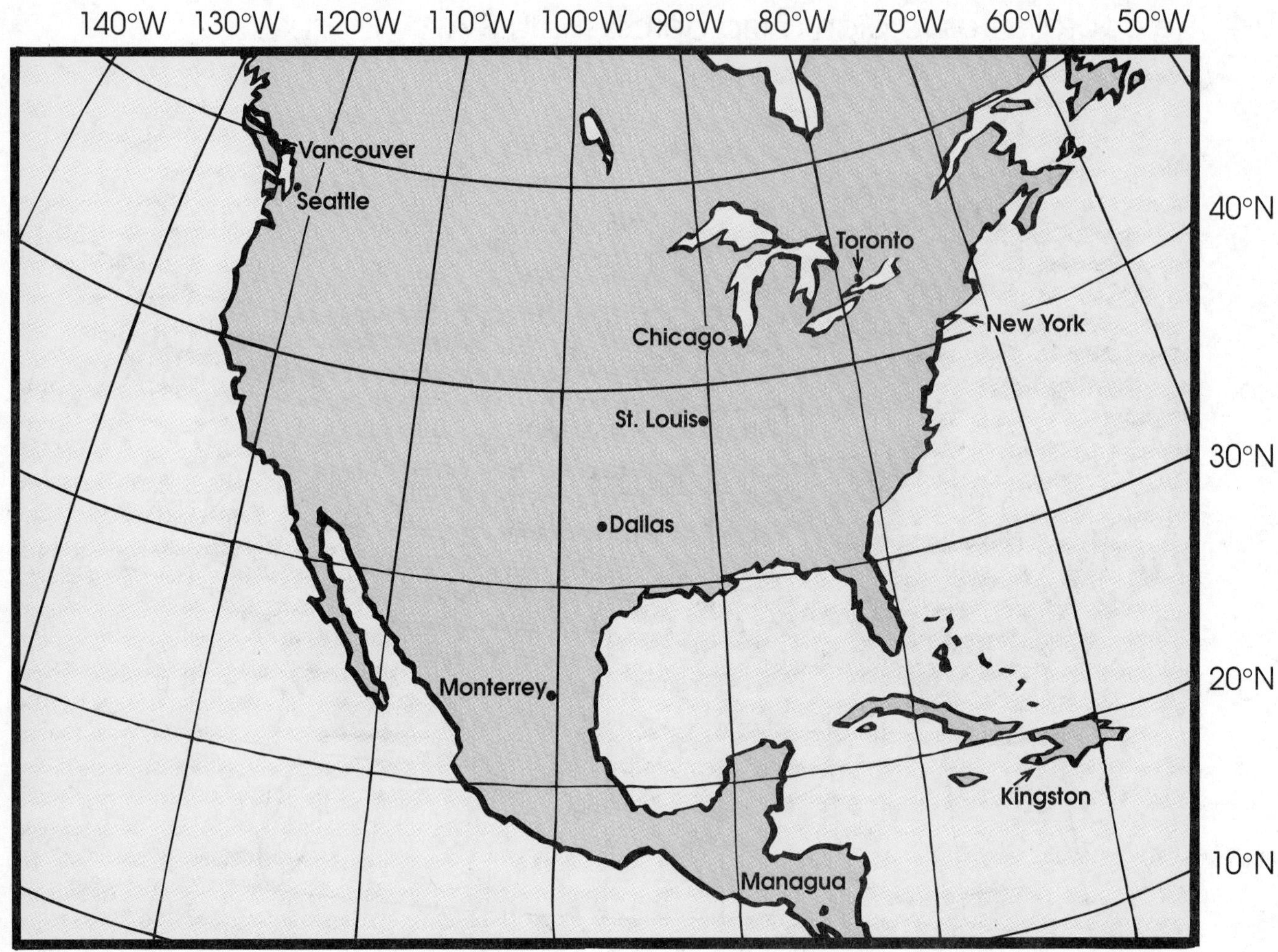

Directions: Use the lines of latitude and longitude to determine the approximate coordinates of the North American cities on the map above. Write the coordinates for each city in the blanks.

	Latitude	Longitude		Latitude	Longitude
1. Seattle	______	______	6. St. Louis	______	______
2. Kingston	______	______	7. Toronto	______	______
3. Dallas	______	______	8. New York	______	______
4. Vancouver	______	______	9. Monterrey	______	______
5. Managua	______	______	10. Chicago	______	______

Name ____________________

Batter Up!

Directions: Use the coordinates below and the map on page 302 to locate these cities. Then, unscramble the words to find out the baseball teams which call these cities "home base."

	Latitude	Longitude	City	State	Baseball Team Names		
1.	41°N	74°W	______	______	(yeesank) or (tmes)	=	______
2.	40°N	105°W	______	______	(ocrkeis)	=	______
3.	34°N	84°W	______	______	(sebarv)	=	______
4.	29°N	96°W	______	______	(satosr)	=	______
5.	39°N	84°W	______	______	(dser)	=	______
6.	38°N	123°W	______	______	(ginsta)	=	______
7.	42°N	88°W	______	______	(cbus) or (twihe xso)	=	______
8.	47°N	122°W	______	______	(raimnesr)	=	______
9.	39°N	90°W	______	______	(rdcailnas)	=	______
10.	42°N	82°W	______	______	(nidaisn)	=	______
11.	43°N	71°W	______	______	(der sxo)	=	______
12.	34°N	117°W	______	______	(ddogesr)	=	______
13.	39°N	76°W	______	______	(rioolse)	=	______

Word Bank

Orioles, Indians, Cardinals, Dodgers, Giants, Rockies, Cubs, White Sox, Yankees, Astros, Mets, Braves, Reds, Mariners, Red Sox

Name ________________________________

Latitude and Longitude

Batter Up!

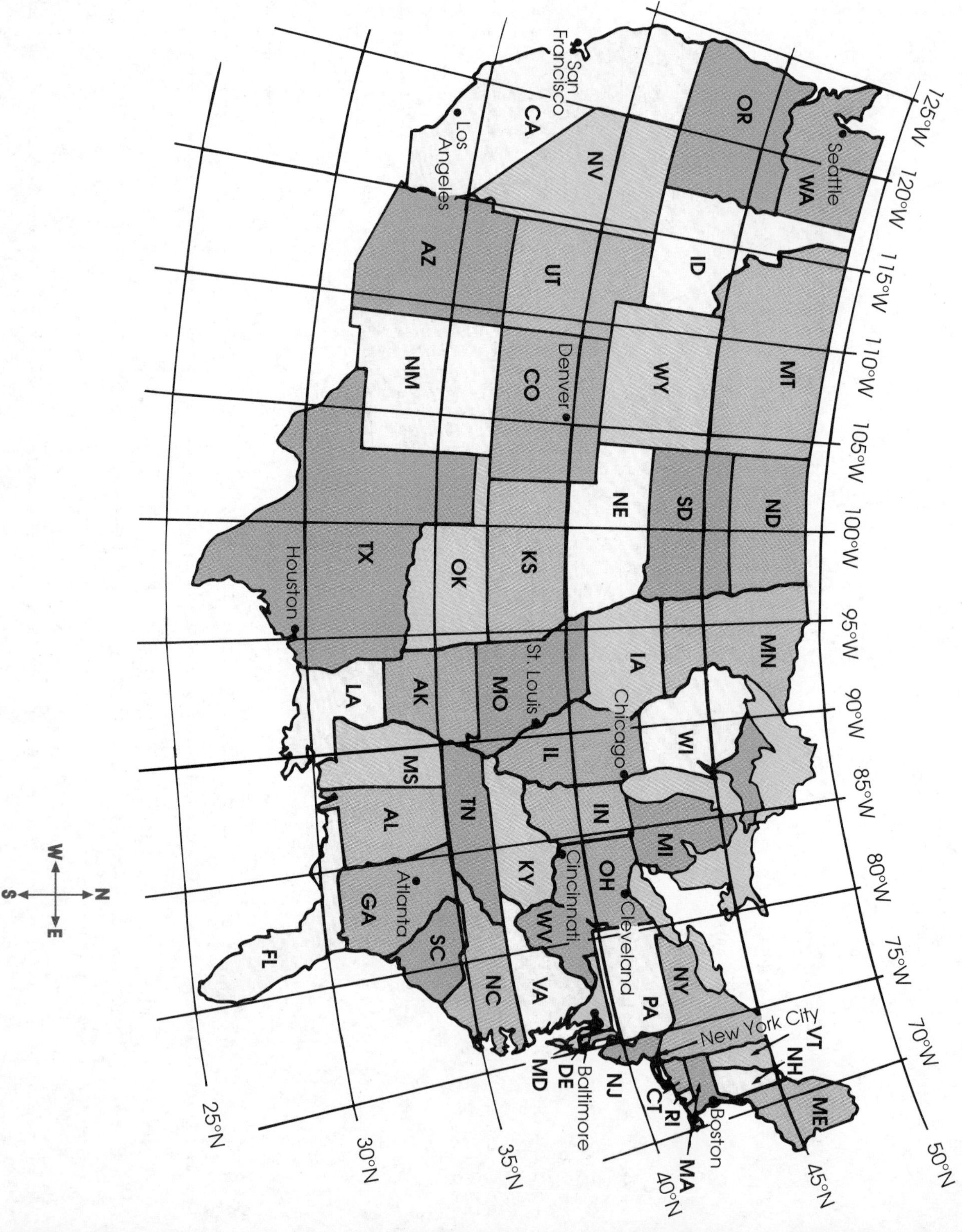

Name ______________________________

Four States

Directions: Use this map to fill in the charts on page 304. Two answers have been filled in for you.

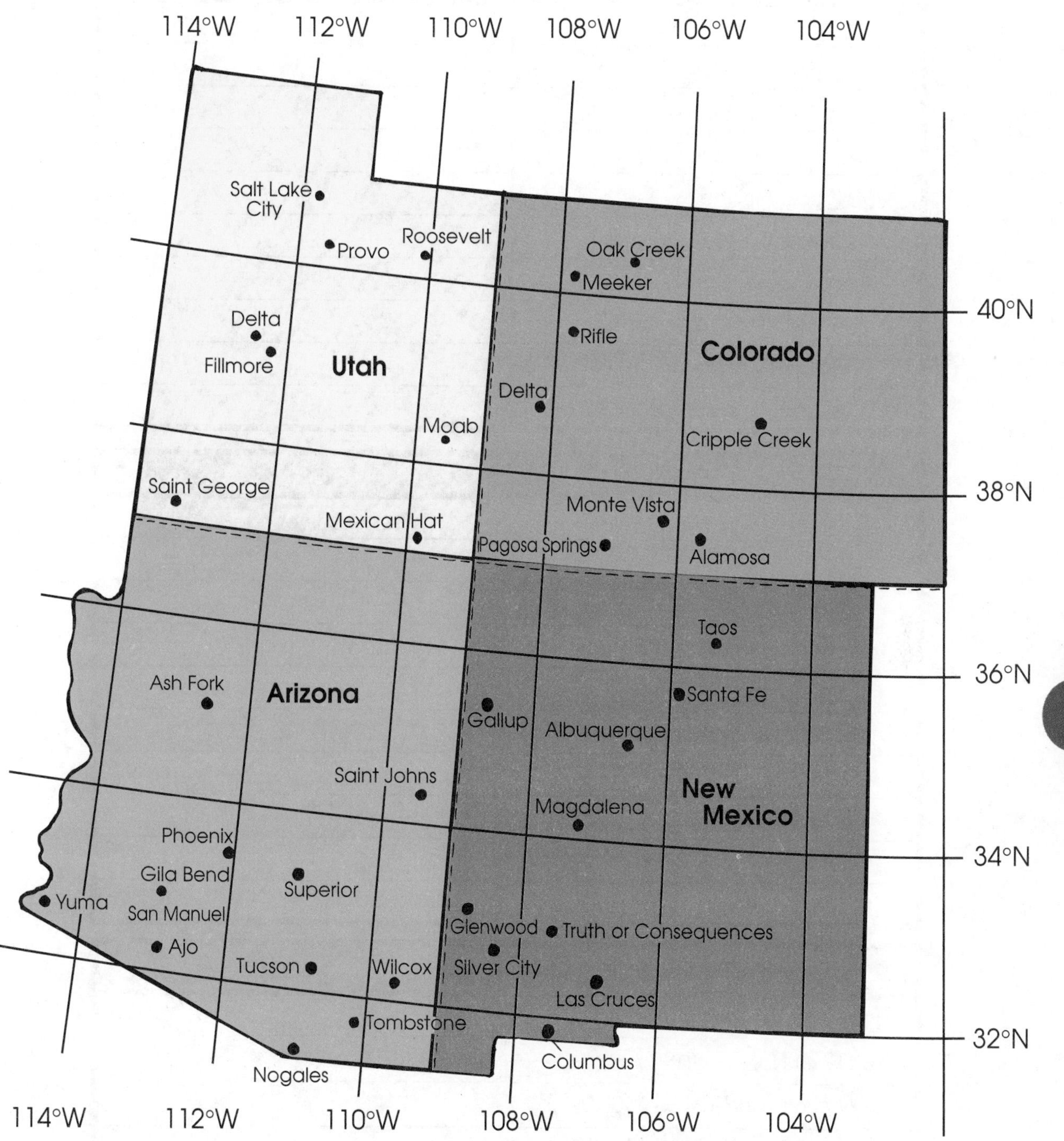

Name____

Latitude and Longitude

Four States

Use with page 303.

City	Coordinates
1. Salt Lake City, Utah	41°N / 112°W
2. Tucson, Arizona	
3. Santa Fe, New Mexico	
4. Oak Creek, Colorado	
5. Wilcox, Arizona	
6. Cripple Creek, Colorado	
7. Las Cruces, New Mexico	
8. Albuquerque, New Mexico	
9. Meeker, Colorado	
10. Saint George, Utah	

Coordinates	City
1. 33°N / 109°W	Glenwood
2. 41°N / 112°W	
3. 39°N / 108°W	
4. 31°N / 111°W	
5. 37°N / 110°W	
6. 40 1/2°N / 110°W	
7. 33 1/2°N / 107°W	
8. 39°N / 112 1/2°W	
9. 35 1/2°N / 108 1/2°W	
10. 33°N / 111°W	

Approximate Coordinates	State
32°N / 36°N and 110°W / 114°W	
36°N / 40°N and 110°W / 114°W	
32°N / 36°N and 104°W / 108°W	
36°N / 40°N and 104°W / 108°W	

Name ____________________

Name the City

Directions: Use the coordinates given below to locate each of the cities. The first one has been done for you.

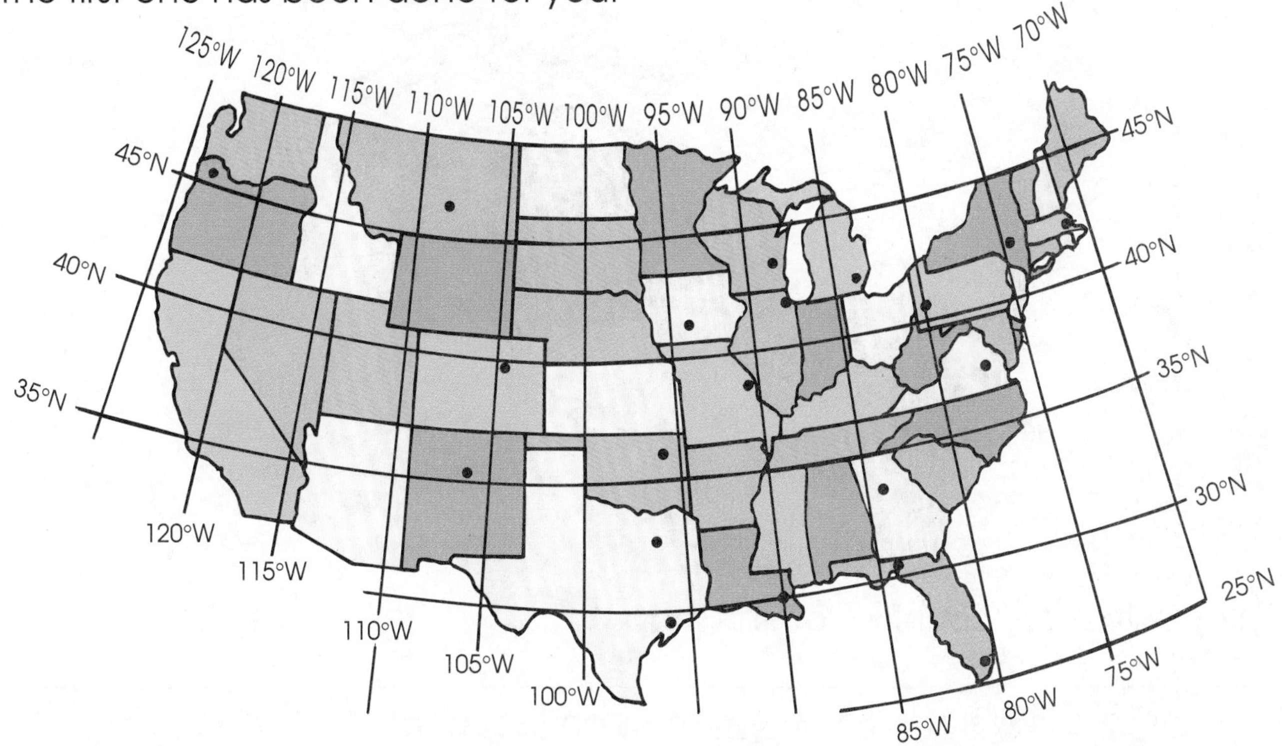

Latitude	Longitude	City
1. 34°N	84°W	Atlanta
2. 26°N	80°W	
3. 40°N	80°W	
4. 36°N	96°W	
5. 37°N	122°W	
6. 33°N	112°W	
7. 39°N	90°W	
8. 46°N	108°W	
9. 43°N	88°W	
10. 42°N	94°W	
11. 43°N	74°W	
12. 45°N	93°W	
13. 33°N	97°W	
14. 30°N	95°W	

Name ______________________________________

Locating Places in Western Europe

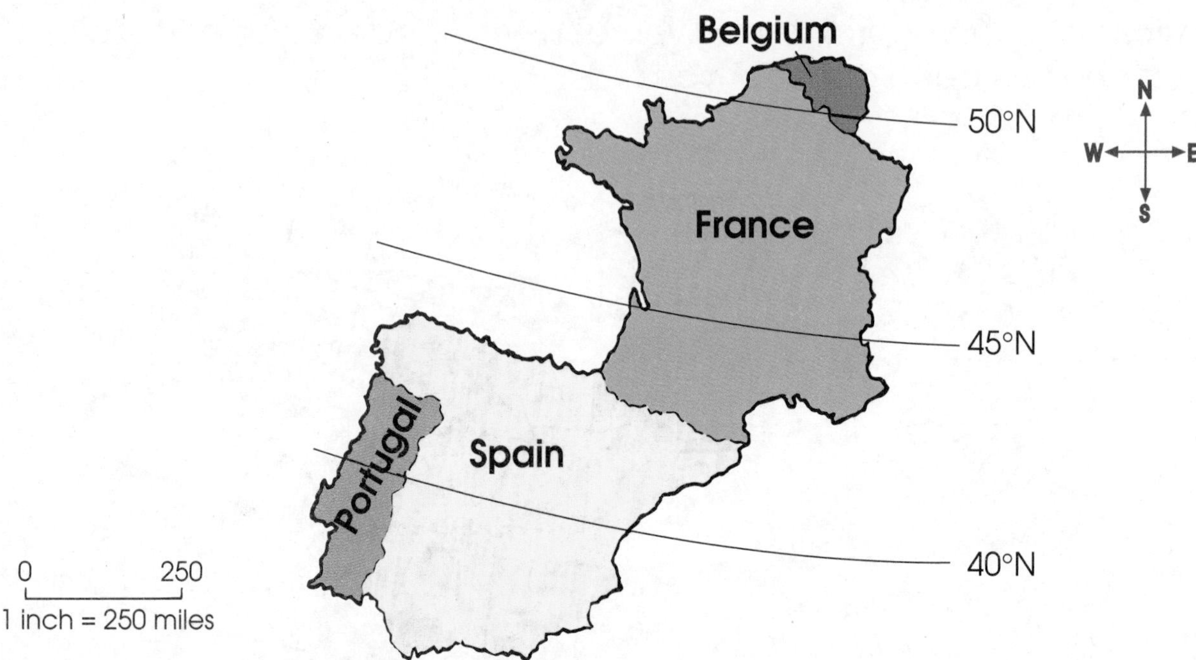

1. Name the four countries on this map.

   ______________ ______________ ______________ ______________

2. One inch equals ____________ miles on the map.
3. Which parallel line crosses both Portugal and Spain? ____________
4. Which two parallel lines cross France? ____________ ____________
5. Name the country directly north of France. ____________
6. Place the city of Barcelona on the northeastern coast of Spain about 225 miles south of the 45°N parallel.
7. Place the city of Paris in the north-central part of France about 75 miles south of the 50°N parallel.
8. Place Lisbon on the western coast of Portugal about 75 miles south of the 40°N parallel.
9. Place Madrid in the center of Spain about 50 miles north of the 40°N parallel.
10. Place Brussels near the northcentral part of Belgium about 50 miles north of the 50°N parallel line.
11. Place Toulouse in the southwestern part of France 100 miles south of the 45°N parallel.

Name____________________

Where in Europe?

Use with page 308.

Name____

Where in Europe?

Directions: Estimate and write the coordinates and countries for these European cities using the map on page 307. The first one has been done for you.

City	Latitude	Longitude	Country
1. London	52°N	0°	United Kingdom
2. Belgrade			
3. Warsaw			
4. Stockholm			
5. Athens			
6. Helsinki			
7. Paris			
8. Munich			
9. Copenhagen			
10. Oslo			
11. Glasgow			
12. Prague			
13. Bern			
14. Hamburg			
15. Dresden			
16. Dublin			
17. Rome			
18. Budapest			
19. Vienna			
20. Amsterdam			

Name________________________________

Latitude and Longitude Lines

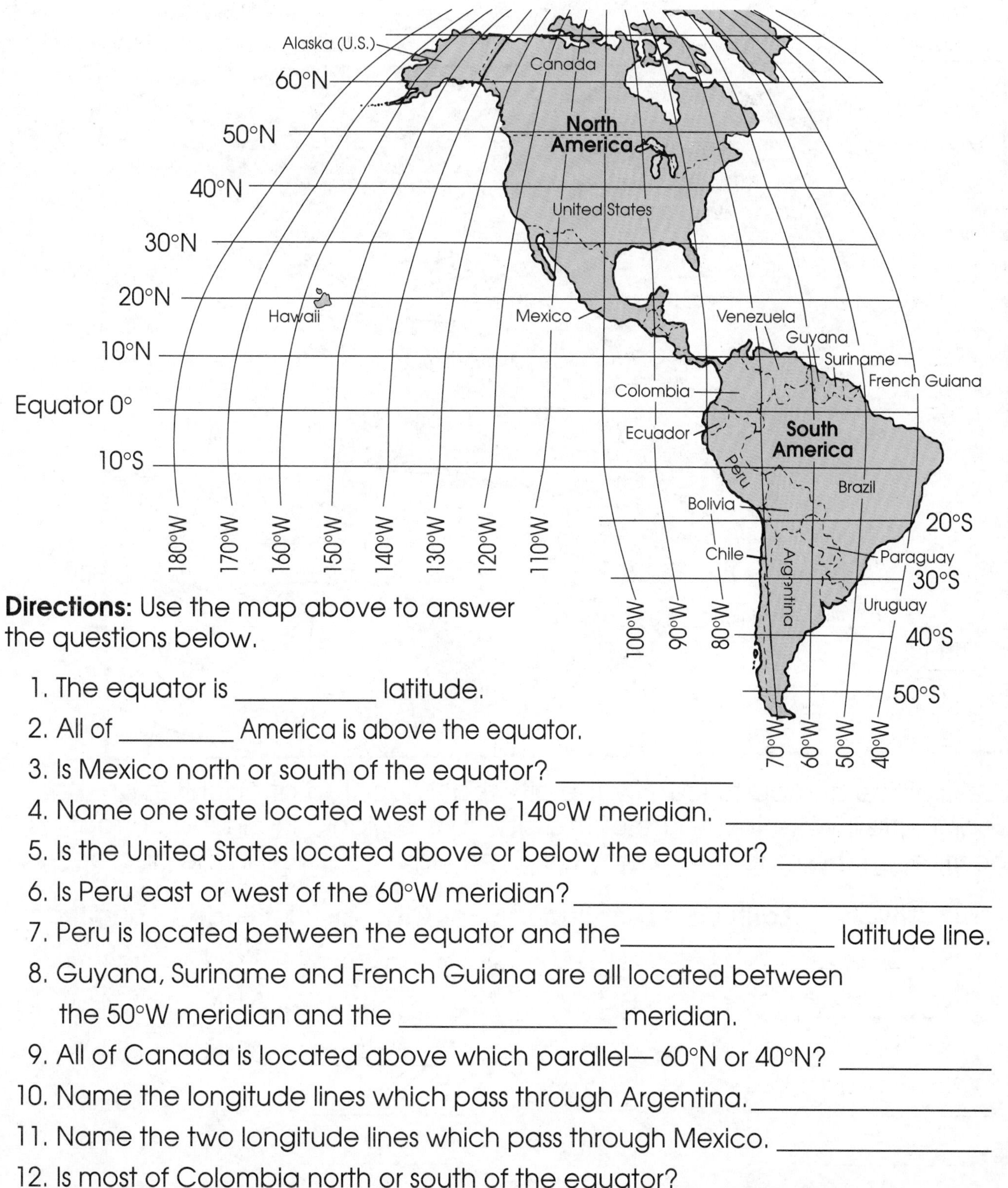

Directions: Use the map above to answer the questions below.

1. The equator is __________ latitude.
2. All of __________ America is above the equator.
3. Is Mexico north or south of the equator? ____________
4. Name one state located west of the 140°W meridian. ____________
5. Is the United States located above or below the equator? ____________
6. Is Peru east or west of the 60°W meridian? ____________
7. Peru is located between the equator and the ____________ latitude line.
8. Guyana, Suriname and French Guiana are all located between the 50°W meridian and the ____________ meridian.
9. All of Canada is located above which parallel— 60°N or 40°N? ____________
10. Name the longitude lines which pass through Argentina. ____________
11. Name the two longitude lines which pass through Mexico. ____________
12. Is most of Colombia north or south of the equator? ____________

Name ______________________________

Pinpointing North American Cities

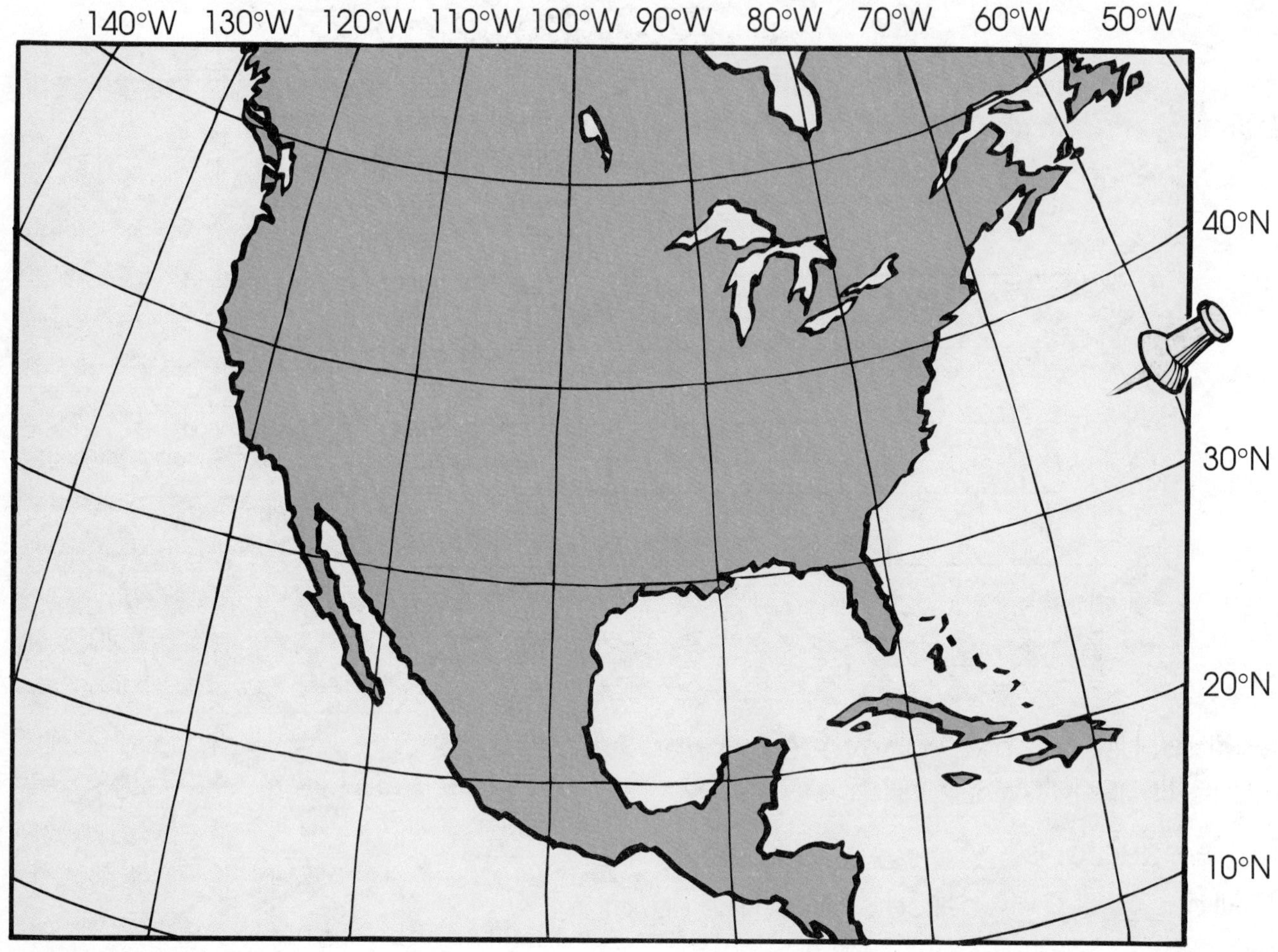

Use a globe or map to identify the city that is located at each set of coordinates. Write the name of the city on the blank and in the correct location on the map. There may be some slight variance in the degrees.

	City	Latitude	Longitude		City	Latitude	Longitude
1.	______________	25°N	80°W	6.	______________	19°N	99°W
2.	______________	39°N	104°W	7.	______________	51°N	114°W
3.	______________	50°N	97°W	8.	______________	33°N	84°W
4.	______________	23°N	82°W	9.	______________	42°N	83°W
5.	______________	37°N	122°W	10.	______________	46°N	71°W

Name ____________________

Night and Day Difference

What causes the daily change from daylight to darkness? Day turns into night because the earth rotates, or spins, on its axis. The earth's axis is an imaginary line that cuts through the earth from the North Pole to the South Pole. The earth spins in a counter-clockwise direction.

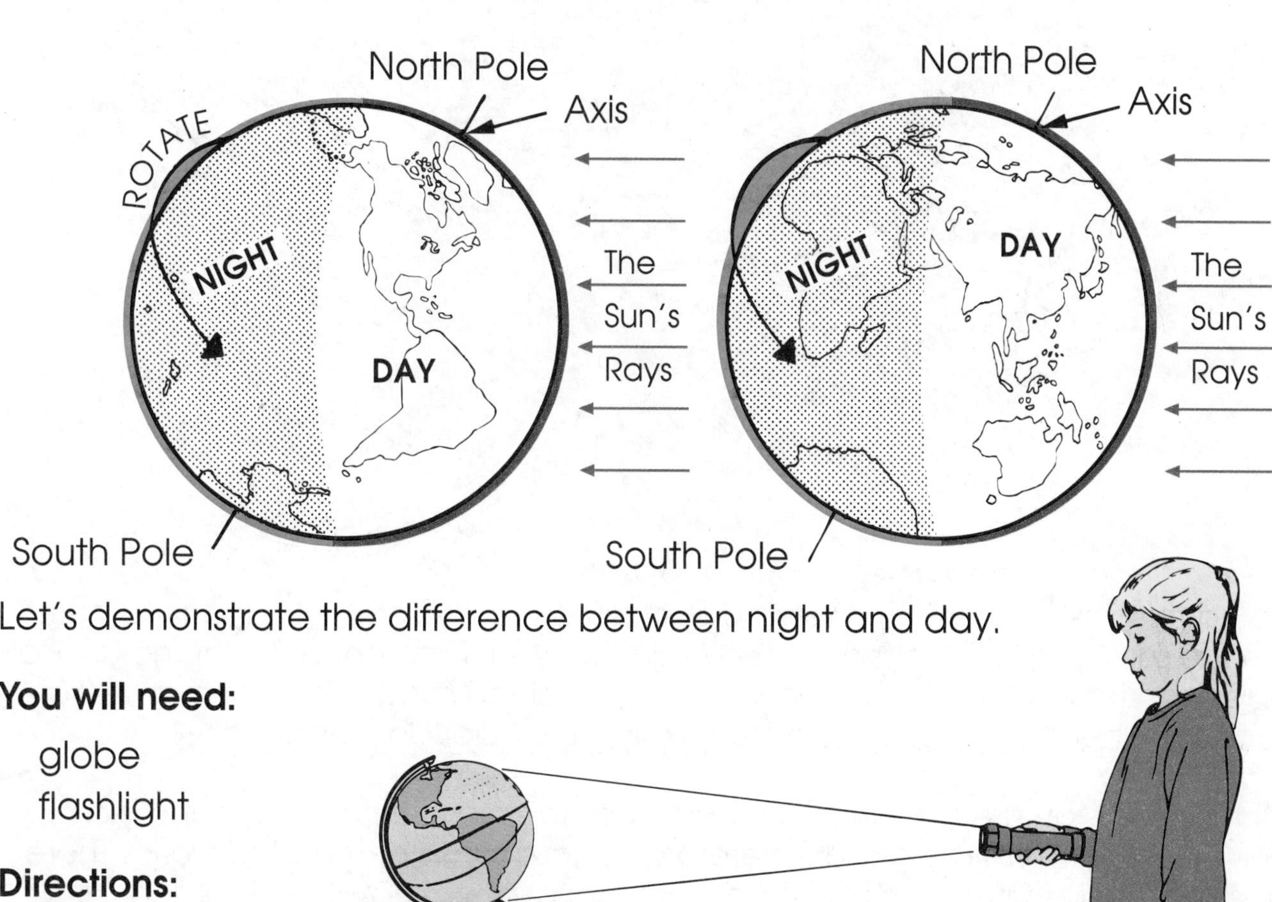

Let's demonstrate the difference between night and day.

You will need:

globe
flashlight

Directions:

1. In a very dark room, set the globe on a table, as demonstrated in the picture.
2. Standing five to ten feet away, aim the flashlight at the globe.
3. Have a friend slowly rotate the globe on its axis.
4. Discover what parts of the world are sleeping when it is daytime in your community.

Name ____________________

Time Zones

Do You Have the Time?

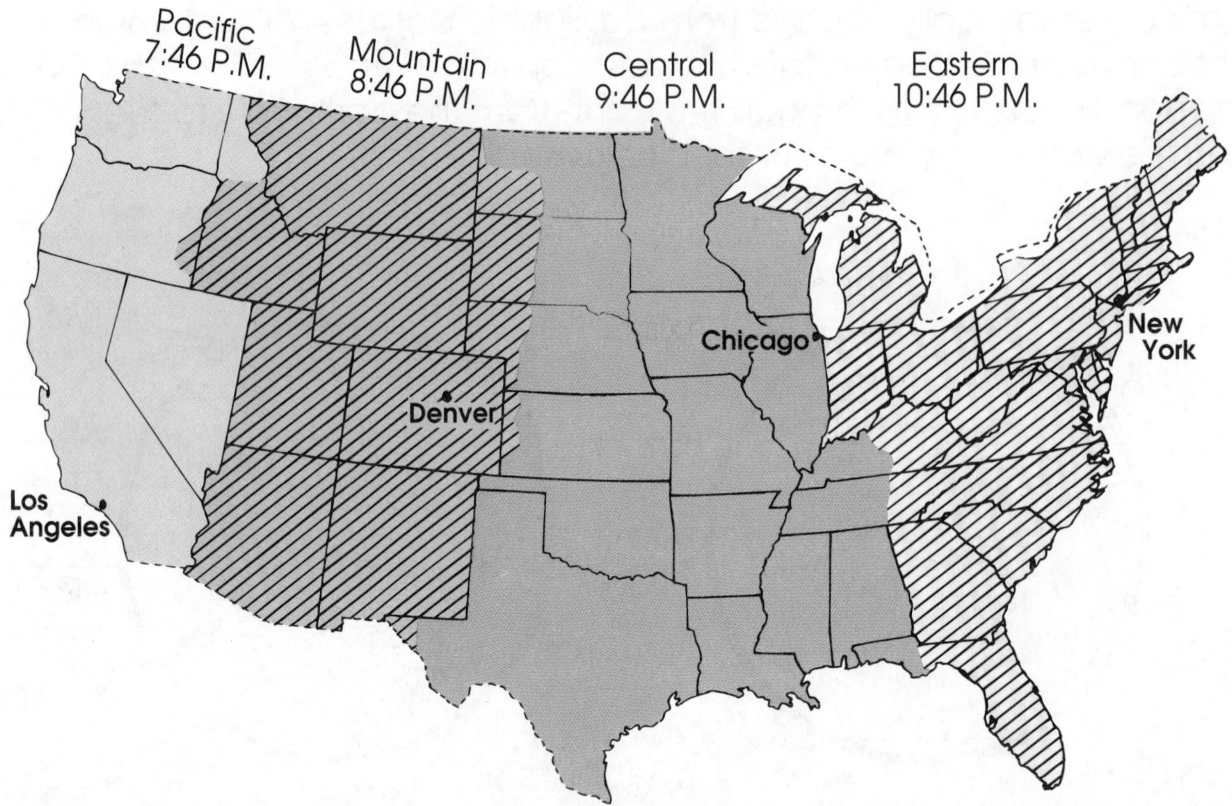

The earth spins on its axis in a west to east direction. This causes our day to begin with the sun rising in the east and setting in the west. Different areas of the United States can have different amounts of daylight at the same moment in time. For instance, when the sun is rising in New York, it is still dark in California.

A **time zone** is an area in which everyone has the same time. Every zone is one hour different from its neighbor. There are 24 time zones around the world. There are six time zones in the United States. The map above shows the four zones that cover the 48 contiguous, or touching, states.

When it is 6 o'clock in New York, what time is it in . . .

Chicago? __________ Los Angeles? __________ Denver? __________

What is the name of the time zone in which you live? __________

Name three other states in your time zone.

__________ __________ __________

Name______________________________________

World Time Zones

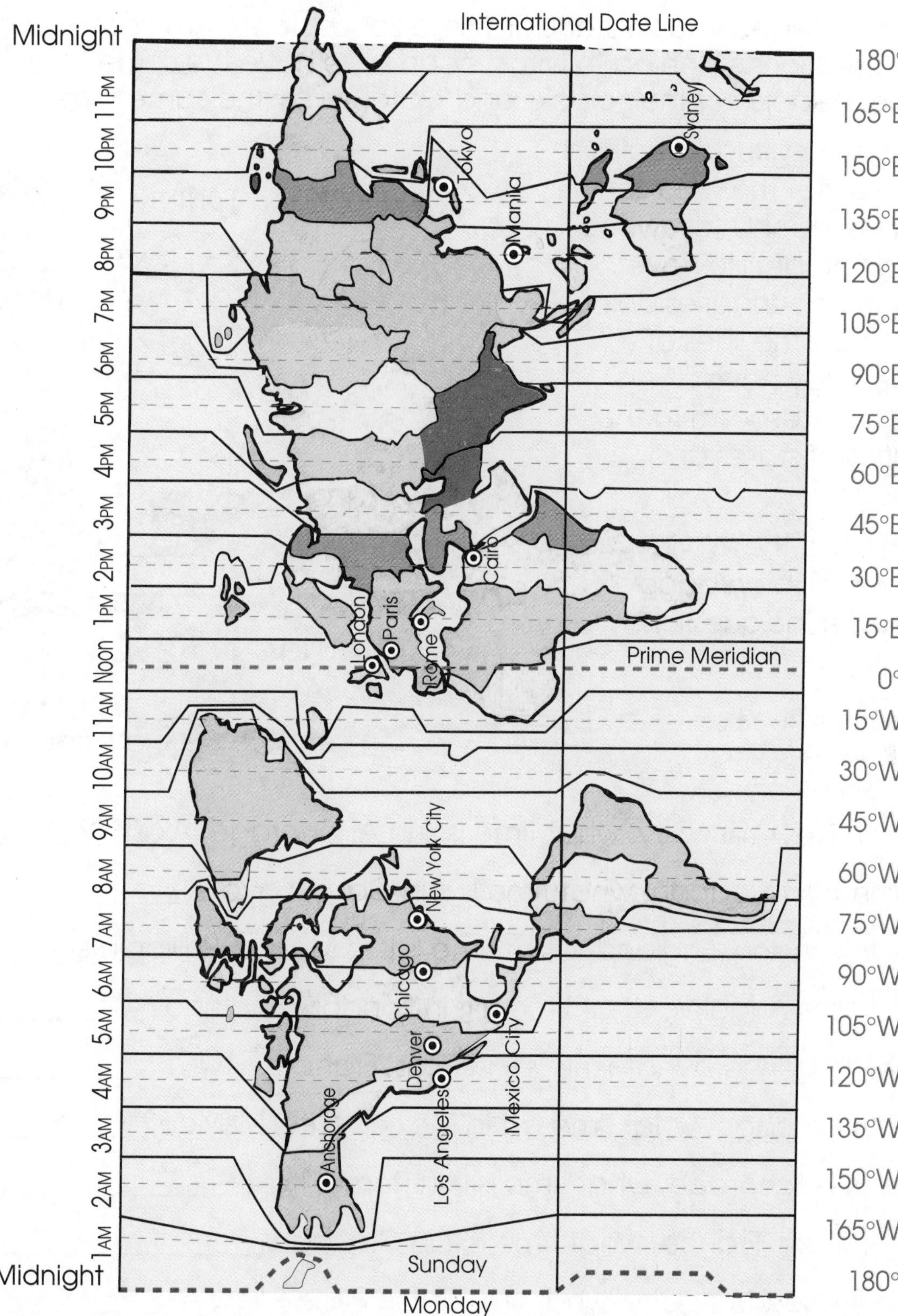

Use with page 314.

Name____________________________________

24-Hour Globe

The earth is divided into 24 standard time zones. These time zones are set so that large sections of the earth within each zone have the same time. In each time zone, people set their clocks and watches by the same time.

Every 15° of longitude begins a new time zone. The time zone boundaries roughly follow the lines of longitude. However, many of the boundaries do not follow exactly the lines of longitude. They have been altered to correspond to the boundaries of states and countries.

Directions: Use the World Time Zones map on page 313 to answer the questions below.

If it is . . .

3 A.M. in New York City, what time is it in Anchorage, Alaska? __________

4 P.M. in Tokyo, Japan, what time is it in Cairo, Egypt? __________

1 P.M. in London, England, what time is it in Manila, Philippines? __________

3 P.M. in Los Angeles, what time is it in London, England? __________

10 A.M. in Denver, what time is it in Paris, France? __________

9 P.M. in Chicago, what time is it in Mexico City, Mexico? __________

4 A.M. in Anchorage, what time is it in Rome, Italy? __________

1 P.M. in Paris, France, what time is it in Chicago? __________

11 P.M. in New York City, what time is it in Paris, France? __________

Name________________________________

Changing Times

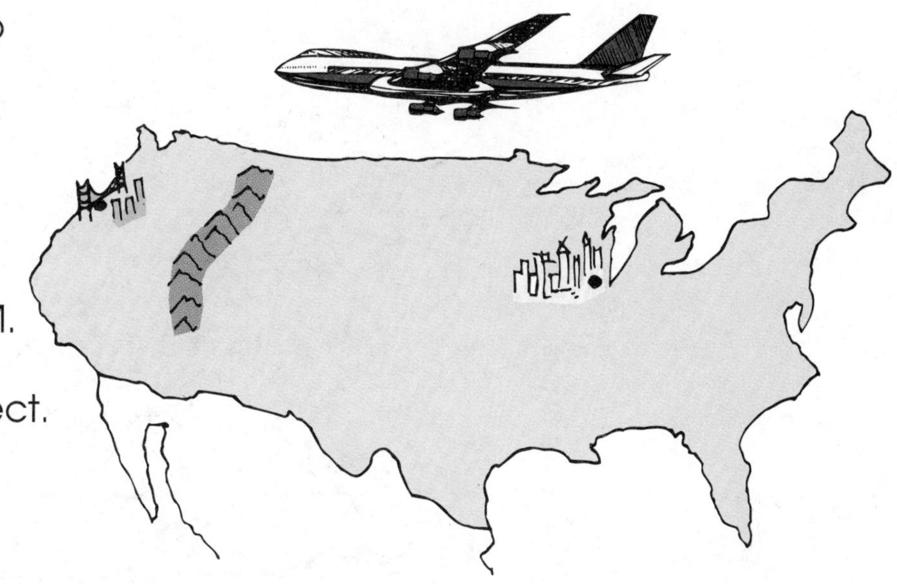

A plane leaves Chicago at 5:30 P.M. heading for San Francisco. The flight takes 3 hours. At what time will it arrive in San Francisco?

If you answered 8:30 P.M. to the above question, you are only partly correct. It would be 8:30 P.M. "Chicago time" but it would be 6:30 P.M. in San Francisco because the plane crossed two time zones.

Examine the time zones of the United States on the map on page 316. Notice that the time-zone boundaries do not always follow the state boundaries. Some states are in more than one time zone.

Directions: Use the United States Time Zones map (page 316) to answer the following questions.

1. How many time zones are there in the United States? ____________
2. How many time zones are there in the 48 contiguous (touching) states?

   ____
3. Name the time zones in all 50 states.____________________

   ____
4. If it is 3:30 P.M. in your state, what time is it in . . .

   California? ____________ Iowa?____________

   New York?____________ Colorado? ____________
5. What time is it right now in . . .

   Miami, Florida? ____________ Portland, Oregon?____________

   Grand Rapids, Michigan? ________ Dallas, Texas? ____________

   Cody, Wyoming? ____________ Richmond, Virginia? ____________

Name________________________________

United States Time Zones

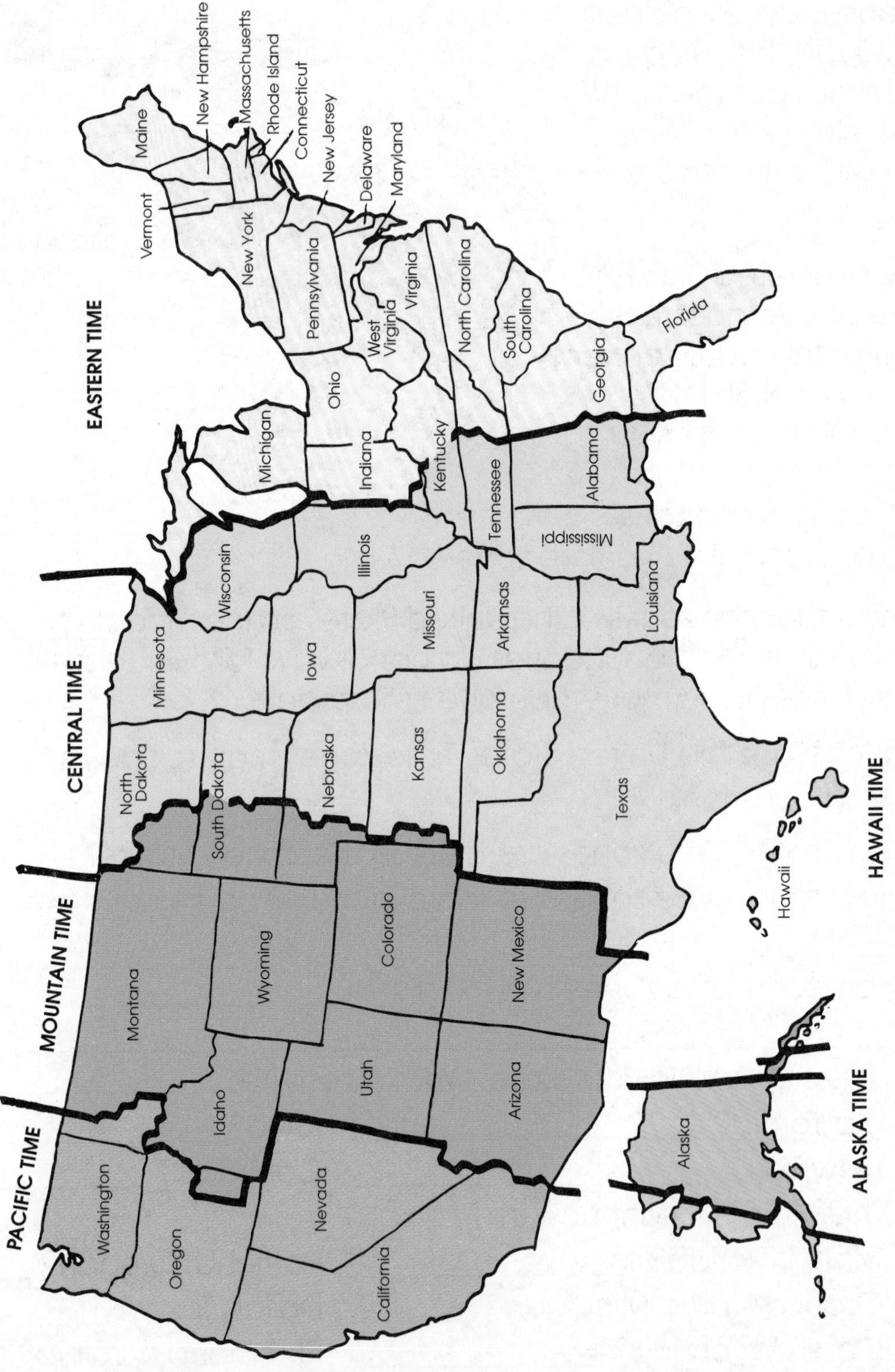

Use with page 315.

Name ______________________________

Map Skills Check-Up

Directions: Fill in the blanks below to show what you know about map skills.

1. Sets of numbers that show where lines of latitude and longitude meet are called ______________.
2. What are meridians? ______________________________
3. What is another name for 0° latitude? ______________________________
4. 0° longitude is called ______________________ and passes through ______________________________.
5. Map symbols are shown in a box called a ______________________.
6. Which kind of map shows capitals, cities and boundaries? __________
7. Which kind of map shows rivers, mountains and plateaus? __________
8. Distance on a map is measured with a ______________________.
9. The earth spins on its ______________ in an west to east direction.
10. A ________ ________ is an area in which everyone has the same time.
11. Name the 7 continents. ____________ ____________ ____________ ____________ ____________ ____________ ____________
12. What is a peninsula? ______________________________
13. Name the 4 oceans. ______________ ______________ ______________ ______________
14. One-half of the earth is called a ______________________.
15. Label this compass rose.

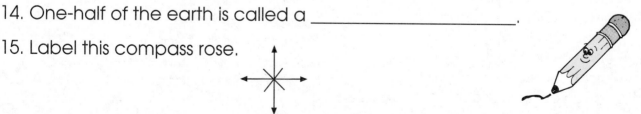

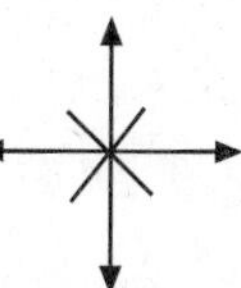

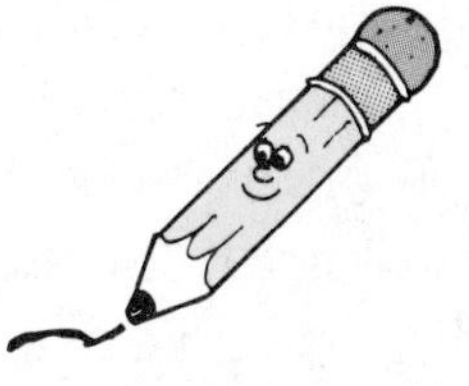

Name________________________________

Globe Puzzle

Directions: Use a world map to solve this puzzle.

Europe
Australia
Africa
Asia
Pacific
Indian
Atlantic
Arctic
equator
axis
north
south
continents
North America
South America
Antarctica

Across:

2. U.S.A.'s continent
3. southernmost continent
5. opposite north
6. continent west of Asia
8. divides the earth into northern and southern hemispheres
9. island continent
11. earth "spins" on it
12. largest ocean
13. ocean east of Africa

Down:

1. large continent northeast of Africa
2. direction of the North Pole from the equator
4. continent between the Atlantic and Indian Oceans
5. Brazil's continent
7. land masses of earth
10. ocean east of North America
11. northernmost ocean

Name______________________________

Carnac the Cartographer

A cartographer is a person who makes maps. Carnac the Cartographer was recently fired from his profession. Can you detect the errors he made on the map on page 320? Place a red **X** on all the mistakes that you see on the map. Then, list corrections in the appropriate sections.

Continents

Mistake	It should be...

Oceans/Seas

Mistake	It should be...

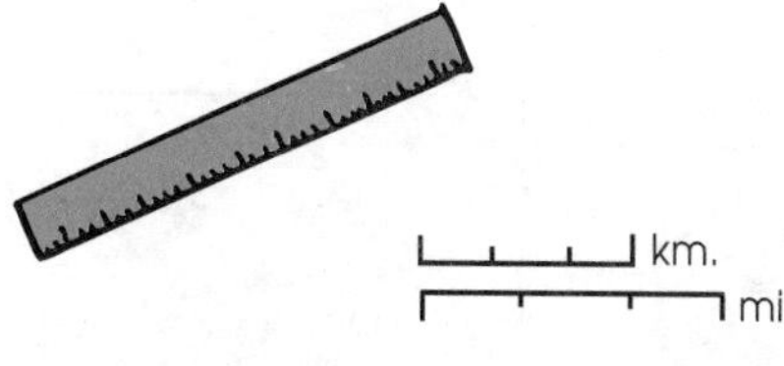

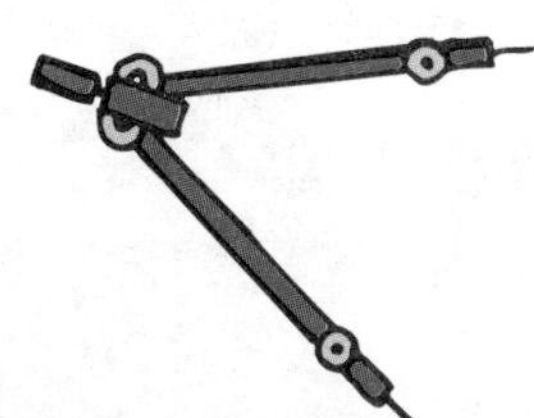

Latitude /Longitude

Mistake	It should be...

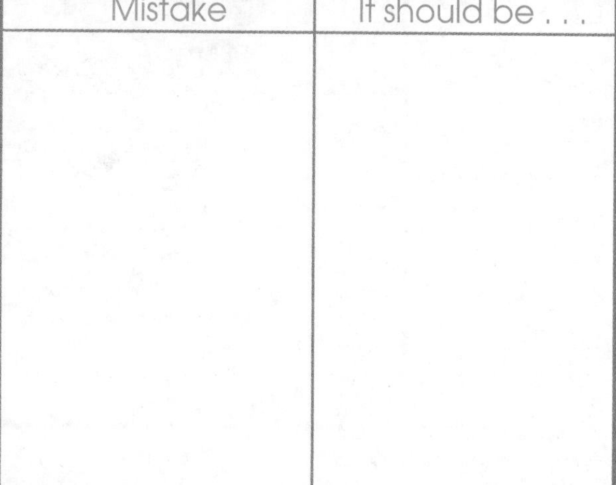

Direction Finder

Mistake	It should be . . .

Name____

Map and Geography Review Sheets

Carnac the Cartographer

Mixed-Up World Map

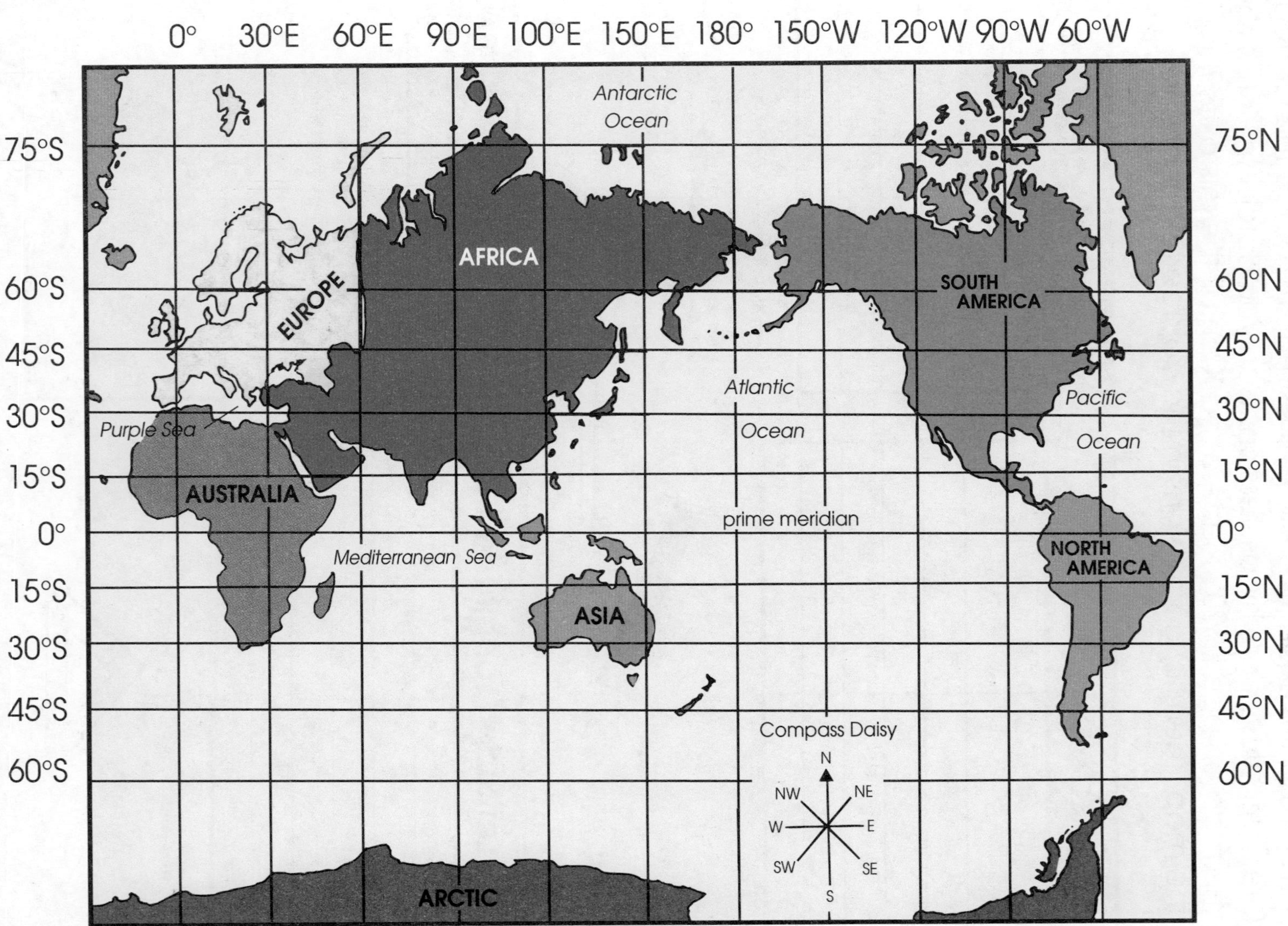

Name______________________________

Map Skills Check-Up

How well do you understand map concepts? Test yourself!

1. Name the 7 continents. ____________, ______________, ____________,

   ______________, ________________, ______________, ______________

2. Circle what is usually the map symbol for a national capital.

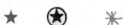

3. Lines of latitude are called ______________.

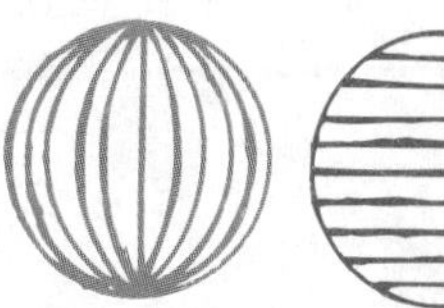

4. Circle the globe which shows lines of latitude.

5. 0° latitude is called the ______________.

6. Name the 4 oceans. ________________, ________________

   ________________, ________________.

7. Lines of longitude are called ________________________.

8. 0° longitude is called the________________________.

9. Draw meridians on this circle. Will they

   be lines of latitude or longitude?

   ____

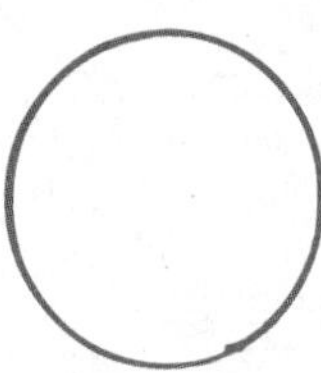

10. What is used on a map to measure distance? ____________

11. A spherical map of the earth is called a ___________.

12. Draw the symbol for degrees. ___________

13. Label the points of the compass rose.

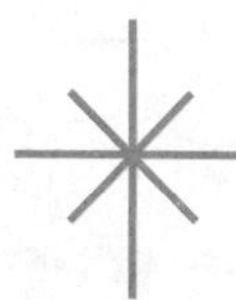

Name ____________________________________

World Map

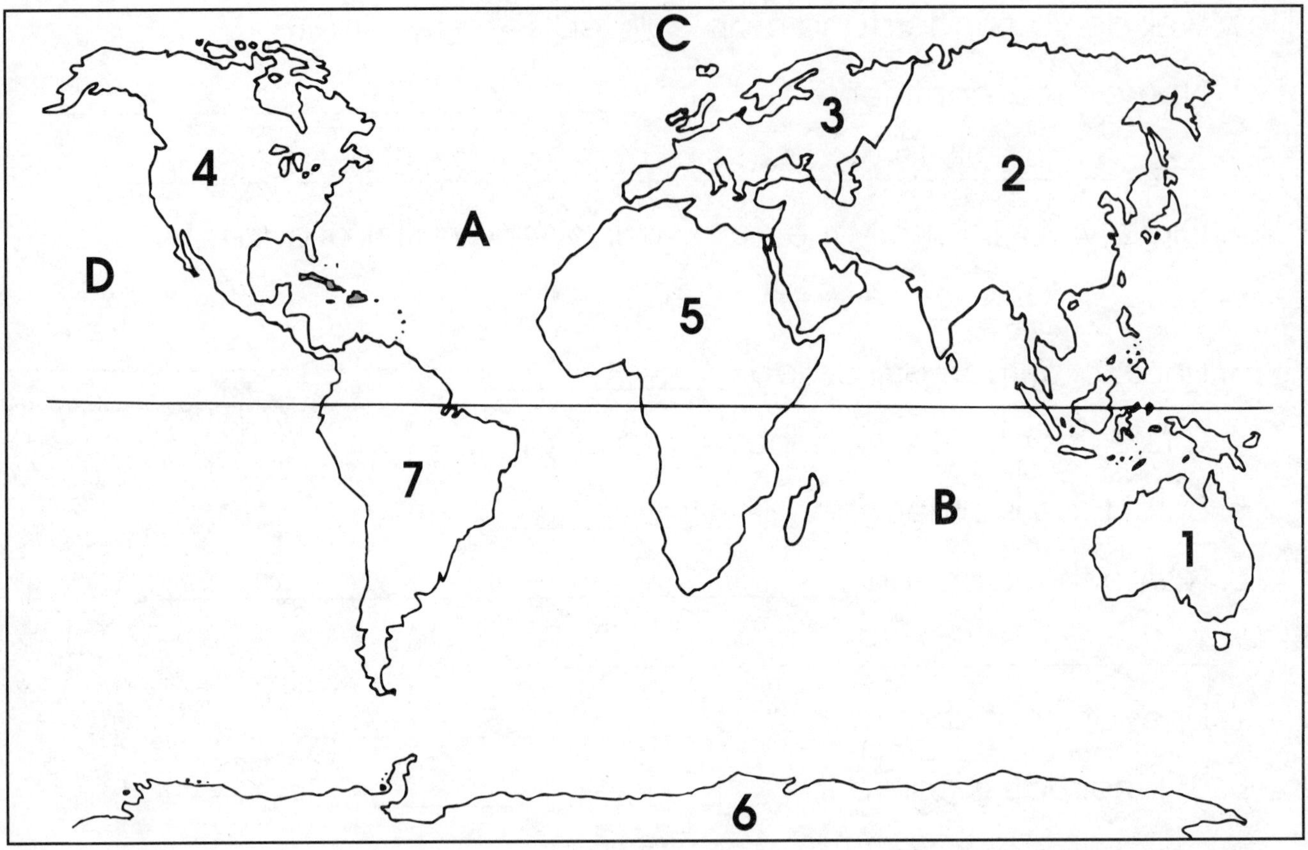

Name the continents as numbered on the map.

1. ______________________________
2. ______________________________
3. ______________________________
4. ______________________________
5. ______________________________
6. ______________________________
7. ______________________________

Outline all of the continents in green.

Draw one blue fish in each ocean.

Name the oceans as lettered on the map.

A. ______________________________

B. ______________________________

C. ______________________________

D. ______________________________

Color the equator red.

The Complete Book of Maps & Geography
Grades 3-6

ANSWER KEY

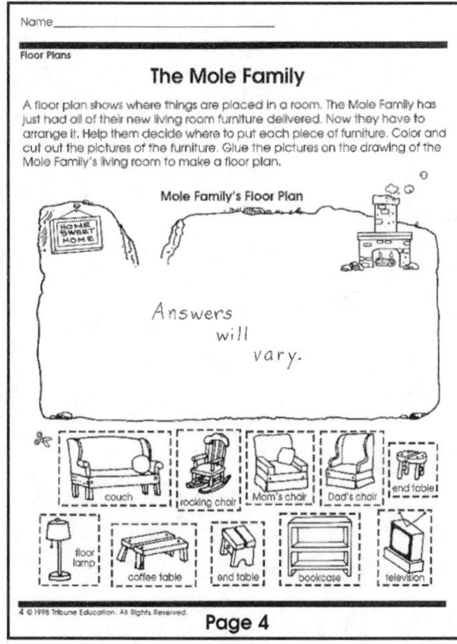

Name____________

Floor Plans

The Mole Family

A floor plan shows where things are placed in a room. The Mole Family has just had all of their new living room furniture delivered. Now they have to arrange it. Help them decide where to put each piece of furniture. Color and cut out the pictures of the furniture. Glue the pictures on the drawing of the Mole Family's living room to make a floor plan.

Mole Family's Floor Plan

Page 4

Name____________

Floor Plans

A Picture From Above

A floor plan looks like a picture someone drew looking down from the sky. It shows you where things are.

Circle the word which correctly completes each statement.

	a.	b.	c.
1. The TV is near the...	a. door	b. (window)	c. bed
2. The dresser is near the...	a. window	b. (door)	c. TV
3. Next to the bed is a...	a. TV	b. window	c. (table)
4. The bench is at the end of the...	a. (bed)	b. bookshelf	c. closet
5. The plant is by the...	a. dresser	b. bed	c. (bookshelf)
6. The bookshelf is next to the...	a. bed	b. closet	c. (door)
7. The lamp is on the...	a. (table)	b. TV	c. dresser

Follow these directions.
1. Draw a red circle around the TV.
2. Draw a black X on the desk.
3. Draw an oval rug in front of the bench using a color of your choice.
4. Draw a stuffed animal in the center of the bed.

Fill in these blanks with the correct word.
1. Between the closet and the TV is a desk.
2. The window is between the plant and the TV.
3. When you walk in the door, the dresser is to your right.
4. There (is) are one lamp(s) in the room.

Page 5

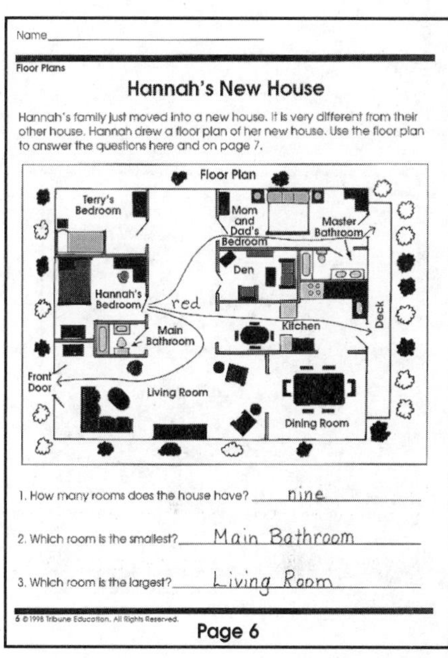

Name____________

Floor Plans

Hannah's New House

Hannah's family just moved into a new house. It is very different from their other house. Hannah drew a floor plan of her new house. Use the floor plan to answer the questions here and on page 7.

Floor Plan

1. How many rooms does the house have? nine
2. Which room is the smallest? Main Bathroom
3. Which room is the largest? Living Room

Page 6

Name____________

Floor Plans

Hannah's New House

4. Who has a room across from Mom and Dad's bedroom? Terry
5. Which rooms does Hannah walk past to go from the living room to her own bedroom? Main Bathroom, Kitchen
6. How many bedrooms are there? three
7. Which rooms have a door leading onto the deck? Kitchen, Mom and Dad's Bedroom
8. The front door opens into what room? Living Room
9. On the floor plan on page 6, use a red crayon to draw the routes Hannah could take from her room to a door leading outside in case of an emergency.

Page 7

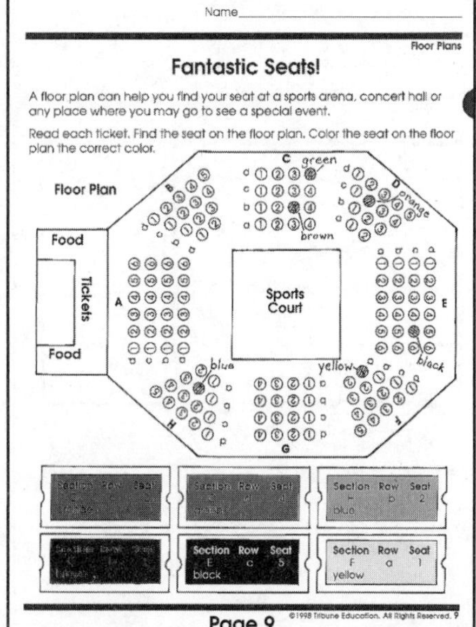

Name____________

Floor Plans

Fantastic Seats!

A floor plan can help you find your seat at a sports arena, concert hall or any place where you may go to see a special event.

Read each ticket. Find the seat on the floor plan. Color the seat on the floor plan the correct color.

Floor Plan

Page 9

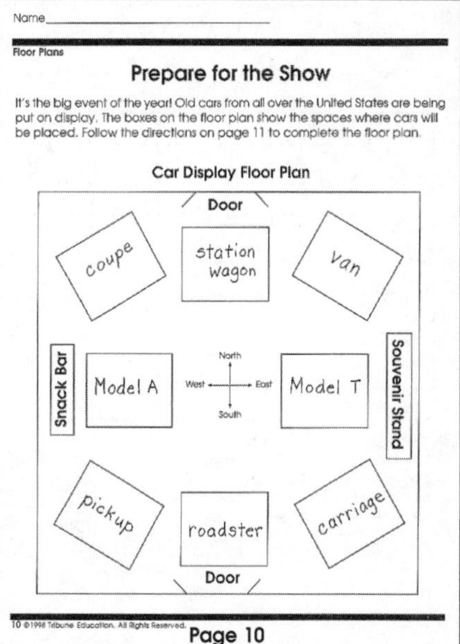

Name____________

Floor Plans

Prepare for the Show

It's the big event of the year! Old cars from all over the United States are being put on display. The boxes on the floor plan show the spaces where cars will be placed. Follow the directions on page 11 to complete the floor plan.

Car Display Floor Plan

Page 10

Name

Floor Plans

Creating a Floor Plan

Pretend you are looking at your classroom or a room in your home from high atop the lighting fixtures. Draw how the room looks.

Answers will vary.

©1998 Tribune Education. All Rights Reserved. 13

Page 13

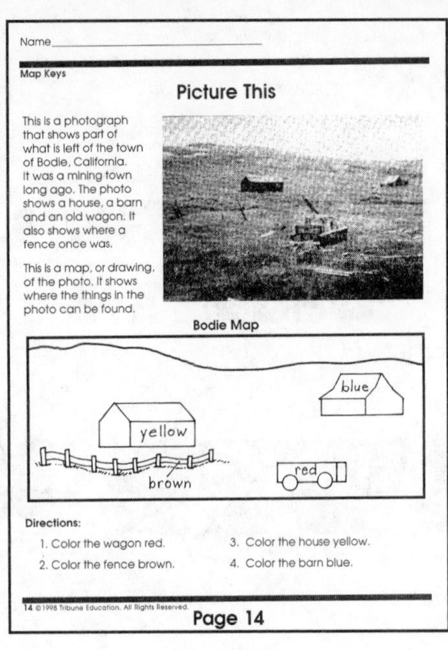
Name

Map Keys

Picture This

This is a photograph that shows part of what is left of the town of Bodie, California. It was a mining town long ago. The photo shows a house, a barn and an old wagon. It also shows where a fence once was.

This is a map, or drawing, of the photo. It shows where the things in the photo can be found.

Bodie Map

Directions:

1. Color the wagon red.
2. Color the fence brown.
3. Color the house yellow.
4. Color the barn blue.

14 ©1998 Tribune Education. All Rights Reserved.

Page 14

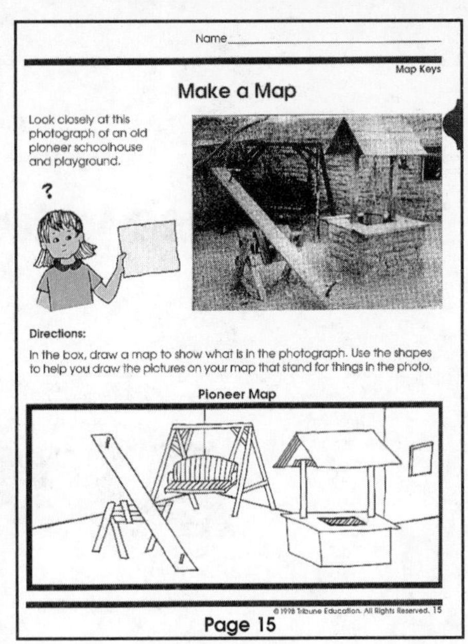
Name

Map Keys

Make a Map

Look closely at this photograph of an old pioneer schoolhouse and playground.

Directions:

In the box, draw a map to show what is in the photograph. Use the shapes to help you draw the pictures on your map that stand for things in the photo.

Pioneer Map

©1998 Tribune Education. All Rights Reserved. 15

Page 15

Name

Map Keys

Symbols on Maps

A symbol is a picture that stands for something that is shown on a map. Symbols used in a map are shown in the Map Key. Look at the symbols. Draw a line from each symbol to what it stands for in the drawing below.

Map Key

16 ©1998 Tribune Education. All Rights Reserved.

Page 16

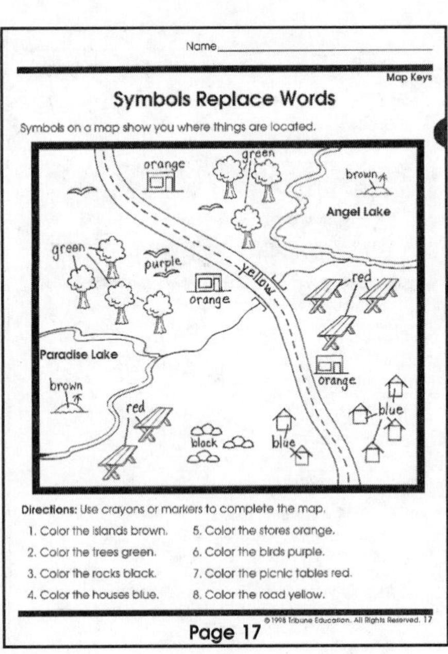
Name

Map Keys

Symbols Replace Words

Symbols on a map show you where things are located.

Directions: Use crayons or markers to complete the map.

1. Color the islands brown.
2. Color the trees green.
3. Color the rocks black.
4. Color the houses blue.
5. Color the stores orange.
6. Color the birds purple.
7. Color the picnic tables red.
8. Color the road yellow.

©1998 Tribune Education. All Rights Reserved. 17

Page 17

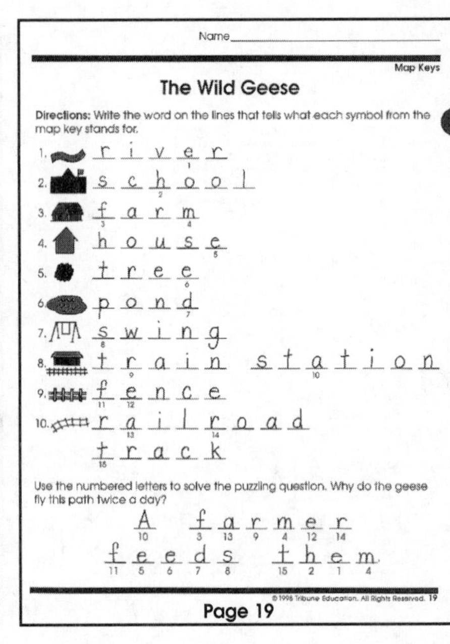
Name

Map Keys

The Wild Geese

Directions: Write the word on the lines that tells what each symbol from the map key stands for.

1. river
2. school
3. farm
4. house
5. tree
6. pond
7. swing
8. train station
9. fence
10. railroad track

Use the numbered letters to solve the puzzling question. Why do the geese fly this path twice a day?

A farmer feeds them.

©1998 Tribune Education. All Rights Reserved. 19

Page 19

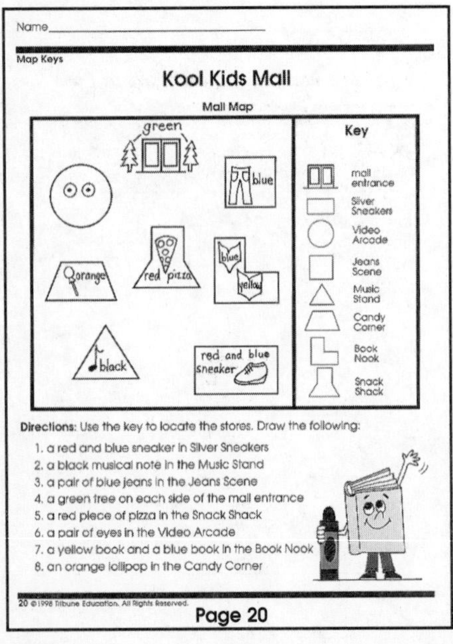
Name

Map Keys

Kool Kids Mall

Mall Map

Key

- mall entrance
- Silver Sneakers
- Video Arcade
- Jeans Scene
- Music Stand
- Candy Corner
- Book Nook
- Snack Shack

Directions: Use the key to locate the stores. Draw the following:

1. a red and blue sneaker in Silver Sneakers
2. a black musical note in the Music Stand
3. a pair of blue jeans in the Jeans Scene
4. a green tree on each side of the mall entrance
5. a red piece of pizza in the Snack Shack
6. a pair of eyes in the Video Arcade
7. a yellow book and a blue book in the Book Nook
8. an orange lollipop in the Candy Corner

20 ©1998 Tribune Education. All Rights Reserved.

Page 20

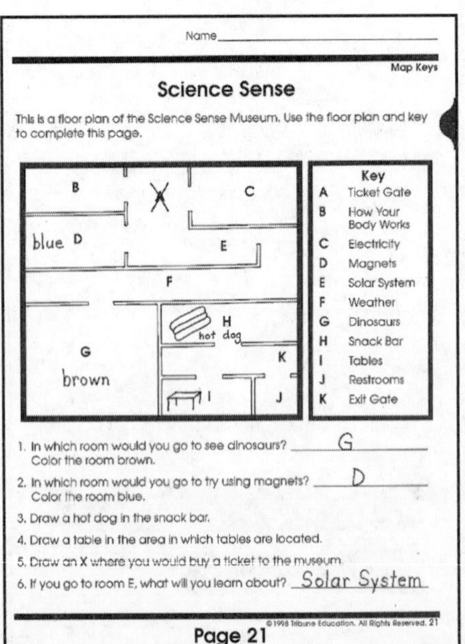
Name

Map Keys

Science Sense

This is a floor plan of the Science Sense Museum. Use the floor plan and key to complete this page.

Key

- A Ticket Gate
- B How Your Body Works
- C Electricity
- D Magnets
- E Solar System
- F Weather
- G Dinosaurs
- H Snack Bar
- I Tables
- J Restrooms
- K Exit Gate

1. In which room would you go to see dinosaurs? G
   Color the room brown.
2. In which room would you go to try using magnets? D
   Color the room blue.
3. Draw a hot dog in the snack bar.
4. Draw a table in the area in which tables are located.
5. Draw an X where you would buy a ticket to the museum.
6. If you go to room E, what will you learn about? Solar System

©1998 Tribune Education. All Rights Reserved. 21

Page 21

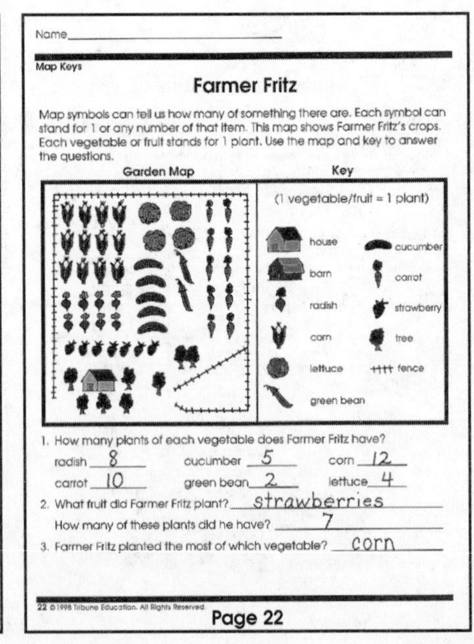
Name

Map Keys

Farmer Fritz

Map symbols can tell us how many of something there are. Each symbol can stand for 1 or any number of that item. This map shows Farmer Fritz's crops. Each vegetable or fruit stands for 1 plant. Use the map and key to answer the questions.

Garden Map

Key

(1 vegetable/fruit = 1 plant)

1. How many plants of each vegetable does Farmer Fritz have?
   radish 8 cucumber 5 corn 12
   carrot 10 green bean 2 lettuce 4
2. What fruit did Farmer Fritz plant? strawberries
   How many of these plants did he have? 7
3. Farmer Fritz planted the most of which vegetable? corn

22 ©1998 Tribune Education. All Rights Reserved.

Page 22

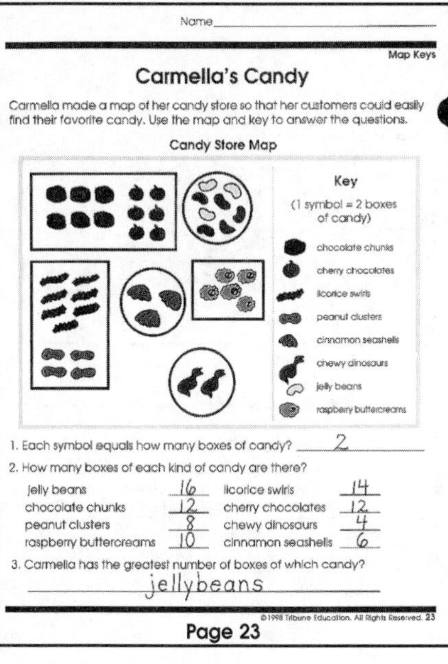

Name___________

Map Keys

Carmella's Candy

Carmella made a map of her candy store so that her customers could easily find their favorite candy. Use the map and key to answer the questions.

Candy Store Map

Key (1 symbol = 2 boxes of candy): chocolate chunks, cherry chocolates, licorice swirls, peanut clusters, cinnamon seashells, chewy dinosaurs, jelly beans, raspberry buttercreams

1. Each symbol equals how many boxes of candy? 2
2. How many boxes of each kind of candy are there?

jelly beans	16	licorice swirls	14
chocolate chunks	12	cherry chocolates	12
peanut clusters	8	chewy dinosaurs	4
raspberry buttercreams	10	cinnamon seashells	6

3. Carmella has the greatest number of boxes of which candy? jellybeans

 23

Page 23

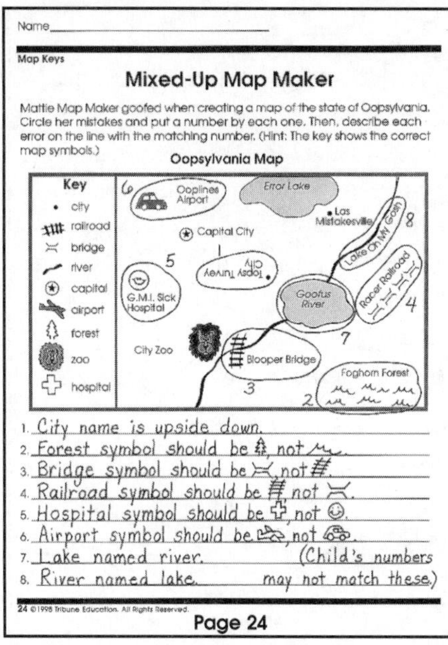

Name___________

Map Keys

Mixed-Up Map Maker

Mattie Map Maker goofed when creating a map of the state of Oopsylvania. Circle her mistakes and put a number by each one. Then, describe each error on the line with the matching number. (Hint: The key shows the correct map symbols.)

Oopsylvania Map

1. City name is upside down.
2. Forest symbol should be [tree], not [grass].
3. Bridge symbol should be [bridge], not [railroad].
4. Railroad symbol should be [railroad], not [bridge].
5. Hospital symbol should be [cross], not [face].
6. Airport symbol should be [plane], not [car].
7. Lake named river. (Child's numbers
8. River named lake. may not match these.)

24

Page 24

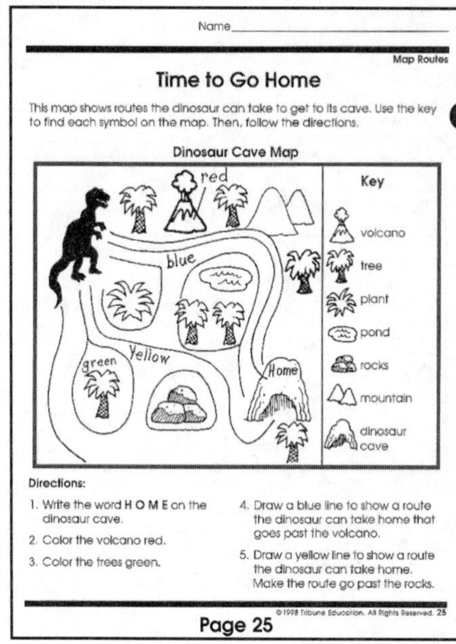

Name___________

Map Routes

Time to Go Home

This map shows routes the dinosaur can take to get to its cave. Use the key to find each symbol on the map. Then, follow the directions.

Dinosaur Cave Map

Directions:

1. Write the word H O M E on the dinosaur cave.
2. Color the volcano red.
3. Color the trees green.
4. Draw a blue line to show a route the dinosaur can take home that goes past the volcano.
5. Draw a yellow line to show a route the dinosaur can take home. Make the route go past the rocks.

 25

Page 25

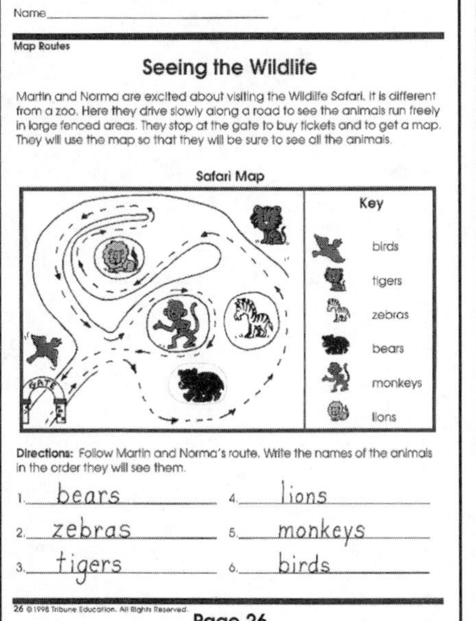

Name___________

Map Routes

Seeing the Wildlife

Martin and Norma are excited about visiting the Wildlife Safari. It is different from a zoo. Here they drive slowly along a road to see the animals run freely in large fenced areas. They stop at the gate to buy tickets and to get a map. They will use the map so that they will be sure to see all the animals.

Safari Map

Directions: Follow Martin and Norma's route. Write the names of the animals in the order they will see them.

1. bears
2. zebras
3. tigers
4. lions
5. monkeys
6. birds

26

Page 26

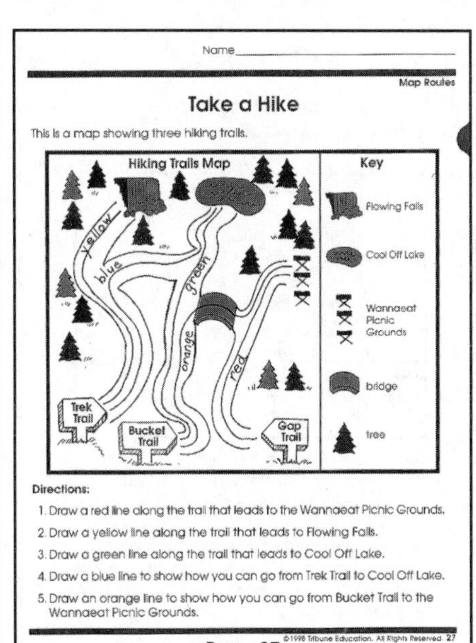

Name___________

Map Routes

Take a Hike

This is a map showing three hiking trails.

Hiking Trails Map

Directions:

1. Draw a red line along the trail that leads to the Wannaeat Picnic Grounds.
2. Draw a yellow line along the trail that leads to Flowing Falls.
3. Draw a green line along the trail that leads to Cool Off Lake.
4. Draw a blue line to show how you can go from Trek Trail to Cool Off Lake.
5. Draw an orange line to show how you can go from Bucket Trail to the Wannaeat Picnic Grounds.

 27

Page 27

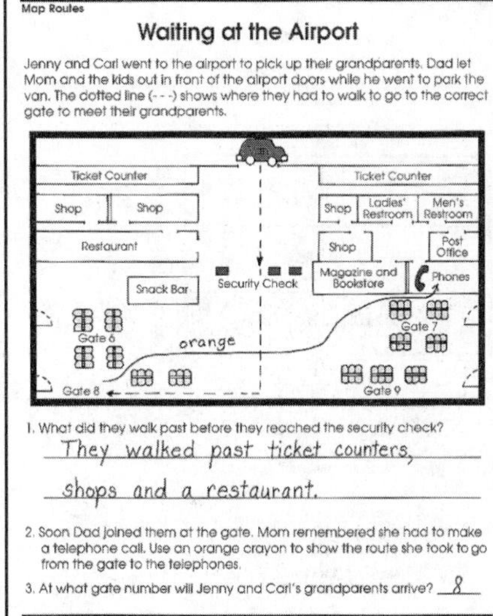

Name___________

Map Routes

Waiting at the Airport

Jenny and Carl went to the airport to pick up their grandparents. Dad let Mom and the kids out in front of the airport doors while he went to park the van. The dotted line (- - -) shows where they had to walk to go to the correct gate to meet their grandparents.

1. What did they walk past before they reached the security check? They walked past ticket counters, shops and a restaurant.
2. Soon Dad joined them at the gate. Mom remembered she had to make a telephone call. Use an orange crayon to show the route she took to go from the gate to the telephones.
3. At what gate number will Jenny and Carl's grandparents arrive? 8

28

Page 28

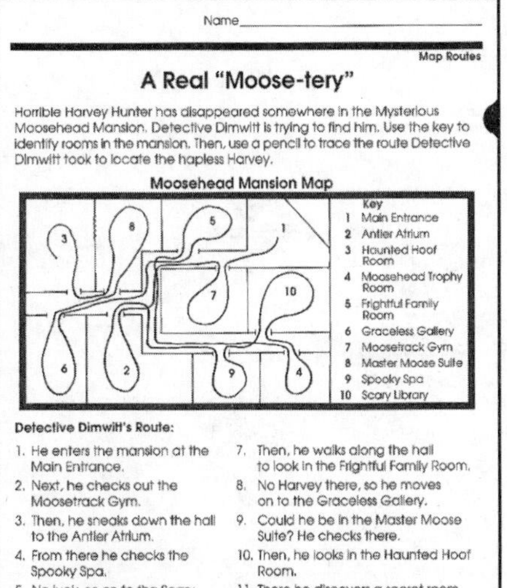

Name___________

Map Routes

A Real "Moose-tery"

Horrible Harvey Hunter has disappeared somewhere in the Mysterious Moosehead Mansion. Detective Dimwitt is trying to find him. Use the key to identify rooms in the mansion. Then, use a pencil to trace the route Detective Dimwitt took to locate the hapless Harvey.

Moosehead Mansion Map

Detective Dimwitt's Route:

1. He enters the mansion at the Main Entrance.
2. Next, he checks out the Moosetrack Gym.
3. Then, he sneaks down the hall to the Antler Atrium.
4. From there he checks the Spooky Spa.
5. No luck, so on to the Scary Library he goes.
6. Next, the detective scans the Moosehead Trophy Room.
7. Then, he walks along the hall to look in the Frightful Family Room.
8. No Harvey there, so he moves on to the Graceless Gallery.
9. Could he be in the Master Moose Suite? He checks there.
10. Then, he looks in the Haunted Hoof Room.
11. There he discovers a secret room. Inside he finds Harvey reading a hunting magazine. The search is over!

 29

Page 29

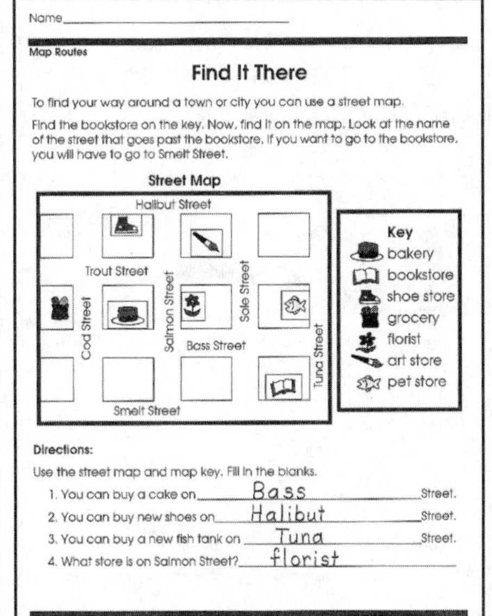

Name___________

Map Routes

Find It There

To find your way around a town or city you can use a street map.

Find the bookstore on the key. Now, find it on the map. Look at the name of the street that goes past the bookstore. If you want to go to the bookstore, you will have to go to Smelt Street.

Street Map

Directions:

Use the street map and map key. Fill in the blanks.

1. You can buy a cake on Bass Street.
2. You can buy new shoes on Halibut Street.
3. You can buy a new fish tank on Tuna Street.
4. What store is on Salmon Street? florist

30

Page 30

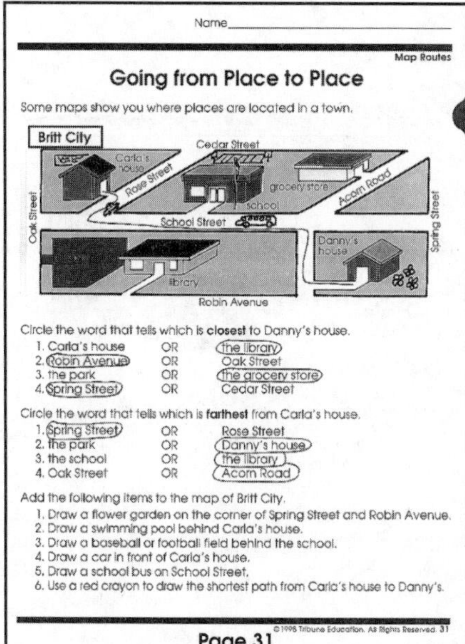

Name___________

Map Routes

Going from Place to Place

Some maps show you where places are located in a town.

Circle the word that tells which is **closest** to Danny's house.

1.	Carla's house	OR	(the library)
2.	(Robin Avenue)	OR	Oak Street
3.	the park	OR	(the grocery store)
4.	(Spring Street)	OR	Cedar Street

Circle the word that tells which is **farthest** from Carla's house.

1.	(Spring Street)	OR	Rose Street
2.	the park	OR	(Danny's house)
3.	the school	OR	(the library)
4.	Oak Street	OR	(Acorn Road)

Add the following items to the map of Britt City.

1. Draw a flower garden on the corner of Spring Street and Robin Avenue.
2. Draw a swimming pool behind Carla's house.
3. Draw a baseball or football field behind the school.
4. Draw a car in front of Carla's house.
5. Draw a school bus on School Street.
6. Use a red crayon to draw the shortest path from Carla's house to Danny's.

 31

Page 31

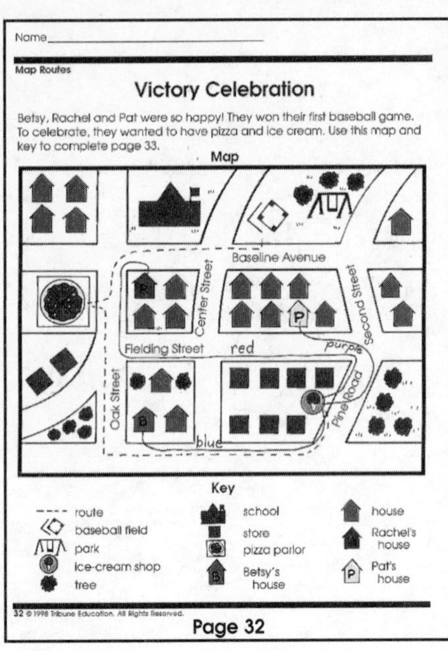

Name________________

Map Routes

Victory Celebration

Betsy, Rachel and Pat were so happy! They won their first baseball game. To celebrate, they wanted to have pizza and ice cream. Use this map and key to complete page 33.

Map

Key

--- route
baseball field
park
ice-cream shop
tree
school
store
pizza parlor
Betsy's house
house
Rachel's house
Pat's house

32 © 1998 Tribune Education. All Rights Reserved.

Page 32

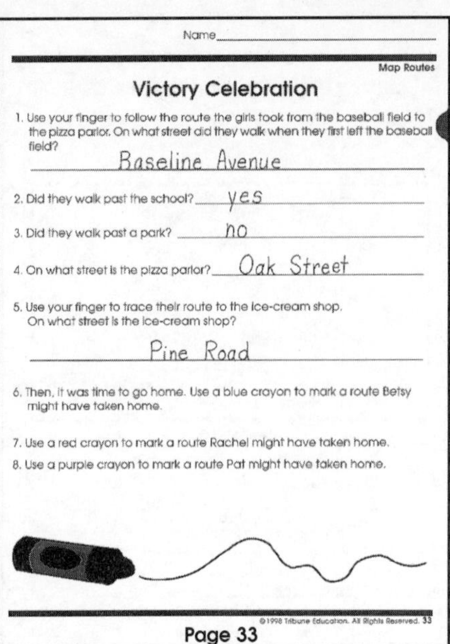

Name________________

Map Routes

Victory Celebration

1. Use your finger to follow the route the girls took from the baseball field to the pizza parlor. On what street did they walk when they first left the baseball field? Baseline Avenue
2. Did they walk past the school? yes
3. Did they walk past a park? no
4. On what street is the pizza parlor? Oak Street
5. Use your finger to trace their route to the ice-cream shop. On what street is the ice-cream shop? Pine Road
6. Then, it was time to go home. Use a blue crayon to mark a route Betsy might have taken home.
7. Use a red crayon to mark a route Rachel might have taken home.
8. Use a purple crayon to mark a route Pat might have taken home.

©1998 Tribune Education. All Rights Reserved. 33

Page 33

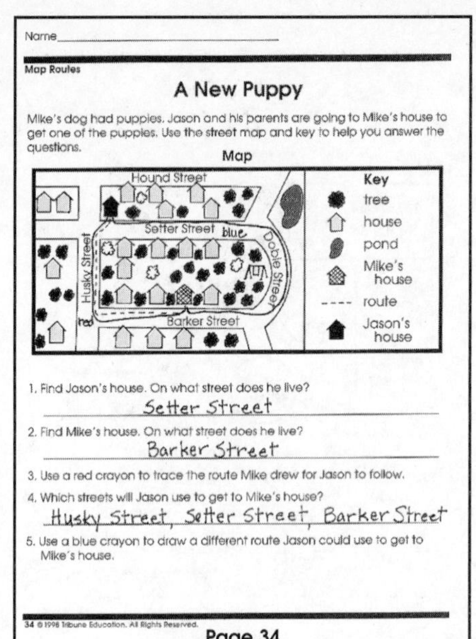

Name________________

Map Routes

A New Puppy

Mike's dog had puppies. Jason and his parents are going to Mike's house to get one of the puppies. Use the street map and key to help you answer the questions.

Map

Key: tree, house, pond, Mike's house, route, Jason's house

1. Find Jason's house. On what street does he live? Setter Street
2. Find Mike's house. On what street does he live? Barker Street
3. Use a red crayon to trace the route Mike drew for Jason to follow.
4. Which streets will Jason use to get to Mike's house? Husky Street, Setter Street, Barker Street
5. Use a blue crayon to draw a different route Jason could use to get to Mike's house.

34 © 1998 Tribune Education. All Rights Reserved.

Page 34

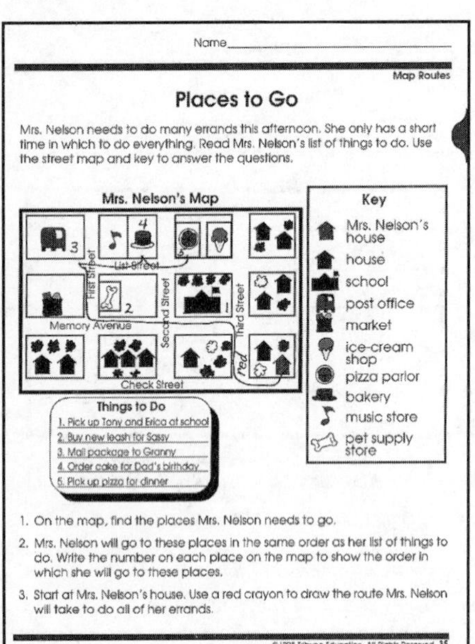

Name________________

Map Routes

Places to Go

Mrs. Nelson needs to do many errands this afternoon. She only has a short time in which to do everything. Read Mrs. Nelson's list of things to do. Use the street map and key to answer the questions.

Mrs. Nelson's Map

Key: Mrs. Nelson's house, house, school, post office, market, ice-cream shop, pizza parlor, bakery, music store, pet supply store

Things to Do
1. Pick up Tony and Erica at school
2. Buy new leash for Sassy
3. Mail package to Granny
4. Order cake for Dad's birthday
5. Pick up pizza for dinner

1. On the map, find the places Mrs. Nelson needs to go.
2. Mrs. Nelson will go to these places in the same order as her list of things to do. Write the number on each place on the map to show the order in which she will go to these places.
3. Start at Mrs. Nelson's house. Use a red crayon to draw the route Mrs. Nelson will take to do all of her errands.

©1998 Tribune Education. All Rights Reserved. 35

Page 35

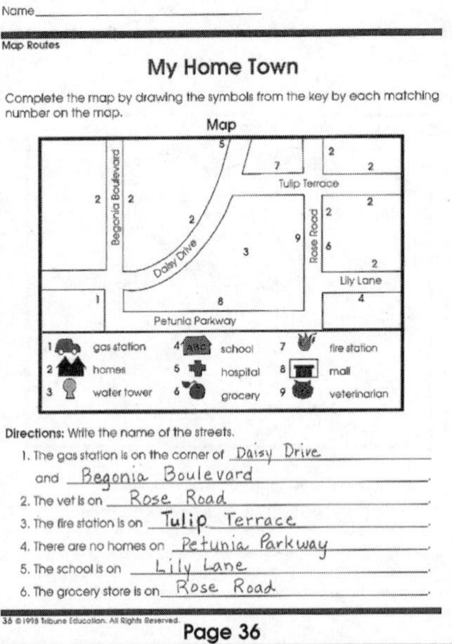

Name________________

Map Routes

My Home Town

Complete the map by drawing the symbols from the key by each matching number on the map.

Map

1 gas station, 2 homes, 3 water tower, 4 school, 5 hospital, 6 grocery, 7 fire station, 8 mall, 9 veterinarian

Directions: Write the name of the streets.

1. The gas station is on the corner of Daisy Drive and Begonia Boulevard.
2. The vet is on Rose Road.
3. The fire station is on Tulip Terrace.
4. There are no homes on Petunia Parkway.
5. The school is on Lily Lane.
6. The grocery store is on Rose Road.

36 ©1998 Tribune Education. All Rights Reserved.

Page 36

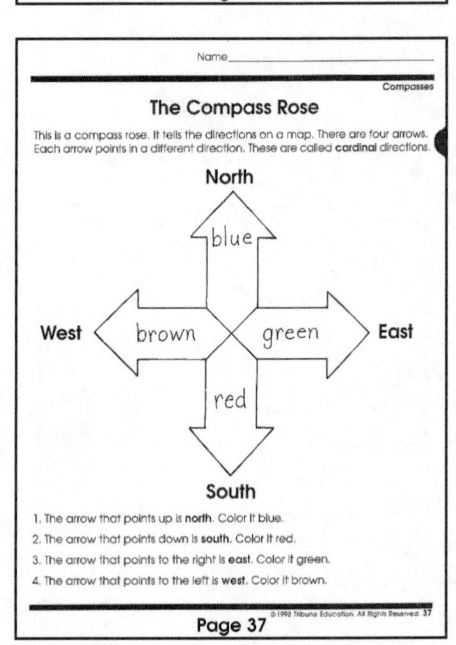

Name________________

Compasses

The Compass Rose

This is a compass rose. It tells the directions on a map. There are four arrows. Each arrow points in a different direction. These are called **cardinal** directions.

1. The arrow that points up is **north**. Color it blue.
2. The arrow that points down is **south**. Color it red.
3. The arrow that points to the right is **east**. Color it green.
4. The arrow that points to the left is **west**. Color it brown.

©1998 Tribune Education. All Rights Reserved. 37

Page 37

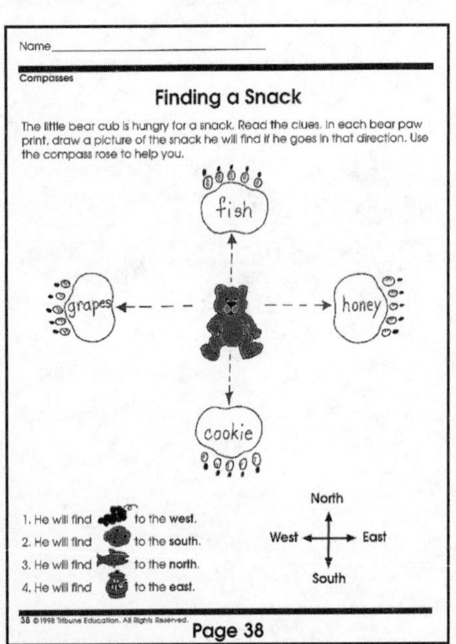

Name________________

Compasses

Finding a Snack

The little bear cub is hungry for a snack. Read the clues. In each bear paw print, draw a picture of the snack he will find if he goes in that direction. Use the compass rose to help you.

1. He will find [grapes] to the **west**.
2. He will find [cookie] to the **south**.
3. He will find [fish] to the **north**.
4. He will find [honey] to the **east**.

38 ©1998 Tribune Education. All Rights Reserved.

Page 38

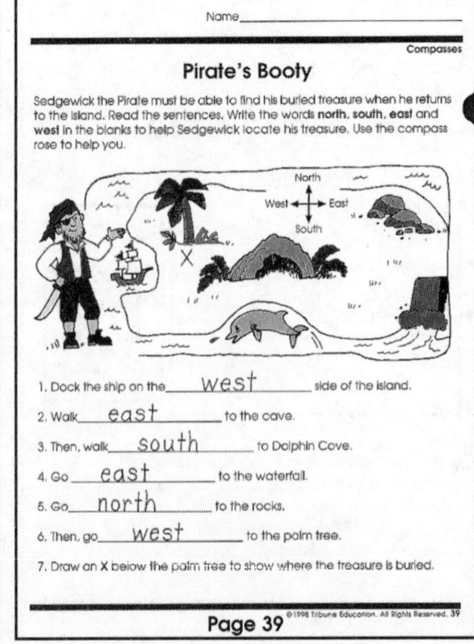

Name________________

Compasses

Pirate's Booty

Sedgewick the Pirate must be able to find his buried treasure when he returns to the island. Read the sentences. Write the words **north, south, east** and **west** in the blanks to help Sedgewick locate his treasure. Use the compass rose to help you.

1. Dock the ship on the west side of the island.
2. Walk east to the cave.
3. Then, walk south to Dolphin Cove.
4. Go east to the waterfall.
5. Go north to the rocks.
6. Then, go west to the palm tree.
7. Draw an X below the palm tree to show where the treasure is buried.

©1998 Tribune Education. All Rights Reserved. 39

Page 39

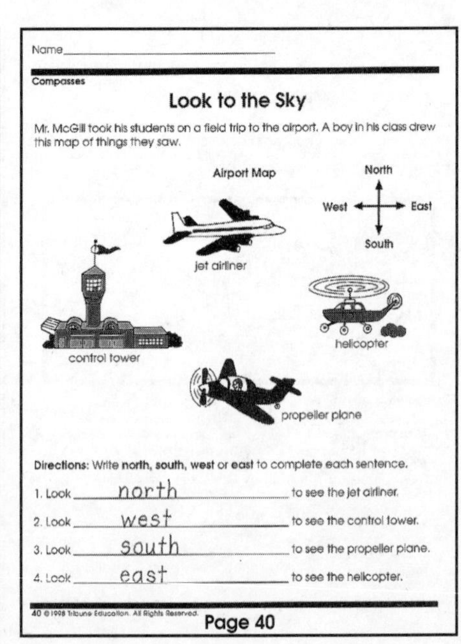

Name________________

Compasses

Look to the Sky

Mr. McGill took his students on a field trip to the airport. A boy in his class drew this map of things they saw.

Airport Map

Directions: Write north, south, west or east to complete each sentence.

1. Look north to see the jet airliner.
2. Look west to see the control tower.
3. Look south to see the propeller plane.
4. Look east to see the helicopter.

40 ©1998 Tribune Education. All Rights Reserved.

Page 40

Name____________________

Compasses

Sign Search

Gina went for a hike. She found a piece of paper. There were strange directions written on it. Then, she looked around and saw pictures drawn on the rocks in the area. Aha! The paper she had found was a route to follow. Read the directions and draw the route on the map.

Map

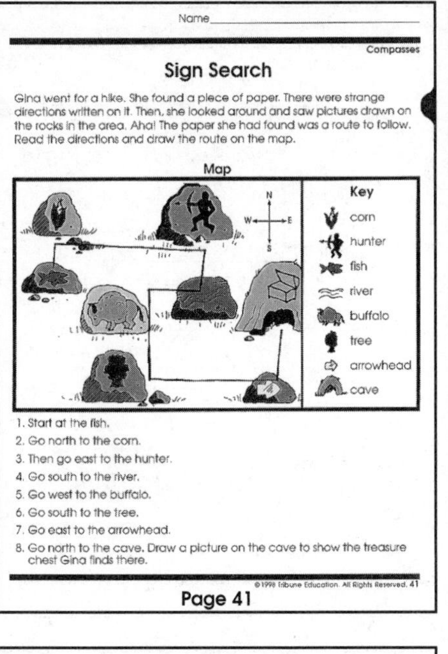

1. Start at the fish.
2. Go north to the corn.
3. Then go east to the hunter.
4. Go south to the river.
5. Go west to the buffalo.
6. Go south to the tree.
7. Go east to the arrowhead.
8. Go north to the cave. Draw a picture on the cave to show the treasure chest Gina finds there.

Page 41

Name____________________

Compasses

What Do Hikers See?

Follow the directions to complete this area map.

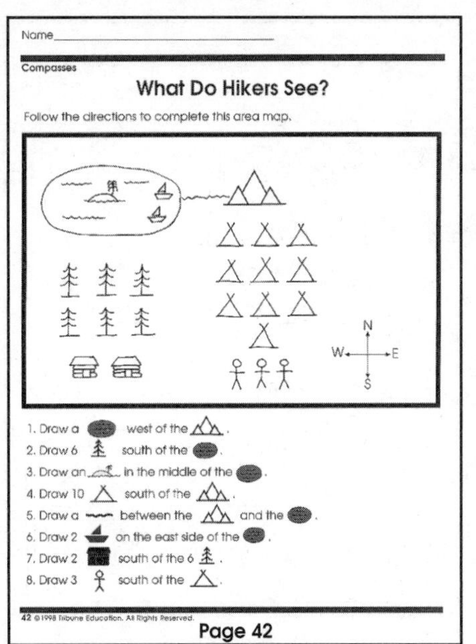

1. Draw a [pond] west of the [mountains].
2. Draw 6 [trees] south of the [pond].
3. Draw an [island] in the middle of the [pond].
4. Draw 10 [tents] south of the [mountains].
5. Draw a [stream] between the [mountains] and the [pond].
6. Draw 2 [boats] on the east side of the [pond].
7. Draw 2 [cabins] south of the 6 [trees].
8. Draw 3 [people] south of the [tent].

Page 42

Name____________________

Compasses

You're Invited

Liz sent out invitations to her birthday party. She drew a map to show how to go from school to her house.

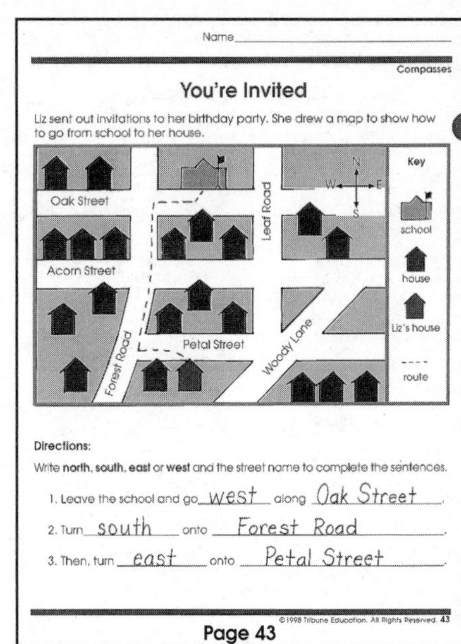

Directions:

Write **north, south, east** or **west** and the street name to complete the sentences.

1. Leave the school and go west along Oak Street.
2. Turn south onto Forest Road.
3. Then, turn east onto Petal Street.

Page 43

Name____________________

Compasses

Missing Diamonds

Mrs. Wently's diamonds are missing. Seth Sleuth has been hired to find them. He listens to Mrs. Wently's story. She had seen the robber run through the library and out onto the balcony. Then, he jumped to the ground and ran away. Seth Sleuth went to search the library. Perhaps the robber had hidden the diamonds in the library and planned to come back later to get them. This is a map of Mrs. Wently's library. Read more about the case on page 45.

Library Map

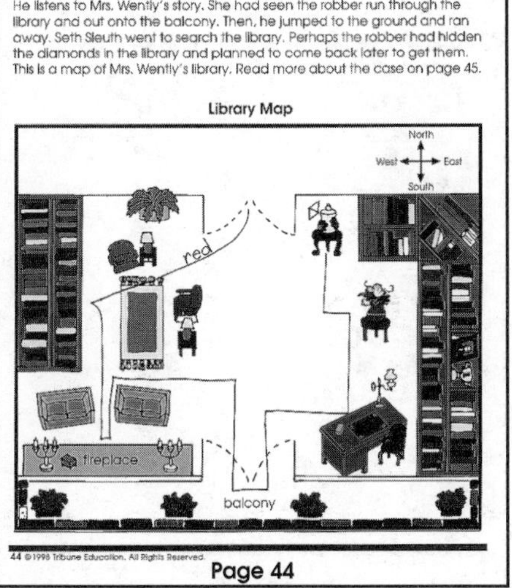

Page 44

Name____________________

Compasses

Ice Cream!

Ding. Ding. Ding-a-ling! Here comes the ice-cream truck. On hot summer days, Stan drives his ice-cream truck around the neighborhood. He takes the same route every day. This map shows the neighborhood where Stan drives. Follow the directions on page 47.

Ice-Cream Truck Route Map

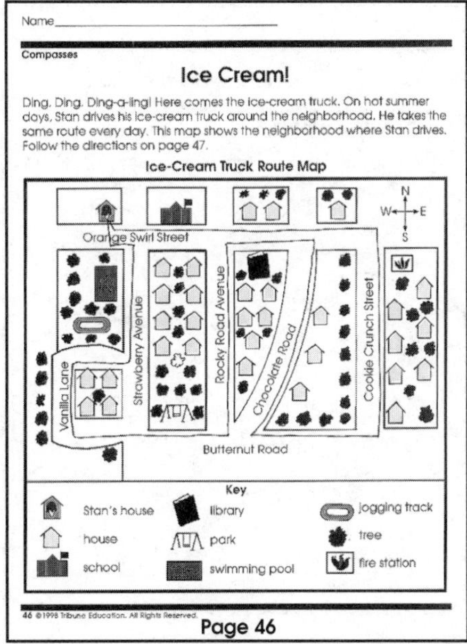

Page 46

Name____________________

Compasses

Secret Mission

Sam Super Spy is on a mission. He must get the secret papers and deliver them to his boss as soon as possible. This is a map of where the mission is to take place. Follow the directions on page 49 to help Sam.

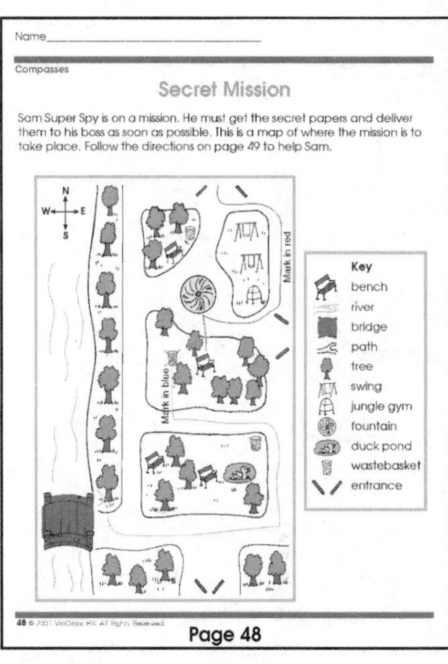

Page 48

Name____________________

Compasses

Connect - A - Dot

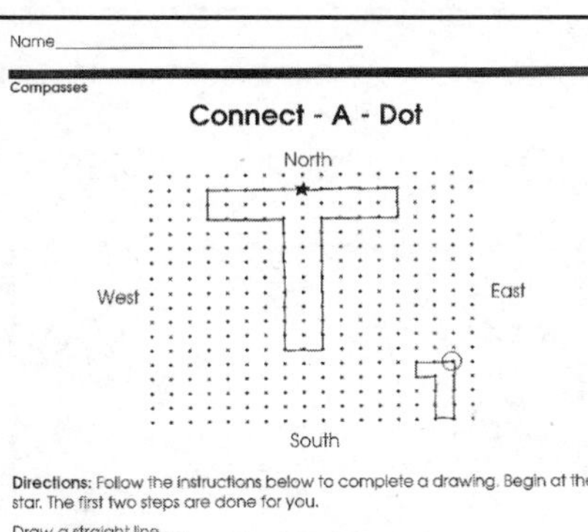

Directions: Follow the instructions below to complete a drawing. Begin at the star. The first two steps are done for you.

Draw a straight line . . .

1. Five spaces west.
2. Two spaces south.
3. Four spaces east.
4. Nine spaces south.
5. Two spaces east.
6. Nine spaces north.
7. Four spaces east.
8. Two spaces north.
9. Five spaces west.

What letter did you draw? T

Begin at the circle to complete another drawing.

Draw a straight line . .

1. Four spaces south.
2. One space west.
3. Three spaces north.
4. One space west.
5. One space north.
6. Two spaces east.

What number did you draw? 7

Page 50

Name____________________

Compasses

Finding Your Way Around Town

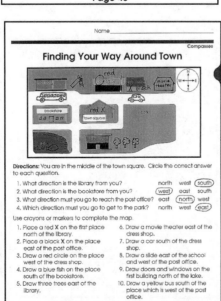

Directions: You are in the middle of the town square. Circle the correct answer to each question.

1. What direction is the library from you? north west (south)
2. What direction is the bookstore from you? (west) east south
3. What direction must you go to reach the post office? east (north) west
4. Which direction must you go to get to the park? north west (east)

Use crayons or markers to complete the map.

1. Place a red X on the first place north of the library.
2. Place a black X on the place east of the post office.
3. Draw a red circle on the place west of the dress shop.
4. Draw a blue fish on the place south of the bookstore.
5. Draw three trees east of the library.
6. Draw a movie theater east of the dress shop.
7. Draw a car south of the dress shop.
8. Draw a slide east of the school and west of the post office.
9. Draw doors and windows on the first building north of the lake.
10. Draw a yellow bus south of the place which is west of the post office.

Page 51

Name____________________

Compasses

A Great Camp!

Read the letter. Then, draw a map to show what the camp looks like. Make a key for the map.

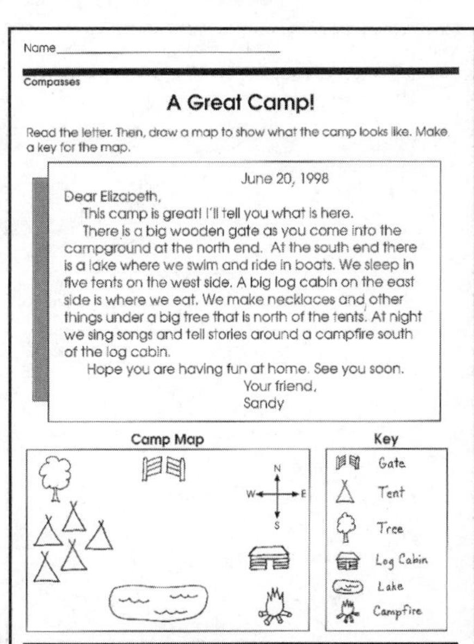

June 20, 1998

Dear Elizabeth,

This camp is great! I'll tell you what is here.

There is a big wooden gate as you come into the campground at the north end. At the south end there is a lake where we swim and ride in boats. We sleep in five tents on the west side. A big log cabin on the east side is where we eat. We make necklaces and other things under a big tree that is north of the tents. At night we sing songs and tell stories around a campfire south of the log cabin.

Hope you are having fun at home. See you soon.

Your friend,
Sandy

Page 52

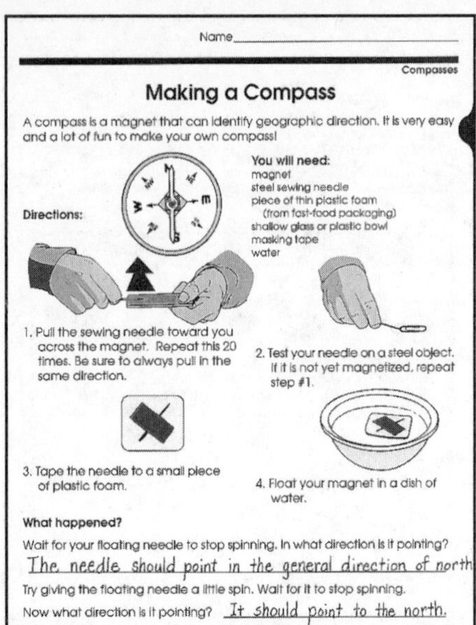

Name______________________

Compasses

Making a Compass

A compass is a magnet that can identify geographic direction. It is very easy and a lot of fun to make your own compass!

You will need:
magnet
steel sewing needle
piece of thin plastic foam (from fast-food packaging)
shallow glass or plastic bowl
masking tape
water

Directions:

1. Pull the sewing needle toward you across the magnet. Repeat this 20 times. Be sure to always pull in the same direction.
2. Test your needle on a steel object. If it is not yet magnetized, repeat step #1.
3. Tape the needle to a small piece of plastic foam.
4. Float your magnet in a dish of water.

What happened?

Wait for your floating needle to stop spinning. In what direction is it pointing? The needle should point in the general direction of north.

Try giving the floating needle a little spin. Wait for it to stop spinning.

Now what direction is it pointing? It should point to the north.

Page 53

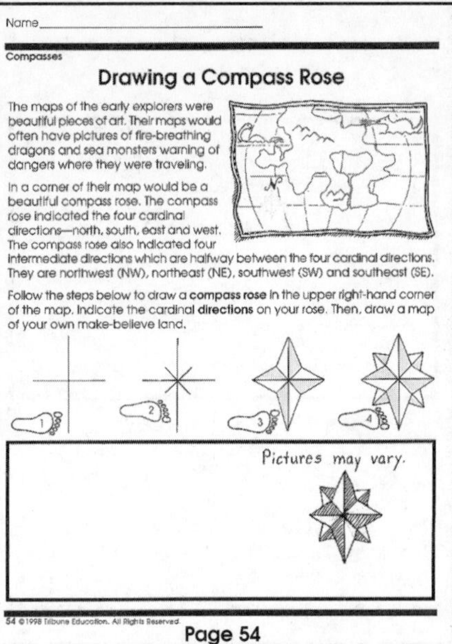

Name______________________

Compasses

Drawing a Compass Rose

The maps of the early explorers were beautiful pieces of art. Their maps would often have pictures of fire-breathing dragons and sea monsters warning of dangers where they were traveling.

In a corner of their map would be a beautiful compass rose. The compass rose indicated the four cardinal directions—north, south, east and west. The compass rose also indicated four intermediate directions which are halfway between the four cardinal directions. They are northwest (NW), northeast (NE), southwest (SW) and southeast (SE).

Follow the steps below to draw a **compass rose** in the upper right-hand corner of the map. Indicate the cardinal **directions** on your rose. Then, draw a map of your own make-believe land.

Page 54

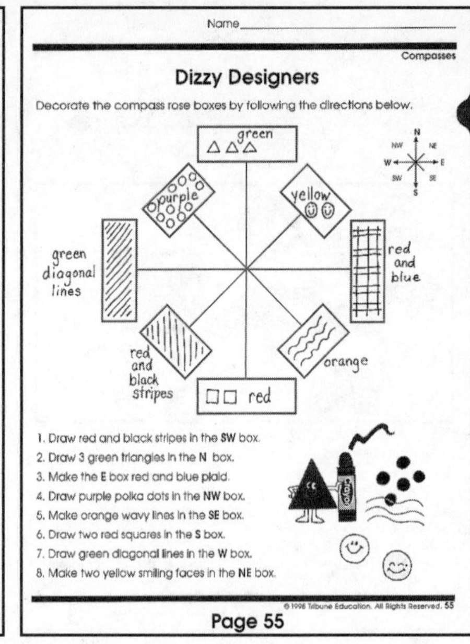

Name______________________

Compasses

Dizzy Designers

Decorate the compass rose boxes by following the directions below.

1. Draw red and black stripes in the **SW** box.
2. Draw 3 green triangles in the **N** box.
3. Make the **E** box red and blue plaid.
4. Draw purple polka dots in the **NW** box.
5. Make orange wavy lines in the **SE** box.
6. Draw two red squares in the **S** box.
7. Draw green diagonal lines in the **W** box.
8. Make two yellow smiling faces in the **NE** box.

Page 55

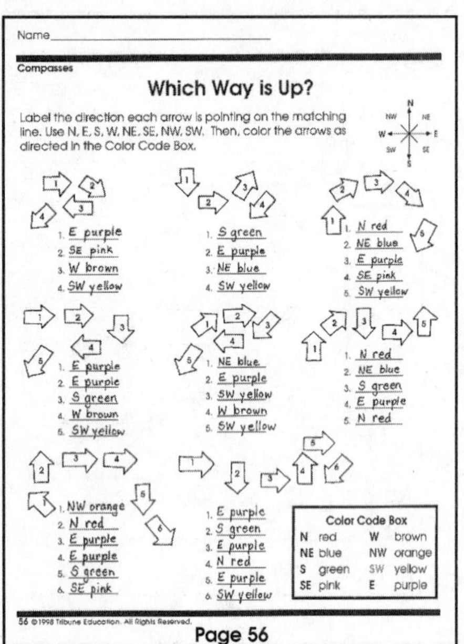

Name______________________

Compasses

Which Way is Up?

Label the direction each arrow is pointing on the matching line. Use N, E, S, W, NE, SE, NW, SW. Then, color the arrows as directed in the Color Code Box.

1. E purple
2. SE pink
3. W brown
4. SW yellow

1. S green
2. E purple
3. NE blue
4. SW yellow

1. N red
2. NE blue
3. E purple
4. SE pink
5. SW yellow

1. E purple
2. E purple
3. S green
4. W brown
5. SW yellow

1. NE blue
2. E purple
3. SW yellow
4. W brown
5. SW yellow

1. N red
2. NE blue
3. S green
4. E purple
5. N red

1. NW orange
2. N red
3. E purple
4. E purple
5. S green
6. SE pink

1. E purple
2. S green
3. E purple
4. N red
5. E purple
6. SW yellow

Color Code Box			
N	red	W	brown
NE	blue	NW	orange
S	green	SW	yellow
SE	pink	E	purple

Page 56

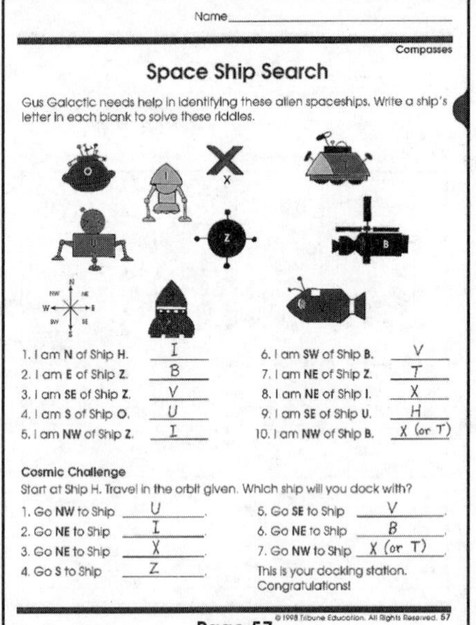

Name______________________

Compasses

Space Ship Search

Gus Galactic needs help in identifying these alien spaceships. Write a ship's letter in each blank to solve these riddles.

1. I am N of Ship H. I
2. I am E of Ship Z. B
3. I am SE of Ship Z. V
4. I am S of Ship O. U
5. I am NW of Ship Z. I
6. I am SW of Ship B. V
7. I am NE of Ship Z. T
8. I am NE of Ship I. X
9. I am SE of Ship U. H
10. I am NW of Ship B. X (or T)

Cosmic Challenge

Start at Ship H. Travel in the orbit given. Which ship will you dock with?

1. Go NW to Ship U.
2. Go NE to Ship I.
3. Go NE to Ship X.
4. Go S to Ship Z.
5. Go SE to Ship V.
6. Go NE to Ship B.
7. Go NW to Ship X (or T).

This is your docking station. Congratulations!

Page 57

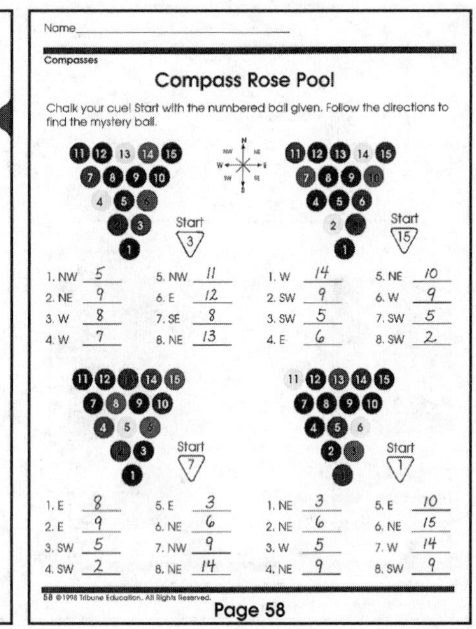

Name______________________

Compasses

Compass Rose Pool

Chalk your cue! Start with the numbered ball given. Follow the directions to find the mystery ball.

Start 3

1. NW 5
2. NE 9
3. W 8
4. W 7
5. NW 11
6. E 12
7. SE 8
8. NE 13

Start 15

1. W 14
2. SW 9
3. SW 5
4. E 6
5. NE 10
6. W 9
7. SW 5
8. SW 2

Start 7

1. E 8
2. E 9
3. SW 5
4. SW 2
5. E 3
6. NE 6
7. NW 9
8. NE 14

Start 1

1. NE 3
2. NE 6
3. W 5
4. NE 9
5. E 10
6. NE 15
7. W 14
8. SW 9

Page 58

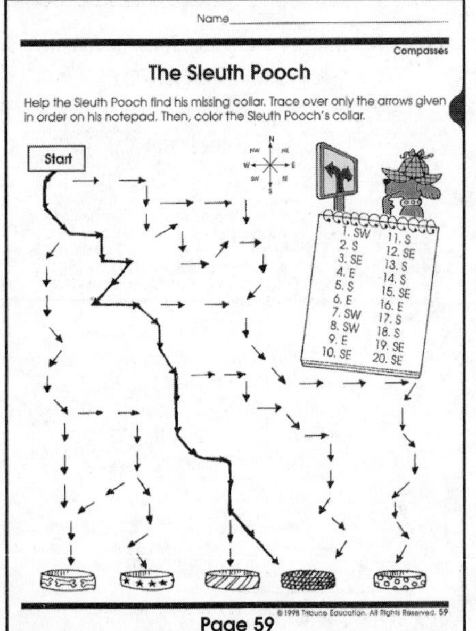

Name______________________

Compasses

The Sleuth Pooch

Help the Sleuth Pooch find his missing collar. Trace over only the arrows given in order on his notepad. Then, color the Sleuth Pooch's collar.

Page 59

Name______________________

Compasses

Draw Your Own Map

A cartographer makes maps. Try your hand at being a cartographer and make your own map by following these directions. Read all directions before you begin.

1. Draw a compass rose using both cardinal and intermediate directions in the bottom right-hand corner of the map.
2. Draw a lake in the center of the map.
3. Northwest of the lake, draw some ducks in flight.
4. Directly south of the lake, draw six trees.
5. East of the ducks, draw the sun.
6. Southwest of the lake, draw a playground area.
7. East of the lake, draw a picnic area.

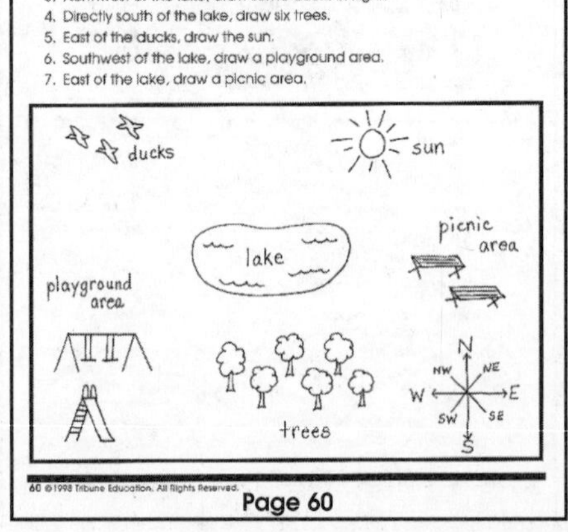

Page 60

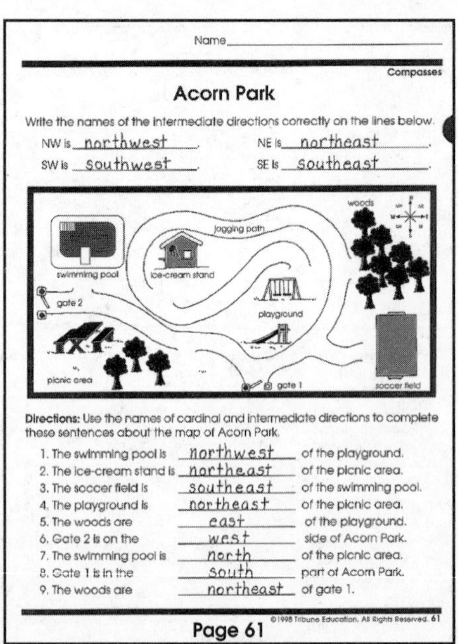

Name______________________

Compasses

Acorn Park

Write the names of the intermediate directions correctly on the lines below.

NW is northwest. NE is northeast.
SW is southwest. SE is southeast.

Directions: Use the names of cardinal and intermediate directions to complete these sentences about the map of Acorn Park.

1. The swimming pool is northwest of the playground.
2. The ice-cream stand is northeast of the picnic area.
3. The soccer field is southeast of the swimming pool.
4. The playground is northeast of the picnic area.
5. The woods are east of the playground.
6. Gate 2 is on the west side of Acorn Park.
7. The swimming pool is north of the picnic area.
8. Gate 1 is in the south part of Acorn Park.
9. The woods are northeast of gate 1.

Page 61

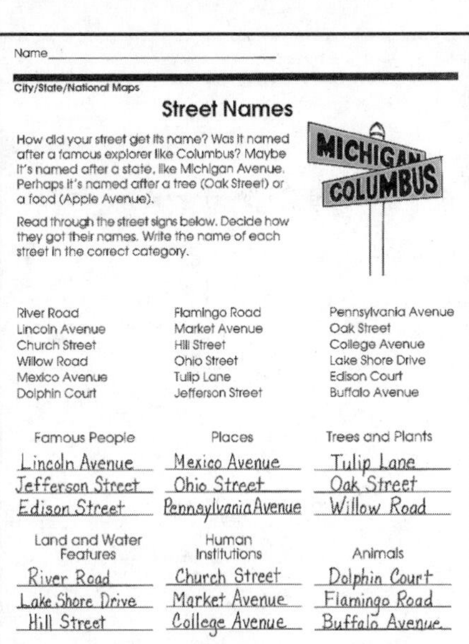

Name

City/State/National Maps

Street Names

How did your street get its name? Was it named after a famous explorer like Columbus? Maybe it's named after a state, like Michigan Avenue. Perhaps it's named after a tree (Oak Street) or a food (Apple Avenue).

Read through the street signs below. Decide how they got their names. Write the name of each street in the correct category.

River Road, Lincoln Avenue, Church Street, Willow Road, Mexico Avenue, Dolphin Court, Flamingo Road, Market Avenue, Hill Street, Ohio Street, Tulip Lane, Jefferson Street, Pennsylvania Avenue, Oak Street, College Avenue, Lake Shore Drive, Edison Court, Buffalo Avenue

Famous People	Places	Trees and Plants
Lincoln Avenue	Mexico Avenue	Tulip Lane
Jefferson Street	Ohio Street	Oak Street
Edison Street	Pennsylvania Avenue	Willow Road

Land and Water Features	Human Institutions	Animals
River Road	Church Street	Dolphin Court
Lake Shore Drive	Market Avenue	Flamingo Road
Hill Street	College Avenue	Buffalo Avenue

Page 62

Name

City/State/National Maps

City Streets

Every town has some interesting street names. Streets can get their names in many different ways. They are often named after presidents, states, trees and flowers. What are some of the interesting street names in your town?

People's Names	Places	Funny Names
Human Institutions	**Natural Features**	**Animals**
	Answers will vary.	
Plants and Trees	**Directions**	**Other**

Page 63

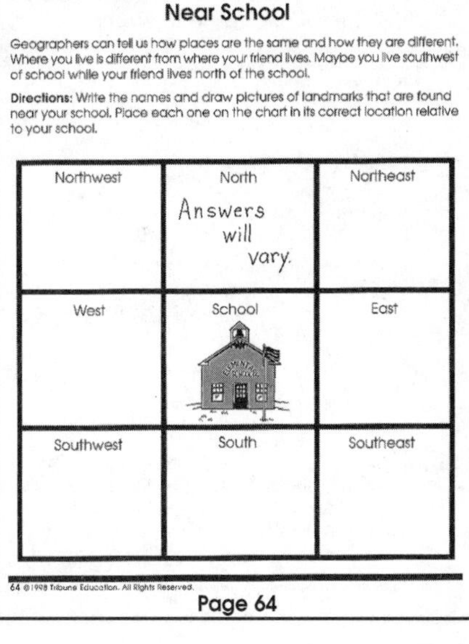

Name

City/State/National Maps

Near School

Geographers can tell us how places are the same and how they are different. Where you live is different from where your friend lives. Maybe you live southwest of school while your friend lives north of the school.

Directions: Write the names and draw pictures of landmarks that are found near your school. Place each one on the chart in its correct location relative to your school.

Northwest	North	Northeast
	Answers will vary.	
West	**School**	**East**
Southwest	**South**	**Southeast**

Page 64

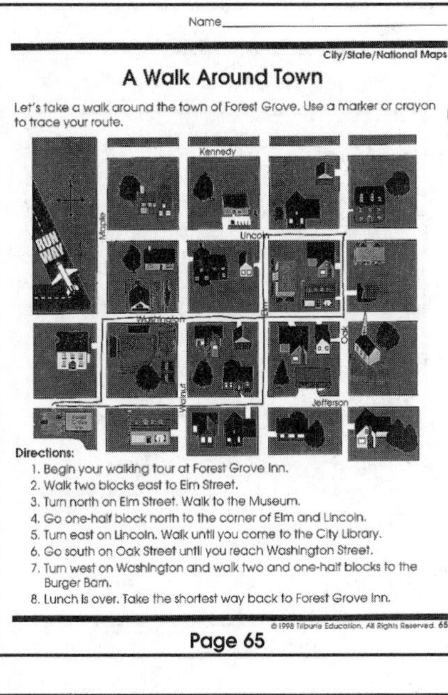

Name

City/State/National Maps

A Walk Around Town

Let's take a walk around the town of Forest Grove. Use a marker or crayon to trace your route.

Directions:

1. Begin your walking tour at Forest Grove Inn.
2. Walk two blocks east to Elm Street.
3. Turn north on Elm Street. Walk to the Museum.
4. Go one-half block north to the corner of Elm and Lincoln.
5. Turn east on Lincoln. Walk until you come to the City Library.
6. Go south on Oak Street until you reach Washington Street.
7. Turn west on Washington and walk two and one-half blocks to the Burger Barn.
8. Lunch is over. Take the shortest way back to Forest Grove Inn.

Page 65

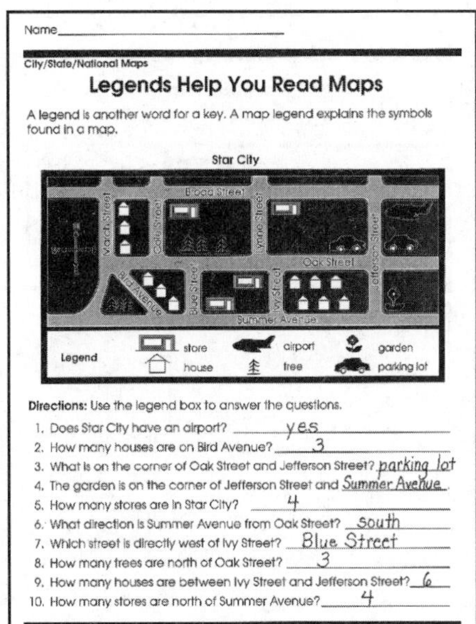

Name

City/State/National Maps

Legends Help You Read Maps

A legend is another word for a key. A map legend explains the symbols found in a map.

Directions: Use the legend box to answer the questions.

1. Does Star City have an airport? yes
2. How many houses are on Bird Avenue? 3
3. What is on the corner of Oak Street and Jefferson Street? parking lot
4. The garden is on the corner of Jefferson Street and Summer Avenue.
5. How many stores are in Star City? 4
6. What direction is Summer Avenue from Oak Street? south
7. Which street is directly west of Ivy Street? Blue Street
8. How many trees are north of Oak Street? 3
9. How many houses are between Ivy Street and Jefferson Street? 6
10. How many stores are north of Summer Avenue? 4

Page 66

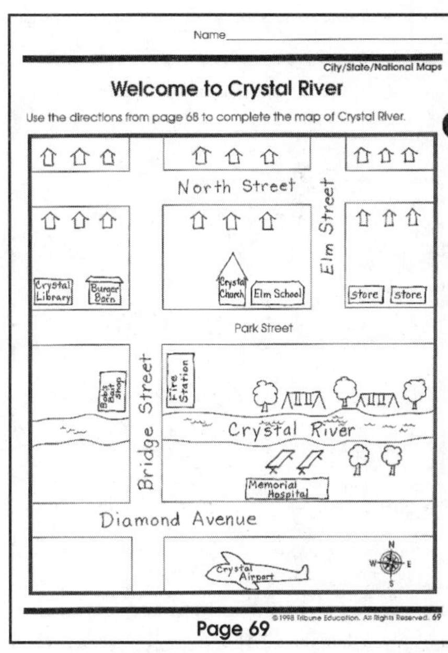

Name

City/State/National Maps

Welcome to Crystal River

Use the directions from page 68 to complete the map of Crystal River.

Page 69

Name

City/State/National Maps

Near My Community

Use a state map to locate your community. Then, write the names of other communities, cities, towns, lakes, places to visit and other well-known landmarks on the chart below. Write each one in its correct location relative to your community.

Northwest	North	Northeast
	Answers	
West	**My Community** will vary.	**East**
Southwest	**South**	**Southeast**

Page 70

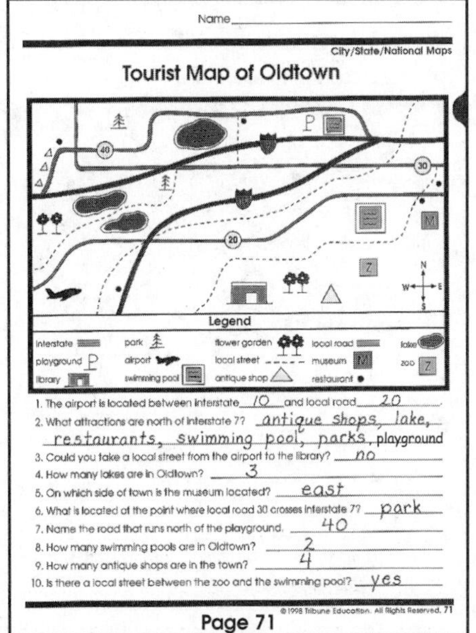

Name

City/State/National Maps

Tourist Map of Oldtown

1. The airport is located between interstate 10 and local road 20.
2. What attractions are north of interstate 7? antique shops, lake, restaurants, swimming pool, parks, playground
3. Could you take a local street from the airport to the library? no
4. How many lakes are in Oldtown? 3
5. On which side of town is the museum located? east
6. What is located at the point where local road 30 crosses interstate 7? park
7. Name the road that runs north of the playground. 40
8. How many swimming pools are in Oldtown? 2
9. How many antique shops are in the town? 4
10. Is there a local street between the zoo and the swimming pool? yes

Page 71

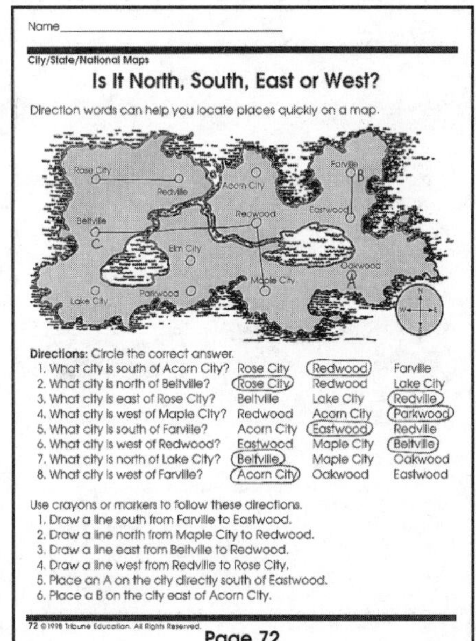

Name

City/State/National Maps

Is It North, South, East or West?

Direction words can help you locate places quickly on a map.

Directions: Circle the correct answer.

1. What city is south of Acorn City? Rose City **(Redwood)** Farville
2. What city is north of Beltville? **(Rose City)** Redwood Lake City
3. What city is east of Rose City? Beltville Lake City **(Redville)**
4. What city is west of Maple City? Redwood Acorn City **(Parkwood)**
5. What city is south of Farville? Acorn City **(Eastwood)** Redville
6. What city is west of Redwood? Eastwood Maple City **(Beltville)**
7. What city is north of Lake City? **(Beltville)** Maple City Oakwood
8. What city is west of Farville? **(Acorn City)** Oakwood Eastwood

Use crayons or markers to follow these directions.

1. Draw a line south from Farville to Eastwood.
2. Draw a line north from Maple City to Redwood.
3. Draw a line east from Beltville to Redwood.
4. Draw a line west from Redville to Rose City.
5. Place an A on the city directly south of Eastwood.
6. Place a B on the city east of Acorn City.

Page 72

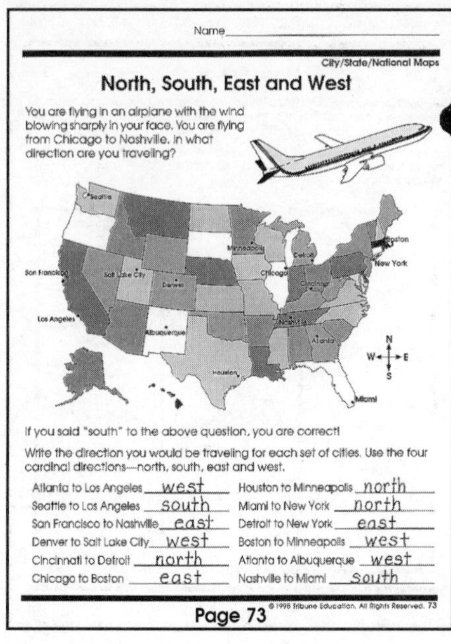

Name____________________

City/State/National Maps

North, South, East and West

You are flying in an airplane with the wind blowing sharply in your face. You are flying from Chicago to Nashville. In what direction are you traveling?

If you said "south" to the above question, you are correct!

Write the direction you would be traveling for each set of cities. Use the four cardinal directions—north, south, east and west.

Atlanta to Los Angeles	west	Houston to Minneapolis	north
Seattle to Los Angeles	south	Miami to New York	north
San Francisco to Nashville	east	Detroit to New York	east
Denver to Salt Lake City	west	Boston to Minneapolis	west
Cincinnati to Detroit	north	Atlanta to Albuquerque	west
Chicago to Boston	east	Nashville to Miami	south

Page 73

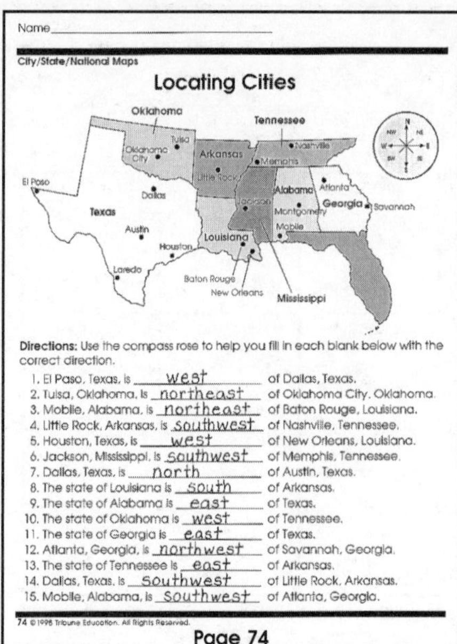

Name____________________

City/State/National Maps

Locating Cities

Directions: Use the compass rose to help you fill in each blank below with the correct direction.

1. El Paso, Texas, is west of Dallas, Texas.
2. Tulsa, Oklahoma, is northeast of Oklahoma City, Oklahoma.
3. Mobile, Alabama, is northeast of Baton Rouge, Louisiana.
4. Little Rock, Arkansas, is southwest of Nashville, Tennessee.
5. Houston, Texas, is west of New Orleans, Louisiana.
6. Jackson, Mississippi, is southwest of Memphis, Tennessee.
7. Dallas, Texas, is north of Austin, Texas.
8. The state of Louisiana is south of Arkansas.
9. The state of Alabama is east of Texas.
10. The state of Oklahoma is west of Tennessee.
11. The state of Georgia is east of Texas.
12. Atlanta, Georgia, is northwest of Savannah, Georgia.
13. The state of Tennessee is east of Arkansas.
14. Dallas, Texas, is southwest of Little Rock, Arkansas.
15. Mobile, Alabama, is southwest of Atlanta, Georgia.

Page 74

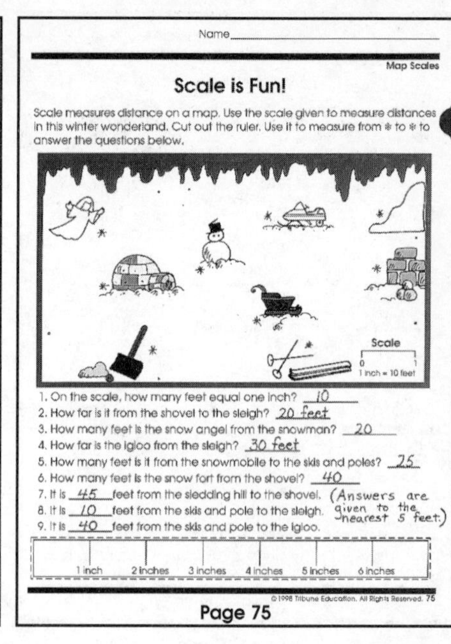

Name____________________

Map Scales

Scale is Fun!

Scale measures distance on a map. Use the scale given to measure distances in this winter wonderland. Cut out the ruler. Use it to measure from * to * to answer the questions below.

1. On the scale, how many feet equal one inch? 10
2. How far is it from the shovel to the sleigh? 20 feet
3. How many feet is the snow angel from the snowman? 20
4. How far is the igloo from the sleigh? 30 feet
5. How many feet is it from the snowmobile to the skis and poles? 25
6. How many feet is the snow fort from the shovel? 40
7. It is 45 feet from the sledding hill to the shovel. (Answers are
8. It is 10 feet from the skis and pole to the sleigh. given to the nearest 5 feet.)
9. It is 40 feet from the skis and pole to the igloo.

1 inch | 2 inches | 3 inches | 4 inches | 5 inches | 6 inches

Page 75

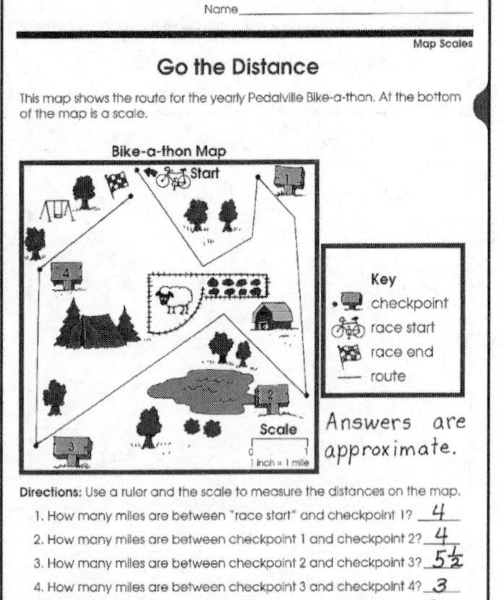

Name____________________

Map Scales

Go the Distance

This map shows the route for the yearly Pedalville Bike-a-thon. At the bottom of the map is a scale.

Answers are approximate.

Directions: Use a ruler and the scale to measure the distances on the map.

1. How many miles are between "race start" and checkpoint 1? 4
2. How many miles are between checkpoint 1 and checkpoint 2? 4
3. How many miles are between checkpoint 2 and checkpoint 3? $5\frac{1}{2}$
4. How many miles are between checkpoint 3 and checkpoint 4? 3
5. How many miles are between checkpoint 4 and "race end"? 2

Page 77

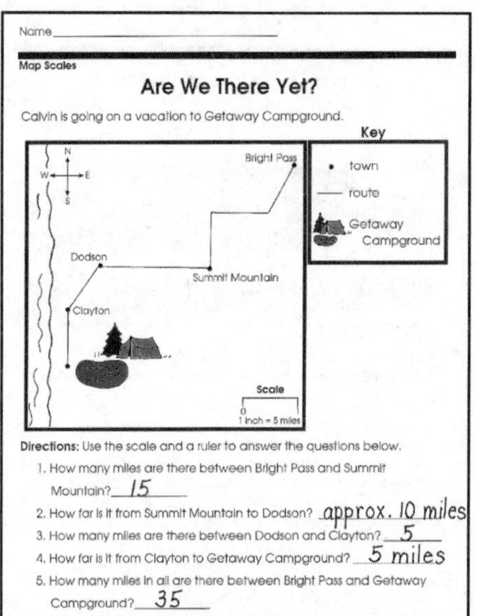

Name____________________

Map Scales

Are We There Yet?

Calvin is going on a vacation to Getaway Campground.

Directions: Use the scale and a ruler to answer the questions below.

1. How many miles are there between Bright Pass and Summit Mountain? 15
2. How far is it from Summit Mountain to Dodson? approx. 10 miles
3. How many miles are there between Dodson and Clayton? 5
4. How far is it from Clayton to Getaway Campground? 5 miles
5. How many miles in all are there between Bright Pass and Getaway Campground? 35

Page 78

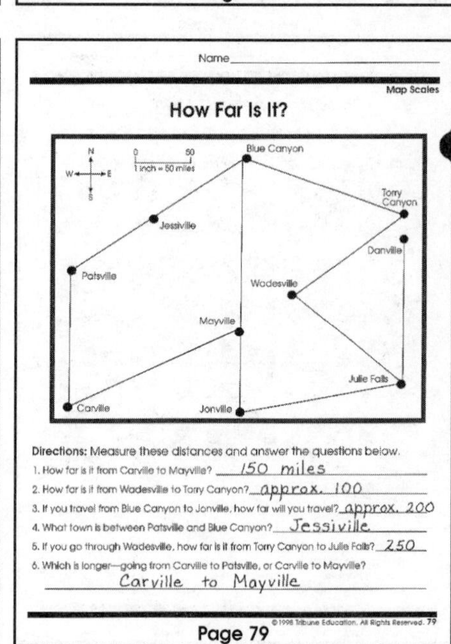

Name____________________

Map Scales

How Far Is It?

Directions: Measure these distances and answer the questions below.

1. How far is it from Carville to Mayville? 150 miles
2. How far is it from Wadesville to Torry Canyon? approx. 100
3. If you travel from Blue Canyon to Jonville, how far will you travel? approx. 200
4. What town is between Patsville and Blue Canyon? Jessiville
5. If you go through Wadesville, how far is it from Torry Canyon to Julie Falls? 250
6. Which is longer—going from Carville to Patsville, or Carville to Mayville? Carville to Mayville

Page 79

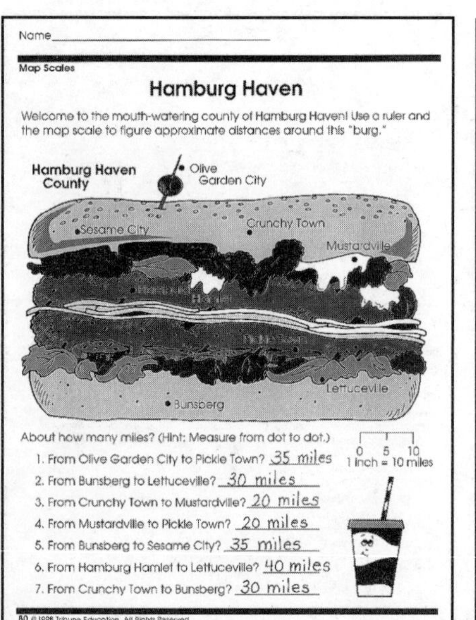

Name____________________

Map Scales

Hamburg Haven

Welcome to the mouth-watering county of Hamburg Haven! Use a ruler and the map scale to figure approximate distances around this "burg."

About how many miles? (Hint: Measure from dot to dot.)

0 5 10
1 inch = 10 miles

1. From Olive Garden City to Pickle Town? 35 miles
2. From Bunsberg to Lettuceville? 30 miles
3. From Crunchy Town to Mustardville? 20 miles
4. From Mustardville to Pickle Town? 20 miles
5. From Bunsberg to Sesame City? 35 miles
6. From Hamburg Hamlet to Lettuceville? 40 miles
7. From Crunchy Town to Bunsberg? 30 miles

Page 80

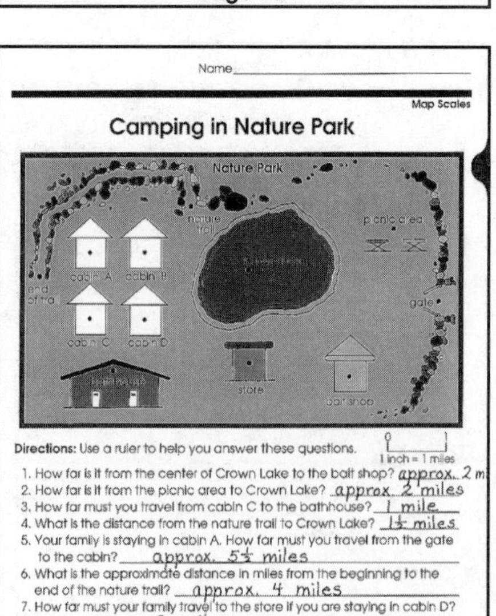

Name____________________

Map Scales

Camping in Nature Park

0 1
1 inch = 1 miles

Directions: Use a ruler to help you answer these questions.

1. How far is it from the center of Crown Lake to the bait shop? approx. 2 m
2. How far is it from the picnic area to Crown Lake? approx. 2 miles
3. How far must you travel from cabin C to the bathhouse? 1 mile
4. What is the distance from the nature trail to Crown Lake? $1\frac{1}{2}$ miles
5. Your family is staying in cabin A. How far must you travel from the gate to the cabin? approx. $5\frac{1}{2}$ miles
6. What is the approximate distance in miles from the beginning to the end of the nature trail? approx. 4 miles
7. How far must your family travel to the store if you are staying in cabin D? 2 miles
8. How far is it from the store to cabin B? approx. 2 miles
9. The end of the nature trail is how far from the picnic area? approx. 6 mil
10. How far is the bathhouse from cabin A? 2 miles

Page 81

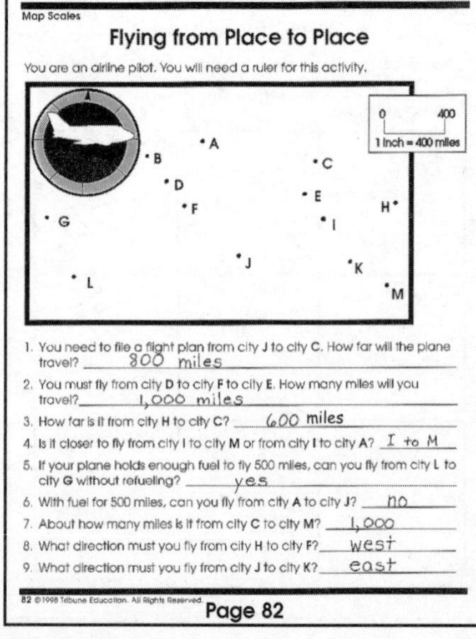

Name____________________

Map Scales

Flying from Place to Place

You are an airline pilot. You will need a ruler for this activity.

1. You need to file a flight plan from city J to city C. How far will the plane travel? 800 miles
2. You must fly from city D to city F to city E. How many miles will you travel? 1,000 miles
3. How far is it from city H to city C? 600 miles
4. Is it closer to fly from city I to city M or from city I to city A? I to M
5. If your plane holds enough fuel to fly 500 miles, can you fly from city L to city G without refueling? yes
6. With fuel for 500 miles, can you fly from city A to city J? no
7. About how many miles is it from city C to city M? 1,000
8. What direction must you fly from city H to city F? west
9. What direction must you fly from city J to city K? east

Page 82

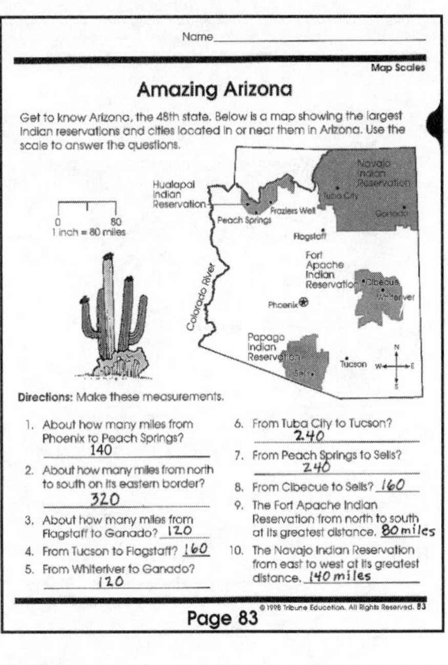

Name________________

Map Scales

Amazing Arizona

Get to know Arizona, the 48th state. Below is a map showing the largest Indian reservations and cities located in or near them in Arizona. Use the scale to answer the questions.

Directions: Make these measurements.

1. About how many miles from Phoenix to Peach Springs? 140
2. About how many miles from north to south on its eastern border? 320
3. About how many miles from Flagstaff to Ganado? 120
4. From Tucson to Flagstaff? 160
5. From Whiteriver to Ganado? 120
6. From Tuba City to Tucson? 240
7. From Peach Springs to Sells? 240
8. From Cibecue to Sells? 160
9. The Fort Apache Indian Reservation from north to south at its greatest distance. 80 miles
10. The Navajo Indian Reservation from east to west at its greatest distance. 140 miles

Page 83

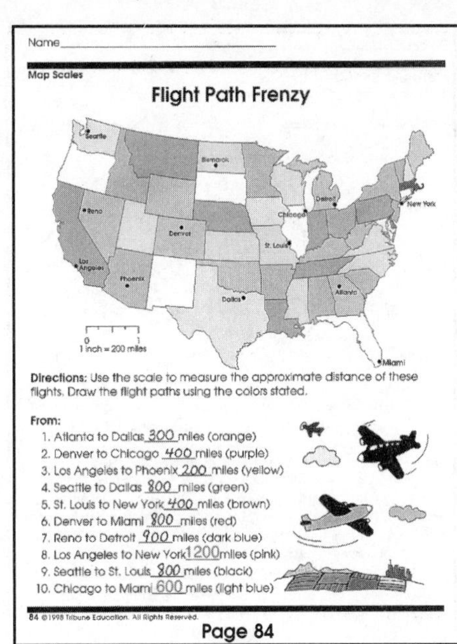

Name________________

Map Scales

Flight Path Frenzy

Directions: Use the scale to measure the approximate distance of these flights. Draw the flight paths using the colors stated.

From:

1. Atlanta to Dallas 300 miles (orange)
2. Denver to Chicago 400 miles (purple)
3. Los Angeles to Phoenix 200 miles (yellow)
4. Seattle to Dallas 800 miles (green)
5. St. Louis to New York 400 miles (brown)
6. Denver to Miami 800 miles (red)
7. Reno to Detroit 900 miles (dark blue)
8. Los Angeles to New York 1200 miles (pink)
9. Seattle to St. Louis 800 miles (black)
10. Chicago to Miami 600 miles (light blue)

Page 84

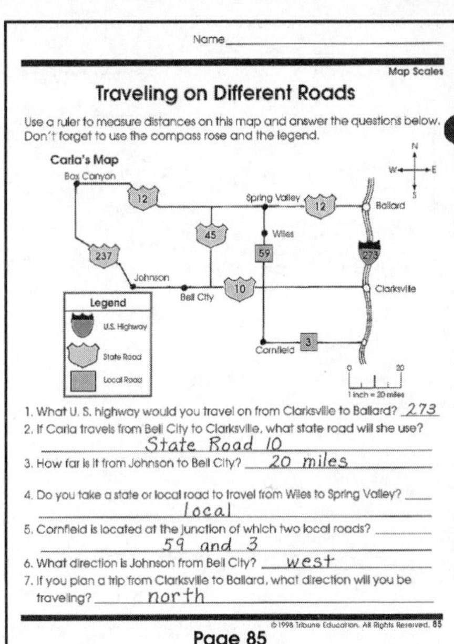

Name________________

Map Scales

Traveling on Different Roads

Use a ruler to measure distances on this map and answer the questions below. Don't forget to use the compass rose and the legend.

1. What U. S. highway would you travel on from Clarksville to Ballard? 273
2. If Carla travels from Bell City to Clarksville, what state road will she use? State Road 10
3. How far is it from Johnson to Bell City? 20 miles
4. Do you take a state or local road to travel from Wiles to Spring Valley? local
5. Cornfield is located at the junction of which two local roads? 59 and 3
6. What direction is Johnson from Bell City? west
7. If you plan a trip from Clarksville to Ballard, what direction will you be traveling? north

Page 85

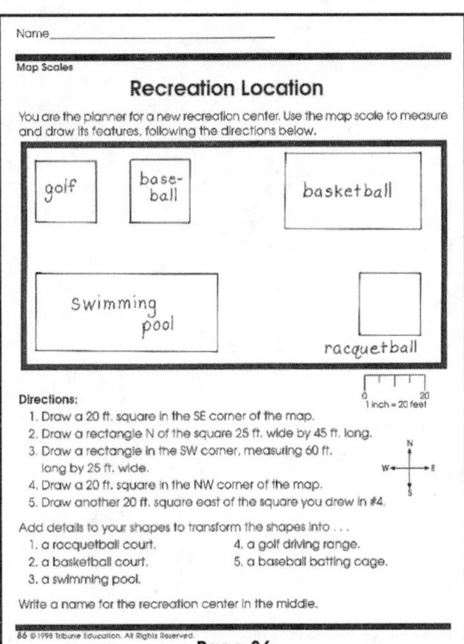

Name________________

Map Scales

Recreation Location

You are the planner for a new recreation center. Use the map scale to measure and draw its features, following the directions below.

Directions:

1. Draw a 20 ft. square in the SE corner of the map.
2. Draw a rectangle N of the square 25 ft. wide by 45 ft. long.
3. Draw a rectangle in the SW corner, measuring 60 ft. long by 25 ft. wide.
4. Draw a 20 ft. square in the NW corner of the map.
5. Draw another 20 ft. square east of the square you drew in #4.

Add details to your shapes to transform the shapes into . . .

1. a racquetball court.
2. a basketball court.
3. a swimming pool.
4. a golf driving range.
5. a baseball batting cage.

Write a name for the recreation center in the middle.

Page 86

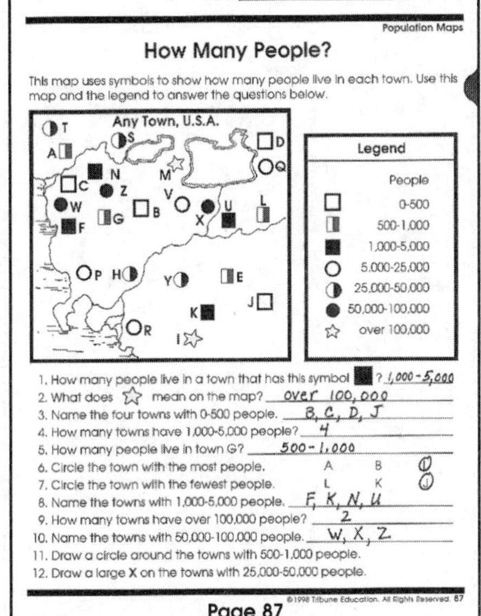

Name________________

Population Maps

How Many People?

This map uses symbols to show how many people live in each town. Use this map and the legend to answer the questions below.

1. How many people live in a town that has this symbol ■? 1,000-5,000
2. What does ☆ mean on the map? over 100,000
3. Name the four towns with 0-500 people. B, C, D, J
4. How many towns have 1,000-5,000 people? 4
5. How many people live in town G? 500-1,000
6. Circle the town with the most people. A B
7. Circle the town with the fewest people. L K
8. Name the towns with 1,000-5,000 people. F, K, N, U
9. How many towns have over 100,000 people? 2
10. Name the towns with 50,000-100,000 people. W, X, Z
11. Draw a circle around the towns with 500-1,000 people.
12. Draw a large X on the towns with 25,000-50,000 people.

Page 87

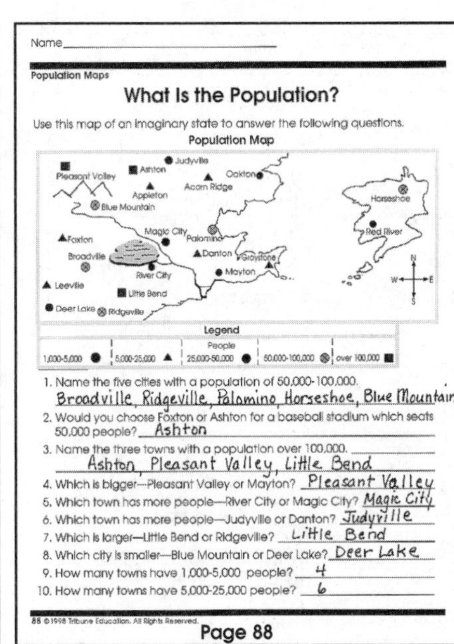

Name________________

Population Maps

What Is the Population?

Use this map of an imaginary state to answer the following questions.

1. Name the five cities with a population of 50,000-100,000. Broadville, Ridgeville, Palomino, Horseshoe, Blue Mountain
2. Would you choose Foxton or Ashton for a baseball stadium which seats 50,000 people? Ashton
3. Name the three towns with a population over 100,000. Ashton, Pleasant Valley, Little Bend
4. Which is bigger—Pleasant Valley or Mayton? Pleasant Valley
5. Which town has more people—River City or Magic City? Magic City
6. Which town has more people—Judyville or Danton? Judyville
7. Which is larger—Little Bend or Ridgeville? Little Bend
8. Which city is smaller—Blue Mountain or Deer Lake? Deer Lake
9. How many towns have 1,000-5,000 people? 4
10. How many towns have 5,000-25,000 people? 6

Page 88

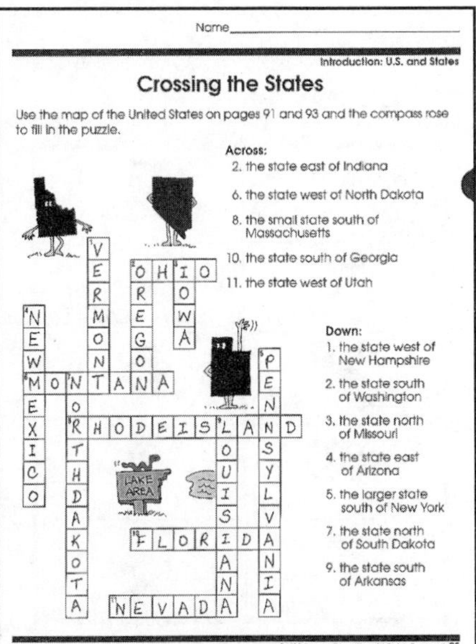

Name________________

Introduction: U.S. and States

Crossing the States

Use the map of the United States on pages 91 and 93 and the compass rose to fill in the puzzle.

Across:

2. the state east of Indiana
6. the state west of North Dakota
8. the small state south of Massachusetts
10. the state south of Georgia
11. the state west of Utah

Down:

1. the state west of New Hampshire
2. the state south of Washington
3. the state north of Missouri
4. the state east of Arizona
5. the larger state south of New York
7. the state north of South Dakota
9. the state south of Arkansas

Page 95

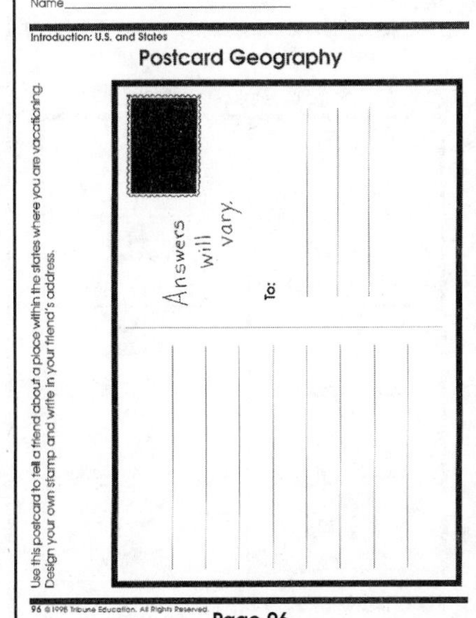

Name________________

Introduction: U.S. and States

Postcard Geography

Use this postcard to tell a friend about a place within the states where you are vacationing. Design your own stamp and write in your friend's address.

Page 96

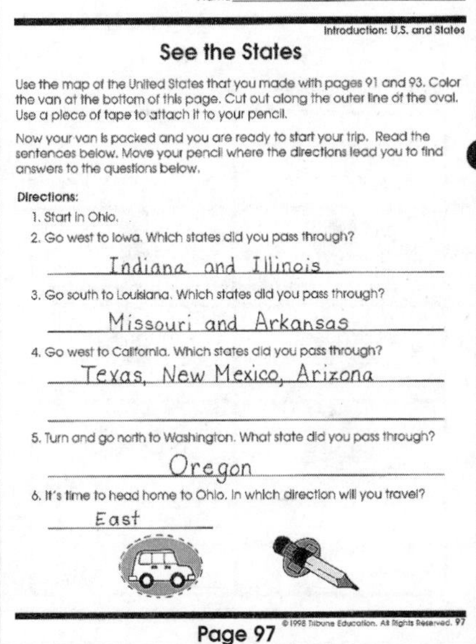

Name________________

Introduction: U.S. and States

See the States

Use the map of the United States that you made with pages 91 and 93. Color the van at the bottom of this page. Cut out along the outer line of the oval. Use a piece of tape to attach it to your pencil.

Now your van is packed and you are ready to start your trip. Read the sentences below. Move your pencil where the directions lead you to find answers to the questions below.

Directions:

1. Start in Ohio.
2. Go west to Iowa. Which states did you pass through? Indiana and Illinois
3. Go south to Louisiana. Which states did you pass through? Missouri and Arkansas
4. Go west to California. Which states did you pass through? Texas, New Mexico, Arizona
5. Turn and go north to Washington. What state did you pass through? Oregon
6. It's time to head home to Ohio. In which direction will you travel? East

Page 97

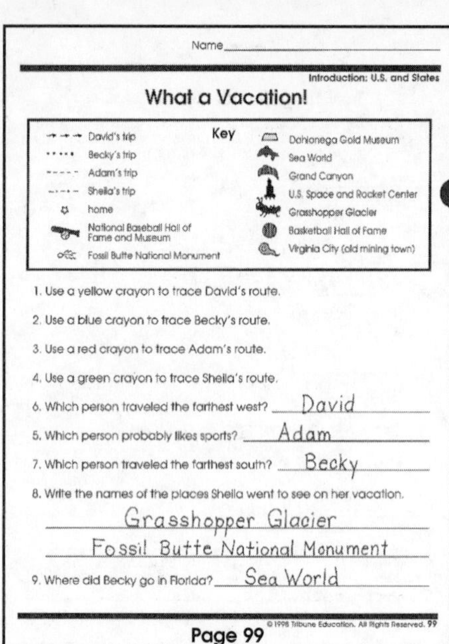

Name ______

Introduction: U.S. and States

What a Vacation!

Key

- David's trip
- Becky's trip
- Adam's trip
- Sheila's trip
- home
- National Baseball Hall of Fame and Museum
- Fossil Butte National Monument
- Dahlonega Gold Museum
- Sea World
- Grand Canyon
- U.S. Space and Rocket Center
- Grasshopper Glacier
- Basketball Hall of Fame
- Virginia City (old mining town)

1. Use a yellow crayon to trace David's route.
2. Use a blue crayon to trace Becky's route.
3. Use a red crayon to trace Adam's route.
4. Use a green crayon to trace Sheila's route.
6. Which person traveled the farthest west? David
5. Which person probably likes sports? Adam
7. Which person traveled the farthest south? Becky
8. Write the names of the places Sheila went to see on her vacation.
   Grasshopper Glacier
   Fossil Butte National Monument
9. Where did Becky go in Florida? Sea World

Page 99

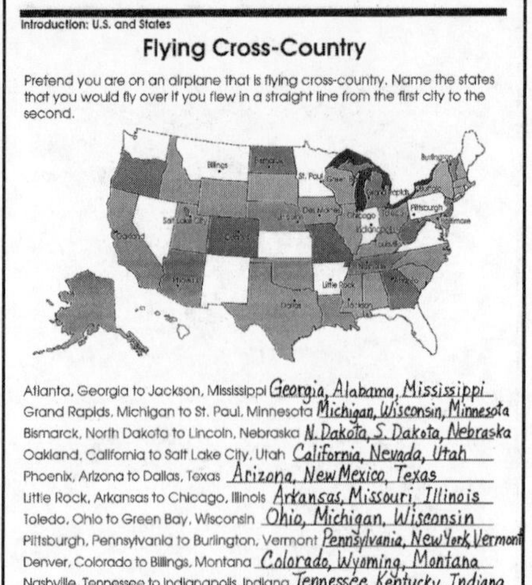

Name ______

Introduction: U.S. and States

Flying Cross-Country

Pretend you are on an airplane that is flying cross-country. Name the states that you would fly over if you flew in a straight line from the first city to the second.

Atlanta, Georgia to Jackson, Mississippi Georgia, Alabama, Mississippi
Grand Rapids, Michigan to St. Paul, Minnesota Michigan, Wisconsin, Minnesota
Bismarck, North Dakota to Lincoln, Nebraska N. Dakota, S. Dakota, Nebraska
Oakland, California to Salt Lake City, Utah California, Nevada, Utah
Phoenix, Arizona to Dallas, Texas Arizona, New Mexico, Texas
Little Rock, Arkansas to Chicago, Illinois Arkansas, Missouri, Illinois
Toledo, Ohio to Green Bay, Wisconsin Ohio, Michigan, Wisconsin
Pittsburgh, Pennsylvania to Burlington, Vermont Pennsylvania, New York, Vermont
Denver, Colorado to Billings, Montana Colorado, Wyoming, Montana
Nashville, Tennessee to Indianapolis, Indiana Tennessee, Kentucky, Indiana
Des Moines, Iowa to Louisville, Kentucky Iowa, Illinois, Indiana, Kentucky
Baltimore, Maryland to Buffalo, New York Maryland, Pennsylvania, New York

Page 100

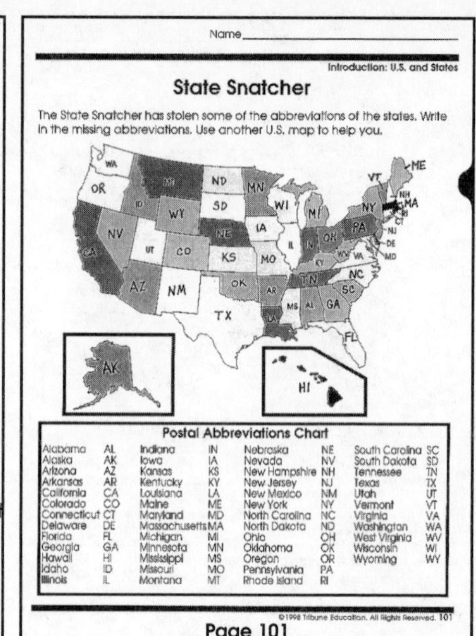

Name ______

Introduction: U.S. and States

State Snatcher

The State Snatcher has stolen some of the abbreviations of the states. Write in the missing abbreviations. Use another U.S. map to help you.

Postal Abbreviations Chart

State	Abbr.	State	Abbr.	State	Abbr.	State	Abbr.
Alabama	AL	Indiana	IN	Nebraska	NE	South Carolina	SC
Alaska	AK	Iowa	IA	Nevada	NV	South Dakota	SD
Arizona	AZ	Kansas	KS	New Hampshire	NH	Tennessee	TN
Arkansas	AR	Kentucky	KY	New Jersey	NJ	Texas	TX
California	CA	Louisiana	LA	New Mexico	NM	Utah	UT
Colorado	CO	Maine	ME	New York	NY	Vermont	VT
Connecticut	CT	Maryland	MD	North Carolina	NC	Virginia	VA
Delaware	DE	Massachusetts	MA	North Dakota	ND	Washington	WA
Florida	FL	Michigan	MI	Ohio	OH	West Virginia	WV
Georgia	GA	Minnesota	MN	Oklahoma	OK	Wisconsin	WI
Hawaii	HI	Mississippi	MS	Oregon	OR	Wyoming	WY
Idaho	ID	Missouri	MO	Pennsylvania	PA		
Illinois	IL	Montana	MT	Rhode Island	RI		

Page 101

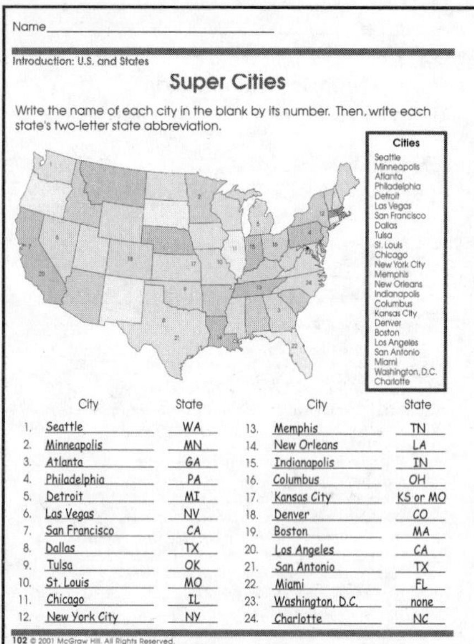

Name ______

Introduction: U.S. and States

Super Cities

Write the name of each city in the blank by its number. Then, write each state's two-letter state abbreviation.

Cities: Seattle, Minneapolis, Atlanta, Philadelphia, Detroit, Las Vegas, San Francisco, Dallas, Tulsa, St. Louis, Chicago, New York City, Memphis, New Orleans, Indianapolis, Columbus, Kansas City, Denver, Boston, Los Angeles, San Antonio, Miami, Washington, D.C., Charlotte

	City	State		City	State
1.	Seattle	WA	13.	Memphis	TN
2.	Minneapolis	MN	14.	New Orleans	LA
3.	Atlanta	GA	15.	Indianapolis	IN
4.	Philadelphia	PA	16.	Columbus	OH
5.	Detroit	MI	17.	Kansas City	KS or MO
6.	Las Vegas	NV	18.	Denver	CO
7.	San Francisco	CA	19.	Boston	MA
8.	Dallas	TX	20.	Los Angeles	CA
9.	Tulsa	OK	21.	San Antonio	TX
10.	St. Louis	MO	22.	Miami	FL
11.	Chicago	IL	23.	Washington, D.C.	none
12.	New York City	NY	24.	Charlotte	NC

Page 102

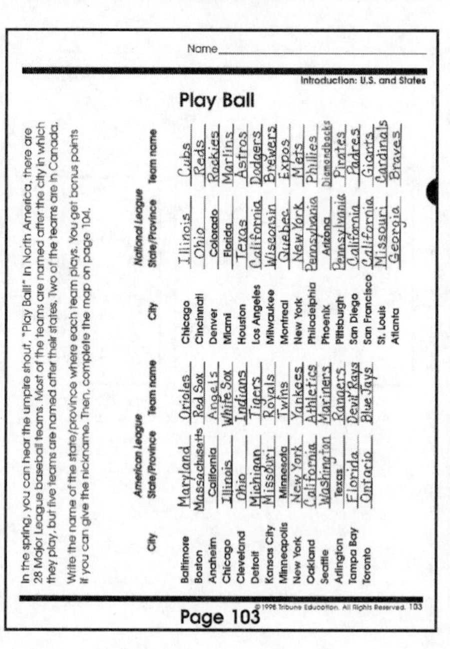

Name ______

Introduction: U.S. and States

Play Ball

In the spring, you can hear the umpire shout, "Play Ball!" In North America, there are 28 Major League baseball teams. Most of the teams are named after the city in which they play, but five teams are named after their states. Two of the teams are in Canada.

Write the name of the state/province where each team plays. You get bonus points if you can give the nickname. Then, complete the map on page 104.

American League

City	State/Province	Team name
Baltimore	Maryland	Orioles
Boston	Massachusetts	Red Sox
Anaheim	California	Angels
Chicago	Illinois	White Sox
Cleveland	Ohio	Indians
Detroit	Michigan	Tigers
Kansas City	Missouri	Royals
Minneapolis	Minnesota	Twins
New York	New York	Yankees
Oakland	California	Athletics
Seattle	Washington	Mariners
Arlington	Texas	Rangers
Tampa Bay	Florida	Devil Rays
Toronto	Ontario	Blue Jays

National League

City	State/Province	Team name
Chicago	Illinois	Cubs
Cincinnati	Ohio	Reds
Denver	Colorado	Rockies
Miami	Florida	Marlins
Houston	Texas	Astros
Los Angeles	California	Dodgers
Milwaukee	Wisconsin	Brewers
Montreal	Quebec	Expos
New York	New York	Mets
Philadelphia	Pennsylvania	Phillies
Phoenix	Arizona	Diamondbacks
Pittsburgh	Pennsylvania	Pirates
San Diego	California	Padres
San Francisco	California	Giants
St. Louis	Missouri	Cardinals
Atlanta	Georgia	Braves

Page 103

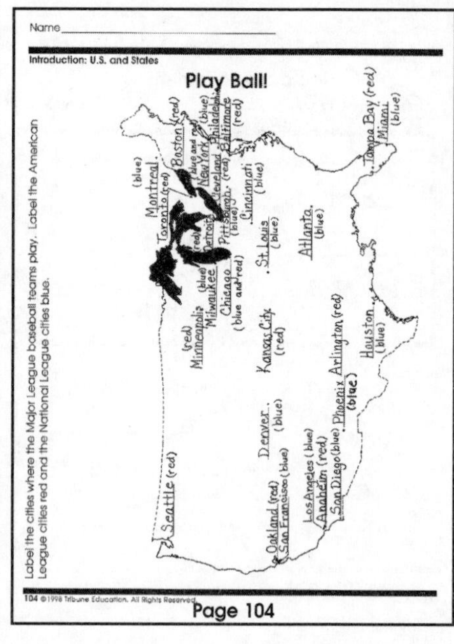

Name ______

Introduction: U.S. and States

Play Ball!

Label the cities where the Major League baseball teams play. Label the American League cities red and the National League cities blue.

Page 104

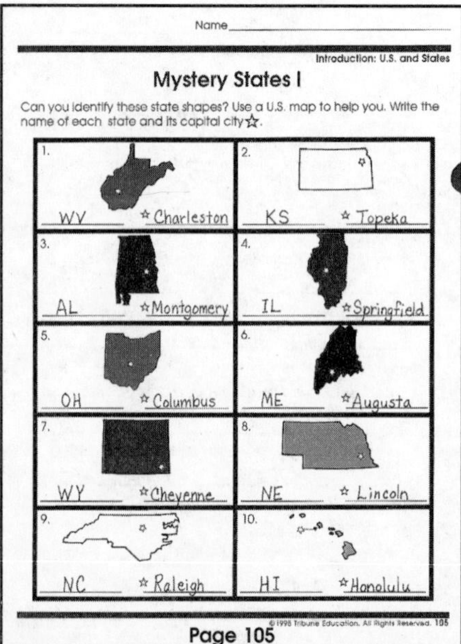

Name ______

Introduction: U.S. and States

Mystery States I

Can you identify these state shapes? Use a U.S. map to help you. Write the name of each state and its capital city ☆.

1. WV ☆ Charleston	2. KS ☆ Topeka
3. AL ☆ Montgomery	4. IL ☆ Springfield
5. OH ☆ Columbus	6. ME ☆ Augusta
7. WY ☆ Cheyenne	8. NE ☆ Lincoln
9. NC ☆ Raleigh	10. HI ☆ Honolulu

Page 105

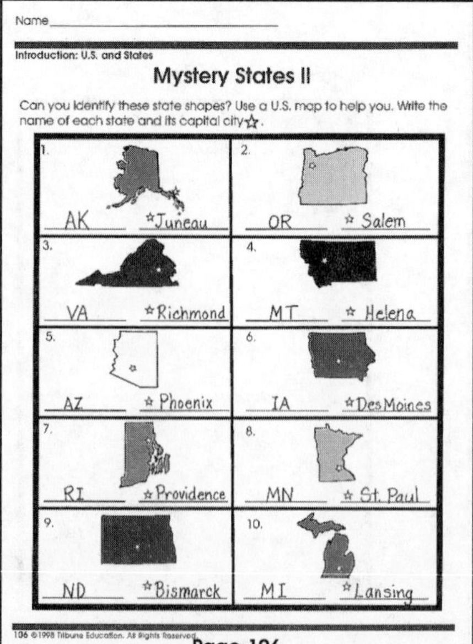

Name ______

Introduction: U.S. and States

Mystery States II

Can you identify these state shapes? Use a U.S. map to help you. Write the name of each state and its capital city ☆.

1. AK ☆ Juneau	2. OR ☆ Salem
3. VA ☆ Richmond	4. MT ☆ Helena
5. AZ ☆ Phoenix	6. IA ☆ Des Moines
7. RI ☆ Providence	8. MN ☆ St. Paul
9. ND ☆ Bismarck	10. MI ☆ Lansing

Page 106

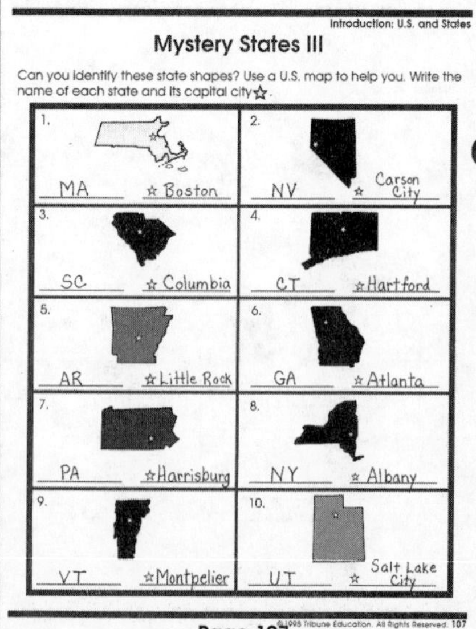

Name ______

Introduction: U.S. and States

Mystery States III

Can you identify these state shapes? Use a U.S. map to help you. Write the name of each state and its capital city ☆.

1. MA ☆ Boston	2. NV ☆ Carson City
3. SC ☆ Columbia	4. CT ☆ Hartford
5. AR ☆ Little Rock	6. GA ☆ Atlanta
7. PA ☆ Harrisburg	8. NY ☆ Albany
9. VT ☆ Montpelier	10. UT ☆ Salt Lake City

Page 107

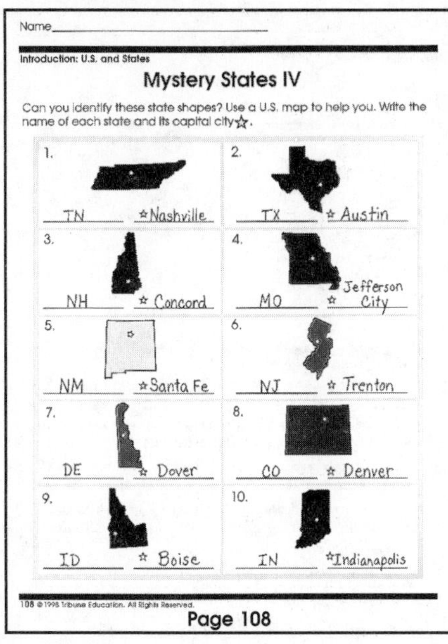

Name___

Introduction: U.S. and States

Mystery States IV

Can you identify these state shapes? Use a U.S. map to help you. Write the name of each state and its capital city☆.

1. TN ☆Nashville	2. TX ☆Austin
3. NH ☆Concord	4. MO ☆Jefferson City
5. NM ☆Santa Fe	6. NJ ☆Trenton
7. DE ☆Dover	8. CO ☆Denver
9. ID ☆Boise	10. IN ☆Indianapolis

Page 108

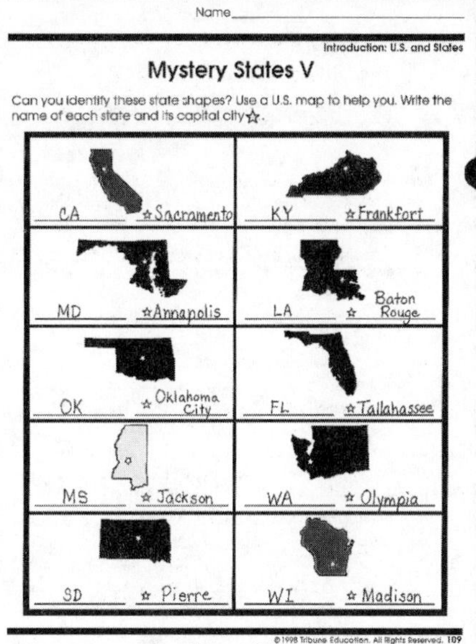

Name___

Introduction: U.S. and States

Mystery States V

Can you identify these state shapes? Use a U.S. map to help you. Write the name of each state and its capital city☆.

CA ☆Sacramento	KY ☆Frankfort
MD ☆Annapolis	LA ☆Baton Rouge
OK ☆Oklahoma City	FL ☆Tallahassee
MS ☆Jackson	WA ☆Olympia
SD ☆Pierre	WI ☆Madison

Page 109

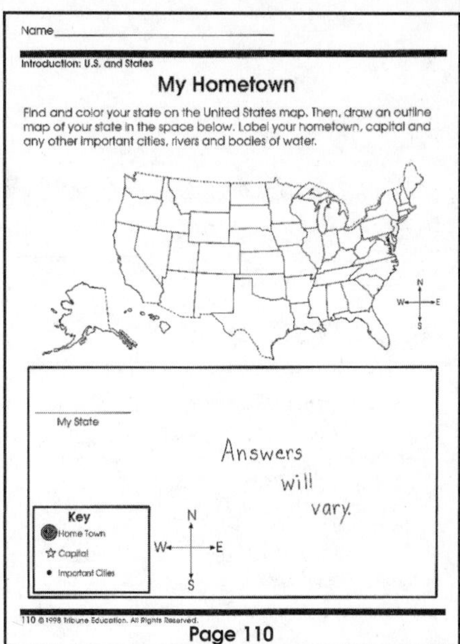

Name___

Introduction: U.S. and States

My Hometown

Find and color your state on the United States map. Then, draw an outline map of your state in the space below. Label your hometown, capital and any other important cities, rivers and bodies of water.

My State

Answers will vary.

Key
Home Town
☆ Capital
• Important Cities

Page 110

Name___

Introduction: U.S. and States

Near My State

Use a map of the United States to locate your state. Write the names of the bordering states/countries and/or bodies of water on the chart below. Write each one in its correct location relative to your state.

Northwest	North	Northeast
	Answers	
West	My State will vary. Draw an outline of your state.	East
Southwest	South	Southeast

Page 111

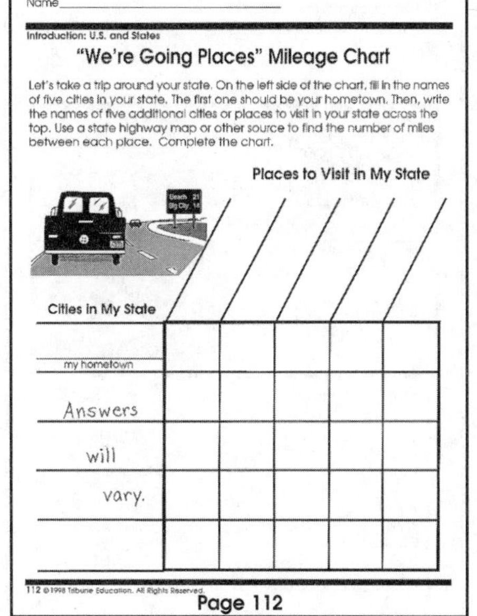

Name___

Introduction: U.S. and States

"We're Going Places" Mileage Chart

Let's take a trip around your state. On the left side of the chart, fill in the names of five cities in your state. The first one should be your hometown. Then, write the names of five additional cities or places to visit in your state across the top. Use a state highway map or other source to find the number of miles between each place. Complete the chart.

Places to Visit in My State

Cities in My State

my hometown

Answers will vary.

Page 112

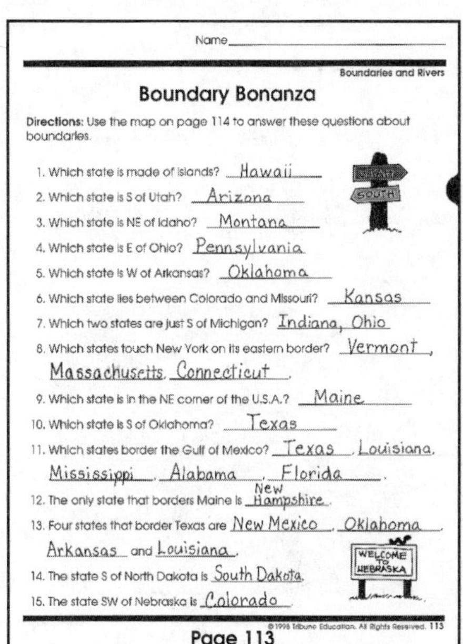

Name___

Boundaries and Rivers

Boundary Bonanza

Directions: Use the map on page 114 to answer these questions about boundaries.

1. Which state is made of islands? Hawaii
2. Which state is S of Utah? Arizona
3. Which state is NE of Idaho? Montana
4. Which state is E of Ohio? Pennsylvania
5. Which state is W of Arkansas? Oklahoma
6. Which state lies between Colorado and Missouri? Kansas
7. Which two states are just S of Michigan? Indiana, Ohio
8. Which states touch New York on its eastern border? Vermont, Massachusetts, Connecticut.
9. Which state is in the NE corner of the U.S.A.? Maine
10. Which state is S of Oklahoma? Texas
11. Which states border the Gulf of Mexico? Texas, Louisiana, Mississippi, Alabama, Florida.
12. The only state that borders Maine is New Hampshire.
13. Four states that border Texas are New Mexico, Oklahoma, Arkansas and Louisiana.
14. The state S of North Dakota is South Dakota.
15. The state SW of Nebraska is Colorado.

Page 113

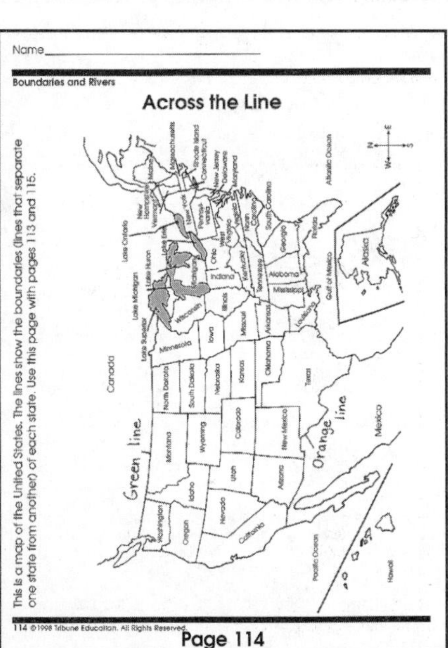

Name___

Boundaries and Rivers

Across the Line

This is a map of the United States. The lines show the boundaries (lines that separate one state from another) of each state. Use this page with pages 113 and 115.

Page 114

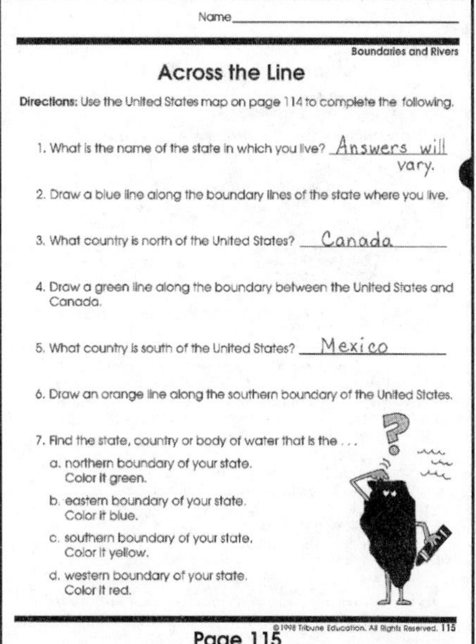

Name___

Boundaries and Rivers

Across the Line

Directions: Use the United States map on page 114 to complete the following.

1. What is the name of the state in which you live? Answers will vary.
2. Draw a blue line along the boundary lines of the state where you live.
3. What country is north of the United States? Canada
4. Draw a green line along the boundary between the United States and Canada.
5. What country is south of the United States? Mexico
6. Draw an orange line along the southern boundary of the United States.
7. Find the state, country or body of water that is the . . .
   a. northern boundary of your state. Color it green.
   b. eastern boundary of your state. Color it blue.
   c. southern boundary of your state. Color it yellow.
   d. western boundary of your state. Color it red.

Page 115

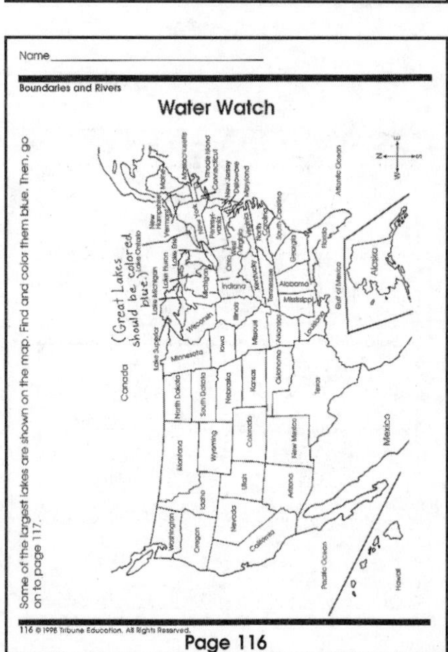

Name___

Boundaries and Rivers

Water Watch

Some of the largest lakes are shown on the map. Find and color them blue. Then, go on to page 117.

(Great Lakes should be colored blue.)

Page 116

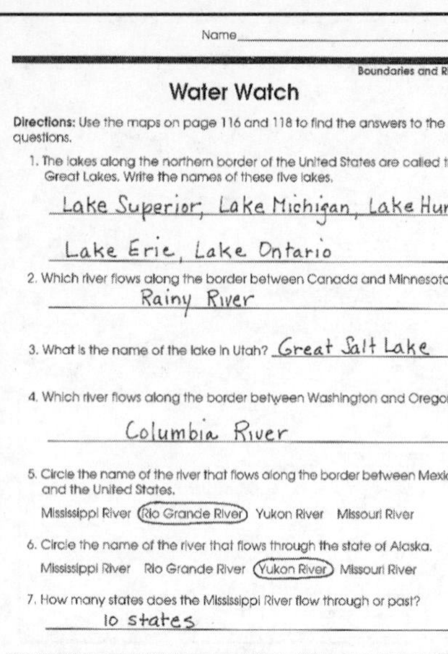

Name______

Boundaries and Rivers

Water Watch

Directions: Use the maps on page 116 and 118 to find the answers to the questions.

1. The lakes along the northern border of the United States are called the Great Lakes. Write the names of these five lakes.
Lake Superior, Lake Michigan, Lake Huron, Lake Erie, Lake Ontario
2. Which river flows along the border between Canada and Minnesota? Rainy River
3. What is the name of the lake in Utah? Great Salt Lake
4. Which river flows along the border between Washington and Oregon? Columbia River
5. Circle the name of the river that flows along the border between Mexico and the United States.
Mississippi River (Rio Grande River) Yukon River Missouri River
6. Circle the name of the river that flows through the state of Alaska.
Mississippi River Rio Grande River (Yukon River) Missouri River
7. How many states does the Mississippi River flow through or past? 10 states

Page 117

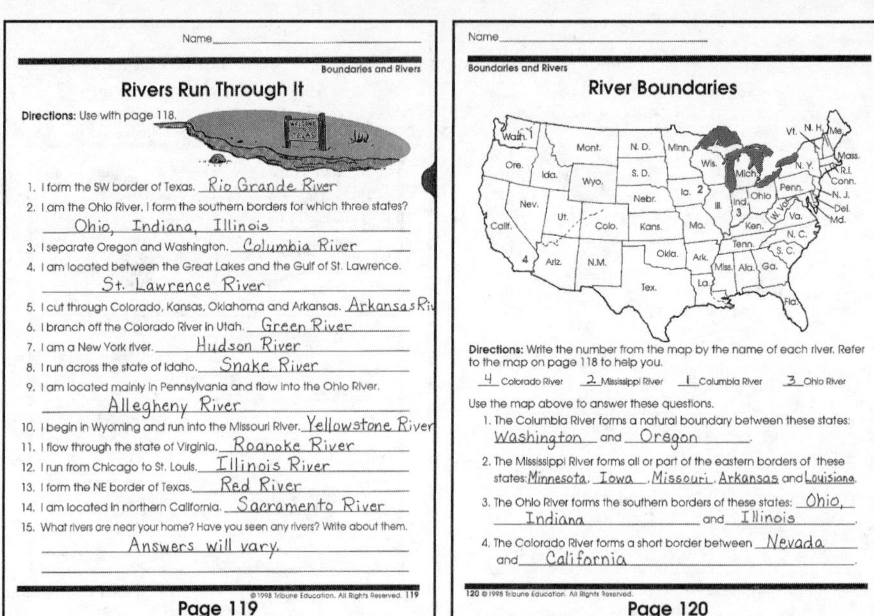

Name______

Boundaries and Rivers

Rivers Run Through It

Directions: Use with page 118.

1. I form the SW border of Texas. Rio Grande River
2. I am the Ohio River. I form the southern borders for which three states? Ohio, Indiana, Illinois
3. I separate Oregon and Washington. Columbia River
4. I am located between the Great Lakes and the Gulf of St. Lawrence. St. Lawrence River
5. I cut through Colorado, Kansas, Oklahoma and Arkansas. Arkansas River
6. I branch off the Colorado River in Utah. Green River
7. I am a New York river. Hudson River
8. I run across the state of Idaho. Snake River
9. I am located mainly in Pennsylvania and flow into the Ohio River. Allegheny River
10. I begin in Wyoming and run into the Missouri River. Yellowstone River
11. I flow through the state of Virginia. Roanoke River
12. I run from Chicago to St. Louis. Illinois River
13. I form the NE border of Texas. Red River
14. I am located in northern California. Sacramento River
15. What rivers are near your home? Have you seen any rivers? Write about them. Answers will vary.

Page 119

Name______

Boundaries and Rivers

River Boundaries

Directions: Write the number from the map by the name of each river. Refer to the map on page 118 to help you.

4 Colorado River 2 Mississippi River 1 Columbia River 3 Ohio River

Use the map above to answer these questions.

1. The Columbia River forms a natural boundary between these states: Washington and Oregon.
2. The Mississippi River forms all or part of the eastern borders of these states: Minnesota, Iowa, Missouri, Arkansas and Louisiana.
3. The Ohio River forms the southern borders of these states: Ohio, Indiana and Illinois.
4. The Colorado River forms a short border between Nevada and California.

Page 120

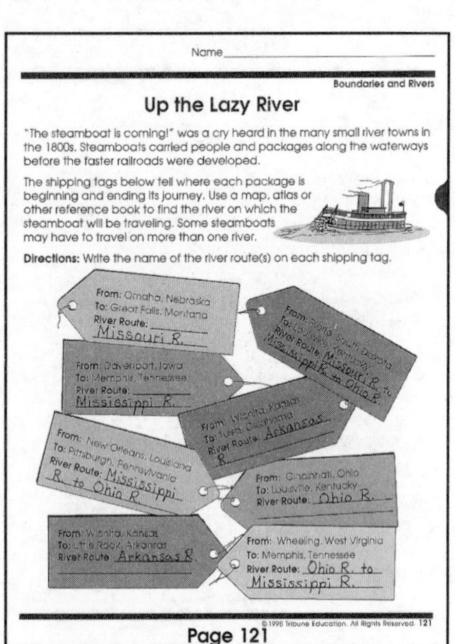

Name______

Boundaries and Rivers

Up the Lazy River

"The steamboat is coming!" was a cry heard in the many small river towns in the 1800s. Steamboats carried people and packages along the waterways before the faster railroads were developed.

The shipping tags below tell where each package is beginning and ending its journey. Use a map, atlas or other reference book to find the river on which the steamboat will be traveling. Some steamboats may have to travel on more than one river.

Directions: Write the name of the river route(s) on each shipping tag.

From: Omaha, Nebraska To: Great Falls, Montana River Route: Missouri R.

From: Pierre, South Dakota To: ... River Route: Missouri R. to Mississippi R. to Ohio R.

From: Davenport, Iowa To: Memphis, Tennessee River Route: Mississippi R.

From: Wichita, Kansas To: Tulsa, Oklahoma River Route: Arkansas R.

From: New Orleans, Louisiana To: Pittsburgh, Pennsylvania River Route: Mississippi R. to Ohio R.

From: Cincinnati, Ohio To: Louisville, Kentucky River Route: Ohio R.

From: Wichita, Kansas To: Little Rock, Arkansas River Route: Arkansas R.

From: Wheeling, West Virginia To: Memphis, Tennessee River Route: Ohio R. to Mississippi R.

Page 121

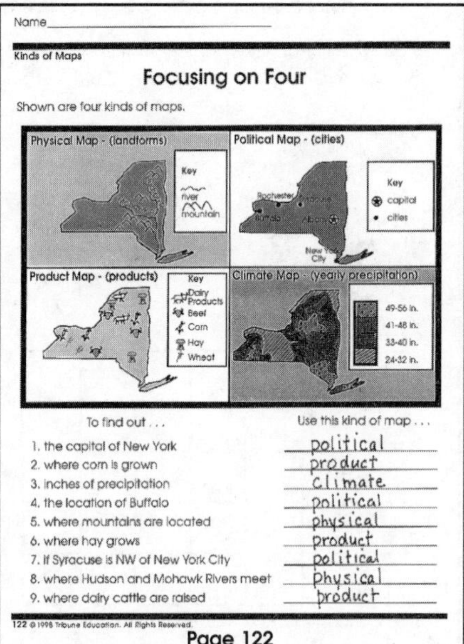

Name______

Kinds of Maps

Focusing on Four

Shown are four kinds of maps.

To find out . . .	Use this kind of map . . .
1. the capital of New York	political
2. where corn is grown	product
3. inches of precipitation	climate
4. the location of Buffalo	political
5. where mountains are located	physical
6. where hay grows	product
7. If Syracuse is NW of New York City	political
8. where Hudson and Mohawk Rivers meet	physical
9. where dairy cattle are raised	product

Page 122

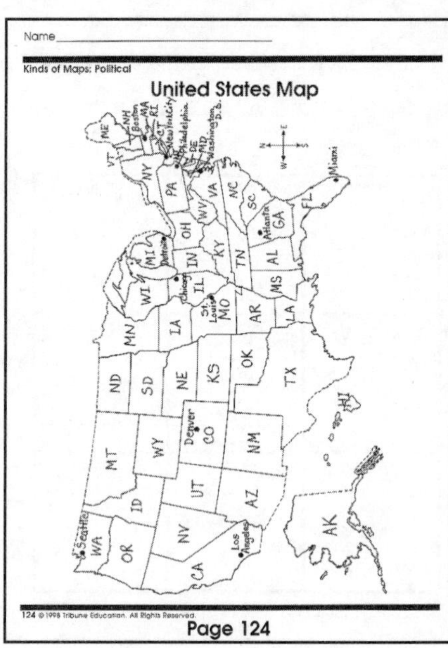

Name______

Kinds of Maps: Political

United States Map

Page 124

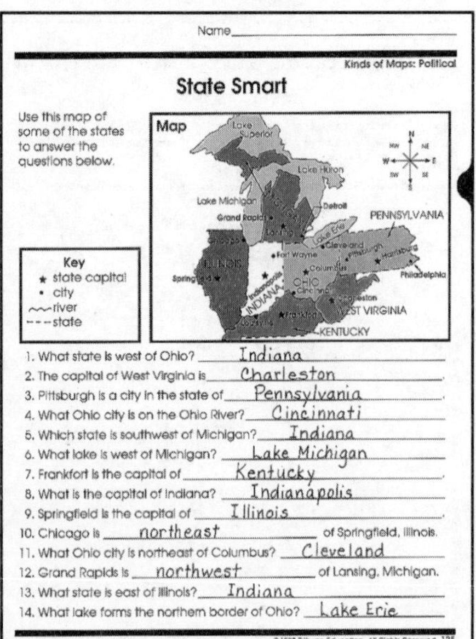

Name______

Kinds of Maps: Political

State Smart

Use this map of some of the states to answer the questions below.

1. What state is west of Ohio? Indiana
2. The capital of West Virginia is Charleston.
3. Pittsburgh is a city in the state of Pennsylvania.
4. What Ohio city is on the Ohio River? Cincinnati
5. Which state is southwest of Michigan? Indiana
6. What lake is west of Michigan? Lake Michigan
7. Frankfort is the capital of Kentucky.
8. What is the capital of Indiana? Indianapolis
9. Springfield is the capital of Illinois.
10. Chicago is northeast of Springfield, Illinois.
11. What Ohio city is northeast of Columbus? Cleveland
12. Grand Rapids is northwest of Lansing, Michigan.
13. What state is east of Illinois? Indiana
14. What lake forms the northern border of Ohio? Lake Erie

Page 125

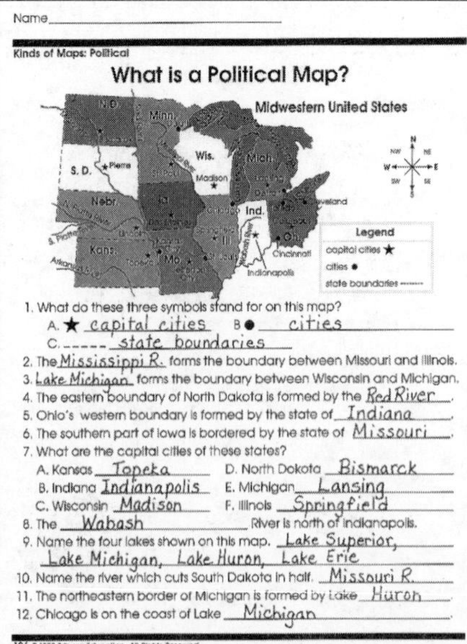

Name______

Kinds of Maps: Political

What is a Political Map?

1. What do these three symbols stand for on this map?
A. ★ capital cities B. ● cities C. ----- state boundaries
2. The Mississippi R. forms the boundary between Missouri and Illinois.
3. Lake Michigan forms the boundary between Wisconsin and Michigan.
4. The eastern boundary of North Dakota is formed by the Red River.
5. Ohio's western boundary is formed by the state of Indiana.
6. The southern part of Iowa is bordered by the state of Missouri.
7. What are the capital cities of these states?
A. Kansas Topeka D. North Dakota Bismarck
B. Indiana Indianapolis E. Michigan Lansing
C. Wisconsin Madison F. Illinois Springfield
8. The Wabash River is north of Indianapolis.
9. Name the four lakes shown on this map. Lake Superior, Lake Michigan, Lake Huron, Lake Erie
10. Name the river which cuts South Dakota in half. Missouri R.
11. The northeastern border of Michigan is formed by Lake Huron.
12. Chicago is on the coast of Lake Michigan.

Page 126

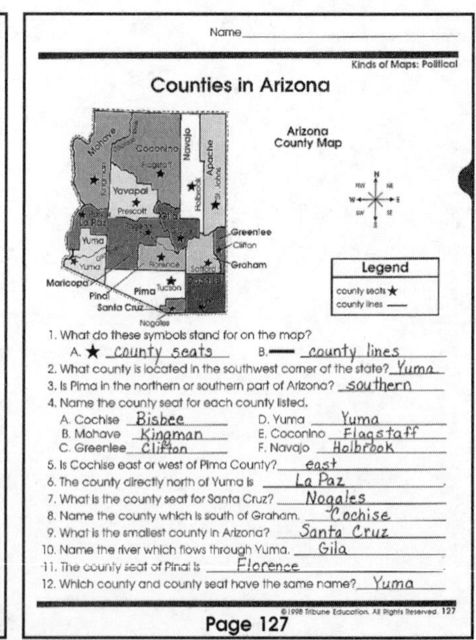

Name______

Kinds of Maps: Political

Counties in Arizona

1. What do these symbols stand for on the map?
A. ★ county seats B. — county lines
2. What county is located in the southwest corner of the state? Yuma
3. Is Pima in the northern or southern part of Arizona? southern
4. Name the county seat for each county listed.
A. Cochise Bisbee D. Yuma Yuma
B. Mohave Kingman E. Coconino Flagstaff
C. Greenlee Clifton F. Navajo Holbrook
5. Is Cochise east or west of Pima County? east
6. The county directly north of Yuma is La Paz.
7. What is the county seat for Santa Cruz? Nogales
8. Name the county which is south of Graham. Cochise
9. What is the smallest county in Arizona? Santa Cruz
10. Name the river which flows through Yuma. Gila
11. The county seat of Pinal is Florence.
12. Which county and county seat have the same name? Yuma

Page 127

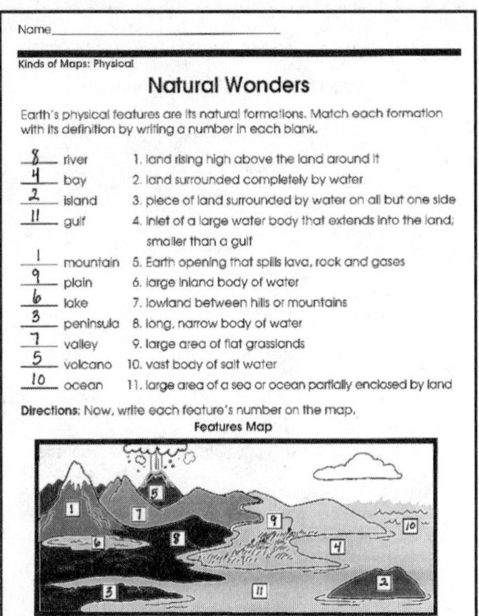
Name________________

Kinds of Maps: Physical

Natural Wonders

Earth's physical features are its natural formations. Match each formation with its definition by writing a number in each blank.

8	river	1. land rising high above the land around it
4	bay	2. land surrounded completely by water
2	island	3. piece of land surrounded by water on all but one side
11	gulf	4. inlet of a large water body that extends into the land; smaller than a gulf
1	mountain	5. Earth opening that spills lava, rock and gases
9	plain	6. large inland body of water
6	lake	7. lowland between hills or mountains
3	peninsula	8. long, narrow body of water
7	valley	9. large area of flat grasslands
5	volcano	10. vast body of salt water
10	ocean	11. large area of a sea or ocean partially enclosed by land

Directions: Now, write each feature's number on the map.

Features Map

Page 128

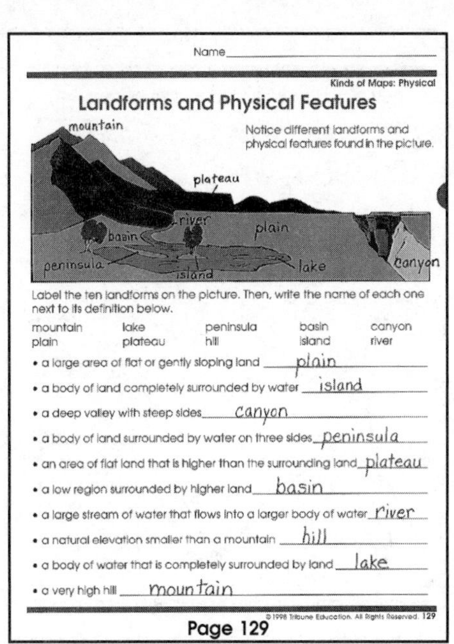
Name________________

Kinds of Maps: Physical

Landforms and Physical Features

Notice different landforms and physical features found in the picture.

Label the ten landforms on the picture. Then, write the name of each one next to its definition below.

mountain lake peninsula basin canyon
plain plateau hill island river

- a large area of flat or gently sloping land plain
- a body of land completely surrounded by water island
- a deep valley with steep sides canyon
- a body of land surrounded by water on three sides peninsula
- an area of flat land that is higher than the surrounding land plateau
- a low region surrounded by higher land basin
- a large stream of water that flows into a larger body of water river
- a natural elevation smaller than a mountain hill
- a body of water that is completely surrounded by land lake
- a very high hill mountain

Page 129

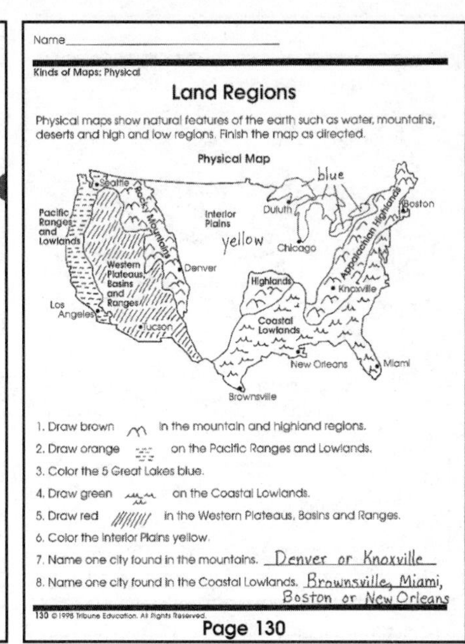
Name________________

Kinds of Maps: Physical

Land Regions

Physical maps show natural features of the earth such as water, mountains, deserts and high and low regions. Finish the map as directed.

Physical Map

1. Draw brown in the mountain and highland regions.
2. Draw orange on the Pacific Ranges and Lowlands.
3. Color the 5 Great Lakes blue.
4. Draw green on the Coastal Lowlands.
5. Draw red in the Western Plateaus, Basins and Ranges.
6. Color the Interior Plains yellow.
7. Name one city found in the mountains. Denver or Knoxville
8. Name one city found in the Coastal Lowlands. Brownsville, Miami, Boston or New Orleans

Page 130

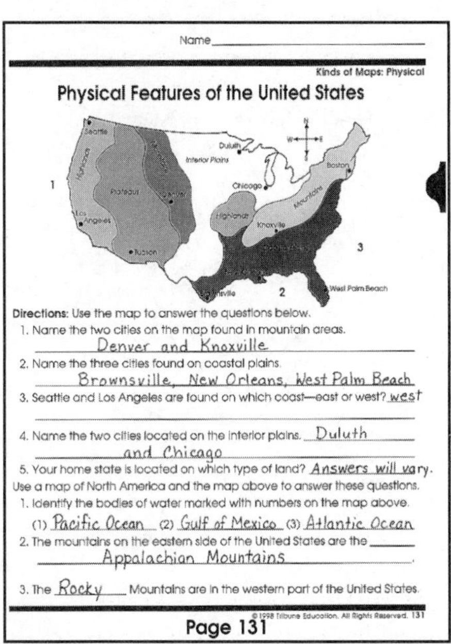
Name________________

Kinds of Maps: Physical

Physical Features of the United States

Directions: Use the map to answer the questions below.

1. Name the two cities on the map found in mountain areas. Denver and Knoxville
2. Name the three cities found on coastal plains. Brownsville, New Orleans, West Palm Beach
3. Seattle and Los Angeles are found on which coast—east or west? west
4. Name the two cities located on the interior plains. Duluth and Chicago
5. Your home state is located on which type of land? Answers will vary.

Use a map of North America and the map above to answer these questions.

1. Identify the bodies of water marked with numbers on the map above. (1) Pacific Ocean (2) Gulf of Mexico (3) Atlantic Ocean
2. The mountains on the eastern side of the United States are the Appalachian Mountains.
3. The Rocky Mountains are in the western part of the United States.

Page 131

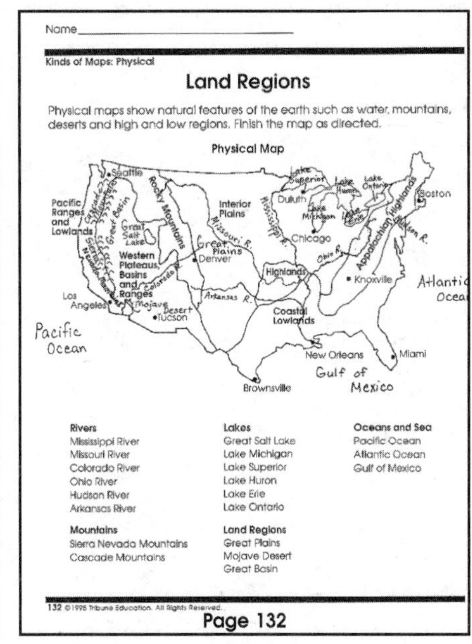
Name________________

Kinds of Maps: Physical

Land Regions

Physical maps show natural features of the earth such as water, mountains, deserts and high and low regions. Finish the map as directed.

Physical Map

Rivers	Lakes	Oceans and Sea
Mississippi River	Great Salt Lake	Pacific Ocean
Missouri River	Lake Michigan	Atlantic Ocean
Colorado River	Lake Superior	Gulf of Mexico
Ohio River	Lake Huron	
Hudson River	Lake Erie	
Arkansas River	Lake Ontario	
Mountains	**Land Regions**	
Sierra Nevada Mountains	Great Plains	
Cascade Mountains	Mojave Desert	
	Great Basin	

Page 132

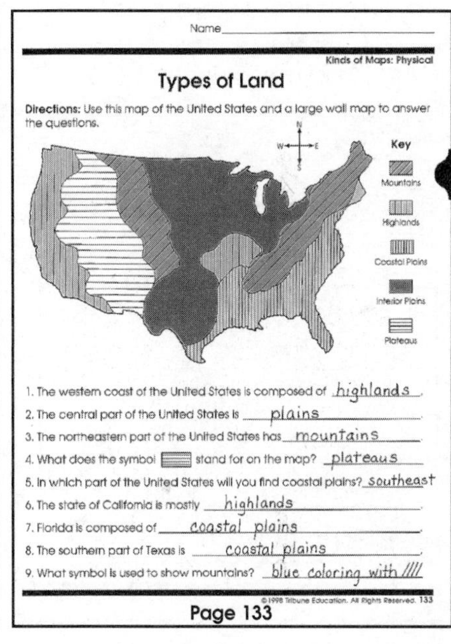
Name________________

Kinds of Maps: Physical

Types of Land

Directions: Use this map of the United States and a large wall map to answer the questions.

1. The western coast of the United States is composed of highlands.
2. The central part of the United States is plains.
3. The northeastern part of the United States has mountains.
4. What does the symbol stand for on the map? plateaus
5. In which part of the United States will you find coastal plains? southeast
6. The state of California is mostly highlands.
7. Florida is composed of coastal plains.
8. The southern part of Texas is coastal plains.
9. What symbol is used to show mountains? blue coloring with ////

Page 133

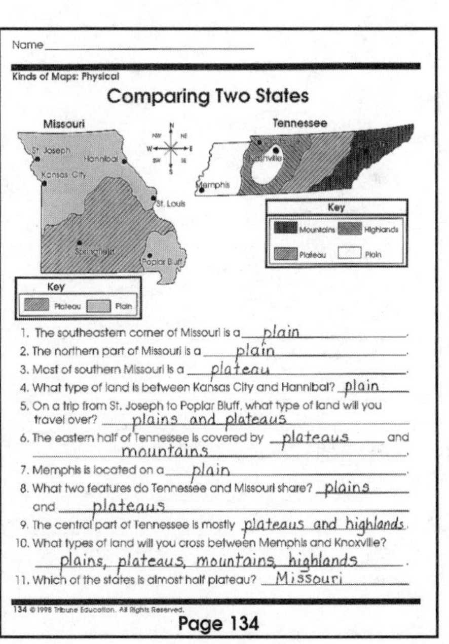
Name________________

Kinds of Maps: Physical

Comparing Two States

1. The southeastern corner of Missouri is a plain.
2. The northern part of Missouri is a plain.
3. Most of southern Missouri is a plateau.
4. What type of land is between Kansas City and Hannibal? plain
5. On a trip from St. Joseph to Poplar Bluff, what type of land will you travel over? plains and plateaus
6. The eastern half of Tennessee is covered by plateaus and mountains.
7. Memphis is located on a plain.
8. What two features do Tennessee and Missouri share? plains and plateaus
9. The central part of Tennessee is mostly plateaus and highlands.
10. What types of land will you cross between Memphis and Knoxville? plains, plateaus, mountains, highlands
11. Which of the states is almost half plateau? Missouri

Page 134

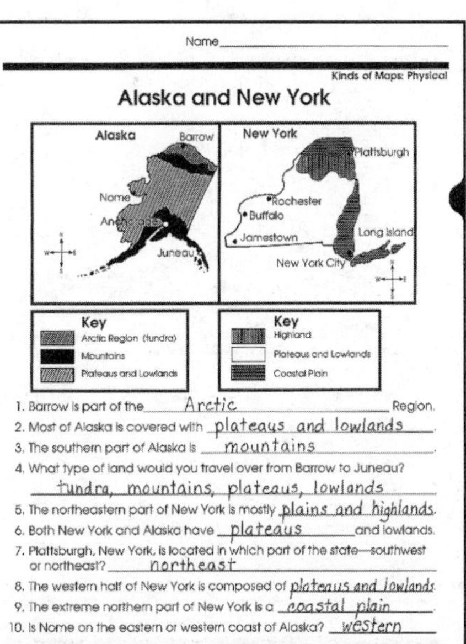
Name________________

Kinds of Maps: Physical

Alaska and New York

1. Barrow is part of the Arctic Region.
2. Most of Alaska is covered with plateaus and lowlands.
3. The southern part of Alaska is mountains.
4. What type of land would you travel over from Barrow to Juneau? tundra, mountains, plateaus, lowlands
5. The northeastern part of New York is mostly plains and highlands.
6. Both New York and Alaska have plateaus and lowlands.
7. Plattsburgh, New York, is located in which part of the state—southwest or northeast? northeast
8. The western half of New York is composed of plateaus and lowlands.
9. The extreme northern part of New York is a coastal plain.
10. Is Nome on the eastern or western coast of Alaska? western

Page 135

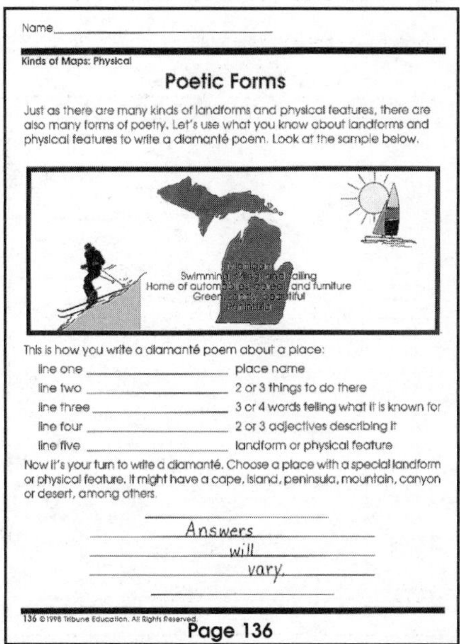
Name________________

Kinds of Maps: Physical

Poetic Forms

Just as there are many kinds of landforms and physical features, there are also many forms of poetry. Let's use what you know about landforms and physical features to write a diamanté poem. Look at the sample below.

This is how you write a diamanté poem about a place:

line one ________	place name
line two ________	2 or 3 things to do there
line three ________	3 or 4 words telling what it is known for
line four ________	2 or 3 adjectives describing it
line five ________	landform or physical feature

Now it's your turn to write a diamanté. Choose a place with a special landform or physical feature. It might have a cape, island, peninsula, mountain, canyon or desert, among others.

Answers will vary.

Page 136

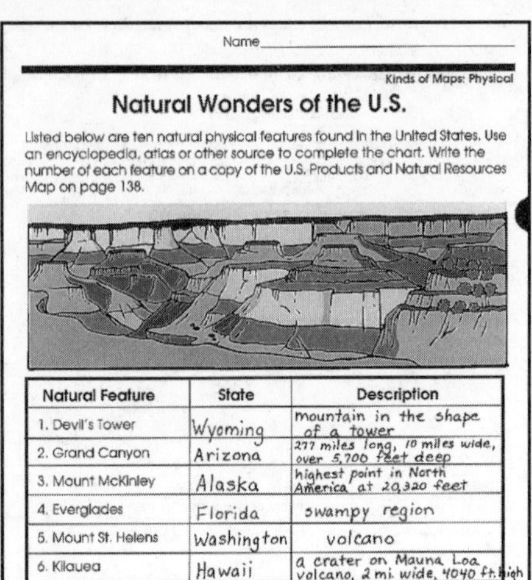

Name________________

Kinds of Maps: Physical

Natural Wonders of the U.S.

Listed below are ten natural physical features found in the United States. Use an encyclopedia, atlas or other source to complete the chart. Write the number of each feature on a copy of the U.S. Products and Natural Resources Map on page 138.

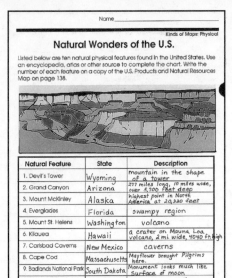

Natural Feature	State	Description
1. Devil's Tower	Wyoming	mountain in the shape of a tower
2. Grand Canyon	Arizona	277 miles long, 10 miles wide, over 5,700 feet deep
3. Mount McKinley	Alaska	highest point in North America at 20,320 feet
4. Everglades	Florida	swampy region
5. Mount St. Helens	Washington	volcano
6. Kilauea	Hawaii	a crater on Mauna Loa volcano, 2 mi. wide, 4040 ft. high
7. Carlsbad Caverns	New Mexico	caverns
8. Cape Cod	Massachusetts	Mayflower brought Pilgrims here.
9. Badlands National Park	South Dakota	Monument looks much like surface of moon
10. Mojave Desert	California	15,000 square miles

 137

Page 137

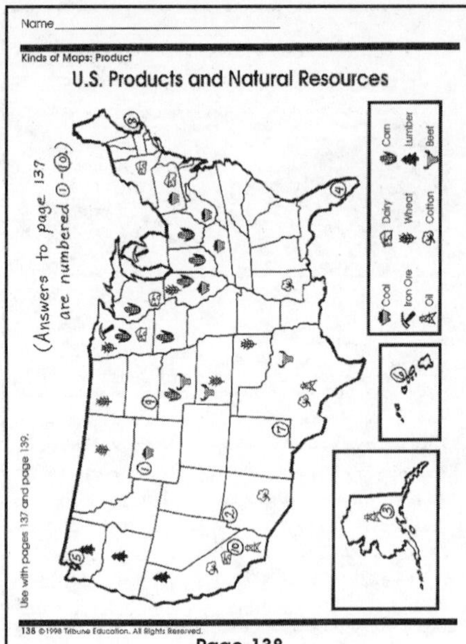

Page 138

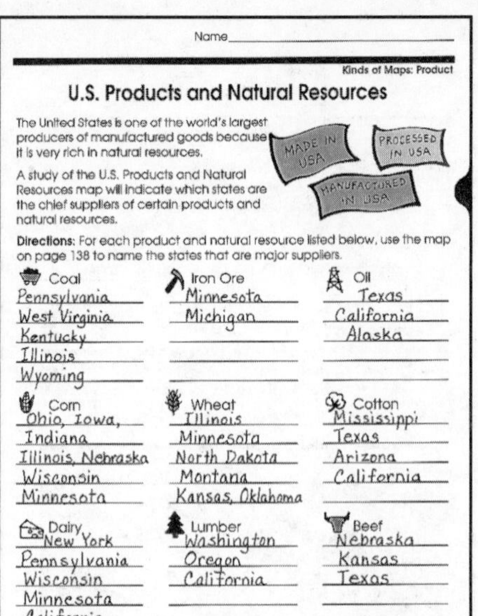

Name________________

Kinds of Maps: Product

U.S. Products and Natural Resources

The United States is one of the world's largest producers of manufactured goods because it is very rich in natural resources.

A study of the U.S. Products and Natural Resources map will indicate which states are the chief suppliers of certain products and natural resources.

Directions: For each product and natural resource listed below, use the map on page 138 to name the states that are major suppliers.

Coal: Pennsylvania, West Virginia, Kentucky, Illinois, Wyoming

Iron Ore: Minnesota, Michigan

Oil: Texas, California, Alaska

Corn: Ohio, Iowa, Indiana, Illinois, Nebraska, Wisconsin, Minnesota

Wheat: Illinois, Minnesota, North Dakota, Montana, Kansas, Oklahoma

Cotton: Mississippi, Texas, Arizona, California

Dairy: New York, Pennsylvania, Wisconsin, Minnesota, California

Lumber: Washington, Oregon, California

Beef: Nebraska, Kansas, Texas

 139

Page 139

Name________________

Kinds of Maps: Product

Grocery Store Geography

Many foods that we eat are not grown in our own community. While some foods come from neighboring states, others come from countries halfway around the world.

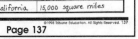

Check some of the foods in your cupboard and refrigerator at home. Check the labels to find out where they came from. Then, go to a grocery store and look at the labels on some other foods. Where did they come from? Look at the fruits and vegetables in the produce area. Many of them probably came from far away. Ask the grocer or produce manager where some of the fruits and vegetables are from.

Directions: Complete the chart.

Food	Where It Was Grown	Kind of Transportation Used to Ship the Product
Answers	will	vary.

On a map, locate where these foods were grown.

Which was shipped the greatest distance? Answers

How far did it have to travel to reach your grocery store? will vary.

 141

Page 141

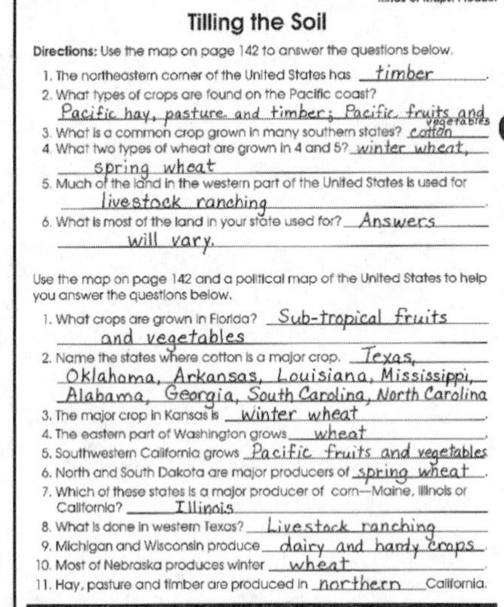

Name________________

Kinds of Maps: Product

Tilling the Soil

Directions: Use the map on page 142 to answer the questions below.

1. The northeastern corner of the United States has timber.
2. What types of crops are found on the Pacific coast? Pacific hay, pasture and timber; Pacific fruits and vegetables
3. What is a common crop grown in many southern states? cotton
4. What two types of wheat are grown in 4 and 5? winter wheat, spring wheat
5. Much of the land in the western part of the United States is used for livestock ranching
6. What is most of the land in your state used for? Answers will vary.

Use the map on page 142 and a political map of the United States to help you answer the questions below.

1. What crops are grown in Florida? Sub-tropical fruits and vegetables
2. Name the states where cotton is a major crop. Texas, Oklahoma, Arkansas, Louisiana, Mississippi, Alabama, Georgia, South Carolina, North Carolina
3. The major crop in Kansas is winter wheat.
4. The eastern part of Washington grows wheat.
5. Southwestern California grows Pacific fruits and vegetables.
6. North and South Dakota are major producers of spring wheat.
7. Which of these states is a major producer of corn—Maine, Illinois or California? Illinois
8. What is done in western Texas? Livestock ranching
9. Michigan and Wisconsin produce dairy and hardy crops.
10. Most of Nebraska produces winter wheat.
11. Hay, pasture and timber are produced in northern California.

 143

Page 143

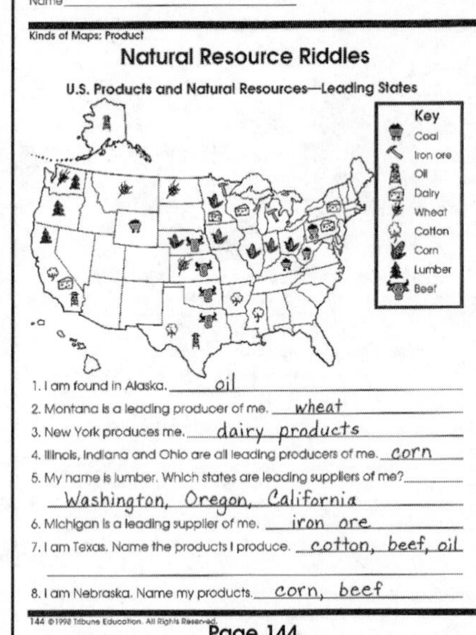

Name________________

Kinds of Maps: Product

Natural Resource Riddles

U.S. Products and Natural Resources—Leading States

1. I am found in Alaska. oil
2. Montana is a leading producer of me. wheat
3. New York produces me. dairy products
4. Illinois, Indiana and Ohio are all leading producers of me. corn
5. My name is lumber. Which states are leading suppliers of me? Washington, Oregon, California
6. Michigan is a leading supplier of me. iron ore
7. I am Texas. Name the products I produce. cotton, beef, oil
8. I am Nebraska. Name my products. corn, beef

144

Page 144

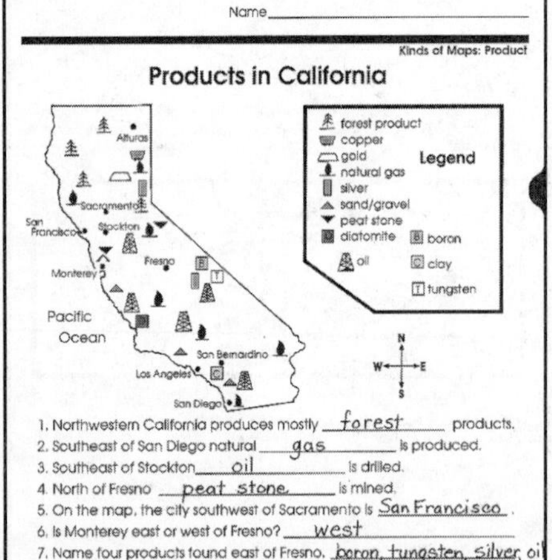

Name________________

Kinds of Maps: Product

Products in California

1. Northwestern California produces mostly forest products.
2. Southeast of San Diego natural gas is produced.
3. Southeast of Stockton oil is drilled.
4. North of Fresno peat stone is mined.
5. On the map, the city southwest of Sacramento is San Francisco.
6. Is Monterey east or west of Fresno? west
7. Name four products found east of Fresno. boron, tungsten, silver, oil
8. Is San Bernardino east or west of Los Angeles? east
9. What body of water is located west of California? Pacific Ocean
10. Is diatomite mined north or south of Los Angeles? north
11. Is copper mined north or south of Alturas? south
12. Is San Francisco north or south of Monterey? north
13. Does California mine any gold near San Diego? no

 145

Page 145

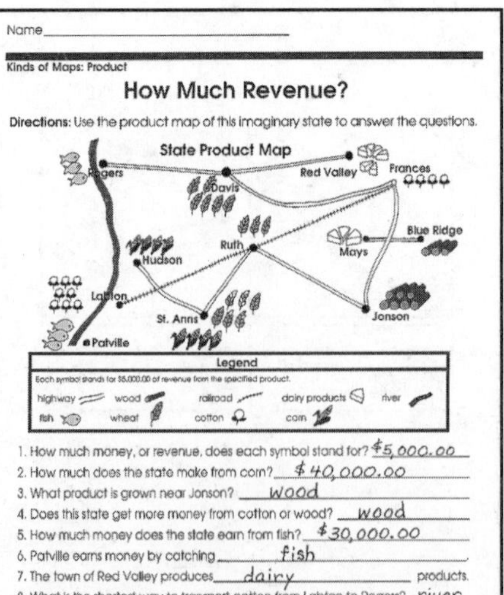

Name________________

Kinds of Maps: Product

How Much Revenue?

Directions: Use the product map of this imaginary state to answer the questions.

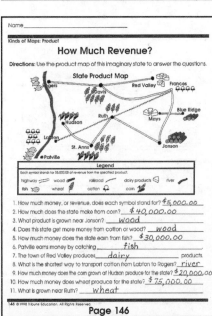

1. How much money, or revenue, does each symbol stand for? $5,000.00
2. How much does the state make from corn? $40,000.00
3. What product is grown near Jonson? wood
4. Does this state get more money from cotton or wood? wood
5. How much money does the state earn from fish? $30,000.00
6. Patville earns money by catching fish
7. The town of Red Valley produces dairy products.
8. What is the shortest way to transport cotton from Labton to Rogers? river
9. How much money does the corn grown at Hudson produce for the state? $20,000.00
10. How much money does wheat produce for the state? $75,000.00
11. What is grown near Ruth? wheat

146

Page 146

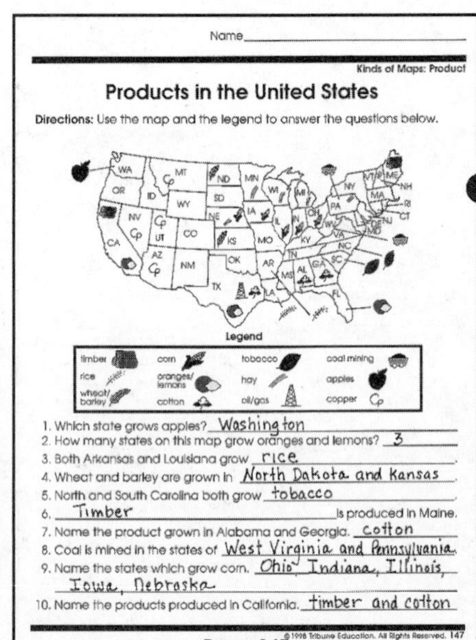

Name________________

Kinds of Maps: Product

Products in the United States

Directions: Use the map and the legend to answer the questions below.

1. Which state grows apples? Washington
2. How many states on this map grow oranges and lemons? 3
3. Both Arkansas and Louisiana grow rice.
4. Wheat and barley are grown in North Dakota and Kansas.
5. North and South Carolina both grow tobacco.
6. Timber is produced in Maine.
7. Name the product grown in Alabama and Georgia. cotton
8. Coal is mined in the states of West Virginia and Pennsylvania.
9. Name the states which grow corn. Ohio, Indiana, Illinois, Iowa, Nebraska
10. Name the products produced in California. timber and cotton

 147

Page 147

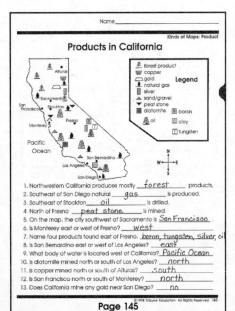

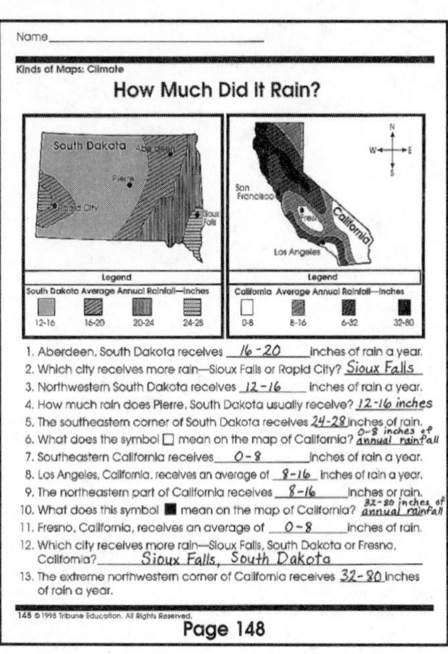

Name____________________

Kinds of Maps: Climate

How Much Did It Rain?

Legend			
South Dakota Average Annual Rainfall—Inches			
12-16	16-20	20-24	24-28

Legend			
California Average Annual Rainfall—Inches			
0-8	8-16	6-32	32-80

1. Aberdeen, South Dakota receives *16-20* inches of rain a year.
2. Which city receives more rain—Sioux Falls or Rapid City? *Sioux Falls*
3. Northwestern South Dakota receives *12-16* inches of rain a year.
4. How much rain does Pierre, South Dakota usually receive? *12-16 inches*
5. The southeastern corner of South Dakota receives *24-28* inches of rain.
6. What does the symbol ☐ mean on the map of California? *0-8 inches of annual rainfall*
7. Southeastern California receives *0-8* inches of rain a year.
8. Los Angeles, California, receives an average of *8-16* inches of rain a year.
9. The northeastern part of California receives *8-16* inches of rain.
10. What does this symbol ■ mean on the map of California? *32-80 inches of annual rainfall*
11. Fresno, California, receives an average of *0-8* inches of rain.
12. Which city receives more rain—Sioux Falls, South Dakota or Fresno, California? *Sioux Falls, South Dakota*
13. The extreme northwestern corner of California receives *32-80* inches of rain a year.

148 ©1998 Tribune Education. All Rights Reserved.

Page 148

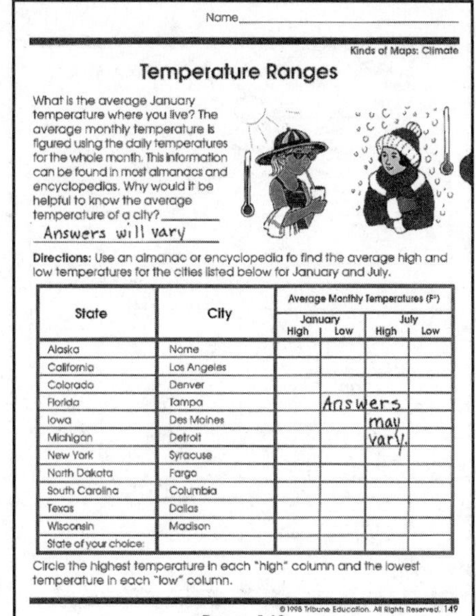

Name____________________

Kinds of Maps: Climate

Temperature Ranges

What is the average January temperature where you live? The average monthly temperature is figured using the daily temperatures for the whole month. This information can be found in most almanacs and encyclopedias. Why would it be helpful to know the average temperature of a city? *Answers will vary*

Directions: Use an almanac or encyclopedia to find the average high and low temperatures for the cities listed below for January and July.

State	City	Average Monthly Temperatures (F°)			
		January		July	
		High	Low	High	Low
Alaska	Nome				
California	Los Angeles				
Colorado	Denver				
Florida	Tampa		Answers		
Iowa	Des Moines		may		
Michigan	Detroit		vary.		
New York	Syracuse				
North Dakota	Fargo				
South Carolina	Columbia				
Texas	Dallas				
Wisconsin	Madison				
State of your choice:					

Circle the highest temperature in each "high" column and the lowest temperature in each "low" column.

©1998 Tribune Education. All Rights Reserved. 149

Page 149

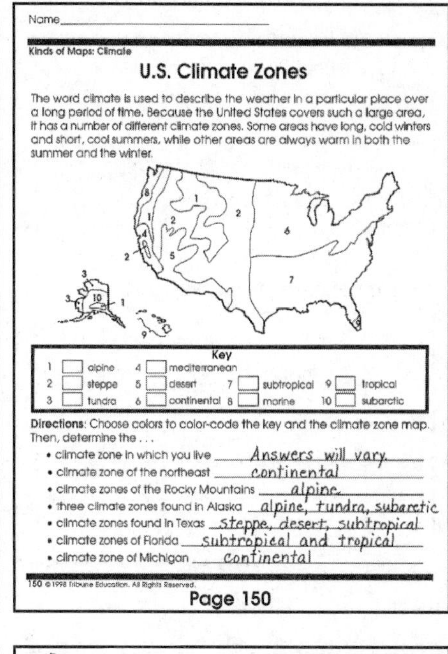

Name____________________

Kinds of Maps: Climate

U.S. Climate Zones

The word climate is used to describe the weather in a particular place over a long period of time. Because the United States covers such a large area, it has a number of different climate zones. Some areas have long, cold winters and short, cool summers, while other areas are always warm in both the summer and the winter.

Key

1	alpine	4	mediterranean						
2	steppe	5	desert	7	subtropical	9	tropical		
3	tundra	6	continental	8	marine	10	subarctic		

Directions: Choose colors to color-code the key and the climate zone map. Then, determine the . . .

- climate zone in which you live *Answers will vary.*
- climate zone of the northeast *continental*
- climate zones of the Rocky Mountains *alpine*
- three climate zones found in Alaska *alpine, tundra, subarctic*
- climate zones found in Texas *steppe, desert, subtropical*
- climate zones of Florida *subtropical and tropical*
- climate zone of Michigan *continental*

150 ©1998 Tribune Education. All Rights Reserved.

Page 150

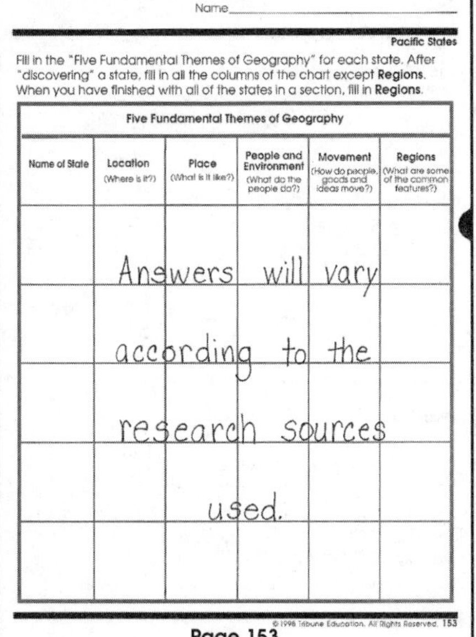

Name____________________

Pacific States

Fill in the "Five Fundamental Themes of Geography" for each state. After "discovering" a state, fill in all the columns of the chart except **Regions**. When you have finished with all of the states in a section, fill in **Regions**.

Five Fundamental Themes of Geography					
Name of State	Location (Where is it?)	Place (What is it like?)	People and Environment (What do the people do?)	Movement (How do people, goods and ideas move?)	Regions (What are some of the common features?)
Answers will vary according to the research sources used.					

©1998 Tribune Education. All Rights Reserved. 153

Page 153

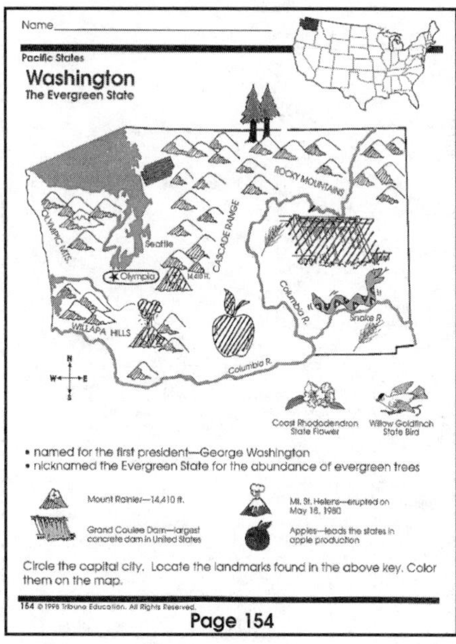

Name____________________

Pacific States

Washington

The Evergreen State

- named for the first president—George Washington
- nicknamed the Evergreen State for the abundance of evergreen trees

Mount Rainier—14,410 ft.

Mt. St. Helens—erupted on May 18, 1980

Grand Coulee Dam—largest concrete dam in United States

Apples—leads the states in apple production

Circle the capital city. Locate the landmarks found in the above key. Color them on the map.

154 ©1998 Tribune Education. All Rights Reserved.

Page 154

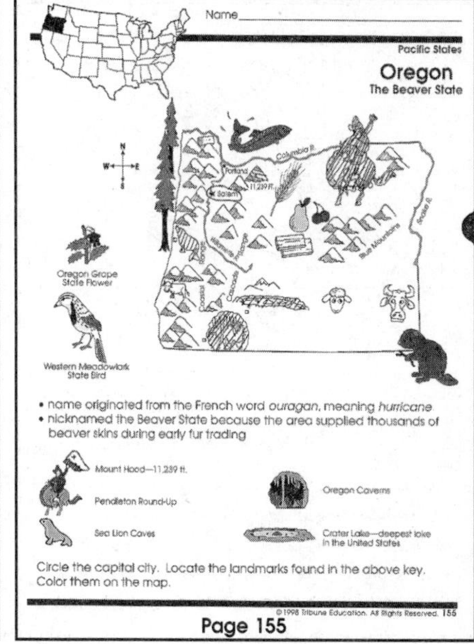

Name____________________

Pacific States

Oregon

The Beaver State

- name originated from the French word *ouragan*, meaning *hurricane*
- nicknamed the Beaver State because the area supplied thousands of beaver skins during early fur trading

Mount Hood—11,239 ft.

Oregon Caverns

Pendleton Round-Up

Sea Lion Caves

Crater Lake—deepest lake in the United States

Circle the capital city. Locate the landmarks found in the above key. Color them on the map.

©1998 Tribune Education. All Rights Reserved. 155

Page 155

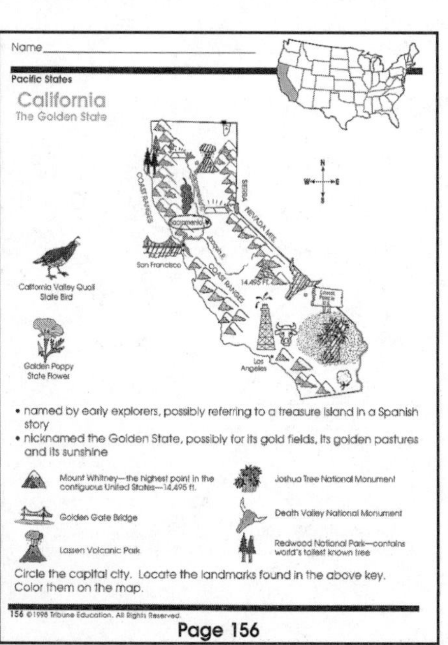

Name____________________

Pacific States

California

The Golden State

- named by early explorers, possibly referring to a treasure island in a Spanish story
- nicknamed the Golden State, possibly for its gold fields, its golden pastures and its sunshine

Mount Whitney—the highest point in the contiguous United States—14,495 ft.

Joshua Tree National Monument

Golden Gate Bridge

Death Valley National Monument

Lassen Volcanic Park

Redwood National Park—contains world's tallest known tree

Circle the capital city. Locate the landmarks found in the above key. Color them on the map.

156 ©1998 Tribune Education. All Rights Reserved.

Page 156

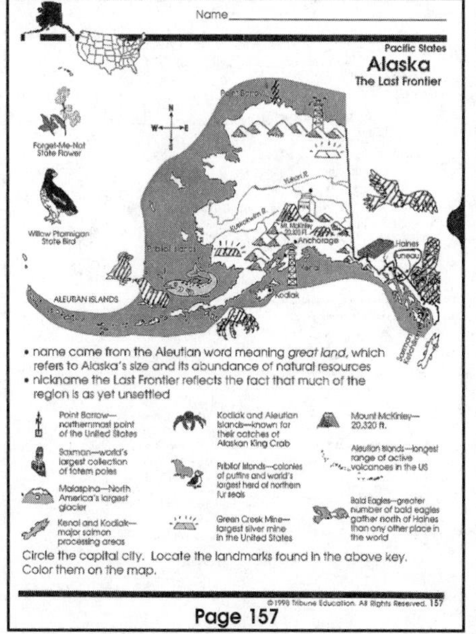

Name____________________

Pacific States

Alaska

The Last Frontier

- name came from the Aleutian word meaning *great land*, which refers to Alaska's size and its abundance of natural resources
- nickname the Last Frontier reflects the fact that much of the region is as yet unsettled

Point Barrow—northernmost point of the United States

Kodiak and Aleutian Islands—known for their catches of Alaskan King Crab

Mount McKinley—20,320 ft.

Saxman—world's largest collection of totem poles

Pribilof Islands—colonies of puffins and world's largest herd of northern fur seals

Aleutian Islands—longest range of active volcanoes in the US

Malaspina—North America's largest glacier

Kenai and Kodiak—major salmon processing areas

Green Creek Mine—largest silver mine in the United States

Bald Eagles—greater number of bald eagles gather north of Haines than any other place in the world

Circle the capital city. Locate the landmarks found in the above key. Color them on the map.

©1998 Tribune Education. All Rights Reserved. 157

Page 157

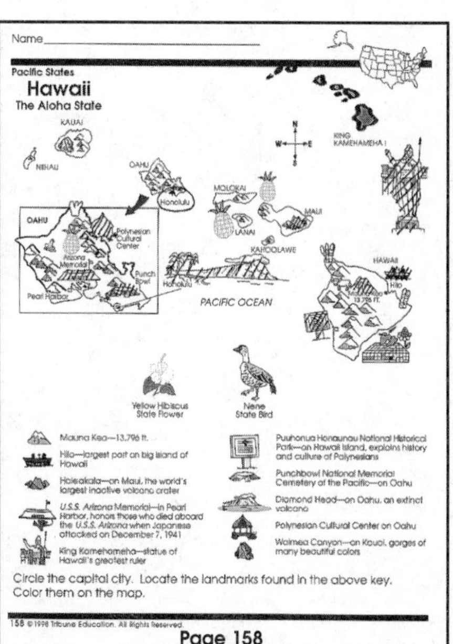

Name____________________

Pacific States

Hawaii

The Aloha State

Mauna Kea—13,796 ft.

Hilo—largest port on big island of Hawaii

Haleakala—on Maui, the world's largest inactive volcanic crater

U.S.S. Arizona Memorial—in Pearl Harbor, honors those who died aboard the *U.S.S. Arizona* when Japanese attacked on December 7, 1941

King Kamehameha—statue of Hawaii's greatest ruler

Puuhonua Honaunau National Historical Park—on Hawaii island, explains history and culture of Polynesians

Punchbowl National Memorial Cemetery of the Pacific—on Oahu

Diamond Head—on Oahu, an extinct volcano

Polynesian Cultural Center on Oahu

Waimea Canyon—on Kauai, gorges of many beautiful colors

Circle the capital city. Locate the landmarks found in the above key. Color them on the map.

158 ©1998 Tribune Education. All Rights Reserved.

Page 158

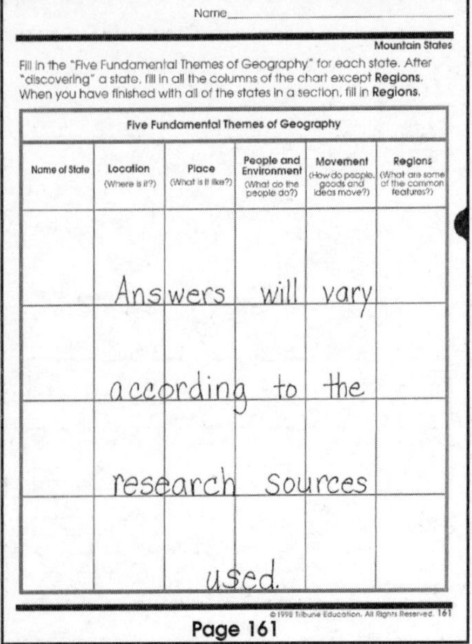

Name________________________

Mountain States

Fill in the "Five Fundamental Themes of Geography" for each state. After "discovering" a state, fill in all the columns of the chart except **Regions**. When you have finished with all of the states in a section, fill in **Regions**.

Five Fundamental Themes of Geography					
Name of State	Location (Where is it?)	Place (What is it like?)	People and Environment (What do the people do?)	Movement (How do people, goods and ideas move?)	Regions (What are some of the common features?)
	Answers will vary according to the research sources used.				

©1998 Tribune Education. All Rights Reserved. 161

Page 161

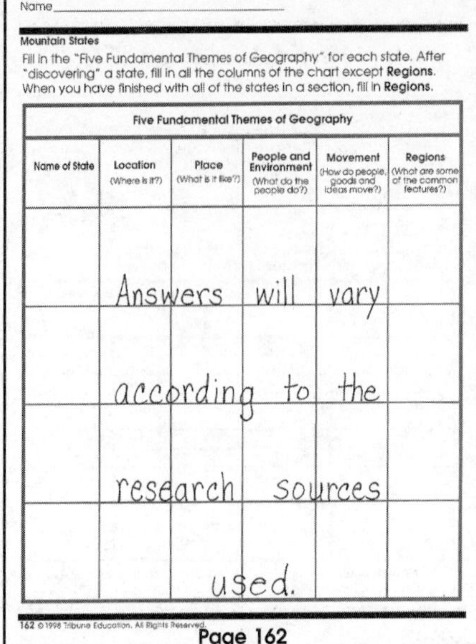

Name________________________

Mountain States

Fill in the "Five Fundamental Themes of Geography" for each state. After "discovering" a state, fill in all the columns of the chart except **Regions**. When you have finished with all of the states in a section, fill in **Regions**.

Five Fundamental Themes of Geography					
Name of State	Location (Where is it?)	Place (What is it like?)	People and Environment (What do the people do?)	Movement (How do people, goods and ideas move?)	Regions (What are some of the common features?)
	Answers will vary according to the research sources used.				

162 ©1998 Tribune Education. All Rights Reserved.

Page 162

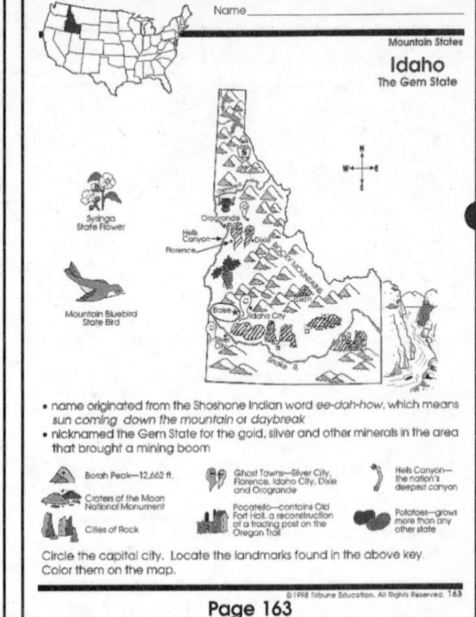

Name________________________

Mountain States

Idaho
The Gem State

- name originated from the Shoshone Indian word *ee-dah-how*, which means *sun coming down the mountain* or *daybreak*
- nicknamed the Gem State for the gold, silver and other minerals in the area that brought a mining boom

Borah Peak—12,662 ft.
Craters of the Moon National Monument
Cities of Rock
Ghost Towns—Silver City, Florence, Idaho City, Dixie and Orogrande
Pocatello—contains Old Fort Hall, a reconstruction of a trading post on the Oregon Trail
Hells Canyon—the nation's deepest canyon
Potatoes—grows more than any other state

Circle the capital city. Locate the landmarks found in the above key. Color them on the map.

©1998 Tribune Education. All Rights Reserved. 163

Page 163

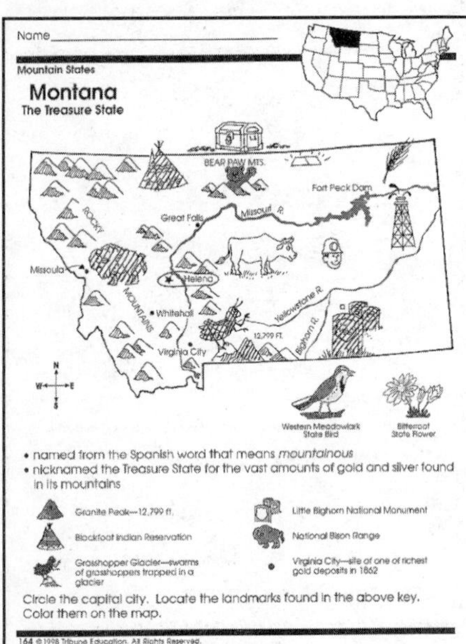

Name________________________

Mountain States

Montana
The Treasure State

- named from the Spanish word that means *mountainous*
- nicknamed the Treasure State for the vast amounts of gold and silver found in its mountains

Granite Peak—12,799 ft.
Blackfoot Indian Reservation
Grasshopper Glacier—swarms of grasshoppers trapped in a glacier
Little Bighorn National Monument
National Bison Range
Virginia City—site of one of richest gold deposits in 1862

Circle the capital city. Locate the landmarks found in the above key. Color them on the map.

164 ©1998 Tribune Education. All Rights Reserved.

Page 164

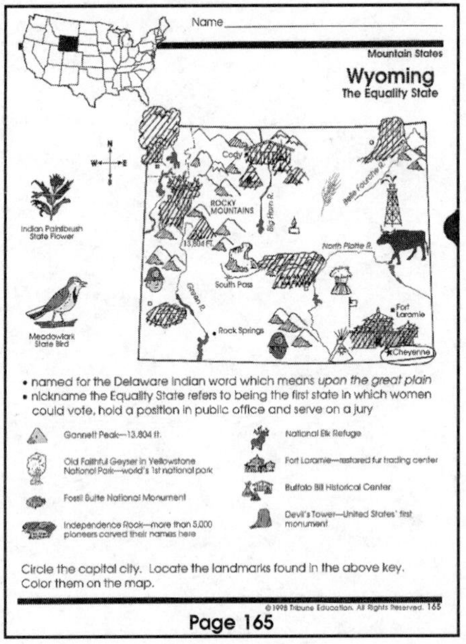

Name________________________

Mountain States

Wyoming
The Equality State

- named for the Delaware Indian word which means *upon the great plain*
- nickname the Equality State refers to being the first state in which women could vote, hold a position in public office and serve on a jury

Gannett Peak—13,804 ft.
Old Faithful Geyser in Yellowstone National Park—world's 1st national park
Fossil Butte National Monument
Independence Rock—more than 5,000 pioneers carved their names here
National Elk Refuge
Fort Laramie—restored fur trading center
Buffalo Bill Historical Center
Devil's Tower—United States' first monument

Circle the capital city. Locate the landmarks found in the above key. Color them on the map.

©1998 Tribune Education. All Rights Reserved. 165

Page 165

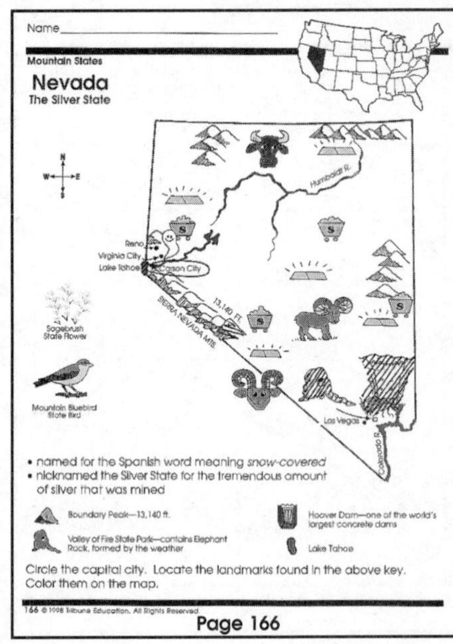

Name________________________

Mountain States

Nevada
The Silver State

- named for the Spanish word meaning *snow-covered*
- nicknamed the Silver State for the tremendous amount of silver that was mined

Boundary Peak—13,140 ft.
Valley of Fire State Park—contains Elephant Rock, formed by the weather
Hoover Dam—one of the world's largest concrete dams
Lake Tahoe

Circle the capital city. Locate the landmarks found in the above key. Color them on the map.

166 ©1998 Tribune Education. All Rights Reserved.

Page 166

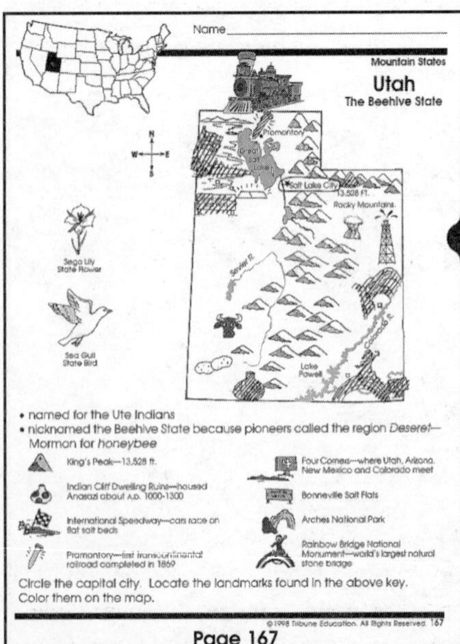

Name________________________

Mountain States

Utah
The Beehive State

- named for the Ute Indians
- nicknamed the Beehive State because pioneers called the region *Deseret*—Mormon for *honeybee*

King's Peak—13,528 ft.
Indian Cliff Dwelling Ruins—housed Anasazi about A.D. 1000–1300
International Speedway—cars race on flat salt beds
Promontory—first transcontinental railroad completed in 1869
Four Corners—where Utah, Arizona, New Mexico and Colorado meet
Bonneville Salt Flats
Arches National Park
Rainbow Bridge National Monument—world's largest natural stone bridge

Circle the capital city. Locate the landmarks found in the above key. Color them on the map.

©1998 Tribune Education. All Rights Reserved. 167

Page 167

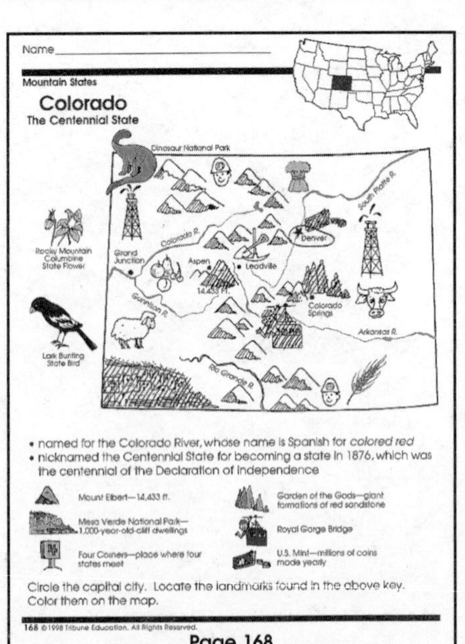

Name________________________

Mountain States

Colorado
The Centennial State

- named for the Colorado River, whose name is Spanish for *colored red*
- nicknamed the Centennial State for becoming a state in 1876, which was the centennial of the Declaration of Independence

Mount Elbert—14,433 ft.
Mesa Verde National Park—1,000-year-old cliff dwellings
Four Corners—place where four states meet
Garden of the Gods—giant formations of red sandstone
Royal Gorge Bridge
U.S. Mint—millions of coins made yearly

Circle the capital city. Locate the landmarks found in the above key. Color them on the map.

168 ©1998 Tribune Education. All Rights Reserved.

Page 168

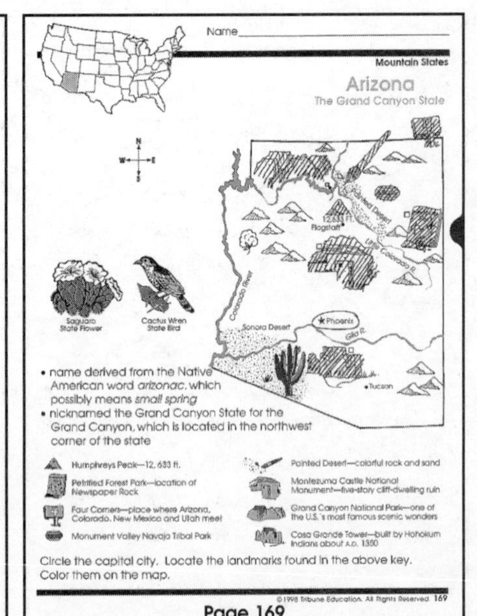

Name________________________

Mountain States

Arizona
The Grand Canyon State

- name derived from the Native American word *arizonac*, which possibly means *small spring*
- nicknamed the Grand Canyon State for the Grand Canyon, which is located in the northwest corner of the state

Humphreys Peak—12, 633 ft.
Petrified Forest Park—location of Newspaper Rock
Four Corners—place where Arizona, Colorado, New Mexico and Utah meet
Monument Valley Navajo Tribal Park
Painted Desert—colorful rock and sand
Montezuma Castle National Monument—five-story cliff-dwelling ruin
Grand Canyon National Park—one of the U.S.'s most famous scenic wonders
Casa Grande Tower—built by Hohokum Indians about A.D. 1350

Circle the capital city. Locate the landmarks found in the above key. Color them on the map.

©1998 Tribune Education. All Rights Reserved. 169

Page 169

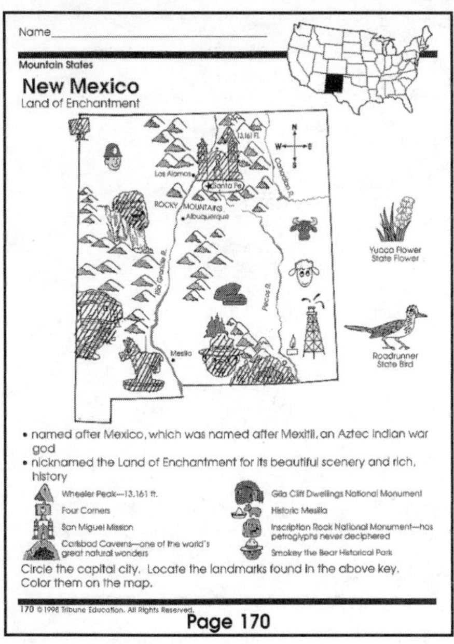

Name______________________

Mountain States

New Mexico

Land of Enchantment

- named after Mexico, which was named after Mexitli, an Aztec Indian war god
- nicknamed the Land of Enchantment for its beautiful scenery and rich history

Wheeler Peak—13,161 ft.
Four Corners
San Miguel Mission
Carlsbad Caverns—one of the world's great natural wonders
Gila Cliff Dwellings National Monument
Historic Mesilla
Inscription Rock National Monument—has petroglyphs never deciphered
Smokey the Bear Historical Park

Circle the capital city. Locate the landmarks found in the above key. Color them on the map.

Page 170

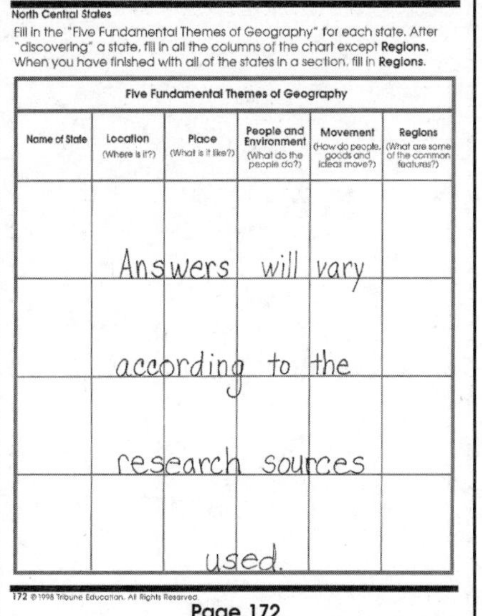

Name______________________

North Central States

Fill in the "Five Fundamental Themes of Geography" for each state. After "discovering" a state, fill in all the columns of the chart except **Regions**. When you have finished with all of the states in a section, fill in **Regions**.

Five Fundamental Themes of Geography					
Name of State	Location (Where is it?)	Place (What is it like?)	People and Environment (What do the people do?)	Movement (How do people, goods and ideas move?)	Regions (What are some of the common features?)
	Answers will vary according to the research sources used.				

Page 172

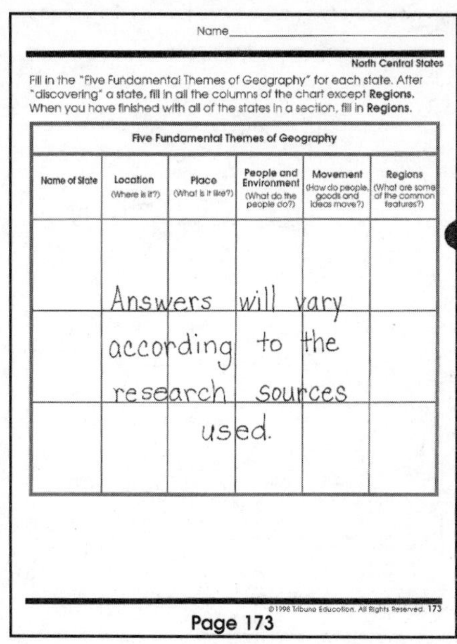

Name______________________

North Central States

Fill in the "Five Fundamental Themes of Geography" for each state. After "discovering" a state, fill in all the columns of the chart except **Regions**. When you have finished with all of the states in a section, fill in **Regions**.

Five Fundamental Themes of Geography					
Name of State	Location (Where is it?)	Place (What is it like?)	People and Environment (What do the people do?)	Movement (How do people, goods and ideas move?)	Regions (What are some of the common features?)
	Answers will vary according to the research sources used.				

Page 173

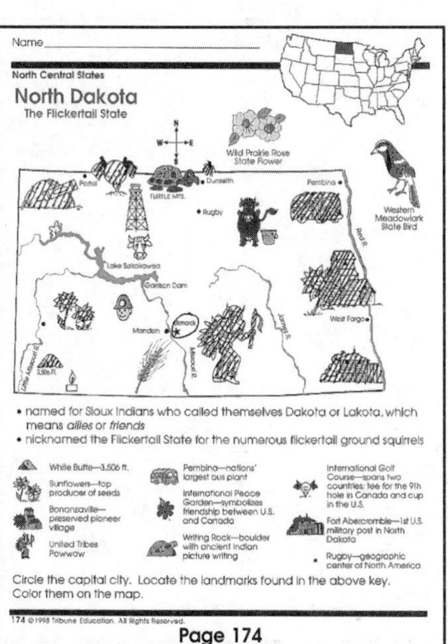

Name______________________

North Central States

North Dakota

The Flickertail State

- named for Sioux Indians who called themselves Dakota or Lakota, which means *allies* or *friends*
- nicknamed the Flickertail State for the numerous flickertail ground squirrels

White Butte—3,506 ft.
Sunflowers—top producer of seeds
Bonanzaville—preserved pioneer village
United Tribes Powwow
Pembina—nations' largest bus plant
International Peace Garden—symbolizes friendship between U.S. and Canada
Writing Rock—boulder with ancient Indian picture writing
International Golf Course—spans two countries; tee for the 9th hole in Canada and cup in the U.S.
Fort Abercrombie—1st U.S. military post in North Dakota
Rugby—geographic center of North America

Circle the capital city. Locate the landmarks found in the above key. Color them on the map.

Page 174

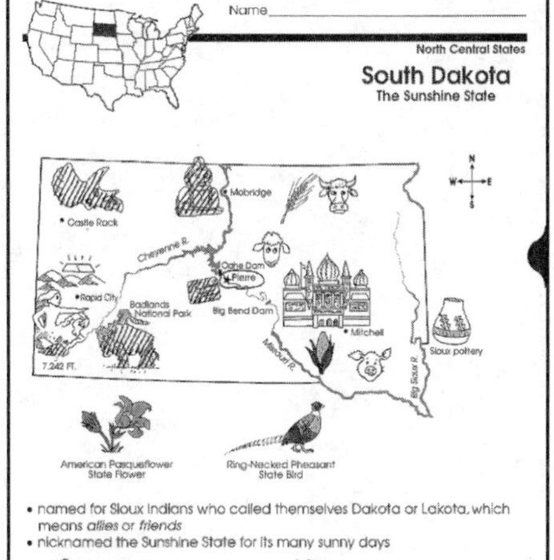

Name______________________

North Central States

South Dakota

The Sunshine State

- named for Sioux Indians who called themselves Dakota or Lakota, which means *allies* or *friends*
- nicknamed the Sunshine State for its many sunny days

Harney Peak—7,242 ft.
Mobridge—sculpture marking the gravesite of Sioux leader Sitting Bull
Triceratops Fossil—found in 1927 in Harding County and now on display
Custer State Park
Castle Rock—geographic center of the 50 United States
Lead Plate—buried by the La Vérendrye brothers in 1743—discovered in 1913

Circle the capital city. Locate the landmarks found in the above key. Color them on the map.

Page 175

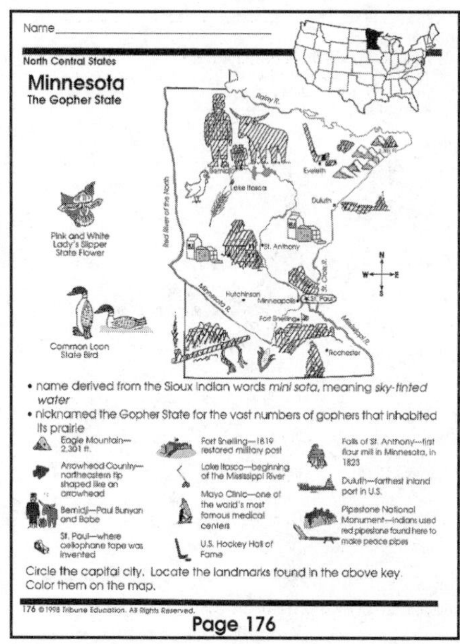

Name______________________

North Central States

Minnesota

The Gopher State

- name derived from the Sioux Indian words *mini sota*, meaning *sky-tinted water*
- nicknamed the Gopher State for the vast numbers of gophers that inhabited its prairie

Eagle Mountain—2,301 ft.
Arrowhead Country—northeastern tip shaped like an arrowhead
Bemidji—Paul Bunyan and Babe
St. Paul—where cellophane tape was invented
Fort Snelling—1819 restored military post
Lake Itasca—beginning of the Mississippi River
Mayo Clinic—one of the world's most famous medical centers
U.S. Hockey Hall of Fame
Falls of St. Anthony—first flour mill in Minnesota, in 1823
Duluth—farthest inland port in U.S.
Pipestone National Monument—Indians used red pipestone found here to make peace pipes

Circle the capital city. Locate the landmarks found in the above key. Color them on the map.

Page 176

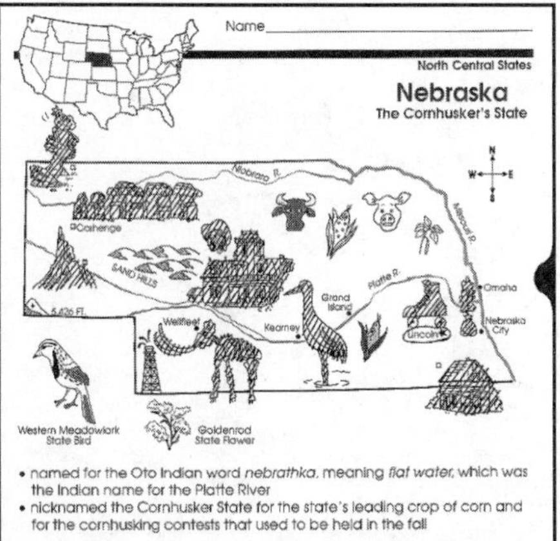

Name______________________

North Central States

Nebraska

The Cornhusker's State

- named for the Oto Indian word *nebrathka*, meaning *flat water*, which was the Indian name for the Platte River
- nicknamed the Cornhusker State for the state's leading crop of corn and for the cornhusking contests that used to be held in the fall

Toadstool Park—in the Badlands, has rock formations resembling toadstools
Wellfleet—largest mammoth fossil ever found
National Museum of Roller Skating
Arbor Lodge—home of Julius Sterling Morton, founder of Arbor Day
Chimney Rock National Historic Site
Carhenge—replica of Stonehenge made of cars
Cranes—about 500,000 stop along the Platte River every spring as they migrate north
Buffalo Bill's home
Homestead National Monument of America—site of the first piece of land claimed under the Homestead Act

Circle the capital city. Locate the landmarks found in the above key. Color them on the map.

Page 177

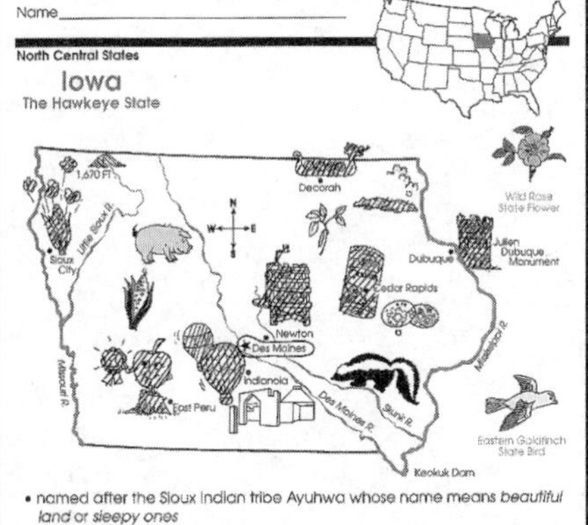

Name______________________

North Central States

Iowa

The Hawkeye State

- named after the Sioux Indian tribe Ayuhwa whose name means *beautiful land* or *sleepy ones*
- nicknamed the Hawkeye State in honor of Chief Black Hawk, a Sauk and Fox Indian leader

Vesterheim Museum—Norwegian culture exhibits
Julien Dubuque Monument—gravesite of the first permanent white settler in Iowa
Indianola—National Balloon Museum
Cedar Rapids—one of the largest cereal mills in the U.S.
East Peru—red delicious apple was developed here in the 1880s
Newton—washing machine capital of the world
Sioux City—largest popcorn processing plants in U.S.
Effigy Mounds—earthen mounds shaped like animals, built by prehistoric Indians

Circle the capital city. Locate the landmarks found in the above key. Color them on the map.

Page 178

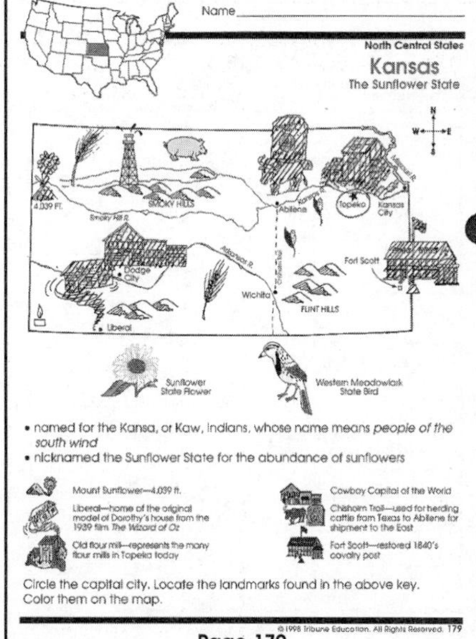

Name______________________

North Central States

Kansas

The Sunflower State

- named for the Kansa, or Kaw, Indians, whose name means *people of the south wind*
- nicknamed the Sunflower State for the abundance of sunflowers

Mount Sunflower—4,039 ft.
Liberal—home of the original model of Dorothy's house from the 1939 film *The Wizard of Oz*
Old flour mill—represents the many flour mills in Topeka today
Cowboy Capital of the World
Chisholm Trail—used for herding cattle from Texas to Abilene for shipment to the East
Fort Scott—restored 1840's cavalry post

Circle the capital city. Locate the landmarks found in the above key. Color them on the map.

Page 179

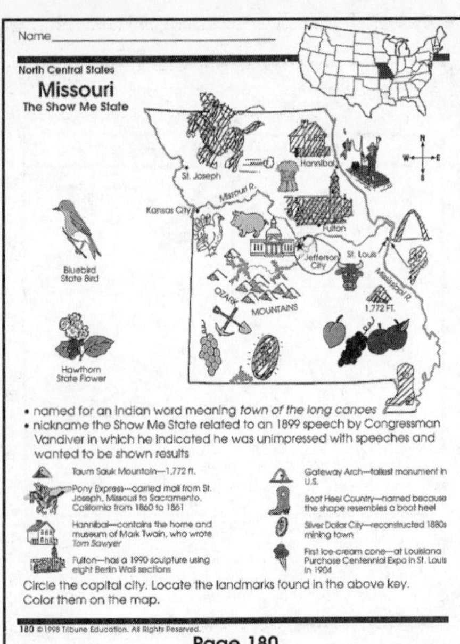
Name________________________

North Central States

Missouri

The Show Me State

Bluebird State Bird

Hawthorn State Flower

- named for an Indian word meaning *town of the long canoes*
- nickname the Show Me State related to an 1899 speech by Congressman Vandiver in which he indicated he was unimpressed with speeches and wanted to be shown results

Taum Sauk Mountain—1,772 ft.

Pony Express—carried mail from St. Joseph, Missouri to Sacramento, California from 1860 to 1861

Hannibal—contains the home and museum of Mark Twain, who wrote *Tom Sawyer*

Fulton—has a 1990 sculpture using eight Berlin Wall sections

Gateway Arch—tallest monument in U.S.

Boot Heel Country—named because the shape resembles a boot heel

Silver Dollar City—reconstructed 1880s mining town

First ice-cream cone—at Louisiana Purchase Centennial Expo in St. Louis in 1904

Circle the capital city. Locate the landmarks found in the above key. Color them on the map.

180 © 1998 Tribune Education. All Rights Reserved.

Page 180

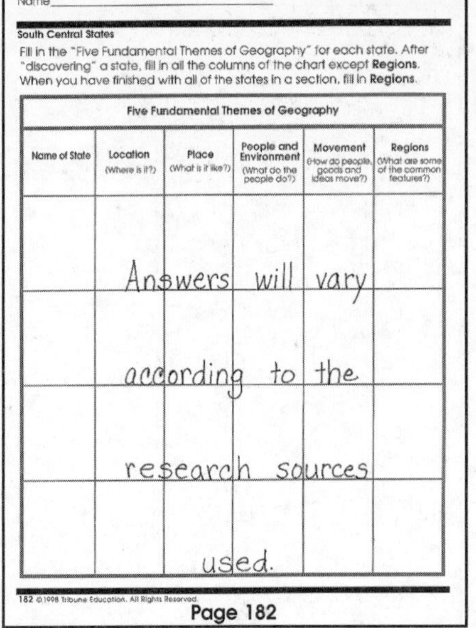
Name________________________

South Central States

Fill in the "Five Fundamental Themes of Geography" for each state. After "discovering" a state, fill in all the columns of the chart except **Regions**. When you have finished with all of the states in a section, fill in **Regions**.

Five Fundamental Themes of Geography

Name of State	Location (Where is it?)	Place (What is it like?)	People and Environment (What do the people do?)	Movement (How do people, goods and ideas move?)	Regions (What are some of the common features?)
		Answers will vary according to the research sources used.			

182 © 1998 Tribune Education. All Rights Reserved.

Page 182

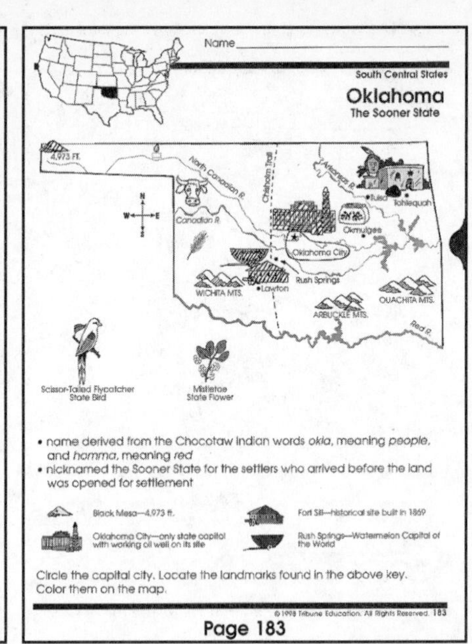
Name________________________

South Central States

Oklahoma

The Sooner State

Scissor-Tailed Flycatcher State Bird

Mistletoe State Flower

- name derived from the Chocotaw Indian words *okla*, meaning *people*, and *homma*, meaning *red*
- nicknamed the Sooner State for the settlers who arrived before the land was opened for settlement

Black Mesa—4,973 ft.

Oklahoma City—only state capital with working oil well on its site

Fort Sill—historical site built in 1869

Rush Springs—Watermelon Capital of the World

Circle the capital city. Locate the landmarks found in the above key. Color them on the map.

© 1998 Tribune Education. All Rights Reserved. 183

Page 183

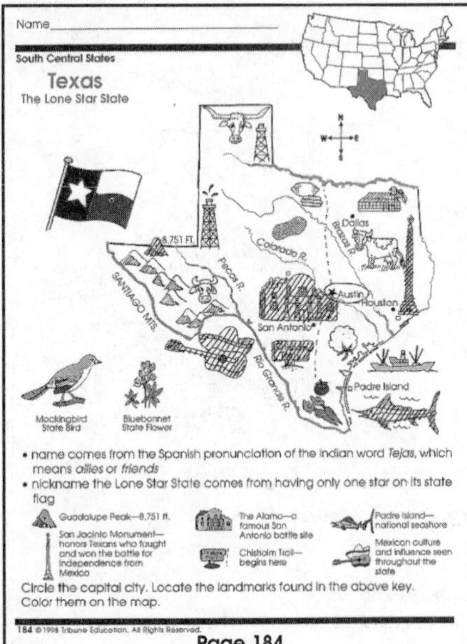
Name________________________

South Central States

Texas

The Lone Star State

Mockingbird State Bird

Bluebonnet State Flower

- name comes from the Spanish pronunciation of the Indian word *Tejas*, which means *allies* or *friends*
- nickname the Lone Star State comes from having only one star on its state flag

Guadalupe Peak—8,751 ft.

San Jacinto Monument—honors Texans who fought and won the battle for independence from Mexico

The Alamo—a famous San Antonio battle site

Chisholm Trail—begins here

Padre Island—national seashore

Mexican culture and influence seen throughout the state

Circle the capital city. Locate the landmarks found in the above key. Color them on the map.

184 © 1998 Tribune Education. All Rights Reserved.

Page 184

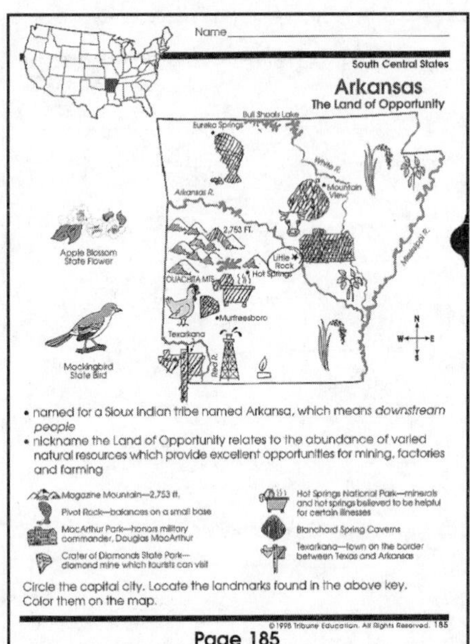
Name________________________

South Central States

Arkansas

The Land of Opportunity

Apple Blossom State Flower

Mockingbird State Bird

- named for a Sioux Indian tribe named Arkansa, which means *downstream people*
- nickname the Land of Opportunity relates to the abundance of varied natural resources which provide excellent opportunities for mining, factories and farming

Magazine Mountain—2,753 ft.

Pivot Rock—balances on a small base

MacArthur Park—honors military commander, Douglas MacArthur

Crater of Diamonds State Park—diamond mine which tourists can visit

Hot Springs National Park—minerals and hot springs believed to be helpful for certain illnesses

Blanchard Spring Caverns

Texarkana—town on the border between Texas and Arkansas

Circle the capital city. Locate the landmarks found in the above key. Color them on the map.

© 1998 Tribune Education. All Rights Reserved. 185

Page 185

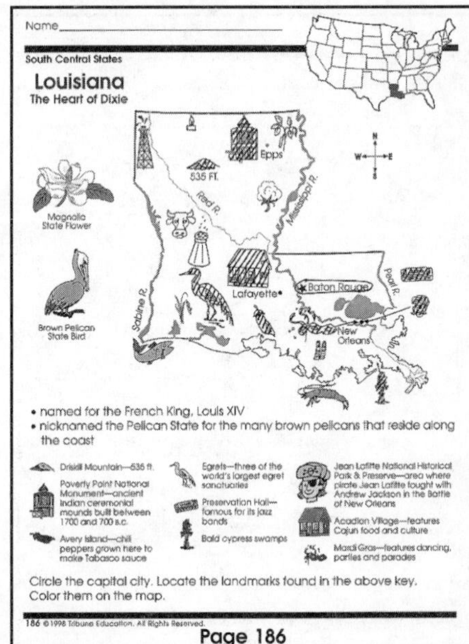
Name________________________

South Central States

Louisiana

The Heart of Dixie

Magnolia State Flower

Brown Pelican State Bird

- named for the French King, Louis XIV
- nicknamed the Pelican State for the many brown pelicans that reside along the coast

Driskill Mountain—535 ft.

Poverty Point National Monument—ancient Indian ceremonial mounds built between 1700 and 700 B.C.

Avery Island—chili peppers grown here to make Tabasco sauce

Egrets—three of the world's largest egret sanctuaries

Preservation Hall—famous for its jazz bands

Bald cypress swamps

Jean Lafitte National Historical Park & Preserve—area where pirate Jean Lafitte fought with Andrew Jackson in the Battle of New Orleans

Acadian Village—features Cajun food and culture

Mardi Gras—features dancing, parties and parades

Circle the capital city. Locate the landmarks found in the above key. Color them on the map.

186 © 1998 Tribune Education. All Rights Reserved.

Page 186

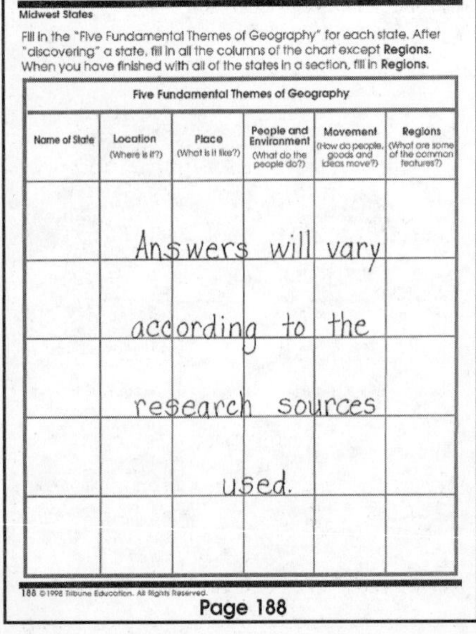
Name________________________

Midwest States

Fill in the "Five Fundamental Themes of Geography" for each state. After "discovering" a state, fill in all the columns of the chart except **Regions**. When you have finished with all of the states in a section, fill in **Regions**.

Five Fundamental Themes of Geography

Name of State	Location (Where is it?)	Place (What is it like?)	People and Environment (What do the people do?)	Movement (How do people, goods and ideas move?)	Regions (What are some of the common features?)
		Answers will vary according to the research sources used.			

188 © 1998 Tribune Education. All Rights Reserved.

Page 188

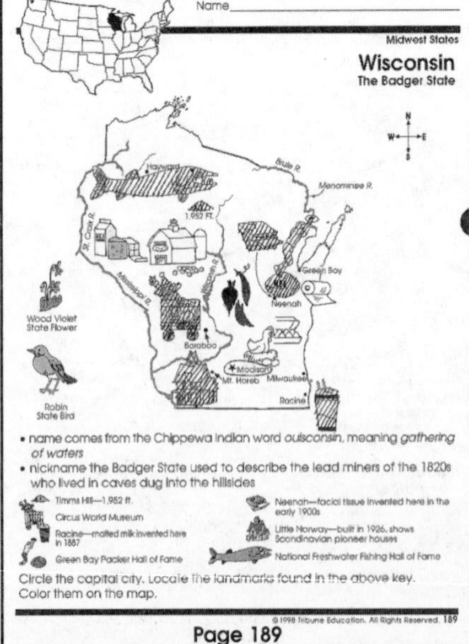
Name________________________

Midwest States

Wisconsin

The Badger State

Wood Violet State Flower

Robin State Bird

- name comes from the Chippewa Indian word *ouisconsin*, meaning *gathering of waters*
- nickname the Badger State used to describe the lead miners of the 1820s who lived in caves dug into the hillsides

Timms Hill—1,952 ft.

Circus World Museum

Racine—malted milk invented here in 1887

Green Bay Packer Hall of Fame

Neenah—facial tissue invented here in the early 1900s

Little Norway—built in 1926, shows Scandinavian pioneer houses

National Freshwater Fishing Hall of Fame

Circle the capital city. Locate the landmarks found in the above key. Color them on the map.

© 1998 Tribune Education. All Rights Reserved. 189

Page 189

Name________________________

Midwest States

Michigan

The Wolverine State

Apple Blossom State Flower

Robin State Bird

- named for the Indian word for Lake Michigan, *Michigama*, meaning *great lake*
- nicknamed the Wolverine State for the once-abundant wolverines that were trapped by fur traders and sold at trading posts

Mount Curwood—1,980 ft.

United States Ski Hall of Fame

Gerber—largest baby food plant in the U.S.

Fayette State Park—iron-ore smelting village from 1866 to 1890

Isle Royale—has one of the largest herds of moose in the United States

Grand Rapids—first carpet sweeper invented here in 1876 by M.R. Bissel

Battle Creek—produces the most breakfast cereal in the world

Sleeping Bear Dunes National Lakeshore—features sand dune shaped like a sleeping bear

Keweenaw Peninsula—one of the world's few sources of pure copper

Windmill Island Municipal Park—has the only authentic and operational Dutch windmill in the U.S.

Detroit—leads the U.S. in car and truck production (nicknamed Motor City)

Circle the capital city. Locate the landmarks found in the above key. Color them on the map.

190 © 1998 Tribune Education. All Rights Reserved.

Page 190

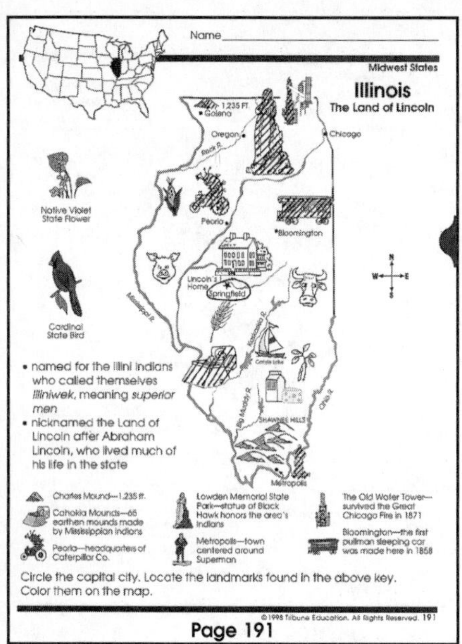
Midwest States
Illinois
The Land of Lincoln

Native Violet State Flower

Cardinal State Bird

- named for the Illini Indians who called themselves *Illiniwek*, meaning *superior men*
- nicknamed the Land of Lincoln after Abraham Lincoln, who lived much of his life in the state

Circle the capital city. Locate the landmarks found in the above key. Color them on the map.

 191

Page 191

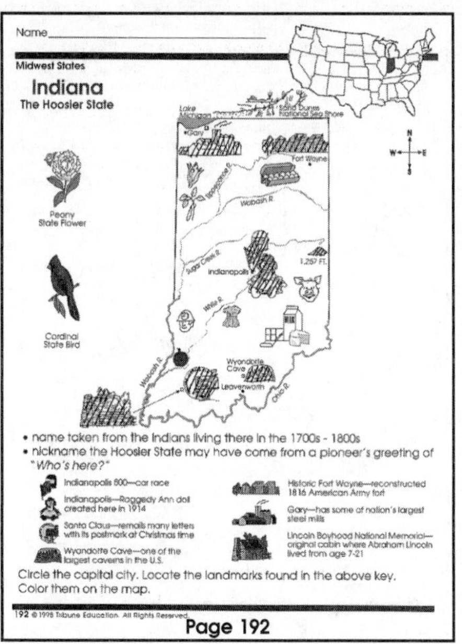
Midwest States
Indiana
The Hoosier State

Peony State Flower

Cardinal State Bird

- name taken from the Indians living there in the 1700s - 1800s
- nickname the Hoosier State may have come from a pioneer's greeting of "*Who's here?*"

Circle the capital city. Locate the landmarks found in the above key. Color them on the map.

192

Page 192

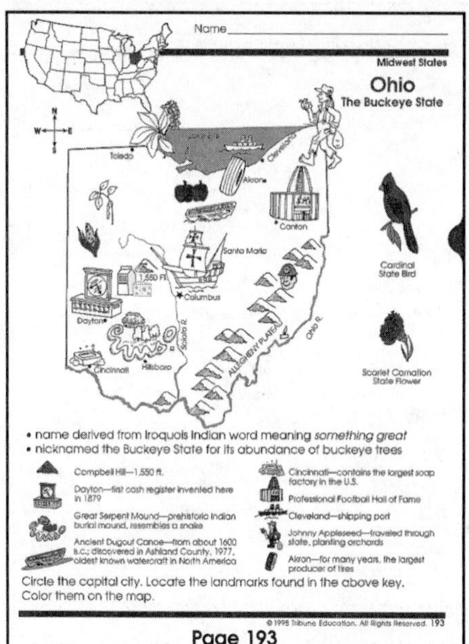
Midwest States
Ohio
The Buckeye State

Cardinal State Bird

Scarlet Carnation State Flower

- name derived from Iroquois Indian word meaning *something great*
- nicknamed the Buckeye State for its abundance of buckeye trees

Circle the capital city. Locate the landmarks found in the above key. Color them on the map.

 193

Page 193

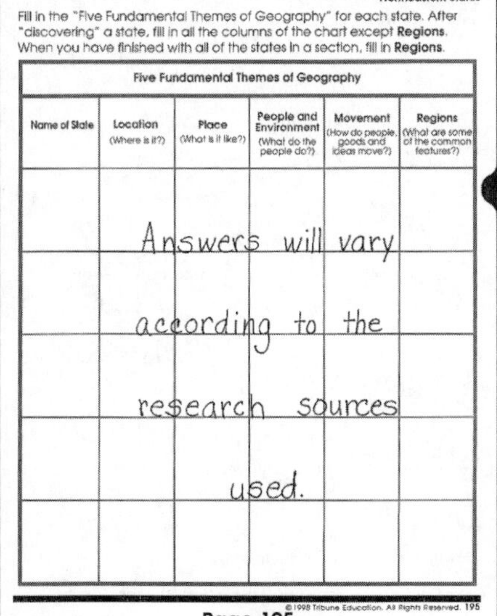
Northeastern States

Fill in the "Five Fundamental Themes of Geography" for each state. After "discovering" a state, fill in all the columns of the chart except **Regions**. When you have finished with all of the states in a section, fill in **Regions**.

Five Fundamental Themes of Geography

Name of State	Location (Where is it?)	Place (What is it like?)	People and Environment (What do the people do?)	Movement (How do people, goods and ideas move?)	Regions (What are some of the common features?)
	Answers will vary according to the research sources used.				

 195

Page 195

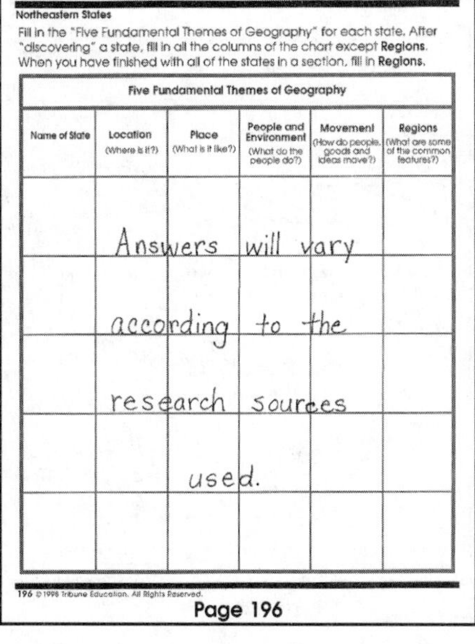
Northeastern States

Fill in the "Five Fundamental Themes of Geography" for each state. After "discovering" a state, fill in all the columns of the chart except **Regions**. When you have finished with all of the states in a section, fill in **Regions**.

Five Fundamental Themes of Geography

Name of State	Location (Where is it?)	Place (What is it like?)	People and Environment (What do the people do?)	Movement (How do people, goods and ideas move?)	Regions (What are some of the common features?)
	Answers will vary according to the research sources used.				

196

Page 196

Northeastern States
Maine
The Pine Tree State

Chickadee State Bird

White Pine cone and tassel State Flower

- name believed to have originated from the English explorers who used the term *main* to refer to the *mainland*, as opposed to the islands
- nicknamed the Pine Tree State for the abundance of pine tree forests

Circle the capital city. Locate the landmarks found in the above key. Color them on the map.

 197

Page 197

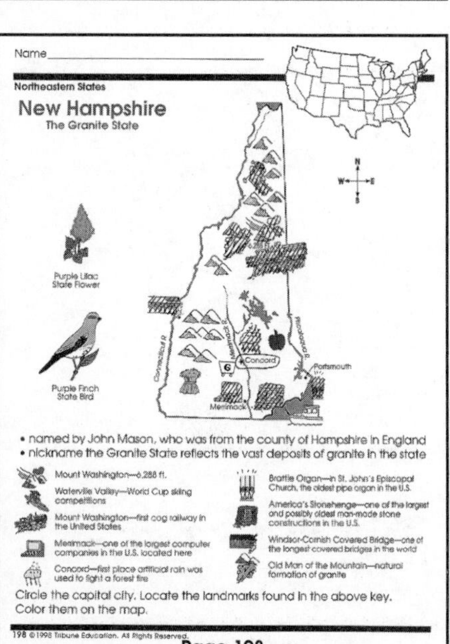
Northeastern States
New Hampshire
The Granite State

Purple Lilac State Flower

Purple Finch State Bird

- named by John Mason, who was from the county of Hampshire in England
- nickname the Granite State reflects the vast deposits of granite in the state

Circle the capital city. Locate the landmarks found in the above key. Color them on the map.

198

Page 198

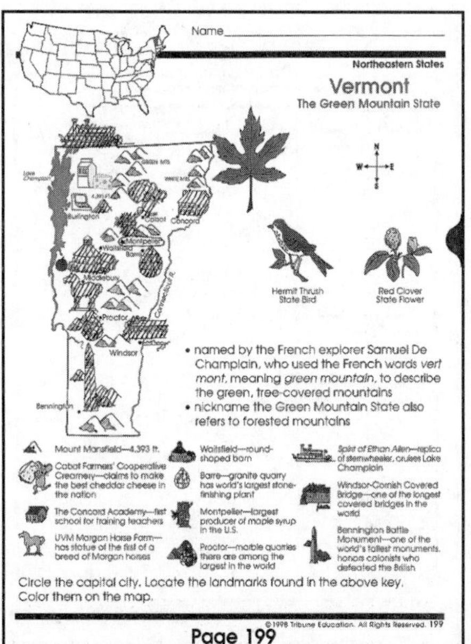
Northeastern States
Vermont
The Green Mountain State

Hermit Thrush State Bird

Red Clover State Flower

- named by the French explorer Samuel De Champlain, who used the French words *vert mont*, meaning *green mountain*, to describe the green, tree-covered mountains
- nickname the Green Mountain State also refers to forested mountains

Circle the capital city. Locate the landmarks found in the above key. Color them on the map.

 199

Page 199

Northeastern States
Massachusetts
The Bay State

Chickadee State Bird

Mayflower State Flower

- name taken from the Massachusetts Indian tribe, whose name means *near the great hill*
- nickname the Bay State refers to Massachusetts Bay, where Puritans established their colony

Circle the capital city. Locate the landmarks found in the above key. Color them on the map.

200

Page 200

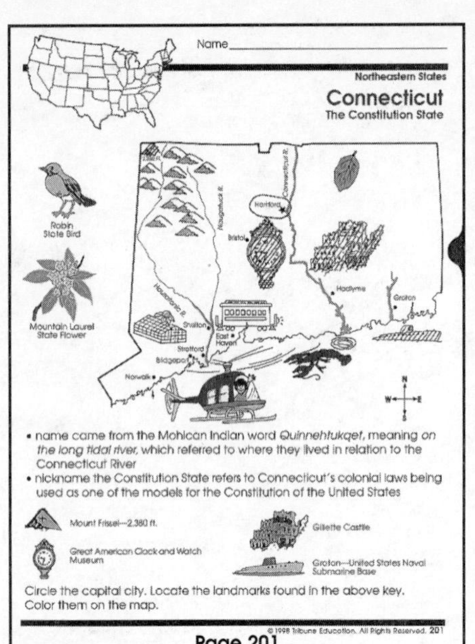

Name________________________

Northeastern States

Connecticut
The Constitution State

Robin
State Bird

Mountain Laurel
State Flower

• name came from the Mohican Indian word *Quinnehtukqet*, meaning *on the long tidal river*, which referred to where they lived in relation to the Connecticut River
• nickname the Constitution State refers to Connecticut's colonial laws being used as one of the models for the Constitution of the United States

Mount Frissel—2,380 ft.
Gillette Castle
Great American Clock and Watch Museum
Groton—United States Naval Submarine Base

Circle the capital city. Locate the landmarks found in the above key. Color them on the map.

 201

Page 201

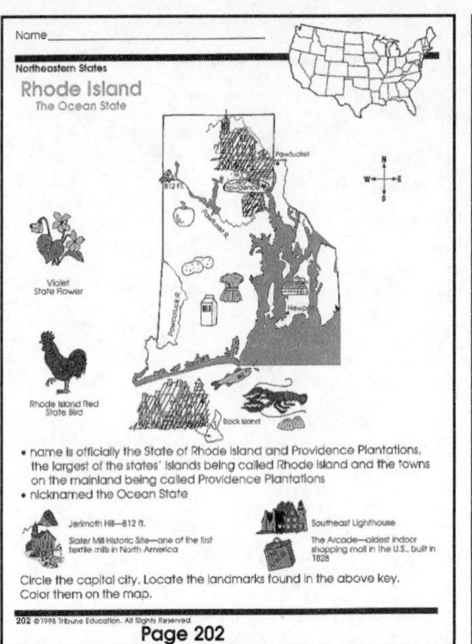

Name________________________

Northeastern States

Rhode Island
The Ocean State

Violet
State Flower

Rhode Island Red
State Bird

• name is officially the State of Rhode Island and Providence Plantations, the largest of the states' islands being called Rhode Island and the towns on the mainland being called Providence Plantations
• nicknamed the Ocean State

Jerimoth Hill—812 ft.
Southeast Lighthouse
Slater Mill Historic Site—one of the first textile mills in North America
The Arcade—oldest indoor shopping mall in the U.S., built in 1828

Circle the capital city. Locate the landmarks found in the above key. Color them on the map.

202

Page 202

Name________________________

Northeastern States

New Jersey
The Garden State

Eastern Goldfinch
State Bird

Purple Violet
State Flower

• named in 1664 by Sir George Carteret after the Isle of Jersey in England
• nicknamed the Garden State for its numerous truck farms, flower gardens and orchards

High Point—1,803 ft.
Margate—a 100-year-old house shaped like an elephant, now a museum
Flemington—leader in machinery and computer assembly
George Washington Bridge—thousands use this to commute from New Jersey to New York City
Old Barracks—British soldiers used these barracks during the French and Indian Wars
Camden—first drive-in theater opened here on June 6, 1933
New Egypt—Ocean Spray first made
Atlantic City—7-mile boardwalk and casinos make this popular for tourists
Waterloo Village—a restored town of the 1700s

Circle the capital city. Locate the landmarks found in the above key. Color them on the map.

 203

Page 203

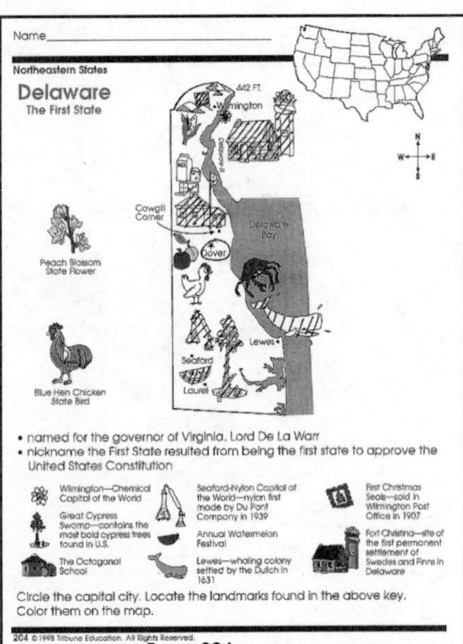

Name________________________

Northeastern States

Delaware
The First State

Peach Blossom
State Flower

Blue Hen Chicken
State Bird

• named for the governor of Virginia, Lord De La Warr
• nickname the First State resulted from being the first state to approve the United States Constitution

Wilmington—Chemical Capital of the World
Great Cypress Swamp—contains the most bold cypress trees found in U.S.
The Octogonal School
Seaford-Nylon Capital of the World—nylon first made by Du Pont Company in 1939
Annual Watermelon Festival
Lewes—whaling colony settled by the Dutch in 1631
First Christmas Seals—sold in Wilmington Post Office in 1907
Fort Christina—site of the first permanent settlement of Swedes and Finns in Delaware

Circle the capital city. Locate the landmarks found in the above key. Color them on the map.

204

Page 204

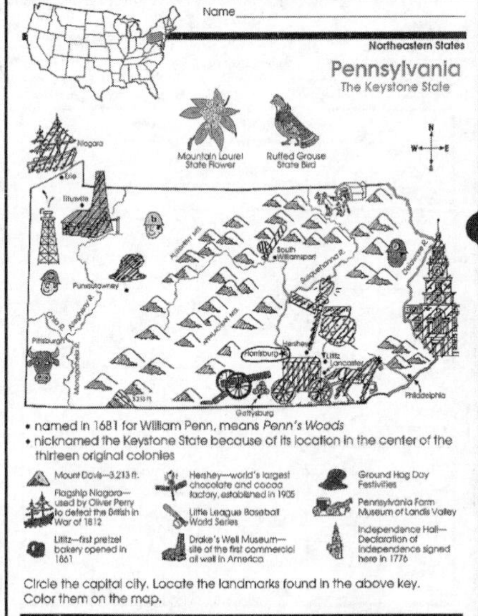

Name________________________

Northeastern States

Pennsylvania
The Keystone State

Mountain Laurel
State Flower

Ruffed Grouse
State Bird

• named in 1681 for William Penn, means *Penn's Woods*
• nicknamed the Keystone State because of its location in the center of the thirteen original colonies

Mount Davis—3,213 ft.
Flagship Niagara—used by Oliver Perry to defeat the British in War of 1812
Lititz—first pretzel bakery opened in 1861
Hershey—world's largest chocolate and cocoa factory, established in 1905
Little League Baseball World Series
Drake's Well Museum—site of the first commercial oil well in America
Ground Hog Day Festivities
Pennsylvania Farm Museum of Landis Valley
Independence Hall—Declaration of Independence signed here in 1776

Circle the capital city. Locate the landmarks found in the above key. Color them on the map.

 205

Page 205

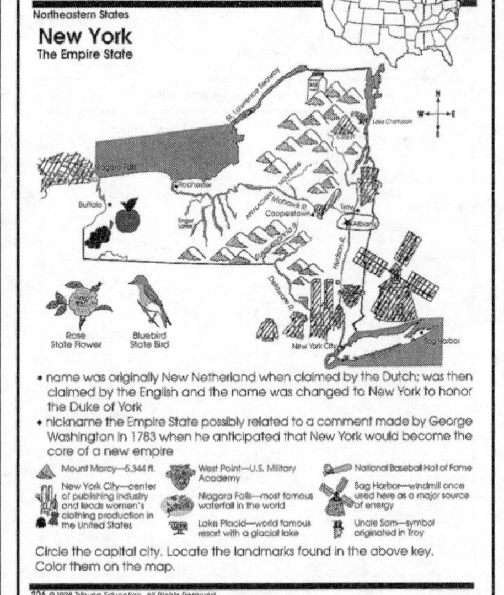

Name________________________

Northeastern States

New York
The Empire State

Rose
State Flower

Bluebird
State Bird

• name was originally New Netherland when claimed by the Dutch; was then claimed by the English and the name was changed to New York to honor the Duke of York
• nickname the Empire State possibly related to a comment made by George Washington in 1783 when he anticipated that New York would become the core of a new empire

Mount Marcy—5,344 ft.
New York City—center of publishing industry and leads women's clothing production in the United States
West Point—U.S. Military Academy
Niagara Falls—most famous waterfall in the world
Lake Placid—world famous resort with a glacial lake
National Baseball Hall of Fame
Sag Harbor—windmill once used here as a major source of energy
Uncle Sam—symbol originated in Troy

Circle the capital city. Locate the landmarks found in the above key. Color them on the map.

206

Page 206

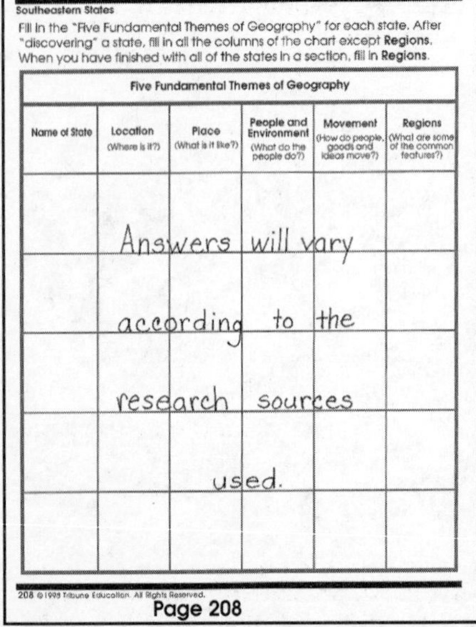

Name________________________

Southeastern States

Fill in the "Five Fundamental Themes of Geography" for each state. After "discovering" a state, fill in all the columns of the chart except **Regions**. When you have finished with all of the states in a section, fill in **Regions**.

Five Fundamental Themes of Geography

Name of State	Location (Where is it?)	Place (What is it like?)	People and Environment (What do the people do?)	Movement (How do people, goods and ideas move?)	Regions (What are some of the common features?)

Answers will vary according to the research sources used.

208

Page 208

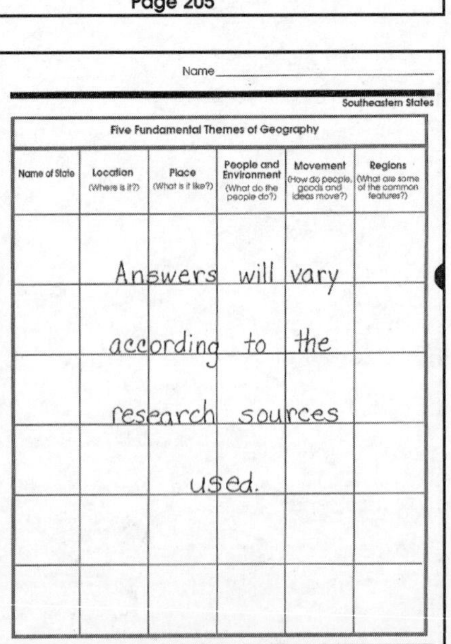

Name________________________

Southeastern States

Five Fundamental Themes of Geography

Name of State	Location (Where is it?)	Place (What is it like?)	People and Environment (What do the people do?)	Movement (How do people, goods and ideas move?)	Regions (What are some of the common features?)

Answers will vary according to the research sources used.

 209

Page 209

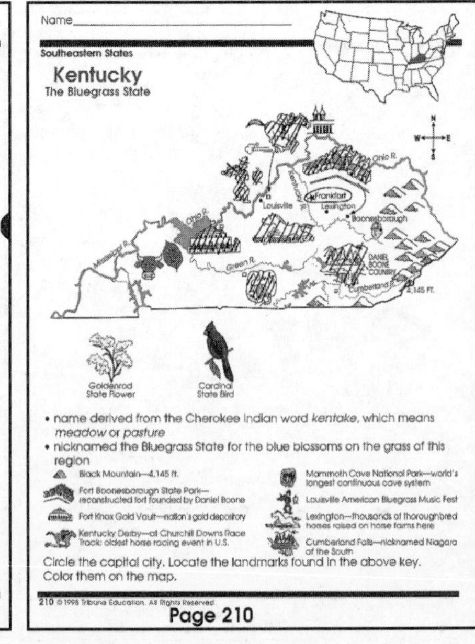

Name________________________

Southeastern States

Kentucky
The Bluegrass State

Goldenrod
State Flower

Cardinal
State Bird

• name derived from the Cherokee Indian word *kentake*, which means *meadow* or *pasture*
• nicknamed the Bluegrass State for the blue blossoms on the grass of this region

Black Mountain—4,145 ft.
Fort Boonesborough State Park—reconstructed fort founded by Daniel Boone
Fort Knox Gold Vault—nation's gold depository
Kentucky Derby—at Churchill Downs Race Track; oldest horse racing event in U.S.
Mammoth Cave National Park—world's longest continuous cave system
Louisville American Bluegrass Music Fest
Lexington—thousands of thoroughbred horses raised on horse farms here
Cumberland Falls—nicknamed Niagara of the South

Circle the capital city. Locate the landmarks found in the above key. Color them on the map.

210

Page 210

Name

Southeastern States

West Virginia
The Mountain State

• named when northwestern counties separated from Virginia during the Civil War and sided with the North
• nicknamed the Mountain State for its rugged mountains, steep hills and narrow valleys

Spruce Knob—4,862 ft.
Grave Creek Mounds—largest conical burial mound, built 2,000 years ago
Marshall County—underground salt mines
Huntington—famous for its glassware and pottery
Shepherdstown—monument to James Rumsay, inventor of the steamboat
Parkersburg—glass marble manufacturing center of U.S.
National Radio Astronomy Observatory

Circle the capital city. Locate the landmarks found in the above key. Color them on the map.

©1998 Tribune Education. All Rights Reserved. 211

Page 211

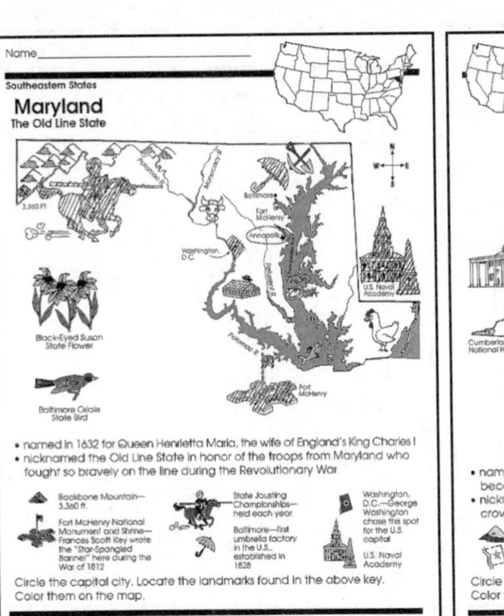

Name

Southeastern States

Maryland
The Old Line State

• named in 1632 for Queen Henrietta Maria, the wife of England's King Charles I
• nicknamed the Old Line State in honor of the troops from Maryland who fought so bravely on the line during the Revolutionary War

Backbone Mountain—3,360 ft.
Fort McHenry National Monument and Shrine—Frances Scott Key wrote the "Star-Spangled Banner" here during the War of 1812
State Jousting Championships—held each year
Baltimore—first umbrella factory in the U.S. established in 1828
Washington, D.C.—George Washington chose this spot for the U.S. capital
U.S. Naval Academy

Circle the capital city. Locate the landmarks found in the above key. Color them on the map.

212 ©1998 Tribune Education. All Rights Reserved.

Page 212

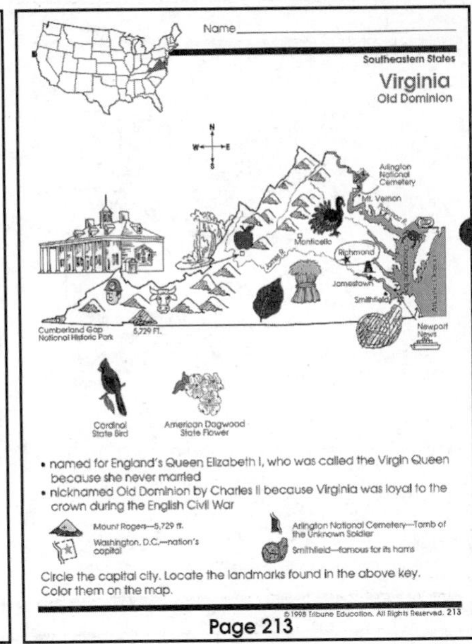

Name

Southeastern States

Virginia
Old Dominion

• named for England's Queen Elizabeth I, who was called the Virgin Queen because she never married
• nicknamed Old Dominion by Charles II because Virginia was loyal to the crown during the English Civil War

Mount Rogers—5,729 ft.
Washington, D.C.—nation's capital
Arlington National Cemetery—Tomb of the Unknown Soldier
Smithfield—famous for its hams

Circle the capital city. Locate the landmarks found in the above key. Color them on the map.

©1998 Tribune Education. All Rights Reserved. 213

Page 213

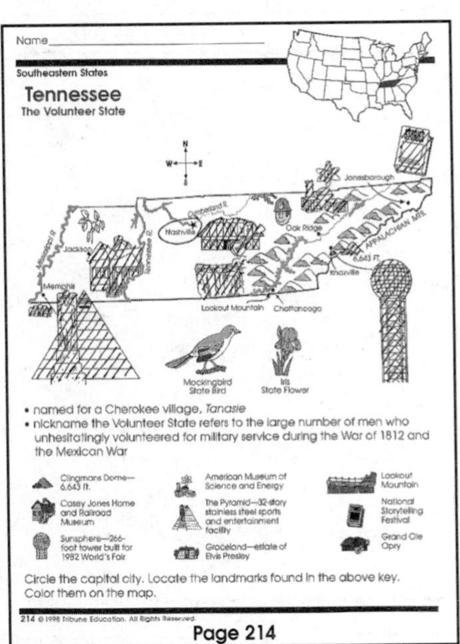

Name

Southeastern States

Tennessee
The Volunteer State

• named for a Cherokee village, *Tanasie*
• nickname the Volunteer State refers to the large number of men who unhesitatingly volunteered for military service during the War of 1812 and the Mexican War

Clingmans Dome—6,643 ft.
Casey Jones Home and Railroad Museum
Sunsphere—266-foot tower built for 1982 World's Fair
American Museum of Science and Energy
The Pyramid—32-story stainless steel sports and entertainment facility
Graceland—estate of Elvis Presley
Lookout Mountain
National Storytelling Festival
Grand Ole Opry

Circle the capital city. Locate the landmarks found in the above key. Color them on the map.

214 ©1998 Tribune Education. All Rights Reserved.

Page 214

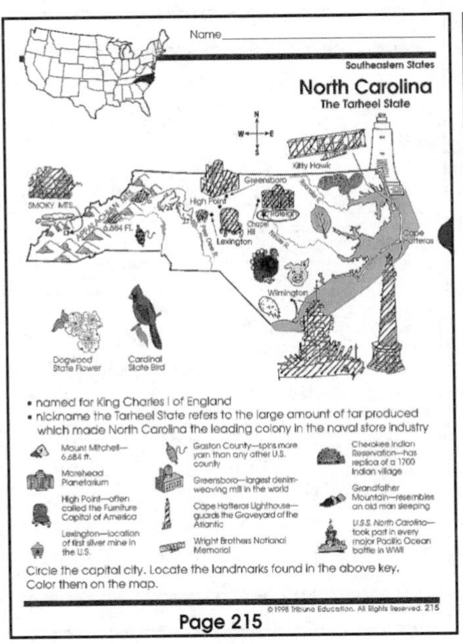

Name

Southeastern States

North Carolina
The Tarheel State

• named for King Charles I of England
• nickname the Tarheel State refers to the large amount of tar produced which made North Carolina the leading colony in the naval store industry

Mount Mitchell—6,684 ft.
Morehead Planetarium
High Point—often called the Furniture Capital of America
Lexington—location of first silver mine in the U.S.
Gaston County—spins more yarn than any other U.S. county
Greensboro—largest denim-weaving mill in the world
Cape Hatteras Lighthouse—guards the Graveyard of the Atlantic
Wright Brothers National Memorial
Cherokee Indian Reservation—has replica of a 1700 Indian village
Grandfather Mountain—resembles an old man sleeping
U.S.S. North Carolina—took part in every major Pacific Ocean battle in WWII

Circle the capital city. Locate the landmarks found in the above key. Color them on the map.

©1998 Tribune Education. All Rights Reserved. 215

Page 215

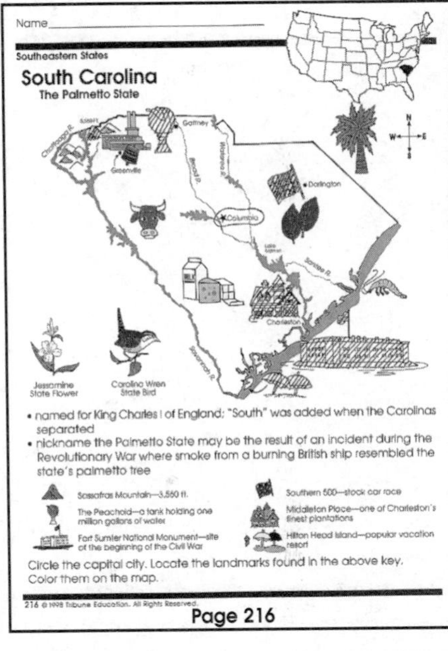

Name

Southeastern States

South Carolina
The Palmetto State

• named for King Charles I of England; "South" was added when the Carolinas separated
• nickname the Palmetto State may be the result of an incident during the Revolutionary War where smoke from a burning British ship resembled the state's palmetto tree

Sassafras Mountain—3,560 ft.
The Peachoid—a tank holding one million gallons of water
Fort Sumter National Monument—site of the beginning of the Civil War
Southern 500—stock car race
Middleton Place—one of Charleston's finest plantations
Hilton Head Island—popular vacation resort

Circle the capital city. Locate the landmarks found in the above key. Color them on the map.

216 ©1998 Tribune Education. All Rights Reserved.

Page 216

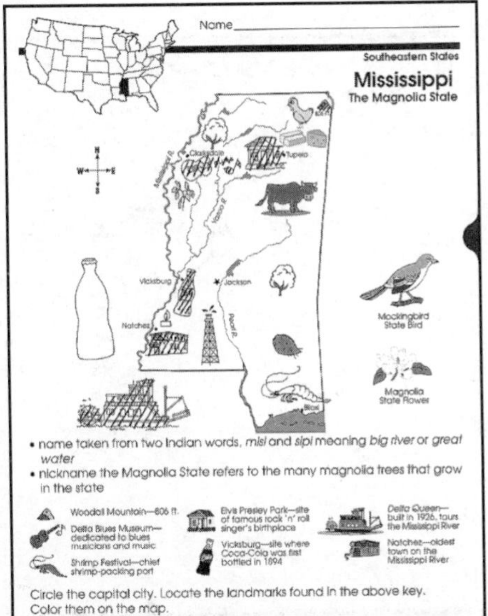

Name

Southeastern States

Mississippi
The Magnolia State

• name taken from two Indian words, *misi* and *sipi* meaning *big river* or *great water*
• nickname the Magnolia State refers to the many magnolia trees that grow in the state

Woodall Mountain—806 ft.
Delta Blues Museum—dedicated to blues musicians and music
Shrimp Festival—chief shrimp-packing port
Elvis Presley Park—site of famous rock 'n' roll singer's birthplace
Vicksburg—site where Coca-Cola was first bottled in 1894
Delta Queen—built in 1926, tours the Mississippi River
Natchez—oldest town on the Mississippi River

Circle the capital city. Locate the landmarks found in the above key. Color them on the map.

©1998 Tribune Education. All Rights Reserved. 217

Page 217

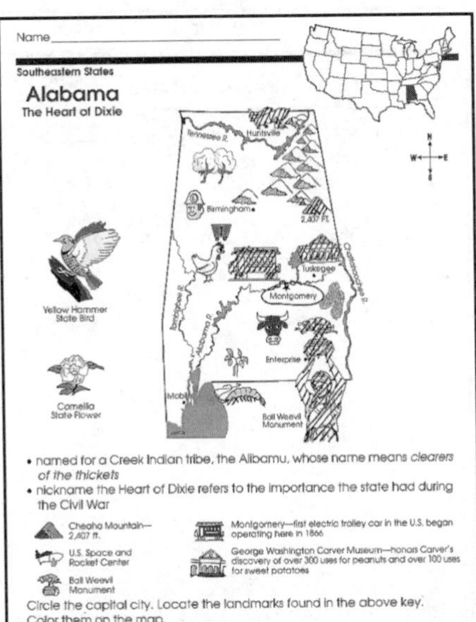

Name

Southeastern States

Alabama
The Heart of Dixie

• named for a Creek Indian tribe, the Alibamu, whose name means *clearers of the thickets*
• nickname the Heart of Dixie refers to the importance the state had during the Civil War

Cheaha Mountain—2,407 ft.
U.S. Space and Rocket Center
Boll Weevil Monument
Montgomery—first electric trolley car in the U.S. began operating here in 1866
George Washington Carver Museum—honors Carver's discovery of over 300 uses for peanuts and over 100 uses for sweet potatoes

Circle the capital city. Locate the landmarks found in the above key. Color them on the map.

218 ©1998 Tribune Education. All Rights Reserved.

Page 218

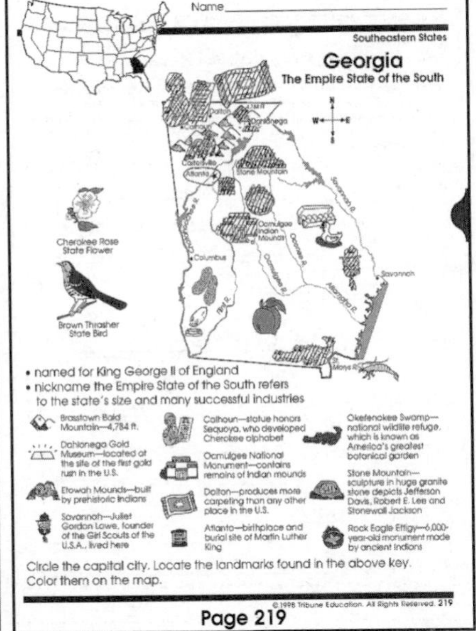

Name

Southeastern States

Georgia
The Empire State of the South

• named for King George II of England
• nickname the Empire State of the South refers to the state's size and many successful industries

Brasstown Bald Mountain—4,784 ft.
Dahlonega Gold Museum—located at the site of the first gold rush in the U.S.
Etowah Mounds—built by prehistoric Indians
Savannah—Juliet Gordon Lowe, founder of the Girl Scouts of the U.S.A., lived here
Calhoun—statue honors Sequoya, who developed Cherokee alphabet
Ocmulgee National Monument—contains remains of Indian mounds
Dalton—produces more carpeting than any other place in the U.S.
Atlanta—birthplace and burial site of Martin Luther King
Okefenokee Swamp—national wildlife refuge, which is known as America's greatest botanical garden
Stone Mountain—sculpture in huge granite stone depicts Jefferson Davis, Robert E. Lee and Stonewall Jackson
Rock Eagle Effigy—6,000-year-old monument made by ancient Indians

Circle the capital city. Locate the landmarks found in the above key. Color them on the map.

©1998 Tribune Education. All Rights Reserved. 219

Page 219

Name______________________

Southeastern States

Florida

The Sunshine State

- name comes from the Spanish word *florida*, meaning *flowery*, which may refer to the many flowers given by Spanish explorer Juan Ponce de León
- nicknamed the Sunshine State for its warm and sunny climate

Sea World—a popular tourist attraction featuring killer whales and dolphins

Pelican Island National Wildlife Refuge—first federal wildlife refuge

EPCOT Center—displays future technology

John and Mable Ringling Museum—Museum of Art and Circus Galleries

Cape Canaveral—space and rocket center

Everglades National Park—largest subtropical wilderness in U.S.

Castillo de San Marcos National Monument—oldest permanent European settlement in the United States

John Pennekamp Coral Reef State Park—first undersea park in the continental United States

Circle the capital city. Locate the landmarks found in the above key. Color them on the map.

Page 220

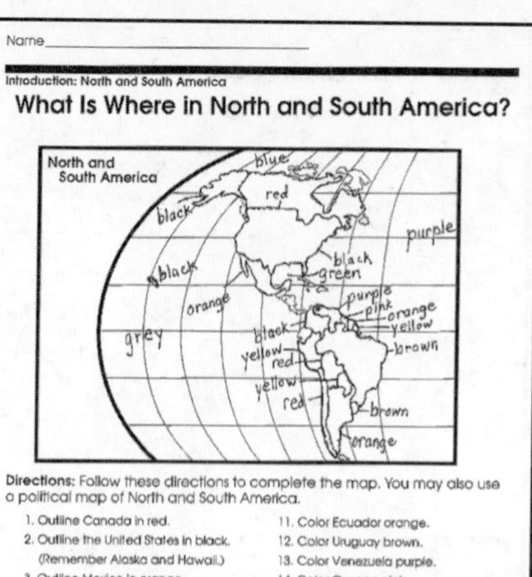

Name______________________

Introduction: North and South America

What Is Where in North and South America?

Directions: Follow these directions to complete the map. You may also use a political map of North and South America.

1. Outline Canada in red.
2. Outline the United States in black. (Remember Alaska and Hawaii.)
3. Outline Mexico in orange.
4. Outline Brazil in brown.
5. Outline Chile in red.
6. Outline Argentina in orange.
7. Outline Paraguay in yellow.
8. Outline Colombia in black.
9. Outline Bolivia in red.
10. Color Peru yellow.
11. Color Ecuador orange.
12. Color Uruguay brown.
13. Color Venezuela purple.
14. Color Guyana pink.
15. Color Suriname orange.
16. Color French Guiana yellow.
17. Color the Gulf of Mexico green.
18. Color the Arctic Ocean blue.
19. Color the Pacific Ocean grey.
20. Color the Atlantic Ocean purple.

Page 222

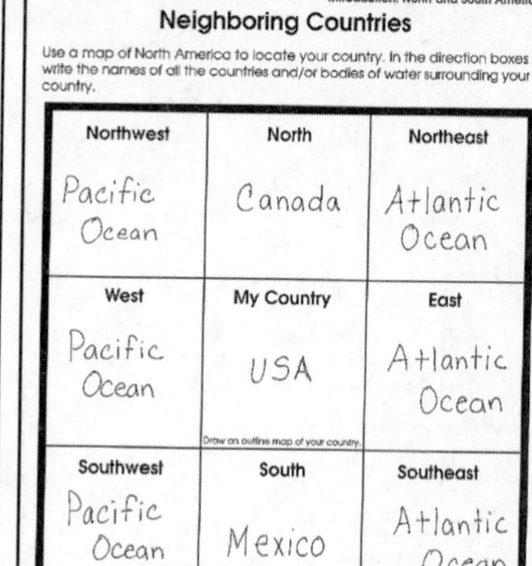

Name______________________

Introduction: North and South America

Neighboring Countries

Use a map of North America to locate your country. In the direction boxes write the names of all the countries and/or bodies of water surrounding your country.

Northwest	North	Northeast
Pacific Ocean	Canada	Atlantic Ocean
West	**My Country**	**East**
Pacific Ocean	USA Draw an outline map of your country.	Atlantic Ocean
Southwest	**South**	**Southeast**
Pacific Ocean	Mexico	Atlantic Ocean

Page 223

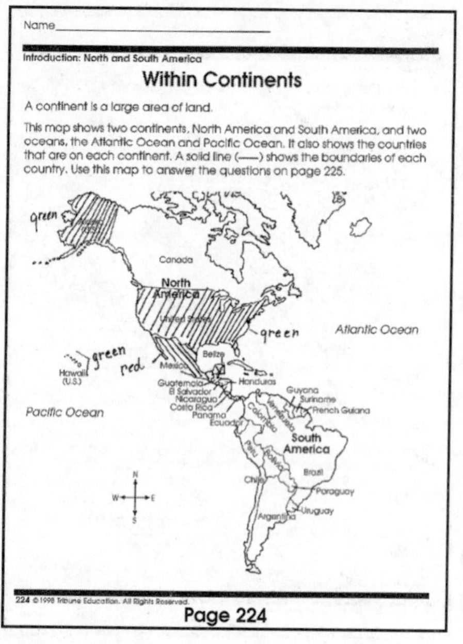

Name______________________

Introduction: North and South America

Within Continents

A continent is a large area of land.

This map shows two continents, North America and South America, and two oceans, the Atlantic Ocean and Pacific Ocean. It also shows the countries that are on each continent. A solid line (——) shows the boundaries of each country. Use this map to answer the questions on page 225.

Page 224

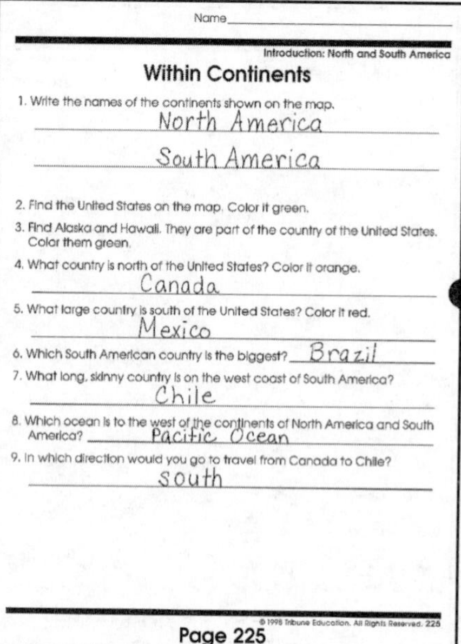

Name______________________

Introduction: North and South America

Within Continents

1. Write the names of the continents shown on the map. North America / South America
2. Find the United States on the map. Color it green.
3. Find Alaska and Hawaii. They are part of the country of the United States. Color them green.
4. What country is north of the United States? Color it orange. Canada
5. What large country is south of the United States? Color it red. Mexico
6. Which South American country is the biggest? Brazil
7. What long, skinny country is on the west coast of South America? Chile
8. Which ocean is to the west of the continents of North America and South America? Pacific Ocean
9. In which direction would you go to travel from Canada to Chile? south

Page 225

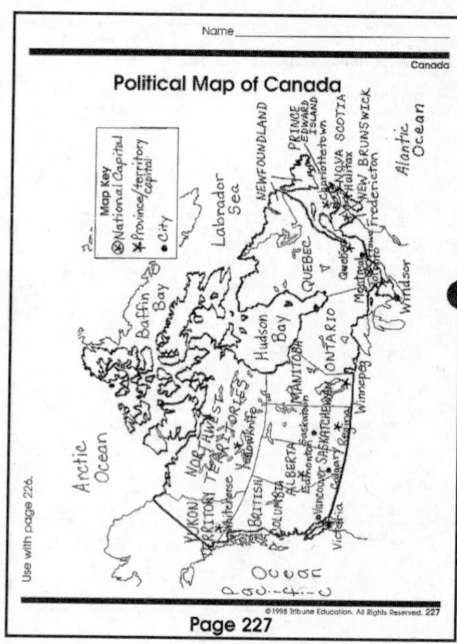

Name______________________

Canada

Political Map of Canada

Page 227

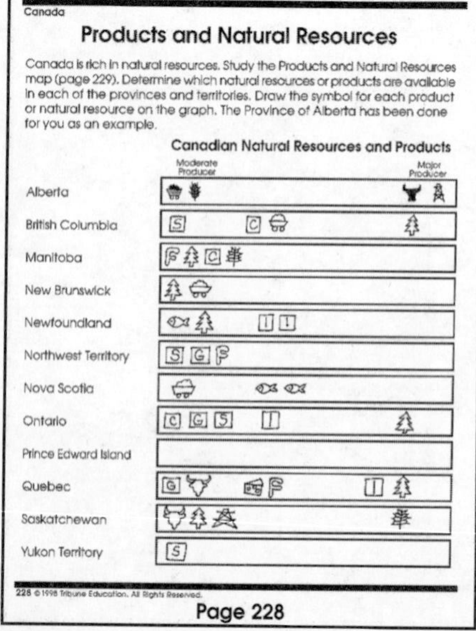

Name______________________

Canada

Products and Natural Resources

Canada is rich in natural resources. Study the Products and Natural Resources map (page 229). Determine which natural resources or products are available in each of the provinces and territories. Draw the symbol for each product or natural resource on the graph. The Province of Alberta has been done for you as an example.

Canadian Natural Resources and Products

Moderate Producer — Major Producer

Alberta

British Columbia

Manitoba

New Brunswick

Newfoundland

Northwest Territory

Nova Scotia

Ontario

Prince Edward Island

Quebec

Saskatchewan

Yukon Territory

Page 228

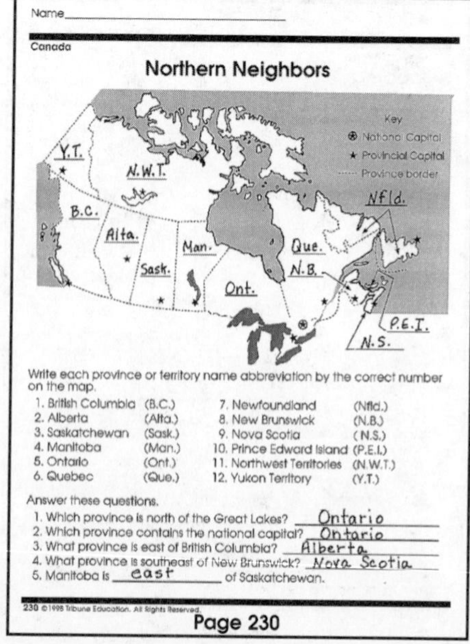

Name______________________

Canada

Northern Neighbors

Write each province or territory name abbreviation by the correct number on the map.

1. British Columbia (B.C.)
2. Alberta (Alta.)
3. Saskatchewan (Sask.)
4. Manitoba (Man.)
5. Ontario (Ont.)
6. Quebec (Que.)
7. Newfoundland (Nfld.)
8. New Brunswick (N.B.)
9. Nova Scotia (N.S.)
10. Prince Edward Island (P.E.I.)
11. Northwest Territories (N.W.T.)
12. Yukon Territory (Y.T.)

Answer these questions.

1. Which province is north of the Great Lakes? Ontario
2. Which province contains the national capital? Ontario
3. What province is east of British Columbia? Alberta
4. What province is southeast of New Brunswick? Nova Scotia
5. Manitoba is east of Saskatchewan.

Page 230

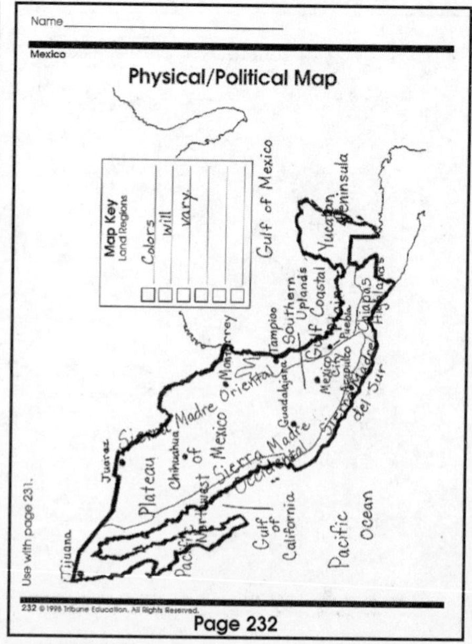

Name______________________

Mexico

Physical/Political Map

Page 232

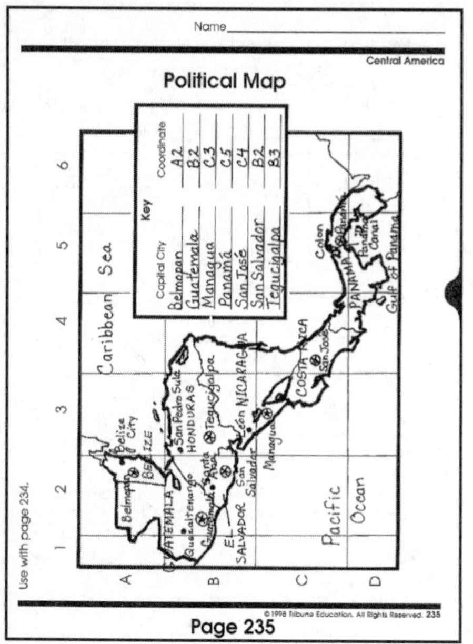
Name________________

Central America

Political Map

Key	
Capital City	Coordinate
Belmopan	A2
Guatemala	B2
Managua	C3
Panamá	C5
San José	C4
San Salvador	B2
Tegucigalpa	B3

©1998 Tribune Education. All Rights Reserved. 235

Page 235

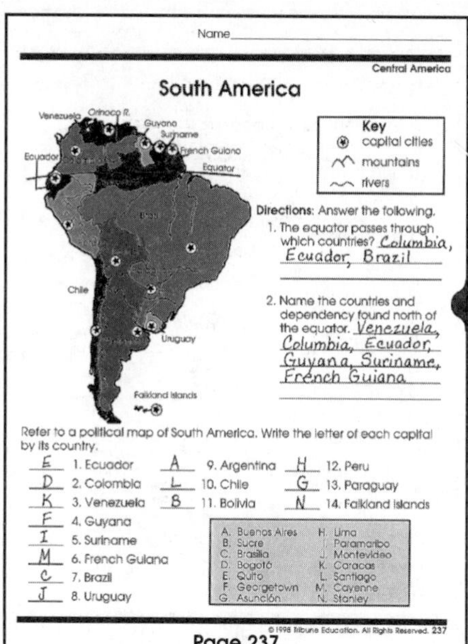
Name________________

Central America

South America

Key: capital cities; mountains; rivers

Directions: Answer the following.

1. The equator passes through which countries? *Columbia, Ecuador, Brazil*
2. Name the countries and dependency found north of the equator. *Venezuela, Columbia, Ecuador, Guyana, Suriname, French Guiana*

Refer to a political map of South America. Write the letter of each capital by its country.

E 1. Ecuador
D 2. Colombia
K 3. Venezuela
F 4. Guyana
I 5. Suriname
M 6. French Guiana
C 7. Brazil
J 8. Uruguay
A 9. Argentina
L 10. Chile
B 11. Bolivia
H 12. Peru
G 13. Paraguay
N 14. Falkland Islands

A. Buenos Aires
B. Sucre
C. Brasília
D. Bogotá
E. Quito
F. Georgetown
G. Asunción
H. Lima
I. Paramaribo
J. Montevideo
K. Caracas
L. Santiago
M. Cayenne
N. Stanley

©1998 Tribune Education. All Rights Reserved. 237

Page 237

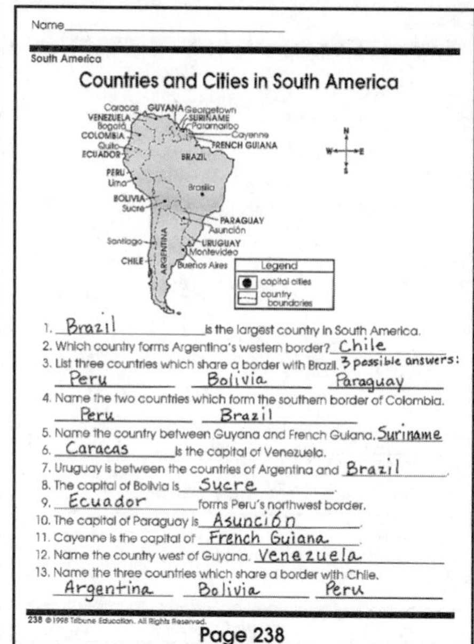
Name________________

South America

Countries and Cities in South America

Legend: capital cities; country boundaries

1. *Brazil* is the largest country in South America.
2. Which country forms Argentina's western border? *Chile*
3. List three countries which share a border with Brazil. *3 possible answers: Peru, Bolivia, Paraguay*
4. Name the two countries which form the southern border of Colombia. *Peru, Brazil*
5. Name the country between Guyana and French Guiana. *Suriname*
6. *Caracas* is the capital of Venezuela.
7. Uruguay is between the countries of Argentina and *Brazil*.
8. The capital of Bolivia is *Sucre*.
9. *Ecuador* forms Peru's northwest border.
10. The capital of Paraguay is *Asunción*.
11. Cayenne is the capital of *French Guiana*.
12. Name the country west of Guyana. *Venezuela*
13. Name the three countries which share a border with Chile. *Argentina, Bolivia, Peru*

238 ©1998 Tribune Education. All Rights Reserved.

Page 238

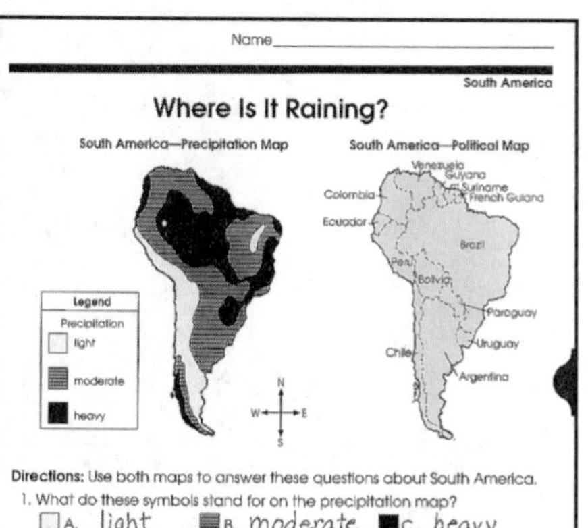
Name________________

South America

Where Is It Raining?

South America—Precipitation Map; South America—Political Map

Legend: Precipitation: light, moderate, heavy

Directions: Use both maps to answer these questions about South America.

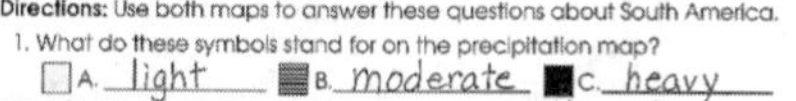
1. What do these symbols stand for on the precipitation map? A. *light* B. *moderate* C. *heavy*
2. The lightest precipitation falls mainly on the *southwest* part of South America.
3. The heaviest precipitation falls mainly in the *northeast* part of South America.
4. The majority of Argentina receives *moderate* precipitation.
5. The majority of South America receives *moderate* precipitation.
6. Most of Chile receives *light* precipitation.
7. The northwestern tip of Colombia receives *heavy* precipitation.
8. The western half of Ecuador receives *heavy* precipitation.
9. Most of Brazil receives *heavy* precipitation.

©1998 Tribune Education. All Rights Reserved. 239

Page 239

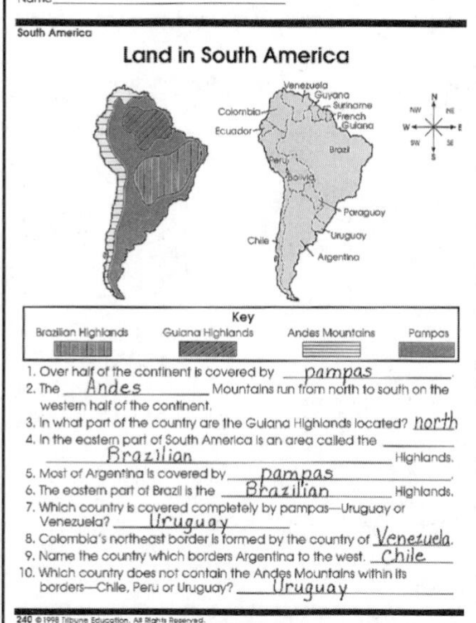
Name________________

South America

Land in South America

Key: Brazilian Highlands; Guiana Highlands; Andes Mountains; Pampas

1. Over half of the continent is covered by *pampas*.
2. The *Andes* Mountains run from north to south on the western half of the continent.
3. In what part of the country are the Guiana Highlands located? *north*
4. In the eastern part of South America is an area called the *Brazilian* Highlands.
5. Most of Argentina is covered by *pampas*.
6. The eastern part of Brazil is the *Brazilian* Highlands.
7. Which country is covered completely by pampas—Uruguay or Venezuela? *Uruguay*
8. Colombia's northeast border is formed by the country of *Venezuela*.
9. Name the country which borders Argentina to the west. *Chile*
10. Which country does not contain the Andes Mountains within its borders—Chile, Peru or Uruguay? *Uruguay*

240 ©1998 Tribune Education. All Rights Reserved.

Page 240

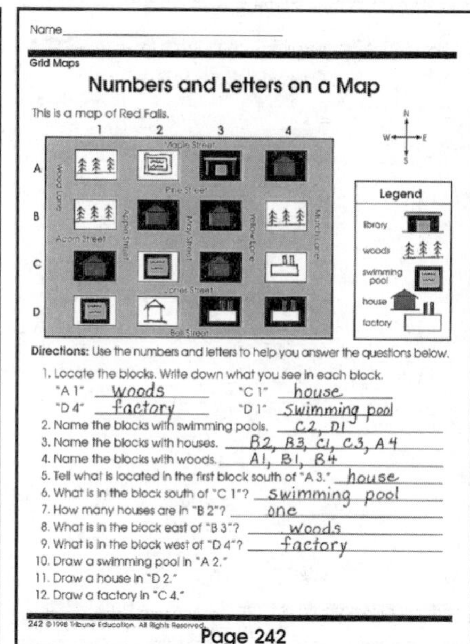
Name________________

Grid Maps

Numbers and Letters on a Map

This is a map of Red Falls.

Legend: library; woods; swimming pool; house; factory

Directions: Use the numbers and letters to help you answer the questions below.

1. Locate the blocks. Write down what you see in each block. "A 1" *woods* "C 1" *house* "D 4" *factory* "D 1" *swimming pool*
2. Name the blocks with swimming pools. *C2, D1*
3. Name the blocks with houses. *B2, B3, C1, C3, A4*
4. Name the blocks with woods. *A1, B1, B4*
5. Tell what is located in the first block south of "A 3." *house*
6. What is in the block south of "C 1"? *swimming pool*
7. How many houses are in "B 2"? *one*
8. What is in the block east of "B 3"? *woods*
9. What is in the block west of "D 4"? *factory*
10. Draw a swimming pool in "A 2."
11. Draw a house in "D 2."
12. Draw a factory in "C 4."

242 ©1998 Tribune Education. All Rights Reserved.

Page 242

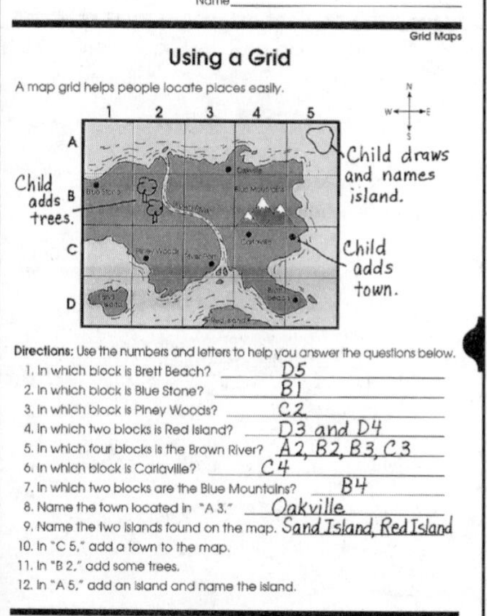
Name________________

Grid Maps

Using a Grid

A map grid helps people locate places easily.

Directions: Use the numbers and letters to help you answer the questions below.

1. In which block is Brett Beach? *D5*
2. In which block is Blue Stone? *B1*
3. In which block is Piney Woods? *C2*
4. In which two blocks is Red Island? *D3 and D4*
5. In which four blocks is the Brown River? *A2, B2, B3, C3*
6. In which block is Carlaville? *C4*
7. In which two blocks are the Blue Mountains? *B4*
8. Name the town located in "A 3." *Oakville*
9. Name the two islands found on the map. *Sand Island, Red Island*
10. In "C 5," add a town to the map.
11. In "B 2," add some trees.
12. In "A 5," add an island and name the island.

©1998 Tribune Education. All Rights Reserved. 243

Page 243

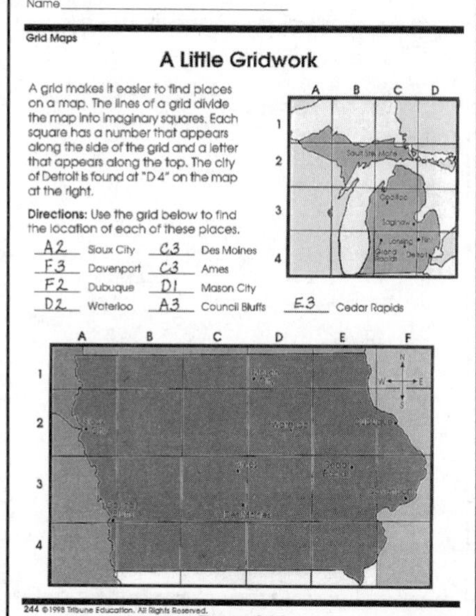
Name________________

Grid Maps

A Little Gridwork

A grid makes it easier to find places on a map. The lines of a grid divide the map into imaginary squares. Each square has a number that appears along the side of the grid and a letter that appears along the top. The city of Detroit is found at "D 4" on the map at the right.

Directions: Use the grid below to find the location of each of these places.

A2 Sioux City
F3 Davenport
F2 Dubuque
D2 Waterloo
C3 Des Moines
C3 Ames
D1 Mason City
A3 Council Bluffs
E3 Cedar Rapids

244 ©1998 Tribune Education. All Rights Reserved.

Page 244

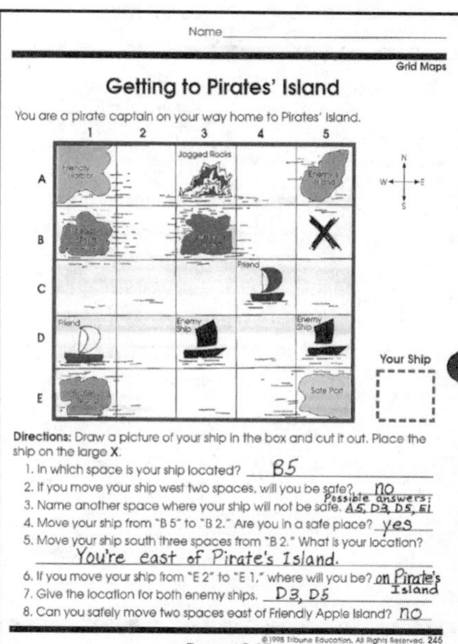
Name________________

Grid Maps

Getting to Pirates' Island

You are a pirate captain on your way home to Pirates' Island.

Your Ship

Directions: Draw a picture of your ship in the box and cut it out. Place the ship on the large X.

1. In which space is your ship located? *B5*
2. If you move your ship west two spaces, will you be safe? *no*
3. Name another space where your ship will not be safe. *Possible answers: A5, D3, D5, E1*
4. Move your ship from "B 5" to "B 2." Are you in a safe place? *yes*
5. Move your ship south three spaces from "B 2." What is your location? *You're east of Pirate's Island.*
6. If you move your ship from "E 2" to "E 1," where will you be? *on Pirate's Island*
7. Give the location for both enemy ships. *D3, D5*
8. Can you safely move two spaces east of Friendly Apple Island? *no*

©1998 Tribune Education. All Rights Reserved. 245

Page 245

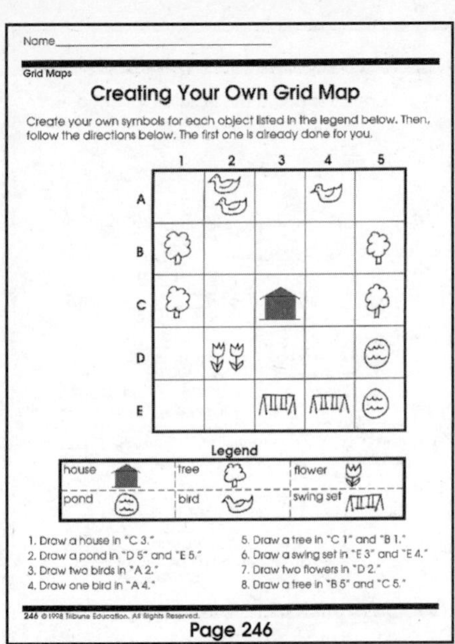
Name________________________

Grid Maps

Creating Your Own Grid Map

Create your own symbols for each object listed in the legend below. Then, follow the directions below. The first one is already done for you.

1. Draw a house in "C 3."
2. Draw a pond in "D 5" and "E 5."
3. Draw two birds in "A 2."
4. Draw one bird in "A 4."
5. Draw a tree in "C 1" and "B 1."
6. Draw a swing set in "E 3" and "E 4."
7. Draw two flowers in "D 2."
8. Draw a tree in "B 5" and "C 5."

Page 246

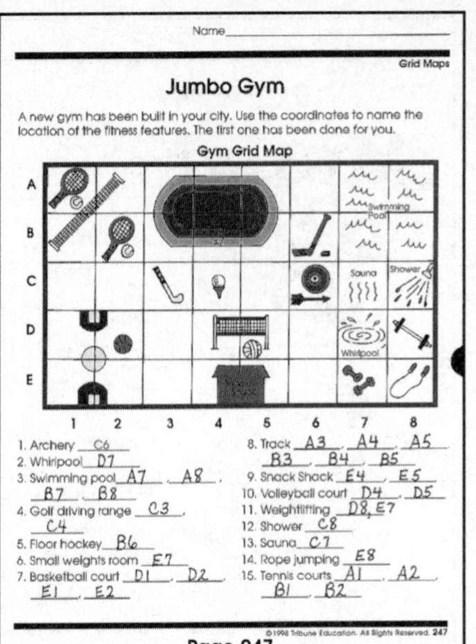
Name________________________

Grid Maps

Jumbo Gym

A new gym has been built in your city. Use the coordinates to name the location of the fitness features. The first one has been done for you.

1. Archery C6
2. Whirlpool D7
3. Swimming pool A7, A8, B7, B8
4. Golf driving range C3, C4
5. Floor hockey B6
6. Small weights room E7
7. Basketball court D1, D2, E1, E2
8. Track A3, A4, A5, B3, B4, B5
9. Snack Shack E4, E5
10. Volleyball court D4, D5
11. Weightlifting D8, E7
12. Shower C8
13. Sauna C7
14. Rope jumping E8
15. Tennis courts A1, A2, B1, B2

Page 247

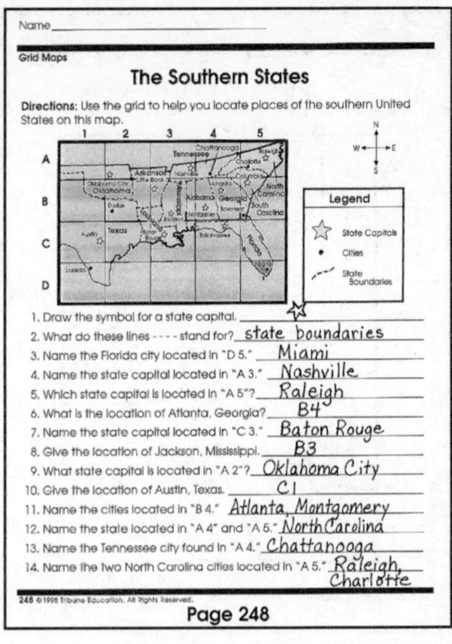
Name________________________

Grid Maps

The Southern States

Directions: Use the grid to help you locate places of the southern United States on this map.

1. Draw the symbol for a state capital. ☆
2. What do these lines - - - - stand for? state boundaries
3. Name the Florida city located in "D 5." Miami
4. Name the state capital located in "A 3." Nashville
5. Which state capital is located in "A 5"? Raleigh
6. What is the location of Atlanta, Georgia? B4
7. Name the state capital located in "C 3." Baton Rouge
8. Give the location of Jackson, Mississippi. B3
9. What state capital is located in "A 2"? Oklahoma City
10. Give the location of Austin, Texas. C1
11. Name the cities located in "B 4." Atlanta, Montgomery
12. Name the state located in "A 4" and "A 5." North Carolina
13. Name the Tennessee city found in "A 4." Chattanooga
14. Name the two North Carolina cities located in "A 5." Raleigh, Charlotte

Page 248

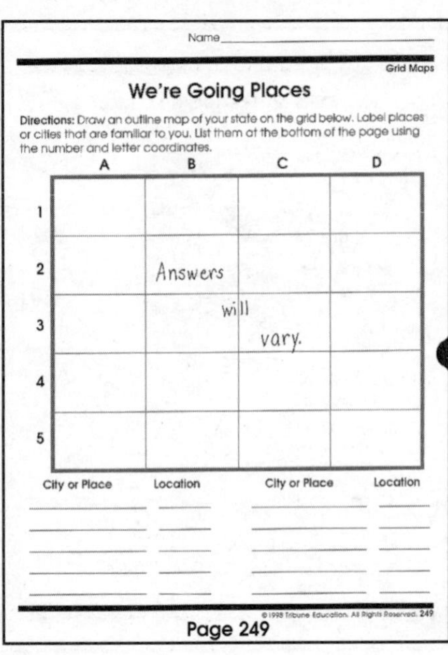
Name________________________

Grid Maps

We're Going Places

Directions: Draw an outline map of your state on the grid below. Label places or cities that are familiar to you. List them at the bottom of the page using the number and letter coordinates.

City or Place	Location	City or Place	Location

Page 249

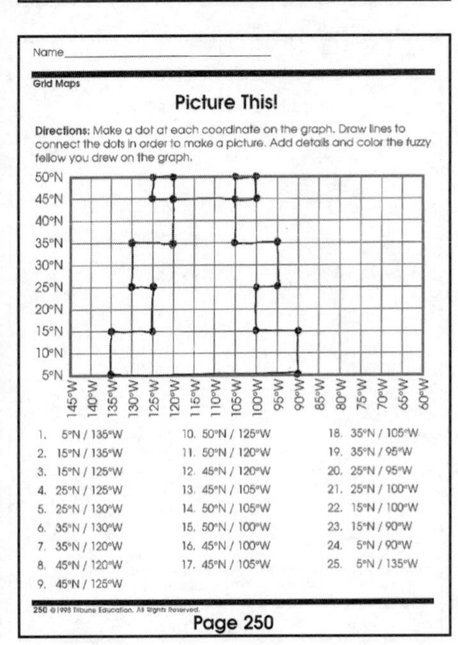
Name________________________

Grid Maps

Picture This!

Directions: Make a dot at each coordinate on the graph. Draw lines to connect the dots in order to make a picture. Add details and color the fuzzy fellow you drew on the graph.

1. 5°N / 135°W
2. 15°N / 135°W
3. 15°N / 125°W
4. 25°N / 125°W
5. 25°N / 130°W
6. 35°N / 130°W
7. 35°N / 120°W
8. 45°N / 120°W
9. 45°N / 125°W
10. 50°N / 125°W
11. 50°N / 120°W
12. 45°N / 120°W
13. 45°N / 105°W
14. 50°N / 105°W
15. 50°N / 100°W
16. 45°N / 100°W
17. 45°N / 105°W
18. 35°N / 105°W
19. 35°N / 95°W
20. 25°N / 95°W
21. 25°N / 100°W
22. 15°N / 100°W
23. 15°N / 90°W
24. 5°N / 90°W
25. 5°N / 135°W

Page 250

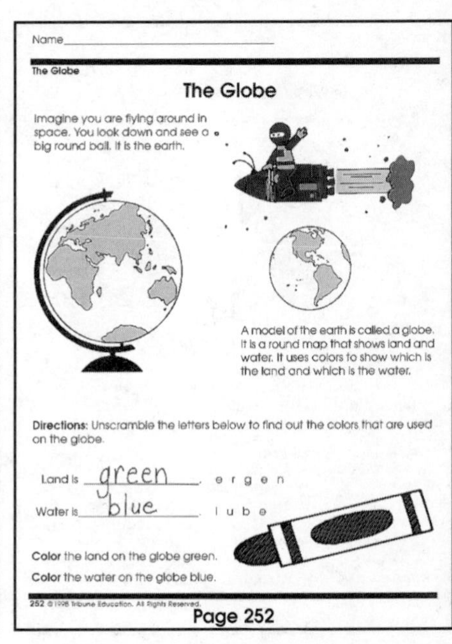
Name________________________

The Globe

The Globe

Imagine you are flying around in space. You look down and see a big round ball. It is the earth.

A model of the earth is called a globe. It is a round map that shows land and water. It uses colors to show which is the land and which is the water.

Directions: Unscramble the letters below to find out the colors that are used on the globe.

Land is green . e r g e n

Water is blue . l u b e

Color the land on the globe green.

Color the water on the globe blue.

Page 252

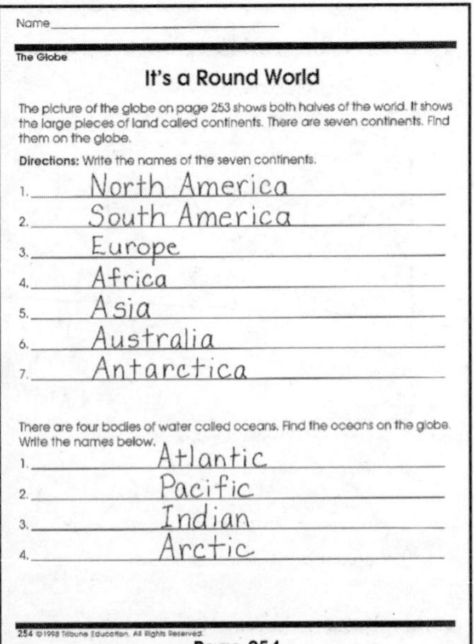
Name________________________

The Globe

It's a Round World

The picture of the globe on page 253 shows both halves of the world. It shows the large pieces of land called continents. There are seven continents. Find them on the globe.

Directions: Write the names of the seven continents.

1. North America
2. South America
3. Europe
4. Africa
5. Asia
6. Australia
7. Antarctica

There are four bodies of water called oceans. Find the oceans on the globe. Write the names below.

1. Atlantic
2. Pacific
3. Indian
4. Arctic

Page 254

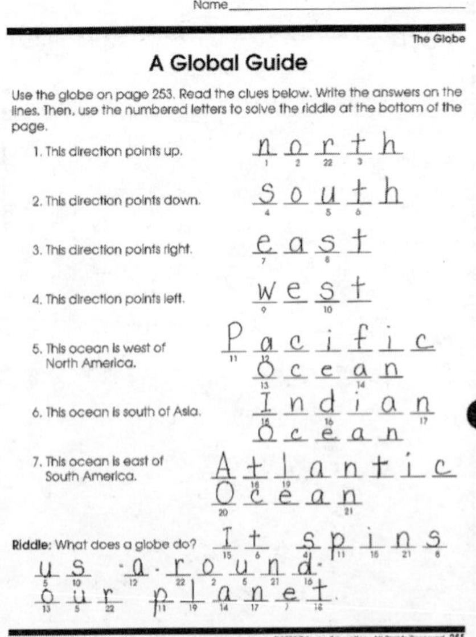
Name________________________

The Globe

A Global Guide

Use the globe on page 253. Read the clues below. Write the answers on the lines. Then, use the numbered letters to solve the riddle at the bottom of the page.

1. This direction points up. north
2. This direction points down. south
3. This direction points right. east
4. This direction points left. west
5. This ocean is west of North America. Pacific Ocean
6. This ocean is south of Asia. Indian Ocean
7. This ocean is east of South America. Atlantic Ocean

Riddle: What does a globe do? It spins us around our planet.

Page 255

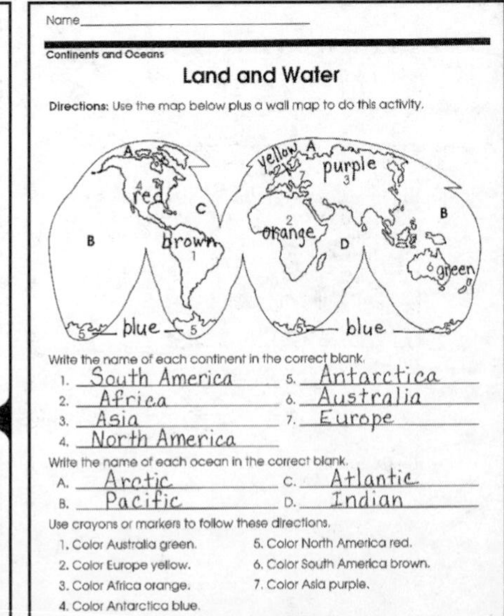
Name________________________

Continents and Oceans

Land and Water

Directions: Use the map below plus a wall map to do this activity.

Write the name of each continent in the correct blank.

1. South America
2. Africa
3. Asia
4. North America
5. Antarctica
6. Australia
7. Europe

Write the name of each ocean in the correct blank.

A. Arctic
B. Pacific
C. Atlantic
D. Indian

Use crayons or markers to follow these directions.

1. Color Australia green.
2. Color Europe yellow.
3. Color Africa orange.
4. Color Antarctica blue.
5. Color North America red.
6. Color South America brown.
7. Color Asia purple.

Page 256

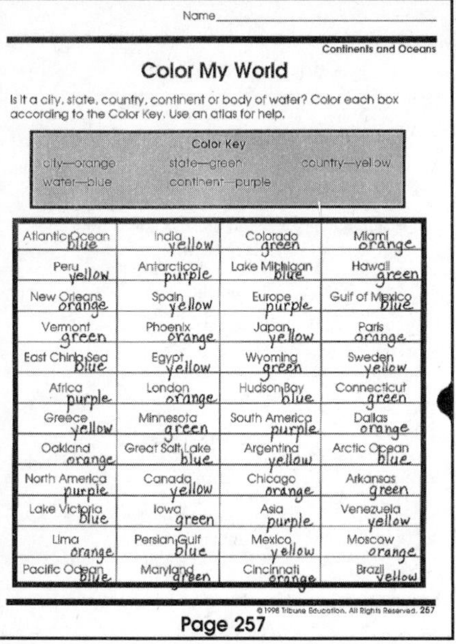

Name

Continents and Oceans

Color My World

Is it a city, state, country, continent or body of water? Color each box according to the Color Key. Use an atlas for help.

Color Key
city—orange state—green country—yellow
water—blue continent—purple

Atlantic Ocean blue	India yellow	Colorado green	Miami orange
Peru yellow	Antarctica purple	Lake Michigan blue	Hawaii green
New Orleans orange	Spain yellow	Europe purple	Gulf of Mexico blue
Vermont green	Phoenix orange	Japan yellow	Paris orange
East China Sea blue	Egypt yellow	Wyoming green	Sweden yellow
Africa purple	London orange	Hudson Bay blue	Connecticut green
Greece yellow	Minnesota green	South America purple	Dallas orange
Oakland orange	Great Salt Lake blue	Argentina yellow	Arctic Ocean blue
North America purple	Canada yellow	Chicago orange	Arkansas green
Lake Victoria blue	Iowa green	Asia purple	Venezuela yellow
Lima orange	Persian Gulf blue	Mexico yellow	Moscow orange
Pacific Ocean blue	Maryland green	Cincinnati orange	Brazil yellow

©1998 Tribune Education. All Rights Reserved. 257

Page 257

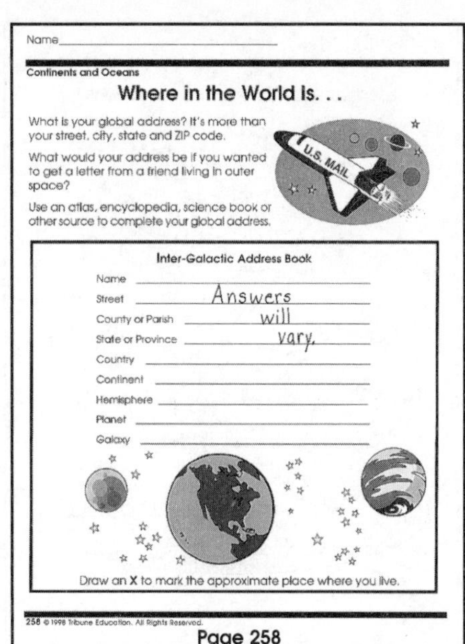

Name

Continents and Oceans

Where in the World Is. . .

What is your global address? It's more than your street, city, state and ZIP code.

What would your address be if you wanted to get a letter from a friend living in outer space?

Use an atlas, encyclopedia, science book or other source to complete your global address.

Inter-Galactic Address Book

Name
Street Answers
County or Parish will
State or Province vary.
Country
Continent
Hemisphere
Planet
Galaxy

Draw an **X** to mark the approximate place where you live.

258 ©1998 Tribune Education. All Rights Reserved.

Page 258

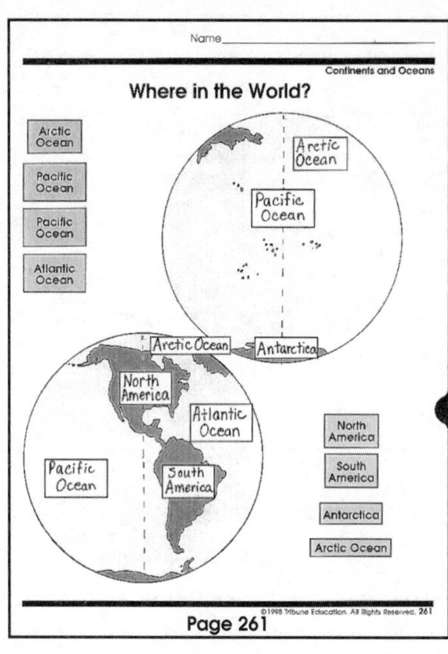

Name

Continents and Oceans

Where in the World?

©1998 Tribune Education. All Rights Reserved. 261

Page 261

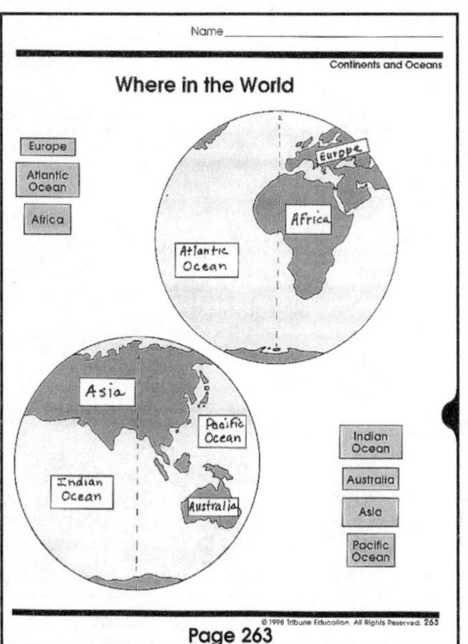

Name

Continents and Oceans

Where in the World

©1998 Tribune Education. All Rights Reserved. 263

Page 263

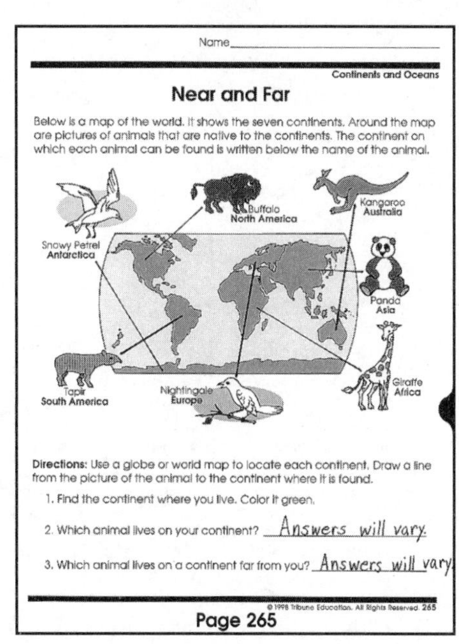

Name

Continents and Oceans

Near and Far

Below is a map of the world. It shows the seven continents. Around the map are pictures of animals that are native to the continents. The continent on which each animal can be found is written below the name of the animal.

Directions: Use a globe or world map to locate each continent. Draw a line from the picture of the animal to the continent where it is found.

1. Find the continent where you live. Color it green.
2. Which animal lives on your continent? Answers will vary.
3. Which animal lives on a continent far from you? Answers will vary.

©1998 Tribune Education. All Rights Reserved. 265

Page 265

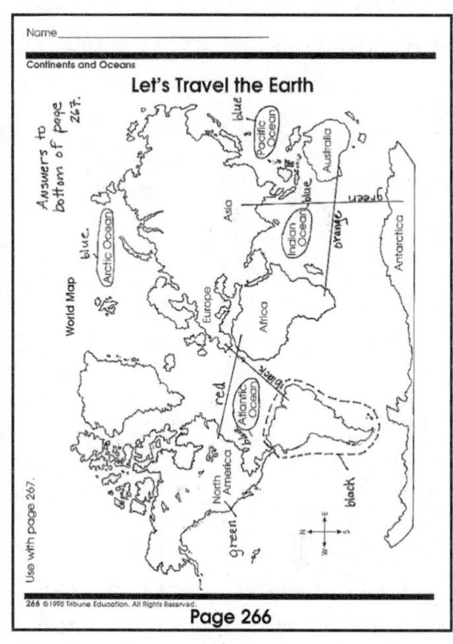

Name

Continents and Oceans

Let's Travel the Earth

266 ©1998 Tribune Education. All Rights Reserved.

Page 266

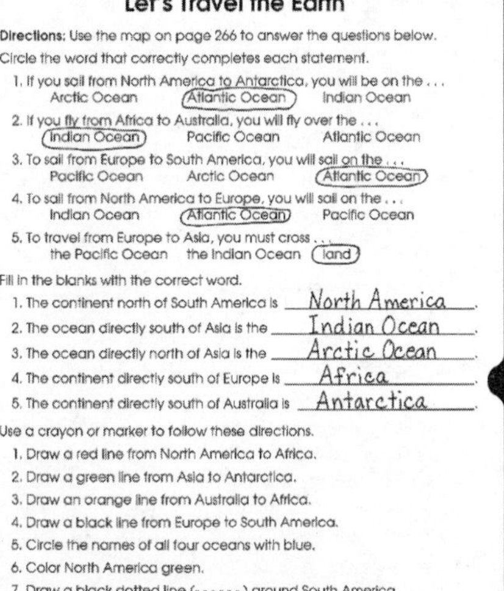

Name

Continents and Oceans

Let's Travel the Earth

Directions: Use the map on page 266 to answer the questions below.

Circle the word that correctly completes each statement.

1. If you sail from North America to Antarctica, you will be on the . . .
   Arctic Ocean (Atlantic Ocean) Indian Ocean
2. If you fly from Africa to Australia, you will fly over the . . .
   (Indian Ocean) Pacific Ocean Atlantic Ocean
3. To sail from Europe to South America, you will sail on the . . .
   Pacific Ocean Arctic Ocean (Atlantic Ocean)
4. To sail from North America to Europe, you will sail on the . . .
   Indian Ocean (Atlantic Ocean) Pacific Ocean
5. To travel from Europe to Asia, you must cross . . .
   the Pacific Ocean the Indian Ocean (land)

Fill in the blanks with the correct word.

1. The continent north of South America is North America.
2. The ocean directly south of Asia is the Indian Ocean.
3. The ocean directly north of Asia is the Arctic Ocean.
4. The continent directly south of Europe is Africa.
5. The continent directly south of Australia is Antarctica.

Use a crayon or marker to follow these directions.

1. Draw a red line from North America to Africa.
2. Draw a green line from Asia to Antarctica.
3. Draw an orange line from Australia to Africa.
4. Draw a black line from Europe to South America.
5. Circle the names of all four oceans with blue.
6. Color North America green.
7. Draw a black dotted line (- - - - - -) around South America.

©1998 Tribune Education. All Rights Reserved. 267

Page 267

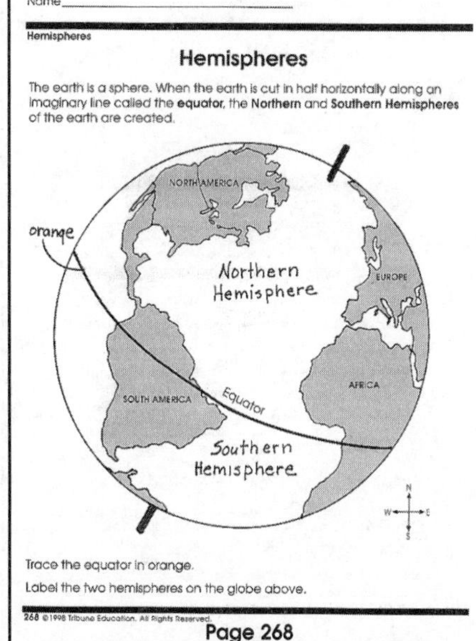

Name

Hemispheres

Hemispheres

The earth is a sphere. When the earth is cut in half horizontally along an imaginary line called the **equator**, the **Northern** and **Southern Hemispheres** of the earth are created.

Trace the equator in orange.

Label the two hemispheres on the globe above.

268 ©1998 Tribune Education. All Rights Reserved.

Page 268

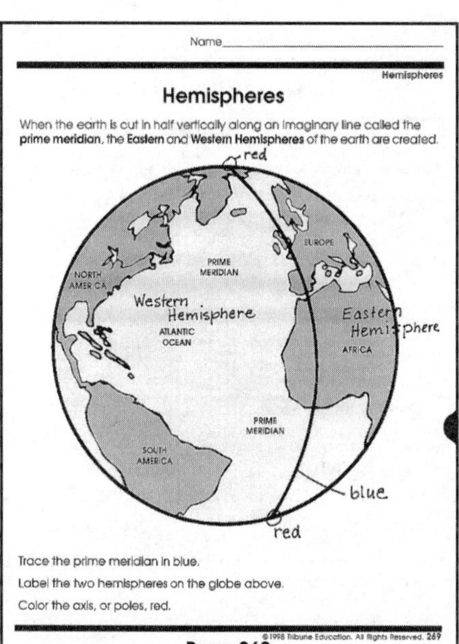

Name

Hemispheres

Hemispheres

When the earth is cut in half vertically along an imaginary line called the **prime meridian**, the **Eastern** and **Western Hemispheres** of the earth are created.

Trace the prime meridian in blue.

Label the two hemispheres on the globe above.

Color the axis, or poles, red.

©1998 Tribune Education. All Rights Reserved. 269

Page 269

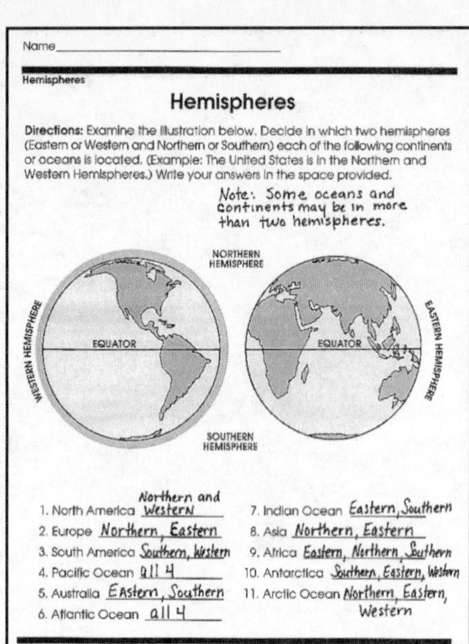

Name

Hemispheres

Hemispheres

Directions: Examine the illustration below. Decide in which two hemispheres (Eastern or Western and Northern or Southern) each of the following continents or oceans is located. (Example: The United States is in the Northern and Western Hemispheres.) Write your answers in the space provided.

Note: Some oceans and continents may be in more than two hemispheres.

1. North America Northern and Western
2. Europe Northern, Eastern
3. South America Southern, Western
4. Pacific Ocean all 4
5. Australia Eastern, Southern
6. Atlantic Ocean all 4
7. Indian Ocean Eastern, Southern
8. Asia Northern, Eastern
9. Africa Eastern, Northern, Southern
10. Antarctica Southern, Eastern, Western
11. Arctic Ocean Northern, Eastern, Western

270 © 1998 Tribune Education. All Rights Reserved.

Page 270

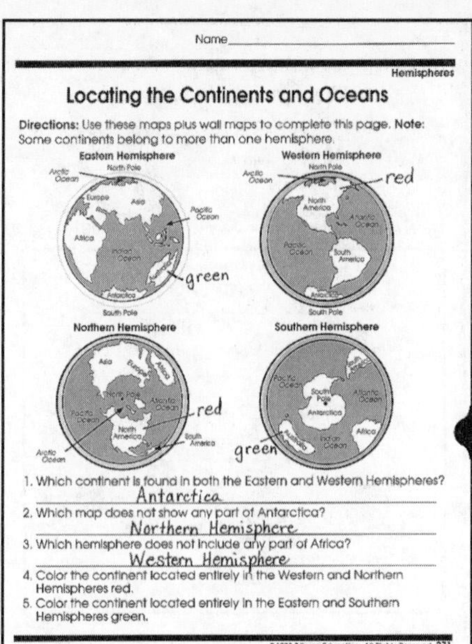

Name

Hemispheres

Locating the Continents and Oceans

Directions: Use these maps plus wall maps to complete this page. **Note:** Some continents belong to more than one hemisphere.

1. Which continent is found in both the Eastern and Western Hemispheres? Antarctica
2. Which map does not show any part of Antarctica? Northern Hemisphere
3. Which hemisphere does not include any part of Africa? Western Hemisphere
4. Color the continent located entirely in the Western and Northern Hemispheres red.
5. Color the continent located entirely in the Eastern and Southern Hemispheres green.

© 1998 Tribune Education. All Rights Reserved. 271

Page 271

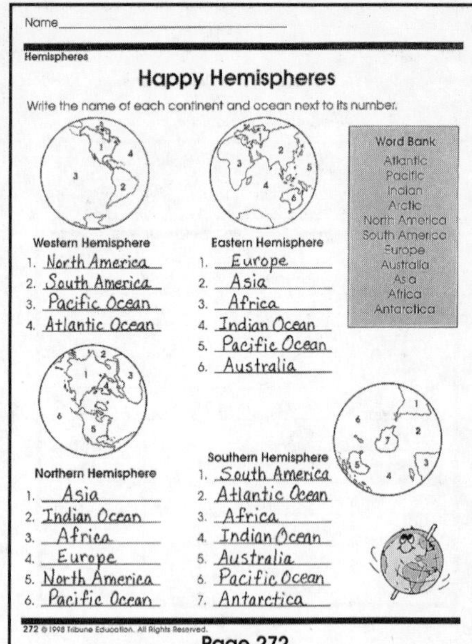

Name

Hemispheres

Happy Hemispheres

Write the name of each continent and ocean next to its number.

Word Bank: Atlantic, Pacific, Indian, Arctic, North America, South America, Europe, Australia, Asia, Africa, Antarctica

Western Hemisphere
1. North America
2. South America
3. Pacific Ocean
4. Atlantic Ocean

Eastern Hemisphere
1. Europe
2. Asia
3. Africa
4. Indian Ocean
5. Pacific Ocean
6. Australia

Northern Hemisphere
1. Asia
2. Indian Ocean
3. Africa
4. Europe
5. North America
6. Pacific Ocean

Southern Hemisphere
1. South America
2. Atlantic Ocean
3. Africa
4. Indian Ocean
5. Australia
6. Pacific Ocean
7. Antarctica

272 © 1998 Tribune Education. All Rights Reserved.

Page 272

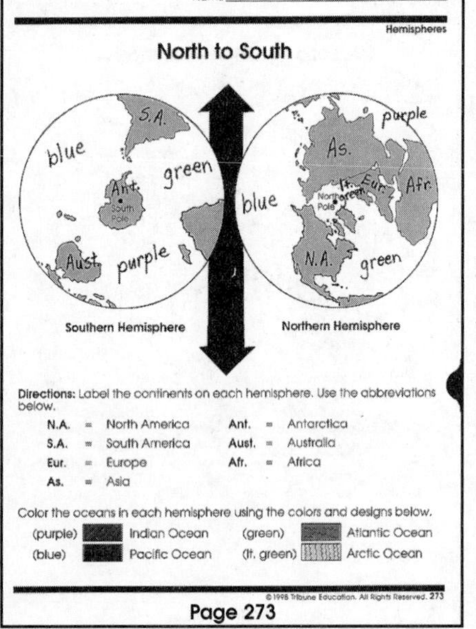

Name

Hemispheres

North to South

Directions: Label the continents on each hemisphere. Use the abbreviations below.

N.A. = North America
S.A. = South America
Eur. = Europe
As. = Asia
Ant. = Antarctica
Aust. = Australia
Afr. = Africa

Color the oceans in each hemisphere using the colors and designs below.

(purple) Indian Ocean
(blue) Pacific Ocean
(green) Atlantic Ocean
(lt. green) Arctic Ocean

© 1998 Tribune Education. All Rights Reserved. 273

Page 273

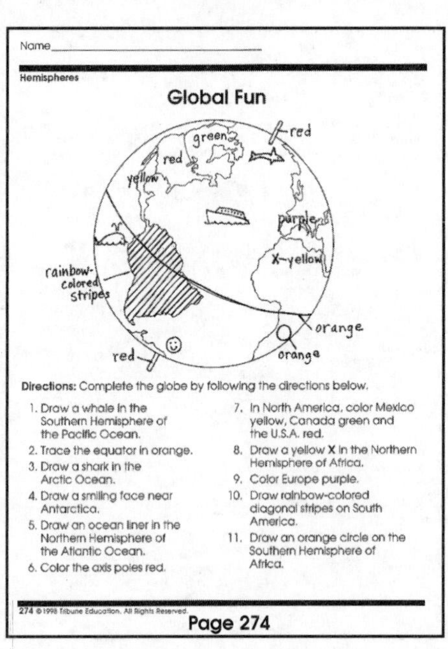

Name

Hemispheres

Global Fun

Directions: Complete the globe by following the directions below.

1. Draw a whale in the Southern Hemisphere of the Pacific Ocean.
2. Trace the equator in orange.
3. Draw a shark in the Arctic Ocean.
4. Draw a smiling face near Antarctica.
5. Draw an ocean liner in the Northern Hemisphere of the Atlantic Ocean.
6. Color the axis poles red.
7. In North America, color Mexico yellow, Canada green and the U.S.A. red.
8. Draw a yellow X in the Northern Hemisphere of Africa.
9. Color Europe purple.
10. Draw rainbow-colored diagonal stripes on South America.
11. Draw an orange circle on the Southern Hemisphere of Africa.

274 © 1998 Tribune Education. All Rights Reserved.

Page 274

Name

Hemispheres

From East to West

Directions: Label the continents using the abbreviations below. Cut out the continents. Glue them onto the correct hemisphere in the proper places. Include Antarctica on each hemisphere.

N.A. S.A. Ant. Eur. As. Afr. Aust. Ant.

Western Hemisphere — Eastern Hemisphere

Abbreviations

N.A. = North America
Eur. = Europe
Aust. = Australia
S.A. = South America
As. = Asia
Afr. = Africa
Ant. = Antarctica

© 1998 Tribune Education. All Rights Reserved. 275

Page 275

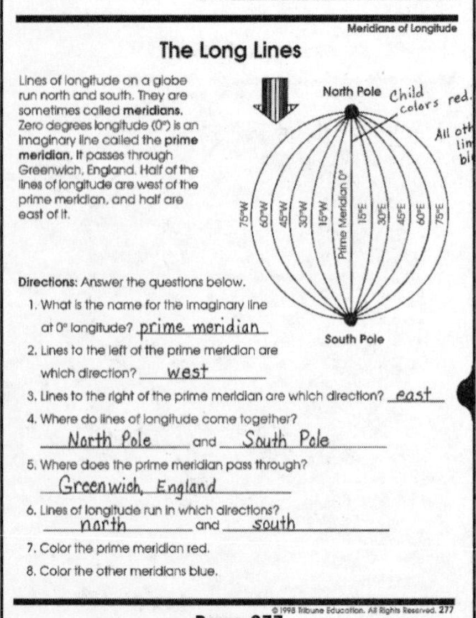

Name

Meridians of Longitude

The Long Lines

Lines of longitude on a globe run north and south. They are sometimes called **meridians.** Zero degrees longitude (0°) is an imaginary line called the **prime meridian.** It passes through Greenwich, England. Half of the lines of longitude are west of the prime meridian, and half are east of it.

Directions: Answer the questions below.

1. What is the name for the imaginary line at 0° longitude? prime meridian
2. Lines to the left of the prime meridian are which direction? west
3. Lines to the right of the prime meridian are which direction? east
4. Where do lines of longitude come together? North Pole and South Pole
5. Where does the prime meridian pass through? Greenwich, England
6. Lines of longitude run in which directions? north and south
7. Color the prime meridian red.
8. Color the other meridians blue.

© 1998 Tribune Education. All Rights Reserved. 277

Page 277

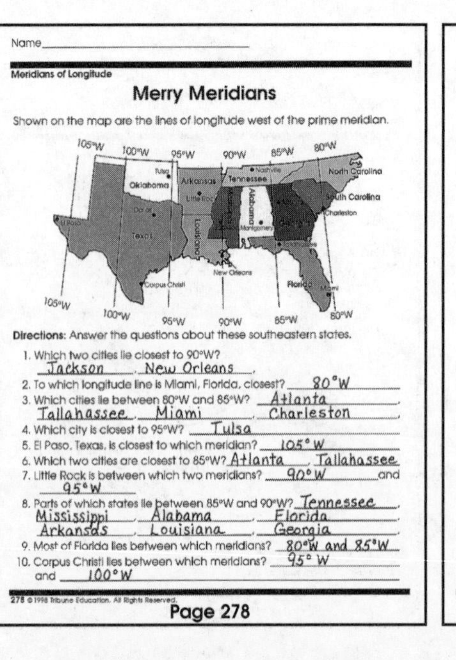

Name

Meridians of Longitude

Merry Meridians

Shown on the map are the lines of longitude west of the prime meridian.

Directions: Answer the questions about these southeastern states.

1. Which two cities lie closest to 90°W? Jackson, New Orleans.
2. To which longitude line is Miami, Florida, closest? 80°W
3. Which cities lie between 80°W and 85°W? Atlanta, Tallahassee, Miami, Charleston.
4. Which city is closest to 95°W? Tulsa
5. El Paso, Texas, is closest to which meridian? 105°W
6. Which two cities are closest to 85°W? Atlanta, Tallahassee
7. Little Rock is between which two meridians? 90°W and 95°W
8. Parts of which states lie between 85°W and 90°W? Tennessee, Mississippi, Alabama, Florida, Arkansas, Louisiana, Georgia.
9. Most of Florida lies between which meridians? 80°W and 85°W
10. Corpus Christi lies between which meridians? 95°W and 100°W

278 © 1998 Tribune Education. All Rights Reserved.

Page 278

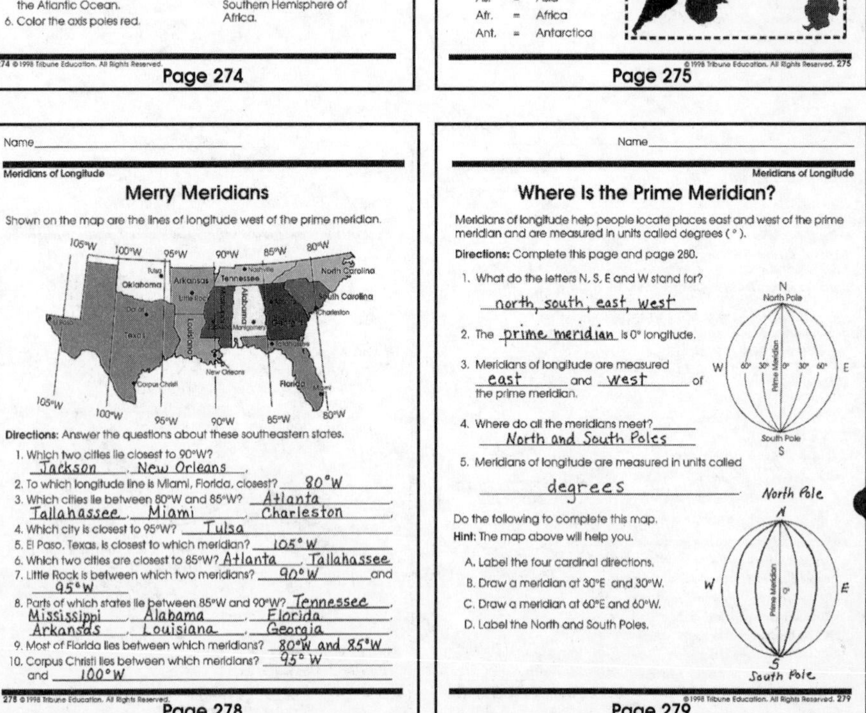

Name

Meridians of Longitude

Where Is the Prime Meridian?

Meridians of longitude help people locate places east and west of the prime meridian and are measured in units called degrees (°).

Directions: Complete this page and page 280.

1. What do the letters N, S, E and W stand for? north, south, east, west
2. The prime meridian is 0° longitude.
3. Meridians of longitude are measured east and west of the prime meridian.
4. Where do all the meridians meet? North and South Poles
5. Meridians of longitude are measured in units called degrees

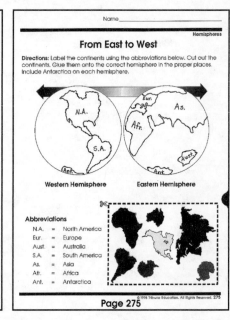

Do the following to complete this map.

Hint: The map above will help you.

A. Label the four cardinal directions.
B. Draw a meridian at 30°E and 30°W.
C. Draw a meridian at 60°E and 60°W.
D. Label the North and South Poles.

© 1998 Tribune Education. All Rights Reserved. 279

Page 279

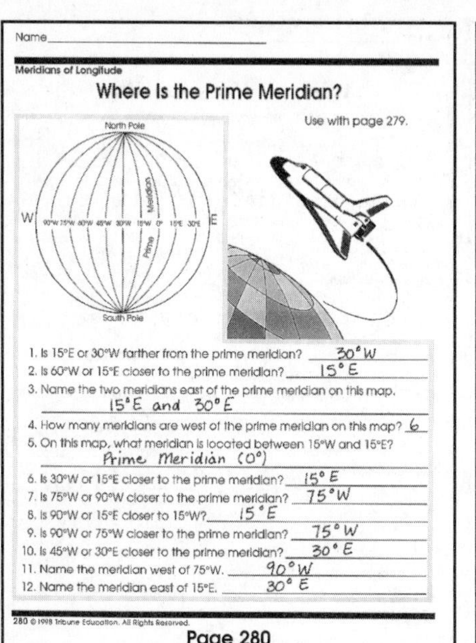

Name____________

Meridians of Longitude

Where Is the Prime Meridian?

Use with page 279.

1. Is 15°E or 30°W farther from the prime meridian? 30°W
2. Is 60°W or 15°E closer to the prime meridian? 15°E
3. Name the two meridians east of the prime meridian on this map. 15°E and 30°E
4. How many meridians are west of the prime meridian on this map? 6
5. On this map, what meridian is located between 15°W and 15°E? Prime Meridian (0°)
6. Is 30°W or 15°E closer to the prime meridian? 15°E
7. Is 75°W or 90°W closer to the prime meridian? 75°W
8. Is 90°W or 15°E closer to 15°W? 15°E
9. Is 90°W or 75°W closer to the prime meridian? 75°W
10. Is 45°W or 30°E closer to the prime meridian? 30°E
11. Name the meridian west of 75°W. 90°W
12. Name the meridian east of 15°E. 30°E

Page 280

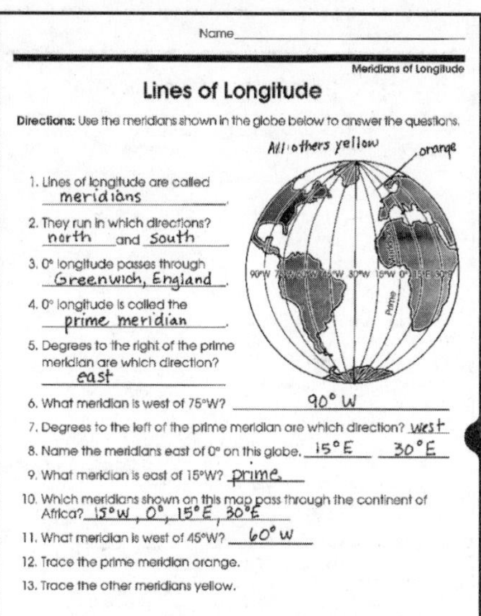

Name____________

Meridians of Longitude

Lines of Longitude

Directions: Use the meridians shown in the globe below to answer the questions.

1. Lines of longitude are called meridians
2. They run in which directions? north and south
3. 0° longitude passes through Greenwich, England
4. 0° longitude is called the prime meridian
5. Degrees to the right of the prime meridian are which direction? east
6. What meridian is west of 75°W? 90°W
7. Degrees to the left of the prime meridian are which direction? west
8. Name the meridians east of 0° on this globe. 15°E 30°E
9. What meridian is east of 15°W? prime
10. Which meridians shown on this map pass through the continent of Africa? 15°W, 0°, 15°E, 30°E
11. What meridian is west of 45°W? 60°W
12. Trace the prime meridian orange.
13. Trace the other meridians yellow.

Page 281

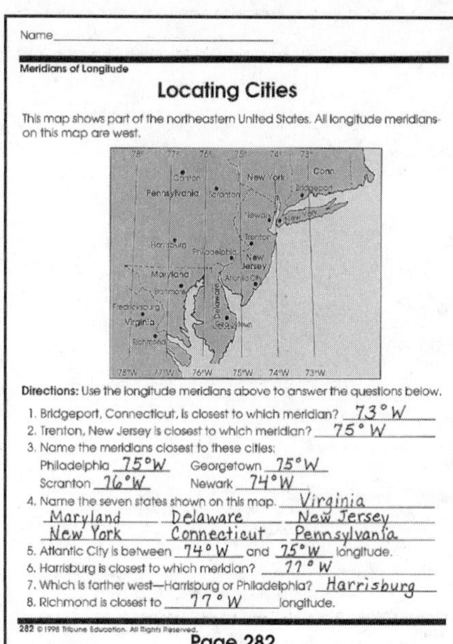

Name____________

Meridians of Longitude

Locating Cities

This map shows part of the northeastern United States. All longitude meridians on this map are west.

Directions: Use the longitude meridians above to answer the questions below.

1. Bridgeport, Connecticut, is closest to which meridian? 73°W
2. Trenton, New Jersey is closest to which meridian? 75°W
3. Name the meridians closest to these cities:
   Philadelphia 75°W Georgetown 75°W
   Scranton 76°W Newark 74°W
4. Name the seven states shown on this map. Virginia Maryland Delaware New Jersey New York Connecticut Pennsylvania
5. Atlantic City is between 74°W and 75°W longitude.
6. Harrisburg is closest to which meridian? 77°W
7. Which is farther west—Harrisburg or Philadelphia? Harrisburg
8. Richmond is closest to 77°W longitude.

Page 282

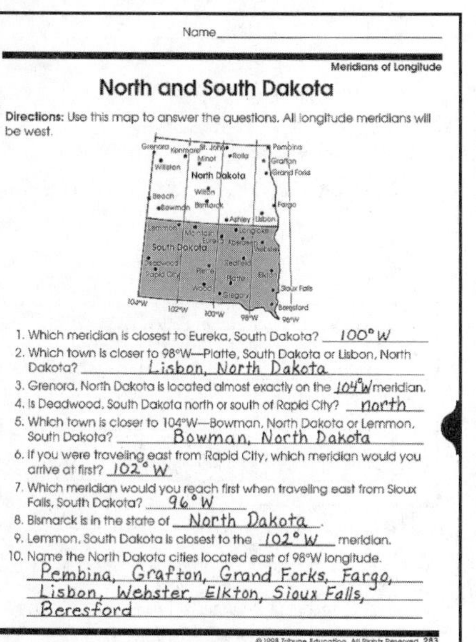

Name____________

Meridians of Longitude

North and South Dakota

Directions: Use this map to answer the questions. All longitude meridians will be west.

1. Which meridian is closest to Eureka, South Dakota? 100°W
2. Which town is closer to 98°W—Platte, South Dakota or Lisbon, North Dakota? Lisbon, North Dakota
3. Grenora, North Dakota is located almost exactly on the 104°W meridian.
4. Is Deadwood, South Dakota north or south of Rapid City? north
5. Which town is closer to 104°W—Bowman, North Dakota or Lemmon, South Dakota? Bowman, North Dakota
6. If you were traveling east from Rapid City, which meridian would you arrive at first? 102°W
7. Which meridian would you reach first when traveling east from Sioux Falls, South Dakota? 96°W
8. Bismarck is in the state of North Dakota.
9. Lemmon, South Dakota is closest to the 102°W meridian.
10. Name the North Dakota cities located east of 98°W longitude. Pembina, Grafton, Grand Forks, Fargo, Lisbon, Webster, Elkton, Sioux Falls, Beresford

Page 283

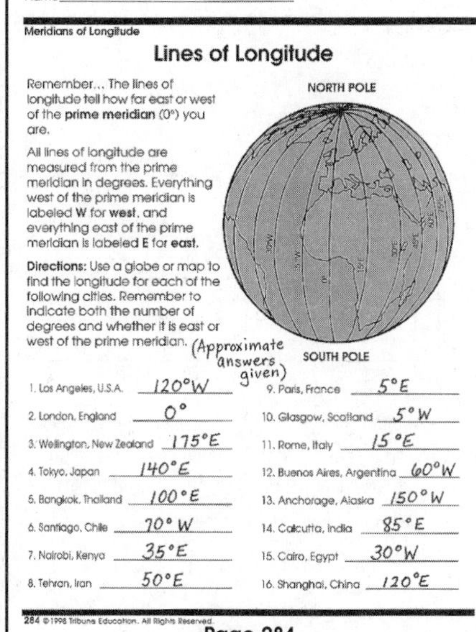

Name____________

Meridians of Longitude

Lines of Longitude

Remember… The lines of longitude tell how far east or west of the **prime meridian** (0°) you are.

All lines of longitude are measured from the prime meridian in degrees. Everything west of the prime meridian is labeled **W** for **west**, and everything east of the prime meridian is labeled **E** for **east**.

Directions: Use a globe or map to find the longitude for each of the following cities. Remember to indicate both the number of degrees and whether it is east or west of the prime meridian. (Approximate answers given)

1. Los Angeles, U.S.A. 120°W	9. Paris, France 5°E
2. London, England 0°	10. Glasgow, Scotland 5°W
3. Wellington, New Zealand 175°E	11. Rome, Italy 15°E
4. Tokyo, Japan 140°E	12. Buenos Aires, Argentina 60°W
5. Bangkok, Thailand 100°E	13. Anchorage, Alaska 150°W
6. Santiago, Chile 70°W	14. Calcutta, India 85°E
7. Nairobi, Kenya 35°E	15. Cairo, Egypt 30°W
8. Tehran, Iran 50°E	16. Shanghai, China 120°E

Page 284

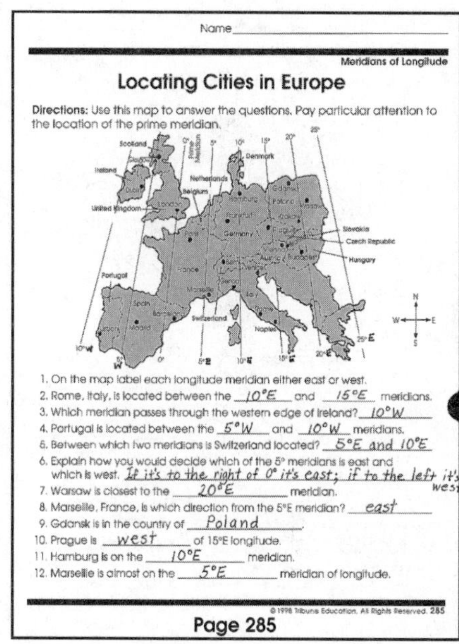

Name____________

Meridians of Longitude

Locating Cities in Europe

Directions: Use this map to answer the questions. Pay particular attention to the location of the prime meridian.

1. On the map label each longitude meridian either east or west.
2. Rome, Italy, is located between the 10°E and 15°E meridians.
3. Which meridian passes through the western edge of Ireland? 10°W
4. Portugal is located between the 5°W and 10°W meridians.
5. Between which two meridians is Switzerland located? 5°E and 10°E
6. Explain how you would decide which of the 5° meridians is east and which is west. If it's to the right of 0° it's east; if to the left it's west
7. Warsaw is closest to the 20°E meridian.
8. Marseille, France, is which direction from the 5°E meridian? east
9. Gdansk is in the country of Poland.
10. Prague is west of 15°E longitude.
11. Hamburg is on the 10°E meridian.
12. Marseille is almost on the 5°E meridian of longitude.

Page 285

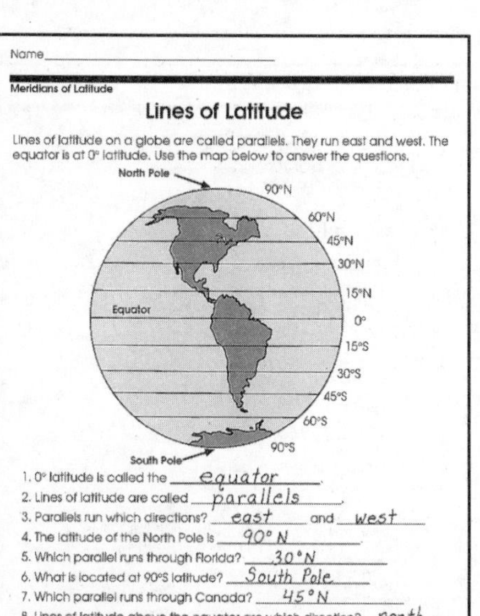

Name____________

Meridians of Latitude

Lines of Latitude

Lines of latitude on a globe are called parallels. They run east and west. The equator is at 0° latitude. Use the map below to answer the questions.

1. 0° latitude is called the equator.
2. Lines of latitude are called parallels.
3. Parallels run which directions? east and west
4. The latitude of the North Pole is 90°N
5. Which parallel runs through Florida? 30°N
6. What is located at 90°S latitude? South Pole
7. Which parallel runs through Canada? 45°N
8. Lines of latitude above the equator are which direction? north
9. Below the equator, the parallels are which direction? south

Page 286

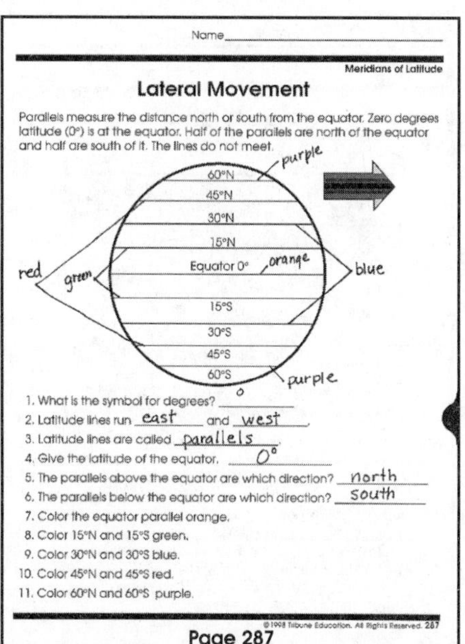

Name____________

Meridians of Latitude

Lateral Movement

Parallels measure the distance north or south from the equator. Zero degrees latitude (0°) is at the equator. Half of the parallels are north of the equator and half are south of it. The lines do not meet.

1. What is the symbol for degrees? °
2. Latitude lines run east and west.
3. Latitude lines are called parallels.
4. Give the latitude of the equator. 0°
5. The parallels above the equator are which direction? north
6. The parallels below the equator are which direction? south
7. Color the equator parallel orange.
8. Color 15°N and 15°S green.
9. Color 30°N and 30°S blue.
10. Color 45°N and 45°S red.
11. Color 60°N and 60°S purple.

Page 287

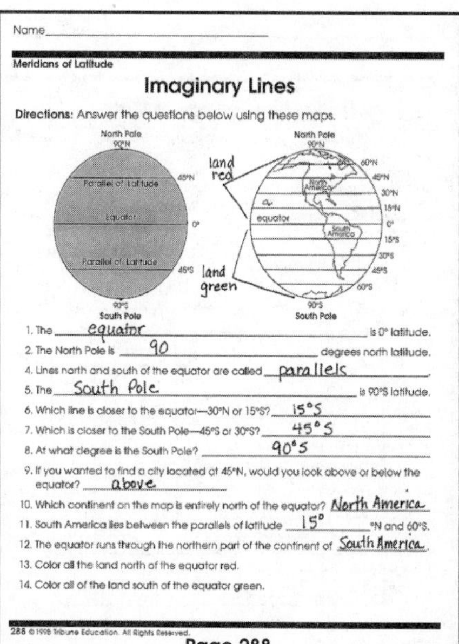

Name____________

Meridians of Latitude

Imaginary Lines

Directions: Answer the questions below using these maps.

1. The equator is 0° latitude.
2. The North Pole is 90 degrees north latitude.
4. Lines north and south of the equator are called parallels.
5. The South Pole is 90°S latitude.
6. Which line is closer to the equator—30°N or 15°S? 15°S
7. Which is closer to the South Pole—45°S or 30°S? 45°S
8. At what degree is the South Pole? 90°S
9. If you wanted to find a city located at 45°N, would you look above or below the equator? above
10. Which continent on the map is entirely north of the equator? North America
11. South America lies between the parallels of latitude 15° °N and 60°S.
12. The equator runs through the northern part of the continent of South America.
13. Color all the land north of the equator red.
14. Color all of the land south of the equator green.

Page 288

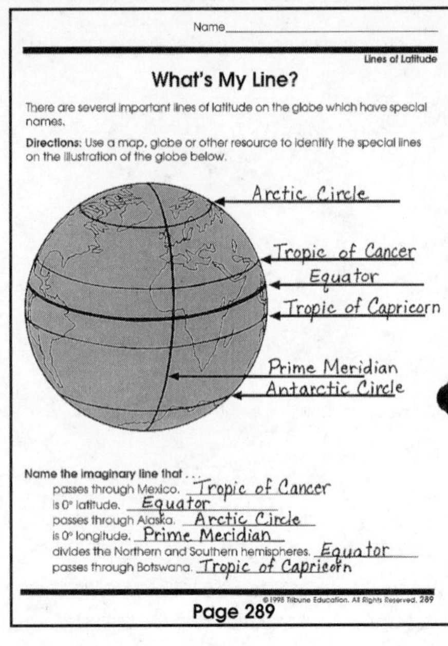
Name ____________

Lines of Latitude

What's My Line?

There are several important lines of latitude on the globe which have special names.

Directions: Use a map, globe or other resource to identify the special lines on the illustration of the globe below.

Name the imaginary line that . . .
passes through Mexico. Tropic of Cancer
is 0° latitude. Equator
passes through Alaska. Arctic Circle
is 0° longitude. Prime Meridian
divides the Northern and Southern hemispheres. Equator
passes through Botswana. Tropic of Capricorn

 289

Page 289

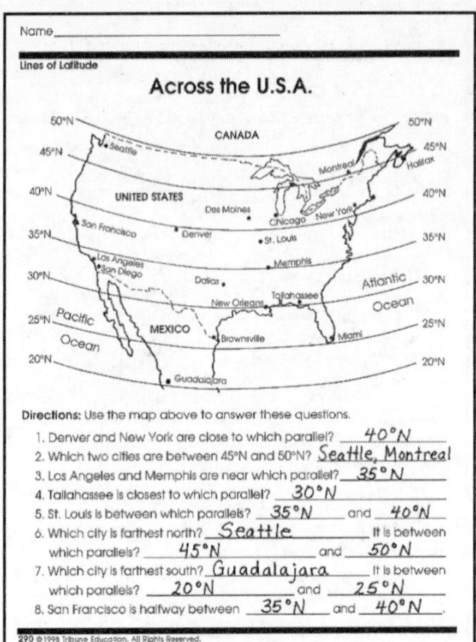
Name ____________

Lines of Latitude

Across the U.S.A.

Directions: Use the map above to answer these questions.

1. Denver and New York are close to which parallel? 40°N
2. Which two cities are between 45°N and 50°N? Seattle, Montreal
3. Los Angeles and Memphis are near which parallel? 35°N
4. Tallahassee is closest to which parallel? 30°N
5. St. Louis is between which parallels? 35°N and 40°N
6. Which city is farthest north? Seattle It is between which parallels? 45°N and 50°N
7. Which city is farthest south? Guadalajara It is between which parallels? 20°N and 25°N
8. San Francisco is halfway between 35°N and 40°N.

290

Page 290

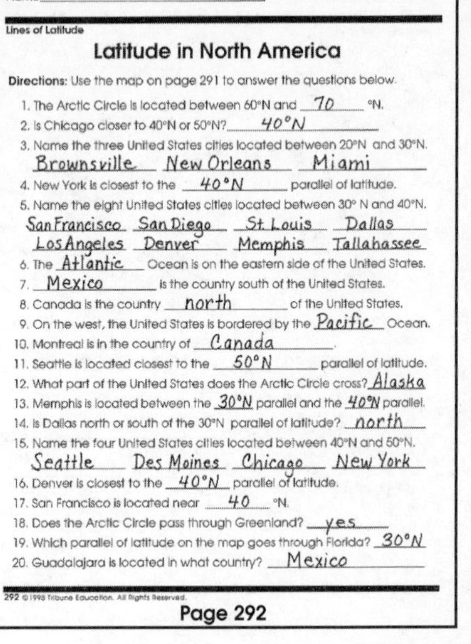
Name ____________

Lines of Latitude

Latitude in North America

Directions: Use the map on page 291 to answer the questions below.

1. The Arctic Circle is located between 60°N and 70 °N.
2. Is Chicago closer to 40°N or 50°N? 40°N
3. Name the three United States cities located between 20°N and 30°N. Brownsville New Orleans Miami
4. New York is closest to the 40°N parallel of latitude.
5. Name the eight United States cities located between 30° N and 40°N. San Francisco San Diego St. Louis Dallas Los Angeles Denver Memphis Tallahassee
6. The Atlantic Ocean is on the eastern side of the United States.
7. Mexico is the country south of the United States.
8. Canada is the country north of the United States.
9. On the west, the United States is bordered by the Pacific Ocean.
10. Montreal is in the country of Canada.
11. Seattle is located closest to the 50°N parallel of latitude.
12. What part of the United States does the Arctic Circle cross? Alaska
13. Memphis is located between the 30°N parallel and the 40°N parallel.
14. Is Dallas north or south of the 30°N parallel of latitude? north
15. Name the four United States cities located between 40°N and 50°N. Seattle Des Moines Chicago New York
16. Denver is closest to the 40°N parallel of latitude.
17. San Francisco is located near 40 °N.
18. Does the Arctic Circle pass through Greenland? yes
19. Which parallel of latitude on the map goes through Florida? 30°N
20. Guadalajara is located in what country? Mexico

292

Page 292

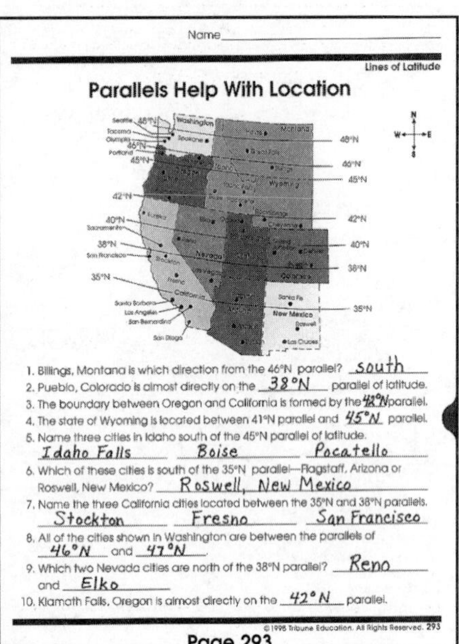
Name ____________

Lines of Latitude

Parallels Help With Location

1. Billings, Montana is which direction from the 46°N parallel? south
2. Pueblo, Colorado is almost directly on the 38°N parallel of latitude.
3. The boundary between Oregon and California is formed by the 42°N parallel.
4. The state of Wyoming is located between 41°N parallel and 45°N parallel.
5. Name three cities in Idaho south of the 45°N parallel of latitude. Idaho Falls Boise Pocatello
6. Which of these cities is south of the 35°N parallel—Flagstaff, Arizona or Roswell, New Mexico? Roswell, New Mexico
7. Name the three California cities located between the 35°N and 38°N parallels. Stockton Fresno San Francisco
8. All of the cities shown in Washington are between the parallels of 46°N and 47°N.
9. Which two Nevada cities are north of the 38°N parallel? Reno and Elko
10. Klamath Falls, Oregon is almost directly on the 42°N parallel.

 293

Page 293

Name ____________

Latitude and Longitude

Picture It!

Directions: Coordinates are sets of numbers that show where lines of latitude and longitude meet. Place a dot at each latitude / longitude coordinate on the graph. Draw lines to connect the dots in order.

1. 30°N / 140°W
2. 25°N / 135°W
3. 20°N / 130°W
4. 15°N / 125°W
5. 15°N / 90°W
6. 20°N / 85°W
7. 25°N / 80°W
8. 30°N / 75°W
9. 30°N / 90°W
10. 45°N / 90°W
11. 45°N / 100°W
12. 30°N / 100°W
13. 30°N / 110°W
14. 45°N / 110°W
15. 45°N / 120°W
16. 30°N / 120°W
17. 30°N / 140°W

Now place a yellow **X** at each coordinate below. Do not connect the Xs.

1. 45°N / 140°W
2. 35°N / 135°W
3. 45°N / 130°W
4. 40°N / 80°W
5. 45°N / 70°W
6. 35°N / 65°W

Color the rest of the picture.

294

Page 294

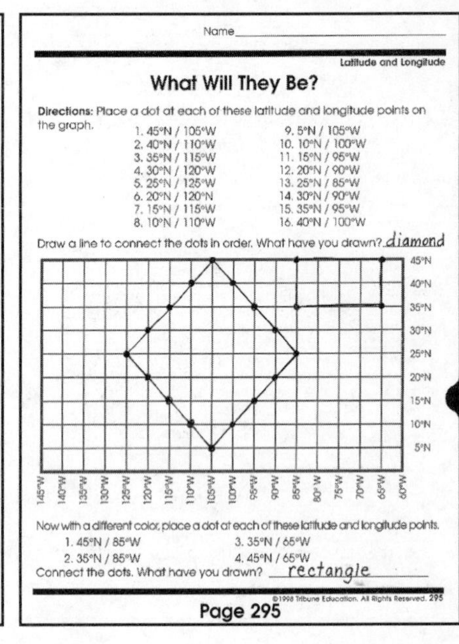
Name ____________

Latitude and Longitude

What Will They Be?

Directions: Place a dot at each of these latitude and longitude points on the graph.

1. 45°N / 105°W
2. 40°N / 110°W
3. 35°N / 115°W
4. 30°N / 120°W
5. 25°N / 125°W
6. 20°N / 120°N
7. 15°N / 115°W
8. 10°N / 110°W
9. 5°N / 105°W
10. 10°N / 100°W
11. 15°N / 95°W
12. 20°N / 90°W
13. 25°N / 85°W
14. 30°N / 90°W
15. 35°N / 95°W
16. 40°N / 100°W

Draw a line to connect the dots in order. What have you drawn? diamond

Now with a different color, place a dot at each of these latitude and longitude points.

1. 45°N / 85°W
2. 35°N / 85°W
3. 35°N / 65°W
4. 45°N / 65°W

Connect the dots. What have you drawn? rectangle

 295

Page 295

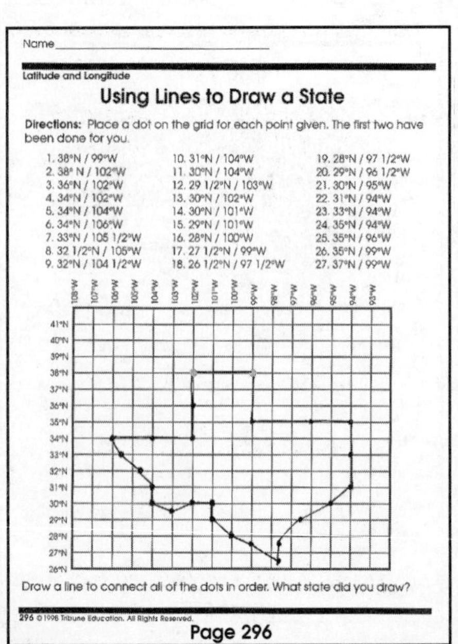
Name ____________

Latitude and Longitude

Using Lines to Draw a State

Directions: Place a dot on the grid for each point given. The first two have been done for you.

1. 38°N / 99°W
2. 38° N / 102°W
3. 36°N / 102°W
4. 34°N / 102°W
5. 34°N / 104°W
6. 34°N / 106°W
7. 33°N / 105 1/2°W
8. 32 1/2°N / 105°W
9. 32°N / 104 1/2°W
10. 31°N / 104°W
11. 30°N / 104°W
12. 29 1/2°N / 103°W
13. 30°N / 102°W
14. 30°N / 101°W
15. 29°N / 101°W
16. 28°N / 100°W
17. 27 1/2°N / 99°W
18. 26 1/2°N / 97 1/2°W
19. 28°N / 97 1/2°W
20. 29°N / 96 1/2°W
21. 30°N / 95°W
22. 31°N / 94°W
23. 33°N / 94°W
24. 35°N / 94°W
25. 35°N / 96°W
26. 35°N / 99°W
27. 37°N / 99°W

Draw a line to connect all of the dots in order. What state did you draw?

296

Page 296

Name ____________

Latitude and Longitude

Casey's Island

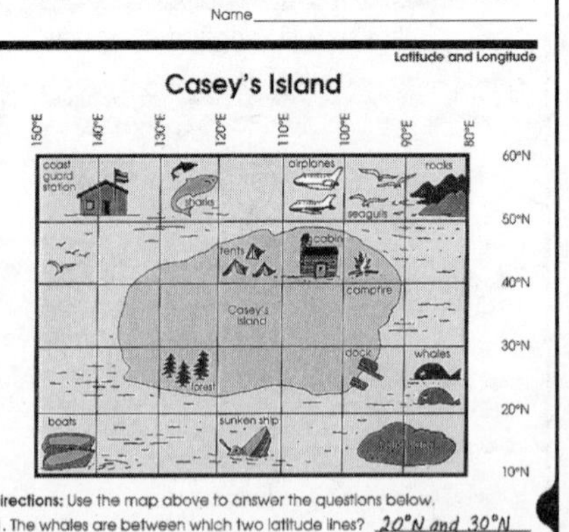

Directions: Use the map above to answer the questions below.

1. The whales are between which two latitude lines? 20°N and 30°N
2. The coast guard station is located between which longitude lines? 130°E and 150°E
3. If the whales go north to 55°N latitude, what will they hit? rocks
4. The boats must cross what longitude lines to get to the sunken ship? 140°E, 130°E, 120°E
5. If you draw a latitude line at 35°N, what will you cross? Casey's Island
6. If the whales cross 90°E longitude, what will they reach? dock
7. Name the items crossed by the 55°N latitude line. coast guard station sharks, airplanes, seagulls, rocks
8. Which longitude lines cross Casey's Island? 100°E, 110°E, 120°E, 130°E

 297

Page 297

Name ____________

Latitude and Longitude

State Search

Which state is roughly between the coordinates given? After locating the state, color it on the map as directed.

	Latitude	Longitude	State	Color
1.	45°N / 50°N	105°W / 115°W	Montana	orange
2.	40°N / 45°N	75°W / 80°W	Pennsylvania	tan
3.	44°N / 50°N	67°W / 70°W	Maine	red
4.	25°N / 30°N	80°W / 85°W	Florida	yellow
5.	40°N / 45°N	90°W / 95°W	Iowa	gray
6.	30°N / 35°N	85°W / 90°W	Alabama	green
7.	43°N / 47°N	87°W / 93°W	Wisconsin	blue
8.	31°N / 36°N	104°W / 109°W	New Mexico	pink
9.	36°N / 38°N	82°W / 89°W	Kentucky	lt. green
10.	36°N / 39°N	75°W / 84°W	Virginia	gold
11.	26°N / 34°N	94°W / 107°W	Texas	purple
12.	41°N / 45°N	104°W / 111°W	Wyoming	lt. blue
13.	36°N / 41°N	90°W / 95°W	Missouri	brown

298

Page 298

Name________________________

Latitude and Longitude

See the U.S.A.

Use the coordinates to plan a trip across the U.S.A.

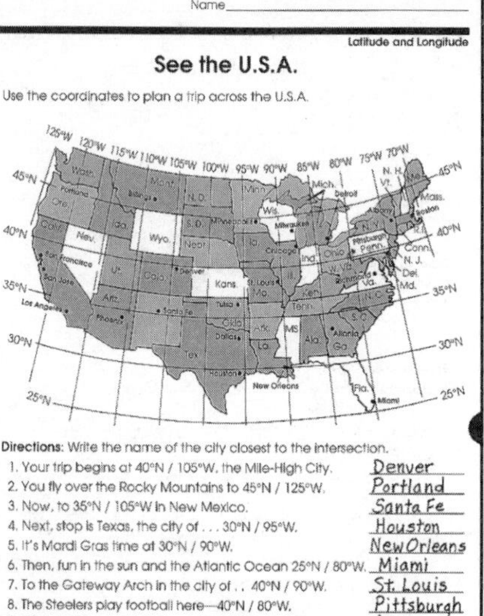

Directions: Write the name of the city closest to the intersection.

1. Your trip begins at 40°N / 105°W, the Mile-High City. Denver
2. You fly over the Rocky Mountains to 45°N / 125°W. Portland
3. Now, to 35°N / 105°W in New Mexico. Santa Fe
4. Next, stop is Texas, the city of . . . 30°N / 95°W. Houston
5. It's Mardi Gras time at 30°N / 90°W. New Orleans
6. Then, fun in the sun and the Atlantic Ocean 25°N / 80°W. Miami
7. To the Gateway Arch in the city of . . 40°N / 90°W. St. Louis
8. The Steelers play football here—40°N / 80°W. Pittsburgh
9. Next, to the capital of New York—40°N / 75°W. Albany

Page 299

Name________________________

Latitude and Longitude

Plotting North American Cities

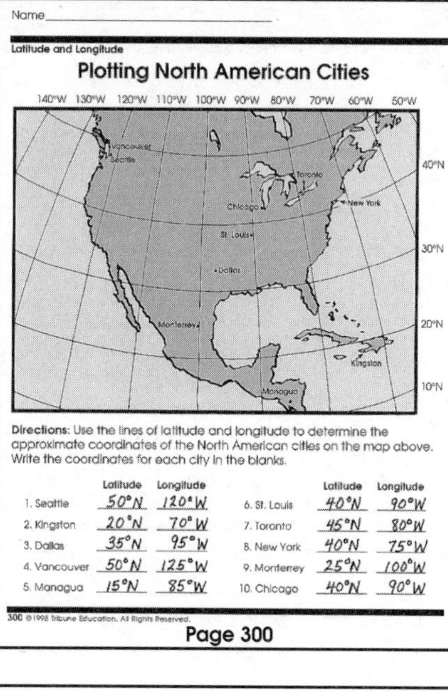

Directions: Use the lines of latitude and longitude to determine the approximate coordinates of the North American cities on the map above. Write the coordinates for each city in the blanks.

	Latitude	Longitude		Latitude	Longitude
1. Seattle	50°N	120°W	6. St. Louis	40°N	90°W
2. Kingston	20°N	70°W	7. Toronto	45°N	80°W
3. Dallas	35°N	95°W	8. New York	40°N	75°W
4. Vancouver	50°N	125°W	9. Monterrey	25°N	100°W
5. Managua	15°N	85°W	10. Chicago	40°N	90°W

Page 300

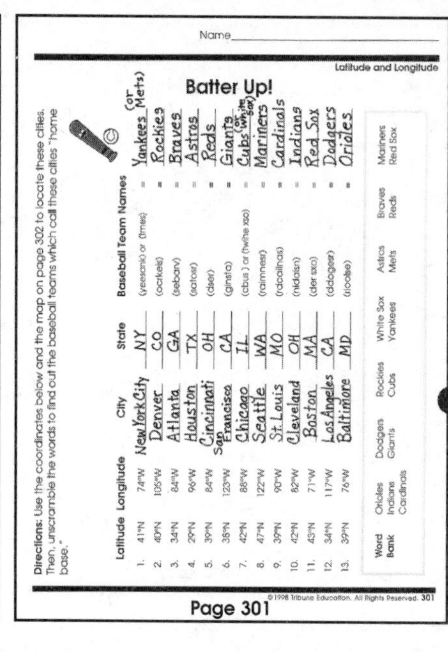

Name________________________

Latitude and Longitude

Batter Up!

Directions: Use the coordinates below and the map on page 302 to locate these cities. Then, unscramble the words to find out the baseball teams which call these cities "home base."

	Latitude	Longitude	City	State	Baseball Team Names	
1.	41°N	74°W	New York City	NY	(yeesnak) or (tmes)	= Yankees (or Mets)
2.	40°N	105°W	Denver	CO	(ockiels)	= Rockies
3.	34°N	84°W	Atlanta	GA	(sebarv)	= Braves
4.	29°N	95°W	Houston	TX	(satosr)	= Astros
5.	39°N	84°W	Cincinnati	OH	(sder)	= Reds
6.	38°N	123°W	San Francisco	CA	(ginsta)	= Giants
7.	42°N	88°W	Chicago	IL	(cbus) or (twihe xso)	= Cubs (or White Sox)
8.	47°N	122°W	Seattle	WA	(raimners)	= Mariners
9.	39°N	90°W	St. Louis	MO	(rdcailnas)	= Cardinals
10.	42°N	82°W	Cleveland	OH	(nidasn)	= Indians
11.	42°N	71°W	Boston	MA	(der sxo)	= Red Sox
12.	34°N	117°W	Los Angeles	CA	(ddoegrs)	= Dodgers
13.	39°N	76°W	Baltimore	MD	(lroioes)	= Orioles

Word Bank: Orioles, Indians, Cardinals, Dodgers, Giants, Rockies, Cubs, White Sox, Yankees, Astros, Mets, Braves, Reds, Mariners, Red Sox

Page 301

Name________________________

Latitude and Longitude

Four States

Use with page 303.

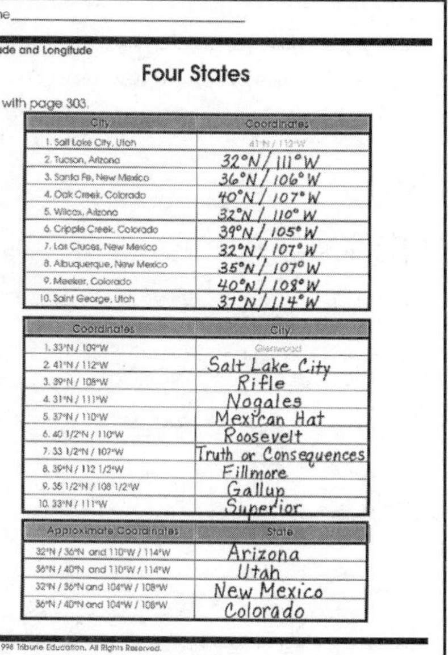

City	Coordinates
1. Salt Lake City, Utah	41°N / 112°W
2. Tucson, Arizona	32°N / 111°W
3. Santa Fe, New Mexico	36°N / 106°W
4. Oak Creek, Colorado	40°N / 107°W
5. Willcox, Arizona	32°N / 110°W
6. Cripple Creek, Colorado	39°N / 105°W
7. Las Cruces, New Mexico	32°N / 107°W
8. Albuquerque, New Mexico	35°N / 107°W
9. Meeker, Colorado	40°N / 108°W
10. Saint George, Utah	37°N / 114°W

Coordinates	City
1. 33°N / 109°W	Glenwood
2. 41°N / 112°W	Salt Lake City
3. 39°N / 108°W	Rifle
4. 31°N / 111°W	Nogales
5. 37°N / 110°W	Mexican Hat
6. 40 1/2°N / 110°W	Roosevelt
7. 33 1/2°N / 107°W	Truth or Consequences
8. 39°N / 112 1/2°W	Fillmore
9. 35 1/2°N / 108 1/2°W	Gallup
10. 33°N / 111°W	Superior

Approximate Coordinates	State
32°N / 36°N and 110°W / 114°W	Arizona
36°N / 40°N and 110°W / 114°W	Utah
32°N / 36°N and 104°W / 108°W	New Mexico
36°N / 40°N and 104°W / 108°W	Colorado

Page 304

Name________________________

Latitude and Longitude

Name the City

Directions: Use the coordinates given below to locate each of the cities. The first one has been done for you.

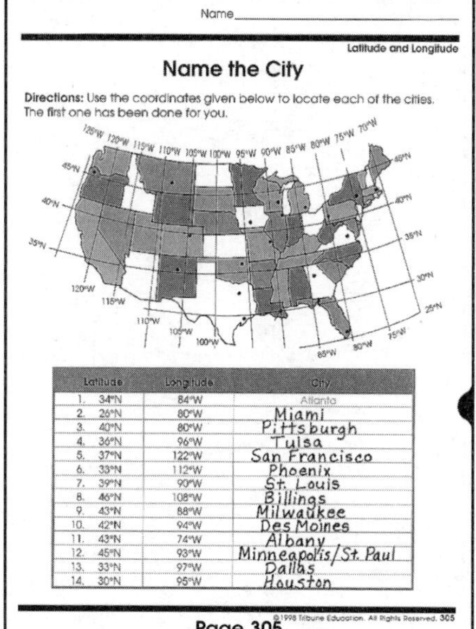

	Latitude	Longitude	City
1.	34°N	84°W	Atlanta
2.	26°N	80°W	Miami
3.	40°N	80°W	Pittsburgh
4.	36°N	96°W	Tulsa
5.	37°N	122°W	San Francisco
6.	33°N	112°W	Phoenix
7.	39°N	90°W	St. Louis
8.	46°N	108°W	Billings
9.	43°N	88°W	Milwaukee
10.	42°N	94°W	Des Moines
11.	43°N	74°W	Albany
12.	45°N	93°W	Minneapolis/St. Paul
13.	33°N	97°W	Dallas
14.	30°N	95°W	Houston

Page 305

Name________________________

Latitude and Longitude

Locating Places in Western Europe

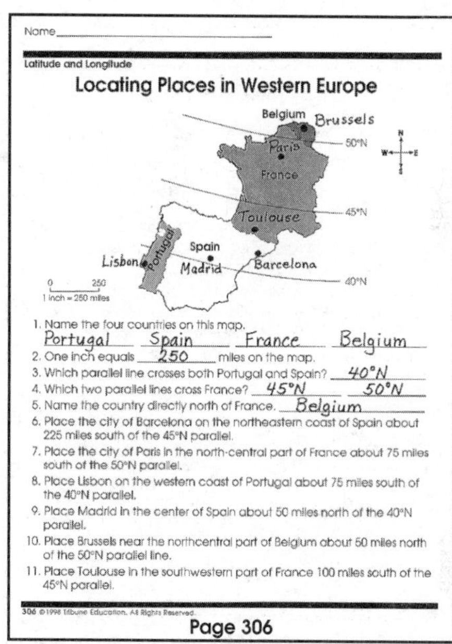

1. Name the four countries on this map. Portugal Spain France Belgium
2. One inch equals 250 miles on the map.
3. Which parallel line crosses both Portugal and Spain? 40°N
4. Which two parallel lines cross France? 45°N 50°N
5. Name the country directly north of France. Belgium
6. Place the city of Barcelona on the northeastern coast of Spain about 225 miles south of the 45°N parallel.
7. Place the city of Paris in the north-central part of France about 75 miles south of the 50°N parallel.
8. Place Lisbon on the western coast of Portugal about 75 miles south of the 40°N parallel.
9. Place Madrid in the center of Spain about 50 miles north of the 40°N parallel.
10. Place Brussels near the northcentral part of Belgium about 50 miles north of the 50°N parallel line.
11. Place Toulouse in the southwestern part of France 100 miles south of the 45°N parallel.

Page 306

Name________________________

Latitude and Longitude

Where in Europe?

Directions: Estimate and write the coordinates and countries for these European cities using the map on page 307. The first one has been done for you.

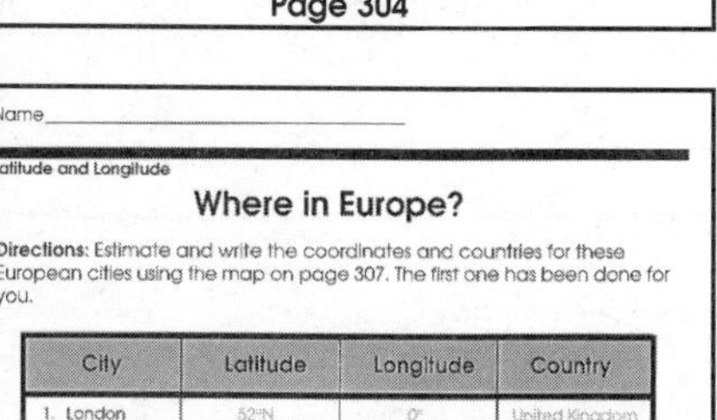

City	Latitude	Longitude	Country
1. London	52°N	0°	United Kingdom
2. Belgrade	45°N	20°E	Yugoslavia
3. Warsaw	57°N	21°E	Poland
4. Stockholm	59°N	18°E	Sweden
5. Athens	38°N	23°E	Greece
6. Helsinki	61°N	25°E	Finland
7. Paris	48°N	3°E	France
8. Munich	47°N	12°E	Germany
9. Copenhagen	56°N	13°E	Denmark
10. Oslo	60°N	11°E	Norway
11. Glasgow	56°N	6°E	United Kingdom
12. Prague	50°N	14°E	Czech Republic
13. Bern	47°N	8°E	Switzerland
14. Hamburg	53°N	10°E	Germany
15. Dresden	52°N	13°E	Germany
16. Dublin	53°N	6°W	Ireland
17. Rome	42°N	13°E	Italy
18. Budapest	43°N	18°E	Hungary
19. Vienna	48°N	16°E	Austria
20. Amsterdam	53°N	5°E	Netherlands

Page 308

Name________________________

Latitude and Longitude

Latitude and Longitude Lines

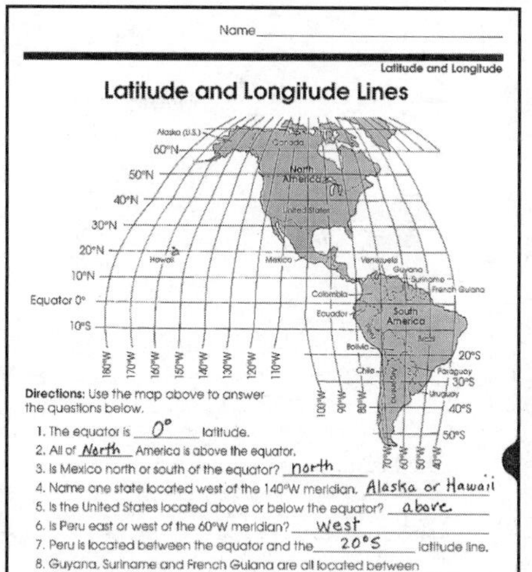

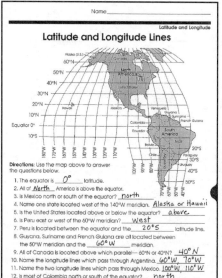

Directions: Use the map above to answer the questions below.

1. The equator is 0° latitude.
2. All of North America is above the equator.
3. Is Mexico north or south of the equator? north
4. Name one state located west of the 140°W meridian. Alaska or Hawaii
5. Is the United States located above or below the equator? above
6. Is Peru east or west of the 60°W meridian? west
7. Peru is located between the equator and the 20°S latitude line.
8. Guyana, Suriname and French Guiana are all located between the 50°W meridian and the 60°W meridian.
9. All of Canada is located above which parallel— 60°N or 40°N? 40°N
10. Name the longitude lines which pass through Argentina. 60°W, 70°W
11. Name the two longitude lines which pass through Mexico. 100°W, 110°W
12. Is most of Colombia north or south of the equator? north

Page 309

Name________________________

Latitude and Longitude

Pinpointing North American Cities

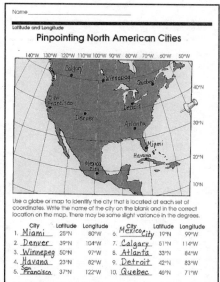

Use a globe or map to identify the city that is located at each set of coordinates. Write the name of the city on the blank and in the correct location on the map. There may be some slight variance in the degrees.

City	Latitude	Longitude	City	Latitude	Longitude
1. Miami	25°N	80°W	6. Mexico City	19°N	99°W
2. Denver	39°N	104°W	7. Calgary	51°N	114°W
3. Winnepeg	50°N	97°W	8. Atlanta	33°N	84°W
4. Havana	23°N	82°W	9. Detroit	42°N	83°W
5. San Francisco	37°N	122°W	10. Quebec	46°N	71°W

Page 310

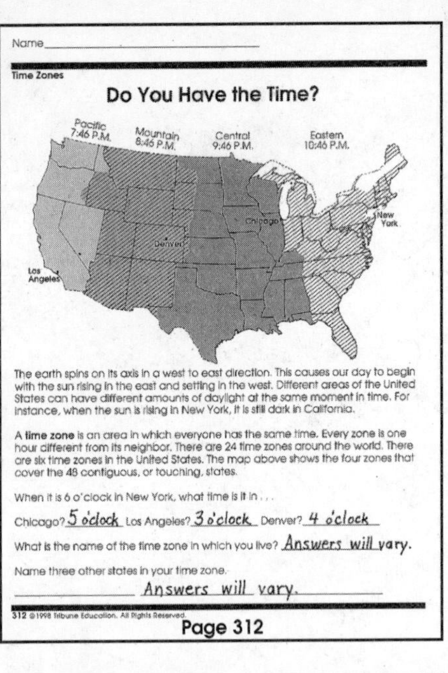
Name________________

Time Zones

Do You Have the Time?

The earth spins on its axis in a west to east direction. This causes our day to begin with the sun rising in the east and setting in the west. Different areas of the United States can have different amounts of daylight at the same moment in time. For instance, when the sun is rising in New York, it is still dark in California.

A **time zone** is an area in which everyone has the same time. Every zone is one hour different from its neighbor. There are 24 time zones around the world. There are six time zones in the United States. The map above shows the four zones that cover the 48 contiguous, or touching, states.

When it is 6 o'clock in New York, what time is it in . . .

Chicago? 5 o'clock Los Angeles? 3 o'clock Denver? 4 o'clock

What is the name of the time zone in which you live? Answers will vary.

Name three other states in your time zone.

Answers will vary.

Page 312

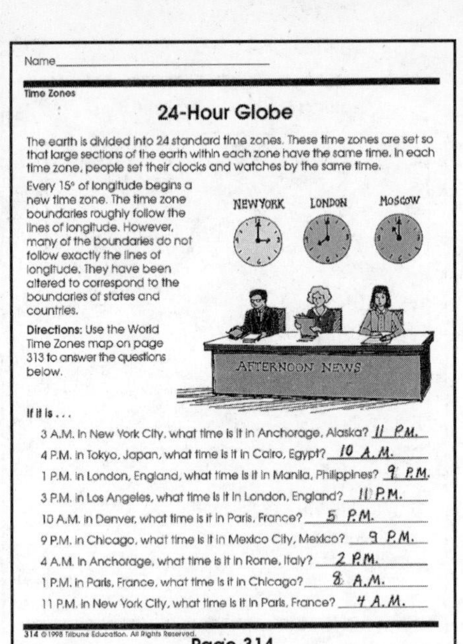
Name________________

Time Zones

24-Hour Globe

The earth is divided into 24 standard time zones. These time zones are set so that large sections of the earth within each zone have the same time. In each time zone, people set their clocks and watches by the same time.

Every 15° of longitude begins a new time zone. The time zone boundaries roughly follow the lines of longitude. However, many of the boundaries do not follow exactly the lines of longitude. They have been altered to correspond to the boundaries of states and countries.

Directions: Use the World Time Zones map on page 313 to answer the questions below.

If it is . . .

3 A.M. in New York City, what time is it in Anchorage, Alaska? 11 P.M.

4 P.M. in Tokyo, Japan, what time is it in Cairo, Egypt? 10 A.M.

1 P.M. in London, England, what time is it in Manila, Philippines? 9 P.M.

3 P.M. in Los Angeles, what time is it in London, England? 11 P.M.

10 A.M. in Denver, what time is it in Paris, France? 5 P.M.

9 P.M. in Chicago, what time is it in Mexico City, Mexico? 9 P.M.

4 A.M. in Anchorage, what time is it in Rome, Italy? 2 P.M.

1 P.M. in Paris, France, what time is it in Chicago? 8 A.M.

11 P.M. in New York City, what time is it in Paris, France? 4 A.M.

Page 314

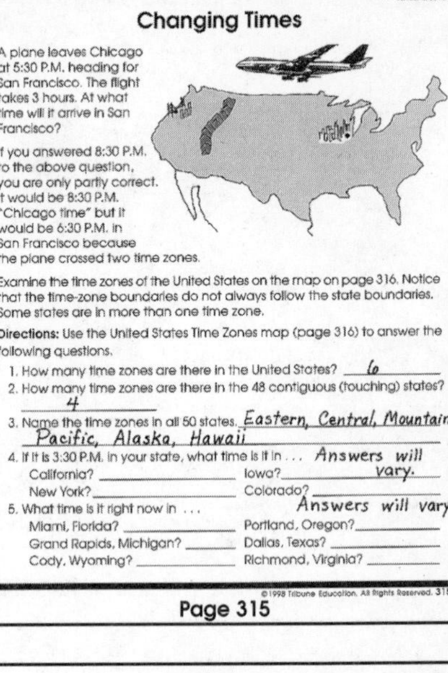
Name________________

Time Zones

Changing Times

A plane leaves Chicago at 5:30 P.M. heading for San Francisco. The flight takes 3 hours. At what time will it arrive in San Francisco?

If you answered 8:30 P.M. to the above question, you are only partly correct. It would be 8:30 P.M. "Chicago time" but it would be 6:30 P.M. in San Francisco because the plane crossed two time zones.

Examine the time zones of the United States on the map on page 316. Notice that the time-zone boundaries do not always follow the state boundaries. Some states are in more than one time zone.

Directions: Use the United States Time Zones map (page 316) to answer the following questions.

1. How many time zones are there in the United States? 6
2. How many time zones are there in the 48 contiguous (touching) states? 4
3. Name the time zones in all 50 states. Eastern, Central, Mountain, Pacific, Alaska, Hawaii
4. If it is 3:30 P.M. in your state, what time is it in . . . Answers will vary.
   California? ______ Iowa? ______
   New York? ______ Colorado? ______
5. What time is it right now in . . . Answers will vary.
   Miami, Florida? ______ Portland, Oregon? ______
   Grand Rapids, Michigan? ______ Dallas, Texas? ______
   Cody, Wyoming? ______ Richmond, Virginia? ______

Page 315

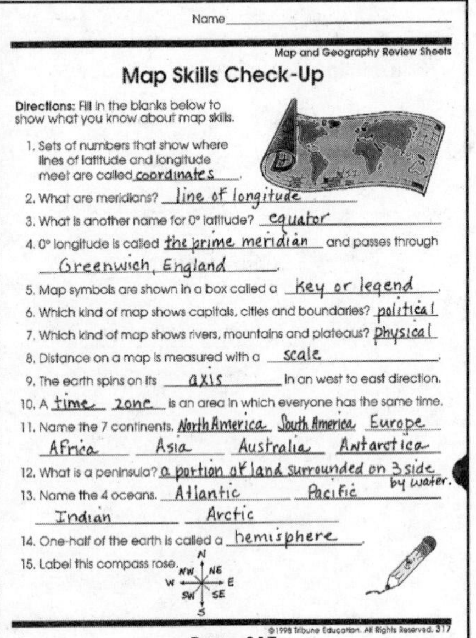
Name________________

Map and Geography Review Sheets

Map Skills Check-Up

Directions: Fill in the blanks below to show what you know about map skills.

1. Sets of numbers that show where lines of latitude and longitude meet are called coordinates.
2. What are meridians? line of longitude
3. What is another name for 0° latitude? equator
4. 0° longitude is called the prime meridian and passes through Greenwich, England.
5. Map symbols are shown in a box called a key or legend.
6. Which kind of map shows capitals, cities and boundaries? political
7. Which kind of map shows rivers, mountains and plateaus? physical
8. Distance on a map is measured with a scale.
9. The earth spins on its axis in an west to east direction.
10. A time zone is an area in which everyone has the same time.
11. Name the 7 continents. North America, South America, Europe, Africa, Asia, Australia, Antarctica
12. What is a peninsula? a portion of land surrounded on 3 side by water.
13. Name the 4 oceans. Atlantic, Pacific, Indian, Arctic
14. One-half of the earth is called a hemisphere.
15. Label this compass rose. N, NE, E, SE, S, SW, W, NW

Page 317

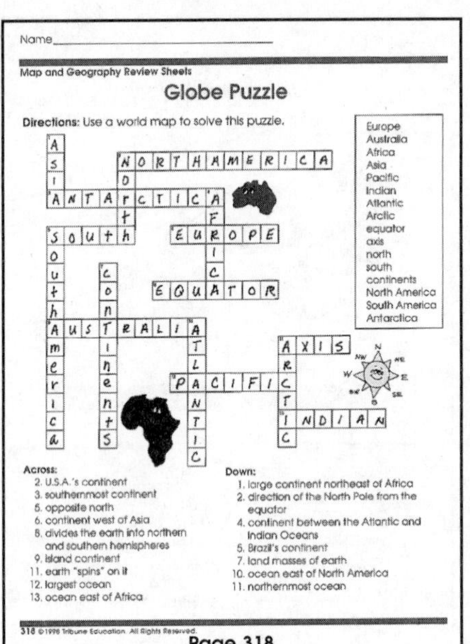
Name________________

Map and Geography Review Sheets

Globe Puzzle

Directions: Use a world map to solve this puzzle.

Word bank: Europe, Australia, Africa, Asia, Pacific, Indian, Atlantic, Arctic, equator, axis, north, south, continents, North America, South America, Antarctica

Grid answers: NORTHAMERICA, ANTARCTICA, SOUTH, EUROPE, EQUATOR, AUSTRALIA, AXIS, PACIFIC, INDIAN, ASIA, SOUTHAMERICA, CONTINENTS, AFRICA, ATLANTIC, ARCTIC

Across:
2. U.S.A.'s continent
3. southernmost continent
5. opposite north
6. continent west of Asia
8. divides the earth into northern and southern hemispheres
9. island continent
11. earth "spins" on it
12. largest ocean
13. ocean east of Africa

Down:
1. large continent northeast of Africa
2. direction of the North Pole from the equator
4. continent between the Atlantic and Indian Oceans
5. Brazil's continent
7. land masses of earth
10. ocean east of North America
11. northernmost ocean

Page 318

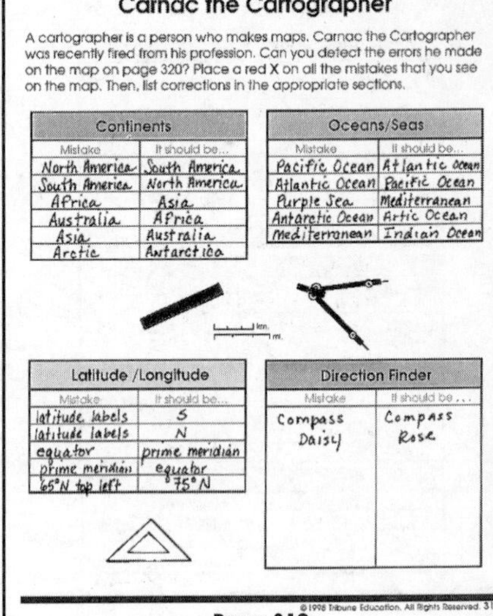
Name________________

Map and Geography Review Sheets

Carnac the Cartographer

A cartographer is a person who makes maps. Carnac the Cartographer was recently fired from his profession. Can you detect the errors he made on the map on page 320? Place a red X on all the mistakes that you see on the map. Then, list corrections in the appropriate sections.

Continents: Mistake	It should be...
North America	South America
South America	North America
Africa	Asia
Australia	Africa
Asia	Australia
Arctic	Antarctica

Oceans/Seas: Mistake	It should be...
Pacific Ocean	Atlantic Ocean
Atlantic Ocean	Pacific Ocean
Purple Sea	Mediterranean
Antarctic Ocean	Artic Ocean
Mediterranean	Indian Ocean

Latitude /Longitude: Mistake	It should be...
latitude labels	S
latitude labels	N
equator	prime meridian
prime meridian	equator
65°N top left	75°N

Direction Finder: Mistake	It should be...
Compass Daisy	Compass Rose

Page 319

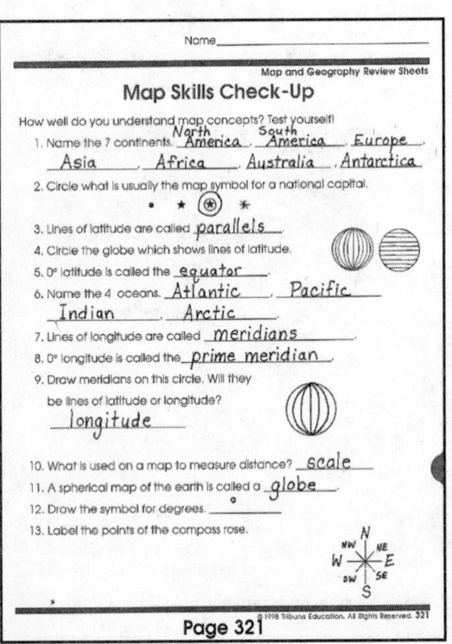
Name________________

Map and Geography Review Sheets

Map Skills Check-Up

How well do you understand map concepts? Test yourself!

1. Name the 7 continents. North America, South America, Europe, Asia, Africa, Australia, Antarctica
2. Circle what is usually the map symbol for a national capital.
3. Lines of latitude are called parallels.
4. Circle the globe which shows lines of latitude.
5. 0° latitude is called the equator.
6. Name the 4 oceans. Atlantic, Pacific, Indian, Arctic
7. Lines of longitude are called meridians.
8. 0° longitude is called the prime meridian.
9. Draw meridians on this circle. Will they be lines of latitude or longitude? longitude
10. What is used on a map to measure distance? scale
11. A spherical map of the earth is called a globe.
12. Draw the symbol for degrees. °
13. Label the points of the compass rose. N, NE, E, SE, S, SW, W, NW

Page 321

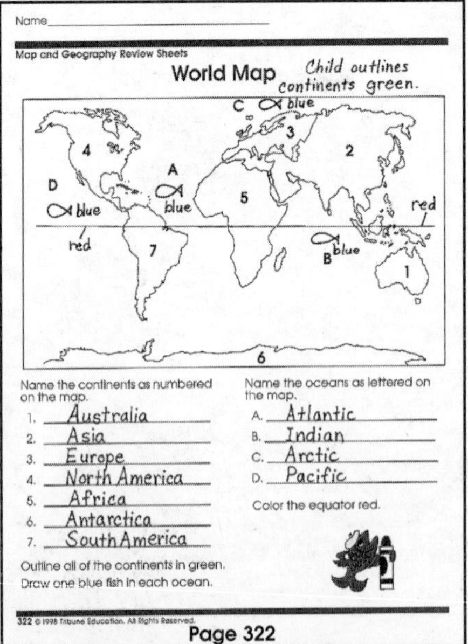
Name________________

Map and Geography Review Sheets

World Map

Child outlines continents green.

Name the continents as numbered on the map.

1. Australia
2. Asia
3. Europe
4. North America
5. Africa
6. Antarctica
7. South America

Name the oceans as lettered on the map.

A. Atlantic
B. Indian
C. Arctic
D. Pacific

Color the equator red.

Outline all of the continents in green.

Draw one blue fish in each ocean.

Page 322